PRINT PUBLISHING

A HAYDEN SHOP MANUAL

Donnie O'Quinn

Hayden
Books

201 West 103rd Street, Indianapolis, Indiana 46290

Print Publishing: A Hayden Shop Manual

Copyright © 2000 by Hayden Books

International Standard Book Number: 0-7897-2102-3

Library of Congress Catalog Card Number: 99-65667

Printed in the United States of America

First Printing: February 2000

02   4   3   2

Trademarks

Warning and Disclaimer

John Pierce
Associate Publisher

Karen Whitehouse
Acquisitions Editor

Beth Millett
Development Editor

Thomas F. Hayes
Managing Editor

Tricia Sterling
Tom Stevens
Project Editors

Victoria Elzey
Linda Seifert
Copy Editors

Angie Bess
Indexer

Jeanne Clark
Proofreader

Matt LeClair
Technical Editor

Julie Otto
Team Coordinator

Donnie O'Quinn
Kevin Spear
Interior Designers

Donnie O'Quinn
Cover Designer

Donnie O'Quinn
Copy Writer

Eric S. Miller
Layout Technician

TABLE OF CONTENTS

Preface 1
  Overview 2
  Visit www.theshopmanual.com 3
  Command Locations 3
  Macintosh and Windows Commands .4
  Contents 4
  Dedication 7
  Acknowledgments 7

1 An Introduction to Digital Prepress 9
  Overview: Conventional Prepress 10
    Concepting and Design 10
    Typesetting 11
    Image Acquisition 11
    Page Composition and Paste-Up 12
    Stripping and Imposition 12
    Proofing and Revising 12
  Overview: Digital Prepress 13
    Concepting 13
    Design and Production 13
    Proofing and Revising 17
  Succeeding in the Digital Age 18
    Computers Are Not Magic 19
    Computers Don't Do Your Work for You 19
    Communicate 19
    Troubleshooting Is Not a Solution 20
    You Cannot Be Passive 20
    Summary 21

2 Creating Your Work Environment 23
  The Hardware 24
    Computer Type 25
    The Processor 30
    Random Access Memory (RAM) 33
    Expansion 35
    Monitors 38
  The Software 42
    The Word Processor 43
    The Vector-Based Graphics Program 44
    The Pixel-Based Editing Program 45

CONTENTS AT A GLANCE

Preface 1

1 An Introduction to Digital Prepress .9

2 Creating Your Work Environment .23

3 Optimizing Your Work Environment 67

4 Font Management 107

5 File Management 149

6 Media Dexterity: Transport and Storage 175

7 Project Planning 219

8 Vector-Based Graphics 231

9 Digital Imaging Fundamentals 311

10 Scanning Line Art and Halftones .349

11 Color Spaces and Printing 409

12 Scanning and Adjusting Color Images 445

13 Photoshop Production Techniques 495

14 Page Layout Issues 565

15 Trapping 627

16 Preflight and File Prep 673

17 Proofing Methods 717

A Image Credits 733

Index 737

The Page Layout Software 45

Fonts 46

Maintenance Utilities 47

Knowledge Resources 48

Training 48

Reference Materials 52

The Human Resource 55

Employees and Co-Workers 55

Print Brokers 57

Service Bureaus 59

Print Shops...60

Freelancers 61

Value-Added Resellers (VARs) 64

Summary..65

3 Optimizing Your Work Environment 67

Optimizing Through Ergonomics 68

Repetitive Stress Injury 68

Preventing RSI 70

Input Devices and Accessories 73

Take Breaks...77

Eye Strain 77

Optimizing Your System 78

Reformat Your Drive...78

Installing the System 81

Customizing the System..81

Using the MacOS Extensions Manager 81

Determining What You Don't Need 83

Configuring Your MacOS Control Panels 85

Font Utilities 91

View Settings 92

Maintaining Your System...95

Your Weekly Maintenance Routine 95

Disk Optimizing Utilities 97

Installing Applications 98

RAM Allocation 99

System Recovery...102

Summary 106

4 Font Management 107

A Brief and Sordid History of Digital Fonts......................110

The Nature of Fonts 113

Screen Fonts..113

Printer Fonts 114

Adobe Type Manager 114

Putting the Pieces Together 115
Weeding Your Font Library 116
Converting Fonts Between Platforms 119
Expert Sets and Multiple Master Fonts 120
Using the Fonts Folder 121
Organizing a Font Library 124
Managing Your Fonts 126
Extensis Suitcase (Mac Only) 127
Managing Fonts with ATM Deluxe (Mac and Windows) 133
Preflight Font Requirements 137
Last-Minute Transport Tips 141
Fonts, Servers, and Networks 143
Fonts and Printing 144
Font Licensing Issues 144
Creating a Font Catalog 145
Summary 146

5 File Management 149
Establishing a File Management System 151
The System Folder 152
The Applications Folder 152
The Type Library Folder 154
The Internet Folder 155
The Utilities Folder 156
The Libraries Folder 156
The To Archive Folder 157
Watched Folders 157
The Personal Folder 158
The Work Folder 159
Backup 166
Manual Backup 167
Automatic Backup 168
Archiving 168
File Naming Conventions 170
FPO, DCS, and Offsite Storage 171
Summary 173

6 Media Dexterity: Transport and Storage 175
Obstacles to Media Dexterity 177
A Brief History of Storage 177
Choosing the Right Media 179
Manufacturer Reputation 179
Product Performance 180
Market Penetration 184

Media Types 187
    Magnetic Media 188
    Optical Media 198
    Magneto-Optical 200
    Magnetic Tape 202
    Final Recommendations 203
Media Dexterity Strategies 203
    Standardize Your In-House Devices 203
    Install a Media Dexterity Station 204
Networks 206
    LocalTalk 206
    Ethernet 207
    Servers 209
    Network Media Dexterity 212
Modems 213
    POTS Modems 214
    ISDN 214
    Cable Modem 215
    T1 215
    Media Dexterity with a Modem 215
Summary 218

7 Project Planning **219**
Project Requirements 221
    Determining Job Requirements 222
    Determining Quality Requirements 223
    Examples of Quality Expectations 224
Assigning Prepress Responsibilities 226
Choosing a Service Provider and Printer 227
    Questions for a Digital Prepress Service Provider 227
    Questions for a Commercial Printer 229
Summary 230

8 Vector-Based Graphics **231**
Using Vector-Based Graphics 235
Understanding Bézier Curves 238
    Points and Segments 239
    Drawing a Straight-Line Path 240
    Curve Handles 241
    Drawing a Curved Path in Illustrator 242
    Drawing a Curved Path in FreeHand 245

Combining Shapes...247
    Using Compound Paths 247
    Using Masks 250
    Merging Shapes 257
Text and Type 265
    Common Vector-Based Type Techniques 266
    Converting Type to Paths...275
Working with Colors 278
    Applying Fill and Stroke in Illustrator 278
    Applying Fill and Stroke in FreeHand...........................280
    Using the Default Colors 281
    Defining Colors...283
    Naming Colors 286
    Creating Tints 287
    Deleting Unnecessary Colors.......................................288
    Converting Colors Between Ink Types 290
Custom Fills 291
    Gradients...291
    Patterns 298
Tracing Pixel-Based Images 299
    Tracing Manually..299
    Tracing Automatically 300
Saving and Exporting...301
    The Native File Format 301
    The EPS File Format 301
Importing into Illustrator and FreeHand 303
Converting Vectors to Pixels 305
    Rasterizing in Illustrator 306
    Rasterizing in FreeHand...307
    Rasterizing in Photoshop 307
Summary 308

9 Digital Imaging Fundamentals **311**
A Brief Overview of the Imaging Process 312
Working with Pixels...314
    Color Mode 315
    Resolution..323
Halftone Screens...325
    Halftone Dots...326
    Screen Angles...332
    Halftone Dot Shapes 334
    Frequency Modulated Screens......................................335

Scanners..337
   Scanner Types...338
   Scanner Features 341
   Choosing the Right Scanner....................................346
Summary 347

10 Scanning Line Art and Halftones **349**
Preparing Your Scanning Environment 351
   Setting Photoshop's Preferences 351
   Readying Your Scanner 359
Scanning Line Art 370
   Step 1: Set the Scanning Mode to Line Art 370
   Step 2: Set the Appropriate Resolution......................371
   Step 3: Preview the Scan 371
   Step 4: Acquire the Scan.......................................372
   Step 5: Evaluate the Image 372
   Step 6: Crop and Clean Up the Image 374
   Step 7: Save the File 376
   Preparing Detailed Line Art 377
Scanning and Adjusting Halftones...............................380
   Step 1: Assess the Original Image 382
   Step 2: Preview, Measure, and Adjust.......................383
   Step 3: Scan and Save 384
   Step 4: Assess the Scan...384
   Step 5: Crop and Fix Any Glaring Problems 385
   Step 6: Sharpen the Image 386
   Step 7: Check and Adjust Endpoints for Press 390
   Step 8: Adjust for Contrast 395
   Step 9: Retouch Any Minor Flaws 400
   Step 10: Compensate for Dot Gain 403
   Step 10: Review, Massage, and Save 407
Summary 407

11 Color Spaces and Printing **409**
The Variability of Color...410
   Color As a Physical Phenomenon.............................411
   Color As a Psychological Phenomenon 413
   Color in the Digital Workflow.................................415
Understanding Color Models.......................................415
   The RGB/CMY Model 416
   The CMYK Model 419
   The HSB Model 420
   The Lab Model 421
   Color Gamut..422

Establishing a Viewing Standard 423

  Using ICC Profiles...423

  Creating a Consistent Viewing Environment.............................425

  Characterizing Your Monitor 426

  Establishing the RGB Workspace 427

Establishing Separation Preferences 431

  CMYK Model 432

  Ink Colors 433

  Dot Gain 433

  Separation Type: UCR 434

  Separation Type: GCR 434

  Black Generation 435

  Black Ink Limit 435

  Total Ink Limit 436

  UCA Amount 436

  Typical CMYK Conversion Setups 436

  Non-Standard Printing Inks 437

Handling Embedded Profiles and Legacy Files 440

  Embed Profiles 441

  Assumed Profiles 442

  Profile Mismatch Handling 442

  Missing and Mismatched Profiles 443

Summary 444

12 Scanning and Adjusting Color Images **445**

Establishing Color Expectations 446

  Any Client Input Is Good Client Input 448

Scanning and Adjusting Checklist 448

  The Conversion Question 451

Elements of Color Quality 452

  Detail...452

  Tone 453

  Gray Balance 454

  Memory Colors 454

Photoshop's Color Adjustment Tools 455

  The Info Palette 455

  The Eyedropper Tools...458

  The Curves Command 460

  The Unsharp Mask Filter 464

Color Adjustment and Correction 470

  Evaluating the Shadows and Highlights 471

  Assessing Gray Balance and Color Casts 472

  Identifying the Endpoints...475

  Setting Neutral Endpoints 477

Neutralization in Practice 483
Adjusting Non-Neutral Colors 485
Summary 493

13 Photoshop Production Techniques **495**
Handling Moiré 496
Cropping Scans 502
Applying Levels-Based Adjustments..504
Selection Techniques..506
Using the Marquee Tools..507
Using the Lasso Tools 509
Using the Quick Mask Command 512
Using the Color Range Command..516
Creating Layer-Based Selections 520
Saving a Selection 520
Loading a Saved Selection 523
Layer Techniques..525
Understanding Layers 525
Layering Fundamentals 528
Copying Layers from Image to Image 532
Flattening the Image 532
Using Layer Effects 533
Creating a Ghosted Image 535
Using Layer Masks 537
Creating a Vignette 538
Using Adjustment Layers 539
Path Editing Techniques 542
Drawing a Basic Path..543
Viewing a Path 545
Continuing an Existing Open Path 545
Converting a Path to a Selection 545
Converting a Selection to a Path 546
Exchanging Paths with Illustrator 547
Using Silhouettes and Clipping Paths 548
Creating a Simple Silhouette 549
Creating a Complex Silhouette 550
Creating a Clipping Path 555
Creating Complex Masks..557
Masking with the Extract Command 558
Masking with an Existing Channel...560
Summary 563

14 Page Layout Issues **565**

    Before You Begin: Setting Preferences 568

        Document and Application Preferences 568

        Recommended QuarkXPress 4.04 Preferences 569

        Recommended Adobe PageMaker 6.5 Preferences 576

        Recommended InDesign Preferences 579

    Setting Up a Document 582

        Page Dimensions 583

        Facing Pages 585

        Adding Pages 586

        Multiple-Page Spreads 587

    Defining and Applying Document Colors 588

        Using Spot and Process Color 588

        Choosing Colors Properly 589

        Defining Colors Accurately 590

        Applying Color Wisely 594

    Working with Text, Type, and Style Sheets 598

        Entering Text 598

        Microsoft Word and Your Prepress Environment 600

        Converting Text into Type 601

        Using Style Sheets 602

    Designing Master Pages 615

        XPress Master Page Issues 617

        PageMaker Master Page Issues 618

        InDesign Master Page Issues 618

    Designing Individual Pages 619

        Importing Graphics 619

        Scaling Graphics 620

        Rotating Graphics 622

        Cropping Graphics 622

        Stacking Graphics 624

    Summary 625

15 Trapping **627**

    Trapping Essentials 630

    Building a Process Bridge 631

    The Limitations of Black Ink 633

        Rich Black 634

        Rich Blacks in Illustrator and FreeHand 639

        Super Black 641

        Super Black in Illustrator and FreeHand 643

        Knockouts and Overprints 645

Vector-Based Trapping Tools 647
    A Simple Trap, Manually Applied 647
    A Simple Trap, Automatically Applied 649
    Complex Vector-Based Traps 651
Page Layout Trapping Tools 651
    Trapping in XPress 652
    Trapping in PageMaker 663
    Trapping in InDesign 666
Trapping in Photoshop...666
    Trapping Vector-Based Artwork Imported into Photoshop 667
Dedicated Trapping Software...668
When and Where Trapping Is Required 669
The Future: Adobe Trapping 670
Summary 671

16 Preflight and File Prep **673**
The History of Preflight...674
Stage One: Gathering Information....................................676
    For the Designer 677
    Service Provider: Using Your Output Request Form.....................686
Stage Two: Reviewing the File 689
    Creating Optimum Preflight Conditions 690
    Opening and Examining the Document 690
Stage Three: Outputting Paper Proofs 698
    Necessary Hardware...698
    Output Laser Proofs 702
    Examining Your Laser Seps 711
Troubleshooting..712
    Billing Practices 713
    Dedicated Preflight Software 714
Summary 715

17 Proofing Methods **717**
Checking Copy 718
Proofing Layout and Composition 720
Proofing Color 721
    Color Proofing Methods...723
    Evaluating a Color Proof 726
    Marking a Proof for Revisions 728
Proofing Spot Colors..729
The Press Check 730
Summary 732

A Image Credits **733**

Index **737**

TELL US WHAT YOU THINK!

As the reader of this book, *you* are our most important critic and commentator. We value your opinion and want to know what we're doing right, what we could do better, what areas you'd like to see us publish in, and any other words of wisdom you're willing to pass our way.

As an Associate Publisher for Hayden Books, I welcome your comments. You can fax, email, or write me directly to let me know what you did or didn't like about this book—as well as what we can do to make our books stronger.

Please note that I cannot help you with technical problems related to the topic of this book, and that due to the high volume of mail I receive, I might not be able to reply to every message.

When you write, please be sure to include this book's title and author as well as your name and phone or fax number. I will carefully review your comments and share them with the author and editors who worked on the book.

Fax: 317-581-4666

Email: hayden@mcp.com

Mail: John Pierce, Associate Publisher
           Hayden Books
           201 West 103rd Street
           Indianapolis, IN 46290 USA

PREFACE

Digital graphics industries, such as print and the Web, have matured to the point where no one works in a vacuum. To accomplish the tasks of any given project, the average worker faces two daunting scenarios:

- **Using multiple software packages.** No one uses a solitary application to get the job done. To achieve any production-oriented goal, the features of many programs and utilities must be successfully combined. As deadlines loom, it's often up to the user to determine the appropriate use of each one.

- **Crossover between trades.** Responsibilities are rarely limited to the title on a business card. A designer must have a functional knowledge of the prepress sciences; a prepress specialist must understand PDF issues; a Web site engineer must grasp not only databases, but the proper distribution of information; an Art Director must understand project management issues specific to print, Web, and multimedia.

But the mainstream computer-book idiom has changed little since the first were published. Most titles focus on a particular application (or programming language, or concept). Whether a book consists of an easily digestible survey or a compilation of hard-core techniques, the only light cast upon the greater context of a production environment is through the limited lens of the subject matter. Although Amazon.com currently lists over 200 items that contain "Photoshop" in the title, I've never encountered a professional who uses the program exclusively. In fact, the typical worker utilizes only 10–15% of any major application's features, as determined by the specific requirements of their work.

A mechanic doesn't learn about automotive repair by reading a book about 5lb slide hammers. A plumber doesn't make a living by reading 800 pages on ratchet-handled pipe-reamers. These professionals have always turned to a time-honored resource: the shop manual. Instead of focusing on a single tool, a shop manual illustrates an entire *trade*, describing all the tools, issues, and goals required to succeed in a given field. The image of a shop manual is somewhat romantic, but accurate. It's easy to picture a tattered, leather-bound book, covered with greasy fingerprints and filled with dog-eared pages, kept within easy reach on a workbench or in a toolbox.

Every *Hayden Shop Manual* treats its target industry—and the people employed within it—with the depth and authority they deserve. A *Shop Manual* evokes the image of a resource to turn to again and again—one that presents the shortest, most efficient distance between concept and execution. You are shown how different resources work together to successfully complete the goals of your industry, and every bit of advice is offered in a profit-oriented context. A *Shop Manual* contains the nuts and bolts of a *trade*, and let's face it: We use this technology not out of love, but to pay the bills.

Overview

This is the book I wished for when I landed my first job in the printing industry. This is the book I've searched for ever since.

Modern technology has made design, prepress, and production techniques available to a huge number of people. It has shortened our turnaround times, increased our design capabilities, and enabled us to produce more work than we ever dreamed possible. What it *hasn't* done is make our jobs any easier. The tools and techniques involved in a typical production environment are innumerable. Every stage of the process is rife with potential mistakes and miscalculations. There are literally thousands of issues that impact your ability to get your work done. Success depends on how well you understand the industry facets that tie into your own responsibilities.

Dozens of books attempt to explain one particular aspect of publishing or another. One might focus on Photoshop techniques; another on QuarkXPress; another on color correcting. Unfortunately, it's always been left up to you to weed through all the text, find the topics that pertain to your work, and then apply the info somehow. But who has time to read 10 or 20 books? Who can afford the luxury of extensive research, when one deadline after another demands your immediate attention? How can you possibly make sense of the most complex industry in the realm of computer graphics?

Print Publishing: A Hayden Shop Manual addresses the entire prepress and file construction process, from purchasing and installing equipment to organizing a managed workflow to the file construction issues that directly impact successful output. If there is one theme that pervades the book, it's that you never work in isolation. It doesn't matter if you're a designer, color corrector, scanner operator, or output technician—if you want to master your trade, you must understand how the remaining facets tie into your own.

This book contains no tutorials. It doesn't hold your hand, or attempt to over-simplify what is at best a difficult and time-consuming process. It doesn't strive to entertain you with pithy prose, pressure you to buy anything (other than the accepted industry-standard products), or waste your time with any info that doesn't affect your bottom line. Instead, it addresses every topic with three no-nonsense goals: saving time, making money, and increasing your skills.

Visit www.theshopmanual.com

Shop Manuals are some of the most thorough references you'll find, but there's never enough space to cover everything we'd like. Some topics are too specific, some utilities change too quickly for accurate coverage, and sometimes there's simply no way to pack another 20 pages into the book at hand. At www.theshopmanual.com, you'll have easy access to updated info, extra chapters, and a continual exploration of the print publishing process. Register your book for free to enjoy immediate access to additional *Shop Manual* content.

Command Locations

Throughout the book, I often refer to a specific command in one application or another. Rather than use a long, wordy sentence to describe its location, I briefly state the command path, separating each item with colons. For example, instead of writing, "Choose the Curves command, located under the Image menu, under the Adjust submenu...," I write, "Choose Image: Adjust: **Curves**."

Macintosh and Windows Commands

Whenever I mention a particular keyboard technique, I include the Macintosh and Windows versions. The Mac keys appear in parentheses, and the Windows keys are in brackets. For example:

- Hold down the (Option)[Alt] key and drag the item to make a duplicate.

- (Option-Command-click)[Alt-Control-click] the item to access the Rotate dialog box.

- Choose (Option-Command-Shift-V)[Alt-Control-Shift-V] to paste into an active selection.

Contents

Each chapter focuses on one facet of the publishing process. Some cover project management issues, others present high-end techniques, others clarify the everyday science that drives a production environment.

Chapter 1, "An Introduction to Digital Prepress"

This chapter presents a brief history of the print publishing industry, explaining how modern prepress techniques are based almost entirely on conventional methods. It also defines the responsibilities and goals of each position in the process.

Chapter 2, "Creating Your Work Environment"

This chapter explores the components of a productive work environment, including your workstation, the required software, training/knowledge resources, and the outside professional resources you may need to incorporate into your workflow.

Chapter 3, "Optimizing Your Work Environment"

This chapter offers techniques in making your work area as efficient and productive as possible, and covers workplace ergonomics, drive formatting, OS and application installation, RAM allocation, recommended system utilities, and emergency backup/recovery.

Chapter 4, "Font Management"

This chapter describes the role of font files in a production environment, including their installation, proper use, and organization. It covers how to establish a professional in-house type library, how to handle client fonts, and how to troubleshoot any conflicts that arise. It includes detailed coverage of two font management utilities: Symantec Suitcase and ATM Deluxe.

Chapter 5, *"File Management"*

This chapter recommends a method of organizing large numbers of files and projects, for both single- and multiple-workstation environments. The importance of job numbering, project tracking, and archiving is stressed.

Chapter 6, *"Media Dexterity: Transport and Storage"*

This chapter gives a detailed rundown of all available media types, offering recommendations based on work methods, storage requirements, client or vendor responsibilities, and overall efficiency. Emphasis is placed on compatibility, expandability, and cost.

Chapter 7, *"Project Planning"*

This chapter details the numerous factors that influence a project's time and cost, and explains how to assign prepress responsibilities and choose output, production, and print vendors.

Chapter 8, *"Vector-Based Graphics"*

This chapter focuses on the production issues you'll encounter when processing vector-based graphics in Adobe Illustrator and Macromedia FreeHand. Emphasis is placed on the techniques that most frequently cause output and reproduction difficulties.

Chapter 9, *"Digital Imaging Fundamentals"*

This chapter introduces you to the issues involved in preparing pixel-based images for on-press reproduction. Topics covered include Photoshop file types, resolution and linescreen requirements, the halftoning process, and choosing an appropriate scanning device for your workplace.

Chapter 10, *"Scanning Line Art and Halftones"*

This chapter takes you through the scanning and Photoshop techniques required to produce print-ready B&W line art and halftones. It includes different examples of each image type, featuring full descriptions of tried-and-true editing strategies.

Chapter 11, "Color Spaces and Printing"

This chapter presents the complex issues surrounding color image acquisition and adjustment. It describes the subjective nature of color itself, the standard color models referenced by Photoshop, and the all-important relationship between RGB and CMYK space. ICC profiles are put into a realistic context, and you're shown how to establish settings that control color separations for different press conditions.

Chapter 12, "Scanning and Adjusting Color Images"

This chapter explains the process of adjusting full-color images in Photoshop. It covers the need to establish client expectations, the proper use of Photoshop's powerful color correcting tools, and critical issues such as neutral grays and memory colors.

Chapter 13, "Photoshop Production Techniques"

This chapter presents an extensive list of production-oriented Photoshop techniques, including handling difficult scans, such as metallic objects and prescreened images; creating complex selections for a wide variety of uses; layer-based techniques such as shadows, clipping groups, and character masks; generating silhouettes and clipping paths; and over 100 more.

Chapter 14, "Page Layout Issues"

This chapter focuses on document construction, addressing the proper use of QuarkXPress, Adobe PageMaker, and Adobe InDesign. Rather than dwell on design-oriented topics, it covers the issues that most frequently cause delays or misprinted files, including setting preferences, using style sheets, defining and applying colors, handling imported graphics, using master pages, and more.

Chapter 15, "Trapping"

This chapter defines the need for trapping, and provides the necessary information to accomplish the task. It discusses design and color considerations, black reproduction techniques, working with a process bridge, manually trapping in Illustrator and FreeHand, and setting trapping preferences in XPress, PageMaker, and InDesign.

Chapter 16, "Preflight and File Prep"

This chapter describes the preflight process, a workflow that ensures successful final output. It describes how to establish such a workflow, the necessary hardware and software, and the client/vendor responsibilities involved.

Chapter 17, "Proofing Methods"

This chapter explains the different proofing methods available, lists their appropriate uses, and guides you through the issues of successfully creating and evaluating a project proof.

Dedication

The book you hold is the result of a dozen jobs, a hundred opportunities, a thousand projects, and a million lessons learned the hard way. To the people who hired me, fired me, rewarded me, threatened me, paid me, stiffed me, trusted me, suffered me, and otherwise taught me about this crazy industry: It only makes sense that I dedicate it to you.

Acknowledgments

If the responsibility for producing a book was left entirely up to the author, we'd live in a world without books. My thanks to the people who helped me with this one: Gina Lewis, who kept the right side of my brain pleasantly distracted so the left side could concentrate; David Rogelberg, Sherry Rogelberg, and the rest of the crew at StudioB, for making sense of an otherwise incomprehensible world; Matt LeClair, for his excellent technical editing; Tom Magadieu and Steve Kurth, for their assistance in conceiving this series; Mr. Kurth again, for his illustrations in Chapter 3 and the inside back cover; Karen Whitehouse, who green-lighted the entire project; Beth Millett (and the rest of the Hayden Books crew), who succeeded in making me appear more intelligent and organized than I really am; and finally, Don, Lois, and Sharon O'Quinn, my family, always ready to cook me a loving hamburger when I need one. Special mention goes out to *Digital Prepress Complete*, that out-of-print first effort, which provided the conceptual foundation for this book.

AN INTRODUCTION TO DIGITAL PREPRESS

Digital prepress technology has transformed the entire print industry. It has increased our capabilities, reduced production costs, and shortened turnaround times. As a result, print publishing has been kicked into overdrive, with over three million professionals generating materials at an unprecedented clip.

Prepress is the science of converting an initial idea into a printed reality. It encompasses any work performed along the way, from the roughest thumbnail sketch to the plates hung on a printing press. To paraphrase Thomas Edison, graphic design is 1% inspiration, 99% production—without an understanding of prepress issues and techniques, even the most brilliant concept will never become ink-on-paper.

Before the advent of desktop computers, prepress existed as a series of well-defined trades. There was little crossover between responsibilities. One department designed a project; another generated the type; another produced artwork; another shot films; another imposed them for printing; another generated plates. The technology was too broad and complex for a person to work beyond the limits of his job description. Today, the paradigm has changed. Powerful computers and software have blurred the lines that once separated these tasks. A single person can create illustrations, scan images, design a multi-page document, and produce print-ready films, often from the same workstation. (Even the word "prepress"—literally, "before the press"—has become somewhat outdated, failing to address film recorders, color printers, high-end copiers, and other modern reproduction options.)

If you're involved in any stage of print publishing—whether as a sales rep or print broker, a graphic designer or scanner operator, a color corrector or output specialist—your business card may as well read "Prepress Operator." To achieve success and profitability, you must understand how your responsibilities tie into the overall process. Consider yourself part of a chain; your choices and actions directly affect every other link. A designer makes an error when constructing a document, and the output specialist can't print films; a scanner operator miscalculates while acquiring an image, and the corrector can't balance the colors. Mistakes weaken the chain, causing blown deadlines and cost overruns—the bane of any print professional.

Computers have radically changed your methods, but your goal is the same as ever: putting ink on paper. The physical factors involved in running a project on-press have not changed, and they permeate every facet of your work. It's not enough to know how to use an application; you must grasp the cause-and-effect relationship between your files and the finished piece. Likewise, if you have conventional printing experience, you must be willing to relearn the process using modern tools. The tasks required to complete a project are no longer isolated; prepress is integrated at every stage of the workflow, and you, your colleagues, and your vendors are more interdependent than ever before.

Overview: Conventional Prepress

Let's take a brief look at a conventional workflow. As recently as a decade or two ago, a publication went through a complex life cycle, involving many artists and tradesmen responsible for each task. Depending on their scope, entire projects could easily take weeks or months to complete.

Concepting and Design

When a project began, an individual or group decided its purpose, how it would look, the number of pages, and the overall budget. This information was handed to the design group, who produced a series of *roughs* (hand-drawn sketches on tissue paper, providing a general idea of text and graphics placement) until they were approved by the concepting group. The roughs might have been crudely rendered, but they had to be accurate in all measurements and specifications.

Typesetting

At the very beginning, concepting, design, and typesetting were handled by the same person: a monk, who hand-lettered every page. Gutenburg's invention of movable type improved things considerably. Here, letters were chiseled from wood, dipped in ink, and pressed onto paper. The process of setting the type was still laborious—every letter of every word had to be placed by hand—but after it was finished, you could print multiple copies of the page. When you think about it, things didn't change much over the next 500 years. Faster and easier methods arose, but until the introduction of the computer, type was strictly a hands-on craft.

Drafts of automated typesetting machines appeared as long ago as the early 1700s, but it wasn't until 1838 that the first hot metal typecaster appeared. (In fact, most type foundries initially resisted the development of mechanized typesetting, regarding any automated methods as a threat to their livelihoods.) By 1900, however, the Linotype and Monotype machines enabled type to be cast and set simultaneously, and found widespread commercial acceptance in the newspaper industry.

As the lithographic process became perfected in the 20th century, the method of reproducing type lagged behind. Printers were still casting type in hot metal, running it on a letterpress, and then shooting the page with a camera to generate the necessary films. Finally, after World War II, the last major conventional type development appeared: the phototypesetter. Here, a machine (loosely based on the Monotype) projected lettershapes onto a photosensitive plate, producing films that could be incorporated more easily with the overall project. Unlike hot metal type, the films could be efficiently stored and readily used again by the print shop.

Phototypesetting remained the standard until the development of digital technology. (In fact, many machines are still in use, primarily by print departments with long-established workflows, with no economic imperative to change.) It wasn't without its flaws. Type was still generated separately from the rest of the project. Typesetters had to format text using a series of proprietary commands, and couldn't evaluate the actual appearance of their work until they generated a physical proof.

Image Acquisition

Like type, images were generated by an independent department or vendor. The process of placing a fine screen over a photograph and shooting it with a camera was developed in the late nineteenth century. With few major changes, the same methods were used until the introduction of desktop scanners. Printers used a *process camera* to capture images, shooting them directly to film. Color images were shot four times, each through a different colored filter, to generate the film separations.

The printed results were essentially the same as you see now, but the entire process was unwieldy in comparison to today's techniques. The operator had to know the precise size of the target image, and adjust for it during shooting. If any changes were required, even the slightest increase or decrease in scale, the image had to be reshot at considerable expense. And because the image only existed as film, the designer had no direct access to its contents— any adjustments or special effects could only be accomplished through extensive communication, and more than a little trial and error.

Page Composition and Paste-Up

For the most part, pages were composed by hand. The typesetter formatted the text in the desired face, size, and spacing, making it fit within the designated areas (as determined by the designer). In turn, the type was handed to the page composition department, where it was affixed with sticky wax in the right place on the paste-up board. People here were also responsible for placing black FPO ("for position only") boxes where each image belonged. After it was completed, the pages were shot with a camera, producing the films required for stripping and imposition.

Stripping and Imposition

The negatives for the pages and images were combined by the stripper, who taped them onto *flats* (sheets of plastic or paper). The stripper ensured the accuracy of the films, and was responsible for the placement of crop, registration, and fold marks. After assembly, the flats were *imposed*, or taped to a larger sheet in the exact signature required for the target press. The imposed flats were made into the lithographic plates, which would soon hang on the printing press and apply ink to paper.

Proofing and Revising

Proofing options were limited. There was no way to evaluate page geometry or color content without first generating films. Less-expensive blueline proofs enabled printers to evaluate the positioning of page elements or the accuracy of imposition. Costly four-color laminate proofs made it possible to evaluate color. When errors were caught, new negatives for the problem areas were made, then carefully stripped in to line up perfectly with the existing text and graphics. The process was repeated until everything was perfect.

Overview: Digital Prepress

Digital techniques haven't completely supplanted the conventional. Despite the growing acceptance of direct-to-plate and direct-to-press technology, printing is still essentially a film-based industry. (Let's not forget that many printing presses are decades old—a good indication that after you generate films, conventional methods are required to finish the job.) The biggest changes have occurred in the work that takes place before films are made.

Concepting

The concepting stage is essentially the same as it ever was. An individual or group determines the need for a project, then determines its overall look, page count, and budget. As soon as this info is handed to the designer (assuming the designer wasn't responsible for it in the first place), changes in method are immediately apparent.

Here's a common scenario. The designer makes a series of roughs, or pages created on the computer using dummy text and FPO clip art or low-res images. These are output to a laser printer and evaluated by the concepting group until an idea is approved. Unlike handmade roughs, these pages provide an accurate representation of the final product. It's easy to experiment with different type formats, page dimensions, and layouts, and checking your progress is as easy as printing the current file. Most often, the approved rough becomes the project document. The dummy text is replaced with actual copy, the FPO images are replaced with illustrations and corrected scans, and the designer applies the necessary tweaks and adjustments to transform the basic idea into the final piece.

Design and Production

The prepress process is thoroughly interwoven with design. Many disciplines that formerly required separate seasoned pros are often handled by the same person. When you enter text into a document, you can freely edit its typeface, size, style, and position on the page. In this sense, you act as a typesetter and page composer. You can scan and adjust your own images, assuming the role of a cameraman. You can crop images and incorporate them into the layout, and even trap colors, impose a press signature, and generate films. Here, you take on the responsibilities of a stripper.

Although computers make it possible to handle all these tasks yourself, few people actually do. The fact that different workflow stages use similar equipment is misleading; it suggests that the science underlying the print process has been simplified. Today's tools make design and prepress more accessible than ever, but a lot of work is best handled by specialists. The typical project involves a series of professionals, whether they're outside vendors or part of another in-house department.

The print industry consists of dozens of job titles and hundreds of responsibilities. The specifics of each one differ slightly from business to business, workflow to workflow. For the purposes of file construction and output, the focus of this book, the areas of specialty can be broken down as follows.

Designer

The designer creates the look and feel of a project. Most often, he is responsible for determining the range of components required to complete the job—including copy, illustrations, and scans—and outsources the work accordingly.

Although most designers farm out the most intensive project elements, their responsibilities aren't limited to the act of page layout. To ensure that their layout document is properly constructed and output ready, they must have a working understanding of all prepress areas. This is perhaps the only position that requires such a broad knowledge base, and it makes sense. The designer is at the center of all activity, maintaining contact with clients, communicating file requirements to vendors, coordinating outsourced work, evaluating proofs, and attending press checks. All the while, they must ensure that the project meets the established time, budget, and press requirements.

If you're a designer, this doesn't mean you have to achieve a level of expertise in these areas; your day is busy enough as it is. Instead, you must be able to base your decisions on an understanding of the print process. For example, you don't have to know how to correct color; you should be able to evaluate a color proof. You don't have to know how to trap a document; you should know how to design with trapping in mind. You don't have to know how to impose pages; you should know that someone ultimately will, what the process involves, and how it will impact your intended design.

Illustrator

Computers have not diminished the role of talented artists. If anything, the proliferation of powerful mainstream software has only increased the need. It's easy to be seduced by the bells and whistles of programs like Photoshop or Illustrator, believing that a few quick filters or commands takes the place of an experienced hand. That's not necessarily so; you might be able to combine images with ease, but software alone doesn't address your inherent skills, artistic background, hand-eye coordination, or ability to choose the most appropriate original scans. Conventional designers relied heavily on illustrators to produce custom artwork for their projects. Today, a new crop of artists have mastered these tools, and their services are just as valuable.

This is not to malign your abilities. If you and your clients are satisfied with your efforts, then continue, by all means. The problem is that many people, designers and non-designers alike, are compelled to create their own artwork. It's a tough idea to avoid—the bold claims of many trade magazines, third-party books, and software manufacturers make it sound like you can create a masterpiece in 10 easy steps. In reality, it's much harder to design when your ideas are more advanced than your skills. When this is the case, consider farming out the work to an artist who can easily reproduce what you have in mind. Also keep in mind that creating your own artwork adds many more hours to your schedule. When deadlines are short, it simply makes sense to invest in outside help.

Production Specialist

Production specialists are the heavy-lifters of the digital workflow. Their tasks depend entirely on where they work, the current project at hand, even the hour of the day. Perhaps someone needs 50 clipping paths drawn; maybe a series of product shots requires drop shadows; the text of an existing file needs to be updated for a client. They probably don't create original documents or artwork, or scan and correct images. Instead, they work behind the scenes, performing the multitude of tweaks and effects that keep the larger project rolling forward.

At smaller companies, these tasks typically fall in the hands of the designers. Some places contract freelancers to handle this work. Others hire production assistants. Larger companies staff an entire department dedicated to production techniques. Whatever the situation, artistic ability is not necessarily required to work in this capacity; more important is an ability to solve problems and work quickly.

Scanner Operator

The scanner operator's responsibilities depend on the workplace and the scanning materials. Many designers handle their own scans, particularly if they're line art, halftones, or color FPOs. Large orders of line art and halftones are often handed off to a trained production specialist, if one is available in-house. Due to their complexity, color scans are usually handled by a full-time scanner operator. These professionals are typically found at service bureaus, larger print shops, and closed-loop, in-house production facilities, where demand is consistent enough to warrant the position. They have access to high-end equipment, and are trained in color science, prescan correction, and press issues. Additionally, they're able to take advantage of different proofing methods to ensure the quality of their scans.

As scanners drop in price and increase in quality, more people are handling their own color scans. Many companies have installed units at their design workstations, assuming they can save the outsourcing costs, and if applicable, bill their clients directly for the service. In some cases, this works well, particularly when printing methods don't require the highest quality. Producing color-accurate images, however, requires investing in more than a pricey scanner. The operator will need extensive training, appropriate proofing devices, and considerable experience before he can produce scans of consistent quality. And then, the right environment must exist for correcting the images onscreen. Too many companies have underestimated the effort involved in switching to a color workflow, and their business has suffered as a result. So do your homework before taking control of your own color scans—and in the meantime, develop a strong relationship with a capable vendor.

Color Corrector

The color corrector adjusts each scanned image to match the originals as closely as the project requires. In smaller companies, the scanner operator and color corrector are often the same person. Larger facilities, particularly service bureaus, employ an entire department. Correctors spend the better part of their day in an image-editing program, such as Photoshop. They're trained in color science and adjustment techniques, and their eyes are sensitive to subtle shifts in color and tone. They're able to determine potential trouble spots in a fresh scan, and can evaluate a color proof for additional corrections.

Color remains the trickiest issue in the industry. Despite the claims of many manufacturers, we're not much closer to "one-click" accurate color than we were five years ago. Due to an extensive list of reasons, you cannot trust the colors that appear on your monitor. To correct color onscreen, you need a rigidly controlled environment, including consistent lighting, calibrated viewing devices, assorted measuring equipment, and appropriate proofing methods—and that doesn't address the training, trial and error, and experience required to develop a hand for color adjustment.

Most places that generate color scans have accounted for these factors. If you routinely outsource your scans to a vendor, you probably don't need to adjust the colors any further. If you're creating your own color scans in an uncontrolled environment, your job is more difficult, but not impossible. In this situation, the only way to correct is to read the numerical color values, and then compare proof after proof.

Output Specialist

In the print industry, every document is output in one way or another. The output specialist ensures that a project meets the requirements of the target printer, makes any necessary adjustments, and evaluates the printed results for accuracy. He uses a variety of output devices, including laser printers, large format printers, color proofers, imagesetters, platesetters, and digital presses.

Outputting is never as simple as choosing the Print command. If you're responsible for preflighting client projects, you flag and communicate (and often repair) file construction problems. If your workflow involves proprietary trapping or imposition software, you prepare each file according to the specs of the target press. If you work with imagesetters and other high-end devices, you're likely responsible for maintaining and calibrating the devices, as well.

Proofing and Revising

Today, as with conventional prepress, the only way to truly see how the final project will appear is to run it on-press. However, digital proofing systems give you near-instantaneous feedback, and many options are extremely close to final printed quality. Black-and-white laser printers enable you to evaluate work at any stage, at extremely low cost. Mid-range color laser and ink-jet printers enable you to get a better feel for how your colors work together. High-end color devices are sensitive enough to reproduce halftone dots and compensate for dot gain, enabling you to create a contract proof without printing a single page of film. Conventional methods such as bluelines and laminate proofs are still commonly used, but the industry is slowly moving away from them as less-expensive digital options prove themselves worthy.

The main advantage offered by modern proofing methods is speed. When you catch an error during the proofing stage, you can edit the document or file and generate a new proof in minutes flat; there's no need to involve a team of people.

Succeeding in the Digital Age

New prepress technology has streamlined the prepress process, but it hasn't reduced the responsibilities. Only the roles and expectations have changed. Tasks that were once the domain of a group of highly trained experts now often fall squarely on the shoulders of a single person. If you're reading this book, that person is probably you.

Many factors work against you, regardless of the power of your tools. First and foremost, you work in a field where there are precious few "experts." Digital prepress has only been viable for a little more than 10 years, hardly enough time to produce a full range of seasoned experts, especially in an industry that changes so rapidly. (Consider the fact that it took at least 10 years to produce an expert *typesetter*, and theirs is a field that changed relatively little over the course of a century.) Instead, the standard bearers of the new age have been pundits and content developers, people only slightly ahead of the Bell curve, who regard the constant change of our industry not as a barrier to productivity, but a phenomenon to exploit for personal profit.

Fortunately, there is hope. You don't work in isolation. There are many people directly involved in bringing your printed materials into physical existence—from your colleagues to the service bureau to the printer—and it's in the best interests of all of them to see that you succeed. The best knowledge resource will always be the people and vendors you work with on a daily basis. You can also feel safe with the knowledge that nearly everything that can go wrong during the development of an electronic file is predictable and avoidable. But first, it helps to dispense with some common misconceptions spawned by the combination of marketing hype and the sketchy understanding that comes with rapid change.

Computers Are Not Magic

Computers are still new to the majority of people living in this country. They're an alien invasion sweeping over the land, transforming our society, our culture, our way of life. Many people have found themselves surrounded by digital technology almost overnight, with little or no choice in the matter, and little of any preparation or training. Never before in the history of human civilization have such extensive and transformative changes affected so many in so short a time.

As a result, the expectations of the public have not caught up with the reality of the technology. Many people, clients and employers alike, will assume that your capabilities have tripled, simply because you use a computer to do your work. It's easy to expect too much of yourself, too. (How many times have you said, "I'll have that done in 10 minutes," only to wrap things up two or three hours later?) It's ultimately up to you to know what tasks you can accomplish with the technology at hand, how long it will take, and if you have the necessary skills to do the job right.

Computers Don't Do Your Work for You

Many a person has experienced frustration and disappointment because they invested thousands of dollars in hardware and software, only to discover that there's no automatic "Make Art" command. Just recently, a friend of mine (in a non-graphic job) looked up in surprise as her boss plopped a new computer onto her desk, expecting her to suddenly produce a company newsletter. When she protested, he replied, "What? You have a *computer*, don't you?"

Your workstation is just a tool. It will do nothing for you that you don't specifically instruct it to. This means you must be aware of the requirements of every stage of the process, and take steps to ensure those requirements are met.

Communicate

It's the rare person indeed who accomplishes every task from design to print. Remember that digital prepress is a complex chain, an endless series of cause-and-effect relationships. No matter what your job is, doing it successfully requires a constant stream of communication between clients, the sales staff, vendors, designers, the print shop, and anyone in between. Ask questions. Make your needs clear. Make sure you understand the requests of other people. Keep a written record of every exchange that transpires, and disseminate that info as needed.

If you're a designer, start every project with a call to the printer, and work backward from there. Many people, fearing that asking obvious questions will undercut their professional standing, simply stay quiet and start working, assuming they'll learn as they go along. Granted, it can be intimidating to continually ask questions, but the alternatives are costly, if not downright damaging.

Consider this example. A designer recently pitched a brochure concept to a client. Without consulting the print shop, she included a complicated seven-fold. When the printer received the job, he called the designer in for some disturbing news. The requested fold was nearly impossible to do in-house. "Look at it this way," he said, and folded a piece of paper in half. "Five hundred dollars." He folded it again. "A thousand dollars." He folded it a third time. "Fifteen hundred dollars." He kept going, with each fold adding another $500 to the project. The folding cost was not included in the estimate, and the design firm had to eat the extra cost. Chalk it up to another problem that could have been avoided with a simple phone call.

Troubleshooting Is Not a Solution

Finding and repairing output-oriented problems in an electronic file is a great idea. So is an emergency tracheotomy performed by a paramedic. In both cases, the damage has already been done. By the time the problem is found, the necessary people are contacted, and the issues are resolved, you've lost precious time and money. This is unacceptable. The only true "troubleshooting" is doing it right the first time, as often as you possibly can. This can only happen with a greater understanding of your role in the prepress process.

You Cannot Be Passive

Unless you're independently wealthy and working in digital graphics for the sheer fun of it, you're in it for the money. Maybe you're freelancing, maybe you're collecting a weekly paycheck, maybe you own the company. Whatever the case, your income—and your career—depend on your ability to get the job done as efficiently as possible. Keep abreast of changing trends and techniques. Always strive to expand your set of skills. For better or worse, the industry will continue to evolve, software will continue to be upgraded, new issues will continue to flood the workplace. As unfair as it may seem, it is up to you to keep up. As long as you keep an eye toward the future, you'll find that it's easier than it sounds.

Summary

The goals of a print professional are simple. Produce your work on time, under budget, at the highest possible quality. But you work in a tricky and counter-intuitive industry; there are many stages, hundreds of tasks, and innumerable things that can go wrong along the way.

But you can take control. At every step along the process, you can take measures to ensure that your work progresses as smoothly as possible. Purchase the appropriate hardware and software. Optimize your workstation for a production environment. Establish font and file management workflows. Develop a strategy for file transport and storage. Properly plan and manage your projects. Master the production-oriented uses of the industry-standard graphics programs. Understand the complexities of a color workflow. Learn to identify output problems and ensure print-ready files. As you'll soon see, your goals and the goals of this book are the same.

It will take time, effort, and commitment, but the rewards are many: decreased frustration; lower costs; faster turnaround; the respect and admiration of colleagues, supervisors, and clients. Most importantly, if you meet the challenges, you become more profitable.

CREATING YOUR WORK ENVIRONMENT

Acquiring the components for a design or prepress workstation is like preparing for a stock-car rally. Invest wisely in the required tools, resources, and know-how, and you'll stay ahead in the race. If you underestimate what you need, you'll be lapped again and again by the competition.

A lot of us got our start by purchasing a second-hand computer, "borrowing" some software from a friend, and subscribing to a couple of how-to magazines. As soon as we designed some one-color, quick-printed business cards, we could promote ourselves as graphics professionals. When digital graphics was a new and unestablished industry, this barebones approach wasn't as bad as it sounds. The design and production standards were lower, and most of the work consisted of simple, one-color projects. It was much easier to hire people with little understanding of output or press issues, as long as they had the sketchiest grasp of the core software. (At my first interview, I didn't know the difference between an 85 and 150 linescreen, and I kept pronouncing "cyan" with a K. Although I managed to get that job in 1991, the Board of Directors would have smiled politely while relegating my résumé to the bottom of the pile if I tried that today.)

As the graphics industry matures, so does its technical and personnel requirements. Software becomes more powerful, enabling you to create more complex and demanding projects. Designers must plan and work in accordance to new, more intricate output and press limitations. Prepress technicians must be able to identify and repair an ever-increasing range of file problems. And everyone, regardless of their tasks, must have the right equipment at their disposal.

This chapter discusses the issues you'll encounter when investing in graphics technology, including the following:

- The hardware you need, from the platform to the processor, RAM, and monitor.

- The industry-standard software you need, including programs for text editing, image editing, vector-based artwork, and page layout, as well as a range of utilities.

- The knowledge resources you have at your fingertips, to keep you and your staff up to date on the latest trends and techniques.

- The professional resources you may need to incorporate into your workflow, including freelancers, service bureaus, print brokers, and value added resellers (VARs).

These areas are ultimately combined to form the basis of an efficient, productive work environment.

The Hardware

It's easy to underestimate how computer-intensive print publishing is. Applications can devour all the processor speed, hard drive space, and memory you throw at them, and still ask for more. Many people responsible for approving the purchase of graphics-based components are not used to this—often, their experience is mainly with word processing, spreadsheets, and databases, which use only a fraction of most computers' resources. Logically, they base their purchasing decisions on their past experiences, which don't apply to the world of print. The demands of design and prepress are different from other business-oriented computer uses. Failure to meet them results in lower capabilities, lost productivity, and wasted time. [1]

Five hardware components immediately affect your capability to get to work more than any others do: The platform, the processor type, the amount of installed RAM, the capability to expand, and the monitor. [2]

Computer Type

When most people think of computers, they think of the *operating system (OS)*, or the software that allows you to organize files, run applications, and otherwise do your work. The OS is driven by the *central processing unit (CPU)*, a series of chips responsible for storing, retrieving, and manipulating data—the computer's brain, if you will. (Your monitor, keyboard, and pointing device enable you to interact with the computer, but the CPU is where all the action takes place.) The combination of the CPU and operating system is known as the *platform*.

FOOTNOTE

[1] Hardware is easily the most costly up-front expense when setting up a new workstation (or adding to an existing one). With the recent release of a whole new range of low-cost, lower-quality, consumer-level products, you may be seduced into using the price tag as the primary basis for your purchasing decisions. For example, you can buy a new iMac, 32MB of additional RAM, a low-end flatbed scanner, and a color ink-jet printer for under $1,600. What a bargain! Or so it seems, until you discover that your monitor is too small for all-day viewing, you have no expansion slots, you can only open one application at a time, your scans lack the required tonal depth for quality reproduction, and you can't output PostScript separations for preflight. What you've really done is put yourself $1,600 in the hole—a bitter pill to swallow while you sell these items to a home-user with less intensive needs and head back to the drawing board.

[2] A productive workstation requires more than these basic components. The remaining functionality comes in the form of *peripherals*, or external hardware that connects to your computer. These devices are covered in-depth elsewhere in this book. For info on hard drives and other storage media, see Chapter 6, "Media Dexterity: Transport and Storage." For info on scanner technology, see Chapter 10, "Scanning Line Art and Halftones," and Chapter 12, "Scanning and Adjusting Color Images."

When investing in computer technology, you must first choose a platform. For the purposes of digital prepress and production, it comes down to two options: a Macintosh (that runs the MacOS) or a PC (that runs Windows). Deciding which to use is an endless source of debate, heated arguments, and political battles.

The MacOS Versus Windows 98

It's almost impossible to compare these operating systems without opening a fat can of worms. People rally around the platform they know best, and thoughtful arguments more often than not descend into finger pointing and one-upmanship. However, the goal of this book is efficient and profitable design and prepress. Years of industry research, testing, and experience has proven time and again that the choice is clear: If the decision-making power is yours, invest in Macintosh-based technology.

True, I've used a Mac since 1987, but my recommendation is not based on personal bias or blind product loyalty. I'm a businessman. I enjoy my work, but in all honesty, my desire to make money is stronger than any need to convert PC users to my favored platform. If a more appropriate platform existed for publishing, I'd switch in a heartbeat. For better or worse, Macintosh is the industry standard for print production and prepress; 80–90% of all digital prepress is Mac-driven. [3]

There is no ignoring the fact that millions of Windows users are actively involved in print publishing, and in no way does this book attempt to leave you out. I would simply be remiss if I glossed over the impact your computer has on the bottom line. If you already use a PC and cannot afford to switch to a new platform, you can still work productively by adhering to the guidelines put forth in the following chapters. (In many ways, this information is

FOOTNOTE

[3] The Macintosh was created to be a graphics machine from its very inception; the PC was created to be a number cruncher. The first PCs couldn't display graphics, and only supported text at one size; Macs supported graphics, fonts, and different type-sizes from the start. Everything that makes digital prepress possible became commercially viable on the Macintosh first, including PostScript (the linchpin of the graphics industry), film output, and support for high-res color images. On the PC, these features were added as afterthoughts in an attempt to compete in the blossoming graphics industry.

more vital to Windows users—your files generally have a much smaller margin for error than work created and processed on a Mac.) Extensive studies have shown, however, that you will not be as productive or profitable using a Windows-based workflow. It's not your fault; responsibility rests squarely on the shoulders of an operating system that was never fully developed to handle the intricacies of print.

Most Windows users are naturally inclined to invest further in the computer platform they already know, assuming it will accommodate the needs of a graphics department. Let's examine some of the more prominent considerations when making such a purchase:

- **Industry market share.** Although most financial statements and stock reports indicate that Apple has a market share of only 8–10%, this figure refers to the *total* installed user base. In the graphics industry, over 60% of us use Macs, while less than 25% use Windows (the rest are divided between UNIX, OS2, and other systems). This means a wider support base for Mac users, and a much greater likelihood that your files will be compatible with the needs of your vendors, freelancers, and new personnel. [4]

- **Print industry focus.** Microsoft has declared in no uncertain terms that its future rests in Internet and multimedia technology. Although Apple actively pursues these areas as well, it has never deviated from its active support of print publishing. Software manufacturers will continue to develop products for Windows, but users can expect few print-oriented enhancements to Windows itself in the future.

FOOTNOTE

[4] Back in the mid-'90s, when Apple's stock plunged to an all-time low, rumors of its imminent demise swept through the industry. Many new graphics departments made their initial investment in PCs (and many existing ones switched over), fearing they would be left without active support. Apple has bounced back, and its market penetration is higher than ever. Many CEOs and supervisors, seeing how their decisions resulted in decreased productivity and higher maintenance costs, are switching back.

- **Output reliability.** For years, service bureaus have had a more difficult time outputting PC files. Because they are unable to predict how the PC is going to handle the PostScript code, they never know how long a file will take to print. Longer, unpredictable processing times mean that service bureaus have to charge extra for Windows-based files—usually on the order of 50–100% more. [5]

- **Established software.** It is widely understood that new software is released for the Windows platform first, because it enjoys such a larger market share. This is true for most business applications, Internet development software, multimedia authoring tools, and games—but not for print publishing. Because the market share for this industry is slanted heavily against Windows, most new and important advances are available for Macintosh first.

- **More speed for less money.** Speed and cost issues have long plagued Apple, and for good reason. For years, PCs were simply cheaper and faster. The new G3 and G4 towers are quickly changing that perception. They now cost the same as a comparably equipped PC, and even *PC Week* magazine reported that a 300MHz G3 is 47% faster than a 400MHz Pentium II when running graphics applications. (Because the main improvement to the Pentium III processor is the addition of the Katmai multimedia extension set, speed increases from the Pentium II are minimal.)

- **Average return on investment (ROI).** According to a number of studies, the average Mac user produces 6.5 times ROI over a three-year period, as opposed to slightly more than 2 times ROI by a Windows user. These studies also claim that the average Mac-based graphics professional generates over $25,000 in annual revenue (and over $13,000 in net profit) more than a Windows-based professional with similar skills, doing the same work on a comparable computer, does.

FOOTNOTE

5 The release of Adobe Acrobat 4.0 and a growing number of PDF workflow solutions offer the hope of true cross-platform output efficiency. If a file is properly converted to PDF, it can be opened, reviewed, proofed, and printed from any workstation—at least in theory. A growing number of success stories is being reported by companies who are shifting to an entirely PDF-based workflow. But until a universal set of standards arises that is accepted and understood by the general production community, PDF will not be an adequate solution for the common masses.

- **True "Plug and Play."** Installing a peripheral device on a Mac is as easy as connecting the cables, plugging it in, and turning it on. Even on Windows 98, the user must manually install a driver that allows the operating system to recognize the device. Depending on the device (and user experience), this may require the services of a consultant.

- **Viruses.** Windows-based Intel computers are more likely to be infected by viruses than any other platform. To date, only one truly destructive virus, "AutoStart," has surfaced on the Mac. (See Chapter 3, "Optimizing Your Work Environment," for more info.)

- **Hardware development standards.** One of the reasons it is so difficult to "master" the PC is that so many different companies manufacture PC clones, each one following a unique set of standards. If you master the intricacies of a particular video card, for example, you know only one of a huge variety available on the market. On the other hand, Apple strictly enforces a series of development standards that determine how hardware will connect to a Mac. All manufacturers adhere to these guidelines.

All this isn't to say that Windows is down for the count. Future versions promise to resolve many of the issues that reduce productivity in a publishing environment, and many major software vendors (such as Adobe) are working diligently to make prepress more viable in a PC-based workflow. In fact, many widely used proprietary software packages for trapping and imposition exist only for Windows. Although we all know someone who swears up and down that he is twice as productive on a PC than anyone on a Mac, this is rare—at least in print, the only industry addressed by this book.

Windows NT

If you're serious about digital prepress in a Windows environment, you should be using Windows NT 4.0 (or higher). This operating system is not only faster than Windows 98, it operates with a stability that makes even hard-core Mac enthusiasts a little envious. Windows NT is also required to take advantage of the full power of the new Pentium chips and multiprocessor systems.

Windows 95 was written to allow users to make the transition from the 16-bit Windows 3.1. As a result, a lot of 16-bit code, which runs far less efficiently than 32-bit, pollutes the system. (Windows 98 offers little relief—it's still a combination of 16- and 32-bit code.) To make matters worse, 16-bit code is processed more slowly on a new Pentium II chip than on an older

Pentium. The code has to go through another step, called *thunking*, which converts the 16-bit code into data the 32-bit processor can use. The architecture of Windows NT was designed from the ground up to be native 32-bit, so it runs faster and more efficiently than Windows 95/98.

Windows NT offers other advantages to the production environment. *Preemptive multitasking* enables the processor to be shared simultaneously by multiple applications. Although the MacOS and Windows 95/98 allow you to open multiple applications, they don't allow for true multitasking. For example, you can't copy a file, format a drive, and edit an image in Photoshop at the same time. Certain utilities may provide this feature, but they result in a significant performance decrease in all of the applications involved. Multitasking in Windows NT results in no overall performance hit.

Windows NT also uses *protected memory*, which means that programs open in their own isolated segment of RAM. If they crash, they don't affect any other open applications. If a program crashes in MacOS or Windows 95/98, there's a good chance you'll lose everything that hasn't been saved in any open application. This rarely happens with Windows NT.

The big drawback to Windows NT is that hardware and software must be configured very precisely in order to work. All communication between software and hardware is controlled by the operating system, as opposed to the hardware/software combination used by MacOS and Windows 95/98. This means that any hardware you want to use must be specifically designed with Windows NT in mind. You must also use 32-bit native software. If you're willing to make the investment in money and configuration, the advantages of NT far outweigh these drawbacks. [6]

The Processor

If you think of the CPU as a brain, the *processor* is the cerebral cortex. This chip is where the active thinking takes place—or in computer terms, where instructions and data are calculated. A seemingly simple rule applies: The faster the processor, the faster the computer. However, the way the processor

---

FOOTNOTE

[6] If you want the advantages of NT but still need to run Windows 95 or 98, you can create a double- or triple-booting system by installing all of these operating systems on your computer. You simply decide at startup which system you want to operate. (You can't change operating systems without restarting the computer.) Consult the manual that came with your system software for more information.

is constructed also affects its performance, which makes any "speed rating" less obvious than it seems. There are two ways to determine the potential performance of a processor: its type and its clock speed. Rather than have you wade through a comparative history of processors (and there have been dozens, dating back to the early '80s and beyond), let's just consider the ones currently in widespread use.

As of this writing, all new Macintosh computers—with the exception of PowerBooks—ship with the G4 processor, Motorola's latest PowerPC chip. Many older computers based on the G3 and PowerPC 604 processors are still in heavy rotation. (Take the term "older" with a grain of salt; new G3s are still readily available, and they only replaced the 604 a little over a year ago.) On the PC side, units are now shipping with the Pentium III processor, Intel's latest chip version. The Pentium III is a modest upgrade from the Pentium II, its predecessor. Certain new multimedia functions have been built into it, but the speed is otherwise pretty much the same. What do all these names mean? Nothing, really. They're just designations that differentiate between chip types, not measures of performance—typically, each new chip type is simply given a higher number than its predecessor. [7]

A number that does mean something is the *clock speed*, a value measured in megahertz (MHz) that states how quickly a particular chip can process a single command. However, many people believe that you can determine which computer is the fastest just by comparing clock speeds. This isn't helped by the fact that ads in computer catalogs blare "450MHz!" in banner-size type, as if it were some definitive measure of performance. When you consider that a 400MHz Pentium II processor runs about 50% slower than a 300MHz G3, you can see that accurate comparison is more difficult than it seems.

F O O T N O T E

[7] Of course, many more chip types are scattered around the industry. Whether you should upgrade depends on how the computer is used. The first PowerMac computers were based on the PowerPC 601—a capable chip in its day, but when compared to the latest models, it is best suited for text entry, accounting, and casual Internet use. The same goes for the original Pentium, which runs at a fraction of the speed of a Pentium II. Other popular (but less-applicable) chips include the PowerPC 603, used in certain pre-G3 PowerBooks and Mac clones, and the Pentium Celeron, a low-end chip used in consumer-oriented PCs. If you're using any of these processors for high-end graphics work, you should upgrade immediately. The speed increase you'll enjoy will quickly repay the investment.

You can only compare clock speeds within the same processor family. For example, you can easily tell that a 450MHz G3 is faster than a 300MHz G3, and a 500MHz Pentium III is faster than a 450MHz Pentium III. When comparing different processors, you must rely on published benchmarks or your own specific tests (if you have access to the computers). It's difficult to give exact speed numbers, because no processor functions in complete isolation. For the most part, in a publishing environment, the following comparisons apply: A G3 runs almost twice as fast as a similarly equipped Pentium III, and 1.5 times faster than a PowerPC 604. A new G4 will run at more than twice the speed of a similarly equipped G3.

What Processor Should You Get?

After you've determined the platform you intend to pursue, choosing the right processor speed is easy. Get the fastest one you can reasonably afford (and don't consider getting anything less than a higher-end G3/G4 or Pentium II/III). If you're using an older computer—anything less than a 150MHz 604 or 200MHz Pentium II—it's time to think about donating it to a school. The increase in performance between the latest chips and their predecessors is so great that if you haven't upgraded yet, you're throwing away time and money.

Fortunately, we live in an age where computers are dirt cheap, and speed increases are becoming a little redundant. Consider the fact that the Mac IIci I bought in 1991 cost over $3,500, but my G3 tower—that runs over 200 times faster—cost only $1,700. To be honest, today's highest-end computers are so fast, only the most intensive users will notice any difference between the 350MHz and 450–500MHz models. Once you've achieved the ability to edit in real-time, it's tough to get any faster. In fact, a colleague recently processed samples of his work on different processor speeds, and found their performance so similar that he chose the "slower" 350MHz unit, opting to spend the leftover $700 on RAM.

Upgradable Processors

When the time comes to upgrade your computer, you may not have to purchase an entirely new unit. Processors exist in one of three ways: They are soldered to the motherboard, attached to a card, or inserted in a removable socket. When the processor is soldered to the motherboard, which usually happens with older computers, you can only upgrade by replacing the entire board, and the expense can easily approach the cost of a new unit. (Upgrade cards for soldered processors are available, but they typically provide only a fraction of the benefits of a complete processor upgrade.) If the processor is on a card or in a socket, you can upgrade cheaply, easily, and with a high degree of compatibility with your existing hardware and software.

All Macs currently in production ship with upgradable processors, as do most higher-end PCs. Many of the low-cost PCs don't. An upgradable processor is worth the extra expense because it extends the useful life of your computer, ensuring that you get the most from your investment.

Random Access Memory (RAM)

If the processor determines how fast a computer can think, the amount of installed RAM determines how much it can think about at one time. Although RAM is memory, you should not confuse it with your hard drive. Instead of storing data, it provides the dynamic workplace you need to run programs and execute commands.

When an application lies dormant and unused, it simply takes up space on your drive, like a car resting in a garage. Launch the program, and it needs a large, fast chunk of memory in which to process files and execute commands—in essence, an open highway. When you open an application, all or part of it loads directly into the computer's RAM. Why? Because RAM is lightning fast. These chips have no moving parts—all activity is a pure dance of electricity through silicon. Even if it were possible to run a program straight from your hard drive, the speed of these mechanisms are measured in milliseconds (millionths of a second). This may seem fast, until you realize that RAM speed is measured in nanoseconds (billionths of a second).

Of course, there's a trade-off. Many people ask, if RAM is so fast, why can't we use it in place of a hard drive? Because it is volatile; you can't save information to these chips. Quitting a program, shutting down the computer, or crashing will purge whatever information may be contained in RAM. [8]

FOOTNOTE

[8] When you launch a program, a copy of the application files are loaded into RAM, leaving the originals untouched. Likewise, when you open a file, the part you work on is loaded into RAM, and the rest remains on the drive until you specifically access it. When you save a file, you actually write the contents of the RAM to the hard drive, which ensures that you can retrieve it later on.

How Much RAM Is Enough?

The most commonly made mistake when setting up a computer is not pur-chasing enough RAM. So many times, I've seen people buy a top-of-the-line model, only to be frustrated by the slow processing times and "Insufficient Memory" alerts when they try to get their work done.

It's long been known that prepress applications are among the most RAM-intensive on the market. Indeed, the latest application versions contain new features that consume monstrous amounts of memory. However, even pro-grams that once required very little RAM have become some of the biggest hogs. (For example, Microsoft now recommends a minimum of 80MB for running Microsoft Office.) Where there was once a predictable amount of memory one would need, there now appears to be no limit. Fortunately, RAM prices are a fraction of what they used to be.

Rather than go point-by-point through specific memory requirements, you can follow a single guideline: The absolute minimum RAM required for pre-press and publishing is 128MB. Anything less, and you make an unfortu-nate compromise in speed and stability. 128MB is the magic number in another way. A side effect of the new range of less-expensive computers is that nearly every model has fewer RAM slots—most contain only two or three, which provides very little room for expansion. For example, if you've already filled your slots with 64MB chips, you'll need to discard some of the RAM you already have when you want to add more. By starting with a sin-gle 128MB DIMM, you can easily install additional chips while retaining your original investment. As of this writing, 128MB DIMMS cost between $200–300—a nominal sum. [9]

Purchasing RAM

Computers ship with a certain amount of RAM already installed—usually 32 or 64MB. You have to add more when you buy a new unit. You can have your computer vendor install the RAM prior to shipping, or you can order it through a third-party mail-order company and install it yourself. Both meth-ods have their advantages.

FOOTNOTE

[9] Installing the necessary RAM is only half the battle. If you're using a Mac, you must manually allocate a specific amount of RAM to each application, which deter-mines how much they will use when launched. (Windows programs automatically take the RAM they need—no user input is necessary.) See Chapter 3 for more info.

Vendor-installed RAM is immediately available when you turn on your computer, relieving you from having to tinker with the insides. You might have to pay a little more, but the work should be guaranteed. Even better, if a stray static spark happens to fry the motherboard during installation, your vendor has to replace it free of charge (if you fry it yourself, you're out of luck). Many computer vendors offer discounts on RAM, as long as you purchase the computer from them as well. Bargain with them; it never hurts to ask.

On the other hand, you can often find a great deal on RAM through catalogs or the Internet. Installing RAM yourself is safe and easy, as long as you follow the instructions provided by the third-party company. (If they don't provide instructions, take your business elsewhere.) However, not all RAM is created equal, and the buyer must beware when purchasing mail-order chips. Some RAM vendors are able to sell their product for ridiculously low prices because their product is either of inferior quality or recycled from the chips of older memory cards. Bad RAM is one of the primary causes of computer malfunction, and unless you know what you're looking for, the cause of the problems will be hard to pin down. If you purchase your own RAM, only buy from a company that offers an unconditional satisfaction guarantee and a lifetime warranty. Or stick with brand names that are known for their reliability, such as Viking (www.vikingcomponents.com) or Kingston (www.kingston.com).

Expansion

The platform, processor, and RAM all affect the potential speed and efficiency of your computer, but this is only part of what you need to consider when setting up a prepress system. You will add many other components, such as internal and external hard drives, scanners, monitors, video cards, and so forth. The number you can add (and how easy it is to add them) depends on three things: your expansion bays, expansion slots, and ports.

Expansion Bays

Expansion bays enable you to insert additional drives inside the CPU. Historically, PCs have featured more bays than Macs, largely because the ports that allow you to daisy-chain devices to the computer—such as SCSI (and more recently, USB or FireWire)—have always been standard on the Macintosh. These ports make it very easy to add external drives to the computer, reducing the need for internal bays.

Many people have tried to buy computers with as many bays as possible, thereby allowing the greatest amount of expandability. However, most people found that they rarely used them. External drives have proven to be much more versatile. They're much easier to change or move around, whereas any time you need to change an internal drive you have to ground yourself (to eliminate static electricity), crack open the case, and muck around inside your computer with a screwdriver. If an internal device breaks, the entire system needs to be taken off-line to fix it. Also, the more internal devices installed inside your CPU, the hotter the computer runs, reducing its life span. The only advantage to internal drives is that their lack of cases or power supplies make them less expensive than external devices. Most people find that the extra $20 to $50 for an external drive is well worth it.

Most often, two expansion bays are quite adequate on any system with an external SCSI, USB, or FireWire port. Use one bay for an internal CD-ROM drive, and the other for a secondary hard drive (or internal zip).

Expansion Slots

On the other hand, expansion slots greatly enhance the usefulness of your computer. Expansion slots hold cards that add specific functionality to the computer, such as internal modems, additional SCSI ports, video cards, and 3D rendering accelerators. Sometimes called *buses*, slots will generally enhance a Windows-based computer more, again because many features that only exist as options on a PC are typically built into a Mac. It is often necessary to purchase and insert additional cards into a PC for features such as sound and increased video capabilities.

It was once possible to go through life without having to add extra cards to your Macintosh, but this is not necessarily the case with newer models. Following in the steps of their PC counterparts, more and more once-standard options are now placed on cards. This results in a less costly, more configurable computer, but features such as serial and SCSI ports—built into Macs for well over a decade—now require extra cards. Soon, ADB ports will follow suit. Eventually, USB and FireWire will replace serial, SCSI, and ADB ports completely, but during the transitional period you may find that you need to invest in a card or two to keep working with your current equipment. [10]

Working with expansion slots is easier than ever. In recent years, both platforms have made the migration to PCI cards. Manufacturers are now able to make one card for both computer types, changing only the software required by the operating system. This means that cards can be produced more cheaply than ever. For example, video cards that once would have set you back thousands are available for just a few hundred dollars.

The two primary types of slots on the PC are ISA and PCI. ISA, like the Mac's older NuBus, is slower than PCI. Just as NuBus has been completely phased out, ISA is currently being phased out of Windows machines in favor of the superior PCI card. ISA cards, however, are much more prevalent than NuBus cards ever were, so it is taking some time to eradicate them completely. ISA cards still have their usefulness because of their lower cost. For the highest degree of compatibility to meet your needs now and in the future, get a computer with a minimum of three ISA slots and four PCI slots.

Ports

Ports enable you to attach peripheral devices to your computer. On older Macs, this is a breeze. The SCSI port is standard, so if you buy a SCSI peripheral that the manufacturer specifies as being compatible with the Macintosh, it's virtually guaranteed you can attach the device to one of the ports and have it work with a minimum of effort. This is more problematic on the new Macs. SCSI is no longer included as a standard feature, although it's *still* the standard in terms of prepress production. (The majority of high-quality production peripherals are SCSI based.) USB and FireWire will eventually replace the need for SCSI, but there are currently no production-quality USB devices available, and FireWire devices are very scarce.

FOOTNOTE

[10] In one of the most infuriating corporate moves Apple ever made, they released their blue G3 towers in January 1999 with no built-in SCSI support, and no prior notice of this change to manufacturers. This meant that anyone who bought one could not connect it to any of their existing SCSI devices (such as external drives, transport media, or scanners) without first purchasing a new SCSI expansion card. The problem was, *every* available SCSI card on the market was incompatible with the architecture of the blue G3s. For over a month, hundreds of thousands of professional users could only sit by and crack their knuckles until the SCSI card manufacturers came out with compatible hardware. Fortunately, a variety of compatible SCSI cards now exist, all for under $100.

PCs use less-expensive EIDE ports—and increasingly, USB ports—instead of SCSI ports. EIDE is inferior to SCSI in many ways, and is generally regarded as unacceptable in a production environment. EIDE controllers can only support two devices, whereas SCSI controllers support up to seven daisy-chainable items. This is important, considering the large number of peripheral devices used in a typical prepress workflow. Also, EIDE controllers use the computer's processor to handle information, while SCSI controllers use their own built-in hardware. This means that EIDE decreases overall computer performance by using up valuable processor time in ways which SCSI controllers do not.

Windows users should consider adding a PCI-based SCSI controller to their PCs, which makes it easier to add and remove peripherals and increases overall computer performance. An additional benefit is that if you are using computers in a mixed Windows and Macintosh environment, you will be able to share drives between the computers with relative ease.

Monitors

The typical graphics professional spends the vast majority of the day staring at his monitor. Connecting a substandard viewing device to a high-end workstation is like wearing three-dollar sunglasses with an Armani suit; you may look good, but you'll always wind up with a headache.

A staggering array of monitor types are available, from ancient 12-inch black-and-whites to Apple's new 22-inch full-color CinemaVision LCD panel, and the costs range from a couple hundred to several thousand dollars. In a design and prepress environment, however, your choices are somewhat narrowed. For the best results, invest in a 21-inch color monitor. (If you're involved in color correcting and intensive image editing, you will likely benefit from an accelerated graphics card. See "Accelerated Graphics Cards," later this section.) Not so long ago, 21-inch monitors were so expensive, only the biggest guns in the industry could afford them. The rest of us had to settle for 15-, 17-, or 19-inch models. Today, the average cost of the typical 21-inch monitor is around $1,300, with some models as low as $800–900. It may be tempting to save a little money by picking up that $400 17-inch unit, but consider the advantages of going full-size:

• You can view letter-sized spreads in page layout programs at actual size, without having to zoom or scroll.

- When working in multiple applications, you can place large document or image windows side by side, enabling you to jump back and forth more easily, and better take advantage of many drag-and-drop features.

- When editing an image in Photoshop, you can see more of the image at once, enabling you to edit more efficiently without forcing the screen to refresh as you navigate to different image areas.

- You can set the resolution of many smaller monitors to a 21-inch equivalent, which theoretically gives you the same workable real estate. Unfortunately, this makes the icons so small, you have to squint to make them out. A true 21-inch monitor gives you over 50% more screen space than a 17-inch, without reducing the size of the onscreen contents.

- Studies indicate that every person who uses a 21-inch monitor claims to work more happily and efficiently than with smaller sizes. Believe it or not, I've even seen users profess an undying love for their specific viewing device. When a small additional investment results in such increased user satisfaction, it can only lead to higher productivity.

Choosing a Monitor

Even when you decide to purchase a 21-inch monitor, there are still over four dozen models from which to choose. It's worth noting that some issues that used to impact overall viewing quality are no longer such a big deal. Cathode-ray tube types (aperture grille and shadow-mask) and screen shapes (flat or convex) are so well-developed now that any difference between them is negligible. Aside from reading published comparisons and reviews, the best way to determine the best one for you is to simply try out a few. Understanding the following issues should help you weed through the available options.

Viewable Image Size

Although a monitor may be labeled "21 inches," the actual size is almost always a little smaller. If you look at most monitors, you'll see that the viewable area doesn't extend all the way to the edges of the screen. On average, the viewable area of a 21-inch monitor is around 19.5 inches, but it varies according to the manufacturer. (All monitors offer controls that enable you to extend the viewable area to cover the entire screen. Unfortunately, doing so usually results in blurred image detail along the outer edges.)

Resolution

All monitors are based on a grid of pixels, similar to a Photoshop image. *Monitor resolution* measures the dimensions of the viewing area, or the number of these pixels that extend vertically and horizontally across the screen. Most new 21-inch monitors can display up to a 1,600×1,200–pixel area. (In comparison, a 17-inch monitor displays at 1,024×768 pixels, and a 13-inch monitor displays at 640×480 pixels.)

Most monitors these days are *multisync*, which means you can change the onscreen resolution on-the-fly. For example, you can set a 17-inch Apple Studio Design monitor (connected to a G3) to seven different resolutions, ranging from 640×480 to 1,600×1,200. This isn't as good an idea as it sounds. When you increase the resolution of a smaller monitor, you decrease the *refresh rate*, or the number of times per second the screen is redrawn. If the refresh rate is too low, the screen will flicker noticeably, which quickly leads to eye fatigue and headaches. When setting a resolution, you'll want a refresh rate of at least 75Hz, though in my experience, 85Hz is best for a flicker-free picture. (See Chapter 3 for more info.)

Dot Pitch

Dot pitch measures the distance between the electron beams that stimulate the phosphors on the monitor's screen. When the beams are closer together—in other words, when the dot pitch is lower—your work will appear more crisp and finely detailed onscreen. For most uses, a dot pitch of .28mm or lower is sufficient. If you're only interested in the sharpest display, some models go as low as .22 or .23mm. Expect to pay slightly more for extra-low dot pitch.

Additional Color Features

Many monitors are sold with bundled color-oriented tools, such as a colorimeter, built-in ColorSync tables, calibration cups, or color matching software. More often than not, these items add to the cost of the unit. Unless you're absolutely certain these tools will contribute to your work—for example, if you're establishing a color-managed workflow—you don't need them.

Accelerated Graphics Cards

Your Mac or PC already has built-in video support, driven by an expansion card or directly from the motherboard. Most new high-end computers can display up to 16.7 million colors on a 21-inch monitor. If the bulk of your work consists of page layout or simple images, you do not need additional support. However, even if your monitor supports high resolutions at high refresh rates (75Hz or more), RAM-intensive programs like Illustrator or Photoshop may max out your computer's built-in video. When this happens, you'll notice that your screen starts to flicker or redraw more slowly when editing very complex artwork or large images.

The solution is a graphics accelerator card, which boosts the signal sent to your monitor from the CPU. This keeps your monitor's refresh rate high, regardless of the complexity of a given file. It's difficult to recommend a particular card, because the one you need depends on the type of computer and monitor. For the best results, though, be sure your card features the following:

- At least 8MB of installed RAM, preferably 16MB.

- The capability to display 32-bit color (millions of colors) at your monitor's highest resolution, at a refresh rate of at least 85Hz.

- A 128-bit graphics engine, which transfers more data at a faster rate between the computer's on-board video support and the accelerator card.

Most video cards cost less than $300, with many exceptional brands (such as ATI's Rage series) available for under $200. If you've ever had the feeling you were waiting needlessly while your screen redrew, you were probably right. Assume that a nonaccelerated system forces you to wait an extra five seconds every time the screen needs to refresh. Say this happens 40 times a day (a conservative estimate for high-end users). Over an average working year, this means you've spent 14 hours staring at the screen, waiting to continue.

Adding a Second Monitor

Not many people realize it, but all Macs (and some PCs running Windows 98) can support as many monitors as you have video cards in your computer. After adding an accelerator card, it's as easy as plugging a second monitor into your computer's built-in video port.

Graphics applications all use a series of floating pallets. They provide handy access to a program's tools and commands, but palettes also obscure your work, and most users are forever opening, closing, and moving them around. You can drag all the palettes over to the second screen, leaving your primary workspace uncluttered and free from obstruction. The palettes will always appear on the second screen whenever you launch an application. Because you'll only use the second monitor for palettes, speed and color fidelity are not critical. I know several people who simply hooked up a 13-inch color monitor, which you can find used for around $50.

The Software

Compared to purchasing and configuring hardware for a prepress environment, determining the software you need is easy. A series of applications is already firmly established as an industry standard, and most of them are covered in this book. To accommodate the different stages of your projects, you'll need to invest in six types of software:

- A universally compatible word processing program for entering and editing text, as well as converting any text files you receive into a usable format.

- A vector-based illustration program, for creating and editing PostScript artwork.

- A pixel-based editing program, for editing and refining scanned images.

- A layout program, for combining words and graphics into a series of printable pages.

- Fonts (and a utility to manage them), so you can have access to a variety of typefaces.

- System and disk maintenance utilities, to optimize the performance of your operating system.

The specific programs you need to purchase depend on your professional responsibilities. If you're a designer, you can safely choose one application from each area, then learn them to the best of your ability. For example, use Word, Illustrator, Photoshop, and XPress. If you're in the position of processing client files, whether as a service bureau, print shop, or quick-print company, you must broaden your range of software packages. For example, a service bureau specializing in high-res film output will require all the major packages described in this section to accommodate the variety of files produced by its clients. On the other hand, a retail quick-print shop usually caters to home-users as well, which requires that it also invest in programs like Deneba Canvas, Microsoft Publisher, and CorelDRAW. [11]

The Word Processor

Word processing programs enable you to enter and edit text before you import it into a page layout. Some people avoid purchasing a word processor, believing they can simply enter all their text directly into a layout document. Page layout programs were intended to format and handle text, not enter it from scratch. Sure, you can enter a few lines here and there, but if you try to write extensive passages, problems arise. The files produced by a word processor are small and easily transported between a series of other word processors, even across different platforms—virtues often lacking in page layout programs. Plus, if you receive text files from a freelancer or copywriter, there's no guarantee that your layout program will recognize the format. Most word processors can extract the text from almost any other file type, which allows you to edit the contents and resave it into a compatible format.

On the flip side, you should avoid trying to perform page layout in a word processing program. This might seem obvious, yet people attempt it with alarming frequency. We have the software manufacturers to blame for this. In the never-ending battle to create a word processor that will dominate all others, software manufacturers add more and more features to their word processors. And so you get 75MB monstrosities like Microsoft Word, which try to do everything but write the actual text, when all you really need is a program that's small, fast, and works without crashing.

FOOTNOTE

[11] This book focuses only on software proven to be reliable and productive additions to a print publishing environment. However, new software and utilities come and go on a near-daily basis. Some manufacturer or another is always promoting what they believe to be the Next Great Thing, and it's easy to be seduced by a well-targeted marketing claim of increased profitability. Hold one piece of advice close to your heart, especially when you're first starting out: Don't be a pioneer. Sure, being the first to succeed with some new program or workflow will win you the respect and admiration of your colleagues, but failure is costly. Can you afford to spend your time mastering an unproven product, one that more than likely isn't supported by a wide user base? If you insist on using an untried, untested, and unproven method, go right ahead—no one will try to stop you. In fact, plenty of people will be there to dissect your experiences (especially your failures) as they make their own future claims about what is right or wrong with the industry. If you want to do your best to guarantee that your files output and print correctly the first time, stick with the industry standards.

Microsoft Word 97/98 is the preferred word processor, mainly because it is the most predominantly used. Other word processors are faster, more reliable, and take up fewer resources than Word, but in this industry, following the crowd is sometimes the key to productivity. Implementing the most commonly used program ensures that the files you create or receive will most likely be recognized and opened by everyone involved in the process. If you don't use Word 97/98, be sure your word processor can open and save Word 97/98 files in their native format. Fortunately, Word 97/98 is such an industry standard that most other word processors can open and save its files.

Microsoft Office 2000 (for Windows) and Office 98 (for Mac) are both available for under $400.

Once you import a text file into a page layout, you still have to format the text and flow it properly throughout the document. See Chapter 14, "Page Layout Issues," for more info.

The Vector-Based Graphics Program

Programs such as Illustrator and FreeHand are vector-based, which means that the image information is mathematically defined, scalable, and geared for high-resolution output. This type of artwork offers several key advantages:

- A production-level illustration program writes true Level 2 or 3 PostScript code that outputs to any PostScript-compatible imagesetter at the highest possible resolution.

- Vector-based artwork can be scaled to any degree, from pin-hole to billboard size, with no loss of resolution, data, or quality. This makes it the standard for producing graphics such as corporate logos and clip art.

- The artwork is infinitely editable. You can make as many changes to it as you want without losing important image information.

The industry-standard vector-based program is Adobe Illustrator, followed by Macromedia FreeHand. The one you decide to use is not just a matter of personal preference—it's also a matter of what your vendors support and what they can output most reliably. CorelDRAW and Deneba Canvas both are fun programs capable of producing fine artwork, but if their files are not supported by your service bureau, you're always at risk. Before investing time, money, and training efforts into a vector-based program, contact your vendors and ask them which one they support most successfully.

Adobe Illustrator 8.0 is available for under $360. Macromedia FreeHand is available for under $400.

For in-depth information on using Illustrator and FreeHand in a production environment, see Chapter 8, "Vector-Based Graphics."

The Pixel-Based Editing Program

Pixel-based images are the flip-side of the graphics coin. Instead of working with individually defined shapes, as with Illustrator or FreeHand, your scans will consist of millions of tiny colored squares, called *pixels*. In the world of print publishing, one pixel-based editing program stands above the rest: Adobe Photoshop, the only one addressed by this book. Several other such programs are available for all platforms, but none come close to matching Photoshop's industry support and reliability when it comes to producing quality color separations. Photoshop users also enjoy wide third-party developer support, nearly unlimited training opportunities, and hundreds of available instructional books. Simply put, it is probably the most important production-oriented weapon in your arsenal. Photoshop 5.5 is available for under $600.

For more information on editing a pixel-based image, see Chapter 9, "Digital Imaging Fundamentals." For info on scanning, see Chapter 10, "Scanning Line Art and Halftones," Chapter 11, "Color Spaces and Printing," and Chapter 12, "Scanning and Adjusting Color Images." For a list of the techniques you'll likely need to know on the job, see Chapter 13, "Photoshop Production Techniques."

The Page Layout Software

Your page layout is where you combine text files, vector-based graphics, and pixel-based scans into a cohesive publication. It is the final stage of your creative process, completed before proofing, outputting, and reproducing a project on-press.

Three standard page layout programs are available: QuarkXPress 4.04, Adobe PageMaker 6.5, and Adobe InDesign 1.0. There are other programs out there, such as Microsoft Publisher and Corel Ventura, but none of them share the same industrywide support. Before you use any other program, check with your vendors to find out what page layout program gives the most consistently reliable separations.

QuarkXPress is available for under $700. PageMaker is available for under $500. InDesign is available for under $700.

For more information on working with a page layout document, see Chapter 14, "Page Layout Issues." For more info on quality-checking and trouble-shooting a completed document, see Chapter 16, "Preflight and File Prep."

Fonts

If you want to use a series of different typefaces in your work (beyond the dozen or two unimpressive options that are automatically installed on each operating system), you must acquire them yourself. Bear in mind that fonts are hands-down the most commonly pirated software in the industry. They're such small, innocuous-looking things, many people don't even realize that giving a copy or two to a friend constitutes theft. Sometimes it happens almost by accident. For example, vendors who process client files routinely accept client font files as well, for the purposes of viewing and output. This is perfectly legal—however, if the vendor's type library is a loosely organized collection of fonts, client type is often mixed in with the legally owned files. As soon as someone uses a font they never paid for, even if they don't realize it, the law has been broken.

Over time, you'll build up a library of hundreds, even thousands of fonts. Font resources include Adobe's Font Folio, a collection of over 2,300 PostScript Type 1 fonts that costs $9,000, to a number of individual font families available for $30–200, to an enormous variety of typefaces you can download for free on the Internet. Large design firms typically benefit from large type libraries; service bureaus, which usually rely on client-supplied fonts, don't need to purchase as many. Take a look around, determine what style of type will best serve your needs, and invest as necessary. [12]

FOOTNOTE

[12] Unless your work immediately demands it, don't feel pressured into purchasing large quantities of fonts up front. Many users start off with a base amount, maybe 40 to 50, then buy new ones only when the need arises. Most online font vendors allow you to download the files immediately on credit card payment. Adobe's Type On Call CD is another fine resource, bundled for free with most Adobe software (or available for under $70). It contains the 2,300-typeface Font Folio, and all you need to do is phone Adobe with the desired font and a credit card number, and you're given a password to unlock the protected CD files and use the font. The beauty of working this way is that the cost of a new font is easily passed on to the client whose work requires it.

After you've amassed your fonts and begin to use them in an active environment, you must still develop a method of organizing them on your hard drive. A font management utility such as ATM Deluxe or Extensis Suitcase will prove indispensable for turning your fonts on and off as you work. For more information on handling your fonts in a production environment, see Chapter 4, "Font Management."

Maintenance Utilities

After your computer, operating system, applications, and fonts are installed and running, you must have a way to keep them all running as smoothly and trouble-free as possible. Your hard drive will become fragmented over time, which slows down overall performance. You must reduce the number of inevitable system crashes, as well as recover from the occasional freeze. You must scan your system for corrupt or incompatible software. You must configure your Control Panels to get as much speed out of your system as possible. You must scan for and repair any viruses that find their way into your workplace.

These are good things for everyone who works on computers to do, but few activities place more demands on your entire system than digital prepress. System maintenance is vital, and you'll find that the solution comes as a series of third-party utilities, improved working methods, and a system configuration that best handles the rigors of print. For more information (and a list of recommended utilities), see Chapter 3. [13]

FOOTNOTE

[13] The temptation to tinker with the system software of a new computer is strong. Therefore, a word of warning: Before tampering with your computer using third-party software, be sure that you know what you're doing, that you use the most current versions of the utilities, and that you've backed up all of your data. Failure to do this can result in lost work, lost hours, and lost hope. For example, a colleague recently discovered the hard way that running an outdated version of Norton Disk Doctor on a system running MacOS 8.6 can permanently destroy all the data on the drive. If you're not sure what to do when your new equipment is delivered—particularly if a new computer is replacing an old one, and you haven't upgraded all your software—enlist the services of a professional.

Knowledge Resources

Getting your investment to work for you day after day is an ongoing adventure, a game of strategy, skill, and a little bit of luck. If using your equipment properly was as easy as buying and installing it, then businesses would have been spared millions in losses due to misprinted materials in the last year alone. It takes years to become an expert in any given field, and graphics is no exception. You can expect to gain a certain amount of knowledge through your own successes and failures. (In fact, you'll always make mistakes—but the more you know, the less costly they'll be, and the more quickly you can recover from them.) Fortunately, you can take advantage of a number of additional knowledge resources that will accelerate your learning curve.

Training

Nothing adds value and retains its worth more than proper training. Even the most expensive cutting-edge hardware and software is of little use if the people who run it don't know what they're doing. A year from now, your hardware will be worth a fraction of what you paid for it, but the know-how acquired from focused training efforts will only increase in value. Considering the potential cost of a typical output or printing error, a training effort that teaches you to avoid even a single mistake will pay for itself with every job you accomplish.

True, training can be costly. A single class for a single person can run you $300 and up, and a dedicated effort for an entire department can approach tens of thousands of dollars. This doesn't even include the time that students must spend away from the workplace. This makes it all the more important that you don't simply choose a training company from the Yellow Pages, or blindly accept the services of some smooth-talking consultant who walks through your door. The training you invest in must pertain directly to your work, delivered by intelligent professionals who understand your specific aspect of the industry.

Finding the right training material requires work on your part, as well as the potential trainer. The following guidelines will assist you when your search for quality training begins.

Assessing Your Needs

You must know what kind of work you intend to pursue, what software you'll be using, and what areas of expertise are most needed by you or your staff.

Explaining Your Needs

Before signing up for any class, call the training facility. Explain to them the current status of your skills and technology, and tell them as best you can what you want to accomplish. This is a highly technical field with very little that is intuitive about it, yet people make the mistake of not asking for additional clarification all the time. The training facility should be able to recommend a course for you. If they can't—or if they only try to shoehorn you into a series of general classes that they already offer—consider taking your training dollars elsewhere. Some training facilities even offer a free onsite consultation, where they send a representative to your work site to further assess your needs and develop a plan of action. [14]

Requesting a Course Outline

A good training facility will provide a course outline on request, which enables you to review the goals and content of the class before signing up. It should also clearly state the specific skills you can expect to walk away with at the end of the session. If you're contracting training materials that will be developed specifically for your company, request samples that were

FOOTNOTE

[14] I know one company who had just started to incorporate digital printing technology into its workflow. Its primary business was creating print advertisements, and because it had just purchased six copies of the program (among other things), it decided to send its staff to a Macromedia FreeHand class. While we should applaud the company for recognizing and acting on the need for training, its failure to contact the training facility beforehand led to a wasted effort for everyone involved. Rather than get thoughtful feedback on the future of its new department, it shelled out $2,000 for a creative illustration class, instead of what it really needed: a production-oriented page layout class. The staff learned how to make a few graphical elements, but not how to incorporate them into a layout document, properly define colors, ensure successful output, and so forth. Any benefits of the training were lost because they couldn't put the new info to immediate use in their production environment.

done for other companies. If that info is confidential, consider paying the trainer a small fee to develop a sample training outline based on your exact needs, which you can refuse if necessary. [15]

Looking for Hands-On Training

Ask the facility if it offers hands-on learning, or follows a strict lecture-only format. Lecture-style classes can be valuable when presenting specific information in a short period of time (no more than 2–3 hours), but experience shows that spending a full day in a comfortable chair listening to someone speak is better suited to taking a nap than a professional step forward. More often, you're better off buying a book on the same subject. Humans are experiential beings. We learn far more by doing than by simply watching.

Determining the Appropriate Time Format

Some classes are intensive day-long workshops. Some meet one night a week for several weeks in a row. Some classes meet all day for a week. Day- and week-long courses may seem like a good idea, but can you absorb all the quantity of information they will present? Night courses can be effective, but can you afford to commit to such an extended period of time? The approach that works best is determined by your personal learning style and professional schedule.

Classroom Versus Onsite Training

Classroom training enables the trainer to work in a rigidly controlled environment that may not look much like your own workplace. This type of training is best suited for closed-loop subject matter such as basic file construction

---

FOOTNOTE

[15] Reviewing an outline will also tell you a lot about the trainer's level of professionalism. If no outline exists (or if the one they give you looks like it was hastily thrown together), look elsewhere. Some classes are taught using a syllabus (or a list of topics and bulleted points) as the only class aid, expecting the student to make up the difference by frantically taking notes during class. A quality class outline should contain references to fully developed materials, real-world examples, class exercises, and supplementary files. Some of the better options include an after-market book in the price of the class, or at the very least, offer discounted prices on a series of recommended texts.

or individual applications. Any training that pertains to your unique work-place, such as workflow issues, networking, proofing, or highly specialized design techniques, will likely benefit from classes that take place at your own facility. Onsite training typically costs more than classroom efforts—custom materials must be created largely from scratch, and you are expected to cover travel and lodging expenses. However, having your staff use their exact work-flow model as the center of training activity quickly recoups any additional payout. [16]

Inquiring About Following Up

Ideally, you want to be able to follow up any training effort with additional training or consulting. After you return to work after taking the class, you start applying the skills and concepts you've learned from the class. If you discover that something you learned was incomplete or unclear, you should be able to phone or email the trainers with focused, applicable questions, and expect a quick response. If the new skills enable a staff to grow to a point where they need additional training, the facility should be prepared to offer a ready solution.

Asking About Industry Ties

A training facility should have the support of the manufacturers of the soft-ware they specialize in. A good training center receives beta software for the classes it teaches, and should be able to test and use any new software months before it is released to the public. By the time a new class is offered,

---

FOOTNOTE

[16] If you choose to pursue onsite training, you must be sure your facility is equipped to handle it. If your workstations are housed in separate rooms, it's almost impossible for a trainer to present the class material efficiently. (Some places try to compensate for this by crowding their staff around one or two computers, which simply doesn't work.) Larger companies, when developing extensive training programs, will set up a temporary classroom. They use a series of new computers connected to the primary network, configured the same as the actual department. When training is completed, the computers are rolled into the regular environment, replacing older models if necessary. If your facility cannot comfortably accommodate onsite training (and can't afford the expense of a private class-room), all is not lost. Many classroom facilities, if the contract is large enough, will temporarily configure their classroom to match your requirements, in essence sim-ulating your workplace.

the trainers should already be advanced users, familiar with any unique feature or problem with the program. These facilities also have insider resources to better answer any questions that might arise.

Requesting a Client List

A good training center will provide you with a list of students and companies who can vouch for the effectiveness of the training. Don't be afraid to contact these people and find out how satisfied they were with their experience.

Reference Materials

Digital prepress is so complicated that you can't afford to overlook any potential source of viable information. Ironically, acquiring the knowledge you need consumes your most valuable resource: your time. You need to learn as much as you can, but you can't afford the time it takes to weed through the piles of information, both good and bad, that glut the industry.

Back when I started learning the tricks of the trade, every written word carried essentially the same weight. A cool type trick in Photoshop seemed as valuable, if not more so, than knowing the difference between RGB and CMYK color. These days, one of the biggest problems you'll face is making the distinction between what info is directly relevant to you, and what is merely interesting. Books, magazines, videos, CD-ROM training, and the Internet can all be worthwhile investments of time or money, but each has its own limitations. Approach every potential knowledge source with the same questions: How advanced are my abilities? Where do I want to be? How will this information help get me there?

If you work for a company, you can easily make a compelling case to your supervisor to buy some of these resources for your department. If you run the company or work independently, you can declare them as a business expense for tax purposes.

After-Market Books

Well-written, process-oriented books can be your most valuable resources. On average, they contain the largest amount of useful information of any resource, and they're relatively inexpensive, to boot. Just like training, if you pick up even one time- or money-saving piece of information, you earn back the cost of the book with every future job.

Although I purchase most of my books via the Internet (where I can usually get a 10–20% discount), I try to check them out in a bookstore first. When choosing a book, review the back cover, table of contents, and chapter summaries for substantive information. Be sure the book is thoroughly indexed and cross-referenced. Read the preface or forward to get a better idea of the book's intentions. Will it enhance your productivity? Does it only focus on one application? Is it intended for designers, prepress operators, or both? Check the author's bio and Web site to learn about his or her background and other books they have written, and search for reviews on Amazon.com or other bookselling resources. More than anything else, be sure the content is clearly written and easily understood, not buried in a sea of author digressions and questionable design.

Try this test: Think of a specific topic you want to learn more about, and see how quickly you can find it in the book. Check the index first, then the chapter descriptions. If you can find pertinent, usable info in under a minute or two, the book is likely a winner. If it leaves you guessing, leave it on the shelf.

Video Training

Studies show that information both seen and heard is retained better than info only seen or only heard. Such is the premise of video-based training, which peaked in the mid-'90s. Although videos are fairly inexpensive and a variety of titles is available, they suffer from more drawbacks than most other resources. Your TV and VCR have to be in close proximity to your workstation (difficult in most environments), and titles tend to focus more on basic approaches to the software than on hardcore industry specifics. Most often, video training is a useful format for non-technical topics, such as project management or team leadership. If you do invest in a video series, read the description carefully to see how it applies to your needs, and be sure you can return it for a full refund if necessary.

CD-ROM Training

CD-based training typically involves a series of QuickTime movies that walk you through various issues and techniques. The content is pretty much the same as its video counterparts, but with smaller screens and lower sound quality. The main advantage is that it takes place on the same computer you work with every day. You can watch a movie, then immediately switch to an open application and apply the lesson. Another plus is that CDs can hold up to eight hours of movies that you can access at will, while videos run around two hours apiece and require that you manually forward and rewind.

CD-ROMs suffer from the pauses and starts of the presenter's speaking voice, but they have many satisfied users. A good place to start looking is VTC, who offers over 70 titles covering graphics, Internet, and business programs. Its CDs range from $50 to $100—more than a book, but far less than a training class. (See www.vtco.com for more info.)

Magazines

To some, computer magazines are standard-bearers of the industry, always striving to redefine the cutting edge. To others, they're the toadying yes-men of the advertisers who pay their bills, and contain no useful (or objective) information whatsoever. The truth falls somewhere in the middle.

Unlike books, videos, and CD-ROMs, magazines come out monthly or weekly, so the information is generally more current and timely. Just as important, magazines also feature advertising and design that can serve as inspiration for your own print projects. Any bookstore worth its salt will have a variety of prepress-related magazines. The best ones will not be found in the computer section, however, but in the art and design sections. *Step-by-Step Design* and *How* are two good examples. Computer technology has become so all-pervasive that it's hard to find any magazine without some sort of computer content these days. Browse for an hour or so, then take the subscription cards and subscribe to as many magazines as you can afford. You'll be glad you did.

The Internet

Many valuable resources are available via the Internet. The trouble is finding them. Information on the Internet comes from two sources: user groups and the World Wide Web.

After you get past the hype, you'll find that the entire World Wide Web is similar to someone learning print publishing for the first time, only worse: Everything carries equal weight. Searching for a subject like "digital prepress" can yield hundreds of responses, but determining which sites contain relevant information and which are merely advertisements for goods and services can be difficult. After you have located a useful site, though, it can make the time and frustration of finding it worthwhile. The Internet is unique in that the information can be updated moment-to-moment, making it possible for its information to be most current.

The other source of information on the Internet is user groups. There are more than 10,000 user groups covering every subject imaginable (and a few that aren't). These areas are totally driven by the people who use them. On a user group, you can post a question, get an answer to it, and browse through other people's questions. The answers may or may not be right, but it's good to know that there are many more people out there seeking knowledge than just you.

Sadly, the Internet is not yet living up to its promise as a provider of useful information. Too much of it is pure marketing hype. The potential is there, though, and some vendors are starting to tap into it. For example, Adobe's site (www.adobe.com) is shaping into a one that can be visited and revisited. It has the potential of becoming a service that adds value to all of Adobe's products by providing not only software updates and plug-ins for its products, but interviews, articles, tips, and techniques. The site is still predominantly an advertisement for Adobe software, but the rewards for visiting are increasing.

The Human Resource

Achieving success in print publishing requires that you establish a series of connections from project concept to final publication. Not just on the computer, but with the industry around you. The prepress process does not happen in a vacuum—you need the right people.

Employees and Co-Workers

Your employees and co-workers fall into one of two categories: Those who got their start in conventional graphics and prepress, and those who got their start on the computer.

Conventional graphics professionals are now required to relearn their trade to adapt to a rapidly changing world. "Rapid change" and "prepress" are two concepts that never met until the advent of computer technology. Thanks to the digital revolution, the print industry has changed more in the past 10 years than in the previous 100. However, those making the change from traditional to digital methods find themselves in an awkward position. After many years of stability, they find themselves forced to change, to learn an entirely new way of production. After working for years at a job known for its consistency, predictability, and tradition, they are faced with the prospect of fitting in or looking for a new career. Most welcome the change with excitement and enthusiasm. Some try their hardest, but find that the traditional methods are so ingrained that they can't make the switch. Some even view it with hostility as an unwelcome hassle and a threat to what they thought were secure jobs. Depending on how well they adapt, those making the change can become a great asset or big liability to a department's future.

On the flip side are those who have tremendous computer skills, but no industry background. These include art and graphic design students who have learned excellent design theory, but only a cursory knowledge of production-oriented file construction; Web and multimedia developers with extensive graphics experience, but none in print publishing; and casual, home, or business-oriented users who are comfortable with a computer, but haven't yet worked in digital graphics.

Utilizing Your Personnel

You can learn just as much from the seasoned prepress pro as the young computer jockey. The question is, will you be able to? I once had a man with 40 years of industry experience gesture to his 23-year-old co-worker and tell me, "I'm not going to let some punk kid tell me what to do!" Meanwhile, the "punk kid" was operating under the assumption that he was already a pre-press expert, simply because he had memorized all the keyboard shortcuts in QuarkXPress. Their conflict illustrates an important point: If the older man wants to adapt to the new technology, he must be open to the tips and advice of the expert computer user. If the younger man wants to thrive in the workplace, he must learn from the prepress veteran's years of acquired experience.

There is no room for a proprietary attitude over your knowledge in a publishing environment. Many people hoard their experience, keeping it to themselves, assuming their job is more secure because their expertise makes them indispensable. In truth, this attitude makes them a detriment. Success in this business requires an ability to learn and a willingness to share what you already know.

As an employee, it is up to you to continually revise and update your skill set. No two people work the same way, nor do they have identical experiences. If you learn something new, turn around and share it with a co-worker. If you're stumped, you should feel equally comfortable turning around and asking for help. There's a good chance someone else has encountered a similar issue, and the two of you working together will find a solution more quickly.

As an employer or supervisor, it is up to you to foster an environment of open communication. Pay attention to your employees, especially if they come from different industry backgrounds, and be sure they are working together to get the most from their collective knowledge. (Don't forget to include yourself in the process!) Many departments set aside a few minutes a day or an hour every week for a "skill session," where employees have the chance to discuss new techniques they've picked up, issues they're unclear about, or specific problems they learned how to solve. This not only enables knowledge to be distributed among your staff, it makes it easier to spot the need for additional departmental training.

When you're under constant deadline pressure, it's easy to look out for Number One, leaving everyone else to fend for themselves. This creates a hostile and stressful work environment, making it much more difficult for people to maximize their skills—and therefore, their productivity.

Print Brokers

A *print broker* is an outside vendor who coordinates and oversees your print projects. His fee takes the form of a markup applied to the original printing cost, usually around 20–30%. Like a stockbroker, a print broker advises you how to spend your money in ways that make you most profitable. His role can range from locating the least expensive print shop to completely managing the project: Taking your files to have proofs made, reviewing the proofs with you, having film separations made, bringing them to the printer, handling all communication with the printer, and so forth.

The best print brokers know the ins-and-outs of the industry, but this is not always the case. Many act purely as a sales representative, who know only what your output looks like and what a project will cost. Either way, it's unlikely that a broker will be an expert in digital design or prepress—that knowledge must come from you. The most valuable service a broker offers is the ability to communicate on a print shop's level, to handle any time-consuming vendor issues that drag your productivity down, and to stay on a printer's back until your project is produced on time and on budget. If you're willing to handle these issues by yourself (and you have the ready time to pursue them), you won't really benefit from the services of a broker. If your production keeps you busy every hour of the day, or if you don't have the depth of experience required to communicate well with a print shop, or if you simply aren't comfortable doing it, a good print broker quickly becomes a valuable ally. [17]

Utilizing a Print Broker

Once you've decided to enlist a print broker, your relationship should be one that increases in value over time. A playing field that remained constant for decades is now redefined yearly. You and your broker need to remain aware of any changing trends and new client or printer expectations, and work with each other through the entire process. If you don't feel comfortable working with your print broker, or if you feel he's just taking you for a ride, find another one. The following guidelines will help make your relationship the most profitable:

- **Define your relationship from the start.** The responsibilities of your broker can vary widely. At the minimum, the broker is just finding you a printer. At most, he oversees every aspect of a job once it leaves your hands. Either way, he gets his markup. Be sure you're getting the most for your money.

- **Make your needs clear.** A broker strives to find you the best deal in printing. Unfortunately, the best deal does not always mean the highest quality. When turning over a job, let your broker know what level of quality you expect, including color fidelity, image clarity, and finishing. You can often get great bargains if you aren't too concerned with the final result. On the other hand, if you demand the cheapest printing without specifying any high-end needs, chances are you'll be disappointed with the results.

FOOTNOTE

[17] The main thing to take into account when enlisting a broker is the markup of printed materials. If you handle your own print work, you can add 20–30% to a project's printing cost when you bill the client, turning an additional profit. (This is a standard practice—unless you're doing someone a favor, always mark up a project's print cost.) If your broker is already marking it up, it becomes difficult to mark it up again without arousing the suspicions of a cost-conscious client, which means you lose the extra percentage. If you're not billing your work to a client—for example, if you work for an in-house design department—the extra markup comes straight out of the company's pocket. Here, you must determine whether a broker's services are worth the additional expense.

- **Make no assumptions.** Your broker is not an output technician, and he will not troubleshoot or repair any problematic files you give him. That responsibility remains on your shoulders. However, if you simply assume that your broker will provide you with a print shop's specific file requirements, and your print broker assumes that you've already contacted the printer, you're both headed for trouble. Keep the channels open and inquire about anything that seems unclear.

Service Bureaus

Service bureaus kick-started the digital graphics revolution. From the start, the technology has cost so much and changed so quickly that individuals and small businesses find it difficult to keep up. Service bureaus typically offer a wide range of services based on the most expensive, high-end equipment, such as drum scanning, imagesetting, calibrated proofing, and quality color correction. Rather than invest in the equipment yourself, you let experienced professionals handle the work on their own gear, and you can pass the production costs along to your client.

A good service bureau is a partner who enhances your capabilities and compensates for any resources lacking in your environment. Need a color scan? A service bureau can provide you with scans sized to your exact specifications and perfectly color corrected. Color proofs? It should offer a variety of options. A service bureau essentially offers every service that isn't cost-effective for you to pursue in-house.

On the other hand, a bad service bureau is like an auto repair shop out to exploit your lack of knowledge. These companies are few and far between. However, as in any knowledge-based industry, some misguided souls will try to take advantage of those who don't know they're being taken, and telling the difference between the two is not always easy. This is particularly problematic in a corporate environment, because the bill is often sent straight to the purchasing department, bypassing the person who requested the services. It's always a good idea to examine the invoices very carefully, even when you're not the person shelling out the cash.

Utilizing a Service Bureau

Once you have found your service bureau, your work should improve dramatically. Your technological capabilities are increased by its in-house equipment. Your relationship with your service bureau, like with your print broker, becomes more valuable as it matures. Invest the time to find a service bureau you like, and you'll be repaid many times over. For more info on finding and utilizing a service bureau, see Chapter 7, "Project Planning."

Print Shops

A printer uses the separation plates generated from your digital files as the basis for applying ink to paper. This much is obvious. What isn't so obvious is the variety of options that are now available at your typical print shop. Digital prepress and new printing technologies have opened up many printing options, from the vibrant colors of high-fidelity printing, to customized print-on-demand, to highly automated form printing. [18]

Print shops range from small Mom-and-Pop businesses that offer limited services and quality at dirt-cheap prices, to giant plants that rarely handle print runs under a million. Some printers have the in-house capability to produce films from your digital files, while others expect you to provide them with films. There is no such thing as a "typical" printer. As many shops exist as there are types of projects, and finding the right resource requires some legwork on your part.

Utilizing a Printer

Communication again is key. You need to be able to work closely with your printer to ensure that your files are reproduced the way you envisioned them. When quality is critical, this can even mean going to the plant and watching while the printer runs your job. A good printer wants you to succeed, and will work with you to be sure your files are prepared so they print properly the first time. Keep the following guidelines in mind:

FOOTNOTE

18 Emerging print technologies are continually transforming the way we do business. Take the simple matter of printing forms. Until recently, businesses would have forms reproduced at a print shop, then take them back in-house to print information sheet-by-sheet from a customer database. Digital printing allows a printer to take the form as well as the info from a database and print them simultaneously. At the same time, the forms are collated, sorted, and mailed from the printing plant, saving a tremendous amount of time and eliminating the need for transportation and storage of the forms. Understanding these new services requires that you make contact with either the print shop, or better yet, a knowledgeable print broker who can point you in the right direction.

- **Begin the prepress process with a call to the printer.** Different printing methods, ink types, and paper stock can all demand unique file requirements. Your printer should be able to tell you what you need to ensure the best possible print quality.

- **Know your printer's requirements.** If the printer will be outputting your digital files, you need to know what programs and versions he supports, as well as what media types he accepts. Find this out *before* you start creating files on your computer. Failure to do this can mean you have to scramble to re-create files or find another printer that can still meet your deadline.

- **Know your printer's capabilities.** Different printers often have reputations for excelling in one specific type of printing. One printer may be great at full-color printing, another may excel in duotones. You may wind up using several different printers to meet all your project needs.

- **Understand turnaround time.** The industry standard turnaround time for a print job is 10 days. If you can find a printer that beats this schedule, consider yourself lucky. Many designers, having pushed their deadline to the breaking point, naively expect that a job can be run in 24 or 48 hours, like having films run at a service bureau. Printers only make money when their presses are running 24 hours a day, and a project backlog is common. The only time you can expect them to bump one job for yours is when you're a big client—and I mean *big*, as in a *million dollars a year* big. Otherwise, you must include a realistic time frame for the print run when you estimate a project's completion date.

For more information on choosing and utilizing a printer, see Chapter 7.

Freelancers

Often, the work you need to complete exceeds the resources of your staff. Rather than invest in additional full-time employees, more companies than ever are turning to freelancers, or professionals who work on a contract-only basis. Freelancers are useful in three areas:

- **Meeting short deadlines.** By employing freelancers, you can make deadlines that you wouldn't be able to by yourself or with your current staff.

- **Enhancing your capabilities.** You may not be an artist, but that shouldn't prevent you from having original artwork in your publications: Hire a freelance illustrator. Likewise, if you suddenly have a need for someone to produce 200 clipping paths or make 100 halftone scans, hiring a freelancer means you don't have to pull in-house employees away from other work in progress.

- **Reducing your costs.** Freelancers reduce the need for permanent additions to your staff in environments with an inconsistent workflow. They don't require benefits, they handle their own taxes, and you don't have to pay worker's comp insurance for them. You can contract a freelancer for a single project and send her away when the project is done. (In fact, I've seen many a design firm staffed primarily by freelancers, who satisfy the demands of only one or two people in charge.)

From a freelancer's point of view, selling yourself as a sort of graphics mercenary has the following advantages:

- **Freelancing can be lucrative.** Depending on the intensity of the project, its duration, and your skill set, you can expect to be paid anywhere from $15 to $100 per hour. Of course, you are responsible for promoting yourself and negotiating your own contracts—and how savvy you are will directly impact your success.

- **You're not tied down.** When you freelance, you're not stuck with one company. You can enjoy a broad range of experiences, meet a larger number of people, and seek gainful (if fleeting) employment anywhere in the country.

- **Freelancing can lead to full-time employment.** Many freelancers are recognized as quality workers by the contracting company. It's sort of like a foot in the door. If you make a strong enough impression, you may well be offered a full-time gig.

- **You can work at home.** If you own a powerful enough workstation, many companies will allow you to complete the contracted work in the comfort of your home office.

Freelancers come in many shapes and sizes. Some are loners who want to work for themselves. Some are already employed and want to supplement their income. Some are paying the bills while they look for steady work. The only thing that matters to both parties is that freelancers have the desired experience and can meet the imposed deadlines.

Utilizing Freelancers

Once a company puts out the word that they're looking for freelancers, they can expect to receive a number of calls. Good freelancers are an aggressive, self-promoting lot that actively seeks out each contract. Most often, you don't even need to spend money on advertising—just talk up your needs with your business associates and vendors. Most professionals are happy to recommend someone they've worked with successfully in the past.

Before contracting someone, you must assess how well they fit your needs. Many people approach hiring a freelancer just as they would a regular employee, asking for a resume, portfolio, and references. In some ways, it's more important to thoroughly evaluate a freelancer before hiring him. Unless he will be working onsite, he will not be under your direct supervision. You must be assured that any freelancer is capable of a high level of communication and trust. Once a freelancer is contracted, the following guidelines will help ensure that things proceed smoothly:

- **Use a written contract.** Responsibilities, deadlines, and payment should be spelled out in advance to avoid any conflict in the future. Be clear about who owns the freelancer's work, and pay attention to any usage rights.

- **Clearly specify your supported programs.** A freelancer must create files that you and your company can open and use. You are responsible for communicating exactly what programs and versions you support. A freelancer is responsible for providing files in the supported formats and programs. If necessary, specify this information in the contract.

- **Clearly specify your supported media types.** The freelancer needs to supply her files on media that you can load and read. Provide each freelancer with a list of the transport media your company uses. (See Chapter 6 for more info.)

- **Be sure the fonts are standardized.** Because so many versions of each typeface exist, you must be sure you provide each freelancer with the exact font files used by your department. Likewise, if a freelancer uses her own typefaces, she must supply copies when she turns in the work. (See Chapter 4 for more info.)

- **Clearly specify your naming conventions.** If your freelancer uses your conventions for naming files, her work can be more easily incorporated into your workflow and file management systems. (See Chapter 5, "File Management," for more info.)

Value-Added Resellers (VARs)

For many people, buying computer equipment means shopping around for the lowest mail-order price. However, the price tag is not necessarily the bottom line. Do you need assistance installing the hardware? If a unit breaks (or doesn't seem to work properly), is there anyone available to help you? When you purchase your equipment from a VAR, a modest increase in price opens the door for a whole range of additional services.

The "value-added" refers to a level of support and technical assistance not offered by a retail computer store or mail-order company. A quality VAR will help determine the exact hardware and software you need, keep you abreast of changing industry trends, and be a ready resource whenever any technical failure occurs. Usually, a VAR is staffed by longtime users who know from experience which tools are appropriate for an intensive workplace, and which can be safely ignored.

Utilizing a VAR

Understanding the role of a VAR can be tricky. They're more than computer vendors, but they're not a full-time tech support hotline. They will be there to help you through a technical crisis, but you should not call them up with Photoshop questions. They will always be ready to evaluate your production environment and system configurations, to be sure you're getting the most from your investment. They won't help you troubleshoot a problematic InDesign document. In essence, a VAR acts as a buffer between you, your hardware, and the manufacturers. Without a VAR, you're left to deal with dozens of faceless corporations on your own. With a VAR, you can direct your questions and issues to a single knowledgeable source. When choosing a VAR, ask yourself the following questions:

- **What is their proximity to your company?** A nearby VAR (within 30–40 miles) means the difference between dropping off a computer for repair or upgrades and shipping it. This difference is critical when time is of the essence.

- **How long have they been around?** Look for a VAR with a long and successful history. You want to be assured that they will be around in the future to assist with upgrades, new purchases, and repairs.

- **How do they treat you?** When you talk to VAR employees, they should treat you with respect and pay attention to your specific needs. They should make perfect sense, regardless of your technical background. If you have the feeling they're hiding their lack of experience with a lot of high-tech mumbo-jumbo, take your business elsewhere.

- **Do they know what they're talking about?** When you ask VAR employees a question, you should get a quick and direct answer. You should have the feeling that they are staying current with the latest technological developments.

- **Do they provide on-site service?** Employees of a good VAR may be willing to come to your site when they know you're in the midst of a crisis. Find out the circumstances under which they'll make an on-site visit, as opposed to requiring that you bring your equipment to them.

- **Is their staff certified?** When service providers are authorized by the major manufacturers, such as Apple, Microsoft, and Adobe, they have access to many resources and tools that unauthorized resellers don't. Also, most companies require that a person pass extensive testing in order to become certified.

Summary

Someday, perhaps, someone will invent a magic box that automatically produces the printed materials you want. Until then, you have to jump and jive within a complex system of hardware and software requirements, personnel issues, and vendor contacts. Establishing your work environment requires a lot more than buying a computer at the local technology store. If you want to hit the ground running, you have to take the following issues into consideration:

- Choose a computing platform that dovetails not only with your own experience, but with the intensive demands of the print publishing industry.

- Your computer must have a processor fast and strong enough to handle high-resolution images and complex files with ease. These days, there is no need to spend any time sitting in your chair, doodling aimlessly, while your computer takes forever to apply a command.

- Purchase enough RAM to run your applications at the efficiency they demand. At minimum, expect to install 128MB in each workstation; more realistically, 196–256MB will do the trick more effectively.

- Your monitor must be big and clear enough to accommodate all-day viewing, and display satisfactory color.

- Acquire a suite of software packages that are proven to be most effective in a production environment. At the very least, most users require a word processor, a vector-based illustration program, a page layout program, a photo-editing program, fonts, and system utilities. Service bureaus and printers, who process a wide range of client files, must invest in all the major packages.

- No one in the industry has a big enough brain to learn and master all the intricacies. Invest in the knowledge resources that will help you most, whether it be training, books, magazines, videos, CD-ROMs, or a combination of all of them.

- Understand the wealth of human resources that surround you, from your own staff to print brokers, service bureaus, print shops, freelancers, and VARs. You do not have to work alone—when you're part of a larger professional community, everyone involved succeeds when you do.

Of course, in the middle of all of this is you. The most expensive technology is nothing more than a paperweight without a knowledgeable operator. It is up to you to always update your skills, learn better and more efficient ways of working, and adapt to this ever-changing world.

OPTIMIZING YOUR WORK ENVIRONMENT

In Chapter 2, "Creating Your Work Environment," I discussed the resources you need to create your work environment. Purchasing is the easy part; pulling it all together and making it work requires a little more effort. In an *optimized* workstation, every element in your environment—from the installed software to the attached peripherals, from your desk to the lights in the room—works together as efficiently and productively as possible.

Ideally, such a workstation works on an almost subliminal level. It should never call attention to itself, never be a conscious obstacle between you and your work. Think about it: generally speaking, you're not consciously aware that you have wrists. You don't have to be. Above and beyond connecting your hands to your arms, they quietly and gracefully add agility and function to your daily routines. If your wrists hurt, you become consciously aware something is wrong. Your mobility is limited; your productivity is diminished. The goal of this chapter is to configure your primary tools to run as smoothly and trouble-free—essentially, as *invisibly*—as possible. You're not computer technicians. You're designers and prepress professionals. Your valuable attention should remain on your work, not on twiddling with controls or being placed on hold, waiting for a tech support representative. You must address your workplace in three ways:

- **Optimize your physical work environment.** Your physical environment includes such noncomputerized elements as your chair, your desk, and the lighting of your workspace.

- **Optimize your computer.** How you configure your system—including the myriad Control Panels, Extensions, and utilities—will greatly affect your productivity.

- **Maintain the operating system.** The Third Law of Thermodynamics essentially states that order descends into chaos, unless you work to prevent it. If it happens everywhere else in the universe, you can bet it will happen on your computer, too. Maintaining and organizing your system on a regular basis will prevent it from *demanding* your attention when you can least afford to give it.

Optimizing Through Ergonomics

It may seem odd to you to see ergonomics in a book so devoted to hardware and software, but I would be negligent if you didn't. Ergonomics are one of the most important factors that consistently affect your work. Throughout this book, I talk about maximizing profits, increasing efficiency, and eliminating wasted production time. Proper ergonomics maximizes the functionality and preserves the usefulness of your most valuable piece of equipment: you. Ignoring the proper methods will result in pain and productivity-loss that can last weeks, months, or even permanently. Many readers will glance at this section, only to flip past it to juicier topics. Take it from me—this is a mistake. I ignored most of this advice for the bulk of my 10-plus years behind a computer. Now, at the tender age of 31, I suffer chronic neck pain, have lousy eyesight, and my wrists sound like Rice Krispies when I roll them around. I've also become a major advocate of ergonomic safety.

Repetitive Stress Injury

One of the more unfortunate contributions of computer technology is our sedentary working style. Where people once moved around as they worked, performing different physical tasks, they now spend much of their time sitting in the same position, repeating the same limited motions. As more people spend more hours in front of the computer, we face a crisis of epidemic proportions, and the medical industry has only recently begun to respond. Fortunately, it is a crisis with obvious, easily preventable causes. The most prominent growing problem is the increase of *RSI*, or Repetitive Stress Injury, which now accounts for nearly two-thirds of all workplace illness.

Carpal Tunnel Syndrome

The most notorious RSI is carpal tunnel syndrome (CTS). Here, the median nerve travelling from the arm to the hand gets compressed by the carpal tunnel, a passageway of ligaments and tendons in the wrist. Nerve tissue is one of the most sensitive and easily damaged tissues in the body. CTS causes pain in the wrist that radiates into the hand, numbness and tingling in the thumb, index, and middle fingers, and loss of strength. Symptoms may also include a tightness that runs up the inner arm to the armpit. There is no cure for this malady; we can only halt its progress, usually by ceasing all the activities that caused it, undergoing physical therapy, splinting the wrist in a neutral position, getting steroid injections, and in some cases, surgery. The surgical procedure is genuinely unpleasant—tendons are removed in an effort to widen the tunnel, and a two- to three-month rehabilitation period is normal. Used only in worst-case scenarios, it's widely regarded as minimally effective.

In 1995, the National Center for Health Statistics estimated there were over 1.89 million cases of carpal tunnel syndrome in the United States, and this is only one form of RSI. Other debilitating forms include upper limb disorders, tendonitis, DeQuervain's Syndrome, Thoracic Outlet Syndrome, tenosynovitis, and back and neck strain. All of them cause pain or discomfort and all of them can result in missed work. This issue goes beyond the idea of losing productivity; it will affect your quality of life. [1]

FOOTNOTE

[1] The advice offered here is based on the best available research and input from physicians and occupational therapists. But it is only advice. It should not replace the personal guidance of a trained physician or therapist, nor should it substitute for medical help.

If you are experiencing pain, damage is already done. Get professional help now. Pause just long enough to fill out an incident/accident report in the Human Resources Director's office. Properly documenting your symptoms will facilitate any worker's comp and insurance claims. These *are* work-related injuries, so call a physician immediately.

Computer-related injuries are so new to the medical world that they may not be diagnosed or treated properly. Many RSIs are incorrectly diagnosed as carpal tunnel syndrome. Doctors are familiar with CTS because it has historically stricken carpenters, warehouse workers, and others who repeat the same motions all day long. There are big differences between these and computer-related injuries. As with any diagnosis, don't hesitate to get a second or third opinion, especially if surgery or any other costly or uncomfortable treatment is involved.

Preventing RSI

Mother always said, an ounce of prevention is worth a pound of cure. A few dollars up front and a few minutes a day will help save thousands of dollars in lost productivity, prevent costly and painful surgery, and avoid months of rehab time. Preventing RSIs is a simple combination of adjusting your environment and changing your work habits.

Posture

Piano teachers and typing instructors have the right idea: posture, posture, posture.

Sit upright in your chair, with your back at a 90° angle to the floor. Keep your head up and face forward comfortably, as you do naturally when walking or having a conversation. Your shoulders should be relaxed, but don't hunch or slouch. Your upper arms should be dropped, keeping a 90° angle with your forearms, which should be parallel to the floor. Your thighs should also be parallel to the floor. Your upper and lower leg should also make a 90° angle, and your feet should be flat on the floor (see Figure 3.1). Your hands should make a straight line with your forearms, and not be tilted up or down (see Figure 3.2).

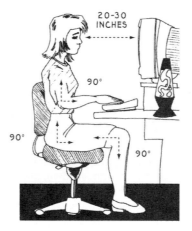

Figure 3.1 *When you sit at your desk, your back, elbows, and knees should be at comfortable 90° angles. The top of your monitor should be at eye level, at least 20 inches away.*

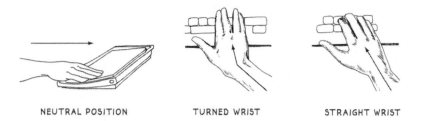

NEUTRAL POSITION   TURNED WRIST   STRAIGHT WRIST

Figure 3.2 *If you aren't careful, you can damage the nerves, ligaments, and tendons in your wrists. You should be able to comfortably hold your hands in a neutral position over the keyboard (left). When you type, don't turn your hands to the side (middle); there should be a straight line from your forearm to your fingertips (right).*

Although it sounds like a geometry quiz, this position should feel comfortable and natural. If any part of you feels strained or tires quickly, don't blame yourself and don't give up. It could be your furniture.

Your Furniture

Many people make the mistake of trying to fit themselves to their furniture. You can't make yourself "fit" to anything. Your bones are a fixed length, and barring growth spurts or unfortunate injuries or diseases, they will remain that way for life. If you sit in the proper position described previously, your arms will be at a height unique to your body type, as will your knees, your eyes, and so forth. You don't buy shoes half your size and expect your feet to miraculously accommodate them, and your furniture should be no different.

Your Chair

Unless you work standing up, you spend more time "interacting" with your chair than any other piece of equipment. More than anything else, your chair affects your physical well-being because it determines the shape of your spine for the eight hours or so a day that you occupy it.

When you sit, your spine (as well as your shoulders, head, and neck) should be in the same position as when you stand (see Figure 3.3). An inexpensive chair twists or overtly straightens the spine. If your back feels tired after sitting all day, or if your neck or shoulders hurt, it's likely your chair doesn't fit properly. In a quality chair, your body naturally maintains a comfortable position.

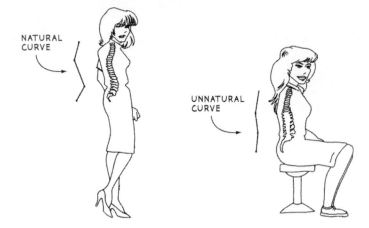

Figure 3.3   *When you stand, your spine curves naturally (left). An ill-fitting chair will force your spine to curve awkwardly or straighten (right), causing fatigue.*

A chair should be fully adjustable, not only in seat height, but in seat angle, arm height, lumbar support, and the amount of recline. The more adjustable the chair is, the more you can tailor it to your body type—but adjustability may come with a price. My chair, a Herman Miller Aeron, cost almost $1,000. The price seemed high at first, but it dawned on me that I'd spend the same amount on a scanner or other piece of equipment without batting an eye. After three years of 14-hour days without a backache, sore neck, or sore shoulders, this chair has become the wisest purchase—and the best bargain—of my professional life.

Your Desk

When you sit in the recommended posture, you should be able to reach the keyboard with your wrists in the neutral position. It's okay if your elbows bend slightly away from 90°, as long as your wrists don't bend and your neck and shoulders don't feel any strain. Elbows are rarely affected by computer-related RSI, but pay attention to how your wrists, neck, and shoulders feel.

This correct posture requires a desk that is easily adjustable. The design of the desk should facilitate, even encourage, adjusting by the user. The best desks have an easy-to-use crank that allows you to adjust the height while fully loaded. You can sit down at the table and adjust it to the exact height that feels comfortable to you at any time. At the very least, look for a desk with a sliding keyboard tray suspended beneath the table. A tray eliminates the need to reach up to access the keyboard and mouse, which bends your wrists unnaturally.

Most often, people "inherit" a desk, whether from a friend, Goodwill, or a past employee. While I can't really fault you for this—desks are expensive, and I used an ill-sized hand-me-down for years—you have to think of such an investment as a way of saving much more later on, in the form of lost work, doctor's bills, or worker's comp claims. Many companies, now aware of the dangers, purchase or build new desks for each new employee.

Stretching

To reduce the effects of repetitive stress, take the time to do some simple stretching exercises. Only one or two minutes of stretches every hour will offer immediate benefits. Some are easy (and discrete) enough to do right at your desk:

- **Arms.** Extend your arms straight out to the sides, as if preparing for a hug, and raise your thumbs. Rotate your arms, turning your thumbs down, until you feel the stretch up the length of your arm. Repeat 10 times.

- **Forearms.** Place your palms together, pointing your fingers toward the ceiling. Slowly lower your hands toward the floor until you feel the stretch. Repeat 10 times.

- **Wrists.** Extend your arms straight in front of you, with your palms facing down. Move your hands up until your fingers point to the ceiling, then down until they point to the floor. Repeat 10 times.

- **Hands.** Make a fist, then spread out your fingers as far as you can. Repeat 10 times.

- **Shoulders.** Shrug your shoulders and relax, rolling them forward and back. Repeat 10 times.

- **Back.** Bend forward in your chair. Clasp your fingers behind your head and slowly draw your elbows back. Repeat 10 times.

Input Devices and Accessories

Although keyboards and pointing devices are essential to computing, they cause pain and damage when used improperly for extended periods. Alternative devices can improve the overall ergonomics of your workplace, but even they can pose certain health problems. While there are no guaranteed fixes, the following tips will help you stay productive.

Keyboards

No current studies conclusively demonstrate that ergonomic keyboards reduce RSI in any way, or even prove the connection between RSI and keyboarding. For now, all we have is anecdotal evidence, which indicates that many RSI sufferers have found their pain reduced or eliminated after switching to a different keyboard design.

A remarkable and exotic array of options are available, from keyboards that follow the standard 105-key layout but are curved and angled to better match human hands, to keyboards that break into several pieces and can be angled to any degree. Other keyboards abandon the 105-key approach altogether in favor of five or seven key stenographer-style pads.

Two of the more interesting concepts are the Comfort Keyboard System and the Datahand. The Comfort Keyboard System is based on the standard 105-key keyboard, but is separated into three sections (see Figure 3.4). Each section is connected to a "custom telescoping universal mount," allowing it to be independently adjusted to a nearly infinite number of positions. This enables users to adjust the keyboard completely in their effort to find the most natural position. (See `www.comfortkeyboard.com` for more info.)

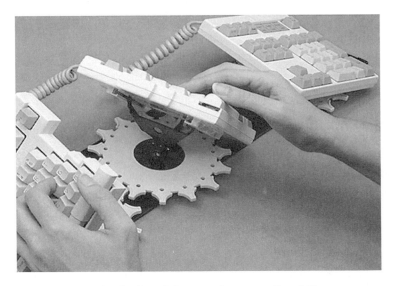

Figure 3.4 *The Comfort Keyboard System takes user-adjustability to a new extreme. Although other ergonomic keyboards can be split and positioned, this one allows you to fully tailor it to match your most comfortable position.*

A solution like the Comfort Keyboard System requires the least amount of learning time. because it's just a modification of a familiar system. On the other hand, the Datahand requires that you learn a new way of typing. It uses two "pods," one for each hand, like a pair of gloves (see Figure 3.5). The four fingers contain five switches each: forward, back, left, right, and down. The thumbs have numerous switches, as well as a built-in pointing device. In spite of the odd appearance, the key layout closely resembles the standard QWERTY and is reported to be easy to adapt to. The idea is that the hands never have to move the whole time that the computer is being used, aside from a twitching of the fingers to click the switches. (Datahand claims that hand movement is reduced by 88%.) The idea has merit. How can repetitive stress injuries occur if there is no motion to cause them? I especially like that the pointing device is included in the Datahand, because the mouse is capable of inflicting much more damage than the keyboard. (See www.datahand.com for more info.)

Figure 3.5   *The Datahand reduces hand movement by up to 88% by eliminating the keyboard and mouse altogether. While it does require learning a new way to type, many sufferers of RSI sing its praises.*

Because no evidence supports one alternative over another, I can't really recommend one specific type of keyboard. My own experience has been with Apple's simple, inexpensive ergonomic keyboard, which I found—once I got used to its unusual feel—to provide a much more comfortable keyboarding experience. Don't hesitate to experiment until you find the perfect fit.

Pointing Devices

The mouse is a far bigger threat to the graphics professional. When keyboarding, stress is divided between ten fingers and two hands. When using a mouse, stress is focused on one hand and one or two fingers. Designers typically run the highest risk of mouse injuries, because they use the mouse almost exclusively, using the keyboard only for limited text entry and file-naming.

Unfortunately, pointing devices are inescapable in our line of work. My advice is to invest in a small variety. There are dozens of options, and most of them are available for under $100. You can string a series of them together, and use any of them as desired. The configuration I use is as follows:

- **The ubiquitous mouse.** Damaging, yes, but I'm still most comfortable using this method. When I purchased a G3 blue tower, however, I immediately discarded that tiny, poorly balanced mouse that Apple now insists on shipping. (iMac users will also know what I'm talking about.) I replaced it with Kensington's $40 Mouse-in-a-Box device, which more closely resembles the traditional mouse shape. (See `www.kensington.com` for more info.)

- **A trackball.** I've been weaning myself from the mouse habit for a couple of years, and I've found Kensington's $60 Orbit trackball the most comfortable option. It has a big, satisfying ball and two programmable, easy-to-reach buttons.

- **A drawing tablet.** I use a tablet for any painting, freehand drawing, or photo-retouching. Any of Wacom's excellent, inexpensive tablets are highly recommended. (See `www.wacom.com` for more info.)

Wrist Rests

Once touted as a way to make keyboarding more comfortable and prevent strain, foam wrist wrests are now viewed as quite the opposite. In fact, a new trauma has arisen: wrist resting syndrome, similar to carpal tunnel. The problem is that many users think they are supposed to actually place their wrists on the pad as they type. Doing so forces the wrists to bend improperly, placing stress directly on the delicate two square inches of tissue surrounding the median nerve. Should you rest your wrists? Absolutely. Just don't do it while you type. I once owned a padded rest, but ultimately threw it away. For the best results, take short and frequent breaks and use the stretching exercises described previously.

Gloves

Several manufacturers offer gloves to wear while working as a way to prevent or help heal injuries, as well as protect the vulnerable median nerve.

Again, according to anecdotal evidence, these help considerably. At the very least, they will help keep your hands warm, which helps more than you might think. Any athlete warms up before engaging in physical activity, to avoid injury. Typing is no exception.

Take Breaks

Far more helpful than anything you can buy are frequent breaks. Get up, walk around, stretch, stare out the window at the beautiful day you're missing, introduce yourself to the new office temp. RSI is caused by doing the same things over and over. When you take a break, you give your body a chance to undo the damage. I don't mean take the federally mandated two 15-minute breaks per day—I'm talking about taking at least two or three minutes every hour, even every half-hour. This goes against the corporate philosophy of keeping your head down and working until dawn, but such an attitude is unhealthy and counterproductive in the long run. A good manager will see to it that her charges take frequent breaks. If you're lucky enough to work for yourself, treat yourself right and you'll be rewarded for a lifetime.

Eye Strain

Staring at the glare of a monitor all day will eventually cause eye strain, pure and simple. Anyone who has ever pulled an all-nighter to meet a deadline knows what I'm talking about. Symptoms include tired eyes, blurred vision, difficulty focusing on distant objects, and impaired night vision. Usually, your eyes are simply tired and need to rest. If these symptoms don't subside when you're away from the computer, then it *is* time to worry—see your optometrist right away.

No scientific evidence conclusively proves that eye strain causes permanent damage. However, in the last year I've encountered an author with two detached retinas and a consultant suffering from what he described as "a hole in his vision." Both were required to spend several months away from their computer. Even minor occurrences of eye strain are unpleasant enough to be avoided, so keep the following in mind:

- **As with RSI, frequent breaks give your eyes a chance to recuperate.** Get away from the computer and stare into the distance. At the very least, try this exercise: every half hour, focus on an object at least 20 feet away for 30 seconds to a minute. Even this little bit is enough to work the muscles surrounding your eyes.

- **Set your monitor at the proper height and distance.** When you sit in the proper position, the top of the screen should be level with your eyes, 20–30 inches away.

- **Blink.** Studies have shown that people blink far less when working at the computer than at any other time (with the exception of playing video games)—sometimes as little as three times a minute. If you don't blink, your eyes dry out and become fatigued.

- **Use a high-quality color monitor.** On a good monitor everything is crisp and in focus, with no discernable flickering. A monitor should be a pleasure to look at.

- **Use proper lighting.** Banish fluorescent and overhead lighting from your work environment, if possible. Also get rid of any lights that glare on your screen. Use low-key, diffused lighting. When doing color-critical work, use a color-balanced light, available at any photography and art supply store.

- **Visit your optometrist.** If you frequently experience eye strain, your eye doctor may have additional methods for reducing the strain, such as a different corrective prescription or tinted eyeglass lenses. Chronic eye strain may be indicative of other problems as well, which should be attended to.

Optimizing Your System

After unpacking your equipment and hooking everything up, your first impulse may be to quickly install the software and start working away. However, taking an hour or two to configure the system before you start to work will save countless hours in the future.

Reformat Your Drive

Before you install anything on your computer, perform a low-level reformat on your hard drive using a utility such as FWB's Hard Disk Toolkit or Apple's free Drive Setup. Reformatting offers the following benefits:

- **Increased capacity.** Manufacturers format hard drives to the advertised size, and that number is often rounded down from the drive's actual capacity. If a drive is advertised at 1,000MB, it might actually hold 1,050MB. Reformatting will gain that extra space.

- **Increased reliability.** Your drive was probably manufactured in a distant third-world country. During its voyage, it was subjected to extreme temperature changes, errant magnetic fields, bumping, and any number of misfortunes that could damage the formatting of the drive. This can result in lost or corrupted data, crashing, and a host of other problems that do not become apparent until you use the drive extensively.

- **Increased predictability.** Formatting utilities install drivers that can only be updated using the same formatting utility. Drivers usually need to be updated when a new operating system is installed. This creates problems if you do not own a copy of the utility used to format the hard drive. For example, if a drive is formatted with FWB's Hard Disk Toolkit, you will get a warning that the drivers cannot be updated whenever you update the OS. At this point, your only options are to purchase the latest version of the utility or reformat the drive. Out-of-date drivers can cause the same problems on an improperly formatted drive.

- **HFS+ (Mac OS Extended).** All new Macs ship with drives formatted to the new, more efficient Mac OS Extended format. Older drives are formatted to the Standard format. Files take up much less space using the new formatting, and this is especially true of fonts. All new drives should be formatted using the HFS+ format.

To reformat a Macintosh drive, you must do two things: start up from the system CD that shipped with your computer (you cannot reformat a drive with an active system), and have a copy of your reformatting software on an external disk. Your startup CD contains Apple's Drive Setup, which allows you to reformat. If you use a third-party utility such as Hard Disk Toolkit, copy it onto a Zip disk, insert it after you boot using the system CD, and run the reformatting from there. (Note that older system CDs don't support Zip drives. However, if the Zip is inserted while the system is booting, it should mount.)

To reformat a PC drive, start up from the system disk that shipped with Windows, then run the FDISK command to format the desired drive. Windows 98 users can now take advantage of FAT32, a file allocation table that allows for larger drive partitions (over 2 GB) and smaller file sizes than the FAT16 used by Windows 95. (FAT32 was available on Windows 95B, but most users found its implementation buggy at best and stuck with FAT16.) If you've upgraded to Windows 98 (as opposed to purchasing a new system with Win98 already installed), chances are your still using the older FAT16. If you want to use FAT32, you must manually convert your disk.

Win 98 includes a utility called Drive Converter, which updates the disk instead of reformatting it. To access this utility, choose Start: Programs: Accessories: System Tools: **Drive Converter (FAT32)**, then maneuver through the Wizard screens that appear. [2]

Partitioning

When you reformat a drive, you have the option of partitioning, which creates the effect of dividing a single unit into multiple drives. If you do not have a separate hard drive to use as a primary scratch disk (which is highly recommended) and are formatting using HFS+, consider splitting the drive into two partitions: one for applications, fonts, work files, and the System Folder, and one of at least 1GB. The second partition can be left empty at all times for use as a scratch disk. [3]

Windows users can create drive partitions using a utility such as Microsoft's free FDISK, or PowerQuest's more robust Partition Magic (available for under $70). FDISK is more widely used, but Partition Magic allows you to add or remove partitions without losing any data currently on the drive.

FOOTNOTES

[2] Before converting to FAT32, you must make sure it suits your environment. While it does provide much more efficient use of your disk space, you should be aware of certain limitations. For example, you will not be able to use any third-party utilities that only work with FAT16, so you'd have to acquire the most recent versions (if they're available). And you won't be able to set up a dual-booting system using older versions of Windows or DOS. Additionally, if you need to revert back to FAT16, you must reformat your entire drive and reinstall everything, including the operating system. If these issues don't deter you, just make sure you back up your entire system before converting and refer to your owner manual for detailed information. If you're confused by any of the settings you see while running the utility, don't be afraid to cancel the operation and seek further assistance.

[3] It may seem a waste to leave an entire gigabyte of storage space empty, but scratch disk space is one of the most utilized areas on your drive. It is accessed constantly by the operating system, Photoshop, Illustrator, and other programs. As these applications operate, they'll write anything that can't be held in RAM to whatever space can be found on the hard drive. Of course, if it has a contiguous space to write files to, it will work much faster. A disk partition specifically designated for this purpose and kept clear of all other files allows programs to work at the fastest possible speed. In addition to the speed gains from having a separate scratch disk, functions will not be available if there is inadequate scratch disk space. When Photoshop runs out of scratch disk space, it ceases to function until its memory is purged.

Installing the System

After reformatting your drive and setting up partitions, you're ready to start creating a clean and efficient prepress machine. For inspiration, turn to the work of Yukio Mishima, Japan's great poet, playwright, and novelist. His writing possesses an elegant simplicity. He used exactly the words he needed to get his point across—no more, no less. This is an ideal to strive for when setting up your system and installing software: Have exactly what you need and no more; have everything where it should be.

Begin with a complete installation of the latest operating system. If there is already an operating system present, *always* perform a Clean Install. This has important advantages over a straight install. First, it preserves all the data in your old system folder, allowing you to retrieve items that you still need. Second, any corrupt or outdated system files are placed in a separate folder and can now be loaded one at a time to check for conflicts.

Also, every new version of the OS contains new features that may make older third-party extensions and Control Panels obsolete.

Customizing the System

The operating system is at the heart of everything you do on the computer. Mastering it enables you to work more efficiently, thereby increasing your productivity. There was a time not long ago when it was possible to configure the operating system once and not touch it again until you installed the latest version. With the power and complexity of the modern OS, maintaining an optimized system is now an ongoing, dynamic, and interactive process. The payoff is a more flexible, customizable system that you can fully tailor to meet your needs. Optimizing requires two things. First, you properly maintain your Extensions and Control Panels. Second, you ensure that you have the software you need, and eliminate whatever you don't.

Using the MacOS Extensions Manager

Extensions and Control Panels add functions to your operating system, like options added to a new car. This functionality may be obvious, such as the addition of a menu item or the capability to toggle through open applications using a key combination, or it might be unnoticeable, such as support for an obscure CD-ROM format. Control Panels are the same as Extensions, with one difference: the options they add to your system can be adjusted using an interactive dialog. Extensions are either active or disabled, and can't be further modified. [4]

The folders for Extensions and Control Panels are located in the System Folder. The contents of these folders greatly determine the behavior of your operating system. Roughly 90% of system configuration involves adding, removing, or adjusting these files.

Extensions management requires more attention than ever before. Not long ago, maintaining a streamlined set of Control Panels and Extensions was easy. These folders were sacred places, and people were outraged when installing an application meant adding an extension to the Extensions Folder. Today, these files have multiplied like viruses. Nearly every application installs at least one. Microsoft Office 98 installs seven Extensions, all of which are necessary to run Office. Netscape Communicator 4.6 installs three, none of which are necessary.

Fortunately, the Extensions Manager has become more powerful than ever. This Control Panel is your most valuable system configuration tool, allowing you to do the following:

- Turn on new Control Panels and Extensions

- Turn off unnecessary Control Panels and Extensions.

- Create different sets of open and closed extensions, allowing you to maintain a series of custom configurations.

- Obtain information about individual Extensions and Control Panels.

FOOTNOTE

[4] The Windows operating systems do not use Extensions or Control Panels like the MacOS. Instead, they use drivers that applications load dynamically when they need them. The MacOS loads Extensions and Control Panels entirely into memory when the computer is started, and they remain there until you turn them off and restart. Therefore, when using a Mac, it is important to thoroughly manage these system files, because they are loaded whether your applications need them or not. Because Windows drivers are only loaded when needed, driver management is not nearly as pressing an issue. If you work exclusively in Windows, skip ahead to "Installing Applications," later this chapter.

You can access the Extensions Manager by choosing the appropriate item from the Control Panels submenu, or by holding down the spacebar during system startup.

Determining What You Don't Need

When you perform a complete installation of your system software, a variety of files are installed, which range from indispensable to superfluous. Remove what you don't need. Back it up onto a removable disk if you're uncertain, but get rid of it. Each file uses a certain amount of RAM, and anything that doesn't help get your job done, that uses up system resources, and increases the chances of conflicts is worth removing. Also, the majority of crashes and freezes come from Extension conflicts, usually caused by outdated or corrupted Extensions. Every file adds a little more instability to the system. Minimize the number of Extensions, and you minimize potential problems.

The first task is to figure out the files you don't need and turn them off. This may take a certain amount of trial and error, but mistakes at this level are easy to recover from. If turning off an Extension results in a loss of important functionality, turn it back on again. The Extensions Manager can help determine what is useful and what isn't (see Figure 3.6). Select an item in the Extension Manager window, then click Show Item Information. A brief description appears, which may help you make an educated guess as to its usefulness. For example, if you click the AppleVision Extension, Item Information reports "Supports AppleVision, ColorSync, and Apple Studio Displays. Provides Additional screen image controls." If you do not have an AppleVision, ColorSync or Apple Studio display, you do not need this Extension and can safely turn it off. Because so many third-party applications add Extensions, you should routinely examine the Extensions Manager and turn off what you don't need.

The following Control Panels and Extensions are often found to be useless:

- **Printer drivers for printers you don't have.** (Extensions) A complete install will install drivers for all the printers Apple makes. You only need drivers for the printers you have.

- **Input sprockets.** (Extensions) Mac OS 8.6 installs some 15 input sprockets to help certain input devices work better with games. If you don't own these devices or play games, throw these away.

Figure 3.6 *Use the Mac's Extensions Manager to review, enable, and disable your system's Extensions and Control Panels. Notice how selecting an item displays a brief description of its purpose.*

- **QuickTime 3D and QuickDraw 3D.** (Extensions) The QuickTime and QuickTime Power Plug extensions are important because, among other things, they allow programs like Photoshop and Illustrator to create file previews in their Open dialog boxes. There are eleven additional extensions in the QuickTime and QuickDraw family that are never used in a prepress environment, and are used very little anywhere else. These include all QuickDraw 3D extensions, QuickTime VR, QuickTime Musical Instruments, and Quick-anything else besides QuickTime and QuickTime Power Plug.

- **Drivers for devices you don't have.** (Extensions) For example, AutoRemounter is a Control Panel that is only used by PowerBooks. Contrast and Brightness is used only by specific, obscure monitors. IrDa is used for infrared communication by certain PowerBooks and iMacs. All of these and many others are typically installed in your system, regardless of the machine you are using.

- **Text-to-Speech.** (Control Panel) This will read System Alert messages and anything that you have written in SimpleText, WordPerfect, or America Online in an odd, emotionless voice of your choice. Amuse yourself with it and throw it away when the novelty wears off.

- **File Sharing Monitor.** (Control Panel) This is a handy way of seeing what kind of activity is going on with your shared computer, such as who is connected to you and how much they are using your files. If you aren't sharing files, or if you don't need this information, then you don't need this Control Panel.

- **Launcher.** (Control Panel) A nice idea—it lets you organize aliases for easy access to files and folders—but poorly executed. It takes up too much RAM and quits in low memory situations. It also takes up considerable monitor space.

- **Map.** (Control Panel) Pinpoint almost any city on a tiny map of the Earth. Remove it.

These are just a few of the most commonly discarded files. Getting rid of the ones you don't require will simplify your life and let you work more quickly and efficiently. Keeping things to a minimum enables things like disk optimizations and desktop rebuilds to work faster. After a little practice, telling the difference between what is useful and what isn't becomes second nature. Things have a way of creeping into your system folder, especially when you install new software. Routinely checking through your Control Panels and Extensions folders will keep things running smoothly. [5]

Configuring Your MacOS Control Panels

The MacOS (and, to a lesser extent, Windows) enables you to customize and personalize your system. The choices you make here will result in either a powerful prepress workstation or a quaint and interesting novelty. On the Mac, the most important system settings are handled through various Controls Panels; on Windows, through a series of Properties dialog boxes.

FOOTNOTE

[5] It can be difficult to determine which Extensions and Control Panels are part of the basic operating system, and which were installed along with your applications. Before installing any software, open the Extensions and Control Panels folders, select all the items, and apply a colored label (by choosing the desired color from the File: **Label** submenu). Any items installed in the future will be unlabeled, making them easy to identify on sight.

Optimizing a system is a much simpler task in Windows than Macintosh. Far fewer settings in Windows will affect your performance in a prepress environment. Practically all the settings that impact performance are automatically set to their optimal values, while the Mac requires additional tweaking. Many additional Control Panels are required by the MacOS for best performance, but I choose not to discuss them here because they have no direct pertinence to a production environment. In this section, I include only the most specific items.

Appearance

Although many settings appear in the Appearance Control Panel, only two directly affect your work. The rest can be set according to taste.

Under Fonts, turn on Smooth All Fonts On Screen to get a more accurate preview of a project. The Desktop settings let you choose many interesting patterns, pictures or solid colors, but none of these are suitable for prepress work. Ignore these options and set a neutral gray background, which offers the following benefits:

- Neutral gray causes the least eye strain of any color or pattern.

- Neutral gray makes it easy to locate files, folders, and windows on the desktop. Patterns make it harder on the eye.

- Color of any sort will affect the way you perceive other colors. For example, a blue background will make images appear more yellow. Neutral gray has the least influence on color perception, which is vital when doing any color work. [6]

FOOTNOTE

[6] Unfortunately, the current MacOS no longer includes a neutral gray background, as previous versions did. You must create your own. In Photoshop, create a new RGB document measuring 128 pixels by 128 pixels. Open the color picker and set the following values: R:128, G:128, B:128. Fill the entire image with the new color. Making sure the Desktop Pattern panel of the Appearances dialog box is open and visible, drag the image from Photoshop to the Pattern window. A new pattern named Untitled Pattern appears in the Pattern list. Select it and click Set Desktop. Windows users can use the same technique to create a neutrally-colored image, then load it as wallpaper.

ColorSync

A common misconception is that specifying the settings in the ColorSync Control Panel will automatically display and print colors accurately. The ColorSync Control Panel is actually a resource used by applications. Like QuickTime, the only time it comes into play is when an application specifically calls upon it. The settings here are important in a color managed workflow, but will not affect overall system performance.

General Controls

There are two relevant settings in the General Controls Control Panel (see Figure 3.7). The first is the Warn Me If Computer Was Shut Down Improperly option. All it does is display an alert if you restart after a system crash, and only causes an unnecessary delay. The effect is similar to being hit by a car, then having someone run over and tell you, "Hey. You just got hit by a car." Leave this box unchecked. Next, choose the Select Last Folder Used in Application option. This will make file management easier, because you will often save things to the same folder over and over again.

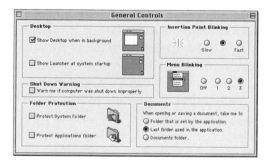

Figure 3.7 *In General Controls, uncheck the Warn Me If Computer Was Shut Down Improperly box and enable the Select Last Folder Used in Application option.*

Memory

The settings in the Memory Control Panel—which determines how your computer handles the installed RAM—can make or break a good system (see Figure 3.8).

Figure 3.8 *Use the Memory Control Panel to set your Disk Cache, enable or disable Virtual Memory, or activate a RAM Disk. For the best results, leave the Disk Cache at the default value, use Virtual Memory to add one more MB of RAM, and avoid the RAM Disk altogether.*

Disk Cache

Disk Cache is something of a misnomer, because caching really takes place in RAM. Disk Cache sets aside a small space to store repetitive calculations, which enables the system to run faster. Leave it at the Default setting, unless you are specifically directed to use a different setting. This setting provides the optimum 32KB for every MB of RAM installed on the computer. The only reason to use a different setting is in extremely low memory situations, because the Disk Cache does use up RAM. (For example, my system has 192MB of RAM installed, and the Disk Cache consumes 6.1MB.) If your RAM is so limited that this setting makes a difference, however, it's time to install more RAM.

Virtual Memory

Virtual memory uses part of the hard drive as RAM. It should be turned on and allotted at least 1MB. Provided you have sufficient hard drive space, the amount of Virtual memory can be taken up as high as 20MB or more without paying a performance penalty. Virtual memory is used intelligently; the operating system and applications will use it to store less frequently used operations, while reserving the much faster physical RAM for the heavy duty actions.

Virtual memory provides three benefits:

- The Macintosh OS has been optimized to work with Virtual Memory turned on. It will work more cleanly and efficiently, leaving parts of the System that aren't being used on the hard drive.

- With Virtual Memory turned on, file mapping can occur. This means that applications will load pieces they need by priority, allowing them to use memory much more efficiently.

- On PowerMacs, applications will require less RAM.

I used to advise people to leave Virtual Memory turned off, but times have changed. Virtual Memory used to make things run much more slowly, but with recent improvements to the System, it no longer results in the same performance hit. Virtual Memory once conflicted with Photoshop, but this has been fixed. Virtual Memory degrades performance if used improperly, so remember the following:

- True RAM is much faster than Virtual Memory. The total RAM used by your applications should not exceed the amount of RAM installed on your computer. Some users attempt to use Virtual Memory as a substitute for true RAM, when they should just make the modest investment in an upgrade.

- The amount you assign to Virtual Memory is hard drive space which will not be available to you as long as the option is turned on. If you raise the value too high, your free drive space will quickly disappear. Most users simply add 1MB of Virtual Memory.

RAM Disk

A RAM Disk is the opposite of Virtual Memory, using a portion of RAM as though it was a hard drive. Applications copied onto a RAM Disk will run very quickly, because all commands will be accessed from lightening-fast RAM. Unless you have hundreds of megabytes of RAM, the RAM Disk option should be left off. The RAM Disk is volatile. Items left in it will vanish when the computer is turned off. Also, it uses up valuable RAM that would be better used elsewhere.

Monitors and Sound

This Control Panel allows you to adjust some simple monitor settings (see Figure 3.9).

Figure 3.9   *Use the Monitor and Sound Control Panel to set your monitor's color depth and resolution. For the best results, set the Color Depth to the highest possible value and choose the Resolution with the highest refresh rate.*

- **Color Depth.** Most recent computers ship with enough video RAM to accommodate thousands or millions of colors. The more colors your monitor displays, the smoother and more photo-realistic onscreen images will appear—an important point when doing any image editing in Photoshop. My advice is simple: set Color Depth to the highest available setting. You may need to occasionally check it, however. Certain software such as games or multimedia presentations may reset this value to 256 colors, which accommodates their limited palette. Not all of them reset the value when they quit, which results in onscreen images appearing dithered or posterized.

- **Resolution.** Many monitors are *multi-sync*, which means that you can change the relative size of their onscreen pixels on-the-fly. For example, a 17-inch monitor typically measures 1,024 pixels wide and 768 pixels high. On a multi-sync monitor, you can increase the resolution to, say, 1,600×1,200 pixels, which approximates the available real estate of a 21-inch monitor. Your actual monitor doesn't change, of course; rather, the icons and images appear to take up much less space in the same area, creating the illusion of a bigger screen. Conversely, you can drop the resolution to 640×480, the same as a 13-inch monitor. The main thing to consider when setting monitor resolution is the refresh rate, measured in Hz (hertz). The higher the rate, the less the screen flickers at it is constantly redrawn by the electrode guns in the CRT. For normal work, choose the highest size with a refresh rate of at least 85Hz. Any less, and the flickering may become noticeable, and can cause quite a headache.

- **ColorSync Profile.** Access this option by clicking the Color button at the top of the dialog box. In this scrolling window, choose the appropriate profile. This only applies to users incorporating a color managed workflow, where the selected profile is typically custom-made.

Font Utilities

As described in Chapter 4, "Font Management," the MacOS and Windows only contain a rudimentary approach for dealing with fonts. To maximize your efficiency when working with these files, you will require the following items:

- **Adobe Type Manager (ATM).** Windows 95/98 users and Mac users with an OS version earlier than 8.5 must acquire a copy of ATM. (Apple now includes this utility with their latest systems, which I highly recommend upgrading to.) This Control Panel renders Type 1 fonts smoothly onscreen, allowing you to work with clean characters at any size or zoom percentage. Note that these features are also included in ATM Deluxe, a font management utility (see the item on font management utilities).

- **Adobe Type Reunion.** This Mac-only Extension organizes the items in your applications' Font menus. Instead of a long, scrolling list of every available typeface, ATR automatically sorts fonts according to family name and typestyle in a submenu under each name. Locating and selecting a font is almost unbearable without it. (Windows users do not require this utility.)

- **Font management utilities.** Production environments benefit greatly from a management utility such as Extensis Suitcase (Mac only) or ATM Deluxe (Mac and Windows), which allow you to open and close fonts on-the-fly. See Chapter 4 for a full description of the benefits.

Antiviral Utilities

Prepress professionals are among the most digitally promiscuous people around, accepting files and disks from anyone who comes along. When you insert that disk into your Zip drive, you link up with every computer that disk has ever been connected to. Catching a virus can be uncomfortable and may result in lost productivity. Giving someone a virus is not only embarrassing, it can almost guarantee a lost client. Always use protection when you mount any media or receive any file from an outside source. [7]

A short time ago, freeware utilities like Disinfectant were more than adequate protection against viruses. But the creators of Disinfectant have thrown in the towel, discontinuing their product, because viruses have become so prolific. Whether working on Windows or Mac, purchase a heavy-duty application that automatically scans every removable device that mounts on your computer, as well as every file downloaded from the Internet. Be sure that your antiviral utility is updated monthly with the latest virus descriptions (via the manufacturer's Web site), as new viruses are continually being identified. Symantec's Norton Antivirus has long been the number-one utility, and it is now available for all major platforms. Network Solutions' Virex has long enjoyed a wide Macintosh user base.

View Settings

In many prepress environments—particularly in a service bureau—each workstation is used by more than one person. As much as possible, these machines should look and feel the same, so each user can quickly find their way around. One of the quickest ways to create consistency between workstations is to set identical View settings.

On both platforms, the View settings control how the computer displays its contents. On the Mac, these settings are established using the Finder's View menu. In Windows, they are found under the View menu of each window. In each, you can choose from a range of options, but certain settings will enable you to work most efficiently.

FOOTNOTE

[7] Until recently, viruses were primarily the scourge of the Windows world, almost unheard of on a Macintosh. The resurgence of Apple Computer has brought increased attention to the Mac not only from consumers and the media, but from virus developers as well. There are now more Mac-based viruses than ever. For example, a new virus called AutoStart made the rounds in summer of 1998. It would hide on a transport medium such as a Zip or floppy. When a fresh victim inserted the disk, the virus would use the AutoMounting procedure to copy an invisible file to the Extensions folder. After the computer was restarted, the extension would run a tiny application every 30 minutes that devoured the data forks of any file over 2MB. The result? Corrupt files, with no tangible reason why presented to the unfortunate user. Even better: the virus would place a fresh copy of itself on every subsequent disk used by the workstation, including mounted server volumes.

Icon, Button, and List Views

The first three View options determine how files appear in open windows:

- **Icon View.** This option displays files as graphical icons. While this may help in terms of instant recognition, it's really only useful when you have very few files on the computer, which is never the case in a prepress environment (see Figure 3.10).

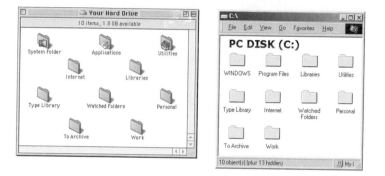

Figure 3.10 *The Icon View setting displays files and folders as full-size icons. Most users use this setting only on the top level of their hard drive.*

- **List View.** This option is something of a misnomer, because it also uses a series of small icons. However, I recommend this choice because items are displayed in an easy-to-read hierarchical list. I prefer setting folders to this option, then choosing By Name in the View: Arrange submenu to make the list alphabetical (see Figure 3.11).

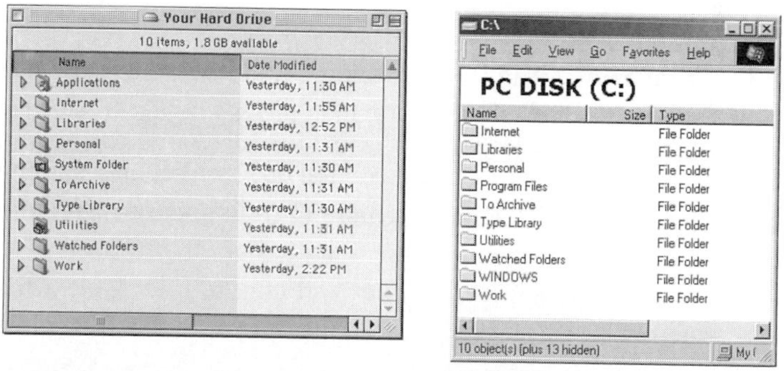

Figure 3.11 *The List View setting arranges the contents of a folder as a scrolling list. I've found that when this list is alphabetical, it's much easier to review folder contents and locate files.*

- **Button View (Mac Only).** This option displays every item into a button. Click the button once and the file opens or the application launches, just like when you double-click a standard icon. The disadvantage to this view is that it is too easy to open something that you were only trying to select (see Figure 3.12).

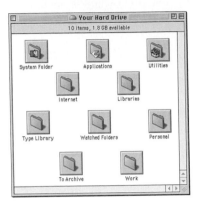

Figure 3.12   *The Mac's Button View displays files and folders as a series of clickable buttons. Because you can't drag items around, it's really more of a novelty than a productive tool.*

To further refine your View settings on a Mac, choose Edit: **Preferences** (in the Finder) and click the View tab. Set the following in the Views Preferences tab (see Figure 3.13):

- **Standard View Options For.** Set List in this pop-up. This way, the following settings will automatically apply whenever you set a folder to By List view.

- **Use Relative Date.** A throwaway option, it simply refers to files with the current date as "Today" and the previous day's date as "Yesterday."

- **Calculate Folder Sizes.** Turn this option off. It calculates folder sizes too slowly to be useful, and serves as more of a distraction. On slower computers, it can actually slow window redraw time. If you need to know the total size of a folder, select the folder and choose File: **Get Info**. This is much faster.

Figure 3.13 *The settings you choose in the Views Preferences tab determine the information that displays when you set a folder to List View.*

- **Icon Size.** Choose the middle option. It displays icons large enough to provide the instant file recognition that icons provide, while being small enough that the information can be displayed efficiently in the window.

- **Show Columns.** These options determine the info listed in the columns of a window. I recommend the following: Size (which lists individual file sizes) and Date Modified (which lists the date of the most recent file changes).

Maintaining Your System

Your computer may be configured properly now, but it will take effort to keep it running smoothly. Fortunately, if you have done things properly from the start, routine maintenance will only require a few minutes a week. Do it while waiting for coffee to brew or returning phone calls on Monday morning. Do it religiously, diligently, and without fail, and you'll avoid a multitude of crashes, corrupt files, and other problems. Preventative maintenance stops problems before they occur, and you already have the basic tools you need.

Your Weekly Maintenance Routine

Most people see their computer as a static device, a tool that simply sits quietly on their desk. However, your system is affected every time you manipulate a file, launch an application, or even open a window. Information is regularly added to or removed from the drive, and the contents of your folders are continually revised. This type of constant activity results in slight wear and tear that will eventually affect your computer's performance, unless you establish a routine maintenance regimen. Every week, perform three tasks to ensure smooth system operation: Rebuild the Desktop, run Disk First Aid, and update your software, if necessary.

Rebuild the Desktop

Whenever you add a file to your Macintosh, a copy of its icon is stored in a special resource called the Desktop file. This file is essentially a simple database that keeps track of file locations, icon graphics, and open window sizes. Because it changes so frequently, it can become so bloated over time that problems occur. Windows open slowly, the computer takes longer to reboot, and overall performance degrades.

Avoid these problems by rebuilding the Desktop file every week. After choosing Restart, hold down the Shift, Command, and Option keys. The Shift key prevents Extensions from loading during startup, which might interfere with the rebuilding. The Command-Option keys trigger the rebuild process—keep the keys pressed until you see an alert stating "OK to rebuild Desktop?" and click OK. Before restarting again—remember, your Extensions are turned off—run your disk repair utility (see the next section).

Run Disk First Aid

When a Macintosh operating system is installed, Disk First Aid is installed into a folder called Utilities. (In Windows, right-click the C: drive, and choose the Tools tab. Run the ScanDisk tool.) It's a fast, easy-to-use utility that detects and repairs most of the simple problems that occur on a hard drive. Third-party repair utilities such as TechTool Pro and Norton Disk Doctor will detect and repair more problems than Disk First Aid, but they do cost money and take longer to run. After rebuilding the desktop and running Disk First Aid, restart your computer.

Update Your Software

The sad truth of today's software industry is that the public is paying to debug software. All software—from the most intensive graphics application to the smallest utility—is incredibly complex. But the industry is highly competitive, forcing production cycles to shorten while software is upgraded with increasing frequency. In this environment, it is impossible for software to be fully debugged before shipping. When buggy software is released, it crashes systems and generally doesn't work right. Users complain to the manufacturers, and the software is updated according to those complaints.

When a new software version is released, most professionals prefer to wait for the incremental upgrade. For example, when Photoshop 5.0 was released, most people waited for *other* users to suffer the bugs, then invested in version 5.0.2. When QuarkXPress 4 was released, it brought many production environments to a halt until version 4.04 was finally made available. Fortunately, these updates are almost always free and can be downloaded from the manufacturer's Web site. Unfortunately, it's up to you to find out if and when the updates exist. This requires research. Every major application and utility has a dedicated Web site maintained by the manufacturer. Scan it routinely for available updates. Check for the following:

- **Application updates.** These typically appear within two or three months after the release of new or upgraded software.

- **Device driver updates.** Locate the page devoted to your peripheral device. New drivers usually appear within a month or two after the release of a new or updated operating system.

- **Third-party extension updates.** These appear a month or two after the release of a new or updated operating system.

Disk Optimizing Utilities

Files are written to the hard drive wherever the disk's read/write head finds the first available space. If that space isn't big enough, it will break the file into pieces until it is written entirely. This is known as *fragmentation*. It may sound odd, but the hard drive is intelligent enough to read files back completely, even if the pieces reside in dozens of spots around the hard drive. As you might guess, this isn't the most efficient method of file storage. When files are stored *contiguously*, or all in one piece, they will open and save much more efficiently.

Defragmentation software pieces these files back together. Optimizing software repositions to the inside or outer edge of the disk, leaving an empty contiguous space for future files. It also allows future defrag/optimization routines to run more quickly, because files are more likely to be written contiguously to wide open spaces. Additionally, provide a separate space for Photoshop, Illustrator, and Virtual Memory to use as a scratch disk; this wide-open space allows both of those things to operate much more efficiently.

Windows ships with a utility called Disk Defragmenter, but Mac users must purchase a third-party utility such as Norton Speed Disk (included in the Norton Utilities package) or MicroMat's TechTool Pro. (See www. nortonutilities.com and www.micromat.com for more info.)

Installing Applications

Thanks to the refinement of automatic software installers, adding applications to your workstation is more painless than ever. RAM allocation is still an important factor (see "RAM Allocation" in the next section), but there are still a few things you can do to make the installation process a little more efficient. Because most applications include dozens of megabytes of files you simply don't need, perform a Custom Install. This will allow you to sidestep the following:

- **Sample files.** These are intended to illustrate how a program is used. If you already know the basics, you don't need them.

- **Tutorial files.** Another attempt to teach you the basics of the program, they're only helpful if you intend to follow a tutorial that shipped with the software.

- **Outdated Control Panels and Extensions.** Many applications require the installation of system software. Photoshop, for example, automatically installs the Adobe Gamma Control Panel. Check to make sure you don't already have more recent versions of whatever the program wants to install. The Install program is supposed to be "intelligent," able to detect earlier versions of this software and not install over it. Unfortunately, I have seen newer versions overwritten by install programs more than once. Often, I didn't even notice until I began experiencing problems.

- **Product demos.** Third-party vendors make deals with other software vendors to include demos of their products on their install disks. Occasionally, they are included in a full installation.

- **Unwanted clip art.** Royalty-free images often ship with software. More often than not, you can see that it's free for a good reason. Never intended for a high-end graphics environment, most free clip art should be ignored.

RAM Allocation

You always have a finite amount of RAM. Before launching an application, you must assign a certain amount of RAM to it, which determines how much memory the program will use while running. RAM allocation is a juggling game. You want each application to have all the RAM it requires, but using up *all* your RAM poses certain system problems. [8]

Recommended allocations depend on your work. If you work primarily in Photoshop, give it all the memory you have, leaving a only few megs left over. But what about when you create an entire publication? Like most designers, you probably prefer to have Photoshop, an illustration program, and a page layout program running simultaneously. If, for example, you only have 96MB of RAM installed on your computer, you must allocate this memory to all three programs in a way that lets you operate most efficiently. Before setting your allocations, keep the following issues in mind:

- Your operating system is actually an application, and requires RAM to run. You don't specifically assign RAM to your system; it simply takes what it needs, and any installed Control Panels and Extensions add to the required amount.

- When assigning RAM, avoid using *every* available megabyte. Your system requires a buffer of about 5MB available at all times. Using all the available RAM results in out-of-memory error messages.

F O O T N O T E

[8] Allocating specific amounts of RAM to an application is only possible on the Macintosh. Programs running in Windows have their RAM allocated dynamically. In theory, an application only takes RAM when it needs it, as opposed to securing a distinct block for itself, which a Mac does. I say "in theory," because this method has proved to be awkward at best, often resulting in application and system crashes.

- When allocating RAM in the Get Info dialogs, always set the Minimum Size and Preferred Size to the same amount. For example, assume the Minimum Size of an application is set to 15000KB and the Preferred Size is 20000KB. This means that when you launch the program, it will use 20MB of RAM *only* if it's available. If only 15MB is currently unused, it will take the entire amount, leaving no buffer for your system. If both values are set to the same amount, you receive an alert stating that not enough RAM is available to launch the application. Close another program or two to free up space, then try again.

To determine how much RAM in installed on your Mac, go to the Finder and choose About This Macintosh from the Apple Menu. This dialog box also displays how much memory the System is using and how much you have left to allocate to applications (see Figure 3.14).

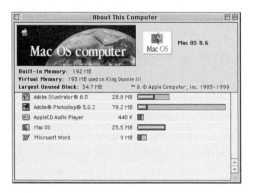

Figure 3.14 *The About This Computer window displays information about the RAM installed in your computer. This screenshot tells you the following: there is 192MB installed; one additional MB is offered by Virtual Memory; 25.5MB is currently in use by the operating system; and 34.7MB is available for opening more applications. The items at the bottom of the window show how much RAM is used by open applications.*

To change an application's current RAM allocation, go to the application's folder and select the application icon. Choose File: Get Info: **Memory**. (If you choose one of the other Get Info options, just select Memory from the Show pop-up.) In the lower-right corner of the dialog, you'll find a sub-section called Memory Requirements. There are three fields (see Figure 3.15):

- **Suggested Size.** This is the minimum amount required to enable a program's basic functionality, as suggested by the manufacturer. This is in no way a recommended amount. For example, the Suggested Size of

Photoshop 5.5 is 16MB; I've allocated 96MB, and I still occasionally run short on memory. It's possible to allocate an amount below the suggested size, but you will likely lose important application features, or even crash. It is almost always a good idea to assign more than the suggested size.

- **Minimum Size.** This value determines the smallest amount of available RAM the program will use. When launching, a program checks the amount of available RAM before it tries to open. If it is less than the Minimum Size, it stops. As described previously, set this value to the same amount as Preferred Size.

- **Preferred Size.** For all intents and purposes, this value determines how much RAM a program will use. Generally speaking, the higher the number, the more efficiently an application runs. However, this rule does depend on the software in question. For example, an email program generally doesn't run any better using 100MB of RAM than it will using 3MB, but the performance of most prepress-oriented applications benefits considerably from amounts higher than the factory defaults.

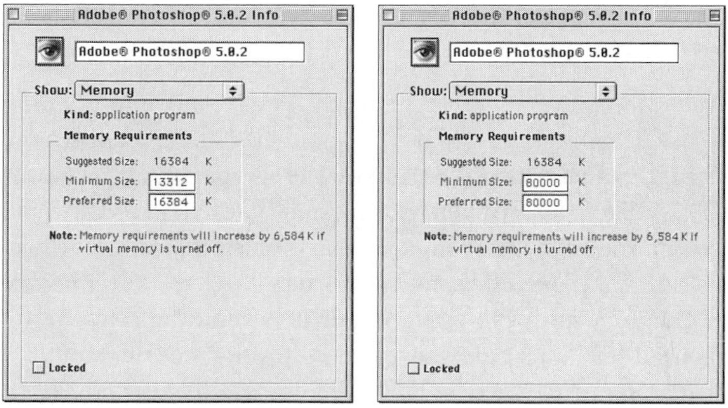

Figure 3.15 *The Get Info dialog box on the left shows the RAM allocations for Photoshop when it's first installed. In the dialog box on the right, the allocation has been raised to 80MB.*

I strongly recommend raising the allocations of the six standard graphics applications. Too many times, I've seen users install hundreds of megabytes of RAM in a high-speed computer, only to leave the allocations at the factory defaults. The original assignments are deliberately low, mainly to accommodate users who install the software on low-RAM computers. In a production workflow, they must be raised: [9]

- **Adobe Photoshop.** This program devours RAM, and any allocation depends on the size of the files with which you work. If you generally work with small images (line art, halftones, even Web graphics), set the value between 25 and 35MB. If you work with large color images, assign as much as you can—usually, a minimum of 80–90MB works best.

- **Adobe PageMaker, Adobe InDesign, and QuarkXPress.** Page layout programs aren't nearly as RAM intensive as Photoshop. I prefer allocating 20MB. When working with large, color-intensive documents, increase the amount to 40MB.

- **Adobe Illustrator and Macromedia FreeHand.** The latest version of Illustrator requires more RAM than ever—20MB usually suffices, but you should raise that amount if you work with very complex graphics. FreeHand typically requires at least 15MB to run smoothly.

System Recovery

Proactively maintaining your system will help avoid many problems, but accidents still happen. As always, it seems like they occur when you can least afford it. Sometimes it seems like your computer can sense stress, like an animal sensing fear. When your system goes down—especially when you're under the gun and your tech support staff has gone home—your response can make the difference between making and blowing a deadline. While a thorough study of system repair is beyond the scope of this chapter, here are a few approaches that can help when your computer is crashing or behaving erratically. Follow these steps, listed here in escalating order of intensity:

F O O T N O T E

[9] Bear in mind that RAM prices are at an all-time low. A couple years ago, RAM cost between $30 and $35 per megabyte, gaining a justifiable reputation as an enormous expense. Today, the price is approaching $2 per megabyte, eliminating any financial excuses against upgrading.

- **Run TechTool Pro, or another diagnostic utility.** This eliminates the possibility that the problems are caused by bad disk information or damaged files.

- **Do some quick research.** With the incredible complexity of today's programs, bugs and conflicts are inevitable. Most of them are known and reported. There are several Web sites devoted to system maintenance and bug reports, with information on how to fix problems. Bulletin boards and discussion groups are also good ways to find out if other people are experiencing the same problems, and what they did about it. If you get error messages, finding out the meaning of the message is a good place to start. If you have issues in one specific program, go to the manufacturer's Web site to see if they've documented the problem. If you have time, email their tech support staff and describe the problem as precisely as you can. You can also try calling the software's tech support team—they usually accommodate registered users.

- **Delete the Application Preferences file.** If you experience problems in only one application, you could have a corrupt Preferences file. With the exception of XPress (which stores its prefs file in the application folder) and Photoshop (which keeps its file in the Settings folder, in the application folder), application preferences are stored in the Preferences folder, which in turn is found in the System folder. This file contains a program's default settings. If it becomes corrupt, the application may behave strangely or crash. Close the application, then delete its preferences file. A new one is created when the application launches again. Just remember that you have to reset any custom defaults.

- **Check the Extensions.** Many crashes are caused by conflicting or corrupted Extensions. Restart your computer, holding down the Shift key to leave Extensions off. Does the problem go away? If so, you have an Extension problem. Start turning off Extensions one by one, starting with the last ones you remember installing. Restart with the remaining Extensions on. Does the problem go away? If so, you've located the problem. Of course, you have a new problem if the Extension was vital to your work. However, chances are if you were having problems, other people were too, and the manufacturer knows about it. Go to their Web site and see if any updates or other solutions are available.

- **Reinstall the application.** If you still experience crashes in one application, then the application itself might be corrupt. Delete the current program files and install a fresh copy using the original disks.

- **Zap the PRAM.** The Mac's parameter RAM is a tiny cache of memory that stores such settings as the time and date. This can become corrupted and adversely affect your system's behavior. "Zapping" the PRAM involves purging its contents, along with any conflicting settings. Restart the computer, holding down the Command, Option, P, and R keys. Before anything appears onscreen, the computer will restart. Let it restart five times. Release the keys and let the computer fully restart. An available freeware utility called TechTool (different than TechTool Pro) will do the same thing with much fewer steps.

- **Do a clean reinstall of the system software.** If crashes and other system-level problems persist, perform a clean install using the most recent OS. A routine system install is typically not enough, because it will only updates the current software. A clean install replaces the entire system.

  On a Macintosh, before installing, choose the Install New System Folder option. This renames your old System Folder, preserving its contents. This way, you can preserve any third-party system software.

  Windows users can use the uninstall option to remove all traces of the OS from the drive, then use the Windows disk to install a fresh system.

- **Back up the contents of the drive and perform a low-level reformat.** A fairly intensive last resort, only try this if you're comfortable with the required tasks. If you're not, skip to the last option. Reinitializing the drive only wipes the drive clean. It will not eliminate bad blocks and other hard drive corruption, like a low-level reformat. You'll need to start up from your emergency disk. [10] When reformatting is complete, install a fresh system. Finally, replace the applications, work folders, and other items you backed up beforehand.

- **Get professional help.** If none of the preceding approaches helped (or if you were uncomfortable attempting any of them), contact a consultant or take your computer in to a repair shop. Finding a good computer shop can be problematic, however, due to the lack of industry standards. Anyone can *claim* to be a qualified computer repair person, regardless of their experience. You are putting your livelihood into someone's hands, so it's okay to ask for credentials. A good technician will provide you with a list of satisfied customers. Additionally, more and more technicians are becoming Apple Authorized or Microsoft Certified. While there are certainly many qualified technicians who have no certification whatsoever, at least you know if they are authorized or certified that they have *some* level of expertise. Before a technician can become Apple Authorized, he or she

---

F O O T N O T E

[10] When you experience system problems, you may have to reboot from an external startup disk. Most people simply use the system CD that originally shipped with computer. Not only can you boot from this disk, you can install a fresh system. However, you may only need to adjust or repair your drive, not reinstall a system. It helps to create a recovery disk (using a zip, Jaz, or other removable medium), which contains the following software:

A system. If your computer doesn't have a CD-ROM drive, install a minimal system onto the recovery disk. This way, you can use it as a startup disk in case of an emergency. If you do have a CD-ROM drive, just use the system CD.

Hard drive diagnostic programs. Place a copy of Norton Disk Doctor or TechTool Pro onto the disk. This way, you can use them to scan a damaged drive.

Disk optimization software. To fully optimize the hard drive, many defrag/ optimization utilities require that you start up using an external system and use a program that doesn't reside on the hard drive.

File recovery software. When you delete a file, you don't really remove it from the drive. You actually tell the computer that the space occupied by the file can be written on. If you accidentally delete a file, you may be able to recover it. The trick is, if you attempt to recover the file to the same drive, you risk overwriting it completely. You stand a better chance of restoring a deleted file when you save it to the recovery disk.

Disk formatting tools. This way, you can reformat the hard drive when necessary— obviously, you can't reformat a drive that contains the reformatting software.

must pass an extensive test. Additionally, an Apple Authorized technician has access to more powerful diagnostic and repair tools than non-authorized technicians, as well as access to information from Apple that is only available to authorized personnel.

Summary

Never forget that you are the most important resource in your production environment. When optimizing your workplace, do whatever it takes to make yourself comfortable, enable yourself to work efficiently, and keep yourself healthy.

An optimized environment is an investment in money and time. With tight budgets and tighter deadlines, maintenance of the workplace is often neglected. This is a mistake. An optimized environment enhances your productivity, and helps avoid any work lost to system crashes, personal illness, and injury. It's an investment, true—but one that always pays off in the long run.

FONT MANAGEMENT

Mention fonts to a designer or prepress professional, and the likely response is what soldiers call "The Thousand Yard Stare," an expression worn only by seasoned veterans of combat. It evokes the image of peering just beyond the horizon, knowing that somewhere out there the enemy lurks, mindless of your humanity, waiting only to carve the next notch on his rifle stock. Largely unchanged since their inception in 1984, fonts still cause a multitude of problems in a production workflow.

Technically speaking, there is a difference between a *typeface* and a *font*. Even though these terms have direct counterparts in the digital world, they've become blurred. We tend to call everything associated with type—from the required files, to their names in a pull-down menu, to their onscreen and printed appearance—as fonts. People usually know what you're talking about, but some conventionally trained professionals may experience frustration when their references to "attractive typefaces" are met with blank stares.

Typeface has always referred to the unified look and feel of an entire character set, such as Futura or Gill Sans. The term *font* originally referred to a single point size of a single style of a single typeface, such as 10-point Futura Bold or 14-point Gill Sans Italic. Each font existed as a series of characters chiseled out of wood (and later cast in lead), which a typesetter would manually arrange as necessary prior to printing.

Today, fonts are files that reside on your hard drive. They contain the information required by your applications to display characters on your monitor, and reproduce them on an output device. A font contains as many as 256 individual characters, ranging from a lowercase b, to a bullet, to a trademark symbol, to special decorative shapes. Different variations of a typeface design are called *typestyles,* which include Italic, Bold, Heavy, Extra Bold, Light, and so forth. All of a font's variations combine to form a *typeface family,* in essence making each typestyle a *member* of that family (see Figure 4.1).

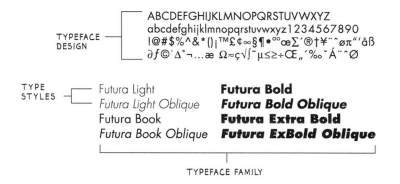

Figure 4.1   *An overall typeface design (top), the variations of typestyles (middle), and the entire family (bottom).*

This chapter is titled "Font Management" because the most pressing problems reside in how you handle the font files, not the typefaces they represent. Even back in the earliest days of printing, fonts posed some ponderous and time-consuming problems. Crafting a font required precision tools to cut each character by hand; it could take years to ready a high-quality typeface for general use. One false move—one bad font—and the print process was compromised.

Fonts can easily cause the most headaches in a production environment. Who hasn't experienced one of the following scenarios:

- The default font Courier prints where your carefully selected typefaces should have appeared.

- Fonts you need are not available in your applications.

- Applications take forever to load.

- Fonts are not included when a client drops off a file (or you receive a call from your printer, who claims that until you supply the missing fonts, your project is dead in the water).

- The tracking or kerning of your carefully adjusted type is inexplicably fouled during output.

- Your printed text reflows throughout your entire document.

- Your boldfaced or italicized words lose their type style during output, printing as regular text.

- Name or number conflicts appear when you try to open new or client fonts.

- A client includes only a suitcase or two, or a couple of screen fonts with his project. Or worse—he includes his entire type library, hoping the printer can sort everything out.

This chapter tells you what fonts are, how they work, and what can go horribly wrong when using them. I'll describe an efficient, flexible, and trouble-free system of working with large type libraries and client fonts. Instead of offering a series of troubleshooting techniques, I'll describe a workflow that handles problems by avoiding them in the first place. My guiding philosophy is simple: You can never be too careful when it comes to fonts. Dealing with all these ancillary files may seem like a waste of time and effort, especially at the end of a project, when deadlines loom. This chapter presents guidelines that ensure as much proactive safety as possible, like dressing warmly to ward off pneumonia.

Read this chapter, and you'll understand the following:

- The convoluted history of fonts and how it impacts your daily work.

- How fonts display and print a typeface.

- The use of Expert sets and Multiple Master typefaces.

- How to create an organized type library.

- How to use a font management utility to maximize the efficiency of your workstation and workflow.

- Preflight font requirements.

- How to establish a system of requesting fonts from your client base, or supplying fonts to your service bureau.

- The applicable licensing issues surrounding the use of fonts.

- The best method of cataloging your type library for your staff and clients.

A Brief and Sordid History of Digital Fonts

If it wasn't for the advent of PostScript fonts back in 1984, the graphics rev-olution would have stalled before it began. With digital typefaces, we could finally exact personal control over the nuances of the words so vital to our communication.

Three kinds of font files circulate throughout the graphics industry: Adobe Type 1, Adobe Type 3, and TrueType. The majority of fonts in the market-place—at last count, well over 100,000 unique typefaces—are Type 1. If you've purchased fonts from a credible vendor in the last nine years, it's likely they're Type 1. These fonts exist in much the same form as the first versions of Helvetica or Times that Adobe ever released: A combination of screen and printer fonts that enable you to manipulate type using onscreen tools and send that information to a high-res output device.

In a perfect world, we would only have to contend with a single font stan-dard. How we wound up with three requires a little background.

By the late-'80s, it was evident that scalable font technology was going to play a major role in the world of personal computing. What remained to be seen was which technology would rise to become the standard. Adobe wanted Apple and Microsoft to license its PostScript code, which would have immediately established Type 1 fonts as the "official" format. However, both corporations balked at the millions in royalty fees they would have had to pay, and Apple was still miffed that Adobe was licensing PostScript to other printer manufacturers, diminishing the appeal of their family of LaserWriters. Apple and Microsoft struck a deal: Microsoft would develop TrueImage, a graphics engine similar to PostScript, and Apple would develop a font platform to compete with Adobe's. Their alliance was announced in 1989—if everything worked, Adobe would be elbowed out of the picture entirely.

Adobe responded with a two-pronged attack. First, they announced Adobe Type Manager (ATM), a program so new it wasn't yet in development. Released in 1990, this utility allowed users to display Type 1 fonts on a Macintosh, smoothly and at any size, with no assistance from Apple soft-ware. Since ATM was cheap—free, when you bought Adobe fonts—it quickly gained widespread acceptance. Second, and more importantly, Adobe made the Type 1 specifications readily available to the public. Although the actual Type 1 code remained encrypted, developers were now free to write and use software that created Type 1 fonts.

Until this point, third-party font developers were given *most*, but not *all*, of the Type 1 secrets to work with. The results were Adobe Type 3 fonts. Most notably, Type 3 fonts were *unhinted*, [1] or did not contain the information needed to print to lower-resolution output devices while maintaining print quality. Also, Type 3 fonts were incompatible with ATM and non-PostScript printers.

Type 3 fonts abounded in the '80s. Before too long, any computer geek with a little patience could produce one in his basement, then release it to the world through bulletin boards and Usenet groups. The differences between Type 1 and Type 3 fonts were subtle, but important. They looked the same onscreen, they both had suitcase files and outline fonts, and they both referenced Adobe. The primary difference arose during output: Type 3 fonts printed *far* more unreliably than Type 1. By unreliable output, I mean that there were more instances of random misprinting, unaccountable text reflow, and awkward tracking and kerning results, just to name a few.

Given the opportunity to produce Type 1 fonts, developers grabbed it in a heartbeat. Who could blame them? This font format had (and still has) the qualities we appreciate most in our type libraries:

- Type 1 printer fonts contain more precise information, allowing them to print with greater detail.

- They can be downloaded to printer ROM, allowing for potentially faster print times.

- They are compatible with Adobe Type Manager (ATM).

FOOTNOTE

[1] *Hinting* is an attribute built into a font by its developer, which tells an output device what lines of a character shape to keep in proportion. This way, type outputs more successfully at smaller sizes, particularly on 300dpi printers.

For example, consider a capital M, where the two vertical stems are intended to be the same width and height. Without hinting, a printer might output one stem at 3 printer dots wide, and the other at 4. Hinting ensures that the printer outputs both stems at the same width. If the character is large—over 30 points, perhaps—you probably wouldn't notice the difference between the stem widths. However, at standard small body text sizes, the difference can be tragically apparent.

- They are compatible with Adobe Type Reunion, which organizes fonts by family in your font menus.

- They typically require less printer memory and download faster than other font types.

In short: predictable system behavior and reliable output.

Meanwhile, Apple and Microsoft were experiencing technical difficulties. TrueImage was wounded on arrival, full of bugs and widely considered unnecessary. Apple released TrueType in March, 1991, and it was marketed as being every bit as revolutionary as Type 1. Indeed, it was a significant departure from what we already knew about Type 1 and Type 3 fonts (for one thing, each font consisted of only a suitcase file—there were no outline fonts). But TrueType was new and unproven; Adobe Type 1, having captured the hearts of developers everywhere, was rapidly becoming the new standard. Nonetheless, Apple began bundling TrueType fonts with their operating system, where they still appear to this day.

In early 1992, Microsoft added TrueType to Windows 3.1. At the time, the computers running Windows 3.1 were based on slow, 16-bit 286 processors. The problem? The TrueType architecture developed by Apple was 32-bit. This meant that simple fonts like Arial, Courier, and Times New Roman worked all right, but more complex characters often wouldn't display, or they would appear onscreen but not print. Developers were frustrated by this inconsistent behavior, and resented having to simplify their character shapes to accommodate the 16-bit restriction. Plus, successful hinting code was almost impossible to write. Quality developers abandoned TrueType, and the Windows market was quickly filled with poorly constructed amateur fonts that only added to TrueType's increasingly bad reputation.

It wasn't until the release of Windows 95 (a 32-bit OS) that TrueType finally found its audience. Microsoft has adopted TrueType as the standard for future Windows versions, and the format now has many of the features normally associated with Type 1 fonts.

But the damage has been done. TrueType fonts never evolved to the same reliable form as Type 1 and never found a niche in PostScript publishing. After all these years, Type 1 still wears the crown.

The Nature of Fonts

A Type 1 font consists of two files: the *screen font* and *printer font*. Screen fonts should always appear in a suitcase file, a specialized folder that can be accessed directly by the operating system. A suitcase always is accompanied by at least one printer font. This does not go in the suitcase file—in fact, if you try to put it there, you'll be denied. This combination of screen and printer font information is at the heart of all font technology. Add to the mix a font utility called Adobe Type Manager, and you have the basis of all font usage, whether you use a PC or a Mac.

Screen Fonts

Screen fonts contain the information that appears on your monitor. They're sometimes called *bitmap fonts* because they contain 72-dpi renderings of every character of a typeface at a particular point size (see Figure 4.2). If you double-click a suitcase, you'll see what I mean: each screen font has a number in its title, such as 10, 12, or 14. These are the point sizes of the bitmapped characters contained in each file. When we first began using digital fonts, the vast majority of us didn't have access to PostScript output devices. We used ImageWriters, or other devices of its ilk: screeching, 72dpi dot-matrix printers. We could only display and print type smoothly at sizes with a corresponding screen font, so if we needed our Avant Garde headline to print at 52 or 13.5 points, we were out of luck.

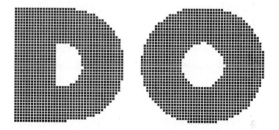

Figure 4.2 *The bitmap characters contained in a screen font are used to display type on your monitor.*

Printer Fonts

Printer fonts have little to do with what appears on your monitor. Rather, they contain the scalable, vector-based information that is sent to a high-res PostScript output device when you print the document. They're sometimes called *outline fonts*, in reference to the resolution-independent character shapes (see Figure 4.3). This information allows fonts to output smoothly at any size. Regardless of the type sizes you've set in your document, the printer automatically calculates what a character shape will look like at that particular size. If you've ever worked with Bézier curves in a program such as Adobe Illustrator or Macromedia FreeHand, you've already worked directly with this type of information.

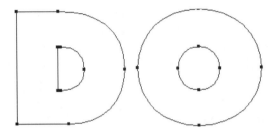

Figure 4.3   *The vector-based outlines contained in a printer font are sent to an output device.*

Adobe Type Manager

The final piece of the digital type puzzle appeared in the form of Adobe Type Manager (ATM), a system file that finally enabled us to work *typographically* on our computers. ATM creates a dynamic onscreen link between your Type 1 screen and printer fonts. By taking a peek into the printer font info, ATM determines what your type should look like at whatever size it appears on your monitor. It then renders the onscreen type as smoothly as possible, regardless of point size, zoom factors, rotation, or scaling (see Figure 4.4). The best part is that it all happens automatically, with no necessary interaction on your part.

ATM *Off* ATM *On*

Figure 4.4 *Onscreen type before (left) and after (right) using Adobe Type Manager.*

All ATM needs to accomplish this feat is a printer font and a suitcase containing a single screen font (regardless of its point size). Theoretically, you could go into all your suitcases and discard all but one screen font for every member of every family—but don't bother. You'll expend countless hours, risk discarding something important, and not save that much room on your hard drive.

ATM also lets you print smooth type to non-PostScript printers, such as StyleWriters, DeskWriters, and low-end personal laser printers. If you've ever purchased Adobe fonts or other Adobe software, ATM came bundled with it, and was automatically placed in your Control Panels folder during installation. (It also ships on Apple's latest system install CD.) Many Mac and Windows users have begun using ATM Deluxe, which includes additional font management features. (See "Managing Your Fonts," later this chapter.) If you use a different utility for opening and closing fonts, you should at least have a version of ATM Lite 4.0 installed, which offers Adobe's latest font smoothing technology.

Putting the Pieces Together

So you have three pieces of software working together to produce type that looks and prints as smoothly and accurately as possible. All you need to do is follow these guidelines:

- Always keep a font's suitcase file and printer fonts in the same folder. Separating them prevents proper output.

- Never remove screen fonts from their suitcases. Consider screen fonts in a suitcase as one file, even though the suitcase may contain an entire series of screen fonts.

- Never combine screen fonts from different families in the same suitcase. Doing so makes it more difficult for both designers and output professionals to keep track of which fonts are available.

- Never change the name of a suitcase. (You cannot change the name of a printer font.) Your type library may be huge, and organization is the key.

Weeding Your Font Library

Now for the big question: "What does this have to do with me?" The short answer is "Use only Type 1 fonts," but it's not always that easy. To successfully remove any TrueType or Type 3 fonts from your system, you have to know how to find them.

Type 3 fonts appeared only on the Mac platform, and millions of these files are still swimming around the marketplace (a friend of mine has over 800 of them stashed away on floppies). When you think about it, a lot of people have been using the same fonts for ten years or more, transferring them from system to system as they upgrade their computers. It's easy to imagine someone unwittingly using those old fonts today, bringing them into the service bureau, and getting surprisingly inaccurate output. To determine whether a particular font is Type 3, you must do one of the following:

- **Compare the printer font icons.** Adobe Type 1 icons always appear as an oblique capital A over a background of horizontal lines. Type 3 fonts always have a different icon, which usually contains a small "3" (see Figure 4.5).

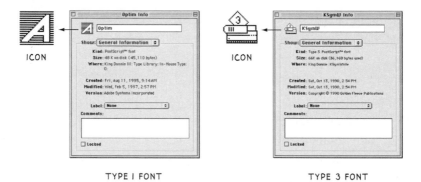

TYPE 1 FONT   TYPE 3 FONT

Figure 4.5 *The standard Adobe Type 1 printer font icon (left) is a skewed capital A, and its Get Info dialog box lists it as a PostScript font. The icon for a Type 3 font (right) is always different and usually contains a small 3. Its Get Info dialog box lists it as a Type 3 PostScript font.*

- **Check for a jagged appearance.** Assuming you have ATM turned on, enter some text in your page layout program and apply a point size that does not have a corresponding screen font, like 49 pt (or, zoom in to a high percentage, like 300–400%). Because ATM does not affect Type 3 fonts, the characters appear jagged.

- **Examine the PostScript code.** Open the printer font file in a text-editing application, such as Microsoft Word (in Word's Open dialog box, be sure All Files is selected in the List Files Of Type pop-up). If the font is Type 1, the document that appears will contain no text. If it does contain text, search for the first occurrence of the word FontType. If it lists the font type as "3 def," the font is Type 3.

- **Examine the resource fork.** Open the printer font file in a resource-editing application, such as ResEdit. To view the resource fork, double-click the POST icon in the window that appears. Type 1 fonts contain a large amount of data in the resource fork; Type 3 fonts contain very little. If only a couple items appear in the POST window, the font is Type 3.

Today's new and improved technology does nothing to address the potential hassles built into every Type 3 font. The best solution is to always throw them away. Peruse your library, choose the fonts you need, and purchase the Type 1 versions. Discard the rest—your work is worth it. And if you receive Type 3 fonts from your client base, kindly but firmly recommend that they do the same.

TrueType fonts are a different story. Most freeware fonts—particularly the ones you download from the Internet—appear in TrueType form. Occasionally, font designers will provide a Type 1 counterpart, but you can't count on it. And let's face it: some of those typefaces are extremely cool. (I like the selection at The Chankstore, at www.chank.com.) Some are virtually impossible to pass up, regardless of their font type. If you must use TrueType fonts, know that the dangers include unpredictable output and incompatibility with new technologies, such as digital presses. Although I say use them at your own risk, understand that many designers do use them, with a fair degree of success.

On a Macintosh, do two things to identify a TrueType font. First, look for any font consisting of only a suitcase—TrueType fonts do not have corresponding printer font files. Next, open the suitcase. If the icon inside has the "triple-A" TrueType mark (see Figure 4.6), discard the font immediately. On a PC, TrueType fonts are single files identified by the .ttf filename extension.

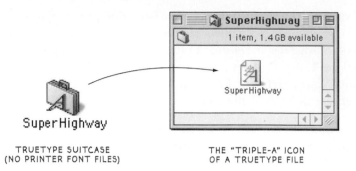

TRUETYPE SUITCASE
(NO PRINTER FONT FILES)

THE "TRIPLE-A" ICON
OF A TRUETYPE FILE

Figure 4.6   *Identifying a Macintosh TrueType font by its "triple-A" icon (visible when you open the suitcase).*

TrueType fonts can sneak onto your system without you even realizing it:

- Every Macintosh ships with a collection of TrueType faces preinstalled in the system's Fonts folder.

- When you reinstall or upgrade your operating system, more TrueType fonts are placed in the Fonts folder, even if you've already stripped them out.

- If you purchase an Apple LaserWriter and run the software installation program from the accompanying disks, TrueType fonts are often automatically installed in the Fonts folder.

In each case, the new items that spontaneously appear in your applications' Font menus are the only indication you receive. If you only intend to use your fonts to output to a relatively low-resolution laser printer, TrueType fonts will work just fine. If you need to output your fonts to an imagesetter or a digital press, they should be sought out and destroyed.

The best bet is to periodically check your Fonts folder for any new and unwanted fonts. There are also utilities available that will perform similar missions. My favorite is FontAgent from Insider Software (www. insidersoftware.com). It searches for different font platforms, regroups misplaced outline fonts with their associated suitcases, searches for corrupt fonts, eliminates potentially troublesome duplicate fonts, and other important tasks. (This utility is bundled with Extensis Suitcase 8.)

Don't succumb to the idea that you're deleting important and valuable software. On the contrary, limiting your font usage to Type 1-only is hands-down the safest bet in the industry, and that should be reason enough. As far as new fonts are concerned, the playing field is pretty safe. As I've said, nearly all fonts sold today are available as Type 1, and many fonts available for free downloading have a Type 1 version. [2]

Converting Fonts Between Platforms

Although Type 1 and TrueType fonts are used by the MacOS and Windows, the files required by both platforms are different. This can cause problems in a production environment, particularly if you're in the position of processing client files. The layout document and graphics may transfer cleanly, but you can't simply copy fonts from a Mac to a PC (or vice versa) and expect them to work. Fonts are system resources, so the data contained in each file has to reside in a location that an OS can recognize. To access a font from a different platform, you must process it with a conversion utility.

The best bet for cross-platform font conversions is Fontographer, Macromedia's font development application. Above and beyond its character editing and font creation features, it allows you to convert TrueType and Type 1 fonts from Mac to Windows, and Windows to Mac. (See www.macromedia.com for more info.) However, its $350 price tag may be too steep for anyone just looking to convert a few fonts. Several available utilities may better suit your needs.

Windows-Based Conversions

Use CrossFont 1.3 (or higher), from Acute Software. This 32-bit program converts Macintosh TrueType and Type 1 fonts to Windows, and converts Windows TrueType and Type 1 fonts to Mac. It runs on Win95/98/NT, allows you to convert entire font families, and successfully maintains hinting and other internal font info, among other features. You can download this shareware utility from www.asy.com, and its registration fee is only $45.

FOOTNOTE

[2] If you have no means to replace your fonts with new versions, another option is to use a font creation program, such as Fontographer or FontMonger, to convert your Type 3 and TrueType fonts to Type 1. This is not the panacea it seems, however: the most delicate font information is not guaranteed to translate accurately, and reading a proof is the wrong time to find that out. The adage for scanning—garbage in, garbage out—applies here, as well. New, honest Type 1 fonts are always the winning choice.

Mac-Based Conversions

For simple TrueType conversions, use TTConverter 1.5 or higher. This simple shareware ($10) has been around for years, and is available for both platforms. There is no primary site for downloading, but a simple search will point you to several options.

For Type 1 conversions as well as TrueType, try TransType 1.0.1 or higher, from the FontLab Developers Group. This utility cleanly converts codepages, encodings, font suitcases, bitmap fonts and other features specific to either platform, and also allows you to batch process a series of fonts. You can download a five-day demo from `www.fontlab.com`, and purchase a full copy for only $50.

Expert Sets and Multiple Master Fonts

Expert sets are additional fonts that accompany certain typefaces as a way of compensating for the limited number of characters each font can offer. They generally contain special characters such as fractions, numerals with descenders, stylized ampersands, and other symbols that don't appear in most standard fonts (see Figure 4.7). Adobe fonts often have additional Small Caps and Old Style Figures (abbreviated as SC&OSF) font sets as well. Not all typefaces have a corresponding expert set. [3]

FOOTNOTE

[3] For the most part, you must manually insert expert set characters into your formatted text. For example, to replace AGaramond's regular numbers with the descending characters of the expert set, you must highlight the desired numerals and choose AGaramond Expert from the font menu. Every time. Fortunately, the latest page layout programs—QuarkXPress 4 and Adobe InDesign—enable you to define and apply character styles, which greatly simplifies this process. In the previous example, a character style would contain AGaramond Expert, at the same size and style as the body text. Apply the expert characters by highlighting the desired numerals and clicking the appropriate item in the Style Sheet palette.

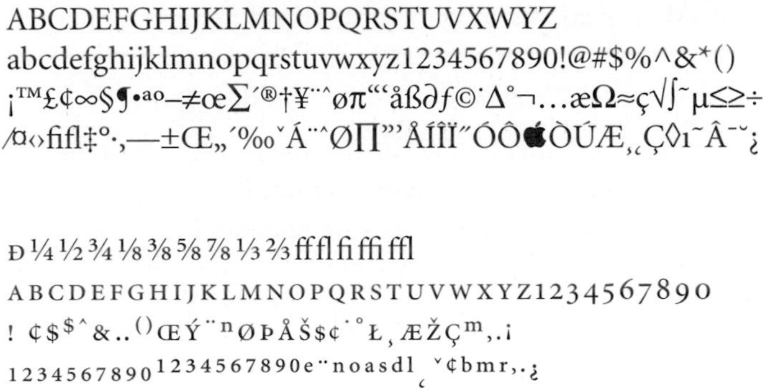

ABCDEFGHIJKLMNOPQRSTUVXWYZ
abcdefghijklmnopqrstuvwxyz1234567890!@#$%^&*()
¡™£¢∞§¶•ªº–≠œ∑´®†¥¨ˆøπ"‘åß∂ƒ©˙∆˚¬…æΩ≈ç√∫˜µ≤≥÷
/¤‹›fifl‡°·,—±Œ„´‰ˇÁ¨˙Ø∏"”ÅÎÏˇÓÔ ÒÚÆ˛Ç◊ı¯Â˘¸¿

Ð¼½¾⅛⅜⅝⅞⅓⅔ff fl fi ffi ffl
ABCDEFGHIJKLMNOPQRSTUVWXYZ1234567890
! ¢$$^&..⁽⁾ŒÝ¨ⁿØÞÅŠ$¢˙°Ł˛ÆŽÇᵐ,.¡
1234567890¹²³⁴⁵⁶⁷⁸⁹⁰e¨noasdl ˇ¢bmr,.¿

Figure 4.7 *Minion Regular and Minion Expert character sets.*

Multiple Master Typefaces allow you to create multiple thicknesses and widths of the same font. Have you ever been setting type and felt that Futura Heavy is just a touch too light, but Futura Bold (the next step up) is way too fat? Multiple Master technology enables you to generate variations of a typeface that range from extremely thin to extremely bold, very condensed to very expanded, and any combination therein (see Figure 4.8). My honest advice is to use them sparingly. Some older laser printers and imagesetter software may be incompatible with Multiple Master fonts. Also, many service bureaus have encountered clients who do not supply the necessary Multiple Master font files when a job is dropped off for output. Again, the purpose of this book is to lower the margin for error as much as possible. Limiting your use of this font platform does just that. If you do use these fonts, ask your output provider if he supports them, and be sure you include the appropriate font files with your job.

Figure 4.8 *Variations of a Multiple Master font.*

Using the Fonts Folder

Before you can access a typeface in an application, you must "turn on" the appropriate font files, or tell your operating system to recognize them. There are two ways to do this. You can use the Fonts folder, a feature built into your operating system, or a font management utility, such as Extensis

Suitcase or ATM Deluxe. Although I recommend using a management utility in nearly every production environment, let's talk about the Fonts folder first: what it does, what it's good for, and its limitations.

On a Macintosh, the Fonts folder is located in the System Folder. In Windows, the Fonts folder is found in the Control Panels folder. It's like a big "Go" button: drop a font into it, and its title appears in the type menu of all your applications. Tired of using the font? Take the files out of the Fonts folder (see Figure 4.9). It seems simple, and in the right circumstances, it is.

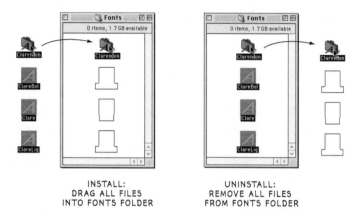

INSTALL:
DRAG ALL FILES
INTO FONTS FOLDER

UNINSTALL:
REMOVE ALL FILES
FROM FONTS FOLDER

Figure 4.9 *Place a font in the Fonts folder to activate it (left); remove the font to deactivate it (right).*

The Fonts folder is an adequate utility if the following are true:

- You own fewer than 50 fonts. If you use more than that regularly, you're a perfect candidate for font management.

- All your printing is done in-house and from your computer.

- You seldom, if ever, need to transport or copy fonts to other locations.

- You seldom, if ever, receive fonts from outside clients.

Some workstations have hundreds of fonts installed in the Fonts folder. Many designers like the idea of having *all* their fonts available to them, and the Fonts folder is an easy way to make this happen. However, this technique can pose the following problems:

- Large numbers of fonts on all the time can radically slow down system and application startups.

- At last count, the Fonts folder has a 128-suitcase limit. So either you'll only have access to the first 128 suitcases in your font library (they'll appear in alphabetical order), or you'll be compelled to combine suitcases to squeak past the limit. The latter technique wreaks havoc on organizing a coherent library, especially if the new suitcases are given names like "Fonts," "A-D," or "Type Suitcase 2."

- You have no easy way to deal with naming or numbering conflicts.

- To access a newly installed font in an open application, you must quit and relaunch the application. To remove a font from Fonts folder, you must quit *all* running applications.

Most people keep a small, core set of fonts in their Fonts folder. They aren't necessarily used for high-res output; they're typically fonts required by the OS, or items sought by certain applications whenever they're launched. Keeping them in the Fonts folder ensures that they are never turned off, and always available.

On a Macintosh, the following items must reside in the Fonts folder: Chicago, Geneva, Monaco, and Symbol (see Figure 4.10). If you use Adobe Acrobat or ATM Deluxe, you must have Adobe Sans MM and Adobe Serif MM turned on at all times. (Acrobat 4 automatically re-installs these fonts if they are missing.) Most Windows users keep at least the following items in their Fonts folder: Arial, Courier, MS Sans Serif, MS Serif, Small Fonts, Times New Roman, and Symbol.

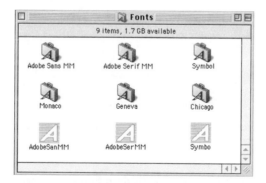

Figure 4.10   *On a Mac, only Chicago, Geneva, Monaco, and Symbol (as well as Adobe Sans MM and Adobe Serif MM, if necessary) should reside in the Fonts folder.*

The Fonts folder is where you put fonts and then forget about them. It has nothing to do with font *management,* an efficient and flexible workflow system. The only time you should manually handle your fonts is when copying them to or from transport media. The more you move these files back and forth on your hard drive, the more likely it is that fonts will become misplaced, deleted, duplicated, and generally disorganized. It's not that I think you're incapable of handling all your fonts this way—I think you shouldn't have to. You're busy enough as it is, without tempting human error.

And that's exactly what font management will help you avoid.

Organizing a Font Library

An organized library is the first step toward true font management. In it, you'll create separate folders for your legally owned fonts, another for your temporarily held client fonts and another for permanently held client fonts. Of course, you'll find it easy to add new folders, depending on the classification of fonts that works best in your production environment.

Setting up a basic library is easy:

1. Create a folder called "Type Library." Don't call it "Fonts." The System Folder already has dibs on that one (see Figure 4.11).

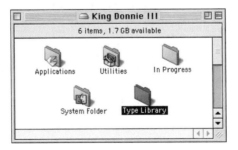

Figure 4.11 *Create a folder called Type Library to contain all the fonts on your system.*

2. Don't keep your library in your System Folder—keep it in plain sight on your main volume with your System Folder, applications folder, utilities, and so forth.

3. In the Type Library folder, create three folders: In-House Type, Client Temporary, and Client Permanent (see Figure 4.12).

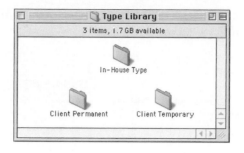

Figure 4.12 *In the Type Library folder, create three folders to complete the basic library set-up.*

4. Place all your legally owned fonts into the In-House Type folder. When you first set up your library, this may involve dragging the contents of the Fonts folder into the new folder (leaving the system fonts listed in the previous note alone, remember). Whenever possible, don't store different sections of your in-house type library in separate folders—keep them all in the same volume.

5. If you routinely hold fonts for client work (if you retain fonts that are not legally yours), place them in the Client Permanent folder. Feel free to create individual client folders within the Client Permanent folder.

6. Use the Client Temporary folder for type that comes and goes on a day-to-day basis.

7. Set each folder to List view, and organize them alphabetically. On a MacOS earlier than 8.5, open each folder and select By Name from the Finder's View menu. On MacOS 8.5 and up, this option appears under the View: **Arrange** menu. In Windows, choose List from the folder's View menu, then choose By Name from the View: **Arrange Icons** submenu. This way, all the font files display as an alphabetical list (see Figure 4.13). By arranging font files this way, you'll notice that nearly every suitcase appears in immediate proximity to the necessary printer fonts. This makes things simple when it comes time to locate specific fonts and copy them onto another disk.

Your type library is now organized. Whenever you purchase new fonts, copy them directly into your In-House Type folder. Even if you have hundreds of fonts in one folder, that's okay. After you begin using a management utility, you'll find that it makes things easier. If your fonts number in the thousands, you may want to subdivide your folders: "In-House Type A-M," "In-House

Type N-Z," and so on. But unless you have that many different fonts, there is no immediate need to do this.

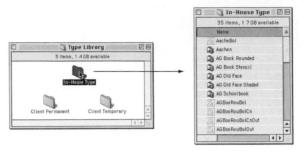

CONTENTS LISTED ALPHABETICALLY

Figure 4.13   *List your fonts by Name to have them appear in alphabetical order.*

If you have an exceptionally large collection of fonts (such as the Adobe Font Folio, which weighs in at over 2,300 typefaces), you may want to arrange the fonts in alphabetical folders. For example, instead of placing all of your fonts into your In-House Type folder, insert a series of folders titled "A", "B", "C", and so forth, and place your fonts appropriately. Fortunately, when you purchase a large font collection, they are typically organized this way already. It can be difficult when you set up your own folders, because suitcase names don't always match up with their printer font names. For example, fonts developed by the International Typeface Corporation (ITC) use a quirky and somewhat inefficient naming convention. If the typeface in question is Souvenir, the suitcase is named "ITC-Souvenir," while the printer font names are conventional, such as SouveLig, SouveMed, SouveBold. So it's possible to inadvertently place the suitcase in the "I" folder, and the printer fonts in "S". Of course, when this happens, every occurrence of Souvenir displays and outputs incorrectly. The best way to avoid this problem is to rename the suitcase, deleting the corporate prefix. In the example above, you would change "ITC-Souvenir" to "Souvenir".

Managing Your Fonts

Your library may be organized, but now that the fonts are out of the Fonts folder, you'll find they can't be accessed in any of your programs. They must be turned on, or recognized by your operating system, which is where your font management utility comes into play. The essence of font management is this: You'll turn fonts on when you need them, and off when you don't. If that sounds too simple to be true, think about it. Accessing only the fonts that you need offers the following solutions:

- Font naming and numbering conflicts are avoided.

- Sluggish system and application startups are prevented.

- You can use only the fonts supplied by a client for outputting a job, avoiding potential misprint and reflow issues.

- Accidental duplication and misplacement of fonts are prevented, because a font will not have to move to be activated.

The circumstances under which you access fonts differ according to your responsibilities, but they all revolve around the basic library set-up I've described. As I offer recommended steps for using three different font management utilities, I'll discuss techniques specific to both designers and output specialists, including:

- Establishing permanent startup fonts.

- Establishing easy-to-access font groupings.

- The most effective workflow systems for working with client font files.

Extensis Suitcase (Mac Only)

The venerable Suitcase has been around for years, originally developed by a company called Fifth Dimension. At about the same time Apple revised the MacOS's font handling (rendering Suitcase incompatible), Symantec took over Fifth Dimension with a threatened forced-leverage buyout. Faced with a hostile takeover that included pay cuts and relocation, the Suitcase programmers quit. (A number went to Adobe, where they created ATM Deluxe.) So Symantec was faced with a problem: Rewrite the core of the program to work with the Mac's new font handling, or just patch it so it could run. Quark had similar issues with XPress's font handling. Unfortunately, both companies took the easy way: They patched their software instead of rewriting it, which explains why there were more problems using Suitcase and XPress than with Suitcase and other programs. Suitcase 8 (now produced by Extensis and available for about $90) and XPress 4.04 are still essentially patch-fixes, but much more successful ones. Be that as it may, many users will simply be happy to be able to use Suitcase's tools on System 8.5 and higher. I know I am.

This section assumes you have already organized a type library, as described previously, and that you have installed Suitcase 8 on your workstation (go to www.extensis.com for a free demo).

Establishing Your Startup Set

When you select Suitcase from the Apple menu, the Sets dialog box appears (see Figure 4.14). This is your primary font management tool. Here, you establish *sets*, or little groups of font names, that you can turn on and off at will.

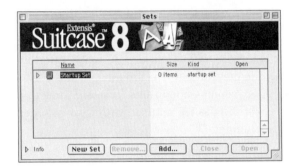

Figure 4.14 *The Sets dialog box of Extensis Suitcase.*

The first listed set is the Startup Set. If you want certain fonts open and available every time you start your workstation, they belong here. And no, don't add your entire library to the Startup Set. This defeats the entire purpose of font management, and you wasted the money you spent on the utility in the first place. Anyway, trying to open huge libraries all at once can freeze your system on startup. Before adding fonts to the Startup Set, make a conscious list of the fonts you want to treat this way. Maybe they're your corporate typefaces, or your personal favorites. Try to keep the number under 30.

To add fonts to the Startup Set, do the following:

1. Select the Startup Set icon.

2. Click the Add button.

3. Find your In-House Type folder in the navigation window that appears. Note that you are only looking for the *suitcases*, not the printer font files (hence the name of the utility).

4. One by one, add the names of the suitcases you want as startup items. Double-click the font name in the upper navigation window, or highlight each item and click Add. Every added font appears in the lower window (see Figure 4.15). If desired, check the Open Immediately box, which will turn on the fonts in the Startup Set as soon as you close the utility.

5. Click Done.

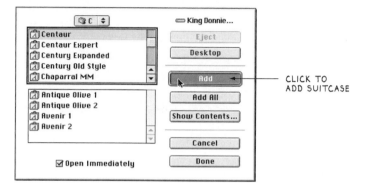

Figure 4.15 *Adding the fonts to be included in the Startup Set.*

As you review the Sets window, it's time to make a very important point. By adding fonts to the set, all you do is make Suitcase aware of the files' existence and location on your hard drive. Until you tell Suitcase to *open* the font, no connection is made between it and the operating system. The font files themselves are never moved—they still reside in the safety of your type library. Regardless of the set to which a font is added, you can select it and click Open to access the font, or click Close to remove access. If desired, you can open or close the contents of an entire set by selecting the set's icon (see Figure 4.16). Choosing Open or Close does not alter the contents of a set.

Establishing Your In-House Set

Here's where Suitcase is most useful, but it gets a little tricky. By creating additional sets in the Sets window, you create groupings of suitcases that you can quickly access. Until you point out to Suitcase that a particular font exists (by either listing it in a set or manually navigating through the Add function every time), you can't turn it on or off on-the-fly. So you'll make additional sets, depending on your needs, that let you work most efficiently. These sets are referred to as Temporary because unlike the Startup Set, these fonts are *not* activated when your workstation starts up. You have to open an entire set or a font within a set to use it in an application.

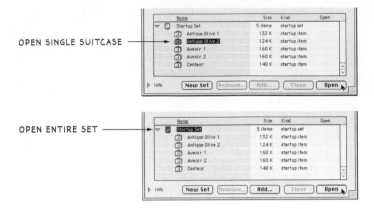

Figure 4.16 *To open an individual font, select the suitcase and click Open (top). To open an entire set, select the folder and click Open.*

The first temporary set contains all your in-house fonts:

1. In the Sets dialog box, click New Set. Name it "In-House Type," the same as your primary type library folder (see Figure 4.17).

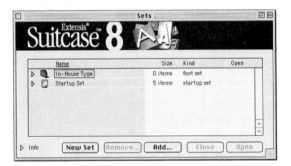

Figure 4.17 *Creating your In-House Type set.*

2. Click Add and navigate to your In-House Type folder.

3. Click Add All to add every suitcase to the set (see Figure 4.18). Be sure that Open Immediately is *not* checked. You don't want all these fonts open at the same time. In fact, trying to do this could lead to a system crash, just as if you added your entire library to the Startup Set.

4. Click Done.

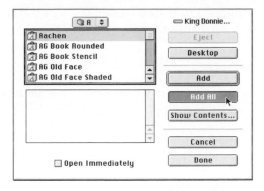

Figure 4.18   *Add all the suitcases in the In-House Type folder, making sure Open Immediately is unchecked.*

All your in-house fonts have been added to a temporary set in Suitcase. Now, to open or close a font, do the following:

1. Launch Suitcase by choosing it from the Apple menu.

2. Open the In-House Type set. Do not double-click the icon to open it (this tells Suitcase to open all the fonts in the set). Instead, click the small triangle to the left of the icon to reveal the list of fonts contained within (see Figure 4.19).

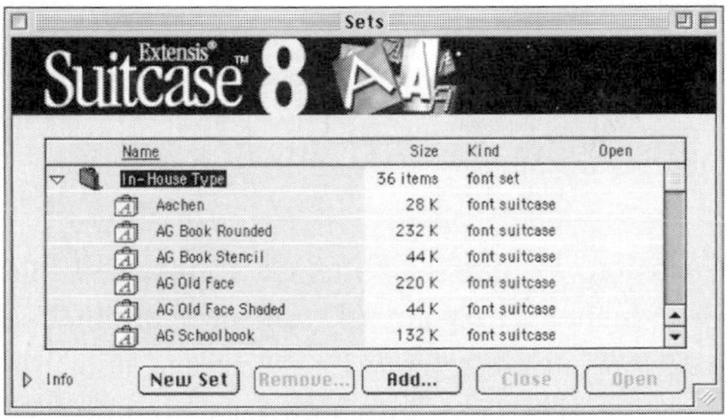

Figure 4.19   *Reveal the contents of the In-House Type set by clicking the small triangle. If necessary, jump to a desired font by typing the first few letters of its name.*

3. Select the desired font and choose Open or Close.

There's no need to move anything around, and no extra navigating through the Add window is required. For designers, this method offers the quickest access to a type library. For output specialists, as I'll discuss shortly, this method also provides the surest way to handle come-and-go client type.

Job and Client Sets

You can create additional sets for job- or client-specific font groupings. The same font can be added to multiple sets, so you can be as organized as you need to be.

A job set organizes fonts specific to a particular project. Let's say you're designing a full-color brochure. Your fonts are Adobe Caslon, Franklin Gothic, and Viking. These fonts are part of your large in-house library, but you don't need to go hunting through your In-House set every time you want to open them up. Instead, make a set dedicated to the project:

1. For this example, create a new set called "Brochure Fonts" (see Figure 4.20).

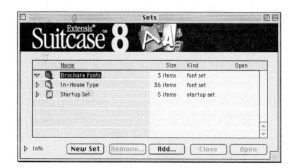

Figure 4.20 *Creating a job set.*

2. Add Adobe Caslon, Franklin Gothic, and Viking to the set (see Figure 4.21). It doesn't matter if they already appear in another set—every occurrence of a font in Suitcase references the same file on your hard drive. If you prefer, you can drag-and-drop suitcases from one set to another and avoid the whole navigational process (the original font doesn't move in Suitcase—this technique simply produces a copy).

3. Whenever you need to open these fonts to work on the project, select the Brochure Fonts set, click Open, and work away.

4. When you're done with the fonts, close them. When done with the entire set, select it and from the Edit menu, choose Remove Selected Items (see Figure 4.22).

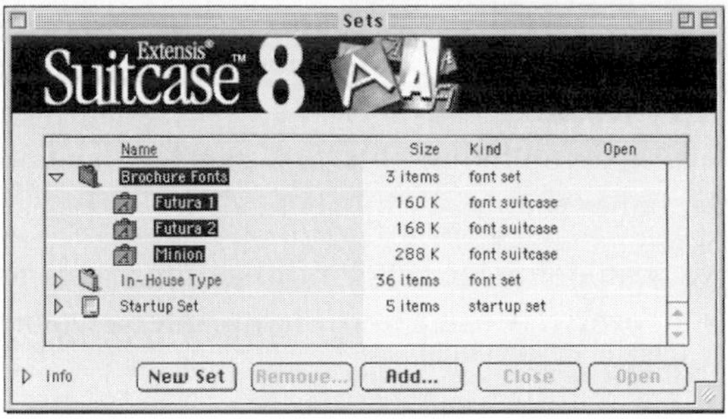

Figure 4.21   *Add only job-specific suitcases to the job set.*

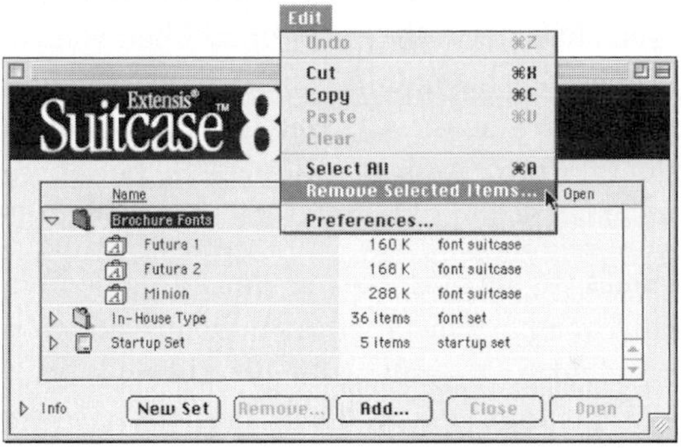

Figure 4.22   *Remove a job set when it is no longer required.*

A client set organizes fonts specific to a particular client. Most designers have clients that they work with again and again. Many of these clients are companies with corporate fonts or typefaces used in any collateral materials based on their corporate identity. Making a client set gives you quick access to their fonts next time you work on one of their projects. To do so:

1. Create a new set, naming it after the client.

2. Add the necessary fonts to the set.

3. Open and close the set whenever required.

Managing Fonts with ATM Deluxe (Mac and Windows)

Adobe finally added a feature to Adobe Type Manager that should have been there from the start: font management. Released in late 1996, ATM Deluxe not only provides all the font-smoothing functions of the standard ATM, it contains a built-in interface that allows the construction and use of font sets. It also ships with an upgraded Type Reunion, which takes font management one step further by enabling you to create custom font menus from within your applications. Imagine being able to organize your font menu by projects and clients, rather than just alphabetically.

Like Suitcase, you can delineate sets for different projects and uses, as well as standard sets for everyday use. However, the interface contains some fundamental differences.

While Suitcase has a single Startup Set, ATM Deluxe allows you to tag a set with different behaviors. The New Set dialog box contains the Upon Restart pop-up, where you can choose from the following: Leave As Is (If the fonts are open when you shut down, they stay open when you start up. If they're closed, they stay closed. This option is not only the default for version 4.5, it's the only option for version 4.); Delete (the set and its contents are removed on system startup); Activate (all fonts in the set are opened on system startup); and Deactivate (all fonts in the set are closed on startup).

This section assumes you have already organized a type library, as described previously, and that you have installed ATM Deluxe 4.5 on your workstation. (Note that the standard ATM—automatically placed in your Control Panels folder when you install an Adobe product—does not have these features. You must purchase ATM Deluxe, which retails for about $100.)

Establishing Sets

Like Suitcase, ATM Deluxe enables you to create a series of sets. From there, you attach font names from your library to the desired set, which allows you to locate and activate fonts as you wish.

When you first open ATM Deluxe, you'll notice that it features three tabs: Sets (which displays all the established sets), Fonts (which displays an alphabetical list of every font added to any of the sets), and Sets & Fonts (which displays both columns at once). Click the Sets & Fonts tab, then forget about the others (see Figure 4.23).

Follow these steps to create a set:

1. Click the New Set button. (Look for the folder icon in the lower right of the ATM Deluxe window. Or, choose New Set from the File menu.)

2. Enter a name in the New Set dialog box and click OK. A folder appears in the Sets column (see Figure 4.24).

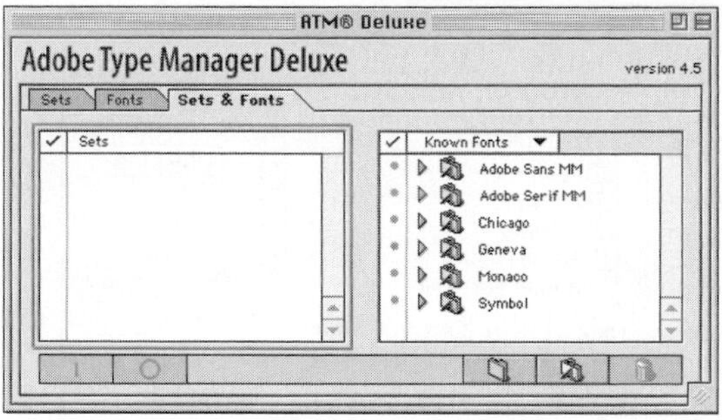

Figure 4.23   *Choosing the Sets & Fonts tab in ATM Deluxe.*

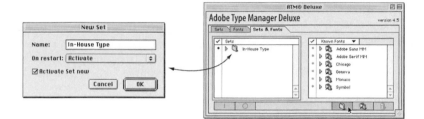

Figure 4.24   *Creating and naming a new set.*

3. Continue as necessary, until all your intended sets are listed.

Unlike Suitcase, which requires that you select a set before you can add suitcases, ATM Deluxe allows you to add fonts without placing them in a set. This is not recommended. If no sets are selected when you add a suitcase, it will simply appear in the Known Fonts column. To activate the font, you have to scroll down a potentially lengthy list. Using sets makes your job easier.

Follow these steps to add fonts to a set:

1. Select the desired set.

2. Click the Add Suitcase button. (Look for the suitcase icon, next to the New Folder button. Or, choose Add Suitcase from the Suitcase menu.)

3. In the Add Fonts dialog box, navigate to your type library (see Figure 4.25).

4. Add suitcases to the set by double-clicking them, or by highlighting the item and clicking Add.

5. Click Done. The set should contain the suitcases you just added.

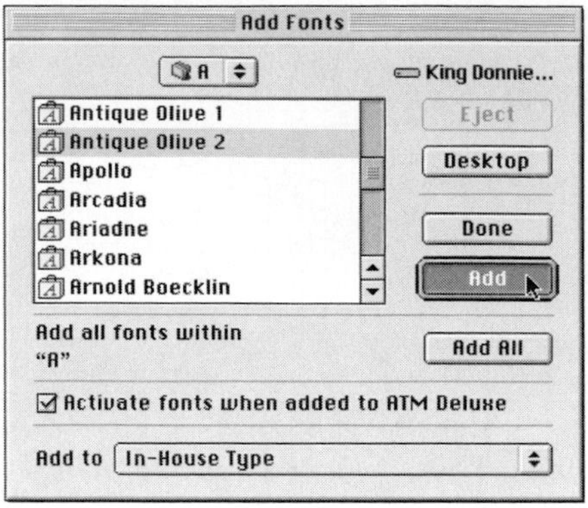

Figure 4.25   *Adding suitcases to a set.*

Activating and Deactivating Fonts

To activate a font in ATM Deluxe, follow these steps:

1.   Open the set that contains the desired font. You can double-click the set to open its contents in a window, or click the small triangle to the right of the folder.

2.   Select the font.

3.   Click the Activate button in the lower-left corner of the window.

You also can activate a font by clicking the small dot in the check mark column, to the left of the suitcase. When the font is turned on, this dot becomes bold. If you click the small dot next to the set folder, every font contained in the set is turned on. You'll notice that if a set has some fonts turned on and some turned off, the dot next to the set folder is gray. To deactivate a font, highlight it and click the Deactivate button in the lower left of the window. Or, click the bold dot in the check mark column (see Figure 4.26).

Also note that you are not restricted to navigating through the set folders to locate a font. After clicking inside the Fonts column (a thin border appears around its edge), you can jump to a font by typing the first few characters of its name. Activate or deactivate a suitcase using the steps described previously.

Figure 4.26 *Evaluating activation status in ATM Deluxe. A black dot next to a suitcase means it's activated. A black dot next to a set means that every suitcase it contains is activated. An open dot next to a set means that it contains activated and deactivated suitcases. A tiny dot next to a suitcase means it's deactivated. A tiny dot next to a set means that it contains no activated suitcases. A gray dot next to a suit-case in the Known Fonts column means that the suitcase is active, but resides in the system's Fonts folder—it cannot be deactivated using ATM Deluxe.*

Preflight Font Requirements

Everything I've discussed so far revolves around a trouble-free system for using fonts. The ultimate purpose of that system is to ensure the most accurate output possible. When it comes time to output a file, the rule is simple: Whenever a job is bundled up and sent for output, every font used during the creation of that job must be supplied. You've undoubtedly heard this before, and there are no exceptions to this rule. Even if the font in question is Helvetica, which *everyone* has a copy of, it must accompany the job to the service bureau or printer.

Here's why. Fonts, like any other software, are upgraded. The only thing is, we aren't notified about it. No version numbers exist, as with applications (we're all aware of the differences between Photoshop 4 and 5.0.2) If you Get Info on a printer font file (single-click the file and press ⌘+I), you'll see creation and modification dates (see Figure 4.27). The changes in the upgrades are minimal: a micron less thickness in the descender of the low-ercase *p*, or a fraction more space in the kern pair of *th*. Even Adobe has released perhaps nine or ten versions of Helvetica, and that does not include any third-party variations. If you create a file using the 1987 version of Helvetica, send the file to a service bureau, and they output the file using the 1994 version, you are using a different font to output your file.

This can easily cause text reflow, unexpected bad kerning, and generally unsatisfactory results. The only way to avoid this is for service bureaus to refuse to accept files that don't have fonts included.

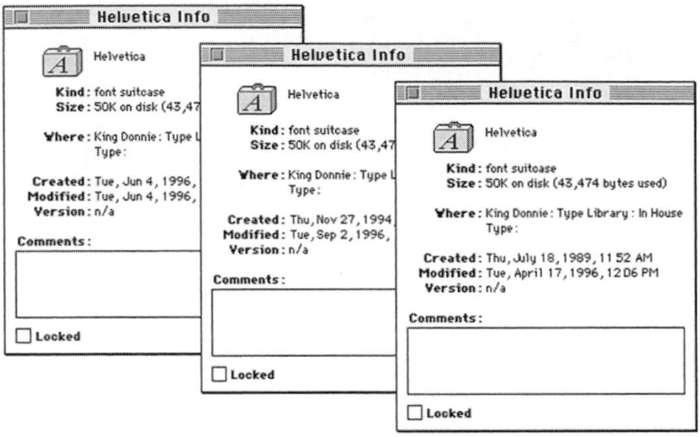

Figure 4.27   *Even though these fonts share the same character set, note the different creation dates.*

Including the appropriate fonts is a breeze:

1. In your page layout program, use the incorporated font utility to determine which fonts need to be supplied. In Quark XPress, click the Fonts tab in the Utilities: **Usage** dialog box (see Figure 4.28). In PageMaker, choose Pub Info under Utilities: **Plug-Ins** (see Figure 4.29). In InDesign, choose File: **Preflight**, and choose Fonts from the pop-up menu (see Figure 4.30).

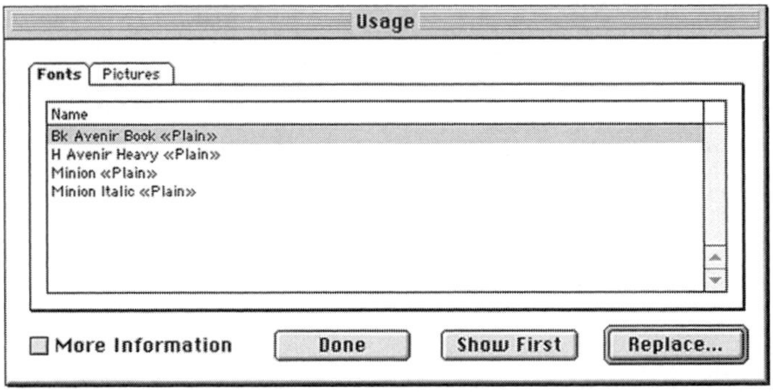

Figure 4.28   *XPress's Fonts Usage panel.*

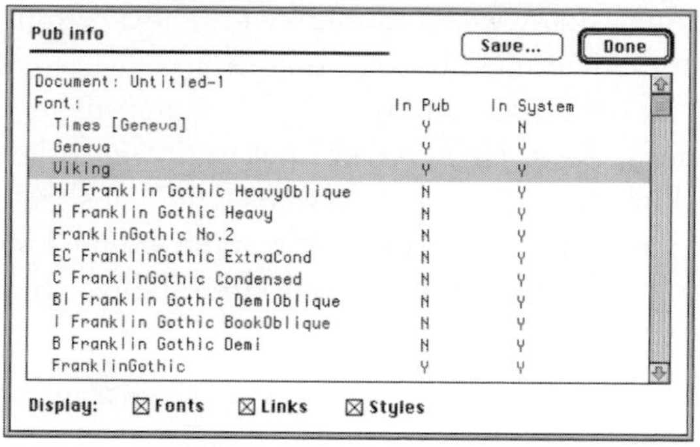

Figure 4.29 *PageMaker's Pub info window.*

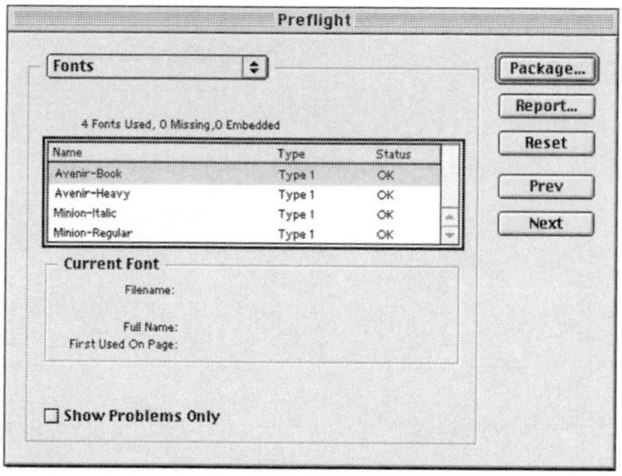

Figure 4.30 *InDesign's Preflight dialog box.*

2. Make a note of the required fonts. Even though some applications allow you to automatically copy fonts to a specified folder, the safest bet is to copy them manually.

3. Open the In-House Type folder in your type library. Select the suitcases and printer fonts for the entire font family of each font used in the publication and copy them to the transport media that contains the document and graphics files (see Figure 4.31).

Another important reason to supply entire font families has to do with the Type Style features in many applications. In days past, if you highlighted text and applied an Italic or Bold style tag, the application itself would force the type to look italic or bold. That way, one only had to supply the Plain version of the font. Today, applications automatically apply a command that substitutes those style tags with the proper font. This means that if you have strategically italicized key words throughout the text of your document, the italic version of the font must be supplied as well. If it's not present, none of the type will be italicized (see Figure 4.32). Unfortunately, if you just use those style buttons, the application will not warn you if the font is missing during output. Including entire font families eliminates that problem. Some people go one step further and use their application's Find and Replace command to swap enforced typestyles with true Italic or Bold text.

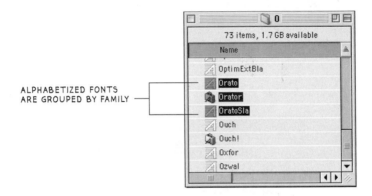

Figure 4.31 *Selecting a font family is simple when the files are listed alphabetically.*

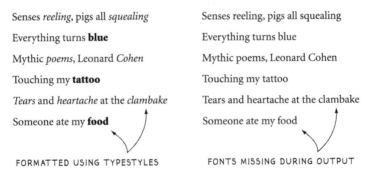

Figure 4.32 *The sample on the left was printed with the entire font family loaded; the sample on the right was printed with only the regular version of the font.*

Now you can output the file while avoiding as many troublesome areas as possible. With the preceding font system in place, the process for loading, outputting, and unloading fonts is as follows:

1. Copy the client fonts to your hard drive. Don't connect to them on the transport media.

2. Close *all* open fonts in your font management utility, even your startup sets. This is critical—it will virtually eliminate naming and numbering conflicts.

3. Create a temporary set and open only the fonts that the client provided (see Figure 4.33). If any fonts have not been supplied, you will be notified when the document is opened.

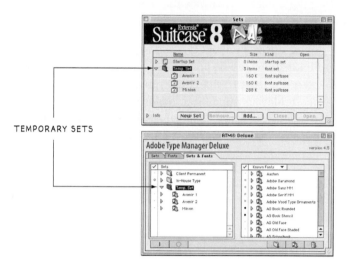

TEMPORARY SETS

Figure 4.33 *When using client fonts, create a temporary output set in Suitcase (top) or ATM Deluxe (bottom).*

4. Output the file.

5. In your management utility, close all client fonts and remove any temporary sets.

6. Decide what needs to happen next: if you have another job to output, go back to step 2 and repeat the process. If you are finished, you can turn your original fonts back on.

Last-Minute Transport Tips

When copying project fonts to your transport medium, keep the following tips in mind:

• Always send entire font families. Even if you're positive that you only used one typeface variation (such as Futura Light), supply the Futura suitcase and *all* accompanying printer fonts. Some fonts, like Futura, may ship with multiple suitcases. If so, provide all of them.

- Don't forget any fonts that may reside in imported vector-based graphics, like Illustrator EPS files. They may not register as being used in your page layout program, but they are required to print. For the best results, convert any type used in FreeHand or Illustrator to outlines before saving and importing the graphic. This way, the font is not required. (See Chapter 8, "Vector-Based Graphics," for more info.)

- When you turn over a project to a service bureau or printer, leave precise contact information, and be prepared to receive a call from the output specialist. Even the most fastidious designer may neglect a typeface, especially when under an impossible deadline. Fortunately, font families are relatively small in size, and one can easily be emailed to the provider. For the best results, include the missing family in a single-file archive (using a utility supported by the provider, such as Stuffit, Compact Pro, or pkZip) before emailing.

- If, heaven forbid, you own TrueType and Type 1 versions of the same font, be sure you send the correct version with your project. Of course, this problem can be avoided by discarding the unwanted font versions before using them in a job.

- Don't send your entire type library, assuming that the service provider can quickly sort things out. It's unfair and time-consuming, and many shops will reject such an effort. Take the few minutes required to send only the project fonts, and your deadline is that much closer to being met.

- Never assume a service provider has retained any fonts you have sent in the past. This only occurs when you make an specific arrangement with them, and the smart shop only does this for their most frequent, consistent, and trouble-free clients.

- If you've modified a font using a program such as Macromedia Fontographer, you must be sure it outputs properly before sending it. If the service provider uses a font management utility that supports font substitution, it may fail to recognize the new font and replace it with another. A good technique is to copy the font to another workstation and output some samples. Better yet, if you use the modified font for custom headlines or logos, set them in a vector-based illustration program, convert them to outlines, and import them as graphics.

Fonts, Servers, and Networks

Many companies store font libraries on central servers and allow systemwide users common access to the font information. Suitcase even enables users to share the same font at the same time. Again, my advice is simple: Don't do it.

I've learned this the hard way. When you open a font and use it in an application, your operating system makes a constantly active connection with the font files. Networks were not intended for that kind of activity. Data transfer? Fine. Font connection? No way. If your font connection is interrupted, it will likely cause your computer to freeze. If someone is sharing the same font you are using, they'll freeze too. And if the server from which everyone is sharing fonts crashes, everybody freezes.

Sharing fonts seems like a good idea. Some people appreciate the space it frees up on their hard drives; after all, my 500-font library consumes about 120MB. Others have libraries so large (or hard drives so small) there's no way to store all the type on individual hard drives. Others simply mistake a program feature for something that can be automatically trusted. Consider first how much time, work, and money is lost every time a computer crashes. Then consider this simple solution: The safest method, hands down, is to install identical type libraries on every workstation. If necessary, configure the type library (as described earlier) on one workstation, copy it to a SyQuest, Zip, or other transport medium, and copy it to all workstations. (Large numbers of fonts don't copy well over networks.)

If your type library is too large to fit on a workstation, here are three options:

- Purchase an external hard drive for each workstation's type library. Connecting to fonts on an external drive is far safer than doing so over a network, and 4GB drives can be purchased for under $300.

- If you store your fonts on a server, do not connect to them with your font management utility. Instead, figure out which fonts you need, copy them from the server to your workstation, and then open them. It's a little extra effort, but it beats re-creating work lost to a system freeze.

- If possible, be sure your hard drive is formatted in Mac OS Extended or FAT32. On a colleague's HFS+ drive, his 2,967-font library takes up only 176MB.

Fonts and Printing

When you send a document to print, it goes through a process of searching for the necessary font information. Because the documents and support files in our industry are so transient—jobs and fonts can be shuffled from workstation to workstation countless times—I recommend manually installing fonts on your hard drive, as discussed in this chapter. The font information is then downloaded to your output device during printing. But for the record, this is the sequence of locations your document searches:

1. Font information manually sent to the printer's RAM.

2. Fonts stored in printer ROM.

3. Fonts stored on a hard drive connected to the printer.

4. Fonts stored in your workstation's operating system and downloaded by the printer driver.

If none of these locations contain the information needed to output a font, a default font such as Courier will be used instead.

Font Licensing Issues

Quite a bit of confusion exists over the licensing of font technology, or your legal rights when using a font you have purchased. I have been frustrated by clients who refused to hand over their fonts out of fear of prosecution, and I have seen the Software Police threaten a local business with $10,000 fines if they didn't purchase legal versions of their software. The rights pertinent to the production environment are

- When you buy a font, you may install that font on all your company's workstations. You do not have to buy one per computer, like other graphics software.

- When you buy a font, you buy the right to use that font to create a printed product. This means that it is perfectly legal to supply a font to anyone involved in the process of designing with, printing, or reproducing the font, like freelance designers, service bureaus, or print shops.

- It is also legal to hold client fonts, provided you do not use them for any other work but the client's. This is the difference between *copying* and *pirating.* It's pirating if you make money by using a font that doesn't belong to you.

- It is legal to change or edit fonts using a program like Fontographer. Legally, typefaces cannot be copyrighted; only the coded information used in creating the font files can be. So, if you make a couple of microscopic changes in a typeface, you have a font you can use freely, or even sell. Unfortunately, every time a font is converted to another platform, a certain amount of information is lost. This eventually impacts how well the font will output, if at all.

Creating a Font Catalog

Designers and service providers alike will find it convenient to keep a catalog of their available type. Usually, this entails a sampling of all the characters of each typeface arranged on an appropriately titled page. Creating something like this by hand is needlessly time-consuming, especially if you have a large type library. Fortunately, a great utility called theTypeBook, from Rascal Software, is available. For about $40, you can automatically inventory, view, catalog, and print your entire font library (see Figure 4.34). It's handy, efficient, and cheap, even including the couple of bucks you'll spend on the three-ring binder.

Figure 4.34 *Catalog sample generated by theTypeBook.*

ATM Deluxe also has a nice built-in cataloging command. Here, you can select the suitcases you want to include, and choose File: **Print Font**

Index. It prints as many pages as necessary, offering lowercase and uppercase alphabets for each item in a each family (see Figure 4.35).

Font File Index: **Avenir 1**

Avenir 35 Light / Avenir-Light
ABCDEFGHIJKLMNOPQRSTUVWXYZabcdefghijklmnopqrstuvwxyz01234567890

Avenir 35 LightOblique / Avenir-LightOblique
ABCDEFGHIJKLMNOPQRSTUVWXYZabcdefghijklmnopqrstuvwxyz01234567890

Avenir 55 Oblique / Avenir-Oblique
ABCDEFGHIJKLMNOPQRSTUVWXYZabcdefghijklmnopqrstuvwxyz01234567890

Avenir 55 Roman / Avenir-Roman
ABCDEFGHIJKLMNOPQRSTUVWXYZabcdefghijklmnopqrstuvwxyz01234567890

Avenir 85 Heavy / Avenir-Heavy
ABCDEFGHIJKLMNOPQRSTUVWXYZabcdefghijklmnopqrstuvwxyz01234567890

Avenir 85 HeavyOblique / Avenir-HeavyOblique
ABCDEFGHIJKLMNOPQRSTUVWXYZabcdefghijklmnopqrstuvwxyz01234567890

Figure 4.35   *Font File Index sample generated by ATM Deluxe.*

Summary

Four out of five designers and output specialists agree: Fonts cause more problems than any other facet of the production process. Missing font files hold up a project. Fonts default to Courier when pages are printed. Tracking and kerning adjustments disappear when a file is output, or entire ranges of text reflow. The fonts you need aren't available in your applications. Boldfaced and italicized type reverts to Regular.

If the list of font-related problems stretched for miles, the list of possible solutions would disappear over the horizon. Fortunately, you can avoid most problems with two words: organization and management. A managed type library establishes the following safeguards:

- By keeping fonts in a separate library, you can maintain an extensive collection without clogging your system's Fonts folder with info you don't immediately need.

- By storing your fonts in clearly marked folders, you can easily access the fonts needed when sending a project to an outside vendor, keep your legally owned fonts separate from any that belong to your clients, and avoid the lost or duplicate files that invariably slow down your work.

- By using a font management utility, you can activate or deactivate your fonts at will, avoiding potential name or number conflicts. Such a utility also enables you to turn off every font on your workstation except those required for outputting a project, being sure that only the proper files are used.

- By fulfilling the essential Preflight requirement of providing the font families for every typeface used in a project, service bureaus are certain to receive all the fonts they need for output. This reduces the number of last-minute phone calls to request any missing files, and also ensures that tracking/kerning values and applied type styles are processed without incident.

It's possible to suffer through project after project without following the guidelines put forth in this chapter. Sooner or later, one way or another, for better or worse, your files will be output, your projects printed. Indeed, if you avoid the simple organizational steps of font management, you'll belong to an elite club: graphics professionals with a tale of woe to tell.

FILE MANAGEMENT

Workflow strategies have existed as long as the printed word. They're even reflected in our everyday lexicon: Back in the days of movable type, for example, *uppercase* and *lowercase* referred to the storage cases that contained the individual characters. Early typesetters had to work smoothly and efficiently, so an appropriate workflow arose: Lowercase letters were used much more frequently than uppercase, so they were kept within easier reach. Although digital practitioners no longer snatch letters out of metal cases when creating printed material, the need for an organized approach to the collective aspects of your work is as important as ever.

Your files are your most valuable property. Every piece of technology you purchase, every hour you toil at your workstation, even the time you spend reading this book is dedicated to producing files of one sort or another. They're your major expense, your prime revenue generator—and the number one source of organizational confusion.

The typical workstation stores thousands of files, from system items, to scans, to applications, and beyond. A poorly managed system causes you to lose jobs, have to rescan or re-create misplaced images, and reproduce updated work from scratch. It also leads to utter confusion when another employee sits down at your computer, which hinders his or her productivity. Proper management maximizes the value of your files, preserving your investment in their creation, storage, and future use. Also, many projects executed on a computer can be produced just as quickly using nondigital methods by an experienced professional. The most important advantages of computer-based production become evident when making edits, updating old jobs, or creating multiple variations of a single project. Without a file management system, you lose the key benefits of working digitally.

A standardized management process tackles three areas: your daily work, file and system backup, and long-term storage. To improve the efficiency of your day-to-day tasks, you must establish an unchanging hierarchy of folders and subfolders on your hard drive. This way, you (and anyone else using your workstation) always know where a file goes and where it resides, and you can quickly identify the status of any work in progress. A routine backup method allows you to recover your most recent files in the event of a disaster, such as a failed hard drive. By archiving your work, you not only free much-needed drive space, you retain easy access to completed projects. This way, you can repurpose existing components such as large scans or page templates, avoiding the time and expense of re-creation. Updated projects such as catalogs, newsletters, and brochures are vastly simplified because you can work from a copy of the existing job.

Your file management system should possess the following qualities:

- **Transparency.** The methods you employ should be so flawlessly integrated into your workflow that you don't even notice them. This means developing a system, sticking to it, and training all employees (especially new hires) to use it properly.

- **Consistency.** Every workstation in your company must adhere to the same organizational guidelines, with no exceptions. Many users treat their workstations like their home computers, arranging things the way they're used to seeing them. Others are simply sloppy, opting to save everything to the desktop, assuming they'll sort it out later. Some devote more time to creating snazzy background images than to organizing their work. A production workstation is a finely tuned tool, just like a printing press; you must treat it like one.

- **Clarity.** Even someone who has never touched your computer before should be able to locate a job or application immediately and intuitively.

- **Redundancy.** Files are safe only when they exist in multiple, easily accessible locations.

- **Accountability.** You must be able to see who creates a file, who makes any edits, and when. This will greatly assist in communication between clients and sales reps, sales reps and designers, designers and production specialists, and so forth.

Establishing a File Management System

There are three places to store files on your hard drive:

- **The desktop.** Although the operating system regards the desktop as a folder, it appears as your fundamental working space, or what you see when all windows are closed. This space is best used for extremely short-term storage of files and constantly used items, such as StuffIt Expander or aliases/shortcuts.

- **The top level.** This refers to the window that appears when you double-click the hard drive's icon. (On Mac, this refers to the startup icon that appears in the upper-right of the desktop. In Windows, this refers to the startup drive in the window that appears when you double-click the My Computer icon.) The top level contains your primary file management folders.

- **Subfolders.** This refers to any folders that reside within the top-level folders.

File management begins on the top level of the hard drive, sometimes called the *macro-level*. Strive for clarity and efficiency when setting up your primary folders. Some of the folders mentioned appear on your drive automatically; others must be created manually. Although the specifics of your workplace may require that you make additions or changes, the most common top-level setup contains the following folders: System folder (or Windows), Applications, Type Library, Internet, Utilities, Libraries, To Archive, Watched Folders, Personal, and Work (see Figure 5.1). [1]

FOOTNOTE

[1] Your top level should contain only the folders that comprise the basis of your management system. Application installations, file downloads, transfers from removable disks, and careless saves can all place files or folders on this level, which will clutter an otherwise efficient setup. Check the top level regularly, at least once a week. It's as easy as double-clicking the hard drive icon and examining the window. Remove or relocate any errant items as needed.

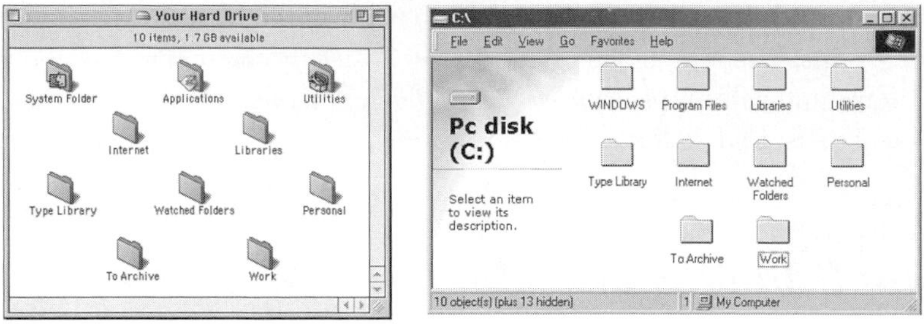

Figure 5.1 *In a file management system, the top level (Your Hard Drive) contains folders that enable you to keep your files and projects in a permanent, well-labeled place. Create enough folders to accommodate all your data—your drive should never contain any loose floating files.*

The System Folder

The operating system is the Id, Ego, and SuperEgo of your workstation. It is the motivating force behind your every action; without it, the computer is reduced to a flashing question mark on an otherwise blank screen. The computer looks for the OS on the top level of the startup hard drive. On a Macintosh, the OS is contained in the *System* folder; on a PC, the OS is contained in the *Windows* folder (see Figure 5.2). The computer will still run if the System folder is moved to a subfolder, but it takes longer to start up (because the computer must search for the files), and overall performance deteriorates. This folder is reserved for only the files required by the operating system. Do not place any files into this folder unless you're specifically instructed to by system or application installation instructions. Even more importantly, don't remove anything from this folder unless you honestly know what you are doing. (Refer to Chapter 3, "Optimizing Your Work Environment," for more info on handling system files.)

The Applications Folder

This folder contains all your production-oriented applications, such as QuarkXPress and Adobe Photoshop (see Figure 5.3). Newer MacOS installations automatically create a folder called "Applications," and you can continue to use this folder if desired. If you use an OS version earlier than 8.5, you may have to create this folder manually and then drag your applications into it. Windows users can continue using the Programs folder, which automatically appears on the top level.

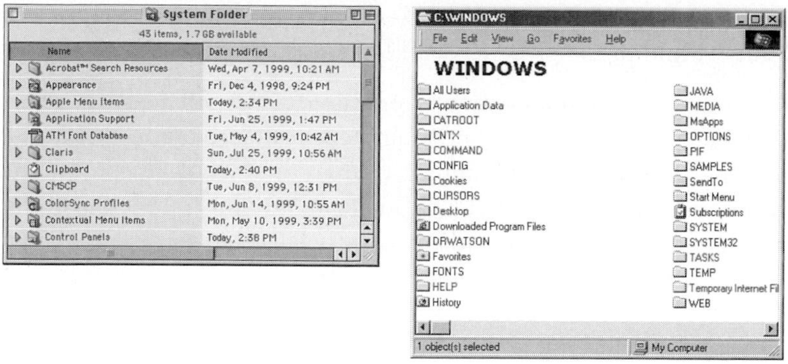

Figure 5.2   *The System Folder used by a Mac (left) and the Windows folder used by a PC (right). Your workstation's System Folder should contain only the files needed by the operating system. Some people (including consultants) stash folders in here, thinking they're safe from accidental deletion. If any consultant or tech support rep wants to add nonsystem files to your workstation, have him or her create a folder elsewhere, such as in the Utilities folder.*

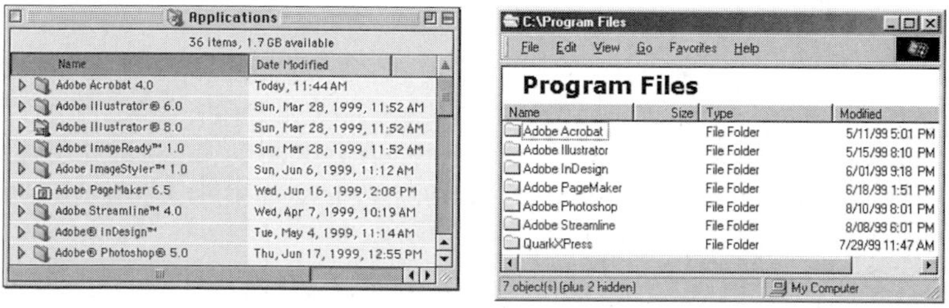

Figure 5.3   *The Applications (or Programs) folder should contain only the full-blown applications used in your production environment. Many users let their app folders float free on the top level, where many installation programs automatically place them. When this happens, you must manually drag the folder into your Applications folder.*

Most applications reside in their own subfolders. An application folder typically contains the application file, plus several required items that support the application (many of which appear in their own subfolders). As with the System folder, removing items from an application folder can degrade performance, or even drag it to a screeching halt. For example, Photoshop's application folder contains a folder called Plug-ins, which holds scanning software, filters, and other items that enhance the program's overall function.

When you launch Photoshop, it scans its own folder for the Plug-ins folder; if it doesn't find it, the plug-ins don't load.

When you install an application, a primary folder is placed on your drive that contains all the necessary program items. After dragging this folder into your Applications folder (if you didn't direct the Install program to place it there automatically), leave it alone. Do not move items into or out of the program folder unless you're specifically instructed to do so. Granted, a greater level of flexibility exists here than with the System folder. Tutorial files, sample images, and readme files generally can be deleted with impunity, but if you're not absolutely certain that an item is nonessential, leave it on your drive. [2]

The only users that really benefit from removing nonessential items from the application folders are large corporate graphics departments. This type of environment typically follows a stringent set of design and production guidelines, which often dovetail with proprietary workflow software. A support staff determines the exact function required of an application and then removes any superfluous items to prevent the possibility of workflow errors or incompatible techniques. For smaller staffs and independent users who aren't affected by such limitations, the only advantage to removing these files is an increase in available hard drive space. You can spend hours deleting every unnecessary item from your hard drive, and you may recover only 100MB of space. If such a small amount makes a difference to you, it makes more sense to invest in a larger drive.

The Type Library Folder

This folder contains your in-house and client font files. (Refer to Chapter 4, "Font Management," for info on creating, organizing, and maintaining this folder.)

FOOTNOTE

[2] Never move an application file out of its native folder. Some users place these files on the desktop (or into the MacOS's Apple Menu Items folder), assuming it makes their applications easier to find and launch. While it does give you easy access, it pretty much disables a program. Because the application cannot find the support items contained in the original folder, it refuses to launch, performs exceptionally poorly, or crashes your system. If you want this kind of access to your applications, make aliases/shortcuts of the program files and place them as desired on your drive.

If possible, copy the subfolder containing your legally owned type onto a large removable disk, such as a Jaz or CD-ROM. This way, you can quickly restore your type library if any fonts are accidentally deleted, or if you start encountering any corrupt files.

The Internet Folder

Many users forego an Internet folder, choosing to place their browser software in the Applications folder and forget about it. Graphics professionals who use the Internet extensively, however, will benefit from a dedicated folder on the top level (see Figure 5.4). This folder should contain all your Internet-specific items, including browsers, email and FTP programs, and compression/expansion utilities. The Internet folder is also the appropriate place to add a Downloads subfolder, as specified in the preferences of your browser and email programs.

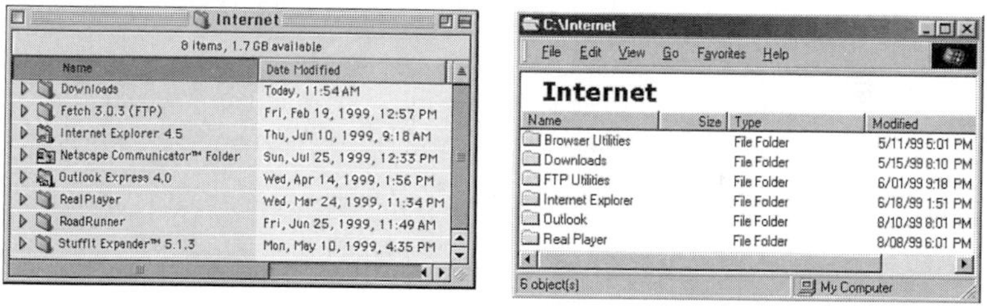

Figure 5.4 *The Internet folder contains every Internet-oriented file on your workstation, from browsers, to email programs, to download folders. This not only makes it easier to access this information, it helps prevent any confusion stemming from the endless copies of these files that are installed with other applications.*

The key benefit of the Internet folder is organization. Without it, your Internet items will be split between your Applications and Utilities folders, making them more difficult to locate and upgrade. Downloads will likely be placed on your desktop, adding clutter to your busy workspace. Because every Internet application ships with a decompression utility (such as Aladdin System's cross-platform StuffIt Expander or PKZip), you may have five or six different copies, each one a different version. Collecting them in one place makes their use much more efficient.

The Utilities Folder

The Utilities folder is a good catch-all location for any applications not used specifically for prepress or the Internet (see Figure 5.5). A typical utility is an application with one specific task, such as Disk First Aid (which diagnoses and repairs hard drive problems) and Virex (which locates and deletes viruses). They are often standalone programs that don't require a native subfolder or support files. [3]

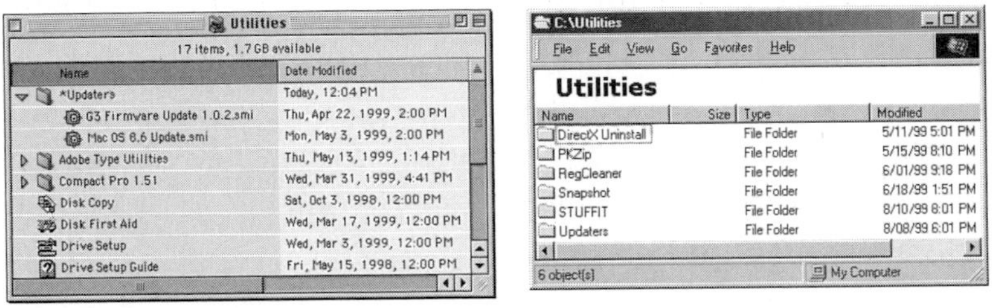

Figure 5.5 *Use the Utilities folder to hold any programs or files that add function to your workflow but aren't full-fledged production applications. Common items include disk repair utilities, formatting software, defragmenting/optimizing programs, and application updaters.*

The Libraries Folder

This folder contains graphics, templates, or other materials that are consistently used on multiple projects (see Figure 5.6). Examples include a folder of client logos created with their specific registered trademark PANTONE or CMYK colors, or templates for mailers in specific post office-approved sizes. It should also contain any library files created in your page layout programs. (See Chapter 14, "Page Layout Issues," for more info.)

FOOTNOTE

3 The Utilities folder is a good place to create an Updaters subfolder. An *updater* is a small installer program that upgrades a specific application, typically made available from the manufacturer's Web site. For example, after QuarkXPress 4.0 was released, Quark posted updaters for each subsequent incremental upgrade: 4.0.1, 4.0.2, 4.0.3, and so forth. To upgrade your version of XPress, all you had to do was download the current updater and launch it from your hard drive. After running an updater, you should keep it someplace on your hard drive. This way, if you need to reinstall an application, you'll have the necessary software right at hand to upgrade it to the current version.

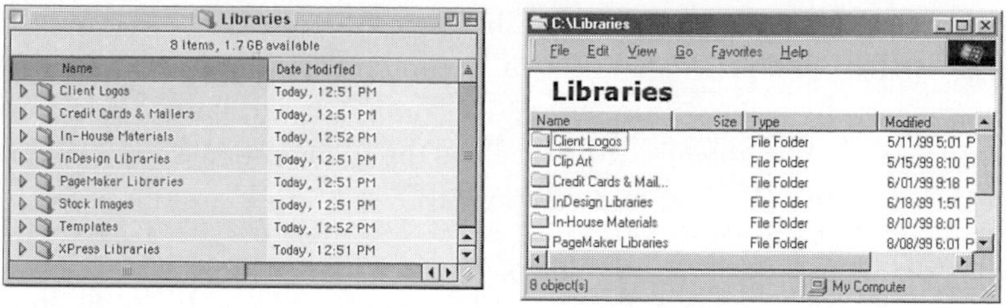

Figure 5.6 *The Libraries folder contains collections of images, layout program libraries, and templates commonly required in your work. Larger design environments usually benefit from having identical Libraries folders maintained on each workstation.*

Like your In-House Type folder, you should consider your Libraries folder sacred and inviolate. If possible, copy the entire folder onto a large removable disk, such as a Jaz or CD-ROM. After adding or changing anything in a library, update this master Library disk as well. This gives you an easy way to restore the information if necessary and will allow you to keep the Library folders on other in-house workstations consistent.

The To Archive Folder

When a project is completed, place its job folder here. Although this folder can be used for short-term storage, its contents should be archived and then deleted on a regular basis. (See "Archiving" later in this chapter for more info.)

Watched Folders

When a folder or directory is *watched*, it is periodically scanned by a specific application. This program executes an action when files of the right type are detected in the watched folder. The most common examples are used by Adobe Acrobat Distiller, which allows you to automatically convert a series of PostScript files into PDFs.

Here is a simple but common scenario: You use Distiller to create a single watched folder, which contains an In folder and an Out folder. As you create PostScript files, you save them directly into the In folder. At an interval you define, Distiller scans the In folder, converts any present PostScript files into PDFs, and places the new items into the Out folder. If desired, you can tell Distiller to delete the PostScript files, in essence cleaning up after itself. In more complex environments, Distiller can watch up to 100 separate folders, allowing you to automatically generate PDF files optimized for digital presses, film output, Web distribution, and so forth.

Distiller is not the only application that can work this way. The Mac-based StuffIt Deluxe compression utility uses watched folders, as does the RIP software used by some service bureaus. There you can have a folder trigger certain imagesetter-specific values before the file is processed, allowing you to set up a highly efficient and customizable output environment.

The needs and methods of a watched folder system depend on the software involved. At the very least, the initial folders should reside on the top level of the hard drive, allowing users to access them consistently.

The Personal Folder

This folder acts as a catch-all for any files not directly related to your work. If more than one person uses a workstation, create individual subfolders named for each employee. The contents of a personal folder may contain program tutorials, experimental images, personally owned fonts, or training materials from a class. Just as often, they may contain humorous email downloads, games, a little freelance work, personal correspondence, or even an updated résumé. Which leads to an important point: In most areas, company computers *and all their contents* are considered the property of the business owner. It's perfectly legal for an employer to search through your personal files and use any incriminating evidence he finds against you. This goes for any email sent using the company server, too.

In a perfect world, privacy wouldn't be an issue. Employees would understand that freelancing on company time poses a conflict of interest, that games detract from paid responsibilities, that copies of their email remain on the internal server, and that keeping a résumé (and maybe a few cover letters) on a company hard drive is just plain crazy. Employers, in turn, would trust their staff members and keep a respectful distance from their personal files. Until that day arrives, users of company equipment can only exercise caution. If you really want to keep games or other doo-dads on hand, store them on a removable disk and keep it with you. If you're compelled to send controversial email, wait until you get home. (A lot of people try to bypass the company email server by using an outside system, such as Hotmail or AOL. Be warned: Many companies invest in "Big Brother" utilities that let the MIS staff monitor your computer activity without you knowing it.)

The Work Folder

From start to finish, every project you create, edit, or output should be stored in the Work folder. This is the most active folder on your hard drive; in comparison, all the others are fairly static. You may occasionally add or remove an item from the rest of your folders, but the contents of the Work folder are dynamic and ever-changing.

The key to its success is the use of individual job folders. Every project you create, no matter how big or small, must reside in a clearly labeled folder, which in turn is stored in the Work folder. When used this way, the Work folder becomes the center of your file management system. It enhances your workflow by allowing you (or another user) to identify the current status of every job. It eases preflighting by storing all project components in a single location, allowing you to copy the whole thing to a removable disk with a single click-drag. It allows entire projects to be backed up, archived, and recovered at once, reducing the risk of lost component files and greatly facilitating future updates.

Job Tracking in the Work Folder

If you place every job folder in the Work folder, you hit an organizational roadblock. How will you know which work is in progress? Or in proofing? Or waiting for client approval? Regardless of your specific environment, the efficiency of your Work folder increases when you add a few subfolders.

These folders should reflect the different stages of your workflow. When a job resides in a particular folder, its current status is immediately identified. This is especially important in a collaborative environment or when multiple jobs are in progress.

A freelance designer working on smaller jobs will typically find two folders adequate: In Progress and Completed. As long as you continue working on a project, it should reside in the In Progress folder. When all is said and done, move it to the Completed folder. From there, you can either leave the job folder alone, in essence using the Completed folder as a storage area, or archive it to free up drive space.

Creative agencies and service bureaus, who typically work on a higher volume of jobs over a longer period of time, require more folders. A few possibilities are shown in Figure 5.7.

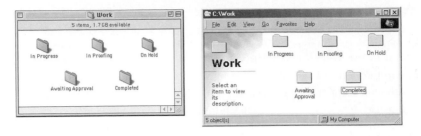

Figure 5.7 *To maximize the efficiency of your Work folder, create a series of sub-folders that reflect the different stages of your workflow. As each job moves to the next stage, move it to the proper folder.*

- **In Progress.** As described previously, this folder contains projects either still in development or in the process of output.

- **In Proofing.** The *proofing loop,* or the length of time spent in this stage, depends on the project. Presumably, the job is completed and undergoing four-color laminate proofs, IRIS or 3M Rainbow prints, bluelines, preflight laser proofs, or whatever method is used to generate a version of the project for the client or other vendors.

- **On Hold.** This folder contains jobs that have been suspended, whether in progress or not. Perhaps the client ran out of money or is dissatisfied with the work to date. Most likely, the project will be discussed in meetings over a period of days, weeks, or months. Keep it somewhere safe and out of the way, but easily accessible for when the project is finally green-lighted.

- **Awaiting Approval.** This folder contains projects that have been completed and proofed. Everyone at the agency has signed off on the work, and it only awaits the final high-sign from the client before being sent to the service bureau or printer.

- **Completed.** In theory, you can bypass the Completed folder in this environment. After a job is finished, you can move it directly into the To Archive folder. But not only is there something deeply satisfying about moving a project into a folder called "Completed," it makes sense to keep a project at hand until it is printed and shipped. There are never any guarantees that a print run will be executed error-free.

Of course, the specifics of your workplace may necessitate different folders. It is up to you to review the different stages of production and manufacture a system, based in part on the above criteria.

Job Folders

Create a new folder for each job. The conventions you use for naming these folders depends on your specific workflow. If your company uses a series of account or project numbers, use the appropriate number as the folder title. This way, you can search for a specific folder by entering the number that appears on a job ticket. If you don't use project numbers, include the client name, start date, and a brief description of the job in the folder name: "MaineLine Catalog May10," for example.

The job folder ultimately holds every element used to create a single project. Many people get as far as creating a job folder, but then they simply dump every file they encounter into it, with no effort to organize any further. This leads to a host of new problems, including the following:

- **Copies of an image file with nearly identical names.** Many users will make small, quick updates to an image and then save it under a slightly different name to avoid overwriting the original. This often results in a confusing series of filenames, such as "Puppy.tif," "Puppy2.tif," "Puppy3.tif," and so forth. If a designer decides to use an earlier version of the image, there is no clear way to tell which one she has in mind.

- **Variations of a layout document, with no clear indication of which one is current.** It's not uncommon to produce several versions of a single document as you make copy edits, test different layouts, or rearrange pages. Many people fall into an unending naming cycle. When they believe they've made the last edit, they add the word "final" to the end of the filename. When a last-minute change is required, they save a copy named "final final." Another change may result in "REAL final," or something similar. This makes it increasingly difficult to identify the version you actually intend to use. You have to either compare modification dates (if you're looking for the most recent copy) or open and examine each file.

- **Files are overwritten.** If you save all your files to the same folder level, they are much more likely to be overwritten by accident. Assume you've received a folder full of fresh scans. If you open, edit, and save the same files without creating copies, you have no originals to refer to if you later discover you've over-corrected an image. Your only option is to rescan. Also, if you overwrite a native Photoshop image that contains layers, you can no longer edit the individual components. If you need to make a change, you have to re-create the entire image.

When properly organized, a Job folder may contain several subfolders and files (see Figure 5.8). [4]

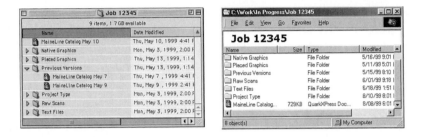

Figure 5.8   *A Job folder contains all the component files used in the creation of a project. Rather than keep all the files on the same level, separate them into clearly labeled subfolders. This prevents you from accidentally overwriting a graphics file or using the incorrect version of a layout document. It also means that all the project components are collected in one place when it's time to send it to a vendor, eliminating the need to frantically search for missing files at the last minute.*

The Page Layout Document

Keep the current version of the layout document on the top level of the Job folder. When more than one designer works on the file, include the date or time of the most recent edits at the end of the filename. If necessary, add the most recent user's initials. This makes it considerably easier to keep track of the most recent version.

F O O T N O T E

4   When a project is properly organized in its Job folder, you no longer need to use any automated preflight utilities or collection commands to prepare a job for transport. After outputting your preflight laser comps and separations, drag the folder to the desired removable media. From there, you may want to open the document that resides on the cartridge and examine for any missing items, as you would with any other job. (See Chapter 16, "Preflight and File Prep," for more info.)

The Previous Versions Folder

Keep earlier copies of the page layout document in this folder. This offers the following benefits:

- You can revert to earlier versions of a layout without having to re-create any elements you may have changed.

- In many design firms and ad agencies, it is important to keep a record of document changes, including who made them and when. The documents in this folder provide a history of a project's evolution; along with printed proofs, they record all changes requested and approved by the client. This is particularly helpful if disagreements arise over the final printed product.

- It offers short-term backup in case a document becomes corrupt. This can occur if your computer crashes when you save a file, if a document's data fork is munched by a virus, or if a file is written to a bad sector on your drive. Most often, you'll never know why—you'll only know you're back to square one if you don't have a backup. Available utilities can often be used to recover a bad file (the Mac-based MarkzTools III from Markzware, for example, opens badly damaged QuarkXPress documents that display "Bad File Format" and "End of File" messages), but they are not 100% reliable.

Some programs enable you to automatically save backup copies of your document. For example, XPress's Auto Backup feature enables you to maintain a specific number of document copies, created at user-defined intervals. For the best results, however, you should create backups manually. Auto-saving gives you little control over the exact content of the backup, and many users find that automated features freeze their system with annoying regularity. To create a backup document, follow these steps:

1. Choose File: **Save** to update the current document, like you normally do.

2. Immediately choose File: **Save As**.

3. Rename the new copy, inserting the current time or some other indicator in the filename.

4. In the Job folder, drag the first document into the Previous Versions folder.

5. Continue editing the second document.

The Raw Scans Folder

This folder contains all the original scans created for a project, whether generated by you, a separate in-house operator, or a service bureau. These files may consume hundreds of megabytes on your drive, but it's in your best interest to retain them. A round of scans may first arrive in perfect condition, but two things are likely to occur: You will perform additional color or tonal corrections, and you will apply edits such as cropping, retouching, sharpening, and so forth. If you edit and save the same files, you can no longer return to the original image if you make a mistake—and rescanning is expensive, especially if you use an outside vendor.

When further editing a scanned image, either duplicate the file before you open it or perform a Save As and rename the file. Completed images should reside in the Placed Graphics folder. If desired, create an additional folder called "Images In Progress" inside the Raw Scans folder, where you can keep edited scans that aren't ready for placement in a page layout.

The Text Files Folder

This folder contains any text files imported into the document. Often, the text used in a project is provided by the client or a contracted copywriter as a word processing file. It's important to retain these files, even after the text is incorporated into the page layout. If any typographical or factual errors slip through, you can track them through earlier stages of the project, which allows you to determine if responsibility lies with a production department or the client.

The Native Graphics Folder

This folder contains copies of your graphics saved in their native file format. Layout documents require that graphics be saved as TIFF or EPS. Unfortunately, these file formats disallow features that are retained only by the native format, such as Photoshop's layers and Illustrator's live blends. Not all of your graphics need to be saved this way, of course—only the ones using application-specific features. For example, the object of a current product shot may be placed against a gradient background. When the client decides he wants you to change the background to solid white and add a drop shadow, you have a choice. If you didn't save a copy of the file with the image layers intact, you'll have to painstakingly remask the product. If you did save a copy, all you have to do is delete the background layer, add the shadow, and save a fresh, flattened version into the Placed Graphics folder.

The Placed Graphics Folder

This folder contains copies of every graphic file imported into the layout document. Some users place new graphics here and then hesitate, knowing that many of their graphics reside in locations all around their drive, such as library folders, personal folders, client file folders, and so forth. Placing copies into this folder may add an extra step in the process, but it saves considerable time and effort as the job progresses. This way, you are free to apply any project-specific edits to a graphic, avoiding the possibility of changing the contents of a file you wish to use again in a different way.

Many users prefer to import their graphics from wherever they normally reside on the drive and then collect the components automatically, using commands such as XPress's Collect for Output or InDesign's Preflight. However, these commands are fairly limited in scope and are better suited for people not establishing a file management system. Most often, they are run at the end of a project, after any graphics have been created, edited, and reedited. Until that point, graphics may be scattered over any number of folders, disks, and drives, making it harder to pinpoint a file for further work.

Collection commands can be useful when initially creating or updating your Placed Graphics folder. After you import the first round of images into a document, use your application's collect feature to place copies of the files into your Placed Graphics folder. Because you have to save the document to run the command, rename it and use it as the current version (as described earlier under "The Page Layout Document"—just remember to drag the copy of the document generated by the collect command from the Placed Graphics folder to the top level of the job folder). You can use the same technique to periodically update the contents of the Placed Graphics folder. (See Chapter 14 for more info on the collection commands of XPress, PageMaker, and InDesign.)

Project Type Folder

As you decide to use specific typefaces in a project, place copies of the font files in the Project Type folder. For the best (and safest) results, copy the entire font family. For example, if you use Minion regular to format the body text of an annual report, place copies of every Minion variation into the folder. (Refer to Chapter 4 for more info on using, copying, and transporting font files.)

Although it means creating duplicate files again, this process offers certain advantages over using the fonts in your primary type library. For example, it allows you to consciously address any typefaces used in vector-based graphics, which may not be identified by your page layout program, but are required for output. Granted, type used this way should be converted to outlines before you import such a file (as described in Chapter 8, "Vector-Based Graphics"), but including these fonts with a project protects you when any unconverted files slip through. Additionally, it can inform you when your document uses fonts that you're not aware of. For example, you can establish a set in your font management utility that uses only the items in the Project Type folder. Before working on the document, you can turn off all the other fonts, using only the ones specified for the project at hand. If you receive any "missing font" alerts, you can determine exactly what they are. From there, you can either remove them from the document or copy the appropriate files to the Project Type folder.

Backup

Bad things happen. The most prevalent belief in the industry is that your computer will die just when you need it most, regardless of what you do to prevent it. This superstition may be unfounded, but many users have stories to tell. Some experienced hard drive failure; some accidentally deleted a job folder; some, in an attempt to repair a disk, reformatted their entire drive, deleting everything. One person I know took his hard drive home, thinking he'd do some work over the weekend, and dropped it down a flight of stairs. You obviously can't plan for all disasters—but by backing up your work, you can keep your profit-generating data safe. When something does occur, you're able to restore your files and keep working.

Backup refers to routinely updated copies of your most commonly used files. When using a management setup similar to the one described in this chapter, you only need to backup the Work folder. Your type library and image libraries should already exist on CD-ROM (or similarly sized media), and your applications and operating system can be restored from the original disks.

Fortunately, backing up your work is easy. It only requires duplicating your files to a location where they won't be affected if something happens to your computer. This could be a removable disk, a company server, or another workstation connected over a network. It can be performed manually (by clicking and dragging) or automatically (using something like Retrospect, a cross-platform utility from Dantz Development). [5]

Manual Backup

Backing up manually is as easy as dragging the Work folder onto a removable disk. Do this as you head to lunch or prepare to go home, letting the files copy as you walk out the door. If you follow this simple routine, you will never lose more than a few hours of work.

When copying, you can replace previous backups with current data. For an extra measure of safety, you can rotate several disks to give yourself a buffer of a few days, allowing you to retain earlier versions of a project. Whatever method you choose, make sure your disk is clearly labeled and that everyone knows not to touch it. Many a backup routine has been compromised by someone who urgently needs a disk and grabs the first one he or she finds.

Always keep in mind the limitations of the media you choose. It must be large enough, reliable, and durable (which makes Zip disks—a common choice for backup—a weaker option). Perhaps the perfect backup media is the rewritable CD. It combines all the durability and convenience of CD-ROM with the ability to be rewritten more than 1,000 times. Rotate five CD-RWs throughout the workweek, and you'll be able to backup your Work folder for almost 20 years for under $75. If you produce more than 650MB of data on a daily basis, consider DVD-RAM, CD-RW's big brother, with more than 5GB of storage space. (See Chapter 6, "Media Dexterity: Transport and Storage," for more info on storage options.)

The advantages to manual backups are the price, the speed, and the ease of execution. The biggest disadvantage is that you have to remember to do it.

FOOTNOTE

[5] Some users back up their work by duplicating folders on the same hard drive. However, the key to successful backup is redundancy. If your computer goes down and you have no off-drive backups, you can't access any of the data, no matter how many copies you've made. Even if the drive is restored, you lost time (and possibly missed deadlines) while waiting for a technician to finish repairs. When your files are properly backed up, you can continue working on another company workstation or even a rental unit. Of course, a widespread disaster—such as your company burning down—can hamstring the most religious backup routine, which is why many users keep their most important data on a disk they carry with them.

Automatic Backup

For those of us who find it difficult to back up every day, there are automatic utilities. The most widely used is Retrospect, which also ships with many new storage devices.

There are several benefits to using Retrospect over copying manually:

- You can set it to back up specific folders at specific times.

- You have the option to compress files during backup, allowing you to fit more on your target storage device.

- Retrospect can be told to recognize whether a file is new or has been modified since the last backup, and it will duplicate only these items.

- Retrospect Remote can perform backups over a network. A single person can back up every workstation on the network, freeing the rest of the staff from backup responsibilities.

There are only two drawbacks to using Retrospect. First, it requires that you master a new application, and it will take time and practice to get it right. Second, the files generated by Retrospect appear in a proprietary format that can be read and restored only by Retrospect. Restoring files this way is significantly slower than working with files that were backed up manually.

Archiving

Archiving is one of the most important stages of the production process— and one of the most overlooked. It preserves all the hard work that goes into any project. However, it isn't seen as a specific revenue-generating step, mainly because it takes place *after* the print run, when the invoice is in the mail.

Archiving is like putting the family jewels in the bank. Your investment is protected. If the client was satisfied with a project, there is a good chance he or she will return later for reprinting with minor modifications. When the job has been properly archived, the old files can retrieved in an instant. The quick turnaround and lower production costs will win you a friend for life. On the flip-side, a client will be rightfully angered when told by an agency that the original project no longer exists. Even worse: Some places, when they realize the files are lost, attempt to cover their tracks by building an exorbitant "de-archiving" fee into the project estimate. This is more than unethical, and it gives the client every reason to take his business elsewhere.

Like backup, archiving is an inexpensive and straightforward process. You can even promote it as a value-added service to your client base—they'll love you for it, never realizing that it cost only pennies and a few minutes of your time.

Archive your work by duplicating finished jobs from your hard drive to a more permanent storage media. If you use the management system described in this chapter, these folders should reside in the To Archive folder. After archiving, delete the job folders from the hard drive. It is important to wait until you're absolutely sure the project is finished. If any last-minute changes are requested—and believe me, a call from the press operator gives new meaning to the term "last-minute"—you'll lose valuable time locating and retrieving the files.

As with backup, you can archive manually or automatically, using Retrospect. For companies with low-volume archiving needs (less than 2GB per week), archiving manually to CD-ROM is the best option. At $2 each, CD-ROMs are affordable enough to allow you to organize disks by client or even archive each project to its own disk.

The only drawback to CDs is that you have to monitor them during copying. If you routinely archive more than 2GB a week, you will spend an inordinate amount of production time copying files and writing CDs. At this point, you need an automated solution such as Retrospect Remote in conjunction with a digital linear tape drive mounted on a server. DLT drives have a well-deserved reputation as the fastest, most reliable, and most cost-effective tape drives currently available. You can set Retrospect to search every computer on the network and archive the contents of any folder it finds named "To Archive." De-archiving using this method may be less convenient than pulling cartridges off the shelf, but the convenience and time savings it provides can't be beat. (See Chapter 6 for more info on storage options.)

Whatever media you use, label them clearly and store them in a well-organized, centrally located area. Establish a list of in-house guidelines on their proper use, and insist that users put them back exactly where they found them. For the most successful archiving, store duplicates offsite to accommodate any worst-case scenarios, such as fire or employee theft.

File Naming Conventions

Develop a consistent system for naming your files. Doing so will allow you to identify your files more readily, and you'll find it much easier to search for any accidentally misplaced items. Also, if any of your files will be processed on a different platform (for example, if your PageMaker document is created on a Mac but will later be opened on a PC), your filenames must adhere to certain requirements. Some suggested conventions include the following:

- When naming a page layout document, include the start date of the job, the project or account number from the job ticket, and if possible, part or all of the client name.

- Add the PC file extensions at the end of the name, such as .tif for TIFF images, .qxd for XPress documents, and so on. Note that even though you can set Windows to hide these extensions (using the View setting under View: **Options**), they are still required when opening files created on a Mac. [6]

- Restrict your filenames to 27 characters or less. This allows you to accommodate the file extensions described previously without hitting the Mac's 31 character limit.

- Don't use the following characters when naming PC-destined files, because they are otherwise used by Windows to structure commands and to separate hierarchical paths: asterisk (*), forward slash (/), backslash (\), colon (:), quotation marks ("), less-than (<), greater-than (>), question mark (?), and pipe (|).

FOOTNOTE

[6] If you add the incorrect extension to a file on a Mac, you may not be able to read it on a PC. Just recently, a colleague created an Illustrator graphic on a Mac, added ".aif" after the filename (assuming it meant "Adobe Illustrator File"), and sent the file to a Windows-based company. Because that extension actually stands for "Audio Interchange Format," the PC recognized it as a sound file. It couldn't be opened, even when they tried from within Illustrator. As soon as they changed the extension, it worked perfectly.

FPO, DCS, and Offsite Storage

If a project involves enough color images, the sheer amount of space required to transport and hold them is daunting. For example, assume you have your service bureau scan 75 full-color, 4×5-inch images. At roughly 6.8MB each, they'll consume 510MB. If you use large, fast disks, or if you know that you will be further editing the scans yourself, accepting the files shouldn't pose any problems. However, if you can't accommodate that amount of data, you can still work with a series of For Position Only (FPO) images.

When the necessary arrangements are made, a vendor can provide a designer with low-resolution versions of the scans, keeping the high-res data required for final output in-house. These images are the same width and height as the originals and can be imported, scaled, rotated, and cropped like any other graphic. The designer incorporates the FPOs into a page layout, and when the job is finished, he or she sends the project back to the same vendor. After replacing the FPOs with their high-res counterparts, the project is output.

The key to this technique is the Desktop Color Separation (DCS) file. This process splits an image into five components: a 72ppi preview (sometimes called the *master file*), plus the individual channels that contain the cyan, magenta, yellow, and black information (see Figure 5.9). Rather than provide the potentially huge image files to the client, the vendor provides the previews, which are roughly 10% of the original file size. In the example used here, each preview might be 610KB. The client would walk away with only 46MB of data—small enough to fit on a single Zip disk. When the vendor receives the final document (with the imported FPO files provided), each image is relinked to its high-res component before further processing.

Yacht.C	1.7 MB	Photoshop® EPS file
Yacht.eps	652 K	Photoshop® EPS file
Yacht.K	1.7 MB	Photoshop® EPS file
Yacht.M	1.7 MB	Photoshop® EPS file
Yacht.Y	1.7 MB	Photoshop® EPS file

Figure 5.9 *A DCS file is a high-res CMYK image split into five parts: a low-res preview and the channels that contain the cyan, magenta, yellow, and black information. A client uses the preview as an FPO, and the vendor retains the high-res components. When the file is returned to the vendor, the files are linked up, and the project is output.*

Successful use of this method requires an understanding of the following issues:

- If you receive an FPO, you cannot open it in Photoshop. It cannot be adjusted or edited in any way; you can only import it into a page layout. This makes it a good choice when using color-corrected scans in a product catalog or brochure. It's a poor choice when you need to add layers, apply filters, or further adjust color.

- If any of the component files are deleted or misplaced by the vendor, the image cannot be relinked or output.

- Don't use this method unless you have a good reason for doing so. If you create DCS files and then keep all the components on your own workstation, you've only succeeded in creating five times as many files to keep track of. Many users have made the mistake of creating their own DCS files and then providing only the previews to the vendor.

- When creating a five-part DCS file, use Photoshop's DCS 1.0 file format. Starting with version 5, Photoshop offers DCS 2.0, which creates only a one-part file. The DCS 2.0 file format exists only to support the use of Photoshop's Spot Color command.

Follow these steps to create a five-part DCS file:

1. Open a CMYK image in Photoshop. (Some color management systems require that you correct an image in RGB and then use an export plug-in to create a DCS file. The image is converted to CMYK in the process.)

2. Choose File: **Save As**.

3. In the Save dialog box, enter the desired name and choose Photoshop DCS 1.0 from the File Formats pop-up.

4. Click Save.

5. When the DCS 1.0 dialog box appears, choose an option from the Preview pop-up (see Figure 5.10). On Windows, choose TIFF (8 bits/pixel); on a Mac, choose Macintosh (8 bits/pixel).

6. Under the DCS pop-up, choose Color Composite (72 pixels/inch).

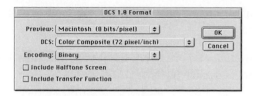

Figure 5.10   *Photoshop's DCS 1.0 Format dialog box. You must use this option to create a five-part file. If you try to use DCS 2.0—which is used only to accommodate a spot color channel—you'll get only a single file.*

7. Select an option from the Encoding pop-up. Mac and Win98 users, choose Binary (for smaller file sizes); Win95 and 3.1 users, choose ASCII (for better compatibility). Avoid the JPEG options—they are known to cause output problems.

8. Click OK. The preview file appears with an .eps file extension; the component files appear with .C, .M, .Y, and .K extensions.

When a designer receives FPO images, he should treat them just the same as any other graphics file. Keep them in the Placed Graphics folder in the project's Job folder. The vendor retains the component files, which should be stored in a well-marked client folder and then either uploaded to the company server or archived for future access.

Summary

It's a safe bet that all of us have experienced a workplace with no file management. Files are kept mainly on the desktop, or in a loose conglomeration of folders scattered throughout a collection of disks and drives. It is difficult at best to collect a project's component files. Jobs are deleted after completion, and often you have no idea until a client returns to update the work. Images are rescanned, illustrations are re-created, documents are reconstructed, time is wasted, profits are depleted, and spirits are broken.

Although I've spent many pages describing the facets of a simple file management system, the work involved is minimal:

• Add a series of clearly labeled folders to the top level of your hard drive.

• Keep the files of each project in separate folders, each one named to accommodate easy identification and searching.

- Name your files consistently, following a simple set of universal guide-lines.

- Back up your current work every day to prevent disaster in the event of some technological mishap.

- Archive your finished jobs for long term storage, freeing up megabytes for future work.

The main reason people avoid setting up a management system is the up-front expenditure of time. We downplay the process of spending hours in a bitter sweat, attempting to recover or re-create work that was lost, deleted, or destroyed. It's a little like surviving a car accident; the brain diminishes the memory, sparing us the pain, allowing us to think it wasn't as bad as we originally thought. A file management system will offer your workflow enough safety and efficiency to avoid those experiences altogether.

MEDIA DEXTERITY:
TRANSPORT AND STORAGE

No one works in a vacuum.

One way or another, you must transport your documents, images, and fonts to a service provider, who in turn must be prepared to accept a variety of disks. You need a way to store your work that allows you to easily retrieve it. You have to archive old projects in a way that can be understood by others. Multiple-user environments require a simple method of distributing files between workstations.

Disorganized media results in lost work, missed deadlines, and wasted money. For example, if you FedEx a job to a service bureau and they can't load your disk, you've lost a day. By the time you resend the file, another day has passed—enough time for your print window to have closed, potentially pushing back a job days or weeks. Archiving a project on unreliable media may mean having to re-create a job from scratch, when you could have otherwise updated existing files. Attempting to send large image files over the Internet can take hours. Sent improperly, they will be unreadable to the recipient, resulting in more wasted time.

We all have experience using transport media. If you've ever successfully inserted a floppy or Zip or sent a file via the Internet, you're ready for the next level. Media *dexterity* involves the capability to flawlessly move files from your station to the service bureau, printer, or other stations in your office. It allows you to receive files from clients and freelancers in a way that gives you immediate, trouble-free access to the information. With media dexterity, you can store vast amounts of data and quickly find what you need, without spending hours searching. Ultimately, your use of removable media should be a transparent process, so automatic that it doesn't need a second thought. Beyond saving time and money, media dexterity allows you to transcend the physical limitations of your computer. Hard drives are finite resources, able to hold only a fixed amount of information. Moving data from one computer to another is only possible using removable media, networks, and the Internet.

Media dexterity was originally dependent entirely on removable disks. Floppies, CD-ROMs, removable hard drives, and Digital Audio Tape (DAT) are just a few examples, and the form you use ultimately depends on your work. Removable media still serves the following purposes: [1]

- **Backing up files.** The files you produce will inevitably surpass your hard disk's capacity, leaving you with a drive too full to work. Deleting files runs the risk of losing work that took hours to create. Backing up files onto removable disks enables you to safely clear nonessential work from the drive. Hard drives can also become corrupt, destroying all the stored data. If your important files are backed up on a removable disk, tragedy is averted.

- **Archiving files.** Completed projects should never be thrown away. A client could want the same ad or catalog next year, with only minor modifications. Parts of one project can always be recycled for another. File creation requires time, effort, and money. Don't throw away that investment—archive everything.

- **Transporting files.** You need a way to move files from one workstation to another. Outsourced scans need to get from the service bureau to you. You need to send work to freelancers, as well as getting finished files to the service bureau or the printer. While networks and the Internet provide additional transport options, most files are still moved on disks.

FOOTNOTE

[1] Two options augment the widespread use of removables: local area networks (LANs) and the Internet. LANs have all but replaced the use of removables for moving files between computers in a small area, such as within a company. Due to the slow speeds of some networks, removables may still be preferable for moving large files, but this is changing as network speeds increase. For smaller files, networks enable files to move from one computer to another with greater ease and efficiency than removables. The Internet has the potential to do for the entire world what LANs did for businesses. In a short time, getting files to the service bureau will require as much effort as it takes to copy them to a removable. In many instances, as we shall see, this is already the case.

- **Maintaining workstation configurations.** Creating a working system on a workstation is a lengthy process involving many applications, system extensions, and other elements. Sometimes it's necessary to reformat the hard drive and restore all this data. Most removable storage media can be made into a bootable system disk, containing everything you need to re-create the working computer. (Refer to Chapter 3, "Optimizing Your Work Environment," for more info.)

Obstacles to Media Dexterity

The following issues can impair an efficient media dexterity system:

- **Too many options.** A variety of options is usually a good thing—here, however, it only adds complexity. New forms of removable media are introduced almost daily. Some, like CD-ROMs, become indispensable. Others, like the Floptical, are all but forgotten a few months after they appear. Others still, like the 120MB iMation SuperDisk, appeal only to a specific audience. Users who don't typically accept many outside files, such as designers, are encouraged to limit their choice of devices to one or two. Service providers are always in the position of investing in a wider array of options, to ensure that they can accommodate work from a wide range of clients.

- **Industry standards change quickly.** A few years ago, 44MB SyQuest cartridges were the disk of choice in the prepress environment. Today, the 100MB Zip disk is almost universal. Next year it may well be something else.

- **Commitment to outdated technology.** It can be hard to let go of the past, especially when you've invested so much money into it. Newer removable storage media is cheaper and faster, and problems arise when you receive a 2GB Jaz disk from an important new client, when you still use an 88MB SyQuest.

A Brief History of Storage

IBM changed the world of computing in the early 1970s—over a decade before digital prepress was ever possible—by creating a technology called Winchester.

The Winchester featured a pair of spinning 14-inch metal platters. A lightweight head floated just above the surface, moved by an actuator arm to wherever information was stored. This head could read and write magnetic charges directly to the platter, and these charges were interpreted by the computer as data. It had distinct advantages over existing devices, which were based on magnetic tape. Not only did it have a much faster data transfer rate, its information was *randomly accessible*. On tape, data is stored linearly. To retrieve information at the beginning of a tape, for example, it had to be completely rewound. The Winchester could jump to information stored on any part of a disk at any time. (Incidentally, because each platter held 30MB of information, the mechanism was named for the Winchester 30-30 repeater rifle.)

The Winchester was the predecessor to the modern hard drive. While modern drives are smaller, faster, and hold more data, the technology is essentially the same. In fact, they're still referred to as Winchester drives.

These storage devices fell largely in the domain of huge mainframe computers. Soon, another innovation made computers a little more "personal": the floppy drive. Before the floppy, programs had to be manually entered whenever you started a computer, unless you were fortunate enough to have an extraordinarily expensive tape system. The floppy was as important to the development of the personal computer as the written word was to the development of the human mind. In both cases, information no longer needed to be discarded and then re-created when needed. It could be remembered, stored, accessed, used, copied, and passed along. Unlike the original Winchester, floppies were inexpensive and transportable.

From the dawn of the industry, digital graphics have pushed personal computers to the limit, and still demanded more. Bitmapped graphics often took so long to print they weren't even cost effective. They were too big to fit on a floppy, and users often had to carry their external hard drives around whenever they needed to move large files. The typical drive was small—my first was only 20MB—so the need quickly arose for flexible storage and a reliable means of transportation.

In 1983, fledgling company SyQuest Technology had a brilliant idea. They separated a Winchester platter from the rest of the drive mechanism, encased it in a dust-free plastic cartridge, and created the first "infinite" hard drive. The platter, which contained the data, could be removed when full and replaced with a fresh disk.

SyQuest drives (and the easy transportation they offered) ultimately led to the creation of the service bureau. The typical desktop publisher could never afford the expensive scanning and output devices their work now demanded. Because service bureaus used this equipment around the clock, they could manage the investment. How were the scans and print-ready jobs transported? Removable disks. This relationship—the ready availability of high-end technology to the common user—was the impetus behind the graphic arts revolution.

Since the creation of removable drives, manufacturers have steadily increased the drive's speed and capacity to keep pace with the growing power of the personal computers. Every increase in processor speed makes it possible to create larger files more quickly, which consumes more space, creating an ever greater need for more storage.

Choosing the Right Media

A staggering array of removable storage options are available, most of which are variations of the Winchester mechanism. Other options include tape media, CD-ROM, magneto-optical, and hot-swappable drives. Several criteria determine the right one for you, which I subsequently describe in full:

- **Manufacturer reputation.** Like when buying a car or a washing machine, if the manufacturer has a good reputation, the chances of getting a quality product improve.

- **Product performance.** Compare the storage device against others. Is it faster? Can it store more information? What is the cost per megabyte?

- **Market penetration.** When a device is more widely used, the more people using a form of storage media, the more useful it is to you in terms of file transportation.

- **Intended use.** Different devices have different optimal uses, which you should be aware of before purchasing.

Manufacturer Reputation

Reputation is everything. Although reputable manufacturers may occasionally release a poorly performing product, it is relatively rare. Beware of inexpensive product knock-offs churned out by some no-name overseas company. If one fails you in a moment of crisis, any amount you have saved will be lost ten times over. Look for the following in a company before buying one of their devices:

- **Tech support.** There should be a toll-free tech support number, as well as some form of email support. Phone support is effective to a degree, but attempting to call during business hours often leads to spending lengthy periods on hold. Email enables you to describe your problem as completely as possible. You shouldn't have to wait more than a day for a response.

- **An extensive Web site.** Device driver or software updates should be free and readily available. Additionally, the Web site should offer technical and troubleshooting information. Due to the number of variables involved in computer technology, the manufacturer may not have found every problem before shipping a product. If so, they won't appear in the accompanying documentation. The Web site should give you these late-breaking answers.

- **Name recognition.** Have you heard of the company before? Can you find reviews of their products in major magazines or Web sites? Do any colleagues recommend the product?

- **A warranty or money-back guarantee.** A warranty should be at least 30 days—time enough to find out if a product works. The sad truth is that in order to keep prices down, the overall quality of computer products is decreasing. Because many lower-end storage devices these days are little more than featherweight plastic toys, you must make sure that you can return or exchange a product if it breaks.

Each of these factors can be easily applied to any piece of hardware or software you plan to purchase. A little research up front saves considerable time and headache later.

Product Performance

Product specifications are easy to find—manufacturers make an abundance of them readily available. Determining which specs are relevant is a tricky business. How expensive is a device? How much are the disks? How fast is it? How long will it last? These are all important issues, but they should not be the sole criteria for your decisions. Performance specs don't indicate how useful a device *is*, but how useful it *might be*.

Many resellers advertise just one measure of performance, such as RPM or seek time. A more useful measure of performance takes many factors into account. As you read on, bear in mind that true performance also depends on the computer to which a device is connected. For example, you can count on a DAT drive working much more efficiently when connected to a G3 tower than to a five-year-old Centris 650.

Storage Capacity

Measured in megabytes, capacity determines how much information the media will hold. Bear in mind that the amount of usable space on a disk is slightly less than the total advertised space, because disk formatting requires some room of its own.

Seek Time

With the exception of tape media, all removable disks store data on *tracks*, which appear as thousands of concentric circles. *Seek time* is the measure of speed required to retrieve information, or the time the actuator arm takes to move its read/write head to the track where the desired data resides. Measured in milliseconds (ms), seek time is an average of many random information requests. If the arm seeks data on adjacent tracks, the seek time can be as short as 2ms. If it has to move a greater distance—for example, from the outermost edge to the innermost edge—it can take 20ms or more. [2]

Because a millisecond is a thousandth of a second, it may seem an irrelevantly small amount of time. (After all, a typical eye-blink takes an entire fiftieth of a second.) Remember that drives are random-access devices. Data can be stored on the disk in any location, in any order. To read a single piece of requested information, the actuator arm may have to move the read/write head hundreds or thousands of times, and the milliseconds add up quickly. The seek times for today's drives average from 6 to 11ms. Lower seek time rates are always better.

Rotational Speed

Because a read/write head only moves back and forth, the disk must rotate for the head to access its entire surface. Each circular track on the disk's surface is divided into sectors. Once the read/write head is in position over the proper track, it must wait for the sector that contains the desired data to

---

FOOTNOTE

[2] Tape media are sequential access, not random-access. Instead of moving the read/write head to the desired track, the media itself must be moved. Here, seek time measures how long it takes the tape to forward or rewind to the location of the desired data.

spin around. This waiting period is called *rotational latency*. The higher the rotational speed, measured in RPM, the lower the rotational latency.

Rotational speed is an important factor in the performance of a drive, but it is only relevant when comparing drives of the same type. When comparing hard drives, for example, higher rotational speeds are clearly better. It's not really useful when comparing different types such as Zip drives and CD-ROM drives. [3]

Originally, hard drives started spinning the moment the computer was turned on and didn't stop until the computer was shut down. In an effort to reduce wear and lower power consumption, today's drives stop spinning or "go to sleep" if they have not been used for a predetermined length of time and then spin up again when they are accessed. Nearly all removable storage media have this feature as well. Therefore, two more items are added to the list of product specs: *time until sleep* and *stop/start time*. Preferably, time until sleep is user definable. For stop/start time, the faster the better, but this is less relevant than other performance measures. The drive sleeps only when it senses inactivity. This feature can often be turned off completely if it causes too many delays.

Transfer Rates

Once the head reads from or writes to the disk, data is transferred between the disk and the CPU. The faster this transfer occurs, the faster the computer can open documents, launch applications, and copy or move files. Transfer rate is measured in megabytes per second (MB/s).

You will likely see an item called *cache buffer* listed among a product's specs. This is a more recent development to improve transfer rates. Often, the CPU processes data much more quickly than the slower drive can provide it. The CPU must wait for the drive to catch up. At other times, the drive provides data faster than the busy CPU can respond. A cache buffer, built into the drive, compensates for these discrepancies by reading information into the buffer before the CPU needs it. It can also store information waiting to be written to the disk. This buffer can boost transfer rates substantially.

FOOTNOTE

[3] Data access time is a combination of seek time and rotational latency. Unfortunately, most product specs omit rotational latency or combine it with seek time. Combining that information is not a bad thing, provided that everyone is doing it. The problem is, how do we know? We can only hope that the major manufacturers use the same system.

Cost-Per-Megabyte

Cost-per-megabyte indicates the total cost of owning a drive. Usually, this amount only considers the cost of the removable media, but I split it into two values:

- **Initial cost.** This value is the amount of the drive with one removable disk, divided by the number of megabytes held by the disk. For example, if a Zip drive with one 100MB disk costs $120, the initial cost is $1.20/MB. If a Jaz drive with one 2GB disk costs $475, the initial cost is $.23/MB.

- **Use cost.** This value is the cost of each removable disk, divided by its number of megabytes. For example, if a 100MB Zip disk costs $12, its use cost is $.12/MB. If a 2GB Jaz disk costs $125, its use cost is $.06/MB.

True cost-per-megabyte is a combination of these values, based on the total amount of space dedicated to a specific drive. To illustrate, I'll use the two drives I've already mentioned. If each drive is ultimately used to store 4GB of information, its costs-per-megabyte is as follows:

- **100MB Zip.** One drive (plus disk) costs $120, and 39 additional disks cost $468. Divide $588 by 4000, and the cost-per-megabyte is almost $.14/MB.

- **2GB Jaz.** One drive (with no disk) costs $350, and two disks cost $250. Divide $600 by 4000, and the cost-per-megabyte is $.15/MB.

Many users, regarding this value as the bottom line, would automatically opt for the slightly less expensive Zip. But you must also factor in the efficiency of the media, as well as how practical it will be to increase the total number of dedicated megabytes. For example, an ad agency I once worked with used Zips as their only means of storage. Five years of ads and projects were stashed away on over 100 half-filled disks. These files were routinely updated, and the two designers would simply wade through the shelves, find the desired disk, update and save the file, and return it to the mix. Forget for a moment the complete logistical, job-tracking, and file-management nightmare this method posed. On a fundamental level, it illustrates what can go wrong when you base a purchasing decision on cost alone. Back then, Zip drives were revolutionary and inexpensive, so the decision to buy a couple was perfectly logical. If they'd only used them for their intended purpose—transporting files—there would have been no problem. As it was, they looked at some other options, decided they didn't want to lay out the extra cash for an additional 3 or 4GB of fast, stable space, and opted to use Zips for storage as well. As their need for storage increased, they simply added more $12 Zip disks to their library, instead of reviewing the need for a more comprehensive archiving system. If they'd only realized that for the cost of their last 80 Zips (about $950), they could have purchased two 6GB external hard drives and the better part of a 2GB Jaz. Compare that to hunting down a misplaced Zip at the last minute.

Media Life

Media life is an estimate of how long stored data remains readable, assuming a cartridge sits on a shelf in a protective case. Manufacturer claims are only estimates, because most disks proclaim a life span that far exceeds the length of time they have been in existence. (For example, CD manufacturers claim that their disks will remain viable for at least 100 years.) It also doesn't consider instances of everyday misuse, such as leaving your disks on your dashboard on a sunny day, stashing them beside the big magnet in one of your stereo speakers, or leaving one in the back pocket of your pants when you throw them in the wash—all of which I've done, and all of which resulted in a horribly foreshortened media life span.

Market Penetration

For better or worse, a good measure of the usefulness of a storage device is how widely it is used. A device's market penetration often has more to do with timing and marketing tactics than with overall performance.

A Tale of Two Standards

The first removable media standard in the graphic arts was the 44MB SyQuest drive. Because it was the first device of its kind (and for quite a while, the only one), sales were high. Shortly after the SyQuest was released, Iomega introduced its Bernoulli drive. Iomega knew that in order to draw users away from the SyQuest, they would have to come out with a superior product. Or so they thought. The Bernoulli was superior to the SyQuest in construction as well as performance, in both the drive mechanism and the cartridge. The reliability of a SyQuest drive was plagued by the fact that its cooling fans sucked dust onto the disk that interfered with the read/write head, a problem avoided by its competitor. The Bernoullis were faster, their disks could be thrown against a wall and still work, and they even had handles for easy portability. They were also a near-complete flop, arriving on the market too late with a higher perceived cost than the SyQuest units. Today, it is difficult to even find Bernoulli cartridges for sale, while an estimated

98.9% of all service bureaus accept 44MB SyQuest disks. It was all a matter of timing.

Perhaps Iomega learned something from this experience. They introduced the 100MB Zip drive in 1995, a few months before SyQuest released their technologically superior 130MB EZ. The cost-cutting performed on the Zip was shameless. It was so light that the weight of SCSI cables could drag it off the table. It had no on/off switch, so you had to unplug it to turn it off. The SCSI ID could only toggle between two settings (5 and 6) and the SCSI connectors were 25-pin instead of the industry-standard 50, forcing users to purchase extra 25-to-50 pin SCSI cables to add a Zip to their existing chain of external devices. The SyQuest EZ was the Zip's polar opposite. It was made of heavy-duty components and had an on/off switch. The SCSI ID switch could be set to any ID, and it used 50-pin SCSI connectors. The disks held a third more data, and the drives had faster seek and transfer times. And it cost about the same as the Zip.

The Zip had several things going for it, but quality was never at the forefront. Its price was revolutionary, making it one of the cheapest external devices of *any* sort ever made. At $20 for 100MB, the disks were a fraction of the cost of any other removable media at the time. Iomega's marketing broke new ground as well, focusing little on the functionality of the device, or even its purpose. The advertising was hip and stylish and actually made removable media seem cool. The drive even looked good—its rich purple case stood out in a world full of dull beige components. Most importantly, the Zip came out first. Everybody bought the colorful Zips and then ignored the ugly gray brick that was the EZ. The Zip is now the prepress industry standard for removable storage. And SyQuest, the company that helped to revolutionize the industry, has gone out of business.

There is a moral to this story: Technical specifications may tell you a lot about the quality of the product you are buying, but they don't determine the industry standard. A product's usefulness is directly related to its market penetration. A standard becomes a standard not necessarily because it's the right choice, but because the majority of people use it. The device you choose must be supported by a wide range of users, from service bureaus to print shops, contractors, and clients. If there is any doubt, pick up the phone. Talk to the people you work with, ask them what media they accept. If necessary, ask them what media is used by a majority of their clients—this will give you a good indication of what people are using in your particular area.

This doesn't mean you have to settle for less than the best when it comes to internal use. Many businesses still use their Bernoulli and SyQuest EZ drives for their internal storage, backup, and transportation needs, and use Zips only when sending data out of house. Different device types will best meet your different needs, and determining what to use is all part of media dexterity. [4]

F O O T N O T E

[4] The Zip drive represented the dawn of an unfortunate new age for the prepress industry. This inexpensive mechanism ushered in the Age of Cheap, where the primary consideration is not how well a device works, but how much it costs.

While price has always been a factor in our buying decisions, it hasn't been the *only* factor until recently. We prepress professionals have been spoiled with quality. The Macintosh computers that have driven the industry from the start are historically well-built machines. For example, it's likely that a Mac SE 30 works just as well now as it did in 1987, requiring little if any repair. But quality has always come with a price, and for years, Macs cost more than comparably equipped PCs. In 1998, Apple addressed this issue with the iMac, which took many cues from the Zip drive. Every expense was spared to make the iMac as cheap (or "affordable") as possible, including cutting out the floppy drive and dropping keys from the keyboard. Its futuristic shape, eye-catching colors, and savvy marketing emphasized style over function. To its credit, the iMac was indeed revolutionary, and superior to anything in its price range; it opened the world of computing to many people who had never touched a computer before, and it single-handedly revitalized the Macintosh platform. The drawback is that professionals now have to contend with something they never had to before: consumers and consumer-level products.

Before the Zip, iMac, and other products of their ilk, prepress professionals (and Mac users in general) could afford a certain level of elitist snobbery. For the most part, the technology they used was genuinely superior, mainly because they demanded professional-quality equipment. It's a consumer market now, which brings regrettable consequences. In an effort to create the inexpensive equipment demanded by consumers, many devices now lack features that meet professional standards. For example, cooling fans, metal cases, and heavy-duty power supplies, once standard for most external storage devices, are now hard to find. Manufacturers are cutting every corner they can to keep prices down, often producing equipment just good enough to make it past the ever-shortening warranty periods.

For professionals, this means you must now be ever vigilant. Trust nothing. It was once easy to ignore backup and archiving procedures. While media failures did happen, it was more a surprise than an expectation. In the new Age of Cheap, you must expect things to go wrong. This makes media dexterity more important than ever. Media failure is increasingly frequent, making backup and archiving absolute necessities.

Intended Use

Before buying, you must have a clear idea of how you will use your new storage device. Each possible use of removable media has special requirements:

- **Transporting files.** Compatibility is of utmost importance. The media is worthless if other people can't read it. Speed is only relevant if you routinely transport jobs of over a gigabyte in total file size.

- **Backing up files.** Compatibility is not an issue because the media only needs to be read by one computer. Speed is a plus, because backing up should be done frequently.

- **Emergency startup disk.** The disk must be bootable, which means that no USB device can be used as an emergency startup disk. The disk must be large enough to contain an operating system and hard disk repair and diagnostic utilities. Ideally, it is large enough to back up the contents of the troubled hard drive before diagnostics begin. Typically this means using an external hard drive. (Refer to Chapter 3 for more info.)

- **Archiving.** Storage capacity and media life are most important. Speed isn't important, unless you plan to access archived files frequently.

- **Alternate hard drive.** Given the speed, reliability, and affordability of hard drives today, don't waste your time using removable storage media as a hard drive—if you need an alternate drive, buy one. No removable device has the combination of speed and reliability of an internal or external hard drive. Also, many users attempt to assign an empty removable disk as scratch disk space for Photoshop or Illustrator, but this is a mistake. Removable media are typically designed to eject at shut down. If a program's primary scratch disk can't be found at startup, it defaults to None and does not change if the disk is mounted later. Using removables this way can cause no end of "scratch disk is full" error messages.

Media Types

The number of options for removable media is downright dizzying. Choosing the right media can be further complicated by the fact that most removable media today are reasonably effective, and all of them have their virtues. [5]

Storage media falls into four basic categories:

- **Magnetic.** This type includes floppy disks, hard drives, and removable hard drives, such as the Zip and Jaz. This is the most common media type.

- **Optical.** Optical drives use a laser to read disks; the most common of these is the CD-ROM.

- **Magneto optical.** As you might guess, this is a hybrid between magnetic and optical. MO drives use a combination of lasers and magnetics to read and write to disks.

- **Tape.** Tape is a throwback to the age before the Winchester mechanism. Data is recorded onto DAT (digital audio tape) or DLT (digital linear tape). Recent advances in the speed, capacity, and reliability of tape have brought about a surprising resurgence of this venerable media type.

Magnetic Media

On this media type, data is stored as a series of electrical charges, written and read by a magnetic head. Even if you're new to computer technology, if you've ever played a VHS or audio cassette tape, you've used magnetic media. This media type has been around for years and is probably more frequently used than any other. Although many quality options exist, they all suffer from a common weakness: Close proximity to a strong magnetic field, such as unshielded stereo speakers, may result in lost or damaged data. The following are the most common magnetic media types.

FOOTNOTE

5 The prices and speeds presented here are estimates based on the latest available data and are given for comparison purposes only. The true performance of any device is dependent on the computer to which it is hooked up. Costs per megabyte are based on single cartridge prices. Prices are often significantly lower when buying in bulk. I only include storage media currently available for sale. This means that some time-honored standards, such as SyQuest drives, have been omitted.

Floppies

Storage Capacity: 720KB to 1.4MB

Avg. Read/Write: 39KB/sec

Avg. Seek Time: 229ms

Est. Cost-Per-MB: $.50

Media Life Span: less than 5 years

At one point in recent history, the floppy was all we had. A single floppy could hold an operating system and application program with enough room left over for saved files. Floppies are the last relics of a time when hard drives and other options were too expensive for all but the largest of institutions, when there was no other choice of media. The only reason they exist now is that almost everyone has a floppy drive, whether they use it or not.

To illustrate how little use the typical graphics professional has for floppies, I'll use myself as an example. Almost two years ago, I bought a PowerBook 3400 with both floppy and CD-ROM modules. I've used the floppy drive once, when I tested it the day I bought it. And my G3 tower? I decided to order the external floppy drive only if I needed it, and six months later, I still haven't. Fortunately, the computer industry is catching on to the fact that the floppy is obsolete. Almost all software manufacturers ship their goods on CD. No computer now shipping from Apple comes with a floppy drive installed, and PC manufacturers are expected to soon follow suit.

Pros

Floppies have the widest market penetration of any storage media. Per-unit price is very cheap. You can usually find floppies for less than 50 cents apiece, with boxes of 100 available for $20 to $50.

Cons

Floppies are the worst possible storage media you can use for these reasons:

- They are slow.

- They are unreliable. Remember, life span estimates are based on media that sits on a shelf in a protective case, not on real use. If you actually use the floppy, expect it to last a few days to a year. In fact, you'll find that many floppies are dead right out of the box.

- Floppies hold very little. When you need to ship more than 1.4MB, you will need to compress the files or break them up to fit on several floppies, both of which will consume time and increase the chances of file corruption.

- They are a marginally supported technology. Now that hard drives and other storage media are available, no research is going into improving drive or disk performance. Computer manufacturers are also using cheaper floppy drives in their computers (if they are using them at all), further reducing their reliability and performance.

- They are ultimately expensive. While the cost per disk may be low, the cost-per-megabyte is more than most other media options. Add to this the cost of waiting for the disk to write, then rewriting the file when the process fails, reformatting the disk, throwing it away when the initialization fails, formatting another floppy, and finally copying the file, and you see a prohibitively expensive storage option that should be avoided.

Recommended Uses

Floppies are okay for transporting small files in noncritical situations. They are also good for giving files to people who have a reputation for not returning things, because floppies are so cheap you won't get upset if they don't come back. They also make good coasters. If a file is small enough to fit on a floppy, it is small enough to send as an attached file through email. Abandon your floppy drive, get a modem, and don't look back.

SuperDisks

Storage Capacity:	120MB
Avg. Read/Write:	100KB/sec
Avg. Seek Time:	50ms
Est. Cost-Per-MB:	$.15
Media Life Span:	5–10 years

The SuperDisk is a beefed-up version of the floppy drive. Not only do these drives read standard floppies, they also use their own 120MB media that looks and feels just like a floppy. Several companies have contributed to the development of this media type, including Hewlett-Packard, Panasonic, and Apple. The first drives in widespread use were released by iMation when the iMac first shipped.

SuperDisks are strictly consumer-level storage media. When someone has to buy a USB floppy drive for a new computer that ships without one, a SuperDisk is the only available option. Every user I know who has purchased one of these drives uses it only to read standard floppies—the 120MB disks that shipped with the unit are still wrapped in plastic. This doesn't mean that SuperDisks are of poor quality or don't have a market somewhere—they just don't dovetail with the demands of a prepress environment. With the exception of capacity, all the restrictions of standard floppy disks still apply.

Pros

Because every floppy drive developed in the future will likely be SuperDisk-compatible, the potential for widespread penetration is good. They do read standard floppies faster than traditional drives, but still much more slowly than other media types.

Cons

The irony of the SuperDisk is that its manufacturer touts its structural similarity to a standard floppy as an advantage. They are still slow, relatively untested in the marketplace, and quite flimsy. The latter is a particular problem, especially when compared to its 1.4MB counterpart—when you're throwing away a disk that cost only a dollar, it barely registers. When you accidentally sit on a $15 disk, it begins to hurt in more ways than one. Reliability is also a big issue, especially for companies who just bought a round of blue G3s, necessitating the purchase of SuperDisk drives. I recently installed five drives at a local shop, and within two weeks, three were shipped back to the manufacturer.

Recommended Uses

These disks are best suited for the nonprofessional home user. They offer the convenience of a standard floppy drive, plus handy 120MB disks for archiving, in case Junior spills his Kool-Aid into the iMac's cooling vent. Designers or prepress professionals looking for cheap, higher-capacity transport media are better off investing in the universally accepted Zip.

If you must purchase an external floppy drive, consider VST's new USB unit. It doesn't support the 120MB disks, which is no great loss, but it's faster and more reliable than a SuperDisk drive.

SCSI Hard Drives

Storage Capacity: up to 40GB

Avg. Read/Write: 4 to 6MB/sec (up to 160MB/sec using Ultra 160/m and adapter card)

Avg. Seek Time: 5 to 9.5ms

Est. Cost-Per-MB: $.04 to $.07

Media Life Span: 5–10 years

Every personal computer since the latter half of the 1980s contains an internal hard drive based on the now-legendary Winchester mechanism. Of all storage media, the hard drive has the best combination of speed, reliability, and cost effectiveness.

On rare occasions, users have been forced to copy files to an external hard drive, power down the computer, disconnect the unit, and carry the drive—with SCSI cables and power cord draped around their necks—to the service bureau. Most likely, an output technician received it with a long-suffering smile that essentially said, "You should know better." External hard drives were created to remain stationary. With a few exceptions, they are not built with the shock-absorbing capabilities possessed by most removable media. Moving it risks damage, and hard drives are too valuable to be treated this way. You are also required to shut down the computer when removing or attaching the drive, and if other SCSI devices are present, they must be reconfigured. For these reasons, never use external SCSI hard drives as removable media. In extreme circumstances, such as if you're creating billboard-sized Photoshop images that no available removable media can contain, it may be necessary to transport a hard drive. In such an event, be sure to contact your service bureau in advance to make sure they are willing to accept it.

Hard drives are available in a wide array of capacities and speeds. It is very difficult to find drives under 2GB, and 4GB is the typical starting point. The traditional Fast/Wide SCSI 2 is the version installed in most Macs prior to 1999, with speeds up to 6MB/sec. These drives work with most Macs created prior to 1999 without requiring special adapter cards. The new Ultra 160/m, combined with a special adapter card, boasts speeds up to an astonishing 160MB/sec. For most prepress purposes, FW SCSI 2 is perfectly adequate.

Pros

Huge price drops in recent years, accompanied by substantial increases in speed and capacity, have made hard drives the fastest, cheapest, and most reliable media for backup and short-term archiving available.

Cons

They are not easily (or safely) transportable.

Recommended Uses

Hard drives are best used as a working space and for short-term file storage.

Additional Hard Drive Types

Although the SCSI hard drives described previously are the most prevalent standard, new drive types are now meeting widespread acceptance.

ATA drives

ATA drives (also known as IDE drives) have been commonplace on the PC for years, but nonexistent on all but the very lowest-end Macintosh until the advent of the iMac and blue G3. ATA drives are slower, not as heavy-duty, and far less reliable than the former Mac-standard SCSI drives. They also cost hundreds of dollars less. Unfortunately, to recover from its recent downward spiral, Apple had to make some unpleasant decisions. One was to cut the cost of its computers by reducing the quality of their components to have more aggressive pricing against PCs, while maintaining an acceptable profit margin.

Again, prepress professionals pay a price for Apple's success. ATAs are not the production-level drives that SCSIs are. Unfortunately, SCSI drives now only come in Apple's highest-end computers. Fortunately, adding a SCSI drive to the new computers is easy and fairly inexpensive. A quality 4GB drive with a controller card can be added for under $400, and it will provide an immediate and substantial performance boost. The already installed ATA drive is still useful for less demanding purposes, such as file storage.

USB and FireWire Drives

Two emerging standards will ultimately replace SCSI drives completely. USB will replace SCSI because it is cheaper and easier to use, and FireWire will supplant USB because it is truly superior.

USB is the consumer-level answer to SCSI. With top speeds of about a fifth of the slowest SCSI, USB drives are not suitable for production-level work.

The benefit of USB drives is that they can be built very cheaply. USB is fully cross-platform, so developers can build and ship one drive for both Macs and PCs, lowering costs even further. Up to 128 devices can be attached to a single USB port, as opposed to SCSI's seven, without the need to set separate IDs. Finally, USB drives are hot-pluggable—you don't have to shut down the computer to install or remove a USB drive. Really, USB is everything a peripheral device should be, and if it weren't for its overall slowness and questionable quality, it would be perfect.

FireWire, on the other hand, is a worthy replacement for SCSI. It has all the advantages of USB (except it supports up to 64 devices instead of 128), and it is stunningly fast. Current speeds are up to 40MB/sec, and 80MB/sec FireWire is expected soon. FireWire devices can also receive their power from the FireWire port itself, eliminating the need for external power supplies, introducing true plug-and-play to computing for the first time. Like Ethernet, FireWire can be used for networking, and a single FireWire device can be shared by multiple computers.

FireWire is certainly impressive, but it is such a new technology that only a handful of devices currently use it. SCSI is still the standard for prepress, but this standard will certainly change in the near future.

RAIDs

RAID stands for *Redundant Array of Independent Disks*. A RAID uses multiple hard drives together to overcome the limitations of a single drive. They are masterpieces of technology that no creative services agency should ignore.

A standard hard drive can't escape a number of built-in limitations. First, while it is faster than most media types, it is terribly slow when compared to the speed of your RAM and CPU. Basic laws of physics determine the maximum speed of a single drive; just think of the difference in time it takes to think of a word, as opposed to writing it down. Second, they have limited space. Currently, a single drive cannot contain more than 40GB of information. Third, they fail, just like any other media type. When this happens, your data may be lost forever, unless you've backed it up.

RAIDs, on the other hand, are faster, larger, and safer than a single hard drive. The main reason why is because they are redundant—all RAIDs use a minimum of two drives working together. There are three levels of RAID, each of which functions differently:

- **Level 1.** These RAIDs overcome the speed limitation by writing data to all drives at once. This is like using each hand to write different words of the same sentence at the same time, in the right order, allowing you to finish the sentence more quickly. Some RAIDs can read/write at up to 200MB/sec. They also overcome the size limitation, because multiple drives are recognized as a single unit.

- **Level 2.** These RAIDs bypass the possibility of failure by writing the same data to several drives, as if you sprouted multiple hands and wrote the same sentence on several different pieces of paper. If one paper caught fire, it wouldn't be a problem—duplicate sentences are written on the others. These setups are remarkably safe. While it is theoretically possible for all data to be corrupted, it would take an extreme act, such as a direct lightning strike or fire.

- **Level 5.** These RAIDs combine all the features of Level 1 and 2 for maximum speed and reliability.

Many RAID arrays are dockable, meaning that if there is a fault in one of the drives, it can be removed instantly and replaced with another. Many feature alarm systems to warn you of possible problems. RAIDs can serve a single computer or an entire network. When installed on a server running AppleShare IP or the Mac OS X and 100BASE-T, data can be accessed with speeds equaling a local hard drive, providing instant access to vast amounts of data to everyone on the network, greatly facilitating backup and archiving.

RAIDs were once the exclusive domain of large businesses, but recent drops in hard drive prices place them well within the reach of small businesses as well. A RAID array can be a technology investment that pays off many times over. They are complex devices that can be configured to meet the exact needs of your organization. While off-the-shelf RAID arrays do exist, it is highly recommended that you find a qualified value-added reseller to help. A qualified reseller will provide you with references from business similar to yours that have successfully incorporated RAIDs into their workflow.

Iomega Zip

Storage Capacity: 100MB, 250MB

Avg. Read/Write: up to 1.4MB/sec, 2.8MB/sec

Avg. Seek Time: 12ms

Est. Cost-Per-MB: $.18, $.07

Media Life Span: 5 years

The current industry standard transport media, the Zip is fast, cheap, and pervasive. The 100MB version has been available for almost five years, and a 250MB counterpart has recently been released. (For more info on Zips, see "A Tale of Two Standards," earlier this chapter.)

Pros

Everyone and his uncle either has a Zip or realizes he needs one, making them the most universally accepted transport option in the industry. And they are inexpensive: New USB Zips are available for under $120, and SCSI models are now under $90. (Although refurbished SCSI Zips can be had for around $50, avoid them. Better to use new flimsy plastic parts than used flimsy plastic parts.)

Cons

The Zip is cheaply made and fairly slow. It's so lightweight it needs to be held in place when inserting disks, and it can be dragged to the floor by the weight of its own SCSI cables. It has no on/off switch, limited SCSI ID capabilities, and 25-pin SCSI connectors instead of the standard 50-pin connectors. The success of the 100MB Zip drive is hindering sales of the new 250MB drive. Either people are content with their current size or they have found ways to work around it. Nobody wants or needs the Zip 250, and few people would trust that much data to one.

Recommended Uses

If there is one "must have" drive, this is it. Its affordability, combined with its widespread acceptance, makes it ideal for transporting files. Its unreliability makes it less useful for anything else.

Iomega Jaz

Storage Capacity: 2GB

Avg. Read/Write: up to 8.7MB/sec

Avg. Seek Time: 10ms

Est. Cost-Per-MB: $.06

Media Life Span: 5 years

The Jaz is the bigger brother of the Zip. It's five times faster, and each disk holds twenty times more data.

Pros

It is very fast, with a low cost-per-megabyte.

Cons

It has a high *perceived* cost. Even though the cost-per-megabyte is less than most other media, the cost of the drive is around $400, and each cartridge costs $125. These prices keep many people away from the drives and prevent as high a market penetration as the Zip.

Recommended Use

The Jaz is a great solution for those who need large, fast, removable storage. Its speed and high capacity make it excellent for just about any purpose. But the Jaz drive never really caught on, and its installed base is rather limited. As with any removable media, call before sending someone a Jaz cartridge.

Castlewood ORB

Storage Capacity:	2.2GB
Avg. Read/Write:	12.2MB/sec
Avg. Seek Time:	10ms
Est. Cost-Per-MB:	$.01
Media Life Span:	5 years

The ORB drive is an astonishing innovation. Sneaking onto the scene with little fanfare or advertising, it is 25% faster than the 2GB Jaz, has 10% more storage space, and costs $150 less. To top it off, the media costs $100 less per disk.

Pros

It is strikingly fast, with a very low cost-per-megabyte.

Cons

It's so new, it's a virtually unknown quantity. Its specifications are the most impressive of any removable storage media on the market, but as you saw in "A Tale of Two Standards" (earlier this chapter), that often means little. A year from now, either the ORB drive will be a new standard, or it will have vanished completely.

Recommended Use

The ORB currently has no market penetration, though its low price is practically throw-away money to most service bureaus. If a few people start using it successfully, it may be adopted by a wider audience. For the time being, its usefulness is limited to backup, archiving, and other in-house tasks.

Optical Media

Optical media is the most widely recognized removable storage media in the world. Most people recognize it as audio CD, video DVD, and even Sony PlayStation games. Regardless of its use, all forms are essentially the same. When optical media is written to, a laser burns the disk, creating spirals of "pits" and "lands" to encode the data. Because optical media is nonmagnetic, it is very reliable. It could withstand an electromagnetic pulse from a nuclear blast without losing data.

CD-ROM Writers

Storage Capacity:	up to 650MB
Avg. Read/Write:	up to 1.4MB/sec
Avg. Seek Time:	50 to 150ms
Est. Cost-Per-MB:	$.003
Media Life Span:	100 years

Speeds of CD-ROMs are defined in terms of the first CD-ROM player, which spun between 200 and 530 RPM. The double speed, or 2x, spins twice as fast. Current speeds go all the way up to 40x. Most CD-ROM readers are 24x to 30x, and most consumer-level writers are 4x or 8x.

Once very slow and very expensive, CD-ROM writers are now a great option for transporting and archiving. They have replaced floppies as disposable media; they cost much less per unit, are very durable, and hold massive amounts of data. CD-ROM burners use *WORM* (write once, read many) media, which means the disks can only be written to once.

Pros

Very low cost per megabyte. CD-ROMs are almost invulnerable, with an extremely long shelf life. Nearly everyone in the graphic arts has a CD-ROM reader. For the price of a single Zip cartridge, you can get 10 recordable CD-ROMs, equivalent in storage to 65 Zips. Despite the low price, it is one of the most reliable and widely used media available. After a job is written to a CD, it can be archived in the same form.

Cons

Once a WORM is burned, that's it. The data is unchangeable. (Fortunately, most CD-ROM burners support multisession writing. Only a portion of the disk is written to, leaving the rest available for more data at a later date.) Data must be written to the disk using Adaptec's Toast or other CD-ROM authoring software. This adds another step that is very different from the drag-and-drop copying method most people are used to.

Recommended Use

The low cost and durability of the media and the market penetration make CD-ROMs an excellent choice for transporting files. Their reliability and longevity make them perfect for archiving as well. Their slower speed and the fact that they can only be written to once make them less suitable for backup purposes.

CD-RW Writers

Storage Capacity:	up to 650MB
Avg. Read/Write:	up to 614KB/sec (4x)
Avg. Seek Time:	50 to 150ms
Est. Cost-Per-MB:	$0.02/MB
Media Life Span:	100 years

CD-RW is virtually identical to CD-ROM, with two exceptions: It uses rewritable disks and files can be copied directly to the CD-ROM without authoring software. CD-RW never really caught on, because the media it uses costs up to 10 times more than CD-ROM (most people simply choose to write 10 CDs and hang onto them, rather than use just one). All CD-RW writers can read and write CD-ROMs, and because the drives aren't all that much more expensive than regular CD-ROM drives, many users opt for the additional functionality.

Pros

They have most of the advantages of CD-ROM. While the media is more expensive, it is still cheaper than many alternatives. They also use standard drag-and-drop file copying.

Cons

The cost is higher than CD-ROM technology.

Magneto-Optical

Magneto-optical disks are among the more interesting of removable media technologies. An MO cartridge is constructed of materials that cause it to be highly resistant to magnetic fields at room temperature. The drive uses a laser to heat the disk to the *Curie point*, the temperature at which metal loses its magnetic properties. At this point, magnetic particles on the disk surface can be realigned by the field generated by the read/write head. This offers advantages over other media. A laser can be focused in a much tighter field than traditional magnetic read/write heads, so data can be written much more densely than on ordinary magnetic media. Because the data can be changed only when the disk is heated to high temperatures, information stored on MO cartridges is incredibly stable.

Traditionally, MO drives have required two passes to write data. Even though rotational speeds of MO disks are comparable to those of magnetic media, until recently they could function at only half the speed of magnetic media. Manufacturers have since developed MO drives that write in one pass, doubling their speed.

3.5-inch MO

Storage Capacity:	up to 650MB
Avg. Read/Write:	3.9MB/sec
Avg. Seek Time:	27ms
Est. Cost-Per-MB:	$.05
Media Life Span:	30 years

3.5-inch MO drives have been around for years, but they haven't caught on. Optical drives were once slow and expensive, but recent improvements in the way the drive writes to the disk have increased speeds substantially. Prices have also dropped considerably. The original 128 and 230MB drives are no longer available, but the newer 650MB drives can read both types of cartridge.

Pros

MO has the advantages of both magnetic and optical media, and none of the disadvantages. Unlike magnetic media, the disks have a high resistance to magnetic fields and are ultra-stable. Unlike CD-ROM, they can be rewritten. Newer MO drives have speeds rivaling that of magnetic media. MO media has a very low cost-per-megabyte.

Cons

Magneto-optical is a technology whose time should have come, but never did. It never received the industry-wide acceptance of magnetic media, making it problematic as a transportation option. With the advent of CD-RW and DVD-RAM, it is doubtful that the technology will ever go anywhere.

Recommended Uses

If the vendor receiving your files can read your MO disks, the disks' stability makes them an excellent transportation option. Their longevity and low cost-per-megabyte makes them great for archiving. Older drives might be too slow for backups and purposes other than archiving, but newer drives are solid all-around storage options.

5.25-inch MO

Storage Capacity:	up to 2.6GB
Avg. Read/Write:	4.3MB/sec
Avg. Seek Time:	19ms
Est. Cost-Per-MB:	$.03
Media Life Span:	30 years

5.25-inch MO media has all the advantages of their 3.5-inch counterparts, with much higher capacity and faster speed.

Pros

These disks are among the lowest cost-per-megabyte of any removable media and have high capacity. They are very fast and very reliable.

Cons

This large media size is old-fashioned, hearkening back to the huge floppies of early computing, and is more difficult to carry and store. A 5.25-inch cartridge is written on both sides, so it has to be periodically flipped when reading or writing data. The high cost has discouraged widespread use.

Recommended Use

An excellent choice for archiving and backup, MO jukeboxes, which can hold in excess of 2.5 terabytes, have been available for a while. Not useful as transportation media.

Magnetic Tape

Magnetic tape was one of the first computer storage options, commonly used on mainframe computers. Remember the wheels of tape spinning round and round on computers in the old sci-fi movies? That's the stuff. Fortunately, today's tape drives are much more compact, and the media can fit into your pocket. Unfortunately, tape technology still has the same major problem it always did. Its access is linear, not random, like disk drives. This means the tape must be fast forwarded and rewound to find data, just like locating your favorite song on an audio cassette. Tape is also subject to more trauma than other media. How many of your favorite tapes were eaten by the tape player before you finally switched to CDs forever? Magnetic tape is a much faster and safer medium than it was just a few years ago. Still, I only recommend it for archiving—the only purpose it was ever intended for.

The two tape media types are DAT (digital audio tape) and DLT (digital linear tape). DAT is slower and generally holds 8GB. On the other hand, DLT is fairly speedy compared to other tape media, and it can hold up to 40GB on a single tape.

DLT has become the new standard for archiving. In addition to being fairly fast, media costs for tape are incredibly low: $.002/MB to $.006/MB, with initial costs as low as $.06/MB. DLT will probably become the archiving medium of choice. For under $2,400, a DLT drive can write 40GB to a tape, which costs under $100. This kind of storage was once available to only the largest of companies who could afford to pay for it. Now it is affordable for small businesses.

A DLT is a must for small- to mid-sized businesses. The key virtue of a DLT archiving system is that it can be automated. Using a utility like Retrospect, it can be set to archive the important data on every hard drive on the network every night. Archiving is like insurance; you do it, but you hope you never have to use it. It should not take the place of performing your own periodic backups. Ideally, every machine on the network should be routinely backed up every day. A workstation can be rebuilt from its archive, and all the hard work that has been done that day will not be lost. This security is worth the cost of an archiving system.

Final Recommendations

Many excellent removable storage options are available. Valid reasons exist for choosing just about every media type I've discussed. Whatever drives you choose for transportation, one of the most important factors to consider is the prevalence of the technology in your locale. Widely accepted disks will prevent the most frustration when dealing with clients, freelancers, and service bureaus.

For personal backup and for emergency startup disks, nearly any of the previously discussed options will do (except for magnetic tape), because speed and compatibility are not as important.

For archiving, I recommend burning your work to CD because of its reliability and low cost. Due to its slower speed and limited space, however, it may not be suitable for archiving large volumes. Here, automated archiving on a 30 or 40GB DLT is preferred.

Media Dexterity Strategies

To fully implement a media dexterity workflow, additional planning is required. Otherwise, you're likely to drift to one of the extremes, both of which I've seen. One company used nothing but Bernoulli drives and had to jump through a frustrating series of hoops whenever they needed to access a client's files or hand their own work to a vendor who didn't support their disks. Another company, striving to avoid those problems, invested in every media type on the market. When the dust settled a few months later, many of the drives were simply collecting dust, never having been used. To determine the drives you intend to support, you must analyze your work methods, client base, and vendor needs.

Standardize Your In-House Devices

Determine the media types that will be supported for all in-house work, such as Zip and Jaz, and install the units on each workstation. This way, every user has the immediate ability to read and write to the chosen disks. Some companies only install drives on one or two workstations, assuming they can copy projects to the station over their high-speed network, and *then* copy to a disk. This method never works—even the fastest network won't top the speed and efficiency of a dedicated removable media drive, and the savings in time and frustration will more than cover the cost of the additional units:

- Digital prepress involves very large files that take a long time to copy over a network. Copying over a network means that the sending station is tied up (unless you are using a copy optimizing utility, such as Connectix Speed Doubler). The network and the receiving station also slow down, decreasing everyone's productivity. Using removable media to transport files between stations ensures that everyone will be able to work at top speed while files are copied for transport.

- Standardizing makes the life of the system administrator less complicated. An administrator can create an emergency startup or maintenance disks for every station and distribute new software and support files more readily.

- Standardizing speeds up the gathering of files to be sent out-of-house. Instead of being copied to one station that has the drive, everyone can copy their files onto the media from their own station.

- Standardizing makes it much easier to receive and use client media if everyone has a station that can read it. Make sure the client knows which media you prefer.

Determining your standardized media requires an analysis of internal workflow issues and the marketplace in which you work. It is easy to recommend Zip drives, for example, but if you routinely create projects larger than 100MB, the disks are too slow and too small. A Jaz, ORB, or higher-capacity MO will better serve your purposes. The drawback to this is that while you gain speed and storage capacity, you may lose compatibility with your clients. If you desire speed, capacity, *and* compatibility, you may require more than one drive type per station. Conduct an informal survey of your clients, as well as the service bureaus and printers you use, to find out what they are using. This will help determine what media is right for you.

Install a Media Dexterity Station

If you receive media from a variety of clients, as service bureaus and printers typically do, establish a media dexterity station. It involves a dedicated high-speed workstation that contains every drive type pertinent to your client base. This way, when jobs come through the door, the disks can be loaded quickly and the files can be copied over and made readily available to the appropriate specialist via the in-house network. Often, this process is performed by the customer service rep responsible for initially accepting the project. When dealing with this number of drives, it is rarely cost-effective to install them on every workstation. Not only will a dedicated media station allow you to efficiently access a wider range of client work, the savings in time will make everyone—clients and output specialists alike—breathe a little easier.

Your media dexterity station works best when you keep a few key issues in mind:

- The more media you support, the more dexterous your company will be.

- Newer, higher-capacity drive types often support older media. For example, the SyQuest 200 reads 88 and 44MB cartridges; a 250MB Zip reads 100MB cartridges; a 640MB MO reads 230 and 128MB disks.

- When using a SCSI chain, you are limited to seven devices (which includes the computer and internal hard drive). If you want to install more than five additional drives, you must add another SCSI card to your computer. A SCSI-2 card can increase the performance of many external drives.

- Do not install DAT drives on the media dexterity station. Optimally, you should have two DAT drives on two separate stations, one for archiving and retrieving in-house files, and one for unloading, archiving, and retrieving client files. DATs are slow, and they will create bottlenecks if placed on a high-volume station. No one can use the station until the DAT is finished.

- Monitor the station. If people consistently wait to use it, productivity is diminished. Redundancy ensures productivity; install a second media dexterity station.

- Don't swap drives back and forth. If you need to use a drive on a second workstation, buy another drive. Consider the costs of swapping. Two computers are shut down, removed from the productivity loop. Cables are disconnected and connected. SCSI IDs and termination issues must be resolved. When finished, the process is repeated to reinstall the drive on the original station.

- Always have devices to accept your clients' disks. Never make them wait needlessly while you hunt for a drive to "borrow," and if you can help it, don't have them bring in their own devices to be hooked up to your equipment. Determining the required media type requires communication with your client, and it may require investing in an additional drive. Remember that a satisfied client will repay the cost of the drive many times over.

Networks

If your workplace has more than one computer, they should be networked. Networks are much more efficient than removables for copying smaller files between computers. To transport a file using a removable, you must first copy the file from the first hard drive to the cartridge and then from the cartridge to the second hard drive. Even though networks copy things more slowly, they need to do it only once because they can copy directly from drive to drive.

When two or more computers are connected by some type of data transmitting wire, you have a network. As you might imagine, a variety of options are available—and the type you choose will determine the overall success of your network.

LocalTalk

A LocalTalk network is the simplest and cheapest kind to set up. It requires only a transceiver for each computer on the network, connected by ordinary telephone cord. Everything needed to connect two computers can be found at your local supply store for less than $30. Bear in mind that LocalTalk is *slow*. It runs at about 230 kilo*bits* per second—too slow for anything but text files and small vector graphics files—but it's still better than no network at all. Most often, this type of network is used to connect ancient workstations, such as Macs from the early '90s, that have no Ethernet capabilities. [6]

FOOTNOTE

[6] KBPS stands for *thousands of bits per second*. BPS is a common measure of *bandwidth*, or the total flow of data over a given time, on a transmission medium such as twisted-pair copper cable, coaxial cable, or optical fiber. Depending on the medium and the method used, bandwidth may also be measured in MBPS (millions of bits, or megabits per second) or GBPS (billions of bits, or gigabits per second).

Ethernet

Ethernet is the most widely installed LAN type. It uses one of two kinds of connecting methods: *coaxial cable* (similar to the stuff used by cable TV and stereo speakers) or *twisted pair* (two insulated copper wires twisted around each other). Ethernet speed is roughly 10 times faster than LocalTalk networks. [7]

Most Ethernet LANs use ordinary telephone twisted-pair wire, known as 10BASE-T. This carrier method supports Ethernet's 10 MBPS transmission speed. Ten-megabit Ethernet is also implemented with the following media types:

- **10BASE-2.** This method uses *thinwire* coaxial cable, a thinner and more flexible wire type. The maximum length of each wire segment, or the distance between connected computers, is 185 meters. (Here, 185 is rounded up to 200, which explains the "2" in the abbreviation.) This type of Ethernet is generally standard on older computer models.

- **10BASE-5.** This method uses *thickwire* coaxial cable, a heavier option that allows a maximum segment length of 500 meters.

- **10BASE-F.** This method uses fiber optic cable, which is generally less subject to electromagnetic interference or the need to retransmit signals. However, installing this cable is expensive and quite labor-intensive, and its installation base is considerably smaller than other methods.

Ethernet compatibility is built-in on most newer computers, and two computers can be connected for as little as $100. If your computer is not Ethernet-compatible, you must install an Ethernet card, available for around $75.

It's important to note that Ethernet cabling is highly subject to electromagnetic interference. When stringing cable through your workplace (or having it professionally installed behind the walls), it must keep a clear distance

---

FOOTNOTE

[7] The abbreviations used for describing Ethernet types were developed by IEEE (the Institute of Electrical and Electronic Engineers). "10" refers to the transmission speed of 10 MBPS. "BASE" refers to *baseband signaling*, meaning that only Ethernet signals are carried on the medium. "T" stands for twisted-pair. "F" stands for fiber optics, another high-speed cabling option. "2" and "5" refer to the maximum cable segment length, in hundreds of meters.

from any power cables. Otherwise, your network activity will be slowed or disrupted.

Fast Ethernet

The speed of Fast Ethernet approaches 100 MBPS, or 10 times the speed of standard Ethernet. 100BASE-T Ethernet is now standard on most new high-end computers. On older models, Fast Ethernet requires an additional card for each computer on the network. The cost of a fast Ethernet can be two to three times the cost of ordinary Ethernet, but if you use your network extensively, the money is well spent. Because Fast Ethernet can still communicate with standard Ethernet (and standard Ethernet can be plugged into Fast Ethernet hubs), you can smoothly transition your existing network over to Fast Ethernet.

Gigabit Ethernet

This new Ethernet standard approaches transfer speeds of 1 GBPS. Gigabit Ethernet is primarily used as a network *backbone*, or a larger transmission line that carries data gathered from smaller connected lines. Fiber optic is the preferred cable type.

Ethernet Hubs

A hub is like the center of a bicycle wheel; it's where all the spokes—or the computers connected to the network—converge. Roughly the size of a book, a hub receives the information sent by one computer and then routes it to the appropriate destination. Hubs greatly reduce the need to use long cable lengths between computers, eliminating the possibility of signal degradation. Smaller Ethernet networks using 10BASE-2 generally forego a hub, particularly if all connected workstations reside in the same room. These network types work by stringing cable between transceivers—one transceiver connects to each computer, and the cable is strung between them. Most twisted-pair networks (such as Fast Ethernet) do require a hub. One end of a 10BASE-T cable, for example, plugs directly into the computer's built-in jack, and the other plugs into a port on the hub. Other computers and devices such as printers and cable modems connect to the same hub, allowing complete network access. Multiple hubs can also be connected this way, allowing you to easily increase the number of ports when necessary.

Servers

A server is a dedicated workstation that connects other computers over a network. Because the typical workflow involves a large amount of data, yours may benefit from the sort of dynamic "holding area" that a server provides. There are four basic server types—file, print, data, and application—but they usually have the following in common:

- They store a large number of files and require large capacity hard drives.

- They are connected to the in-house output devices.

- The are connected to long-term storage devices, such as a DAT drive, creating a central location for archiving and recovery.

- They are driven by server software that launches immediately upon startup.

Endless debate exists over which computer makes the best server. It is impossible to recommend one over the other. Instead, the demands of your specific workplace will determine the right choice. Some companies use a stock Mac or PC as a dedicated server, simply adding the necessary third-party software. Others may configure a PC with a network-specific OS, such as Windows NT. High-volume environments may opt for a proprietary server—or a machine specifically designed for workgroup server capabilities—which can range from Pentium III rack units to UNIX-based or Silicon Graphics workstations. Establishing a server is a complex task, regardless of the type you choose; maintaining one in a larger company can require at least one full-time employee. If you're unsure where to turn, it's time to enlist the services of a network consultant.

File Servers

This server stores files and job folders in a central location. This way, you can back up work on a short-term basis, yet make it available to every workstation on the network. Your workplace will likely benefit from a file server when the following issues apply:

- If you maintain extensive file libraries that are too large to efficiently store on each workstation.

- If you routinely process files, such as color scans, that are too large to efficiently copy back and forth between workstations.

- If more than one person in the company will routinely need to access the same files.

Some companies set up a basic file server by repurposing an older, slower workstation no longer used in production. They add an 8 or 9GB hard drive, connect it to the network, set up an organized system of folders, and make them available to the appropriate people. It can be this simple, but once network traffic increases to a certain point, bottlenecks will hinder its effectiveness. Keep an eye on your overall network speed; if the file server is the source of any slowdowns, it may be time to upgrade to a more powerful unit.

Print Servers

A print server receives and processes jobs during the output process. Without a print server, each project is output directly from a workstation. Because true multitasking doesn't yet exist in a digital production environment, some or all your system's resources are occupied when you print a file. On operating systems without a built-in print spooler (which allows printing to occur in the background), you cannot use the computer while it prepares a file to be sent to an output device. Even when your system does feature a spooler, printing a medium-to-large file is usually enough to drag overall system performance to a crawl. When you use a print server, you copy the file to a separate workstation, letting it handle any processing while you get back to work as quickly as possible.

The key to a print server is the *print queue*, or a list of jobs waiting to print. When multiple users send jobs to the same printer, they generally output in the order they were sent. With a server, multiple users copy jobs to the same workstation before they are processed. This allows you to reorder them according to priority, as well as put jobs on hold for future printing. A server can also manage queues for every in-house printer, allowing you direct control over the output process of your entire workflow.

Print servers are partially automated by a series of watched folders. For example, the queue for each printer may contain the following folders:

- **Active.** Jobs in this folder are processed as soon as the target output device is available.

- **On Hold.** Jobs here will be moved to the Active folder as soon as they are released by the output manager or administrator.

- **Printed.** Jobs are moved here after printing, ready for archiving or any necessary reprints.

- **Error.** Jobs that misprint are moved here, ready for additional review or preflighting.

Most print server software gives you a great deal of freedom to manage the individual jobs. Each queue should be able to contain output settings specific to each device, which range from resolution to custom screen values. You should be able to redirect jobs from one queue to another; to cancel printing and delete jobs; to change the order of the print list; to enable, disable, or password-protect any of the queues; to instantly view the status of a job at every stage of printing.

In high-volume environments, the need for a print server is clear. Smaller companies should review their workflow. If the biggest drain on your production time is waiting for print jobs to process and clear, your environment will benefit from this technology.

Data Servers

A data server uses a database to track jobs and manage workflow. Many companies use an electronic job ticketing system, which can be reviewed and updated by any employee involved with a project. The key advantage here is the immediate access to the information. A client can call a company with a question and get an immediate answer; account reps are always kept in the loop; records are kept of file locations, specific problems, and new changes.

Standard production workstations are usually not used to handle this information—it typically requires a UNIX- or NT-based PC. However, some companies have begun using Web site-based job tracking systems with considerable success. The data on a Web site is accessible by any computer with an Internet connection, making a tracking system platform-independent. Pertinent employees can be notified of any changes or issues with an automatic email flag, as opposed to routinely checking a central database. It can also be accessed by account reps on the road—clients, too, if they're given a password.

Application Servers

An application server is a workstation dedicated to the use of a single program. The most common example is a trapping station. When a print shop or service bureau uses intensive, proprietary trapping software (such as iMation TrapWise), they never know how long it will take to process a single job. By using a dedicated computer, they can enter the desired settings, drop the job in the appropriate folder, and walk away. Otherwise, one of the other production workstations—which rely on quick turnaround in order to remain profitable—will be consumed with the task.

Network Media Dexterity

More than ever, people working in a graphics department must access files stored on a different workstation. When you connect to another computer over a network, a few simple steps will ensure that you are working as efficiently as possible when retrieving or copying files.

Connect and Disconnect

Connect to another workstation, copy the files you need, and disconnect immediately. Computers, particularly Macs, are notoriously "chatty." When connected, they constantly send information to each other, even when they're not actively copying files over the network. This steals processor time from both connected workstations, and also slows down the network. Always disconnect when you are not specifically accessing another computer.

Share Just a Folder, Not the Whole Computer

Whenever possible, don't share the entire contents of your hard drive. Instead, designate a single folder to be accessed by other users. This way, other users will only have access to files that you specifically place inside this folder. This method offers several immediate benefits:

- It decreases network traffic, because only one folder needs to be addressed, rather than all the folders on all the hard drives on your computer.

- It provides more security, because users cannot access any confidential files, applications, fonts, or system files on your hard drive.

- When properly set up, users can connect to that folder without wasting time entering a password. If desired, share your entire drive as well, allowing authorized users password-access.

Don't Work Over a Network

Copy the file you need to work with to your hard drive and disconnect from the network. *Do not* open up the file over the network and try to work on it from your station. This can slow you down almost to a complete standstill. Ethernet moves data at a fraction of the speed of a slow hard drive. Working on even small text files is slow if you try to do it over a network. To make matters worse, the increased network traffic bogs down your entire network. Not only will you decrease your own productivity, but other users are affected as well.

This is one of the most common mistakes made by people who are new to networks, also one of the worst. It's an easy one to make. Once you connect to another computer, its shared folders and files appear exactly as they do when they are on your own computer. Always remember to copy the files you need to copy and then disconnect. This will keep you out of trouble.

Networks *can* be configured to allow you to work over them freely. A file server with a RAID array running 100BASE-T Ethernet would definitely provide this capability, and the emerging FireWire networks blur the distinction between what is remote and what is on the computer. For example, a Mac OS X Server even provides net-booting capabilities—a computer can start up using the operating system on an entirely different workstation. These systems are complex, however, and should be installed only by a qualified professional.

Modems

The final way to move files from your computer to another is via modem. Traditionally, modems have been too slow and unreliable for routine use of moving files that are more than a few kilobytes in size. As with every other computer technology, however, modems are getting faster and better. It will still be a few years before modems replace removable storage media, but it will happen. If you start using the technology now, you will be in a position to take advantage of it in the future.

How useful modems are to you right now largely depends on who receives your files. More businesses than ever are relying on modems to receive files from remote clients, mainly because they transcend distance. A file can be sent from Tokyo to New York faster and cheaper than if it was sent on a removable.

Larger print shops have already been combining modem and digital print technologies. For example, a bulk mailing company in the Midwest, who distributes color advertisements all over the country, discovered low printing rates in the Northeast. They send ad templates to printer via modem. Copy comes from Missouri, and graphics arrive from Ohio. All are received on the same workstation, and the ads are composed, printed, sorted, and mailed from the plant. Modem transfers provide faster turnaround time than overnight delivery (same-day, in some cases) and eliminate the need to find local printers, writers, and designers.

Modems come in many speeds and styles, but the majority fall into four categories: POTS, ISDN, cable, and T1.

POTS Modems

POTS modems use the "plain old telephone system" and are the most common and inexpensive type. They are also the slowest and least reliable. This is because their carrier medium, the phone lines, was installed decades ago, when such a thing as a modem existed only in the minds of science-fiction writers. Everyone has experienced noise on the telephone line: static, other voices, bad connections. While this is an annoyance to us, to the modem it means slowed or lost connections and corrupted data.

These modems are best suited for recreational use, but if you can't afford a faster ISDN or T1 connection (and your area doesn't yet offer cable modem access), get at least a 56 kilobits per second (Kbps) modem. Under ideal circumstances, which are rare, a 56Kbps modem transfers data at roughly 28.8Kbps. The speed of a 56Kbps modem hovers just above the frustration level. Use a slower modem for anything other than email, and you will go mad waiting for anything to happen.

ISDN

ISDN (Integrated Services Digital Network) provides higher-speed access with a price. ISDN requires that a special digital phone line be installed on your premises. Depending on where you live, this can cost as little as a standard phone line or several times more. ISDN modems are available for under $400. For the price, ISDN delivers far greater performance than POTS modems. At 128Kbps, they deliver almost five times the speed of the fastest POTS modems. Digital phone lines are far more reliable than standard phone lines. There is virtually no noise, which eliminates the slowdowns and errors associated with POTS modems.

Cable Modem

The cable modem is the bargain of the century. Using the same coaxial cable used to transmit video signals, they are considerably faster than ISDN, attaining speeds of up to 500Kbps—all for only $40 to $50 a month. This technology is still relatively new, and widespread availability is still a couple years away. As soon as it becomes available to your area, contact your cable company and sign on immediately. I've been using TimeWarner's Roadrunner service for more than two years, and I've never looked back.

T1

For businesses that rely on the Internet for transferring files, a T1 line offers the highest performance available. The cost of using a T1 line can run into thousands of dollars a month, so it is used primarily by larger businesses with the most intensive need. Unlike POTS and ISDN lines, T1 lines are generally used to connect entire companies to the Internet, not just one computer.

A T1 line uses 24 64Kbps ISDN lines for a total throughput of 1.544 megabits per second. The throughput is divided amongst the people using the line. Twelve people could be connected at 128Kbps, or two people at 772Kbps. If your business requires that all your employees have fast connections to the Internet, or if you are an international magazine publisher receiving advertisements, articles, and images from all over the world, T1 is the only way to go.

Internet service providers typically use one or more T1 lines. Because one line typically offers more bandwidth than a single company needs, many businesses choose to share a line to lower their costs.

Media Dexterity with a Modem

Faster modems and Internet connection speeds have finally enabled us to efficiently transmit large amounts of data to a vendor, partially eliminating the need to ship our work on disks. Unfortunately, this isn't as easy as sending a 100MB attachment to a service bureau. Your ability to send files via the

Internet largely depends on the system set up by a vendor. After finding out whether or not they accept files this way in the first place, you must determine their connection speed, maximum file size, and supported compression methods. There are two common methods of sending and receiving data via modem. You can send information as an email attachment or use an FTP site.

Transferring Via Email

Sending files over the Internet is often less expensive than dialing directly. If you have a local dial-in for Internet access, you only have to pay for a local call. If you dial directly, you may have to pay long-distance charges. Sending files via modem can be very slow (depending on your modem type), but if you are using a local dialup with unlimited access, this can be an acceptable solution. This way may be slow, but it can be done in the background, enabling you to work while files upload. Be aware that if a transfer is interrupted, you will have to upload the entire file all over again, even if you were only a few seconds from finishing.

You can send files as email attachments or via FTP. Sending files as email can be a problematic solution. Minimize problems by paying attention to the following:

- If sending from a business using email as part of its network services, check with your network manager first. Businesses often have strict size limits to the size of attachments that can be sent with email. Exceeding these size limitations can crash the entire network.

- If you use an Internet service provider, your service provider may also have restrictions on transferred file sizes. Call or email them to be sure. Tell them exactly how large the files you want to send are. Don't just tell them "large files" because if they are not in the digital graphics industry, they have no idea how large the files can be.

- Always check with the person receiving your files. It's very bad form to send someone large files, which they will have to download at their own expense, without asking first.

- Most email programs will automatically compress an attachment before transmitting it, creating smaller file sizes that take less time to send. You also have the option of using your own compression utility to convert your files to an archive, which you can then send as an attachment. Whether sending via email or FTP, you must make sure the person receiving your files can recognize your compression type. [8]

Transferring Via FTP

FTP (File Transfer Protocol) transfers are a better way to transfer files. On a hard drive of a destination computer, a space is set aside for the express purpose of receiving files. This space is usually divided into several folders, which can be freely accessed by the public or password-protected. FTP has several advantages over sending files as email attachments:

- It uses a designated space, so you know where the file should be, and that it is welcome there.

- FTP programs monitor the transfer and alert you if there is a problem. They also prompt you to resend the file. Email often does not do this.

- Typically, there are no limits on file size, although the larger the file, the more likely its transfer can be interrupted, forcing you to resend it.

- It does not interfere with regular email messaging.

Check with the person you want to send files to in order to find out if they have FTP capabilities. If so, he or she will provide you with an address and a password.

F O O T N O T E

[8] When transmitting data over the Internet, you must use some sort of file compression. This can be more difficult than it sounds. You must make sure that the person on the receiving end not only can decompress the attachment, but can read the expanded files afterward. If there was one universal compression utility, this wouldn't be a problem. Unfortunately, many utilities and standards abound, and cross-platform transmissions can be particularly problematic. Before you start sending files, arrange a small test with your vendor. Send the same archive using a variety of encoding methods to find out which one arrives successfully; use that method for all future transmissions.

For example, a couple of years ago I was sending book chapters to a publisher who had difficulty opening them. I was writing on a Mac, and my editor was reviewing them on a PC running Windows 95. After a series of tests, we discovered that the only way I could send the chapters intact was to save them as .rtf files, compress them into a Zip archive (using ZipIt), and transfer them using my email program's Base 69 encoding. It only took an hour or two to figure out, but I use the same method to this day.

If you want to receive files via FTP, you have two options:

- If you have an Internet account through a local access provider, chances are you already have space on its server to use as an FTP site. Call your ISP to ask how to utilize this space. An FTP site at your access provider does have one drawback: You must download the files to your own computer to work with them.

- Set up your own computer that allows people to upload files directly to you. Using a program like FTPd, you can allow people to connect to your computer and download or upload data. People will still need to go through the Internet to get to you, and your computer must be constantly connected to the Internet. This will be pricey unless you have unlimited access.

Summary

Media dexterity has nothing to do with design, project planning, proofing, or output. In fact, it doesn't even involve opening a single file. Without it, however, you cannot move a project from your workstation to the many outside resources required by today's graphics professional. It revolves around the need to communicate:

- You use a compatible, reliable transportation media for moving files back and forth between your vendors.

- You have enough removable drives installed to accommodate the needs of your client base.

- You use media systems that allow you to back up large amounts of daily work, as well as archive gigabytes of completed projects.

- You connect your in-house workstations with a fast and easy-to-use networking type.

- You are able to successfully transmit files over the Internet.

Although it requires an investment in technology, the dividends paid by media dexterity are obvious. The only alternative is a closed loop, designing on isolated workstations for your own enjoyment.

PROJECT PLANNING

Two dangerous myths abound in the digital graphic arts industry.

The first is that PostScript publishing is a straightforward and automated process simply because it is computer-based. We've all seen movies where The Computer is elevated to the level of a technological messiah, where all you have to do is make the keyboard go clickety-clack, and miracles occur: Funny faces appear on counterfeit twenties; an adolescent hacks into NORAD and creates a global nuclear threat; a bad guy squints and sweats for a second or two and then says, "I'm in!" as the bank vault door swings open.

Or this one: an account rep, maybe even your boss, reviews the specs of a new project and proclaims, "Forty-eight pages? Critical color? How does day after tomorrow sound?"

Today, your work is subject to all the same planning, attention, and laws of physics as a project produced using conventional techniques. In a perfect world, you could stand in front of a stainless steel box, type in some flowery adjectives, press a few buttons, and watch perfectly printed results roll out on a conveyor belt. In real life, the computer is just another tool used in the process, like rubylith tape or a Heidelberg press. It's powerful, but no miracle cure.

Don't get me wrong. Computer technology has given us incredible design and production capabilities, and project turnaround times are shorter than they have ever been. But this phenomenon has resulted in the second dangerous myth: that all project tasks can be handled by a single person.

All the tasks of a typical project—stripping, scanning, color correcting, design, typesetting, and so forth—used to be areas of *craft*, requiring years of disciplined training and experience to master. Today, most people assume these areas have become *sciences*, or a mere topic to be broken down into steps that anyone can successfully follow. This is true to a certain degree: The hardware is inexpensive, the software is fairly easy to learn, and more how-to documentation is being written than ever before. However, the context for these tools—producing quality ink on paper—hasn't changed in 100 years. The issues are just as complex and demanding as they ever were, and graphics hardware and software simply provide a new way to deal with the same tasks. A colleague of mine likes to say, "It's not rocket science. Rocket science deals with known, finite quantities: force of gravity, coefficient of friction, explosive force. Prepress is nothing but variables and unpredictability." How could we expect one mere mortal to handle all the responsibilities of prepress and publishing?

Planning the details of a project *before* design and production is just as important now as it ever was. Unfortunately, good project planning is one of the first tasks cut in the interests of saving time (a tip of the hat to what's quickly becoming the third dangerous myth: that computers enable us to slash already outrageous deadlines in half). Deluded by the sweet-tasting marketing pap asserting that computers actually do the work for us, many of us simply open a page layout program, turn on a few fonts, and tear into the project, figuring we'll take care of any other details if and when the need arises.

Any commercial printing project consists of a dizzying array of variables, and project planning lays the foundation for design and prepress tasks that await. The earlier you consider and plan for those variables, the more control you have over quality, cost, and time.

At the start of any project, the first thing to do is evaluate your own skills. Can you honestly handle a six-color annual report with custom folds and die-cuts if your most intensive experience is with two-color business cards and letterhead? Can your equipment come through under the same circumstances? Chances are, probably not. Few things can overwhelm designers like biting off more than they can chew. If you're bidding on work that involves new, more complex, and more expensive techniques, consult with your service providers, printers, and colleagues before accepting the job. Get an honest assessment of the time and know-how required. The three biggest mistakes a designer can make have nothing to do with software techniques:

- **Promising a product you're unable to deliver.** The more individual elements a project has—high-res images, pages, ink colors, and so forth—the more intensive your expertise must be. Make sure you're familiar with the requirements of *every* aspect of a project before you commit yourself. In my younger days, I struck a more cavalier pose, believing that biting off more than I could chew was the only *real* way to learn. As a result, my primary lessons were in crisis management, not prepress techniques.

- **Submitting a ridiculously low project estimate.** You do yourself and your client a great disservice by lowballing an estimate, whether intentionally or unintentionally. Nothing upsets a client more than a request for more money halfway through the production schedule, and nothing hurts a designer more than having to foot the bill for any surprise expenditures. By articulating every aspect of a job, you can predict the appropriate number of design hours and account for all associated production costs. Also bear in mind that experienced clients typically regard a low bid as a sign of shoddy work or inexperience.

- **Letting a client nickel-and-dime you to death.** When a client signs off on a project estimate, they agree to conform to the specifications you've spelled out. This way, if they request major changes later on (or even a multitude of minor ones), you can bill for the extra time with a clear conscience. And beware the "Just One More Tiny Thing" syndrome. It's probably okay to make one or two small allowances, but if you're too giving, people will take advantage of you. (And who could blame them? This stuff is expensive, and smart clients try to save money any way they can.) Another big problem is failing to account for even the smallest expenses, such as a quick flatbed scan or laser proofs.

The remaining variables fall under two categories: project requirements and project tasks.

Project Requirements

Every printed project is a combination of budget, schedule, and quality. Although these issues don't apply to personnel or project content, working through each one of the following items ensures that your printed result takes best advantage of the money available, the time allocated, and the ultimate printing process.

Determining Job Requirements

In this industry, there are two basic rules concerning project cost:

- Everything costs something.

- No one likes to be surprised by the final cost of a project.

Budget is by far the strongest influence on design and production. As much as everyone would like four-color logos, brochures, and catalogs, it is just too expensive for most projects. Therefore, you must keep the project parameters within the limits of what you are able to spend.

The final cost of a project is the total of the following:

- **Design hours.** This includes content development, page layout, photo editing, and illustrations.

- **Production/prepress hours.** This includes scanning, color correcting, trapping, page imposition, proofing, and final output.

- **Client meetings.** Often considered a free service, a series of organized meetings to overview a project's status, brainstorm new changes, or simply keep the client in the loop should be included in the project estimate and billed at the standard design rate.

- **Materials.** This includes lithographic film, paper, plates, and ink.

- **Press run.** This includes press setup, inking, printing, and cleaning.

- **Finishing.** This includes binding, cutting, and folding.

- **Distribution.** This includes shipping and/or mailing.

You must consider all these issues when estimating a job. For designers, this process is as simple as describing the nature of your project as clearly as possible and getting estimates from different service bureaus and printers.

Most people, however, get burned in one of two places. First, they didn't include enough design hours in their estimates. At the end of a project, it feels good to receive, say, $2,000 for design time (based on an estimate of 40 hours at $50 per hour). If you actually put in two solid weeks of 12-hour days—plus ten hours of unbilled client meetings—the realization that your hourly rate has dipped to almost $10 will be a sad one indeed. If you're unsure of how long a specific project may take, turn to the graphic arts community for counsel. Ask your service bureau for advice. Consult other graphic designers you've met. Join an online graphic arts newsgroup. You'll find that the majority of industry professionals are willing to share their knowledge—or at very least, their opinions.

Second, they allowed the parameters of a job to change without reevaluating the original estimate. Even the smallest deviation from your original estimate can make a big difference in cost. In terms of physical design, the final cost of a typical project is increased by the following:

- Increasing the number of colors

- Increasing the number of pages

- Increasing the page size

- Adding bleeds and crossovers

- Adding multiple folds

- Adding custom die-cuts

- Building graphics that require trapping

- Using higher-quality paper

- Demanding critical color

- Short deadlines and rush charges

- Last-minute changes or corrections

- Last-minute file repair or "massaging"

Every publication must be discussed with your service bureau and printer. All your vendors should be involved in even the most preliminary decisions. They are the only ones who can tell you exactly what the costs are, what the potential printing problems are, and ultimately who the best people are to handle specific prepress tasks.

Determining Quality Requirements

Aside from content and design—which I gladly leave in your able hands— the perceived quality of your final project is greatly affected by the printing process. Sure, everyone wants the finest stochastically screened Hexachrome color on the best paper, but the trick is finding the most appropriate degree of quality for the specific project at hand. Doing so is vital for

both the designer creating the project and the printer preparing to reproduce it.

The following issues determine your quality requirements:

- **Market longevity.** How long will the publication remain viable and useful? Is it promoting an event that happens on a certain date? Or is it an
  item that will be used again and again?

- **The intended audience.** How must the publication present itself? For
  example, newsletters often have a built-in audience, whereas other printed
  pieces compete with similar items for audience attention. Other pieces
  must live up to an audience's discerning standards, and others must communicate a company's solidity, worth, and well-being.

- **Image clarity.** How important are the detail and color of your scanned
  images to the printed result? A textbook of screen shots requires little
  attention to image clarity, but a furniture catalog might require detailed
  reproduction of woodgrains, fabrics, and textures.

- **Color accuracy.** This usually comes down to a choice between color
  matching and color *balance*. Clothing and furniture catalogs often require
  pinpoint color matching, so customers know exactly the color of the items
  they desire. On the other hand, images of food usually just need to be
  balanced or made to appear pleasing instead of matching the original
  objects. [1]

Examples of Quality Expectations

This section lists some examples of different publication types to illustrate
how quality expectations change from project to project. Although these
descriptions are not carved in stone, they give some insight into the issues

---

FOOTNOTE

[1] I can't overstate the importance of communicating color expectations to a client.
Clients (and sometimes, unfortunately, account reps) often don't realize the difference between a flatbed scan and a drum scan, or 85lpi on newsprint and 150lpi
on gloss paper. They will naturally assume the same quality from all methods of
scanning and printing, unless you patiently take the time to refine their expectations. Even if they choose not to listen, cover your assets and leave a paper trail.
Email and fax them at every stage of production about the most pressing color
issues. I've seen jobs refused because the color of a client logo shifted almost
indiscernibly on-press.

that determine your print expectations: paper stock, the discerning nature of our audience, shelf-life, and color.

One-Color Newsletter

Here, the product is short-lived, intended for one or two readings before being replaced or discarded. The paper is usually inexpensive "photocopier" stock. Images are reproduced only fairly, and fine details (often highlights) are lost. Quick-printed or quick-copied publications fit into this category as well.

Two-Color Newsletter

The product may be a one-shot deal but may be intended to be used for a few months. These jobs are typically run on presses that hold up to a 150 linescreen. Halftones reproduce well, holding more detail. Newsletters may continue to use cheaper paper, but two-color corporate identity pieces—business cards, brochures, and similar pieces—require better stock.

Computer Wholesaler Catalog

This item is in full color and printed on less expensive, lower-grade paper kept in stock by most printers. Color fidelity is not an issue because customers are not using color as criterion for purchasing a product. Image reproduction is clear, and registration is usually to within .5 pt. The expected life span of this item ranges from a week to a couple of months.

Furniture or Clothing Catalog

The color in this catalog must match the actual items so customers can make informed and accurate purchasing decisions. Although the life span of these publications may be short (three to four months), premium paper and inks are used to create the impression of quality. The publication is fully trapped, and the press registers to within .3 pt.

It's interesting to note that the number-one cause for returning mail-order clothing is that the colors don't match what appears in the catalog.

The No-Holds-Barred Annual Report

Often the design adventure of a lifetime, this one-shot publication has the responsibility of communicating the company's entire image through design and print. Color matching may not be required, but color reproduction is of the highest quality. Images are crisp, often screened at 175 or 200lpi, with no apparent flaws.

Assigning Prepress Responsibilities

You can handle any prepress task in one of three ways:

- Do it yourself, digitally.

- Assign it to someone else to do digitally.

- Have it done conventionally.

If you're new to commercial printing and PostScript publishing, it's wise to turn the majority of prepress tasks over to an outside resource. The ability to accommodate this work in-house takes time, training, and experience. Assume new responsibilities one at a time, allowing yourself enough time to absorb the last aspect of the prepress process before launching into the next. As you gain experience and make contacts in the industry, consider investing in classes and new equipment that better enable you to handle these tasks.

I advise anyone new to these tasks to be aware of the major downside of doing it yourself: accountability. The overriding reason to perform your own prepress work is to save money, but it can cost more to repair a bad file than it would have to farm out the work in the first place.

You may already be at the point where you perform all your own prepress tasks, delivering a ready-to-output electronic document to your service provider. Even so, communication with your printer and service provider is paramount in making your decisions.

The following tasks are most frequently farmed out to specialists:

- **Scanning/color correcting.** It's uncommon for most facilities to have the scanners and rigidly calibrated systems needed to acquire and correct critical color. Even if your color isn't critical, scanning and correcting is time-consuming and most flatbed scanners, which many designers possess, don't really generate a high-enough quality color scan for good reproduction. Service providers can also provide FPO images rather than complete scans, holding the high-res information in-house until it's time to output films.

Many designers I know have everything scanned out-of-house, even non-critical pieces. This offers two benefits: They're not responsible for guaranteeing accurate color, and they can simply mark up the cost of the scans, allowing them to make more profit with less effort.

- **Trapping.** Some service providers use dedicated trapping software to take care of this task, and others just manipulate the tools found in QuarkXPress and PageMaker. Often, the specialists are most familiar with the issues involved in creating a successful trap.

- **Film output.** Imagesetters are expensive and need constant adjustment and chemical balancing. An in-house film-based output device requires a huge investment in training, materials, and testing. Because most freelancers, graphic departments, and design firms do not produce the volume of film necessary to make such an investment pay off, they send their files to either a service bureau or the printer running the actual job for output.

- **Stripping.** Here, the printer uses conventional techniques to arrange and impose the page films before shooting the job to plates. Most printers prefer setting up the job this way, rather than imposing a file digitally, prior to output.

Choosing a Service Provider and Printer

Most print shops and service providers are happy to offer a tour, samples of their work, and lists of customer references. To better help you in your eternal search for capable facilities, I have included a list of questions to ask print shops and service providers. Their answers should determine whether they possess the level of commitment and expertise your work requires.

Questions for a Digital Prepress Service Provider

1. **What formats and platforms do you accept for digital work?** Ask about their supported software and transportation media. (Refer to Chapter 6, "Media Dexterity: Transport and Storage," for more info on transport media.)

2. **What are your rates?** Many service bureaus have increased their processing fees for Windows-based files by 50–100%, while keeping their Macintosh margins razor-thin to remain competitive.

3. **Do you offer any training or technical support?** Some service bureaus have their own in-house training facility and offer clients free or reduced-rate training.

4. **What type and size imagesetters do you use?** Some facilities can output only letter- and tabloid-sized page films. If your work is larger than this, you'll have to look elsewhere.

5. **How often are your imagesetters calibrated?** Look for a service bureau that calibrates at least every day, as well as whenever the film is changed. Calibration consists of checking emulsion density and halftone dot consistency. Someone on staff should also be checking the film processing chemicals to ensure they are not depleted or diluted. If a shop has invested in imagesetter technology but not the requisite training to use it successfully, your work will suffer.

6. **What screening options are available?** More and more establishments are offering stochastic screening and other types of custom screening. Ask for samples and a description of the steps involved in getting the most out of such technologies.

7. **Do you offer scanning and color correcting services?** Ask to see samples of their work, as well as their scanning equipment. Be leery of any facility offering critical color if their only device is a flatbed scanner. Also inquire about using Desktop Color Separation files. (See Chapter 10, "Scanning Line Art and Halftones," Chapter 11, "Color Spaces and Printing," and Chapter 12, "Scanning and Adjusting Color Images," for more info on scanning issues and requirements.)

8. **What color proofing systems are available?** Viable systems include laminate systems, IRIS inkjet, calibrated Fiery (or another color laser printer), and bluelines. (See Chapter 17, "Proofing Methods," for more info on proofing.)

9. **What trapping services are available?** Some service bureaus use dedicated trapping software but charge considerably more for the service. Others use a combination of dedicated software and manual techniques. Others include a certain amount of trapping in the overall cost of output. (See Chapter 15, "Trapping," for more info.)

10. **Who will be the primary contact?** Will you communicate only with a salesperson? Or are you encouraged to contact the people responsible for processing your file? Choose a system that makes you most comfortable.

11. **Do you have your own print shop?** Many service bureaus, in order to remain competitive, have "closed the loop" by acquiring or merging with conventional print shops. This can be a great benefit, especially if you choose to have your project printed at their facility. It is likely that their production specialists can optimize their film output for reproduction on their presses.

Questions for a Commercial Printer

1. **Do you accept digital files?** If so, see the previous section "Questions for a Digital Prepress Service Provider." No one should feel obliged to hand over files to a printer for processing if you don't feel comfortable with his level of digital experience. Also note that some printers, under the auspices of providing digital services, merely farm out the work to a service bureau and then mark up the cost by 20–30%.

2. **What are your rates?** If possible, ask about cost breakdowns for representative samples of your work to get a better idea.

3. **Do you offer any training or technical support?** Most printers encourage designers to call with even the tiniest inquiries. Find out the proper people to contact with such questions.

4. **What prepress services do you offer?** Ask for input on what prepress services might be more cost-effective if performed conventionally.

5. **Are both sheet- and Web-fed presses available?** By describing the nature of your projects to your printer, you can determine how these best suit the needs of your work. (Refer to Chapter 1, "An Introduction to Digital Prepress," for more info about different printing presses.)

6. **How many colors can be printed in a single run?** Many print shops run four-color jobs on two-color presses, which make press-checks almost impossible without using a densitometer. Stochastically screened images and five- or six-color jobs are also more difficult to print successfully and take more time to complete.

7. **Do you offer high-fidelity color printing?** Typically, only shops possessing six-color presses offer this service. Ask for samples printed on their presses.

8. **What is your average turnaround time?** The industry-standard turnaround time is 10 days, from the day the printer receives the films. Ask about their typical press schedule, and inquire about rush rates (or if they even accept rush jobs).

Summary

For today's designer, good project planning means meeting your deadlines, getting the highest quality for your budgeted dollars, and ensuring that you make a profit—all without driving yourself crazy. This takes more than learning how to write a good project estimate. It means that you hold the following truths to be self-evident:

- **The responsibilities of producing a color publication are vast and complex.** You're encouraged to turn to outside resources—freelancers, service bureaus, and printers—for assistance.

- **You must recognize new, unaccounted-for changes in your project.** Recognize how they affect final deadlines and cost.

- **You must understand the issues that determine the final printed quality of your work.** These include everything from paper stock to the target audience to color requirements.

- **Let your service providers know of your willingness to learn.** Try saying, "Please tell me if there was anything wrong with the file, or anything I can do better." This approach often results in a tremendous amount of free training and valuable information.

- **You keep an objective, global view of your work at all times.** It's easy to get caught up in the smaller details, like scanning images or physically designing a page layout, while other issues are ignored until the last minute.

Call it greasing the skids, laying the groundwork, or pounding the beach with artillery before the invasion. All the strategies that lead to a successful project are born before the actual project begins.

VECTOR-BASED GRAPHICS

When vector-based graphics are combined with pixel-based images and page layout documents, they form an unrivaled trinity of design and pre-press power. Adobe Illustrator and Macromedia FreeHand are among the most powerful and useful graphics applications, but their artwork is often the most misunderstood and misused. To further guide you through the production process, this chapter presents the features and techniques you're most likely to encounter when designing or troubleshooting a vector-based graphic.

Vector-based graphics have their origin in the earliest days of the Macintosh. Early Macs shipped with three programs: MacWrite, MacPaint, and MacDraw. MacWrite was the father of today's word processing programs, and the uncle of layout programs like PageMaker and XPress. MacPaint allowed you to create images by editing pixels, simulating the effect of pen on paper. The mathematical shapes offered by MacDraw established the starting point for vector-based graphics programs—in fact, the essential technology, Bézier curves, has changed little since then. The influence of these simple programs is felt to this day; pixel-based applications are commonly known as *paint programs*, and vector-based applications are referred to as *draw programs*.

The fundamental difference between paint and draw programs is the same now as it was then. Paint programs (like Photoshop) use pixels, or tiny colored squares, to construct an image. The effect is similar to painting on a piece of graph paper, filling each cell with a single color. The *resolution*, or the exact size of the pixels, depends on the intended use of the image. For this reason, pixel-based images are *resolution dependent*; successfully displaying or outputting such an image depends largely on its fixed pixel size. (See Chapter 9, "Digital Imaging Fundamentals," for more information.)

On the other hand, vector-based graphics have no resolution. They don't use pixels. Instead, their shapes are comprised of points and segments, like a connect-the-dots puzzle (see Figure 8.1). Only here, you can reposition the points, curve the segments, and create a series of overlapping shapes virtually at will. These graphics are *resolution independent*—they have no resolution until they're printed, and the final value depends on the output device used. For example, assume you have a 300-pixel-per-inch Photoshop image of a black circle. If you output it to a 300dpi printer, of course, it reproduces at 300dpi. If you send the same image to a 2400dpi imagesetter, its resolution doesn't change—it still outputs at 300dpi. The resolution is fixed. Now assume you have an Illustrator image that contains a vector-based circle. On a 300dpi printer, it outputs at 300dpi; on a 600dpi printer, it outputs at 600dpi; on a 2400dpi imagesetter, it outputs at 2400dpi. The resolution depends solely on the output device used to reproduce the image.

PIXEL-BASED IMAGE   VECTOR-BASED ARTWORK

Figure 8.1 *Pixel-based images are actually a grid of tiny colored squares, which become evident as you zoom in on the graphic (left). Because vector-based shapes are resolution independent, you could zoom in forever and never find a pixel (right).*

To look at it another way, when you use a vector-based graphics program, you write code. In the case of Illustrator and FreeHand, the code is PostScript, the output engine that drives our industry. You don't have to write PostScript by hand, or even know how it works; the interface of both programs lets you create shapes much more intuitively than that. However, it's at the heart of every vector-based graphic, enabling them to output at such high and flexible resolutions. In fact, you can view the code if you open a graphic as text in a word processing program. For example, a black circle is described like this:

```
%%BoundingBox: 95 528 189 622
%%HiResBoundingBox: 95.2319 528.8613 188.2549 621.8843
%%DocumentProcessColors: Black
%%DocumentSuppliedResources: procset Adobe_level2_AI5 1.2 0
%%+ procset Adobe_ColorImage_AI6 1.3 0
%%+ procset Adobe_Illustrator_AI5 1.3 0
%%+ procset Adobe_cshow 2.0 8
%%+ procset Adobe_shading_AI8 1.0 0
%%BeginData: 3460 Hex Bytes
%00003300006600009900 00CC00330000333300336600339900 33CC0033FF
%006600006633006666006699 0066CC0066FF0099000099330099660099 99
%0099CC0099FF00CC0000CC3300CC6600CC9900CCCC00CCFF00FF3300FF66
```

And so on, for another 11 pages. Essentially, these lines contain a set of XY coordinates that determine the location of a series of points. Other commands draw curved lines between the points and fill the space with black.

The magic of PostScript drawing is that it's all done with text. If you want to increase the size of a pixel-based image, you have two choices. You can add more pixels, which involves creating new data, increasing the file size and potentially blurring the existing image detail. Or you can make the pixels bigger, which lowers the overall resolution, perhaps more than the target output method can tolerate. However, if you increase the size of a vector-based shape, the code is simply changed to move the XY coordinates farther apart. The quality of the shape stays the same no matter how much bigger you make it, and the file size is unchanged. This approach gives all vector-based graphics the following qualities:

- **They're infinitely editable.** You can keep changing a vector-based graphic as much as you want to, just as you would with text in a word processing file. Unlike Photoshop images, there are no layers to flatten, and no process required that combines all your different elements into one. Nothing is permanent until it appears on the printed page or film plate.

- **They don't degrade.** Every production-oriented command that you apply to a pixel-based image results in some degree of lost detail. For example, unsharp masking forces certain pixels in detailed image areas to become lighter or darker, only creating the illusion of increased clarity; rotating or scaling forces Photoshop to recalculate the color and position of every pixel, which it never does with 100% accuracy; adjusting an image using Levels or Curves compresses the tonal range, reducing the number of colors. In normal use, you don't notice the loss of detail—in fact, when done properly, these commands enhance the printed appearance of an image. Over-manipulation—one incorrect value or command—degrades an image to the point of uselessness. However, you can apply thousands of commands to a vector-based graphic without compromising its output quality whatsoever.

- **They print at the highest possible resolution.** As described previously, the mathematics of a vector-based graphic enable it to be output on any PostScript-compatible printer at the highest possible resolution.

- **They're infinitely scalable.** Whether in the original application or imported into a layout document, you can increase or decrease the size of a vector-based graphic to any degree, and it will still appear and print at the highest quality. For example, assume you've imported two black circles into a layout document, scaling one to 10% and the other to 1000%. If you output the file to a 2400dpi imagesetter, both shapes print at the same crisp resolution.

- **Their file sizes are small.** The size of a vector-based graphic is usually measured in kilobytes, while the size of a pixel-based image with a resolution high enough to meet print requirements is usually measured in megabytes. For example, the logo on the front of this book, created in Illustrator, measures 220KB. If converted to a 300ppi, CMYK Photoshop image, the size balloons to over 5MB. An extremely complex vector-based graphic can be as large as a pixel-based image, but this is rare.

- **They are easily "stacked" in a layout document.** When you import a vector-based graphic, you only import the shapes contained in the file. If you've ever placed a pixel-based silhouette (part of an image isolated on a white background) in a layout, you've noticed that the white area surrounding the element imports with the rest of the image. If you try to place the element on top of a colored box or another image, the background info is partially obscured by the white information. Here, the only alternative is to create a clipping path, or a vector-based mask. (See Chapter 13, "Photoshop Production Techniques," for more info.) No such white information appears in a vector-based graphic, unless you add it on purpose.

- **You can Undo almost endlessly.** Unlike page layout programs and earlier versions of Photoshop (where you can only undo the most recent command), you can choose Edit: **Undo** dozens, even hundreds of times while editing a vector-based graphic. This enables you to quickly remove a lengthy series of commands without having to save multiple copies of the file. In Illustrator, you can undo up to 200 times. (Set this value in the Minimum Undo Level field, in the File: Preferences: **Units & Undo** dialog box.) In FreeHand, you can undo up to 100 times. (Set this value in the Undo's field, in the File: Preferences: **General** dialog box.) Be aware that higher undo values require more RAM. If you intend to set the maximum amount, you must increase the program's RAM allocation. (See Chapter 3, "Optimizing Your Work Environment," for more info.) Most users set this value between 30 and 50.

Using Vector-Based Graphics

The more you use a program like Illustrator or FreeHand, the better you'll understand the type of artwork for which they're best suited. Understanding when to use these programs is just as important as knowing when to put them aside for more appropriate software. Their unique qualities make them an excellent choice for the following:

- **Logos.** Often-used graphics such as corporate and credit card logos need to be portable, easily edited, and consistent—all of which PostScript artwork provides.

- **Stylized type.** The points and paths used in vector-based artwork are virtually identical to the shapes used to create the characters of your favorite typefaces. This makes Illustrator and FreeHand the perfect tools for editing and enhancing customized type.

- **Refining traced images.** It's possible to convert a pixel-based image to vector-based shapes. This is done by tracing an element with paths, either by hand or using an automated program like Adobe Streamline. This technique is not suitable for every pixel-based image; simple black and white shapes work best, like a line art scan of a logo that only exists in printed form. By converting the image to outlines, you can edit, scale, and output it just like any graphic created in Illustrator or FreeHand. Both tracing methods, however, rarely turn out perfect artwork the first time around. Most often, you need to open the graphic in your vector-based editing program, use its Bézier toolset to refine the shapes, and resave before incorporating it into your layout. (See "Tracing Pixel-Based Images," later this chapter.)

- **Fonts and specialized font characters.** Most font designers use Illustrator or FreeHand at least in part when creating new digital typefaces. After drawing the characters (or tracing a scanned set), they can import or copy and paste the outlines into a font development utility, such as Macromedia Fontographer. Additionally, some people use this process to create font-based versions of any specialized characters that don't appear in standard fonts. For example, the phonorecord copyright symbol (a tiny "P" in a circle) isn't included in most typefaces. CD cover designers often create the symbol in Illustrator or FreeHand, save it as an EPS file, then place it as an anchored graphic whenever they need it. Many go one step further by creating a one-character font containing only this symbol, enabling them to enter it at will like any other text element.

- **Graphs.** Illustrator features a fairly robust toolset for creating updateable graphs, similar to the ones found in programs like Microsoft Excel. You can choose from different graph types, dynamically change the represented values, and most importantly, prepare the image for output in a high-res print environment. [1]

Despite their flexibility and crisp, high-res output, vector-based programs are not the right choice for a wide range of other graphic types. This isn't to say that you *can't* perform some of these tasks in Illustrator or FreeHand— your time will just be better spent using the proper tools:

FOOTNOTE

[1]   Many production specialists find themselves in the position of incorporating an Excel graph into a page layout. Because you can't import the file, copy and paste it into another graphics program, or open it directly in Illustrator or FreeHand, many people resign themselves to re-creating the graph in the program of their choice. There is a solution. From Excel, save the graph as a PostScript file. (In the Print dialog box, set the Destination pop-up to File instead of Printer.) Use Adobe Acrobat Distiller to convert the PostScript file to a PDF file. Open the PDF from within Illustrator or FreeHand—when you do, the graph appears as a series of editable objects, which you can color, trap, and refine as needed. (Unfortunately, it doesn't appear as an editable Illustrator graph—only shapes.) When finished, save the file as an EPS and import it into your layout.

- **Photo-realistic images.** In a pixel-based graphic, every single pixel can have a different color. Even areas that appear to possess the same value, such as a flesh tone, are actually the result of thousands of slightly varying pixel colors. When applied to an image like a full-color scan, this phenomenon can reproduce the same subtle shades and tones found in nature. In fact, Photoshop's color adjustment tools enable you to target and edit specific parts of an image's tonal range, relieving you from the impossible duty of attacking pixels one by one. In a vector-based graphic, every colored element has to be defined as a separate shape (with the exception of gradients and patterns, which offer limited functionality). Attempting to reproduce a continuous tone image with points and paths would require so many shapes that the file wouldn't print, and so much time that the deadline would surely pass before you finished. The effect is similar to reproducing a photograph using nothing but stencils.

- **Extremely complex images.** The more shapes a vector-based graphic contains, the more time it requires to create, the harder it is to edit, and the longer it may take to output. There's really no limit to the number of objects you can build into your artwork. Some designers even auto-trace finely detailed line art or color images, in an effort to create illustrations with a distinctly "computerized" look. When working this way, proceed with caution; they may result in PostScript errors during output, especially on older printers.

- **Drawing by hand.** Even though these applications are often called drawing programs, they really aren't well-suited for the free and natural style associated with the concept of drawing. Although the tools and commands separate you from the knowledge that you are writing PostScript code, PostScript has very strict parameters that the program won't (and shouldn't) let you violate. This prohibits you from being freely expressive, a must when drawing by hand. If you want to incorporate hand drawings in your designs, you have two choices: draw on paper and scan it, or invest in a pressure-sensitive tablet.

- **Page layout.** Each new version of Illustrator and FreeHand offers more enhanced page layout features. They now support tab settings, spellcheckers, and many other functions normally associated with page layout programs. FreeHand even allows you to create multipage documents. For the best results, however, ignore these features and use the applications for their intended purpose: creating supplementary graphics. The page layout tools in a vector-based program are like the can opener on your Swiss Army knife. The puny blade may seem like enough when you have nothing else, but when you compare it to using a full-fledged electric can opener, the choice is easy. (See Chapter 14, "Page Layout Issues," for more info.)

Understanding Bézier Curves

If you're new to Illustrator or FreeHand, it may seem like they fly in the face of any approach to graphics you've ever experienced. Indeed, these programs are the least intuitive in the design and prepress environment, and therefore have the sharpest learning curve. Don't despair; they do use a consistent logic, and once you understand a few basic guidelines, you can use them with relative ease.

At the heart of every vector-based program is a geometric modeling algorithm called Bézier (BAY-zee-ay) curves, originally developed in the 1960s to assist in computer-aided automobile design. A colleague once explained curves to me like this: "...the parameter values are points in three-dimensional space, blended together by polynomial functions." True, perhaps, but hardly appropriate. Put simply, drawing with Bézier curves involves working with a series of points and segments. The points are like dots, the segments are like lines that extend between them. The dots can be moved, the segments can be curved. Together, they form a series of shapes that you can color, combine, refine, and otherwise turn into a printable graphic. [2]

FOOTNOTE

[2] For anyone wondering, vector-based curve technology was developed independently by two men: Pierre Bézier, an engineer for Rénault, and Paul de Casteljau, an engineer for Citroën. Because they were employed by competing auto makers, their efforts were largely cloaked in secrecy. De Casteljau's work was actually finished first, but it was never published. Bézier's was, so the field subsequently bears his name. The math that forms the basis of today's Bézier curves, however, is widely attributed to de Casteljau.

As I discuss the different components, Bézier curves may sound more complex than they really are. Don't worry. Although you can create elements by placing points one by one, most people use more simplified techniques. For example, each program offers tools for creating geometric shapes; at the click of a button, you can merge simple items into complex objects; a single command converts type into editable outlines. Quite often, you'll create graphic after graphic without manipulating a single control point. Understanding what makes a vector-based graphic tick will only enable you to get the most out of each program, whether designing original artwork or troubleshooting a problematic file.

Points and Segments

The fundamental building block of a vector-based shape is a *point*. A single point is invisible; it only serves as an XY coordinate, or a position on the page. A series of points form the basic outline of a shape, which in turn is fully realized by the *segments*, or the lines that extend between points (see Figure 8.2).

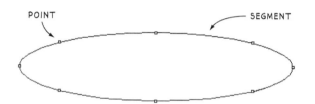

Figure 8.2 *Points, like the numbered dots in a child's puzzle, create the rudimentary outline of a shape. Segments are the lines that connect the dots.*

A series of points and segments is a *path*. When a path has a visible start and endpoint, such as a straight line, it's known as an *open path*. When a path starts and ends on the same point, it becomes a *closed path*, often referred to as a *shape* (see Figure 8.3).

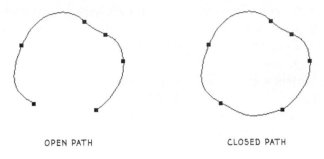

OPEN PATH   CLOSED PATH

Figure 8.3 *When a path has a separate starting and ending point, it's considered open (left). When a path starts and ends on the same point, it is closed.*

Drawing a Straight-Line Path

The easiest path to create is made entirely out of straight lines. [3] The steps are the same in Illustrator and FreeHand:

1. Select the Pen tool.

2. Position the tip of the cursor where you want the straight line to begin, then click to place the first point.

3. Move the cursor to where you want the segment to end, and click again. (Shift-click to constrain the tool to 45-degree increments.)

FOOTNOTE

[3] Many people create all their paths by placing hundreds of tiny, straight segments. You can't really blame them—sometimes, when time is tight, it's better to rely on the methods you know, than to learn a whole new process. Be aware, however, that anyone with a reasonably trained eye can spot straight lines where curves are supposed to exist. If such a client is presented a series of geometric polygons instead of smooth, curving shapes, there's a good chance someone will be doing the work over again. Besides, when you use tiny straight lines, the artwork contains far more points—and therefore, more data—than if you'd used curves. Depending on your output devices, the files may take much longer to process.

Working with curves is not magic; it only takes practice. If you find them awkward, allow yourself 30 minutes a day to mess around with some sample shapes and paths. After two or three weeks, you'll be using them like a pro.

4. Continue clicking to place additional straight segments (see Figure 8.4).

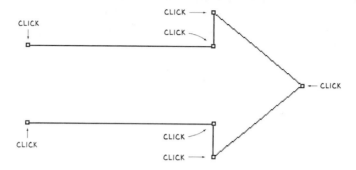

Figure 8.4 *You can create a path that consists entirely of straight lines by clicking with the Pen tool. Refine the shape by moving the individual points.*

Complete the path by doing one of the following:

- To end an open path, (Command-click) [Control-click] anywhere away from the path.

- To create a closed path, place the cursor over the first point. Click or click-drag to close the path.

Curve Handles

Each point contains two handles, used to add curve to the connected segments. Their concept is simple: the first handle affects the segment on one side of the point, the second handle affects the segment on the other (see Figure 8.5). It's not necessary to reveal the handles, but without them, you can only create straight lines.

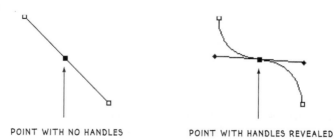

Figure 8.5 *Every point contains two curve handles—even if they are hidden (left). When revealed, one handle curves the segment on one side of the point, and one curves the segment on the other (right).*

After creating a curved path, you can manipulate the handles to refine the amount of curve in each segment. In FreeHand, click a point with the Pointer tool; in Illustrator, click a point with the Direct Selection tool. When a selected point has visible curve handles, you can drag the handles to reduce or enlarge the amount of curve.

Successfully creating curves may involve using a series of tools and techniques to properly adjust the handles. When you automatically create curved shapes, like when you use the Ellipse tool to click-drag a circle, the handles are manipulated by the program. When creating an open path or refining an existing shape, you'll have to edit the points by hand.

Drawing a Curved Path in Illustrator

Follow these steps to create a simple curved path:

1. Select the Pen tool.

2. Place the tip of the cursor where you want the curve to begin. Press (but do not release) the mouse button. The first anchor point appears, and the cursor changes to an arrowhead.

3. Drag in the direction you want the curved segment to appear. As you drag, you reveal one of the point's two handles. The length and angle of this handle will determine the amount of curve applied to the next segment.

4. Release the mouse button.

5. Position the pointer where you want the curved segment to end. Press the mouse button to place the point, then drag to reveal the handles, which further defines the shape of the segment (see Figure 8.6).

Figure 8.6 *As you place the first point, drag the handle in the desired direction of the next segment (left). As you place the next point, drag the mouse to reveal the handles again, which enables you to further edit the curve of the segment.*

As you add segments to the path, use the following techniques:

- To draw a continuous curve, move the cursor to where you want the next segment to end. Then click-drag away from the curve.

- To reposition a point while you draw, hold down the spacebar after you click, without releasing the mouse button. Release the spacebar to drop the point and continue editing the handles, if necessary.

- After creating a smooth point, you can hide the second handle by clicking directly on the most recent point. This enables you to add a straight segment after a curved one (see Figure 8.7).

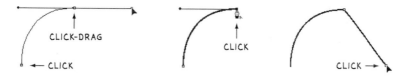

Figure 8.7 *To apply a straight segment after a curved one (left), click once on a point after placing it (center). This hides the second handle, enabling you to start fresh when you place the next point. Many people use this technique alone when creating curves—by placing your points closer together, you can curve each segment with only one handle, allowing a little more control.*

- To break the link that initially appears between curve handles, hold down the (Option) [Alt] key and reposition the second handle to the desired location. Release the key, move the cursor to where you want the next segment to end, and place a point.

- If you want to create a series of open paths, you must deselect the most recent path before starting the next. Otherwise, the end of the last path will automatically connect to the start of the new one. Do this by (Command-clicking) [Control-clicking] on an empty part of the page, or by selecting another tool.

- As you're creating a path, you can select and move points, reposition handles, and drag segments by holding down the (Command) [Control] key, which changes the cursor to the Direct Selection tool. When you've completed the edits, release the key and continue placing points.

- If you accidentally deselect the path (usually by (Command-clicking) [Control-clicking] on the page instead of the path), click the most recent point with the Pen tool before continuing.

Adding Points in Illustrator

To continue adding points from the end of an existing path, follow these steps:

1. Select the path with one of the two selection tools.

2. Select the Pen tool.

3. Click the endpoint you want to start from.

4. Continue adding points.

Occasionally, you may need to add points to an existing segment. This gives you increased flexibility in refining the segment's shape. Whether adding points to an open or closed path, the steps are the same:

1. Select the Add Anchor Point tool.

2. Click on the segment where you want to add a point.

3. Choose the Direct Selection tool.

4. Select the new point and edit as desired.

Note that if you add a point to a segment that's already curved, its handles are revealed as necessary to maintain the current shape.

Deleting Points in Illustrator

To delete a point you have just placed with the Pen tool, press the Delete key. Watch out: if you accidentally press Delete a second time, you remove the entire path. (Choose Edit: **Undo** if this happens.)

If you delete a point by selecting it with the Direct Selection tool and pressing the Delete key, you remove the point as well as the segments on either side. To remove a point from a path without removing any segments, follow these steps:

1. Select the Delete Anchor Point tool.

2. Click the point you want to remove.

Note that when you delete a point with exposed handles, you affect the curve of the remaining segment.

Drawing a Curved Path in FreeHand

Follow these steps to create a simple curved path:

1. Select the Pen tool.

2. Place the tip of the cursor where you want the curve to begin. Press (but do not release) the mouse button. The first anchor point appears.

3. Drag in the direction you want the curved segment to appear. As you drag, you reveal the point's two handles. The length and angle of the handle beneath the cursor determines the amount of curve applied to the next segment.

4. Release the mouse button.

5. Position the pointer where you want the curved segment to end. Press the mouse button to place the point, then drag to reveal the handles, which further defines the shape of the segment (see Figure 8.8).

Figure 8.8 *As you place the first point, drag the handle in the desired direction of the next segment (left). As you place the next point, drag the cursor to reveal the handles again, which enables you to further edit the curve of the segment.*

As you add segments to the path, use the following techniques:

- To draw a continuous curve, move the cursor to where you want the next segment to end, and click+drag away from the curve.

- To reposition a point while you draw, hold down the (Command) [Control] key after you click, without releasing the mouse button. Release the key to drop the point and continue editing the handles, if necessary.

- After creating a smooth point, you can hide the second handle by clicking directly on the most recent point. This enables you to add a straight segment after a curved one (see Figure 8.9).

Figure 8.9 *To apply a straight segment after a curved one (left), click once on a point after placing it (center). This hides the second handle, enabling you to start fresh when you place the next point. Many people use this technique when creating curves—by placing your points closer together, you can curve each segments with only one handle, allowing you to work with a little more control.*

- To break the link that initially appears between curve handles, you must convert the point type. After placing a smooth point with linked handles, click the Corner Point button in the Object Inspector palette. Immediately afterward, hold down the (Command) [Control] key to access the Pointer tool, and reposition the second handle as desired. Then move the cursor to where you want the next segment to end, and place a point.

- To create a series of open paths, you must deselect the most recent path before starting the next. Otherwise, the end of the last path will automatically connect to the start of the new one. Do this by (Command-clicking) [Control-clicking] an empty part of the page, or by choosing Edit: Select: **None**.

- You can select and move points, reposition handles, and drag segments of a path in progress by pressing the (Command) [Control] key, which changes the cursor to the Selection tool. When you've completed the edits, release the key, click the most recent point, and continue.

- If you accidentally deselect the path (usually by (Command-clicking) [Control-clicking] on the page instead of the path), click the most recent point with the Pen tool before continuing.

Adding Points in FreeHand

To continue adding points from the end of an existing path, follow these steps:

1. Select the path with the Pointer tool.

2. Select the Pen tool.

3. Click the endpoint you want to start from.

4. Continue adding points.

Occasionally, you may need to add points to an existing segment. This will give you increased flexibility in refining its shape. When adding points to an open or closed path, follow these steps:

1. Select the path with the Pointer tool.

2. Hold down the (Option) [Alt] key.

3. Click on the segment where you want to add a point.

4. Release the key, select the new point, and edit as desired.

Before you can add a point to a geometric box (created with the Rectangle, Ellipse, or Polygon tools), you must select the shape and choose Modify: **Ungroup**. If you add a point to a segment that's already curved, its handles are revealed as necessary to maintain the current shape.

Deleting Points in FreeHand

To delete a point, select it with the Pointer tool and press the Delete key. If you do this while using the Pen tool, you remove the most recent point; keep pressing Delete to remove points one by one, in reverse order.

Combining Shapes

One of the most common ways to produce a complex element in Illustrator or FreeHand is to combine a series of simple shapes. There are two approaches to this method. First, you can force one or more items to behave in a way that ordinary shapes do not. The most common examples are *compound paths*, where multiple shapes are recognized as a single item by the program, and *masks*, where a single shape is used to reveal only a portion of any underlying information. Second, you can use the programs' *merge* commands to make a new object from a series of overlapping shapes. Merging relieves you from the arduous task of creating many complex elements by hand.

Using Compound Paths

Many people confuse compound paths with *grouped* items. When a series of shapes are grouped together, it means you can select, position, and transform them at the same time. When shapes are converted into a compound path, they are treated by Illustrator and FreeHand as a single entity, which opens the door for some new editing possibilities. Compound paths are commonly used for the following:

- **"Punching holes" in a shape.** Let's say you're designing a donut. It actually consists of two shapes: a large circle for the donut, and a smaller circle for the hole. The problem is, you can't apply a simple color value that allows you to see through the hole. (Many people attempt to color the inner shape with None, which has no effect on the larger circle.) Instead, you must select the two items and create a compound path, which uses the smaller shape to punch a hole in the larger one, allowing you to view any underlying info (see Figure 8.10).

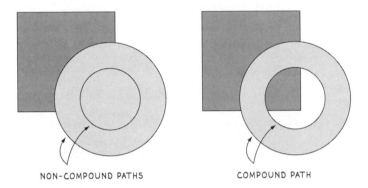

NON-COMPOUND PATHS   COMPOUND PATH

Figure 8.10 *Normally, when shapes overlap, they appear as a series of stacked items (left). When you create a compound path, the overlapping areas are "punched out," creating the effect of a see-through hole.*

- **Editing customized type.** Many font characters automatically use compound paths as described in the previous item. For example, a capital "P" consists of two shapes: the primary outline, and the smaller loop. Because you can always see through the loop when you place it over a colored background, the shapes already exist as a compound path. This relationship remains when you convert type to editable outlines. (See "Converting Type to Paths," later this chapter.)

- **Combining separate shapes for custom fills and masks.** For example, if you attempt to apply a gradient fill to a series of selected shapes, each one is filled separately. By converting them to a compound path, the same gradient flows through every shape (see Figure 8.11). You must employ the same technique when using separate shapes as a single masking element. (See "Using Masks," later this chapter.)

- **Facilitating merge commands.** Because many of the merge commands result in "holes" or separate items, they automatically convert to compound paths. (See "Merging Shapes," later this chapter.)

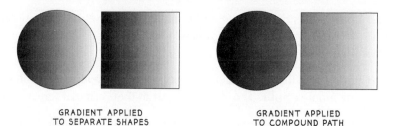

GRADIENT APPLIED
TO SEPARATE SHAPES

GRADIENT APPLIED
TO COMPOUND PATH

Figure 8.11 *When you apply a gradient to separate shapes, each one is uniquely filled (left). After converting to a compound path, you can run a single gradient through all of them (right).*

Creating a Compound Path in Illustrator

To create a compound path in Illustrator, select the desired shapes and choose Object: Compound Paths: **Make**. Where any of the shapes overlap, a transparent "hole" results. If no shapes overlap, the compound path still exists; the items can be filled, transformed, and used to mask other objects as a single item. Be aware of the following issues:

- You can remove the compound path command by selecting the item and choosing Object: Compound Paths: **Release**. The shapes revert to their original form.

- You can select the individual items of a compound path by clicking them with the Direct Selection tool. To edit the items' path shape, make sure you click directly on the outline.

- The fill and stroke of the bottom-most shape is applied to every component of a compound path.

- If you use very complex shapes in a compound path, or if you use a large number of compound paths in a graphic, you may experience difficulty printing. If so, simplify the shapes or remove some of the items.

- To reverse the effect of a single shape within a compound path, select it with the Direct Selection tool, choose Show Attributes from the Windows menu, and click the available Reverse Path Direction button.

Creating a Compound Path in FreeHand

To create a compound path in FreeHand, select the desired shapes and choose Modify: **Join**. Where any of the shapes overlap, a transparent "hole" results. If no shapes overlap, the compound path still exists; the items can be filled, transformed, and used to mask other objects as a single item. Be aware of the following issues:

- You can remove the compound path command by selecting the item and choosing Modify: **Split**. The shapes revert to their original form.

- You can select individual items that comprise a compound path by (Option-clicking) [Alt-clicking] them with the Selection tool. To edit their path shape, make sure you click directly on the outline. (Make sure to release the key after selecting a shape—if you attempt to edit while holding it down, you'll create a duplicate shape.)

- The fill and stroke of the bottom-most shape is applied to every component of a compound path.

- If you use very complex shapes in a compound path, or if you use a large number of compound paths in a graphic, you may experience difficulty printing. If so, simplify the shapes or remove some of the items.

Using Masks

When you create a mask, you use a single shape to crop a series of shapes and colors. The artwork itself isn't affected; the masking element acts as a sort of clipping path, revealing only the information that falls within its outline. The hidden paths still exist, and can be restored at any time. [4]

FOOTNOTE

[4] To a certain degree, masking in Illustrator and FreeHand is like cropping a graphic in a page layout program. If you mask a large amount of information with a small shape—for example, a 9×6-inch scan with a two-inch box—you may experience output problems. At the very least, the graphic will take a lot longer to process. Avoid this by keeping the amount of masked information to a minimum. If masking a pixel-based image, crop it as much as possible in Photoshop before importing and using it. If masking vector-based shapes, delete any items you know will not be visible in the mask. If necessary, you can crop the unnecessary info using the programs' merge commands before creating the mask. (See "Merging Shapes," later this chapter.)

Creating a Mask in Illustrator

Follow these steps to create a mask in Illustrator:

1. Create the information you want to include in a mask. In this example, I use a series of lines.

2. Create the shape that will act as the masking element. Here, I use an ellipse (see Figure 8.12).

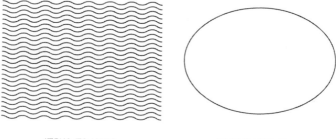

ITEMS TO MASK   MASKING ELEMENT

Figure 8.12   *A mask consists of two items: the shapes you want to partially conceal (left), and the element you intend to mask them with (right).*

3. Make sure the masking element is the top-most object. If necessary, select it and choose Object: Arrange: **Bring to Front**.

4. Place the masking element in the desired position over the remaining items.

5. Select all the items involved in the mask. If any other shapes already exist on the page, don't choose Edit: Select All—if you do, they'll be included in the mask as well. Just drag a marquee with the Selection tool that touches the appropriate items.

6. Choose Object: Masks: **Make**. As you can see, the information falling outside the ellipsis is hidden; the information falling inside remains visible (see Figure 8.13).

Locking a Mask

After creating a mask, its shapes are not grouped or locked. You can continue dragging and editing the items with the selection tools, which becomes annoying when you're trying to work on a larger graphic. (For example, you can select the items inside the mask by accidentally clicking on one of the "invisible" parts.) Avoid this by choosing Object: Masks: **Lock** immediately after creating the mask, which enables you to treat the mask as a single item. Choose Object: Masks: **Unlock** to regain access to the component shapes.

BEFORE MASKING   AFTER MASKING   SELECTING THE MASK

Figure 8.13   *Before creating the mask, make sure you've placed the masking element in the correct position (left). After masking, the shapes appear to be clipped by the element (center). However, when you select the mask (right), you can see that all the data still exists.*

Selecting Masked Items

There are two ways to select the masking element. You can click its outline with the Direct Selection tool, or you can choose Edit: Select: **Masks**, which selects all the masking elements in the graphic.

Coloring a Masking Element

The masking element always loses its fill and stroke colors when you apply the command. To reapply them, select the shape and set the desired values in the Colors palette.

Creating a Compound Mask

To create a *compound mask*, or a masking element that consists of more than one shape, you must first convert the shapes into a compound path. If you don't, only one of the shapes is used as the masking element (see Figure 8.14).

Creating Character Masks

A *character mask* uses type as the masking element. Follow these steps:

1. Create the information you want to include in a mask.

2. Use the Type tool to enter and format the desired text.

3. Position the text as desired over the remaining info.

4. Choose Object: Masks: **Make.**

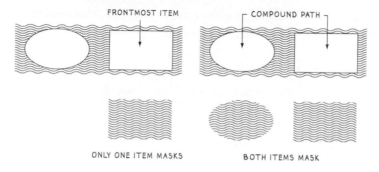

Figure 8.14   *When you want to mask items with several shapes instead of a single element, position them as desired (top). If you don't convert the masking elements to a compound path first, only the topmost shape masks the underlying info (bottom left). Only by using a compound path can you mask items with more than one shape (bottom right).*

At this point, you can still edit the type, adjusting the kerning, size, font, and characters as much as you want. Sometime before you save and import the graphic, however, you must convert the type to outlines—otherwise, you'll have to provide the necessary font when you turn the project over to an output vendor. This can be a little tricky, so follow these steps:

1. Select the type with the Selection tool.

2. Choose Type: **Create Outlines** to convert the type to editable outlines. You'll notice that the type no longer masks the underlying info.

3. Leave the outlines selected and immediately choose Object: Compound Paths: **Make**. The mask effect is restored, and you no longer require the original font. (See "Converting Type to Paths," later this chapter.)

Adding Items to a Mask

When you need to add another shape to an existing mask, you don't have to release, edit, and re-create the entire element. Instead, you can use Illustrator's Paste in Front and Paste Behind commands:

1. Create the item that you want to add to the mask.

2. Place the item over the mask in the desired position.

3. Choose Edit: **Cut**.

4. Use the Direct Selection tool to select an element inside the mask.

5. To place the new item above the current selection, choose Edit: **Paste in Front**. To place it behind, choose Edit: **Paste Behind**.

Releasing a Mask

To separate the shapes from the masking element, select the mask and choose Object: Masks: **Release**.

Creating a Mask in FreeHand

Follow these steps to create a mask in FreeHand:

1. Create the shape that will act as the masking element. In this example, I will use a rectangular box.

2. Create the information you want to include in the mask. In this example, I will use a series of colored shapes.

3. Place the shapes as desired over the masking element. This is important—when you create the mask, the shapes initially appear in this position.

4. Choose Edit: **Cut**.

5. Select the masking element.

6. Choose Edit: **Paste Inside**. The shapes now appear inside the masking element (see Figure 8.15).

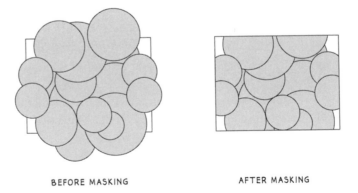

BEFORE MASKING   AFTER MASKING

Figure 8.15 *When creating a mask in FreeHand, you must position your shapes over the masking element exactly where you want them to appear (left). After cutting them, select the masking element and choose Edit:* **Paste Inside**. *The shapes are placed inside the mask in the same position (right).*

Selecting Masked Items

To select the entire mask, click it with the Pointer tool. To select an individual shape within a mask, (Option-click) [Alt-click] it.

Moving Masked Items

When you select a mask, a blue "handle" appears in the center. To reposition the entire contents within the mask, click-drag this handle. To temporarily release of the objects for individual editing, double-click the handle.

Coloring a Mask

To change the fill and stroke of the masking element, select it and set the desired values. To color all the shapes inside the mask, double-click the blue handle to temporarily release the items, then set the values. To color a single shape, (Option-click) [Alt-click] it before setting the values.

Creating a Character Mask

Follow these steps to create a mask using type characters:

1. Use the Type tool to enter and format the desired text.

2. Convert the type to editable outlines by choosing Text: **Convert to Outlines**.

3. Leave the text selected and immediately choose Modify: **Join** to create a compound path.

4. Create the information you want to include in the mask.

5. Place the shapes as desired over the type. This is important—when you create the mask, the shapes initially appear in this position.

6. Choose Edit: **Cut**.

7. Select the type outlines with the Pointer tool.

8. Choose Edit: **Paste Inside**. The shapes now appear inside the masking element (see Figure 8.16).

Because you have to convert the type to outlines before creating a mask, you don't have to supply the original font to the output vendor.

ARRANGE CONVERTED TEXT OVER THE DESIRED ITEMS

CUT THE ITEMS AND PASTE INSIDE

Figure 8.16 *FreeHand only allows you to create a character mask using type you've converted to outlines—you cannot continue editing or formatting the text. After converting the type, convert it to a compound path, then paste your shapes inside of it.*

Transforming a Mask

When scaling, rotating, skewing, or otherwise transforming a mask, be sure the Contents box is checked in the Transform palette. This ensures that the mask contents are transformed as well. Otherwise, only the masking element is affected (see Figure 8.17).

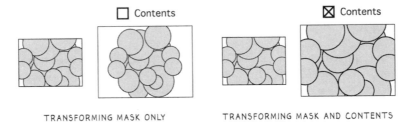

TRANSFORMING MASK ONLY   TRANSFORMING MASK AND CONTENTS

Figure 8.17 *When transforming a mask in FreeHand, make sure the Contents box is checked in the Transform palette. This way, the masked shapes will be affected along with the masking element (right). If you leave the box unchecked, you only transform the masking element (left).*

Adding Items to a Mask

When you need to add another shape to an existing mask, you don't have to release, edit, and re-create the entire element. Follow these steps:

1. Create the new item that you want to add to the mask.

2. Place the item over the mask in the desired position.

3. Choose Edit: **Cut**.

4. Select the mask and choose Edit: **Paste Inside**. The new item initially appears above the remaining shapes, but you can (Option-click) [Alt-click] it and use FreeHand's Arrange commands to move it backward and forward.

Releasing a Mask

To release the shapes inside a masking element, select the mask and choose Edit: **Cut Contents**.

Merging Shapes

In Illustrator and FreeHand, you can generate a new shape by combining a series of overlapping items. When used properly, the merge commands allow you to create complex artwork even if you have no idea how to use the Pen tool or edit Bézier curves. This is particularly useful when you find yourself in the position of producing a complex item at the request of a client. Illustrator refers to its merge commands as *Pathfinder* features; in FreeHand, they're known as the *Combine* commands.

Illustrator's Pathfinder Options

The Pathfinder options are found in the Pathfinder palette. (In earlier versions, they were available as filters.) You must make sure that every shape you want to affect is selected before applying a command.

Unite

The Unite option affects every selected item (see Figure 8.18). When items overlap, the multiple shapes are converted to a single path. If any items do not overlap, the result is a compound path. (See "Using Compound Paths," earlier this chapter.)

Intersect

The Intersect option creates a new shape based on any overlapping information (see Figure 8.19).

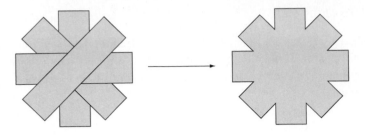

Figure 8.18 *When you apply Unite, all overlapping shapes are converted into a single outline.*

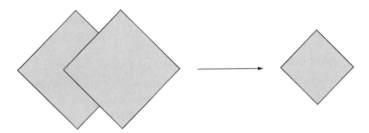

Figure 8.19 *When you apply Intersect, only the overlapping areas of your selected shapes remain.*

Exclude

The Exclude option removes the overlapping areas of any objects from the bottom-most item, converting the rest of the info into a compound path (see Figure 8.20).

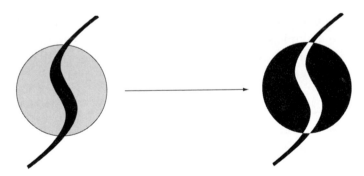

Figure 8.20 *When you apply Exclude, the overlapping areas of the frontmost items are removed from the bottom object. The effect is the same as choosing Object: Compound Path: **Make**.*

Minus Front

The Minus Front option removes the shape of any overlapping elements from the the bottom-most item (see Figure 8.21).

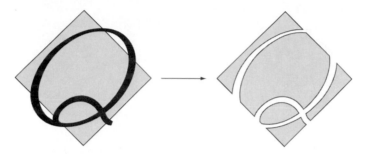

Figure 8.21 *When you apply Minus Front, the upper items are removed, along with any overlapping areas from the bottom shape.*

Minus Back

The Minus Back option only affects the topmost item. Any underlying info is removed from its shape (see Figure 8.22).

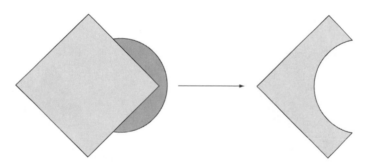

Figure 8.22 *When you apply Minus Back, the shapes of the underlying objects are removed from the topmost item.*

Divide

The effect of the Divide option depends on whether you use open or closed paths. If you've selected overlapping shapes, they are split at whatever point they intersect. If you've selected a shape with a series of overlapping open paths, the shape is split along the exact line of the paths (see Figure 8.23). (The new shapes are automatically grouped; to move them independently, you must choose Object: **Ungroup.**)

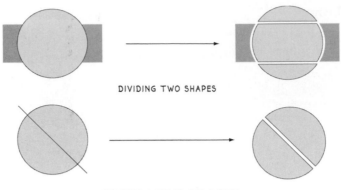

DIVIDING TWO SHAPES

DIVIDING A SHAPE AND A PATH

Figure 8.23 *When you apply Divide to overlapping items, they are split at the points of intersection, creating a series of individual shapes (top). When one of the overlapping items is an open path, applying Divide uses the path to split the under-lying shape (bottom).*

Trim

When you apply the Trim option, it removes the hidden portions of any over-lapping shapes (see Figure 8.24). (The new shapes are automatically grouped; to move them independently, you must choose Object: **Ungroup**.)

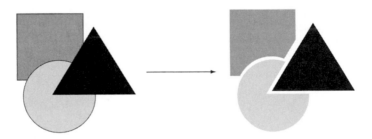

Figure 8.24 *When you apply Trim to a series of overlapping shapes, the portions hidden from view are removed.*

Merge

The Merge option does the same thing as Trim, with one exception: if any of the overlapping shapes have the same fill color, they are combined into a single shape (see Figure 8.25). (The new shapes are automatically grouped; to move them independently, you must choose Object: **Ungroup**.)

Figure 8.25 *Applying Merge is the same as applying Trim, with the exception that any shapes with the same fill color are combined into a single outline.*

Crop

The Crop option uses the top-most shape to crop the underlying info (see Figure 8.26). (The new shapes are automatically grouped; to move them independently, you must choose Object: **Ungroup**.)

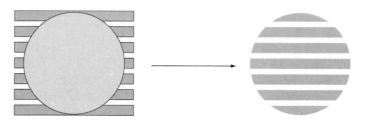

Figure 8.26 *When you apply Crop, the topmost shape is used to trim away any underlying items it doesn't overlap.*

Outline

The Outline option converts any overlapping shapes to very thin paths, split at every point they intersect (see Figure 8.27). The fill color of each shape is applied to the new path; any stroke color is discarded. (The paths are automatically grouped; to move them independently, you must choose Object: **Ungroup**.) [5]

F O O T N O T E

[5] The Trap options of the Pathfinder palette are covered in-depth in Chapter 15, "Trapping."

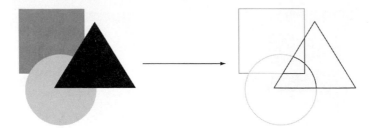

Figure 8.27   *When you apply Outline, the shapes are converted to very thin, stroked paths.*

FreeHand's Combine Options

These commands are found under the Modify: **Combine** submenu. They also appear as icons in the Operations palette, enabling you to apply them with a single click. (Display the palette by choosing Window: Xtras: **Operations**.) [6]

Union

The Union command affects every selected item. When multiple shapes overlap, they are converted to a single shape. If any items do not overlap, the result is a compound path (see Figure 8.28). (See "Using Compound Paths," earlier this chapter.)

Divide

The effect of the Divide command depends on whether you use open or closed paths. If you've selected overlapping shapes, they're split at whatever point they intersect. If you've selected a shape with a series of overlapping open paths, the paths are used to split the shape (see Figure 8.29). (The new shapes are automatically grouped; to move them independently, you must choose Object: **Ungroup**.)

F O O T N O T E

[6]   When applying the Combine options, you can retain a copy of the original shapes by holding down the Shift key as you choose the desired command.

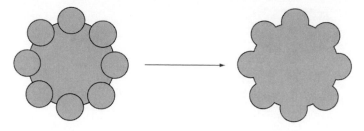

Figure 8.28 *When you apply Union, all overlapping shapes are converted into a single outline.*

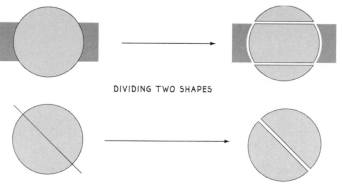

DIVIDING TWO SHAPES

DIVIDING A SHAPE AND A PATH

Figure 8.29 *When you apply Divide to overlapping shapes, they are split at the points of intersection, creating a series of individual objects (top). When you place a series of open paths over a closed shape, they're used to split the object (bottom).*

Intersect

The Intersect command creates a new shape based on any overlapping information (see Figure 8.30). The new shape retains the fill and stroke of the bottom-most object.

Punch

The Punch command only works when two items are selected. When applied, the top shape is removed from the bottom (see Figure 8.31).

Crop

The Crop option uses the topmost shape to crop the underlying info (see Figure 8.32).

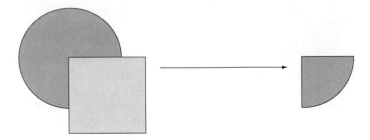

Figure 8.30   *When you apply Intersect, only the overlapping areas of your selected shapes remain.*

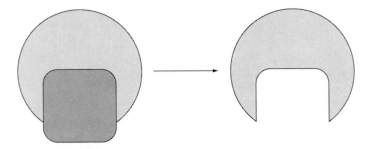

Figure 8.31   *When you apply Punch, the shape of the upper item is removed from the lower object.*

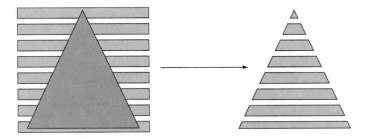

Figure 8.32   *When you apply Crop, the topmost shape is used to trim away any underlying items it doesn't overlap.*

Text and Type

One of the most important uses of Illustrator and FreeHand is the creation of stylized type. With relative ease, you can flow text along a curved path, apply separate fill and stroke values, even edit the actual character shapes. Incorporating this information into a page layout is as easy as importing any other graphic.

Working with vector-based type is a lot easier—even a lot of fun—if you remember one thing: you're using Illustrator or FreeHand to manipulate the text, not to perform page layout. If you're using the programs to simply create columns of text, or to create some sort of page geometry, you really should be working in XPress, PageMaker, or InDesign. Many users, upon shelling out three or four hundred dollars for a graphics program, try to save a little money by using Illustrator or FreeHand to design pages as well as artwork. But the text-handling controls of a true page layout program are far more powerful, their ability to construct multi-page documents is so advanced, that your investment in the software will return with the first few projects you bring to successful completion.

Many people do use a page layout program, but because they're more familiar with their vector-based program, they set up their text blocks there, then import them into a larger layout. If this is the case, consider the following issues:

- **Page layout programs have the most powerful text handling tools.** Layout programs were created to make handling large amounts of text as easy as possible. They feature paragraph and character style sheets, advanced hyphenation algorithms, and a host of other tools that enable you to edit and refine document text. The text tools in Illustrator and FreeHand, although they have become much more robust in recent years, are simply not as thorough.

- **Large ranges of text are handled more efficiently in a layout program.** If you lay out lengthy blocks of text in a vector-based program then import it into a page layout as an EPS graphic, editing that text is a real pain. You have to open the graphic file, make your changes in the original program, save it, then re-import it into the layout. When you enter the text in the layout program, it's a simple matter of highlighting and changing it (or editing a style sheet). Plus, if you've converted the type to outlines, you will not be able to edit the text at all. (See "Converting Type to Paths," later this chapter.)

- **Font handling becomes more complex.** When you import larger text ranges into a layout, the program is *supposed* to keep track of any fonts that reside in an imported EPS graphic, and warn you when they're not present during output. Too often, this doesn't happen. If you don't supply the fonts to your vendor, your project will either misprint or be delayed. (See Chapter 14 for more info.)

Common Vector-Based Type Techniques

The most straightforward type effect is text on a horizontal baseline, possible in both programs with a single click.

In Illustrator, click once on the page with the Type tool. A flashing cursor appears, enabling you to enter the desired text. To select the text block, click any of the characters with the Selection tool. To highlight characters or enter additional text, click an existing block with the Type tool.

In FreeHand, click once on the page with the Text tool. A flashing cursor appears beneath a small text ruler, ready for you to start typing. To select the text block, click it once with the Selection tool. To edit the contents, click the box with the Text tool.

In both applications, you don't need to highlight any characters if you want to edit all the text at once. Simply select the entire block with either program's Selection tool and apply the desired values. However, if you want to create the effects that these programs are famous for, you must use some more intensive techniques. [7]

FOOTNOTE

[7] FreeHand features a set of automated type effects, which I don't describe in this book. Found under the Text: **Effect** submenu, they include such popular items as Inline, Shadow, and Zoom. The reason I don't cover them is simple: you cannot convert the text to outlines. If you try, the applied effect is removed. This means that in order to import one of these effects into a page layout, you must leave the font information embedded in the EPS file. If you don't remember to include the necessary fonts when you turn the project over to a vendor, the image may misprint, or output will be delayed while he hunts down the missing files. Avoid this problem by creating these effects using manual techniques, or by using a different design approach altogether. (I recommend the latter—the effects are a little heavy-handed and obvious, anyway.)

Type Within a Shape

You can flow text into any closed shape (see Figure 8.33). Use simple shapes for the best results, because it is difficult to flow text properly into a complex outline with lots of twists and turns.

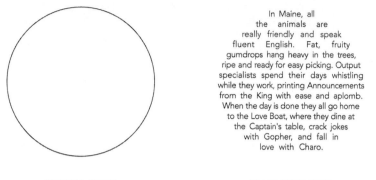

In Maine, all the animals are really friendly and speak fluent English. Fat, fruity gumdrops hang heavy in the trees, ripe and ready for easy picking. Output specialists spend their days whistling while they work, printing Announcements from the King with ease and aplomb. When the day is done they all go home to the Love Boat, where they dine at the Captain's table, crack jokes with Gopher, and fall in love with Charo.

ORIGINAL SHAPE   FILLED WITH TEXT

Figure 8.33 *When placing text inside a shape, smaller point sizes in simpler shapes work best. Otherwise, the text might not flow properly. To make the text flush with all sides of the shape, apply the Justify alignment option.*

Type Within a Shape in Illustrator

In Illustrator, follow these steps:

1. Create the desired shape.

2. Select the Area Type tool.

3. Click directly on the outline of the shape with the tool. If you try to click inside the shape, an alert appears, stating "You must click on a non-compound, non-masking path."

4. Enter your text when the flashing cursor appears at the top of the shape.

You can continue manipulating the shape by clicking it with the Direct Selection tool—the text within automatically reflows. It's important to note that you cannot apply a fill or stroke to a shape that contains text. If you want to continue using the shape, create a duplicate before clicking it with the Area Type tool.

Type Within a Shape in FreeHand

In FreeHand, follow these steps:

1. Enter the desired text using the Text tool.

2. Create the desired shape.

3. Select both of the items.

4. In the Text toolbar, click the Flow Inside Path button.

To continue manipulating the shape, choose Modify: **Ungroup,** then click the shape with the Selection tool.

Type Along a Path

Normally, text follows a horizontal baseline. To create a curved baseline, you must apply text to an existing open path.

Type Along a Path in Illustrator

In Illustrator, follow these steps:

1. Create the desired path.

2. Select the Path Type tool.

3. Click directly on the path where you want the text to begin (see Figure 8.34).

TEXT ALONG A PATH   DRAG "HOT POINT" TO REPOSITION

Figure 8.34 *To flow text along an Illustrator path, click directly on the path with the Path Type tool. As you enter text, it flows along the shape of the path (left). To slide the text along the path, drag the bar that appears at the click-point (right).*

You can continue manipulating the path by clicking it with the Direct Selection tool—the text automatically reflows. Note that you cannot apply a stroke to a path that contains text. If you want to continue using the path, create a duplicate before clicking it with the Path Type tool.

It is possible to reposition text along the path. When you select the path with one of the arrow tools, the original click-point appears as a blue horizontal bar (sometimes known as the "hot point"). Drag the bar left or right to move the text back and forth. If you drag it below the path, the text flips to the opposite side of the path, reading upside-down.

Type Along a Path in FreeHand

In FreeHand, follow these steps:

1. Enter the desired text using the Text tool.

2. Create the desired shape.

3. Select both of the items.

4. In the Text toolbar, click the Attach to Path button (see Figure 8.35).

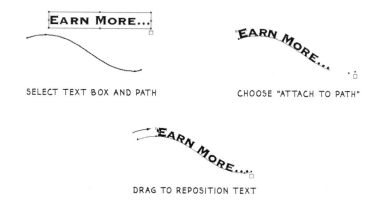

SELECT TEXT BOX AND PATH   CHOOSE "ATTACH TO PATH"

DRAG TO REPOSITION TEXT

Figure 8.35 *In FreeHand, create the path and the text separately (top left), then click the Attach to Path button (top right). To slide the text along the path, drag the small blue triangle that appears at the click-point (bottom).*

You can continue manipulating the shape by clicking it with the Selection tool—the text automatically reflows. Note that you cannot apply a stroke to a path that contains text. If you want to continue using the path, create a duplicate before clicking it with the Path Type tool.

To reposition text back and forth along the path, drag the small blue triangle that appears at the original click-point. Unlike Illustrator, you can't flip it to the opposite side of the path. Achieve this effect by rotating the entire path 180 degrees.

Type Around a Shape

Type can flow around a closed path. The most common example is text around a circle, but you can use any shape.

Type Around a Shape in Illustrator

In Illustrator, follow these steps:

1. Create the desired path.

2. Select the Path Type tool.

3. Click directly on the path where you want the text to begin (see Figure 8.36).

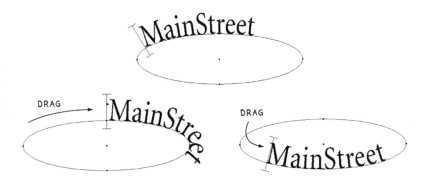

Figure 8.36 *Flow text around a shape by clicking directly on its outline with the Path Type tool (top). Start typing when you see the flashing cursor. To slide the text around the shape, drag the bar that appears at the click-point (bottom left). To place the text inside the shape, drag the bar inside its outline (bottom right).*

To center the text on the top of a circle, make sure you click directly on the topmost point, then choose the Center Alignment option in the Paragraph palette. If you want the text to flow along the inside, drag the blue bar that appears at the click-point into the center of the shape.

Type Around a Shape in FreeHand

In FreeHand, follow these steps:

1. Enter the desired text using the Text tool.

2. Create the desired shape.

3. Select both of the items.

4. In the Text toolbar, click the Attach to Path button (see Figure 8.37).

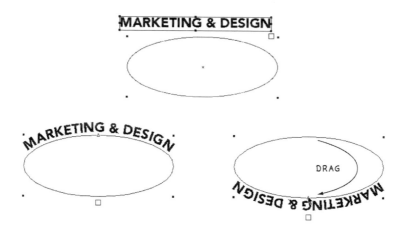

Figure 8.37 *In FreeHand, create the shape and the text separately (top), then click the Attach to Path button (bottom left). To slide the text around the shape, drag the small blue triangle that appears at the click-point (bottom right).*

The text is automatically placed on the top of the shape. If you want the text to flow across the bottom, enter a single paragraph return before the text in the original box, prior to applying the command.

Type Around Both Sides of a Circle

A popular technique involves flowing text above and below the same circle.

Circular Type in Illustrator

In Illustrator, follow these steps:

1. Draw a circle at the desired size.

2. Select the Path Type tool, and click the top-most point of the circle. When the flashing cursor appears, enter and format the text.

3. Choose the Selection tool. The entire circle is selected. In the Paragraph palette, click the Align Center button. The text should center itself along the top of the circle (see Figure 8.38).

Figure 8.41   *Using the centerpoint as a guide (left), you can (Option-Shift-drag) [Alt-Shift-drag] with the Ellipse tool to add concentric circles that complete the effect (right).*

Circular Type in FreeHand

In FreeHand, follow these steps:

1. Draw a circle at the desired size.

2. Use the Text tool to enter the text you want to appear above and below the circle. Separate the two lines with a single paragraph return (see Figure 8.42).

Figure 8.42   *When entering the text, make sure you separate the lines intended for the top and bottom with a paragraph return.*

3. Select both the items.

4. In the Text toolbar, click the Attach to Path button. The first line of text flows across the top of the circle; the second line flows across the bottom (see Figure 8.43).

Unfortunately, no centerpoint automatically appears inside the type circle, which makes it a little more difficult to add concentric circles. You can see a centerpoint, however, if you switch to Keyline view and double-click the circle's outline with the Selection tool. When it appears, immediately choose the Ellipse tool and (Option-Shift-drag) [Alt-Shift-drag] the desired circles (see Figure 8.44).

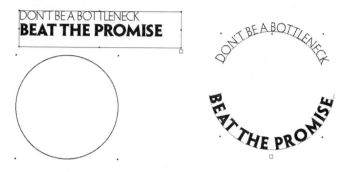

Figure 8.43   *Create the effect by selecting the items and clicking the Attach to Path button (left). The first line of text flows along the top of the circle; the second line flows along the bottom (right).*

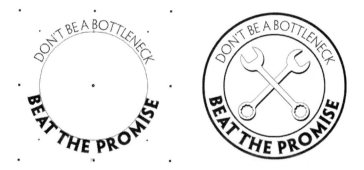

Figure 8.44   *No visible point appears in the center of the effect. However, you can temporarily see one if you switch to Keyline view and double-click the circle with the Selection tool (left). (Option-Shift-drag) [Alt-Shift-drag] from this point with the Ellipse tool to add concentric circles (right). If necessary, you can adjust them with the Align palette.*

Converting Type to Paths

When you enter and format text in Illustrator and FreeHand, it exists as editable type. Similar to text in a layout document, you can highlight the characters, apply a different typeface, set a new point size, change the alignment, and so forth. However, Illustrator and FreeHand also feature a powerful command that converts these characters to editable Bézier shapes.

After converting type to outlines, you can no longer adjust it with any text editing commands—the shapes appear exactly as if you drew them with the Pen tool.

You can edit converted type in an entirely new way. You can reposition and transform individual letters. You can apply a series of commands that only affect shapes, like Distort filters or Merge options. You can edit the points and segments that comprise each shape, enabling you to create highly stylized custom characters (see Figure 8.45).

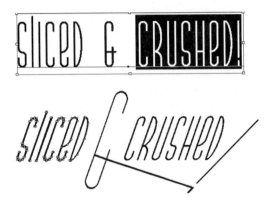

Figure 8.45 *Before type is converted to outlines, you can highlight and format text like any word processing or page layout program (top). After converting, you can edit the individual character shapes (bottom).*

More importantly, converted type does not require the original font in order to output. Because the font data is no longer referred to, you can simply save and import the graphic without worrying about providing any particular font files to an output vendor. This concept leads us to one of the most important rules of working with vector-based graphics: Whenever you create type, you *must* convert it to outlines before you save and import the graphic. This eliminates the possibility of missing font files during output, easily the most common preflight-oriented issue when using this software. Even if you don't need to convert it for the sake of editing, do it as the last step before saving the file. [8]

Converting Text in Illustrator

To convert a text item to editable paths, select it with one of the arrow tools and choose Type: **Create Outlines**. Keep the following issues in mind:

- You can't convert highlighted text. Make sure the entire item is selected with an arrow tool.

- After applying the command, all the individual characters are selected. However, they're not grouped. If you try to reposition the entire item later on, you'll only drag one of the shapes. Avoid this by choosing Object: **Group** immediately after converting.

- If you want to convert all the text in a graphic at once, you don't have to select the individual items. Instead, choose Edit: **Select All**. When you apply the command, it only affects the type.

- If you want to treat the converted text as a single shape—for example, if you want to fill it with the same blend or use it as a mask—choose Object: Compound Paths: **Make** immediately after converting.

Converting Text in FreeHand

To convert a text item to editable paths, select it with one of the arrow tools and choose Text: **Convert to Paths**. Keep the following issues in mind:

- You can convert text whether it is selected with an arrow tool or highlighted. However, even if you've only highlighted a few characters, all the text in the box converts.

FOOTNOTE

[8] Many people avoid converting text to outlines, fearing that they won't be able to edit its contents later on. The solution is simple: save a copy of the graphic before converting. If you need to make any changes, open the unconverted file, make the edits, then save a new converted copy. Re-import the newly converted graphic into your layout document. This method relieves you from having to reenter any text from scratch, while enabling you to import only converted files into your layouts. Don't think of it as an extra step—it's an extra layer of security.

- After applying the command, all the characters are grouped. If you want to edit individual shapes, either (Option-click) [Alt-click] one with the Selection tool, or select the item and choose Modify: **Ungroup**.

- If you want to convert all the text in a graphic at once, you don't have to select the individual items. Instead, choose Edit: **Select All**. When you apply the command, it only affects the type.

- If you want to treat the converted text as a single shape—for example, if you want to fill it with the same blend or use it as a mask—choose Modify: **Join** immediately after converting.

Working with Colors

Vector-based objects can be colored in two ways (see Figure 8.46). You can apply a *stroke*, or a line thickness that straddles the exact contour of the path. You can also apply a *fill*, which colors the area inside of a path. Fill and stroke can be any color or tint, using spot or process inks. (See "Defining Colors," later this section.) Applying color is as easy as selecting an object and clicking a few options in the appropriate palette.

FILL ONLY   STROKE ONLY   FILL AND STROKE

Figure 8.46   Fill *refers to the colored area inside a shape (left).* Stroke *is a colored thickness that straddles the actual path (center).*

Applying Fill and Stroke in Illustrator

To apply a colored fill, follow these steps:

1. Select an object with one of the arrow tools.

2. Click the Fill option in either the toolbox or the Color palette. (When you activate an option in one location, it automatically activates in the other.)

3. Click the desired item in the Swatches palette, or enter CMYK values in the Colors palette. You can also apply a gradient or patterned fill. (See "Gradients" and "Patterns," later this section.)

To apply a stroke, follow these steps:

1. Select an object with one of the arrow tools.

2. Click the Stroke option in either the toolbox or the Color palette. (When you activate an option in one location, it automatically activates in the other.)

3. Click the desired item in the Swatches palette, or enter CMYK values in the Colors palette. You can also apply a gradient or patterned fill.

4. Determine the line thickness by setting a value in the Weight field of the Stroke palette.

When setting fill and stroke in Illustrator, keep the following in mind:

- To simultaneously apply the same fill or stroke to multiple shapes, select them all before choosing your colors.

- You can apply a color by dragging it from one of the palettes directly onto the shape. Whether it affects the fill or stroke depends on the option currently active in the toolbox.

- You cannot apply a gradient as a stroke. If you try, it automatically appears as a fill.

- You can copy the fill and stroke of one object onto another. Select the shape you want to affect, choose the Eyedropper tool, and click the shape that contains the desired colors.

- Illustrator allows you to apply a fill to an open path. It does this by drawing an invisible line between the endpoints, and filling the "closed" spaces accordingly (see Figure 8.47). This often proves to be an annoyance, especially when using the Pen or Pencil tools to create a path manually. If desired, you can eliminate the fill by applying a value of None.

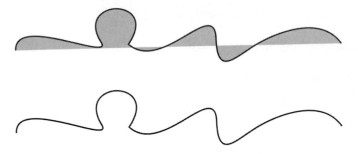

Figure 8.47 *If an open path contains a Fill color, Illustrator draws an imaginary line between the endpoints (top). To remove the fill, apply a value of None (bottom).*

Applying Fill and Stroke in FreeHand

To apply a colored fill, follow these steps:

1. Click an object with the Selection tool.

2. Click the Fill option in the Colors palette.

3. Click the desired color swatch in the Colors palette.

To apply a stroke, follow these steps:

1. Click an object with the Selection tool.

2. Click the Stroke option in the Colors palette.

3. Click the desired color swatch in the Colors palette.

4. Determine the line thickness by setting a value in the Width field of the Stroke Inspector palette.

When setting fill and stroke in FreeHand, keep the following in mind:

- To simultaneously apply the same fill or stroke to multiple shapes, select them all before choosing your colors.

- You can apply a color by dragging it from one of the palettes directly onto the shape. Whether it affects the fill or stroke depends on the option currently active in the Colors palette.

- You cannot apply a gradient as a stroke. If you try, nothing happens.

- To apply the fill and stroke of one shape to another, select the shape with the desired colors. Choose Edit: **Copy Attributes**. Select the shape you want to affect and choose Edit: **Paste Attributes**.

- FreeHand does not allow you to apply a visible fill to an open path.

Using the Default Colors

Illustrator and FreeHand both ship with a selection of default colors: None, White, Black, and Registration. To use them successfully, you must understand the values that they represent. [9]

None and White

It's easy to confuse None and White. In the CMYK printing lexicon, they mean the same thing: an area with no applied ink. The white of the underlying paper provides the white that appears in a graphic.

FOOTNOTE

[9] Whenever you create a new file in Illustrator, the Swatches palette is filled with a series of colors, gradients, and patterns. Because you have no control over the printed appearance of these items, you should simply avoid them in favor of the colors you've already chosen for your project.

However, they will always be in your way as you create a color list specific to a particular file. You have a choice. First, you can delete all the items from the Swatches palette when you create every file. Do this by choosing Select All Unused, then Delete Swatch from the Swatches palette submenu. (Black and Registration remain untouched.)

If this sounds repetitive, you can change the default settings entirely. This info is actually stored in a separate file called "Adobe Illustrator Startup," located in Illustrator's Plug-ins folder. Although this file contains the colors, gradients, patterns, custom brushes, and so forth that the program loads as defaults during startup, none of them are essential. Follow these steps:

1. Open the Adobe Illustrator Startup file in Illustrator.
2. Choose Edit: **Select All** and delete the items.
3. Choose Select All Unused in the Swatches palette submenu.
4. Choose Delete Swatch from the same location.
5. Choose File: **Save** and close the file.

The changes are apparent the next time you launch Illustrator. If you want to add new default colors, you must define them *and* apply them to a shape before saving and closing the Adobe Illustrator Startup file.

In Illustrator and FreeHand, there's a difference (see Figure 8.48). When an object is colored None, it contains no color information whatsoever. You can see right through it to any underlying data. When an object is colored White, it obscures any underlying colors; wherever the white shape appears, no ink is applied there during printing.

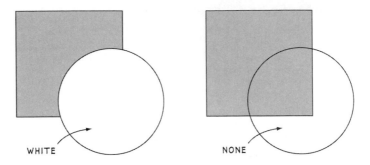

WHITE   NONE

Figure 8.48   *Illustrator and FreeHand consider white a color that obscures any underlying shapes (left). When a shape is colored None, it is transparent (right).*

The difference becomes more apparent when you apply None as a stroke color, which results in no stroke at all. When you apply a white stroke, you can add a varying thickness, just like any other color.

Black

The default black is always 100% process black, with no additional components. This value often differs from the blacks found in a high-res scan, which usually contain additional cyan, magenta, and yellow information as well. More often than not, the default black is perfectly suitable for your work. Different uses (such as four-color linework or large black objects) may require an *enriched black*, or a black beefed up with one or more process inks. (See Chapter 15 for more info.)

If you're using black when working with spot colors, continue using the default. For example, if you're creating a two-color logo with black and Pantone Reflex Blue, you don't have to define a new black item.

Registration

Items tagged with Registration output at 100% of all document colors, which makes it a highly specialized color. Do not use this option to color any objects in your artwork. Instead, it is used to color such items as registration marks, trim and fold marks, and crop marks—production-oriented items that must appear on every plate of a separated project.

Defining Colors

Illustrator and FreeHand allow you to define a list of colors specific to each file. Before you do, however, you must remember one simple rule: know the colors you want to use. Although both programs enable you to access an extensive series of color libraries, you cannot make accurate decisions by viewing these colors onscreen. One of the fundamental stages in planning your work is choosing the project colors before you begin. (See Chapter 7, "Project Planning," for more info.) The only accurate method is to refer to a printed spot or process swatchbook, like Pantone Coated or Trumatch. These books are available at any graphics supply store. (See Chapter 14 for more info.)

When you have selected your colors, just access the appropriate library in Illustrator or FreeHand, and add the necessary items to the program's Swatches palette for future use.

Creating a Color List in Illustrator

To access a color from an existing library, follow these steps:

1. Make sure the Swatches palette is visible. If not, choose Windows: **Show Swatches**.

2. Choose the desired color library from the Window: **Swatch Libraries** submenu. A palette containing the library appears onscreen.

3. Scroll through the library and click the colors you want to use. (They should automatically appear in the Swatches palette (see Figure 8.49). If they don't, select the color and choose Add to Swatches from the library palette submenu.)

To add your own colors to the Swatches palette, follow these steps:

1. Choose New Swatch from the Swatches palette submenu. The New Swatch dialog box appears (see Figure 8.50).

2. Enter the desired color name. (See "Naming Colors," later this section.)

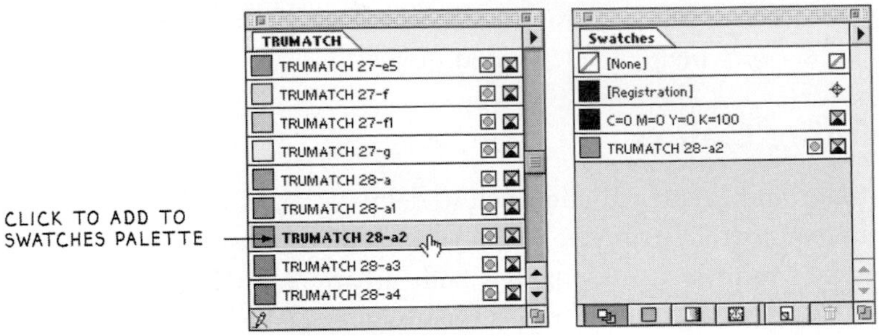

CLICK TO ADD TO
SWATCHES PALETTE

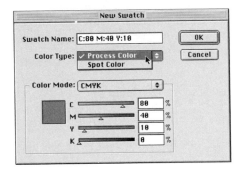

Figure 8.49 *When adding a color from a predefined library, choose the desired item from the Window: Swatch Libraries submenu. (In this example, I accessed the Trumatch library, then chose By Name in the new palette's submenu.) Select the colors you want from the palette that appears—as you click, they automatically appear in the Swatches palette.*

Figure 8.50 *The New Swatch dialog box allows you to name and define a new spot or process color.*

3. In the Color Type pop-up, choose Spot Color or Process Color. When you choose Spot Color, the available color bars only adjust the color's onscreen appearance. When you choose Process Color, you must enter the desired values for cyan, magenta, yellow, and black.

When you close the dialog box, the new color is available in the Swatches palette. Apply these colors by selecting an object (targeting its stroke or fill) and clicking the correct palette item. [10]

Creating a Color List in FreeHand

To access a color from an existing library, follow these steps:

1. Make sure the Colors palette is visible. If not, choose Window: Panels: **Color List**.

2. Choose the desired color library from the Options pop-up menu.

3. In the dialog box that appears, scroll through the color list and select the first color you want.

4. Click OK to add the color to the Colors palette.

5. Repeat steps 2 through 4 to add the remaining colors.

To add your own swatches to the Colors palette, follow these steps:

1. Make sure the Mixer palette is visible. If not, choose Window: Panels: **Color Mixer**.

2. To define a process color, click the CMYK button and enter the desired process percentages. To define a spot color, click the RGB button and use the color sliders to define the color's onscreen appearance (see Figure 8.51).

3. Click the Add to Color List button. In the Add to Color List dialog box, determine whether the color is Process or Spot, and enter an appropriate name. (See "Naming Colors," later this section.)

4. Click OK to add the new item to the Colors palette.

FOOTNOTE

[10] If you want to access the same colors again in the future, you can use an existing file as a color library. Instead of opening a library from the Windows: **Show Swatches** submenu, choose Other Library. When you locate and open the file, its colors appear in a new palette. Click the colors that you want to add to the current Swatches palette.

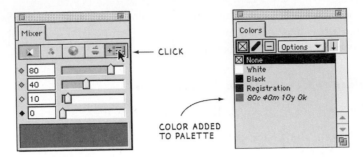

Figure 8.51 *Use the Mixer palette to define your own colors in FreeHand. After adjusting the sliders, click the Add to Color List button to name the color and add it to the Colors palette.*

In the Colors palette, spot color names appear in regular type; process color names are italicized.

Naming Colors

Spot colors should only use the name that appeared in the original library. If you change the name, a new color may be added to the list when you import the graphic, especially if you've already defined your project colors in the target document. Process colors, because they're always based on the same four inks, don't have the same requirement. You can name them anything you want. (See Chapter 14 for more info.)

Incorrectly named spot colors generally result in additional ink plates when a project is separated. When this occurs, you must open the graphic in the original program, reapply the catalog color name, and resave the file. If you're unsure of which name to use, either refer to the original swatchbook, or jot down the color name you already defined in your layout document.

Renaming a Color in Illustrator

Rename a color by double-clicking it in the Swatches palette. Enter a new name in the Swatch Options dialog. If you've created any tints based on this color, you'll notice that they are renamed as well.

Renaming a Color in FreeHand

Rename a color by double-clicking its name in the Colors palette. The field highlights, enabling you to enter a new one. Any tints based on this color are renamed as well.

Creating Tints

A *tint* is a reduced screen value of an existing color, which results in a lighter tone. For example, when you simply apply black, at appears at 100%, or total ink coverage. When you reduce the screen to 50%, you create a shade of gray; reducing the screen to 20% creates an even lighter gray.

Although Illustrator and Freehand enable you to create a tint of any spot or process color, this technique is more suitable for spot inks. You can create a dozen different tints, but they are still based on the same ink, which ensures a certain degree of color fidelity. When you create a tint based on a process color, the programs take the easy way out. For example, if you reduce C:60, M:30, Y:80, K:10 by 50 percent, their component values are simply cut in half, resulting in C:30, M:15, Y:40, K:5. This may be mathematically correct, but you'll have no real idea what the color really looks like until the proofing and printing stage. The new color may be too yellow, or may need more black, to look like a real tint of the original. For this reason, many people use a color library like Trumatch, which displays a series of accurate tints along with each color.

Creating a Tint in Illustrator

To create a tint of an existing spot color, follow these steps:

1. Make sure the Swatches and Colors palettes are both visible.

2. Click the desired spot color in the Swatches palette. It appears in the Colors palette.

3. In the Colors palette, move the tint slider to the amount you want, or enter a value from 0–100 in the percentage field (see Figure 8.52).

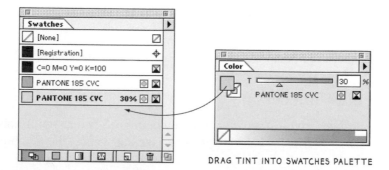

DRAG TINT INTO SWATCHES PALETTE

Figure 8.52 *To create a tint based on a solid ink, select the base color in the Swatches palette and adjust the slider in the Colors palette.*

4. As you enter the value, the new color appears in a small swatch in the upper left of the Colors palette. Drag this item from the Colors palette directly onto the Swatches palette. A new swatch appears, with the tint percentage included in its name.

This method can also be applied to any process color you have accessed from a color library, such as Trumatch or Pantone Process.

To create a tint of a process color that you define yourself, follow these steps:

1. Click the desired spot color in the Swatches palette. It appears in the Colors palette.

2. In the Colors palette, hold down the Shift key and drag one of the process color sliders. The values change proportionately, resulting in an even-handed tint.

3. Drag the new color from the Colors palette directly onto the Swatches palette. It appears as New Color.

4. To rename the color, double-click it in the Swatches palette. Enter a new name in the Swatches Options dialog box and click OK.

Creating a Tint in FreeHand

To create a tint of any existing color, follow these steps:

1. Open the Tints palette. (Choose Windows: Panels: **Tints**.)

2. The pop-up menu contains all the colors currently available in the Colors palette. Choose the one you want to tint.

3. Move the tint slider to the desired amount, or enter a value in the percentage field (see Figure 8.53).

4. Click the Add to Color List button to add the tint to the Colors palette.

Deleting Unnecessary Colors

As you design a file, it's easy to add a number of colors that you ultimately don't need to your color lists. Before you save and import the graphic, it's wise to double-check your color usage to make sure only the project colors are contained in the file. This eliminates the possibility of importing any unwanted colors into your page layout.

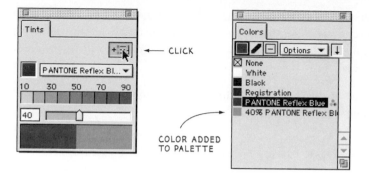

Figure 8.53 *To create a tint based on any color, select it in the Color palette and enter the desired value in the Tints palette. Click the Add to Color List button to add the tint to the Color palette.*

The easiest way to weed your color list is to automatically delete all the unused colors. If any unwanted colors remain in the list, you can locate the shapes they're applied to, then either delete or recolor them.

Weeding Illustrator's Color List

Follow these steps to remove any unused colors:

1. In the Swatches palette, choose Select All Unused from the Palette sub-menu.

2. Choose Delete Swatch from the same submenu.

3. Examine the Swatches palette. It should only contain your project colors, along with any tints.

Weeding FreeHand's Color List

FreeHand does not have a command to automatically select or delete any unused colors. However, you can perform this step manually:

1. Open the Colors palette.

2. Select the first color in the list.

3. Hold down the Shift key and click the last color in the list. This selects every item in the palette.

4. Choose Remove from the Options pop-up menu.

5. An alert appears, asking whether to remove just the unused colors, or every color. Click the Unused button. (If you click All, you convert all the applied colors to process percentages—unwise, if you're working with spot colors.)

6. Examine the Colors palette. It should only contain your project colors, along with any tints.

Converting Colors Between Ink Types

Occasionally, a designer defines a spot color instead of process, and vice versa. This often isn't noticed until the file is being preflighted. You must open the file in the original program and convert the ink type.

Converting Ink Types in Illustrator

To change a color from spot to process (or vice versa), double-click it in the Swatches palette. Choose the correct item from the Color Type pop-up menu. After making sure the Non-Global box is *not* checked (which ensures that the change is applied throughout the graphic), click OK.

Converting Ink Types in FreeHand

To change a color from spot to process (or vice versa), select it in the Colors palette. In the Options pop-up menu, choose Make Spot or Make Process, whichever is appropriate.

Specifying Knockout and Overprint

When one shape overlaps another in Illustrator or Freehand, its color *knocks out*, or doesn't mix with any underlying inks. The only exception is black type, which automatically *overprints*, or combines with any underlying info. Both programs allow you to determine whether a shape's fill and/or stroke knocks out or overprints. In Illustrator, use the Attributes palette. In FreeHand, use the Fill and Stroke Inspector palettes.

There are only two reasons to force an object to overprint. First, you can create different color effects by combining colors this way, which unfortunately are not visible until a project is run on-press. Usually, it's done for the sake of *trapping*, which compensates for the misregistration that naturally occurs in the printing process. Trapping issues and techniques are described in full in Chapter 15.

Custom Fills

You are not restricted to applying solid-color fills in Illustrator and FreeHand. Both programs feature a variety of tools for defining gradient and patterned fills. Although this section provides some basic steps for applying these effects, understand that knowing how to use them is not the same as knowing how to use them *properly*. Pay close attention to the lists of guidelines.

Gradients

A *gradient* is a blend from one color to another. For example, if you apply a black-to-white gradient to a shape, its color fades from black to white in a smooth transition of increasingly lighter gray tones. There are two basic types of gradient: *linear*, where the tones move in one direction, and *radial*, where the tones extend outward from a centerpoint (see Figure 8.54).

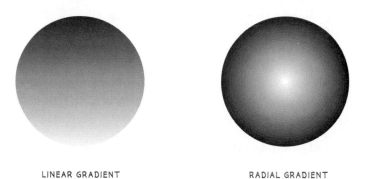

LINEAR GRADIENT   RADIAL GRADIENT

Figure 8.54   *The tones of a linear gradient run back and forth in one direction (left). A radial gradient starts at a midpoint and extends outward (right).*

When used in a complex, photo-realistic graphic, gradients enable the artist to apply subtle tonal variations that create the illusion of shadows, light, and depth. In fact, one of the most impressive uses of vector-based gradients can be found in your newspaper's Automotive Classifieds. Check out the tiny black and white graphics of the latest models. Although they look like a scanned image, they are painstakingly constructed of thousands of shapes, each one filled with exactly the right gradient to produce the desired effect.

More often, gradients are used as stylistic flourishes, applied to simple shapes or customized type. Not so long ago, gradients were one of the most misused design elements in the industry. Many artists, appreciating the easy, high-tech look of a gradient, would pack the white space of their graphics and layouts with blend after blend. (Many designers now refer to them as "blands.") Should you avoid using them? Of course not. Simply strive for a level of taste and restraint, as you would with any other element. Not only will your designs be executed much more cleanly, you will greatly reduce the likelihood of production- and output-related problems.

Keep the following issues in mind whenever you work with gradients:

- **Avoid "banding."** A gradient produces a specific number of tonal steps from beginning to end. If a gradient is too long, the individual steps may become visible, a phenomenon known as *banding* or *shade-stepping*. For example, if you apply a blend that ranges from 50% black to white, the program fills the space between with every output value from 49% to 1% black. If the blend is five inches long, each tonal step is about seven points wide—thin enough to create a smooth transition when you output the file. However, if the same blend only runs from 20% black and white, each step is 18 points wide—at that size, it's entirely possible that each shade will be visible after output (see Figure 8.55). Avoid banding by being sure your gradients don't extend further than its tones can accommodate. A full gradient, which runs from 100% ink value to white, can extend up to seven or eight inches. As you reduce the number of tones, you must reduce the length of your shape. Also note that outputting at higher linescreen values will increase the likelihood of banding. [11]

- **Beware of color-to-color blends.** When you blend from one color to another, you have little control over the appearance of the in-between colors. When blending between process colors, the varying CMYK combinations may result in unpredictable values when you run the job on-press. When blending between spot inks, the combined values are typically muddy. These inks are opaque, and not intended for mixing on-press. The only way to be sure of how a printed gradient will appear is to use a single color, blending it into either a lighter tint or white.

FOOTNOTE

[11]   The type of output device you use also determines whether banding occurs. Older printers based on the first version of PostScript successfully reproduce only the shortest gradients. PostScript Level 2, the most common version, can easily accommodate the values I described previously. The advent of PostScript Level 3 promises to eliminate banding altogether, regardless of the length of your gradients. Until PS3 is in widespread use, however, use gradients with caution.

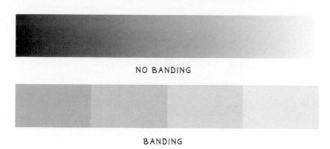

NO BANDING

BANDING

Figure 8.55   *If a gradient doesn't contain enough tones to accommodate its length, banding (or shade-stepping) may occur.*

- **You cannot blend into None.** Many people try to blend a color into None, thinking they can create a semitransparent effect. You cannot do this in Illustrator or FreeHand; you can only create an effect like this in Photoshop. (See Chapter 13 for more info.) If you want to incorporate such a blend into vector-based artwork, you must convert the graphic to Photoshop-editable pixels, and continue from there. (See "Converting Vectors to Pixels," later this chapter.)

Creating a Gradient in Illustrator

To create a simple gradient in Illustrator, follow these steps (in this example, I create a blend from 100% black to white):

1. Make sure the Gradient, Color, and Swatches palettes are visible.

2. In the Gradient palette, choose Linear or Radial from the Type menu.

3. To define the first color in the gradient, click the Starting Color slider (the small tab in the lower left of the Gradient palette). Click an existing color in the Swatches palette, or enter new values in the Colors palette. In this example, I selected Black.

4. To define the second color, click the Ending Color slider (the small tab in the lower right of the Gradient palette). In this example, I set White in the Colors palette (see Figure 8.56).

5. Drag the thumbnail in the upper left of the Gradients palette directly onto the Swatches palette. This way, you can access the gradient whenever you want. To name the gradient, double-click it and enter a name in the Swatch Options dialog box.

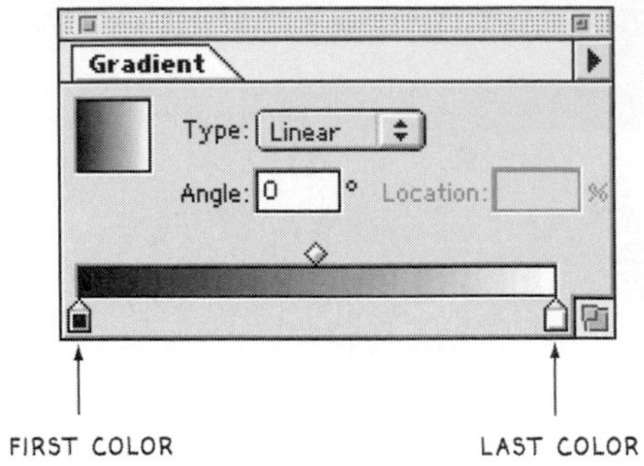

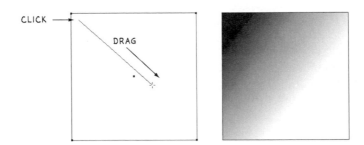

FIRST COLOR   LAST COLOR

Figure 8.56 *When defining a gradient in Illustrator, set each base color by clicking the sliders and choosing an item from the Swatches palette.*

To apply a gradient, follow these steps:

1. Select the shape you want to fill.

2. Click the desired gradient in the Swatches palette.

3. To further adjust how the gradient initially appears, select the Gradient tool.

4. Leaving the shape selected, click-drag with the Gradient tool to reposition the blend. The starting color begins at the point where you initially click, and the ending color stops wherever you release the mouse button (see Figure 8.57).

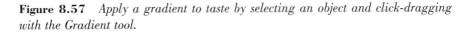

Figure 8.57 *Apply a gradient to taste by selecting an object and click-dragging with the Gradient tool.*

When editing the contents of a gradient, keep the following in mind:

- To reposition the midpoint between the gradient colors, move the small diamond that appears above the preview, between the sliders (see Figure 8.58).

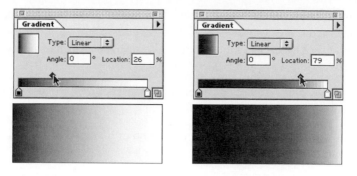

Figure 8.58 *By moving the diamond-shaped slider in the Gradient palette, you reposition the midpoint between the start and end colors.*

- To incorporate more than two colors, you must add more color sliders in the Gradients palette. Do this by clicking directly between the existing sliders, or by dragging a color from the Swatches palette onto the gradient preview. A new one appears, allowing you to click a color from the Swatches palette, or enter values from the Colors palette (see Figure 8.59). Whenever you add a another slider, new midpoint diamonds appear.

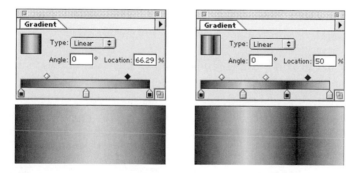

Figure 8.59 *Add more colors to a gradient by clicking between the color sliders in the Gradient palette. After placing a new slider, choose a color from the Swatches or Colors palette.*

- To remove a color from a gradient, drag its slider off the Gradient palette.

Gradient Mesh Issues

Illustrator 8 features a new gradient mesh command. Instead of applying a single gradient to a shape, you can convert the shape to a *mesh object* (by selecting it and choosing Object: **Create Gradient Mesh**), which applies a grid of editable points and segments. By selecting points, you can apply new colors from the Swatches or Colors palettes. By manipulating the grid with the Direct Selection and Gradient Mesh tools, you can apply unique, curved transitions between colors.

Unfortunately, mesh objects have proven to be problematic at best in a production environment:

- When output to a PostScript Level 1 printer, the mesh object is converted to a bitmap image.

- When output to a PostScript Level 2 printer, the mesh object is converted to a 150ppi JPEG image.

- Even if you print to a PostScript Level 3 printer, you will experience problems if the PostScript option in the Print dialog box is set to Level 1 or Level 2. For the best results, make sure this value is set to Level 3.

- Earlier versions of Illustrator cannot read mesh objects. If you attempt to open the Illustrator 8 file, the object will not appear. If you backsave the file to an earlier version, the object will appear as a 150ppi JPEG image. This makes it impossible for anyone using an earlier version of the program to edit or successfully output such a file.

- You cannot rasterize a mesh object in Photoshop 4.

In an attempt to avoid many of these issues, Illustrator allows you to convert a mesh object to pixels using the Object: **Rasterize** command. However, because the new pixels reside only the Illustrator file, it becomes difficult to edit them any further. If desired, you can save the converted object as an EPS and open it in Photoshop. (See "Converting Vectors to Pixels," later this chapter.)

Because gradient meshes only function successfully in a specific loop, it is difficult to recommend their use in a general environment. If you still intend on using them—for example, if you know you are outputting to Level 3 printers—simply be aware of the issues discussed previously.

Creating a Gradient in FreeHand

To create a simple gradient in FreeHand, follow these steps (in this example, I create a blend from 100% black to white):

1. Make sure the Color and Fill Inspector palettes are visible.

2. Select the shape you want to fill.

3. In the Fill Inspector palette, choose Gradient from the Fill Type pop-up menu.

4. Click the Linear or Radial button.

5. In the pop-up menu next to the top color, set the first color in the gradient. The pop-up contains the same items as the color list. If desired, double-click the small swatch to access the Mixer and Tint palettes. (In this example, I set it to Black.)

6. In the pop-up menu next to the bottom color, set the last color in the gradient (see Figure 8.60). The pop-up contains the same items as the color list. If desired, double-click the small swatch to access the Mixer and Tint palettes. (In this example, I set it to White.)

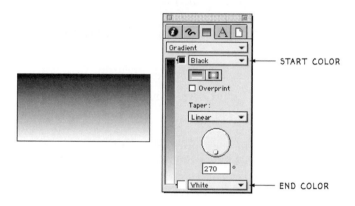

Figure 8.60 *When creating a FreeHand gradient, choose Gradient from the Fill Type pop-up in the Fill Inspector palette. Set the start and end colors in the available pop-up menus.*

7. If creating a linear gradient, set its angle by entering a value in the Fill Inspector palette's Angle field, or by rotating the small Angle wheel. If creating a radial gradient, set its starting point by clicking in the small grid.

When working with gradients, keep the following in mind:

*   To incorporate more than two colors in a blend, drag a color from the Colors, Mixer, or Tints palettes directly onto the gradient preview in the Fill Inspector palette. A new color swatch appears, which you can reposition and recolor as needed (see Figure 8.61).

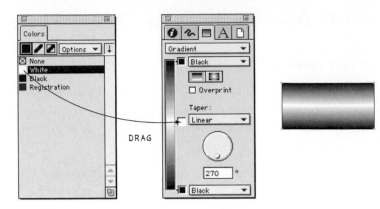

Figure 8.61 *To incorporate an additional color into a gradient, drag it onto the gradient preview bar in the Fill Inspector palette.*

- To remove a color from a gradient, drag its small swatch away from the Fill Inspector palette.

- You cannot add a gradient to the Colors palette. To apply the same value to another shape, use the Edit: **Copy Attributes** and Edit: **Paste Attributes** commands.

- You can further edit the appearance of a linear gradient with the options in the Fill Inspector palette's Taper pop-up menu. When you choose Linear, the tones between each color are equally sized. When you choose Logarithmic, the tones increase in width from the start color to the end.

Patterns

When you apply a *pattern*, you fill a shape with the same repeating tile, creating an effect similar to wallpaper. Illustrator and FreeHand use different approaches to this effect, each with their own output-related issues.

Using Illustrator Patterns

Illustrator patterns are entirely vector-based. You also have the capability to apply *pattern brushes*, which enable you to apply a repeating series of shapes as a brush stroke. However, you should avoid the default items at all costs, because you have no control over the colors in a predefined pattern. For the best results, create your own patterns based on the colors specific to the project at hand.

Using FreeHand Patterns

In FreeHand, the rule is simple: do not use the options that appear when you choose Patterns from the Fill Inspector palette's Fill Type pop-up. These items are actually pixel-based patterns, similar to the ones used by the earliest paint programs. They do not scale, can only be edited in an 8×8-pixel grid, and will not separate properly. Plus, they immediately make a graphic look like it was created in 1985.

The Custom and Textured options in the Fill Inspector pop-up menu also enable you to apply a predefined fill. Although these are essentially vector-based patterns, similar to those used in Illustrator, they suffer from a number of restrictions. Most importantly, you can't preview them onscreen, which makes it difficult to see the effect of any applied colors or transformations. They are also known to produce exceedingly long print times. Most people rightfully avoid them.

Tracing Pixel-Based Images

Pixels and vectors exist in completely different forms. The process of producing vector-based outlines from a pixel-based image is known as *tracing*. There is no easy way to convert a pixel-based image, such as scanned line art, into shapes that you can edit in Illustrator or FreeHand.

You trace an image because you want to be able to edit it with the tools of Illustrator or FreeHand. Perhaps you need to create a crisp, scalable version of a company logo that only exists in a printed form. Or maybe you want to apply a black stroke and gradient fill to a sketch that you've made. Once they hear about this technique, many users feel they have to trace *every* image they scan, and this simply isn't required. If you want to incorporate a hand-drawn image into a page layout, for example, there is no reason to trace it. Just scan it at the right size and resolution, then import it like any other graphic. Once you've determined the need for tracing an image, you must choose the right technique.

Tracing Manually

When you trace an image manually, you use the Pen tool to literally trace its outline by hand. The resulting path can be edited further in Illustrator or FreeHand (see Figure 8.62). There are two ways to do this.

Figure 8.62 *I traced the primary image with the Pen tool (left), creating a path I can continue editing in Illustrator or FreeHand.*

First, you can trace the image directly in Photoshop. After creating the desired paths, you can copy and paste them directly into Illustrator or export the paths into a separate file that you can open later in Illustrator or FreeHand. (Export the paths by File: Export: **Paths to Illustrator**, setting the paths you want to include in the Write pop-up.)

Second, you can import an image into Illustrator or FreeHand, lock it, and trace it there. When you're finished, unlock the image, delete it, and continue editing the path.

Tracing Automatically

The most popular auto-tracing program is Adobe Streamline, available for under $150. You can use it to convert black and white, grayscale, or color images to vectors, and it features several commands that control the frequency of points, the number of included shades, and overall smoothness. After converting, you can save the paths in a variety of formats, including Illustrator and FreeHand.

However, Streamline does not produce the flawless results that you may be hoping for. Even simple tracings usually require further tweaking in your preferred graphics program (see Figure 8.63).

Figure 8.63   *Auto-tracing an image with Adobe Streamline does not usually give you picture-perfect results. In this example, I auto-traced the image on the left. As you can see in the artwork on the right, much of the fine detail is lost or obscured. More often than not, you'll have to continue editing the shapes in Illustrator or FreeHand.*

Saving and Exporting

Even though Illustrator and Freehand allow you to save artwork in a number of different file formats, the print industry is only interested in two: Native and EPS.

The Native File Format

The native format refers to the file structure most readily recognized by a particular application. When you save a graphic in its native file format, you ensure that all the effects and objects you created remain intact when you open the file for future editing. Saving as a different format may convert some of these elements into a noneditable form.

In Illustrator, the native file format is called "Illustrator," as found in the Format pop-up menu of the Save As dialog box. In FreeHand, the native format is called "FreeHand Document," as found in the Format pop-up menu of the Save As dialog box.

While a graphic is in development, you may wind up saving, closing, and reopening the file many times. As you do, save it in the native format, preferably into the Native Graphics folder, in a project's job folder. (See Chapter 5, "File Management," for more info.)

The EPS File Format

If you intend to import Illustrator or FreeHand artwork into a page layout, you must save it as an Encapsulated PostScript (EPS) file. Otherwise, you will not be able to recognize the file using a layout program's import command.

An EPS file differs from a native file in that it contains a low-res preview of the graphic, as well as the PostScript code required for proper output. When you import an EPS file, you actually import the preview, which allows you to position, rotate, and scale the artwork as needed. The preview is linked to the rest of the graphic's info, which is downloaded to an output device during printing.

Saving an EPS File from Illustrator

Saving an Illustrator graphic as an EPS file is easy:

1. Choose File: **Save As**.

2. In the Save As dialog box, choose Illustrator EPS from the Format pop-up menu.

3. In the file's Name field, add ".eps" at the end of the current filename. This is not really required on a Macintosh, but it helps to identify the file. If the file will be processed on the Windows platform, the extension is mandatory.

Saving an EPS File from FreeHand

Saving a FreeHand graphic as an EPS file requires a different method:

1. Choose File: **Export**. (You cannot create an EPS file using FreeHand's Save As dialog box.)

2. In the Export Document dialog box, choose Macintosh EPS or MS-DOS EPS from the Format pop-up menu.

3. The ".eps" file extension automatically appears at the end of the filename. Leave it there, changing the rest of the name as desired.

4. Check the Include FreeHand Document in EPS box. This way, you can open the exported EPS file in FreeHand, in case you or your vendor needs to make any last-minute changes. [12]

Importing into Illustrator and FreeHand

You can import graphics in dozens of different formats into Illustrator and FreeHand. Only add an external graphic to your artwork when you specifically need to. Common reasons include masking a high-res image, or combining a scanned graphic with vector-based text to produce a single-file logo. If it's not imperative to import a graphic into an Illustrator or FreeHand file, don't—combine them in your page layout instead. If you must embed a graphic, keep the following rules in mind.

Provide Every Graphics File

Just because you've imported one graphic into another, it doesn't mean you can ignore the imported file when it's time to print. In one of the most common output-oriented problems, many people fail to provide *both* graphic files when they send a project to an output vendor. If the embedded graphic isn't available, your layout document won't print properly. Even worse, some programs do not alert the output technician if an embedded graphic is missing.

F O O T N O T E

[12] Many users neglect to check the Include FreeHand Document in EPS box when they export an EPS file. Maybe they forget to do it, maybe they like that it results in a considerably smaller file size. Whatever the reason, leaving this box unchecked is a big mistake. For example, if the file is misprinting at the service bureau, the output technician will not be able to open and troubleshoot the file. If he tries, he can only access an uneditable preview of the entire graphic. The designer will likely get a phone call, asking for a fresh, editable copy of the file. When the document info is built in, any other user can access the data.

Just remember that when you open and edit a FreeHand EPS, you cannot simply save it and expect it to work. You must export a new EPS file—with the Include FreeHand Document in EPS box checked, of course.

Use TIFF and EPS Files

Just like in a layout document, you should only import TIFF and EPS images in your Illustrator and FreeHand artwork. These file formats are the only ones proven to work consistently in a print environment.

Heed the Scaling Restrictions

In a page layout, you can scale an imported vector-based graphic with wanton abandon. If that graphic contains an embedded pixel-based image, however, the rules change. Many people assume that because the pixel-based data exists in an EPS file, it somehow converts it to scalable shapes. This simply isn't the case:

- Images imported into Illustrator and FreeHand follow the same resolution requirements as the images you import into a page layout program. (See Chapter 9 for more info.)

- In Illustrator or FreeHand, you should only scale pixel-based images by as much as 25% in either direction. Any more than that, and you run the risk of pixelized output or PostScript errors. If you need a larger or smaller image, create or scan a new one.

- If you've already scaled the pixels in Illustrator or FreeHand, try not to scale the graphic again when you import it into your layout document. Doing so actually scales the pixels twice. For example, if you enlarged an image by 20% in Illustrator, then scaled the Illustrator graphic by another 20% in XPress, the pixels are actually scaled by 40%. Depending on its original resolution, the image may output poorly (see Figure 8.64).

Avoid "Matryoshka"

A Matryoshka is a Russian toy. An ornately painted figurine opens up to reveal a smaller one, which opens to reveal another, and so forth. This is an interesting novelty, but when the concept is applied to documents and graphics, you add a level of complexity and risk.

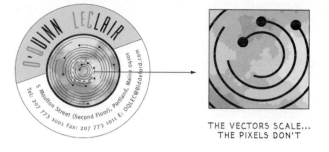

THE VECTORS SCALE...
THE PIXELS DON'T

Figure 8.64 *When a vector-based graphic contains an embedded pixel-based image, you must make sure you don't over-scale it after importing it into a page lay-out. The image on the left hasn't been scaled, and outputs at the desired appearance. When I greatly increase the scale percentage, the vectors still output smoothly, but the pixel-based info becomes jagged (right).*

For example, if you place a Photoshop image into an Illustrator file, then place the Illustrator file into an XPress document, everything should output properly (assuming they're set up right, and you've provided all the files). However, if you place a Photoshop file into a FreeHand file, import the FreeHand file into another FreeHand file, import that one into an Illustrator file, and *then* import it into your document, there are no guarantees that your document will even be processed, let alone print successfully. In some instances, your computer will even crash. None of your programs will warn you when Matryoshka is detected—it's up to you to avoid it. [13]

Converting Vectors to Pixels

It is possible to *rasterize* vector-based information, or convert it to editable pixels. As with any conversion, you should only do this when you have a deliberate reason. Most often, people rasterize objects when they want to apply pixel-specific effects such as semiopacity, soft drop shadows, or Photoshop filters.

FOOTNOTE

[13] There is rarely a reason to import one Illustrator or FreeHand file into another. For example, if you want to incorporate artwork from one Illustrator file to another, don't import it. Instead, open both files and copy/paste the desired shapes. This removes a level of complexity, because every shape resides in the same file, removing the need to link to another graphic.

Illustrator and FreeHand both feature rasterizing commands, but you should refrain from using them whenever possible. Because the new pixels will reside only in the vector-based file, your editing options are extremely limited. You're able to apply some filters and a few other effects, but for the most part, you're limited to the results of the command. The only time you should rasterize in Illustrator or FreeHand is when you don't have access to Photoshop—easily, the most powerful pixel-editing program. [14]

Regardless of which program you use, you must determine the following information when rasterizing vector-based shapes (see Chapter 9 for more info):

- **Color mode.** You must establish whether the new pixels will exist in Bitmap, Grayscale, RGB, or CMYK mode. Choose the option that dovetails with your target print requirements.

- **Resolution.** If you recall, vectors have no resolution until they are output; pixel-based images are defined in large part by the size of their pixels. You must establish the resolution at which you want the new shapes to exist.

- **Anti-aliasing.** Anti-aliasing provides a thin, smoothing transition between the converted shapes. Always apply this option, unless you have a specific reason for not using it.

- **Width and height.** In Photoshop, you can apply larger or smaller dimensions to the artwork, essentially scaling it to the appropriate size as you convert. (In Illustrator and FreeHand, you must manually scale the artwork before applying the rasterize command.)

Rasterizing in Illustrator

To rasterize Illustrator shapes, select them and choose Object: **Rasterize**. In the Rasterize dialog box, set the desired options and click OK (see Figure 8.65).

FOOTNOTE

[14] Converting from pixels to vectors typically results in an imperfect tracing that you must edit further in Illustrator or FreeHand. However, rasterizing almost always gives you a picture-perfect rendition of every shape. It's important to realize that once you rasterize artwork, there is no easy way to convert it back to vectors. (Refer to "Tracing Pixel-Based Images," earlier this chapter.)

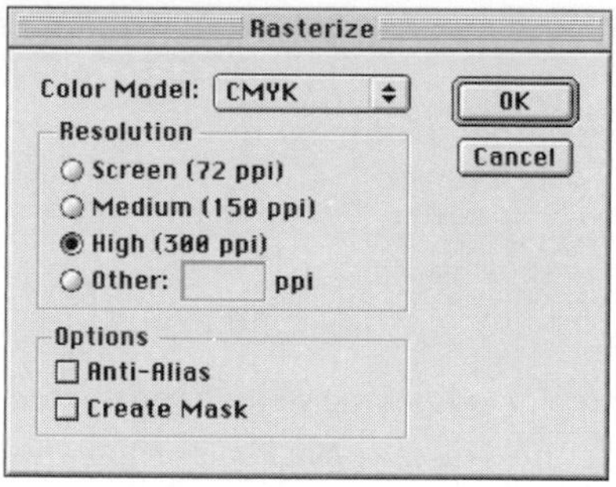

Figure 8.65 *Use Illustrator's Rasterize dialog box to determine the color mode and resolution of any shapes you convert to pixels.*

Rasterizing in FreeHand

Although FreeHand allows you to export a pixel-based version of a file, you should avoid this option. It gives you no control over resolution or anti-aliasing, and only produces a 72ppi image. Instead, select the items you want and choose Modify: **Rasterize**. Set the desired options in the Rasterize dialog box and click OK (see Figure 8.66).

Figure 8.66 *Use FreeHand's Rasterize dialog box to determine the resolution of any shapes you convert to pixels.*

Note that FreeHand does not allow you to set a color mode—it simply converts the shapes using the currently applied color values.

Rasterizing in Photoshop

Converting vectors to pixels in Photoshop is the preferred method. Not only does it give you the most satisfactory results, you can immediately begin editing the information with a wide range of tools and commands. Even better, the rasterized shapes are automatically placed on a transparent image layer, allowing you to combine it seamlessly with other images. Just remember that sooner or later, you'll have to flatten the image in order to save it as a TIFF or EPS. (See Chapter 13 for more info.)

Illustrator files can exist in either native or EPS file format. FreeHand graphics, however, must be exported to an EPS file before you can rasterize it. For the best results, convert any existing type to outlines before rasterizing.

To rasterize, select a file by choosing File: **Open** from within Photoshop. Set the desired values in the Rasterize EPS Format dialog box and click OK (see Figure 8.67).

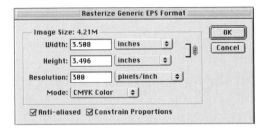

Figure 8.67 *When you open a vector-based EPS file in Photoshop, the Rasterize EPS Format dialog box enables you to set the width, height, resolution, and color mode.*

Summary

The hardest part of using a vector-based graphics program is often deciding when to use one in the first place. Because Illustrator and FreeHand tend to fall in the middle-ground between Photoshop and your page layout programs, it's easy to make the mistake of trying to use them for one or the other. Don't fall into this trap.

Illustrator and FreeHand serve you best when you use them to create simpler graphics such as logos, clip art, and creative type manipulations. These items tap into the power of vector-based illustrations most successfully: infinite scaling, infinite editability, and highest-quality PostScript output.

However, even simple artwork is subject to an important series of production-oriented guidelines:

- To refine the outline of any shape, you must have at least a rudimentary knowledge of how to manipulate Bézier points and segments. As bizarre as it may seem at first, path editing only requires a little practice.

- You're not restricted to creating all your artwork by hand. Illustrator and FreeHand both feature a series of merge options that enable you to create complex shapes by combining simple items. In fact, many users get through the day without having to touch a single curve handle.

- Whenever you incorporate type into your artwork, you must ultimately convert it to outlines before saving and importing. Not only does this remove the need to provide any additional fonts to a vendor, it allows you to edit the outlines of individual character shapes.

- When working with spot or process colors, you must define and apply them with the same care and accuracy of any page layout document.

- To import any Illustrator or FreeHand graphic, you must save or export it as an EPS file. Otherwise, your layout program will not recognize it.

- Above all, strive for simplicity as you work. The more complexity you add to a file, the longer it takes to produce, the longer it takes to process, and the more likely it is that problems will crop up during output.

To be sure, each program features many more design-oriented tools and commands than I've described in this chapter. However, you can apply these guidelines to any illustration you endeavor to create. Even the most beautifully rendered artwork is worthless if you can't get it to print.

DIGITAL IMAGING FUNDAMENTALS

If you want to incorporate a physical item into a printed project, such as a photograph or hand-drawn sketch, it must be re-expressed as digital information. As with any print-oriented undertaking, there are literally thousands of issues that seem to conspire against your images printing correctly. Therefore, it's important to understand the core concepts of digital imaging *before* you start working. If you accidentally disregard any facet of the process, you'll wind up with either inferior, unprofessional results or hours of costly last-minute repairs.

This chapter examines the basics of converting noncomputerized materials into a format you can refine, import into a page layout, and output in a way that will reproduce successfully on-press. Before you start generating your own scans (or ordering them from a vendor), you must have a working knowledge of the following issues:

- How pixels display tones and colors.

- The different resolution types you'll encounter in a production environment.

- The relationship between pixels, halftone dots, and the tiny spots of ink that a printing press lays down on paper.

- The issues involved in choosing the input device most appropriate for your work.

The information covered in this chapter will act as a foundation for the info presented in Chapter 10, "Scanning Line Art and Halftones," Chapter 12,

"Scanning and Adjusting Color Images," and Chapter 13, "Photoshop Production Techniques."

A Brief Overview of the Imaging Process

Before getting into specifics, let's take a look at a typical imaging workflow to give you a better feel for the context of this chapter. In this example, a scanned photograph is prepared for on-press reproduction.

When you scan something, its tonal information is converted to pixels, or a grid of tiny colored squares (see Figure 9.1). The effect is similar to a mosaic or a needlepoint sampler—one color for each square. The pixels, which exist only inside a computer, create a sort of map that software and output devices refer to during printing. Keep this grid in mind as we move along. [1]

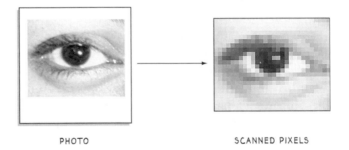

PHOTO   SCANNED PIXELS

Figure 9.1 *In the first stage of the image process, a piece of artwork—a photograph, drawing on paper, film negative, or slide transparency—is converted to pixels, which enables the colors and tones to display on a computer.*

FOOTNOTE

[1] Because this example is only a cursory illustration of a production workflow, I skip what is probably the most important and complex aspect of pixel-based editing: adjusting the image tones and colors for optimal reproduction. This stage takes place after an image is scanned, but before it's imported into a page layout. The issues involved in image enhancement are covered in-depth in Chapter 10 and Chapter 12.

You import an *image*, a single file that contains the pixel data, into a layout document created in QuarkXPress, Adobe PageMaker, or Adobe InDesign (see Figure 9.2). When the document is output, the page layout program translates the pixels into PostScript code that a printer can understand.

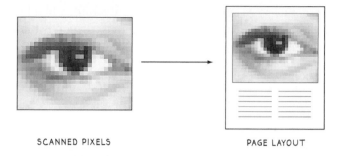

SCANNED PIXELS   PAGE LAYOUT

Figure 9.2 *In the design stage, the image is imported into a layout document, where you incorporate it into your page design.*

During output, the pixels are replaced with a series of *halftone dots*, which enable tones to be reproduced on a printing press (see Figure 9.3). These dots are usually round, and each one takes the place of several pixels. Unlike pixels, they do not appear in any particular color (on lithographic film, for example, they exist as tiny areas that were stimulated with a laser and exposed when the film was processed), nor do they cover the entire image area. Halftone dots appear in varying sizes, creating the appearance of tone when viewed with the naked eye. The size of each dot is directly based on the original colors of the pixels.

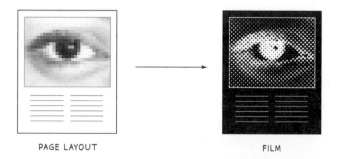

PAGE LAYOUT   FILM

Figure 9.3 *In the output stage, you print the document, converting the continuous tones to a series of tiny halftone dots, which simulate the appearance of the image. In this example, the image is output as a lithographic film negative.*

For most offset printing purposes, the dots printed onto film appear as a *negative* (or opposite) of the original image. At the print shop, the film is placed over a metal plate covered with a photosensitive layer and exposed to ultraviolet light. After the plate is processed, the exposed areas are lightly etched into the plate, and the image again appears in positive form. On a printing press, this plate is used to apply ink to a rolling blanket (the image briefly appearing as a negative again), which in turn applies the ink to paper in a form you can recognize as the original item (see Figure 9.4).

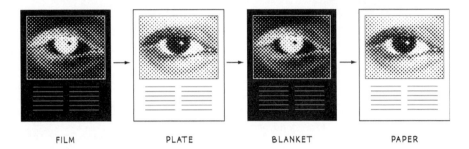

FILM   PLATE   BLANKET   PAPER

Figure 9.4 *In the printing stage, the film containing the halftone dots is used to create a metal plate. On-press, the plate applies ink to a rolling blanket, which in turn applies the ink to paper.*

This example is common, but it's not the only workflow model. You might use a digital camera to capture the image instead of a scanner. Perhaps the job will be printed to a digital press, which doesn't require film. Maybe you're creating artwork that you'll output only on a high-quality inkjet printer, such as an Iris, which doesn't generate halftone dots. Whatever other variables change, one element remains constant whenever you convert photographic information to a format that you can process digitally: the pixels.

Working with Pixels

Pixels are the fundamental building blocks of every image. They're different from the vector-based shapes used by Illustrator or FreeHand. In those programs, every graphical element exists as a separate object—for example, if a graphic consists of a circle sitting atop a square, you can select one shape by clicking it with an arrow tool, and then rearrange, or edit it independently of the other. If the same image is pixel-based, however, the individual pixels have no sense of the big picture. For all intents and purposes, they have no idea that they're arranged to create the appearance of a circle and a square. Each pixel is firmly ensconced in its own square in the grid, which necessitates an editing approach entirely different from any vector-based or page layout program. Instead of working with independent image elements—such as a circle, square, or the eyeglasses of a corporate executive—you must work with a range of colored pixels that combine to create the illusion of those shapes.

In a print production environment, pixels exist for two reasons: to describe complicated tonal space and to reproduce extra-fine details. It is almost impossible to create a photorealistic image using vector-based shapes, and unless you have a supernatural talent, Illustrator and FreeHand are not appropriate for reproducing fine linework such as a pen-and-ink drawing. Because each pixel can potentially contain a different color, they can replicate all the minuscule changes in color and texture found in nature. And because you can increase the *resolution*, or the size of each pixel in an image, you can create pixels small enough to capture the smooth appearance of black-and-white line art. (The differences between pixels and vectors are described further in Chapter 8, "Vector-Based Graphics.")

Of course, pixel-based images enter a new set of issues and file requirements into your workflow. Each image is defined by its color mode and resolution. If you satisfy the requirements of each variable, your images will output in a form that can reproduce successfully on-press.

Color Mode

In the world of print publishing, each image exists in one of three forms: black-and-white line art, a one-color halftone, or full "hi-res" color. The *color mode* determines the range of colors that an image can display and ultimately output. More than anything else, color mode is a file structure that determines the following:

- **Pixel depth.** Each pixel can be only one color, so you must be sure that an image can display the number of colors you need. The color potential of each pixel, or the number of colors it can possibly display, is known as pixel depth. Your computer defines color values in terms of binary data, or strings of 1's and 0's. Each one of these characters is called a bit. The number of bits available to describe each pixel depends on an image's color mode. ²

- **The number of color channels.** Every Photoshop image contains at least one *channel*, a file component that enables the program to keep track of the multitude of pixel values. There is a maximum amount of information that a single channel can contain, so in order to display the vast amounts of data of a full-color image, Photoshop requires additional channels—one for each color. For example, an image in Grayscale mode contains one channel. An image in RGB mode contains three channels, one each for Red, Green, and Blue. An image in CMYK mode contains four channels, one each for Cyan, Magenta, Yellow, and Black. When you edit an image, you actually edit the contents of its color channels. ³

The color modes you encounter most often are Bitmap, Grayscale, RGB, and CMYK. Depending on the specifics of your production environment, you might come across lesser-used color modes such as Duotone, Lab Color, or Indexed Color. Duotones, which reproduce a one-color halftone using multiple inks, are covered in Chapter 13. Lab Color (a device-independent color model) and Indexed Color (a mode that features a greatly reduced number of colors) are covered in Chapter 11, "Color Spaces and Printing."

FOOTNOTE

² Don't confuse pixel depth with a scanner's *bit depth*. Pixel depth refers to the color capacity of an existing file; bit depth refers to the color sensitivity of an input device. For example, an RGB image might be limited to 8 bits of information per color channel, but many scanners acquire up to 16 bits per channel (which translates into a 48-bit scanner). This extra information is not written directly into the file, but it almost always results in a higher-quality scan. See "Scanners," later this chapter, for more info.

³ The concept of color channels can be tricky to understand, especially when you're first starting out. When you open a color image, you're not immediately made aware of the existence of separate channels—all you see is a color image that you can edit at will. By default, Photoshop displays a *composite view*, or an onscreen representation of the values contained in the color channels. When you edit the composite view, any changes are automatically applied as needed to the component channels. (See Chapter 12 for more info.)

Bitmap Mode (1-Bit Color)

Images in Bitmap mode are used to reproduce black-and-white line art. Here, pixels are one of only two colors: black or white. The reason we refer to these files as "1-bit color" is because only one bit is available to describe each pixel. Black pixels are described with a "1"; white pixels are described with a "0" (see Figure 9.5). Because so little information is required to display these colors, 1-bit images have the smallest relative file sizes. (See Chapter 10 for info on preparing line art scans for print.)

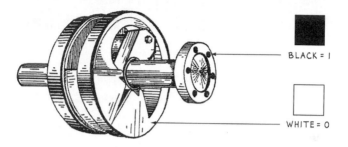

BLACK = 1

WHITE = 0

Figure 9.5 *In a 1-bit color image, pixels can only be black or white. Think of the two bits as an on/off switch. When a pixel has a value of 1, it's turned on, or colored black. When a pixel has a value of 0, it's turned off, or receives no color info at all.*

Grayscale Mode (8-Bit Color)

Grayscale images can display a *tonal range*, or an entire series of gray tones from black to white. Here, eight bits are available to describe each pixel. There are 256 possible combinations of 1's and 0's in a string of eight characters, which results in 256 possible levels of gray (including pure black and pure white) (see Figure 9.6). Because each pixel contains eight times more data in an 8-bit image than in a 1-bit image, similarly configured images are eight times as large. (See Chapter 10 for info on preparing Grayscale scans for print.)

RGB Mode (24-Bit Color)

RGB is the most commonly used color mode. All scanners acquire images in RGB (even if some scanning software automatically converts them to CMYK). The reason an RGB file can display so many colors is because 24 bits are available to describe each pixel. As you know, an RGB file consists of three color channels: one for red data, one for green data, and one for blue data. In every channel, just like a Grayscale file, eight bits are available to describe each pixel (see Figure 9.7). Eight bits times three equals 24 bits per pixel, or 16.7 million possible colors.

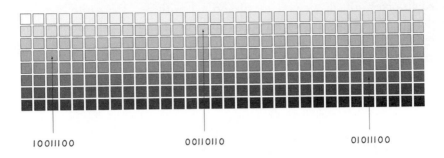

100111100   00110110   01011100

Figure 9.6 *In an 8-bit color image, each pixel is described by a string of eight 1's and 0's. Each combination produces a unique tone. There are 256 possible combinations, so a Grayscale image can display 256 possible tones. (Incidentally, the 256 tones that exist from pure black to pure white are known as the "gray scale," hence the term "Grayscale.")*

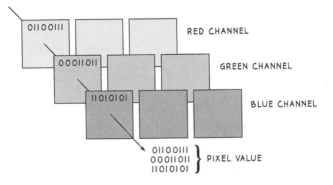

RED CHANNEL

GREEN CHANNEL

BLUE CHANNEL

01100111
00011011 } PIXEL VALUE
11010101

Figure 9.7 *An RGB image is similar to three overlapping Grayscale images. Each pixel is defined by three sets of eight bits, which produce 16.7 million possible combinations. Because each channel is used to control the red, green, or blue data generated by your monitor, the combinations result in different colors.*

Although some output methods enable you to create CMYK separations from an RGB file, most workflows require that you convert these files to CMYK mode before importing them into a page layout and printing.

Because an RGB image contains three times more information than a similarly configured Grayscale image, the files are three times as large. (For more info on working in RGB color space, see Chapter 11. For more info on preparing an RGB scan for print, see Chapter 12.)

CMYK Mode

Images in CMYK mode contain the information necessary to produce four-color process separations. Each image consists of four channels, one each for the cyan, magenta, yellow, and black data (see Figure 9.8). Although CMYK channels contain just as much data as those of a Grayscale or RGB file, it doesn't mean you can tally up the bits and say, "Aha! 32-bit color! 4.2 billion possible values!" If only that were true. The number of colors a CMYK image will display is limited by the printing process, which only accommodates a much smaller range of possibilities.

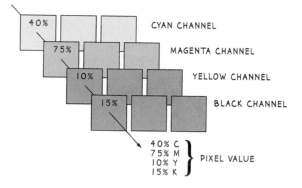

Figure 9.8 *A CMYK image consists of four 8-bit channels. Unlike the math used by an RGB image, the 32 bits per channel don't result in billions of color combinations. Instead, each channel contains the cyan, magenta, yellow, and black info that will be printed to each plate when the image is separated during output.*

Because a CMYK image contains four channels, it is 33% larger than an RGB file (and four times larger than a Grayscale file) with similar dimensions. (For more info on working in CMYK color space, see Chapter 11. For more info on preparing a CMYK image for print, see Chapter 12.)

Choosing the Right Color Mode

An image doesn't simply appear in the correct color mode—you must make that distinction yourself, based on the following criteria:

- **The ultimate use of the image.** Just as an image must be saved in the right file format, it must also exist in the right mode. If the image you need will be output as line art, it must be in Bitmap mode. If you intend to reproduce a photograph as a one-color halftone, it must be in Grayscale mode. If an image will be reproduced in full color, it must be scanned in RGB mode, and ultimately converted to CMYK.

- **The number of available colors.** One-color images require a mode that displays only one color. On the other hand, when you work with full-color images, you usually edit in a mode with a wide range of colors (like RGB) before converting to a mode with a smaller range (like CMYK).

- **The editing tools available to that mode.** Not all commands are available to all modes. This largely depends on the number of colors in an image. If you're editing an RGB image, which can contain 16.7 million colors, you have access to all filters and color adjustment tools. In CMYK, you lose access to a number of artistic filters that can only be used on RGB images. If you're editing a Bitmap image, which contains only one color, you can't use any of those commands.

People working in Photoshop quickly learn that they can convert an image from one mode to any other. However, doing so will always change the color values of the image. As you read more about working in the different modes, I'll present a series of guidelines that describe the appropriate times to convert, along with warnings about what will happen if you convert at the wrong point.

Reading Pixel Values

It's never enough to stare at the monitor, rub your chin, and think, "That looks pretty good." Successfully editing an image in Photoshop will depend on your ability to read the values of the pixels. Pixel colors are measured in two forms: brightness levels and output values.

Brightness levels measure the intensity of the red, green, and blue electron guns inside your monitor. The pixels in your Grayscale images and color channels are not the only items that can display one of 256 possible tones.

To reproduce those tones onscreen, each electron gun must stimulate the phosphors of your monitor at one of 256 possible strengths. A brightness level of 0 means that no light is projected by the gun. A brightness level of 255 means that the gun is firing at full intensity. Because all three electron guns are firing at once, every color you see onscreen consists of three brightness levels, one for each color.

When you're working in print, the only values that matter are *output values*, which appear as percentages from 0 to 100. These values tell you the size of the halftone dots that will appear on paper or film when the image is output. A value of 0% results in no color info, and a value of 100% results in total coverage. (See "Halftone Screens," later this chapter, for more info.) In most environments, these values are the only indication you have of how an image will ultimately appear.

In Photoshop, you can read the values of your pixels by displaying the Info palette and moving the cursor over the image. Whether you read brightness levels or output values depends on an image's current color mode:

- **Bitmap mode.** The values of 1-bit pixels display as output values. White pixels are 0% K (or black) and black pixels are 100% K (see Figure 9.9).

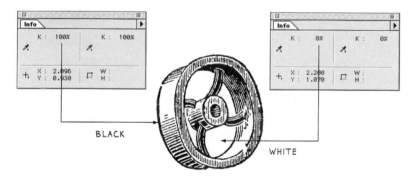

Figure 9.9 *When you read the pixels values of a Bitmap image, they appear as either 0% or 100% black.*

- **Grayscale mode.** The values of Grayscale pixels display as output values, or the screen values that will be used to represent the varying tones when you output the image as a halftone (see Figure 9.10). You'll notice that darker pixels are closer to 100% K, and lighter pixels are closer to 0% K.

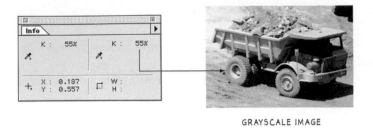

GRAYSCALE IMAGE

Figure 9.10 *When you read the pixel values of a Grayscale image, they appear as tints of black.*

- **RGB mode.** RGB files were never intended for printing, so their colors display as brightness levels. Each pixel is described with three levels, one each for the intensity of its component red, blue, and green values (see Figure 9.11). For example, black appears as R:0, G:0, B:0. White appears as R:255, G:255, B:255. Burgundy appears as R:128, G:32, B:65.

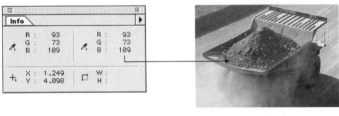

RGB IMAGE

Figure 9.11 *When you read the pixel values of an RGB image, they appear as brightness levels. These units measure how intensely your monitor stimulates the onscreen phosphors that represent the pixel with red, green, and blue light. A value of 0 is the lowest level of intensity (no light). A value of 255 is the highest intensity (full power).*

- **CMYK mode.** Because CMYK files are always created with the print process in mind, their colors are measured in output values (see Figure 9.12).

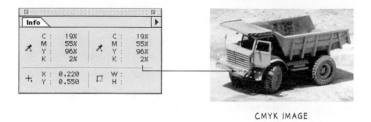

CMYK IMAGE

Figure 9.12 *When you read the pixel values of a CMYK image, you read the percentages of cyan, magenta, yellow, and black inks that will be used to reproduce that part of the image on-press.*

Resolution

The *resolution* of an image determines the size of the pixels. This value is important—depending on your color mode and the linescreen at which you intend to print a project, your resolution requirements might change from image to image.

Resolution is a measurement of linear frequency. For example, when an image's resolution is 300 pixels per inch, it's not 300 pixels per *square* inch. Instead, 300 of these pixels placed side by side measure exactly one inch across. (In turn, this means the image contains 9,000 pixels per square inch—a big difference.) The target resolution of an image depends on whether or not it will be screened during output.

Line Art Resolution Requirements

Line art that exists in Bitmap mode will not be halftoned. Rather, every single pixel will output as it exists in the file. If the resolution is too low, the pixels become visible as jagged edges. To ensure that the pixels are small enough to avoid being detected by the human eye, these images are scanned at very high resolutions—typically, between 900–1,200ppi.

Halftone Resolution Requirements

Grayscale and color images are converted to a series of halftone dots when you print them, and this changes the resolution requirements. [4] Before scanning any of these images, you must first determine the linescreen at which your project will be output. For example, an image reproduced on newsprint might output at 85 lines per inch; an image intended for glossy, coated paper might output at 150 lines per inch. The industry standard approach is this: After determining the linescreen value, double that number and scan your images at that resolution. Therefore, you would scan the preceding newsprint image at 170 pixels per inch, and the coated paper image at 300ppi. (The reasons underlying this equation are further explored in the section "Halftone Screens," later this chapter.)

Other Resolution Types

"Resolution" has become one of the most misused and ill-defined terms in the graphics industry. Not only does it pertain to pixel size, it's used to describe scanner sensitivity, printer dots, halftone screens, and the viewable area of your monitor, as well. Most often, resolution is referred to as "dots-per-inch," which is not entirely correct. Understanding the proper terminology goes a long way toward achieving accurate communication with your service bureau, printer, or clients. In the sections that follow, I clarify the different resolutions you'll encounter in the workplace.

Monitor Pixels Per Inch (ppi)

Your monitor uses a fixed grid of pixels to display information onscreen. These pixels are completely separate from the pixels of an image—instead,

---

FOOTNOTE

[4] When people first begin making scans, one of the most common errors is the belief that extra-high resolutions result in extra-high quality. Sometimes this notion stems from the fact that the marketing materials for a scanner might boast a maximum resolution of 4,800ppi; sometimes a fledgling scanner operator is confused by the fact that his scans will be output on a 600, 1,200, or 2,400dpi printer. The only thing you gain by exceeding the basic resolution requirements is file size. For example, a 5×7-inch RGB scan at 300ppi has a file size of 9MB. If you tried to scan the same image at 1,200ppi (which I actually tried to do, the first time I ever tried to make a color scan), the size balloons to over 144MB. Assuming your output device could even handle a file this big, it would appear no different than its 300ppi counterpart.

the electron guns inside the monitor stimulate the phosphors in each tiny square, causing it to display a particular color. Most monitors have 72ppi grids (the very reason most Web graphics exist at 72ppi), although some multisync models and color laptop computers can approach 80–85ppi. (Refer to Chapter 2, "Creating Your Work Environment," for more info.)

Samples Per Inch (spi)

This resolution type refers to the number of times a scanner "looks" at an image during scanning. It's sometimes referred to as *optical* or *native* resolution. Sampling is a true measure of how much information a scanner can read. Most scanners can interpolate, or further increase the resolution of an image after scanning. The distinction between spi and ppi is an important one, because the two are not always the same. Scanner manufacturers often advertise scanner resolution in ppi, rather than spi. For example, a scanner might be advertised as capable of 1,200ppi, when it really samples the image only 400 times per inch. Therefore, the scan quality is probably not as high as a scanner with an optical resolution of 800spi. (See "Scanners," later in this chapter, for more info.)

Dots Per Inch (dpi)

The most often-used term, dpi, refers only to the tiny dots produced by an output device. These have nothing to do with image resolution—rather, they are a printer's smallest reproducible dot size. With this in mind, it's easier to understand why higher-resolution printers produce more attractive results. A low-res device—say, a 300dpi laser printer—produces jagged lines, and cannot create very small halftone dots. On the other hand, a 2,400dpi imagesetter can produce halftone dots measured in microns, resulting in a smoother, almost continuous-tone appearance. (For more info, see "Halftone Screens," later this chapter.)

Spots Per Inch (spi)

A rarely used term, spots per inch, refers to halftone dots that have been reproduced on a printing press, and exist as ink-on-paper.

Halftone Screens

A printing press cannot reproduce continuous tones; it can only lay down one color at a time. But the majority of projects are printed using only one, two, or four different inks—how, then, are you able to reproduce the vast tonal transitions of your Grayscale and full-color images? The answer is a time-honored optical illusion: halftone screens.

Screening first appeared in the mid-nineteenth century. Back then, a printer would reproduce an image by placing a photograph over a glass plate etched with a series of ultrafine lines, which in turn was placed over a sheet of photosensitive paper. When light was projected through the photograph, tiny exposed areas appeared on the underlying sheet. Darker parts of the image appeared as larger dots, and lighter parts appeared as smaller dots. These varying dot sizes, when combined with the surrounding whitespace, created the appearance of tone.

Over time, photographic elements and light sources improved, platemaking materials became more advanced, the glass plate was replaced with a sheet of film. The screening method, however, has changed little. Even in today's thoroughly digitized workflow, you'll use the same grid of variable dots to reproduce any tints and tones.

Halftone Dots

Like pixels, halftone dots are arranged in a grid of squares, or *cells*. Every dot is printed in the middle of a cell. Although the dot sizes might vary, the center of the dots are equidistant. This ensures that larger dots are placed closer together and smaller dots are spaced farther apart, which better conveys the appearance of smooth tones (see Figure 9.13).

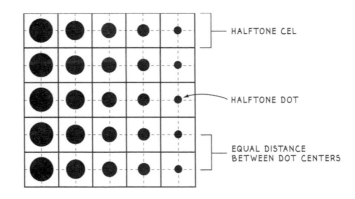

Figure 9.13 *To create the illusion of continuous tones, halftone screens employ a series of equally spaced dots of varying sizes. The dot sizes combine with the surrounding white space, resolving in your eye as tone.*

Each dot takes up a certain percentage of a cell, a process known as *tinting* or *screening*. For example, when a printed dot occupies 80% of the cell, it's known as an *80% tint* (or *80% screen*). When a dot occupies only 10% of the cell, it's a *10% tint*. You might recall this terminology from the description of output values, earlier in this chapter; colors and tones are described as percentages so you'll know the size of the halftone dots that will be output to reproduce them (see Figure 9.14). [5]

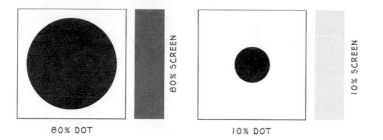

80% DOT   80% SCREEN   10% DOT   10% SCREEN

Figure 9.14 *The value of a halftone dot is directly related to how much space it occupies in the halftone cell. When it occupies 80% of the space, you call it an 80% dot. When it occupies 10% of the space, it's a 10% dot.*

The size of each dot is determined by three factors: the applied linescreen value, the pixel values of the image, and the resolution of the output device.

Establishing Halftone Cell Size: LPI

Although the plate of etched lines has gone the way of the Linotype machine, its terminology remains: The grid of halftone cells is still referred to as the *linescreen*, and the overall dot size is measured in *lines per inch* (lpi). Don't be fooled by the word "lines." There are no actual lines involved, and there haven't been for a long time. Instead, this value refers to the size of the halftone cells. Like resolution, lines per inch is a linear unit, measuring how many cells placed side by side comprise an inch.

FOOTNOTE

[5] Images are not the only items that receive this treatment. For example, if you've ever applied "20% Black" to a box or headline in a page layout document, you've applied a tint of black ink. Although the box or text might look gray as you view it onscreen, the element is actually reproduced using a series of dots that occupy 20% of each halftone cell.

Lower linescreen values result in larger cells, which means the dots are spaced farther apart. Higher values result in smaller cells, which places the dots closer together. When you print with higher linescreen values, the individual dots become more difficult to see, giving the printed image a more "photographic" appearance (see Figure 9.15).

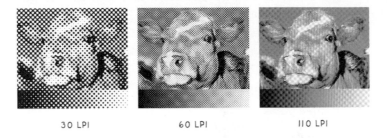

<table>
<tr><td>30 LPI</td><td>60 LPI</td><td>110 LPI</td></tr>
</table>

Figure 9.15 *Lower linescreen values use larger dots to reproduce an image, resulting in a coarser appearance. Higher linescreen values use smaller dots, resulting in a finer, more photographic appearance.*

In a perfect world, you could always use the highest value possible. The reason you must cope with different linescreen values is because of the variety of paper stock used throughout the industry. Lower-quality paper such as newsprint or uncoated photocopier stock is highly absorbent. When you print dots onto absorbent paper, the ink spreads slightly, a phenomenon known as *dot gain*. [6] If the dots are spaced too closely together, the ink might spread so much that the dots run into one another, destroying any attempt to reproduce tones. Therefore, when printing a project on absorbent paper, you must use a lower (or *coarser*) linescreen value. For example, most newspapers use a value between 85 and 100lpi. Uncoated paper can usually tolerate values between 110 and 133lpi.

FOOTNOTE

[6] Dot gain is an issue you must grapple with whenever you reproduce images on-press. Because ink absorption results in larger dot sizes, dot gain might result in printed images that appear darker than you expected. At one point or another during scanning and image editing, you must compensate for the expected dot gain by lightening the image tones most likely to spread during printing. For more info on how dot gain affects one-color halftones, see Chapter 10. For more info on how dot gain affects color images, see Chapter 12.

Higher-quality paper stock is still absorbent, but much less so. Therefore, it can tolerate much higher (or *finer*) linescreen values with less risk of the printed dots running together. For example, news magazines printed on basic coated stock are usually printed at 133 or 150lpi. Projects such as company brochures or product catalogs are typically run at 150 or 175lpi. [7] Specialty items, such as annual reports, printed on the highest-quality paper, are sometimes printed at linescreens as high as 200lpi.

Establishing Halftone Dot Size: Pixel Values

Even though the size of your halftone cells might vary from project to project, the concept of halftoning remains constant: Each dot occupies a specific percentage of a cell. The value of a dot is directly related to the corresponding pixel-based information in the image.

When you output an image, your printer compares the image pixels to the intended halftone grid. It examines the pixel values that fall into each cell, averages their percentages, and produces a halftone dot at that size. To illustrate, assume that you're reproducing a 300ppi image at 150lpi (following the guidelines set forth under "Resolution," earlier in this chapter). In this scenario, four pixels fall within each halftone cell. To generate a single halftone dot, the output device tallies up the percentages, divides them by four, and applies the resulting value (see Figure 9.16). [8]

FOOTNOTE

[7] These linescreen values are not arbitrary numbers. For example, you don't have to ponder the differences between 87 and 89lpi. A set of standard values are used throughout the industry, and the one you need is largely determined by the intended paper stock. For newsprint, the values are typically 60, 85, or 100lpi. For uncoated paper, the values are 85, 110, 120, or 133lpi. For coated paper, the values are typically 120, 133, 150, or 175lpi. Exceptions to these rules commonly occur. For example, high-quality uncoated paper might tolerate a value as high as 150lpi, and some printing methods have their own built-in restrictions. The safest bet is to consult your print shop—they can help you choose the right stock and determine the appropriate linescreen.

[8] The math used by your printer is rarely this cut and dried. If you scale the image, scan at a lower resolution, change the linescreen value, or apply a different screen angle, it's unlikely that *exactly* four pixels will appear in each halftone cell. The basic concept still applies, though; the printer recognizes that smaller parts of some pixels fall within the cell, and adjusts the ratio of pixel values to cell space accordingly.

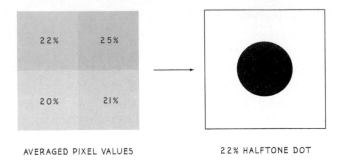

AVERAGED PIXEL VALUES   22% HALFTONE DOT

Figure 9.16   *When pixels are converted to halftone dots, your output device reviews the pixel values that fall within each cell, and then uses the average value to produce the dot.*

Constructing Halftone Dots: Printer Resolution

After your output device determines the size of the halftone dots it must reproduce, it must construct them using the smallest fundamental particles of any printed project: printer dots.

Printer dots (sometime called *machine dots*) are tiny squares, and are the only elements an output device can produce. Anything you've ever sent to a laser printer or imagesetter is comprised completely of printer dots. Dot size is determined by a printer's resolution (see Figure 9.17). For example, a 600dpi laser printer can generate a dot measuring 1/600 of an inch. A 2,400dpi imagesetter can generate a dot measuring 1/2,400 of an inch. [9]

The rule regarding printer resolution is simple. The smaller the dot, the more finely detailed information you can produce. Think about it this way: Imagine you have four floppy disks, and you're asked to arrange them into as many different shapes as possible. Obviously, you don't have that many options. Now imagine a handful of Scrabble tiles. How many more shapes can you arrange?

FOOTNOTE

[9] The resolution of a laser printer is set in stone. For example, you cannot force a 600dpi printer to somehow print a smaller dot. Imagesetters, on the other hand, can usually print at resolutions of 1,200, 2,400, and 3,600dpi, and this value is set using the software that drives the RIP. At higher resolutions, the output device must produce more printer dots, which results in longer processing times. The majority of imagesetter output is produced at 2,400dpi. When a higher resolution is required— for example, a project output at 200lpi requires a resolution of 3,600dpi—service bureaus usually charge an additional fee.

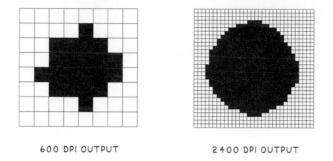

600 DPI OUTPUT   2400 DPI OUTPUT

Figure 9.17 *The resolution of an output device will determine the range of halftone dot sizes it can accurately produce. Low-resolution printer dots can be arranged only to form larger halftone dots (left). To produce the fine halftone dots required for high-linescreen printing, you must use a high-resolution output device, such as a 2,400dpi imagesetter.*

When you reproduce a halftone, particularly at high linescreen values, you must be sure the target output device is capable of reproducing the subtle differences that exist between the halftone dots. If you try to output a high linescreen on a lower-resolution printer, you cannot successfully reproduce all the image tones—essentially, you're trying to make small shapes using those big floppy disks. When the number of tones is reduced too far, the result is *posterization*, or blotchy areas of solid tints (see Figure 9.18). [10]

It's possible to set up a complex equation that compares printer resolution and linescreen values to give you the number of reproducible tones. However, this approach is too unwieldy to be of much use on a day-to-day basis. Suffice it to say that each printer resolution is capable of successfully reproducing a certain range of linescreen values. The table that follows lists

FOOTNOTE

[10] To explore this effect on your own, try this simple test. Import a Grayscale image into your page layout program and output it at 75lpi to your 600dpi laser printer. Output it again, resetting the linescreen value to 150lpi. Compare the two. Because the device's dot size is too large to reproduce all the tones of 150lpi output, the tones of the second printout are severely posterized.

a series of standard printer resolutions and the linescreens they can toler-ate before visible posterization occurs. [11]

Resolution	Linescreen Tolerance
300dpi	Up to 53lpi
600dpi	Up to 75lpi
1,200dpi	Up to 110lpi
2,400dpi	Up to 150lpi
3,600dpi	Up to 200lpi

133 LPI
OUTPUT AT 2400 DPI

133 LPI
OUTPUT AT 600 DPI

Figure 9.18 *If you attempt to output a high linescreen using a low-resolution printer, the number of reproducible tones is greatly reduced (right).*

Screen Angles

If you imagine a halftone screen as a physical grid, its cells must exist at a specific rotational orientation, or *screen angle*. The standard angle for one-color screens is 45°. Industry experience has proven that this angle makes the halftone grid least noticeable to the eye, further tricking you into seeing tones instead of dots (see Figure 9.19).

FOOTNOTE

[11] Very few graphics professionals use laser printers to generate their final out-put. If the resolution of your in-house laser printer isn't high enough to accommo-date your target linescreen value, don't worry. It's perfectly acceptable to output preflight composites and separations at a lower linescreen—just be sure your ven-dor is made aware of the desired lpi when you turn over the project for final output. (See Chapter 16, "Preflight and File Prep," for more info.)

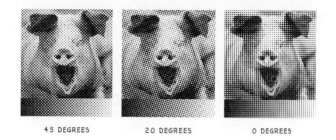

45 DEGREES   20 DEGREES   0 DEGREES

Figure 9.19 *All halftone dots appear in a grid, and every grid is printed at a specific angle. One-color halftones are always printed at 45°. Other angles make the arrangement of dots much more noticeable to the eye.*

Things get more complicated when you start working in color. When you reproduce a full-color image, you're actually printing four different halftones, one directly on top of another. One halftone consists of cyan ink, one is magenta, one is yellow, and one is black. If each halftone is printed at the same screen angle, the component dots would simply overlap on-press. Instead of colors, you'd see a murky, ill-defined, inky mess. Print shops avoid this problem by outputting each color at a different angle. Fewer dots overlap this way, enabling inks to be printed in a way that our eye interprets as photographic colors.

The screen angles used in a typical printing environment are as follows. Black is the most dominant color, and therefore receives the optimal angle: 45°. Cyan, the next most dominant color, is printed at 15° (or 105°, the same relative angle). Magenta is printed at 75° (or 165°). Yellow is the least visible ink, so it is printed at the most noticeable angle with the least jarring effect: 0° (see Figure 9.20).

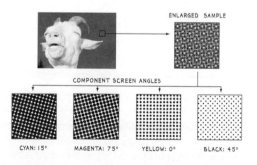

ENLARGED SAMPLE

COMPONENT SCREEN ANGLES

CYAN: 15°   MAGENTA: 75°   YELLOW: 0°   BLACK: 45°

Figure 9.20 *When a full-color image is separated, each color is printed at a different screen angle to prevent the halftone dots from completely overlapping.*

These angles are firmly established standards, and they're applied automatically by the software of your printer's RIP. Unless a special printing issue demands it, you won't have to define any particular screen angles. [12] Understanding the angles and the underlying reasons, however, is helpful whenever you work with process colors.

Moiré

If any of the screen angles deviate from the established values, a phenomenon called *moiré* occurs. Improper screen angles cause the halftone grids to conflict, which produces a distracting interference pattern. As long as you leave the CMYK angles to the default values used by the output device (or you follow specific instructions given to you by the print shop), moiré shouldn't appear. Most often, this pattern results when a person attempts to override the defaults and define their own screen angles. If this need arises, don't estimate an angle and hope for the best—consult with your print shop. [13]

Halftone Dot Shapes

By default, PostScript screens use slightly varying dot shapes. The dots are round in the lightest tonal areas, change to squared shapes in the midtones, and revert to round in the darkest areas. (Square dot shapes are known to

---

FOOTNOTE

[12] Two occasions where you need to define your own screen angles are when you work with duotones and to define spot colors in QuarkXPress. When you create a duotone, you specify that two or more inks be used to reproduce a one-color halftone. You must determine the angle of the additional inks. (See Chapter 13 for more info.) When you define a spot ink in XPress, you have the option of attaching a specific screen angle. It normally defaults to Black's angle (45°), but if you intend to combine spot colors using the program's Multi-Ink option, you must apply different angles. (See Chapter 14, "Page Layout Issues," for more info.)

[13] More often, people encounter moiré during the scanning process. If you attempt to acquire a *prescreened* image—for example, a photograph printed in a magazine—most scanners cannot successfully interpret the halftone dots. When you output the image again, it is converted to another set of halftone screens, which only increases the moiré pattern. Most scanners feature descreening software that resolves the dots and spaces into solid colors, and most do a fairly decent job of avoiding moiré. If not, you can employ a number of techniques to eliminate the pattern yourself. (See Chapter 13 for more info.)

produce sharper details in the tones between 45% and 65%.) Most applications enable you to change the overall shape of the halftone dots, using squares, ellipses, or even varying line widths instead. By far, the most common reason to do this is to create a special effect at very low linescreen values (see Figure 9.21).

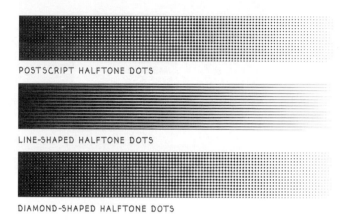

POSTSCRIPT HALFTONE DOTS

LINE-SHAPED HALFTONE DOTS

DIAMOND-SHAPED HALFTONE DOTS

Figure 9.21 *For most printing purposes, the halftone dot shapes generated by PostScript output devices are perfectly adequate. However, you can still reproduce tones using a variety of specialized shapes, such as squares, ellipses, or lines. Unless you're doing this for a special effect, consult with a printer before attempting to use special shapes—he might not reproduce your tones as well as you think.*

Frequency Modulated Screens

The halftoning methods I've described at length are by far the most commonly employed, but they're not the only ones. Conventional halftoning is also known as *amplitude modulated* (AM) screening. The hallmark of AM screening is that it requires a series of dots spaced evenly apart. Another method is enjoying a growing support base: *frequency modulated* (FM) screening. Instead of a grid of halftone dots, FM screening uses much smaller dots, arranged randomly on the page to reproduce image tones (see Figure 9.22). (In fact, this method is often referred to as *stochastic*, stemming from the Greek word for "random.")

FM screening is superior to AM in a number of ways. Because you aren't working with screen angles, you will not encounter moiré. The finest image details are not obscured by rosette patterns or overlapping halftone dots. Many users claim that they can achieve a higher level of color fidelity.

Overall, images are reproduced with a much finer grain, approaching the look and feel of an actual photograph. Finally, because the screen angle restrictions are removed, you can better utilize printing processes that use more than four inks, such as PANTONE's six-color Hexachrome method.

AM SCREEN   FM SCREEN

Figure 9.22 *Unlike AM screening, which uses a series of equally spaced dots of varied size, FM screening reproduces tones using extremely tiny dots of the same size, dithered randomly.*

However, FM screening is not for every person, nor for every project. First, you are restricted to using specific output products that deliver the randomized dots, such as Agfa's CristalRaster or Linotype-Hell's Diamond Screening RIPs. Second, you enter a minefield of new problems. Most proofing systems were developed to accommodate conventional halftone printing, making it difficult to check your images before going to press. (Most last-minute adjustments take place on-press, spectrophotometer in hand, as the job is run.) You have no control over the actual dot size, beyond changing the resolution of the output device, making it difficult to ensure the proper distribution of tones. Finally, FM screens have proven to be a poor option for reproducing flat screens and solid colors. If a project contains images and solid colors, you must resort to a complex solution such as embedding FM screens in your images, and importing them into a document, and outputting with a combination of AM and FM screens.

If you're new to FM screening, don't assume you can simply make a smooth transition from your current way of working. It will take considerable research on your part, as well as plenty of input from your service bureau and printer. To be sure, the time and effort can well be worth it. I rank the few FM-screened jobs I've sent to press among the most successful I've ever created.

Scanners

A variety of input devices are available for the graphics arts professional—so many, you might have difficulty determining the one most appropriate for your work.

On one end of the spectrum, you can purchase a consumer-level flatbed scanner for under $100. On the other end, the price tags of some high-quality flatbed and drum scanners can exceed $40,000. With the cheapest devices, you get exactly what you pay for; they capture an extremely limited range of tones and colors (most Grayscale and all color scans are inadequate for offset printing purposes), and they wear out after a couple hundred scans. The most expensive options capture the most viable range of image information, but you would have to be generating scans for at least 10 hours a day—every day—to justify the high cost.

Choosing the right input device is a balancing act. You must consider the expected use of the scans, your preferred printing methods, and your over-all quality expectations, and then weigh your conclusions against what you're willing or able to spend.

Your specific work environment will also affect the decision. If you're a designer, for example, you need only a midrange flatbed scanner, which enables you to scan line art and one-color halftones with enough quality for print. However, most designers neither have nor want the responsibility of generating full-color scans. These items are handed to a service bureau or other vendor who will scan them on a higher-quality device, and usually include a round of color correction in the price. In turn, the scanning costs are included in the production fees passed on to the client.

In-house production departments will benefit from more costly scanners that capture more information and include more features in the operative soft-ware. These devices will ensure that the images used in your publications reproduce successfully, without the need to farm color work to an outside vendor. Because these departments typically aren't able to bill anyone for scans, the cost of a scanner (along with the operators and the training they'll require) must be weighed against the cost of having your scans performed out-of-house.

Traditionally, service bureaus and print shops have invested in the highest-quality scanning devices. Because they cater to a steady client base, they receive a constant stream of revenue to offset the high costs of their equipment. Also, they're usually staffed by highly trained operators and supplemented by experienced color correctors, which helps ensure that scans are produced right the first time.

In this section, I describe the different types of input devices from which you can choose, and the scanner features that are most important in a graphics environment. At the end, I've provided a list of common image requirements along with their most suitable scanner type.

Scanner Types

Although you can choose from hundreds of different input devices, they fall into four categories: flatbed scanners, transparency scanners, drum scanners, and digital cameras. [14] The primary differences between these devices are cost, image quality, and the method of use.

Flatbed Scanners

Flatbed scanners are the most inexpensive input devices. They sit on top of your desk, enabling you to place the item you want to digitize on top of a sheet of glass, under a cover. When you scan, a mechanism slides beneath the glass, shining bright light that reflects off the artwork to be interpreted by an array of tiny sensors. Most often, these devices are used to scan *reflective artwork*, such as a photograph, ink on paper, watercolor paintings, and so forth. Some scanners can be fitted with a *transparency unit* that enables you to acquire images from slides, photographic negatives, and other types of film. Here, instead of bouncing light off the artwork, the unit shines light through it, which is then interpreted by the sensors. [15]

F O O T N O T E

[14] There are other ways to capture information for digital processing, such as sheetfed scanners for dedicated optical character recognition (OCR), add-on cards that capture video stills, and tiny handheld devices that enable you to scan by sweeping them over a page. Because these devices aren't capable of capturing the ranges of tone and color required for quality reproduction, they're not included in this book.

[15] Scanners are an example of a *SAD* system, which stands for *source, attenuator, detector*. SAD is a method of measuring change. In a scanner, the source is light. When light bounces off or shines through the artwork being scanned, the amplitude of its signal is attenuated, or slightly reduced. This change is then detected by the scanner sensors, which measure the difference between the light values.

The sensors appear in two forms. Most flatbeds use *charged-coupled devices* (CCDs) to convert light to pixels. Each scanner contains thousands of CCDs, arranged in a row across the scanning mechanism. (This arrangement is known as the *linear array*.) A smaller number of flatbeds use *complementary metal-oxide semiconductor* (CMOS) sensors, which first appeared in digital cameras. These differ from CCDs in that they exist as a single unit, similar to a processor or memory card.

CCD and CMOS sensors work the same way. As you scan, they compare the electrical charge of light before and after it hits the artwork. The difference is translated into a tone, and pixels are born. Historically, flatbed scanners have not been capable of producing high-quality color images. Recent technological advances, however, enable high-end units to generate scans almost as well as any other method.

Transparency Scanners

Although you can install a transparency unit to a flatbed scanner, it does not guarantee a quality scan. The sheet of glass that exists between the artwork and the CCDs will slightly distort the scanning light, detracting from transparency's inherent tonal depth. Also, most flatbed units require that you remove the transparency from its protective covering before placing it on the bed, increasing the chances of fingerprints and dirt sullying the process.

A dedicated transparency scanner is designed to handle only film, which offers certain advantages. They capture a deeper tonal range, and scan at much higher resolutions than flatbeds (enabling you to scale those tiny 35mm slides with little or no loss of detail). Also, most units use a *fixed* array of CCD or CMOS sensors. This means that during the scanning process, the artwork is moved instead of the sensors, decreasing the likelihood of vibration or distortion.

The prices vary according to the film size that a unit accepts. Entry-level units such as Nikon's CoolScan III, which handles 35mm and APS film, are available for under $1,000. Because professional photographers often use larger film sizes (2×2-inch and 4×5-inch are most common), you must use a scanner with a larger capacity. Scitex's LeafScan 45 (no longer produced, but still available and fully supported) handles film sizes up to 4×5, but costs over $15,000.

Drum Scanners

With a drum scanner, artwork is affixed to a Plexiglas cylinder. Reflective pieces use an opaque drum, and transparencies use a clear drum. During scanning, the cylinder rotates at a very high speed. An ultrafine light source inside illuminates the artwork point-by-point, which is interpreted by the scanner optics that convert the values to pixels.

The sensors used by drum scanners are *photomultiplier tubes* (PMTs). Functioning similar to a vacuum tube, they are extremely sensitive to incoming light signals. The highest-end PMTs recognize an extremely wide range of tones, particularly between subtly varying shadow detail. When you scan, light is distributed to three separate PMTs, one each for the red, green, and blue components.

For years, drum scanners were the sole domain of high-volume service providers and production facilities. Their prices range from tens of thousands to millions of dollars, but without a doubt, they can generate the highest-quality scans possible. They feature the highest scanning resolution (up to 9,600spi), handle films of practically any size, and support batch processing. In recent years, high-end flatbeds have successfully challenged the quality of lower-priced drum scanners by such as those produced by Scitex and Linotype-Hell.

Digital Cameras

Digital cameras enable you to acquire images using techniques similar to traditional photography. They function virtually the same as a scanner, with one important exception: You can focus a digital camera to acquire images over a range of distances; scanners can only recognize artwork a fraction of an inch away.

One of the main attractions of digital cameras is that they eliminate an entire stage of the imaging process. In theory, the images they capture can be opened directly in a program such as Photoshop for further editing, without the need to process film or scan. In practice, the quality you can achieve depends on the capabilities of the unit. Although you can find cameras for well under $1,000, their images are too compressed and blurred for printing purposes. The more expensive units can produce images so clear and well-defined, you can't tell them apart from an image that was professionally photographed and scanned.

There are two types of digital camera. *Instant-capture* models are self-contained units, storing the captured images on a tiny hard disk or memory card. You can find these cameras for as little as a few hundred dollars, but their resolution and bit depth is too low, and their exposure time too long for print-quality imaging. The more expensive options can range from a couple thousand to more than $25,000, but these devices guarantee enough data for successful output. *Scanning-back* models attach to the back of a standard high-quality camera, and are designed for studio use only. They are typically hard-wired to a computer, so the large images they acquire are written directly to a high-capacity hard drive. The resolution of higher-end scanning-back cameras can rival drum scanners, and their price tag shows it. They start around $9,000, and can cost more than $50,000.

Scanner Features

All scanners are not created equal. Four issues will make or break any scanner's ability to create images that reproduce successfully on-press: resolution, bit depth, dynamic range, and the scanner interface. If you consider these features a chain, a scanner is only as strong as the weakest link.

Resolution

When you read a scanner's marketing write-up, you'll find two types of resolution listed. The *optical* resolution measures how many samples per inch a scanner can read. This is often referred to as a scanner's *true* resolution, and it determines how many times a scanner is able to "look" at an image as it acquires it. To illustrate, consider the CCDs of a flatbed scanner's linear array: If 600 of these tiny sensors appear side by side every inch, the scanner's optical resolution is 600spi. [16]

FOOTNOTE

[16] Although scanner resolution is a measure of samples per inch, manufacturers use the less accurate "dots per inch" designation to describe it. Instead of listing an optical resolution as 600spi, for example, they publish the value as "600dpi," This measurement has no bearing on true dpi, which pertains to printer resolution, but what can you do? Just be aware of the difference when researching a scanner.

Each scanner also has an *interpolated* resolution. (You might have seen scanner ads that boldly proclaim "4,800dpi!" with "interpolated resolution" printed in tiny letters underneath.) Here, the scanner mimics a higher sensitivity. When you scan at a resolution higher than the optical value, the scanner interpolates the additional pixels, or estimates what their values should be. On one hand, interpolation is helpful; without it, you couldn't generate a 1,200ppi line art scan using a 600spi scanner. On the other hand, you shouldn't be seduced into buying a scanner simply because it features a high interpolated resolution. True pixels are better than educated guesses; if you need the additional tonal depth, invest in the higher optical resolution.

Flatbed scanners generally feature optical resolutions from 300 to 1,200spi. (If you're scanning color images, you'll need 600spi at the very minimum.) Transparency scanners generally feature resolutions between 2,000 and 4,000spi. Drum scanners can attain up to 9,600spi.

Bit Depth

Bit depth refers to how much information your scanner gathers as it reads the artwork. Essentially, it determines how many unique tonal variations it is capable of reading. For example, a 24-bit RGB scanner uses 8 bits per color channel, making it sensitive enough to recognize 16.7 million different tones. (This is similar to the method used to describe pixel-based images in general. For more info, refer to "Color Mode," earlier this chapter.) Most scanners available these days can recognize even more information. A 30-bit scanner, for example, uses 10 bits per channel, enabling it to recognize a billion variations; a 36-bit scanner uses 12 bits per channel, enabling it to recognize over 68 billion; 48-bit scanners use 16 bits per channel, enabling them to recognize over 300 trillion. [17]

FOOTNOTE

[17] These numbers are more theoretical than they let on. Although a scanner might have the built-in capability to recognize that many tonal variations, the actual number depends on the quality of the CCDs. For this reason, a $99 36-bit scanner will *not* recognize as many variations as a $1,500 36-bit scanner—another reason to set aside a few more dollars for that higher-quality input device.

Of course, after an image is scanned, each pixel in an RGB image is defined by only 24 bits of data. So does the additional information of a 30, 36, or 48-bit scanner help? Absolutely. The more information a scanner initially has at its disposal, the more likely the resulting image will contain the proper distribution of tones.

Dynamic Range

If bit depth refers to the number of possible tonal variations, the *dynamic range* refers to the range of tones that a scanner can read. Picture an image as a ladder: The dynamic range determines the ladder's height, and the bit depth determines the number of rungs. In this sense, you can see how the two concepts are interdependent. A long ladder is of little use if it has only a few rungs. Conversely, if a ladder is too short, it doesn't matter *how* many rungs it contains.

The dynamic range is often referred to as *density*, which measures the scanner's sensitivity as it acquires detail in the lightest and darkest image areas. For scanning purposes, density has two slightly different meanings. First, it describes the opacity of the materials you scan: how much light is able to pass through a film negative or transparency, or how much light reflects off a print. It uses an algorithmic scale from 0.0 (perfectly clear) to 4.0 (99.99% of light is blocked). For example, newsprint has a typical density of 1.8; high-quality coated paper is rated around 2.0; a photographic print measures between 2.0 and 2.8 (depending on the substrate); photographic transparencies are rated around 3.0.

Second, density describes a scanner's ability to capture a tonal range. Because dark image tones are the most difficult to acquire accurately, density values rate the darkest end of the scanner's range. What this means for you is simple: Your scanner should have a density rating higher than the materials you need to scan. For example, if your scanner has a density of 2.2 and you try to scan a chrome transparency, there's no way you can acquire enough shadow detail to successfully reproduce the image. No amount of post-scan correction can replace tones that were lost during the scanning process. Flatbed scanners typically offer density ratings between 3.0 and 3.7. High-end flatbeds and drum scanners can approach 4.0. For most purposes, a density rating of 3.2 is adequate.

Software

The features described so far are hardware-based, or dependent on the mechanical structure of the unit. But this is only half the battle; every scanner is driven by a software package that ultimately determines how well detected tones are converted to editable pixels.

There are almost as many scanning applications as there are scanners. Usually, each manufacturer develops its own interface, so you're likely to see some differences as you work with different devices. For the best results, you should choose a package that delivers the following features:

- **An Onscreen Densitometer.** This option enables you to read pixel values directly from an onscreen scanning preview, making it easier to determine any corrections that need to applied at the time of the scan.

- **Multiple Scan Modes.** Every scanner should produce more than RGB scans. At the very least, look for Line Art and Grayscale options. Most high-end units enable you to scan in a variety of color modes, including CMYK and Lab Color.

- **Transparency Adapter.** These units enable you to acquire images from slides and film transparencies. They're often pointless on lower-cost units, which simply cannot generate enough information to scan and scale film-based artwork. If your work demands it, a transparency adapter on a higher-end scanner will prove to be a boon. (If most of your work revolves around film, however, consider purchasing a dedicated transparency scanner.)

- **Application Support.** Because you'll edit your images further in Photoshop, you need to make sure the scanning software can be driven straight from the application. Most software packages ship with a TWAIN device (for Windows) or a plug-in (for Mac) that enables you to access the scanner interface from within Photoshop. When you scan, the image opens directly in the program, awaiting further edits. The only other option is a dedicated scanning application, which produces images independently of any other program. Unless you need to do something such as batch process a series of scans, this usually results in a waste of precious seconds as you close the scanning software and open the image manually in Photoshop.

- **Intuitive Tonal Correction.** Most scanning software ships with a range of color editing controls, enabling you to make a round of color corrections at the time of the scan. These tools should be easily accessed, easily understood, and not produce hard tonal jumps in the image.

- **Endpoint Placement.** Your scanner should be able to locate the lightest and darkest points of an image. However, it might occasionally require some assistance on your part, and you should be allowed to override the automatic settings whenever necessary.

- **Sharpening Features.** Sharpening is a process that reduces some of the slight blurring that naturally occurs during the scanning process. Good scanning software enables you to set the intensity of any sharpening, as well as when and where the values are applied. One-touch auto-sharpening features should be avoided.

- **Channel-Specific Settings.** Scanners might not produce analogous results in all three color channels. The ability to address individual channels in the scanning software is a must.

- **Savable Settings.** After perfecting an extensive range of settings for a specific film type, for example, you'll want to be able to save them for future use.

- **Optical Character Recognition (OCR).** OCR software scans pages of printed words and converts them to editable text characters. It's not always a flawless process, but it's faster and cheaper than doing it yourself or out-sourcing the work to a freelance typist.

- **Descreening Function.** After an image has been printed, it is referred to as "screened." Ordinarily, you cannot rescan these images without producing a blotchy moiré pattern. If your scanner has a descreening function, it will be able to interpret the halftone dot shapes and convert them to a smoother range of continuous tones.

- **Batch Scanning.** Batch scanning is the ability to set up and acquire several images at once. For example, you can place a dozen small images on a flatbed unit (or wrap them around the cylinder of a drum scanner), establish your base settings, press a button, and walk away while the scanner generates the different images. Historically, this option was available only on drum scanners. Recent advances in high-end scanning software now enable this process to be executed on flatbed scanners.

Choosing the Right Scanner

It's no easier to recommend a specific scanner than it is to recommend a monitor. Ultimately, you have to try them out and process some samples of your work to get an accurate idea of how well they'll perform for you. Most often, the only places you can test a variety of scanners is at a trade show, such as Macworld or Seybold. If this isn't feasible, consider asking your vendors for input. If they've scanned your work before and you were satisfied with the results, find out what device they used and ask a few questions. If you simply pick a scanner out of a catalog, there's no guarantee you'll be satisfied with the tonal range, color, or software options, regardless of the technical specs you researched.

The following table will give you a head start on choosing a scanner based on your work and its capabilities. After you've determined the basic technical requirements, use the information to locate a few scanners to take for a test-drive.

Items to Scan	Printing Method	Reflective/ Film	Max. lpi	Scanner Type
Text only (OCR)	N/A	Reflective	N/A	Low-end flatbed, 300dpi, 24 or 30-bit color
For Position Only (FPO)	N/A	Both	N/A	Mid-range flatbed with trans. unit, 300dpi, 30-bit color
FPO	N/A	Film only	N/A	Low-end film scanner, 2,000+dpi, 30-bit color
One-color halftones	Newsprint	Both	100	Mid-range flatbed with trans. unit, 300dpi, 30-bit color
One-color halftones	Quick-printing on uncoated stock	Reflective	133	Mid-range flatbed, 600dpi, 30-bit color
Full color	Offset	Reflective	133	Mid-range flatbed, 600dpi, 36-bit color
Full color	Offset	Reflective	175	Mid to high-end flatbed, 600 to 1,200dpi, 36-bit color

Items to Scan	Printing Method	Reflective/ Film	Max. lpi	Scanner Type
Full color	Offset	Film only	175	Mid-range film scanner, 4,000dpi, 36 or 48-bit color
Full color	Offset	Both	175	High-end flatbed with trans. unit, 600 to 1,200dpi (refl.), 4,000dpi (film), 36 to 48-bit color
Full color	Offset	Both	200 or FM	Highest-end flatbed with trans. unit, 1,200dpi (refl.), 4,000dpi (film), 48-bit color Or Mid to high-end drum, 4,000+dpi, 48-bit color

Summary

It's easy to underestimate what you're getting into when you assume the responsibility for generating your own scans. It's not hard to understand why. Many people get their start by handling scans that were produced by an outside vendor. As far as they were concerned, they handed over some photos or slides, and then received a zip full of viable images they could import directly into a page layout. No problem.

When you're the one scanning, the world changes. Too many people make the mistake of picking up a $100 scanner at the local discount store, assuming it'll somehow generate the necessary image quality with little or no user input. In the real world, you must understand the following issues before you even produce the first scan:

- Every printed image undergoes a series of conversions: A photograph is converted to pixels; pixels are converted to halftone dots; halftone dots are converted to ink on paper. The decisions you make at every stage directly affect the final image quality.

- The most important image elements are pixels. Unless you know how they display color, how to read their values, and how they relate to halftone dots, you will not be able to develop a successful scanning strategy.

- Halftone screens are the universally accepted method of reproducing tones on-press. The values and output methods used to generate them are based on factors that must be determined before an image is scanned.

- You can choose from an exceptionally wide range of scanning devices. Before you start your search, you must understand the work you need to scan, your printing methods, and the tonal and color quality you must attain.

- As you wade through the multitude of scanner options and technical specs, you must understand the ones that pertain most to your work: scanner resolution, bit depth, density, and the software interface.

After you've grasped the information covered in this chapter and acquired the right equipment, you're ready to start scanning. More importantly, you're ready to learn the techniques involved in adjusting and refining a scanned image for optimal printing.

SCANNING LINE ART AND HALFTONES

Not long ago, I toured the production facility of a weekly newspaper as part of a workflow evaluation. When I asked how they handled photographs and halftones, the department supervisor waved a dismissive hand toward his desk. "We have Photoshop and a scanner," he said, "but the images we get are so dark and clogged, we don't use them." The entire paper was composed digitally except for the photographs, which were conventionally shot with a stat camera and stripped in before printing.

I reviewed their scanning process, and his conclusion made sense. No one in the department had been trained how to optimize an image for print. They'd simply make a quick Grayscale scan, and then save the file. The resulting tones were flat, somewhat blurred, and too dark for newsprint. As far as they were concerned, Photoshop was nothing more than a static extension of the scanning software—if the image that automatically appeared didn't work out, the equipment obviously didn't satisfy their needs. Meanwhile, additional steps and hours of extra work were bloating their production process, as thousands of dollars of viable, timesaving technology collected dust.

I told him that Photoshop had powerful tools he could use to tweak and enhance each image. Using the same scan, I adjusted the endpoints, lightened the midtones, added some contrast, and sharpened the overall image. Two minutes of off-the-cuff edits, and the scan met the requirements of his printing press. Thinking the supervisor was on the verge of a workflow epiphany, I further explained that digital halftoning was a simple process, one that would save time and material costs, empower their onscreen layout capabilities, and even open up new design options. In the end, he only shook his head, and declared that they didn't have the time to learn new technology—even though every week, their workaround consumed more time than it would have taken to learn the basic techniques.

What can you learn from this experience? First, no scanner is sensitive or accurate enough to give you perfect results straight off the glass. To generate the tones required for your printing method, you have to follow a strict set of scanning guidelines, and then apply a series of adjustments in Photoshop. Next, understand that learning these techniques (and the underlying issues) will indeed require an initial investment of time and effort. Your editing decisions will be based on a thoughtful evaluation of the original artwork, the paper stock you'll print to, and the limitations of the target press.

The process might seem unnecessarily complex at first, and you're bound to make a few mistakes as you develop a confident hand. But the effort pays off many times over. Whether scanning line art or halftones, you'll be able to complete each image in minutes flat. Instead of relying on costly outside vendors or conventional shooting techniques, you'll produce images that are combined easily with other artwork, quickly incorporated into page layouts, and output in a way that successfully reproduces on-press.

This chapter focuses on black-and-white line art and one-color halftones, the two most basic and commonly required scanning methods. [1] If you're comfortable with the material covered in Chapter 9, "Digital Imaging Fundamentals," you're ready to delve more deeply into the following:

- Preparing your scanning environment, which involves setting the appropriate production-oriented preferences in Photoshop and performing a round of basic tests on your scanner.

- Scanning, cleaning up, and saving 1-bit line art, including techniques for handling any highly detailed information your scanner might have trouble acquiring.

FOOTNOTE

[1] The info in this chapter focuses on the proper use of flatbed scanners, the most commonly used input device in the print publishing industry. However, the subsequent issues and adjustment techniques apply to every image, regardless of the device used to acquire them.

- Developing a strategy for scanning and adjusting Grayscale images, based on a set of scanner, paper stock, and press-related issues.

- Using the Photoshop tools most appropriate for optimizing print images, including the Crop and Rubber Stamp tools, the Levels and Curves commands, and the Unsharp Mask filter.

Preparing Your Scanning Environment

Whenever you acquire an image, Photoshop and your scanner work side by side—you won't use one without the other. Take some time to prepare your scanning environment. By customizing some production-oriented settings in Photoshop and running some simple tests on your scanner, you'll go a long way toward establishing a consistent, efficient workflow.

Setting Photoshop's Preferences

Photoshop has a vast and complex interface. Because there are so many variables and so many different uses for the program, it contains certain base settings that you can adjust to better suit your specific requirements. They're called Preferences (or "prefs"), and you can change them on-the-fly whenever Photoshop is open. [2]

These settings are stored in a file called "Adobe Photoshop Preferences." Photoshop 5.5 and 5.0.2 place the file inside the application folder, in the "Adobe Photoshop Settings" folder. If you ever want to restore the factory-default settings, delete the Preferences file and let Photoshop create a new one the next time the program is launched. Also, if the program ever begins

---

FOOTNOTE

[2] This isn't the only time you'll be required to establish application preferences. In Chapter 14, "Page Layout Issues," I discuss the production-specific settings for QuarkXPress, Adobe PageMaker, and Adobe InDesign. You'll notice at least one difference between those values and Photoshop's. In a page layout program, you work with *application* prefs (values set with no documents open, that affect every new document you create) and *document* prefs (values set with a document open, that override the application prefs and are built directly into the individual file). Photoshop doesn't make this distinction. Here, it doesn't matter whether an image is open when you set your preferences, nor are any values built into an image. Photoshop's preferences affect only the interface of your specific copy of the program.

acting inconsistently—for example, if certain values inexplicably reset or color definitions change—deleting the Preferences file will often solve the problem.

The preferences are contained in eight separate panels. In the next sections, I explain only the settings that have the strongest impact on a print production workflow. Wherever I have a specific recommendation, I include it in parentheses after the title.

The General Panel

This panel appears when you access the Preferences dialog box by choosing File: Preferences: **General**, or pressing (Command-K) [Control-K] (see Figure 10.1).

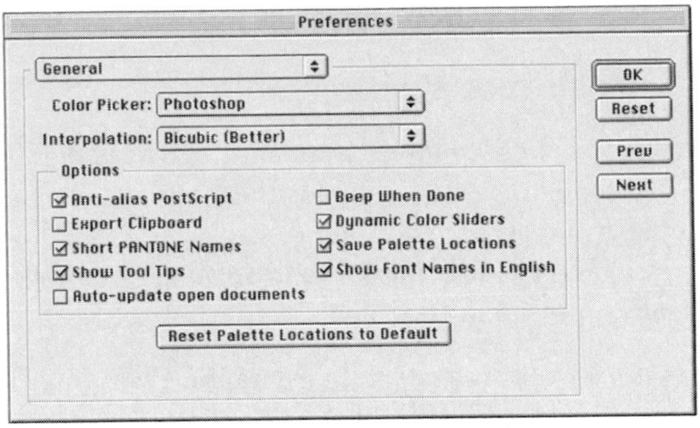

Figure 10.1   *The General preferences panel.*

Color Picker (*Photoshop*)

This option is available only on Mac systems. Here, you choose between Photoshop's robust color picker and the rudimentary one developed by Apple. The Apple color picker is found in many other programs, but defines only a limited range of color types. Photoshop's picker can define Lab colors, displays a gamut warning, and enables you to select custom colors from libraries such as PANTONE or Trumatch.

Interpolation (*Bicubic*)

When Photoshop resizes an image or processes a transformation (such as scaling or rotating), it has to figure out how to rearrange the pixels. To do this, it must interpolate the new pixels, or make an educated guess about how they should appear. The best option is Bicubic, the factory default. It forces Photoshop to "read" the highest number of pixels before making its decision, producing the highest-quality results. Nearest Neighbor offers the lowest quality, not attempting to interpolate the pixels at all. Bilinear falls somewhere in the middle.

Anti-Alias PostScript (*On*)

When you import a vector-based graphic using the File: **Place** command, this option tells Photoshop to automatically *anti-alias*, or smooth the edges of the shapes. Note that it has no impact on any images that you rasterize by opening them into Photoshop, or by copying and pasting from Illustrator. When this happens, anti-aliasing is a clickable option in the dialog box that appears. (Refer to Chapter 8, "Vector-Based Graphics," for more info.)

Export Clipboard (*Off*)

This option tells your computer to hold any copied information in memory when you quit Photoshop. However, in a print publishing environment, it's unlikely that you'll be pasting pixel-based data into another program. The copied info can be megabytes in size; simply leaving it there can result in system slowdowns.

Short PANTONE Names (*On*)

There are two ways to include spot ink data in a Photoshop image: Create a duotone, or add a spot color channel. When this option is turned on, Photoshop uses the short version of any PANTONE ink names—for example, "PMS 287 CV" instead of "PANTONE 287 CV." The short names are recognized by more print-related graphics programs.

Show Tool Tips (*On*)

When you place the cursor over an item in the Tools palette, this option displays a tiny, single-letter keyboard shortcut. When you place the cursor over a palette button, it displays the button's name. Not a huge timesaver, but it does help you memorize names and shortcuts.

Beep When Done (*Off*)

When this option is turned on, Photoshop sounds an alert whenever it finishes processing a command. It's useful if you're applying intensive edits using a low-end computer, where some commands take several minutes to finish. Otherwise, it's an annoyance.

Save Palette Locations (*On*)

This option tells Photoshop to remember where you've placed any visible floating palettes. When it's turned off, the palettes revert to their default positions whenever you launch the program. To automatically reset the palette positions, click the "Reset Palette Locations to Default" button at the bottom of the Preferences dialog box.

The Saving Files Panel

These preferences affect the way that Photoshop saves an image (see Figure 10.2).

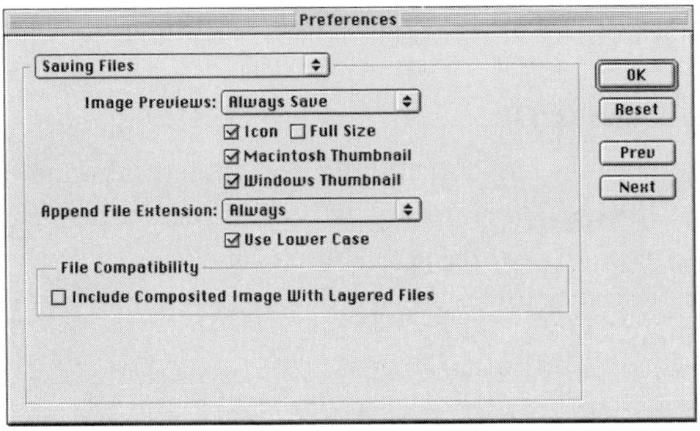

Figure 10.2   *The Saving Files preferences panel.*

Image Previews (*Always Save, Icon, Thumbnail*)

A *preview* is a small rendering of an image that Photoshop build into a file when you save it. The Icon option inserts a 32×32-pixel version of the image as the file's icon, which makes it slightly easier to identify a file without opening it. The Thumbnail options create a slightly larger preview that will appear in the Open dialog box. If you check Full Size, Photoshop will include an actual-size 72ppi preview that your page layout program can use when you import the image, enabling it to appear onscreen a little more quickly. (However, this option results in a notably larger file size, and the larger preview really isn't required if you're using a reasonably fast computer.)

Append File Extension (*On*)

This option tells Photoshop to automatically add the appropriate three-letter extension at the end of each filename. For example, TIFF images are labeled ".tif," EPS images are labeled ".eps," and so forth. There are two reasons to turn this option on. First, it enables Windows users to access images created on a Macintosh. Second, it makes it a lot easier for anyone processing the files to understand the image contents when they can easily discern the file format. (Refer to Chapter 5, "File Management," for more info.)

Include Composited Image with Layered Files (*Off*)

This option includes a flattened version of an image whenever you save it in the native Photoshop file format. The only reason to do this is if you'll be handing over files that contain image layers to someone using Photoshop 2.5 or earlier, and that isn't very likely these days. This option will increase your file size by as much as 200%, and should be turned off. If you need backward compatibility, save a flattened copy of the file.

Display & Cursors

These preferences affect the onscreen appearance of Photoshop's colors, channels, and tools (see Figure 10.3).

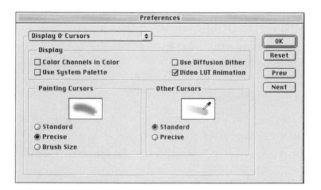

Figure 10.3   *The Display & Cursors preferences panel.*

Color Channels in Color (*Off*)

When this option is turned on, the separate channels that comprise a color image appear in the colors they represent. For example, in an RGB image, the channels are actually colored red, green, and blue. Some people prefer this effect, believing that it enables them to approach a color image more intuitively, and it helps reduce the likelihood of editing the wrong channel when they select one in the Channels palette. However, I prefer leaving it off. The colors it shows are misleading, and have no bearing on the file structure Photoshop uses to display color. Also, the colored versions display with less contrast and clarity than the standard Grayscale approach, making it more difficult to read the contents of an individual channel. (Refer to Chapter 9 for more info.)

Use System Palette (*Off*)

This option applies to people using 8-bit monitors, which display only 256 colors. It tells Photoshop to refer to only one color palette when you're editing more than one image at once, which results in images that display more quickly. Use it on a more capable monitor, and you'll severely skew your onscreen color values. No one in the industry uses 8-bit monitors anymore—if you do, you're better off upgrading your equipment than trying to fudge faster display times.

Video LUT Animation (*On*)

When the Video LUT (Look-Up Table) option is turned on, adjustments made in dialog boxes such as Levels or Curves affect the entire screen instead of just the image pixels. On slower models (or when you edit large images), this enables you to preview the effect of a command much more quickly. Color accuracy will be slightly impeded, but if you need to see the actual pixel values, you can check the Preview box that appears in any adjustment command's dialog box.

Painting Cursors (*Precise*)

This option determines the appearance of your cursor when you use a Photoshop tool that implements a brush, such as the Pencil, Airbrush, or Rubber Stamp tools. When you choose the Standard option, the cursor appears as a fairly descriptive but wholly inaccurate tool shape. When you choose Precise, the cursor is replaced with a more accurate crosshair, which enables you to pinpoint the exact center of the current brush shape. When you choose Brush Shape, the cursor appears as a circle that matches the size of the current brush.

The Brush Shape option is usually the best choice, because you'll always know which pixels are about to be affected by your next edit. However, set the preference to Precise. This way, you'll get the crosshairs by default, but you can toggle to the Brush Shape option on-the-fly by pressing the Caps Lock key.

Other Cursors (*Standard*)

This option determines the cursor shapes used by the remaining items in the Tools palette. Although the Standard option gives you the same clunky icon as a cursor shape, it enables you to toggle to Precise mode by pressing the Caps Lock key.

Plug-Ins & Scratch Disks

These preferences determine how Photoshop handles plug-in files and the empty drive space it requires as a scratch disk (see Figure 10.4).

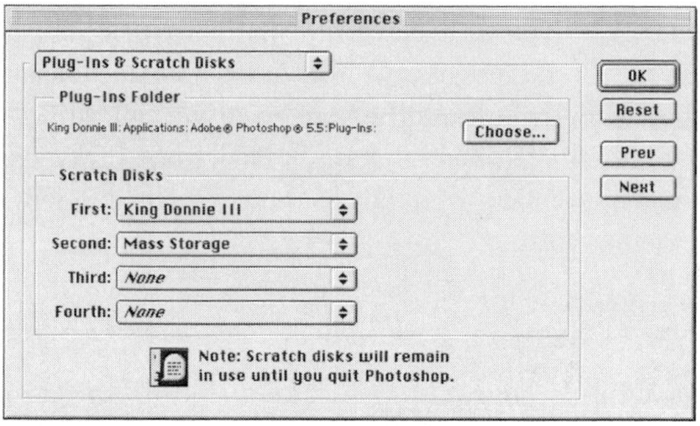

Figure 10.4 *The Plug-Ins & Scratch Disks preferences panel.*

Plug-Ins Folder

Plug-ins are auxiliary files that add features to Photoshop, such as the Extensions and Control Panels used by your operating system. For example, Photoshop's filters and the driver used to access your scanner exist as plug-ins. By default, Photoshop installs a folder called "Plug-Ins" inside the application folder, and it automatically knows to refer to this folder and load the contents when you launch the program.

Photoshop can also recognize plug-ins used by other pixel-based editing programs, such as MetaCreations Painter and Adobe After Effects. To access these files, you can redirect Photoshop to use *their* Plug-Ins folder instead of its own. However, if you frequently use other plug-ins this way, consider creating one central Plug-Ins folder that each program is told to read. This way, each program has access not only its own plug-ins, but to all the rest as well.

To specify a new Plug-Ins folder, click the Choose button, which brings up a navigation window. Locate and highlight the desired folder and click the Select button at the bottom of the window. Pressing Return or Enter will not automatically choose the folder. It's fairly easy to choose the wrong folder, but it's also easy to see when it happens: None of the filters or other features you want are available. When this happens, return to this preferences panel, reset the Plug-Ins folder, and relaunch Photoshop. [3]

Scratch Disks

When Photoshop runs low on available RAM, it resorts to using the *scratch disk*, or empty space on your hard drive, to store the data it requires to process commands. If you only have one hard drive, Photoshop automatically searches out the largest chunk of free drive space. If you have multiple drives, Photoshop defaults to the startup drive, but allows you to use as many as four additional drives as scratch disk space. For example, if the drive set in the First pop-up runs out of room, Photoshop will switch to the second drive, and so forth. [4]

Image Cache

The *image cache* preferences are a way to speed up the onscreen refresh time of very large images (see Figure 10.5). They enable Photoshop to hold lower-resolution versions of an image in memory. When you decrease the zoom percentage, the program refers to any cached info to display the new view more quickly.

FOOTNOTE

[3] Some power-users have hundreds, if not thousands, of plug-ins. Loading this many modules at once can take a prohibitively long time, especially on older computer models. If this is the case, consider dividing your plug-ins into multiple folders, rather than one primary folder. This way, you hold down the (Option-Command) [Alt-Control] keys while launching Photoshop, which enables you to select the desired Plug-Ins folder on-the-fly.

[4] Photoshop uses only the largest contiguous space as a scratch disk—if even one tiny file fragment resides in the middle of the space, the available scratch disk is cut in half. To keep this space constant, consider creating a 100MB partition on one of your hard drives. This partition will be available in the First pop-up, just like a separate hard drive. As long as no files are ever copied into this partition, the space always remains contiguous and fully available. (Refer to Chapter 3, "Optimizing Your Work Environment," for more info.)

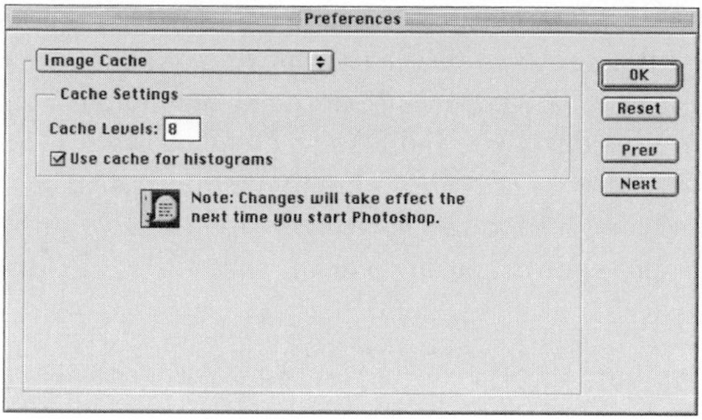

Figure 10.5 *The Image Cache preferences panel.*

Cache Levels

Setting a Cache Levels value determines the number of low-res previews that Photoshop holds in memory. The default is 4, which means that previews for four zoom percentages from 100% on down are maintained in RAM. The image redraws faster when editing at these zoom percentages, but it comes at a cost: Photoshop will require more RAM. Therefore, users with large amounts of RAM (96MB and above) can safely increase the number of Cache Levels to 8, the maximum amount. Workstations with less RAM should reduce the value.

Use Cache for Histograms

When you check this option, Photoshop uses the data in one of the stored cache levels to generate the tonal graphs found in the Levels and Histogram dialog boxes. The information won't be totally accurate, but histograms are rarely used for anything more than a general overview of an image's tonal range. This option requires a little more RAM, so turn it off if your Cache Level is set below 4.

Readying Your Scanner

As useful as flatbed scanners are, they're amazingly inconsistent devices. When you compare scanners made by different manufacturers, the results differ. When you compare the different models made by a single manufacturer, the results differ. On a single scanner, when you acquire the same image placed in various locations on the glass, the results might very well differ. Even images scanned in the same location will differ over time as your scanner ages.

You can't assume that a scanner will automatically give you the results you expect, even with artwork as simple as line art and halftones. You can, however, find out the limitations of your particular scanner, maximize the range of information it can acquire, and take steps to ensure it gives you consistent results scan after scan. For basic scanning purposes, your goal isn't to grab press-ready images straight off the glass—instead, you want to be able to capture enough information so you can make the necessary adjustments in Photoshop.

Before incorporating a scanner into your workflow, evaluate how it handles the images you need to scan. The idea is that if you can determine how your scanner behaves every day, you can determine which of its software settings (if any) will produce the most effective results for each image type. For example, if you have a reasonably clean piece of line art, which settings will capture it most successfully, in a way that requires the least amount of additional effort? Any work you can front-load at the time of the scan saves you valuable time down the road. [5]

Testing Line Art Scans

Testing how well your scanner captures line art is easy. For the best results, use a clean, clear sample of finely detailed black-and-white artwork. [6] Scan the image at the desired resolution (800–1,200ppi), using your scanner software's Line Art setting. Immediately after scanning, output the image to your laser printer. Compare the printout to the original and look for the following (see Figure 10.6):

FOOTNOTE

[5] This section focuses entirely on line art and Grayscale scans. For more information on establishing base settings for color scans, see Chapter 12, "Scanning and Adjusting Color Images." For information on profiling your scanner as part of a color-managed workflow, see Chapter 13, "Photoshop Production Techniques."

[6] Service bureaus and other vendors with in-house imagesetters frequently print test strips to gauge and calibrate the performance of their output devices. Most of them contain a *resolution tester*, or a series of starbursts constructed of delicate, micron-thin lines. It's unlikely you'll be scanning any detail finer than these lines, which makes them perfectly suited for testing the sensitivity of your scanner. If you don't have a test target handy, ask your service bureau to make a positive of their test film. (If they routinely output to RC paper, there's a good chance they'll have a recent round of strips sitting in or near their trash barrel.)

- Does it appear too dark, with areas of fine detail filling in to solid black?

- Does it appear too light, with areas of fine detail blowing out to solid white?

- Is there an abundance of stray pixels, giving the artwork an overall "dirty" appearance?

TOO LIGHT   TOO DARK   WELL-BALANCED

Figure 10.6 *Whenever you scan line art, you must be sure it contains enough detail. The scan on the left is too light, with blown-out details. The scan in the middle is too dark, with clogged details. The scan on the right has an acceptable balance of black and white data.*

If the scan looks perfect, you're ready to move on. If the scan is cluttered with a lot of stray pixels, your scanner might have a dying light source or faulty CCDs (for more info, see "Mapping Your Scanner Bed," later this chapter). If the scan is too light or dark, you might be able compensate by tweaking some settings in your scanner software.

When your scanner interprets line art, it applies a *threshold*, or a line of demarcation that separates black pixels from white. Normally, the threshold is placed at the halfway point—when your scanner perceives any tones over 50% black, they are converted to black; any tones under 50% are converted to white. [7] However, your scanner is not smart enough to know what's supposed to be black and what's supposed to be white. When light is reflected

F O O T N O T E

[7] The default position of the threshold varies from scanner to scanner. The manufacturers are aware of their devices' different sensitivities to light, and will attempt to set the threshold accordingly. Some might default to 30%, some as high as 60–70%. More often than not, you should regard the initial setting as a starting point, not a value set in stone. As you test different values, move in small increments from the original threshold.

off the artwork and read by the linear array, the very edges of the black information are seen to possess a slightly blurred fringe. If these "gray" tones appear dark enough to your scanner, they're converted to black pixels, which might result in finer detail becoming clogged. If the tones appear light enough, they're converted to white pixels, which might result in a loss of finer detail.

The trick is to reposition the threshold so it retains enough detail in the lightest and darkest areas of the artwork. Most scanner software contains a setting called "Threshold" or "Brightness/Contrast," available whenever you choose Line Art as a scanning type. There, you'll either be able to set a new threshold percentage or manipulate a slider that ranges from 0 to 255. (The slider is in reference to the 256 brightness levels of a Grayscale image. Most often, it is positioned at 128, or the midpoint between black and white.)

If your test scan was too dark, increase the threshold percentage (or move the slider closer to 0). This way, you specify that more of the gray fringe is converted to white pixels. If your test scan was too light, decrease the threshold percentage (or move the slider closer to 255), which converts more of the fringe pixels to black. Work in small amounts. For example, adjust the percentage in 5% increments, scan the image again, and compare a printout to the original. When you pass the point of optimal quality, work backward in 1% increments until you nail the balance between black and white.

Of course, it's unfair to assume that your scanner is sensitive enough to capture the most complex and difficult line art scans. In these cases, you might need to employ some additional scanning techniques (see "Preparing Detailed Line Art," later this chapter). You just need to get as close as possible, which will give you acceptable results for the majority of your scans.

If your scanner software enables you to save settings, save the adjusted threshold value and load it whenever you scan line art. If not, document the value in a notebook, or on a piece of tape affixed to the bottom of your monitor.

Testing Grayscale Scans

When you scan halftones, your scanner must be able to capture a wide enough range of tonal values to accommodate on-press reproduction. Just because a Grayscale file can display output values from 0% to 100% black, it doesn't mean your scanner is capable of recognizing the same range.

To test your scanner, use a black-and-white photograph with a full range of tones: dark shadows, bright highlights, and plenty of information in between. [8] Your goal is not to get picture-perfect results off the glass—instead, you want to capture enough information as possible, so you can adjust the image as necessary in Photoshop.

Setting the Right Scanning Mode

The first issue crops up when you set the scanning mode. Most older devices offer only one option: Grayscale. This means that the scanner is an 8-bit device, capable of generating a maximum of only 256 tones. Newer scanners, even the least expensive ones, usually offer a 10- or 12-bit scanning option for Grayscale images. (Usually, it's listed as "1000s of Shades of Gray," with the 8-bit option listed as "256 Shades of Gray.") It's important to choose the highest number of values. If you scan at only 256 levels, there's a good chance you won't be able to capture a full range of tones. When this happens, the image is more likely to appear thin, washed out, or posterized after you apply any adjustments using Photoshop's Levels or Curves commands.

On the other hand, the higher-bit option will recognize up to 4,096 levels, and then select the 256 tones of the target image from a much broader range. This offers two advantages. First, most scanner software has controls that enable you to adjust for contrast, sharpness, and dot gain at the time of the scan. If you scan at a higher bit depth, you can use the controls to compensate for certain scanner limitations, such as an inability to recognize the darkest tones. Second, even if you bypass the scanner controls, you'll have

---

F O O T N O T E

[8] Your testing will also benefit from a scanning target. You can order one directly from the Graphic Arts Technical Foundation (GATF), or you can buy a perfectly suitable target from your local photographic supply store. Targets are available in transparent and reflective forms, and come in different emulsion types (for film scanning). They typically feature a neutral gray strip, intensity scales for cyan, magenta, yellow, and black, and a series of CMYK combinations that produce a variety of reds, blues, and greens. There will often be some other test swatches, such as flesh tones and a photograph to test for sharpness. The main advantage of a scanning target is that you'll always be able to use the same rigidly calibrated information whenever you run tests or make profiles in the future.

a much fuller range of tones to start with as you apply future adjustments in Photoshop. [9]

Evaluating the Tonal Range

To get an idea of the tones you'll be able to work with, scan your high-quality photograph or scanner target at 300ppi. When the image opens in Photoshop, choose Image: **Histogram**. This dialog box contains a graph that displays the image's tonal range as a series of vertical lines (see Figure 10.7). There are 256 possible lines, which extend from left to right; one for each tone, from the darkest to the lightest. The height of each line indicates how many pixels of that particular tone exist in the image.

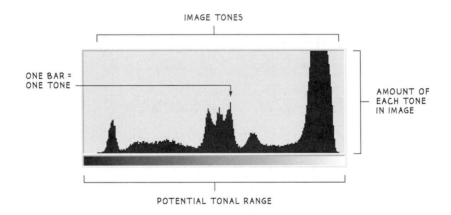

Figure 10.7 *The histogram is a graph that displays the tonal content of an image. It's similar to the graph found in the Levels dialog box, but slightly more accurate. After you become familiar with the layout of the vertical bars, you'll be able to evaluate the range of an image at a single glance.*

FOOTNOTE

[9] Sooner or later, a 10- or 12-bit scan has to be converted to an 8-bit image. Some scanners do this automatically, applying the conversion after they acquire the image. Others do not, and this might lead to some confusion. When this happens, the scan appears in Photoshop as a 16-bit image. It will look the same as any other file—in fact, you can apply Levels and Curves adjustments, save the image as a TIFF, and import it into a page layout. However, many editing options will seem mysteriously available. You can't access any filters. Most of the items in the Image: Adjust submenu are grayed out. You can save only in the Photoshop native and TIFF file formats. To regain access to these controls, manually convert the image to 8-bit Grayscale by choosing Image: Mode: **8 Bits/Channel**.

As you evaluate the test image, check for the following:

- Because you've scanned an image with a full range of tones, the bars in the histogram should extend almost all the way across the graph. If there is a severe drop-off on the far left or right of the graph, the scanner is not adequately picking up the shadow or highlight detail (see Figure 10.8). (A short drop-off is common, and easily compensated for in Photoshop.)

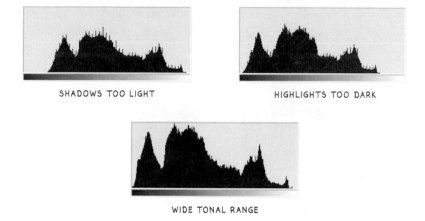

Figure 10.8   *Here, the same image was acquired on three different scanners. The top-left histogram indicates that the scanner is not picking up shadow information, or interpreting the values as far too light. The top-right histogram indicates that the scanner isn't picking up the highlight details, or interpreting them as far too dark. The bottom histogram shows a wide range of tones.*

- If the graph spikes at either end, the highlights or shadows might be getting *clipped* by the scanner. This means that large areas of all-white or all-black pixels exist in the image, which hinders the reproduction of light or dark detail (see Figure 10.9). (If the original image does, in fact, contain a large amount of white or black info, the histogram doesn't necessarily indicate a problem.)

- The bars should rise and fall fairly smoothly across the histogram, which indicates that the scanner is successfully reading the continuous image tones. If the image is predominantly dark, the bars will appear more prominently on the left side of the graph; if it's predominantly light, they'll appear more prominently on the right (see Figure 10.10). There should be no large, blocky areas in the graph.

CLIPPED SHADOWS   CLIPPED HIGHLIGHTS

Figure 10.9 *The histogram on the left shows that the shadows are being clipped by the scanner, which results in too many black (or nearly black) pixels. The histogram on the right shows that the highlights are being clipped, which results in too many white (or nearly white) pixels.*

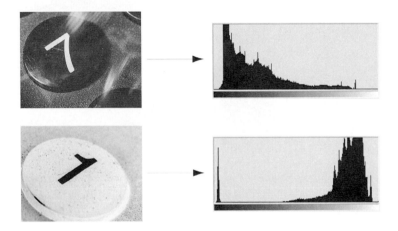

Figure 10.10 *When you scan a dark original, the tones are concentrated in the shadows (top). When the original is mostly light, the tones are concentrated in the highlights (bottom).*

- There should be no missing bars, which appear as thin gaps on the graph. This indicates that entire tones are being dropped at the time of the scan. There is no way to regain this information in Photoshop—in fact, as you further adjust the image, the gaps will only increase. If the gaps are wide enough, the image becomes posterized (see Figure 10.11). [10]

FOOTNOTE

[10] As you edit an image and reexamine the histogram, gaps will invariably appear. This is a natural byproduct of the editing process, which makes it all the more important to capture as many tones as you possibly can up front.

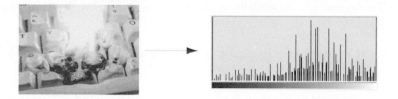

Figure 10.11 *When gaps appear in the histogram, it means that tones are already missing from the image. Future adjustments will increase the size of the gaps, which might result in posterization and lost detail. (If you're not sure whether an image has already been adjusted, this type of histogram is a good indication that someone has already had their hands on it.)*

- There should be no spikes, or random bars that extend all the way to the top of the graph. This indicates that the scanner is generating noise, or including too much of a single tone in the image.

If your scanner produces an acceptable tonal range, you're ready to move on. If gaps appear in your histogram, your scanner more than likely isn't sensitive enough for the demands of print publishing. If the histogram contains spikes, your scanner might have a dying light source or faulty CCDs (for more info, see "Mapping Your Scanner Bed," later this chapter). If you're losing highlight or shadow tones, you might be able to compensate using your scanner software.

Compensating for Lost Highlights and Shadows

Most scanning software enables you to reposition the *endpoints*, or the values of the darkest and lightest acquired pixels. This feature is often called "Brightness/Contrast" or "Shadows & Highlights." (Your software might use a series of dialog boxes similar to Photoshop's Levels and Curves commands. If so, read the image adjustment section of this chapter before manipulating these controls.) Whatever form they take, use the following approaches: [11]

FOOTNOTE

[11] This process will work only on a scanner that uses a 10- or 12-bit Grayscale option. If you try to apply prescan adjustments using an 8-bit scanner, the results are essentially the same as if you simply scan the image and adjust it in Photoshop—only with less accuracy and control. If you use an 8-bit scanner, bypass these controls and do your all of your work in Photoshop.

- If the scanner is clipping the darkest tones, try reducing the overall brightness.

- If the scanner is clipping the lightest tones, try increasing the overall brightness.

- If the scanner is clipping the lightest and darkest tones, try reducing the overall contrast.

- If the scanner is recognizing the lightest and darkest tones, but isn't adequately representing the remaining tonal range, try increasing the overall contrast.

The results produced by these effects might not look very appealing onscreen, but you'll be able to fix that in Photoshop. The entire purpose of a scanner is to acquire as many tones as possible; the entire purpose of Photoshop is to adjust them appropriately for printing.

Mapping Your Scanner Bed

As a rule, flatbed scanners don't read information uniformly across the glass. Light leaking under the cover, an aging light source, and mechanical imperfections can all introduce variances that adversely affect image quality. Before you start scanning, create a *scanner map* to pinpoint which areas are inadequate for scanning, and which will offer the best results. In essence, you're finding the scanner's "sweet spot." Follow these steps:

1. Place a large sheet of highly reflective white paper in your scanner. The resin-coated (RC) paper used by some imagesetters works best.

2. Scan the entire bed as a 72ppi RGB image. Leave the remaining scanner settings at their defaults.

3. Open the image in Photoshop. In theory, the image pixels should be entirely white. However, any imperfections in your scanner will result in light areas of tone throughout the image.

4. Exaggerate any existing tones by choosing Image: Adjust: **Equalize**. (This command completely expands the existing tonal range, turning the darkest pixel value black.) Any areas that did not scan as fully white appear as dark splotches (see Figure 10.12).

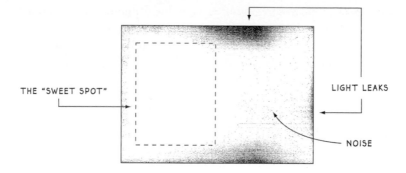

THE "SWEET SPOT" LIGHT LEAKS NOISE

Figure 10.12 *When you map your scanner bed, you can determine which areas will give you the cleanest scans off the glass. Pinpoint the noise-free spots represented by the map, and place your artwork there only when you scan. Some people even print out a copy of the map, trim away the clean parts, and tape it to their scanner as a sort of mask.*

5. As you scan in the future, avoid placing artwork on the parts of the scanner bed that resulted in blotchy areas.

Optimally, this technique should produce only a few dark pixels. If light is leaking under the cover, blotches will appear around the image edges. When your scanner's light source starts to wear out, the entire image will turn dark. If a brand-new scanner produces an image full of dark pixels, you might have a defective (or simply low-quality) unit.

Keeping It Clean

Nothing compromises the detail of your scans more than dirt, whether it's dust, fingerprints, or smudges. You should clean your scanner at least once a day. (Experienced high-volume users do it as many as 10 times a day.) Pull together a cleaning kit that includes the following items:

*   An antistatic brush

*   Glass cleaner (some scanners require nonammonia cleaners)

*   Scanner wipes

*   Photo wipes

*   Film cleaner

*   A can of compressed air

Most of these items are available at your local photographic supply store. Use the brush, glass cleaner, and scanner wipes to clean the scanner plate. The photo wipes and film cleaner will get rid of fingerprints and gunk on the face of your photographic originals. If the scanner or the originals get dusty, spray them with compressed air.

Scanning Line Art

Assuming you've tested your scanner's capability to interpret black-and-white artwork (as described earlier in this chapter), you can follow the same step-by-step process whenever you scan line art:

1. Set the scanning mode to Line Art.

2. Set the appropriate resolution.

3. Preview the scan.

4. Acquire the scan.

5. Evaluate the image.

6. Crop and clean up the image.

7. Save the file.

Let's take a closer look at the issues involved in each step.

Step 1: Set the Scanning Mode to Line Art

When you scan as Line Art, you don't scan tones. Instead, you acquire an image based entirely on all-black and all-white pixels. (Refer to Chapter 9 and "Testing Line Art Scans," earlier this chapter, for more info.) [12]

FOOTNOTE

[12] More and more people are using the Line Art scanning mode only for the most basic artwork, such as simple shapes, rudimentary lines, or images that won't necessarily be printed from a high-resolution output device. If your artwork contains any sort of fine detail, consider scanning it as a Grayscale file first, which gives you many more options to manipulate and enhance the image before converting it to 1-bit color. (For more info, see "Preparing Detailed Line Art," later this chapter.)

Figure 11.2 *The same color appears to change when placed against differently colored surroundings.*

Figure 11.3 *These three images contain a slightly different colored sky. Which one is correct? They all are. As long as a memory color is well-balanced and isn't contrary to what you expect to see, your eyes and brain accept it as natural.*

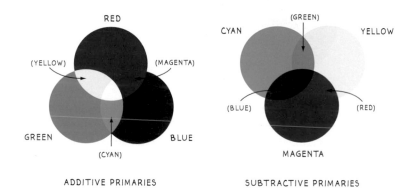

ADDITIVE PRIMARIES   SUBTRACTIVE PRIMARIES

Figure 11.4 *When you combine full values of the additive primary colors (the basis for transmitted light), the result is white. When you combine full values of the subtractive primary colors (the basis for reflected light), the result is black. Note how two primaries of one model combine to produce a primary in the other.*

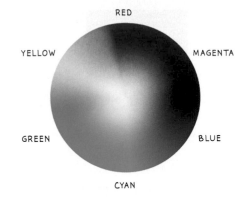

Figure 11.5 *The RGB/CMY color wheel alternates between the additive and subtractive primaries. To determine a color's complement, look for the value directly across from it.*

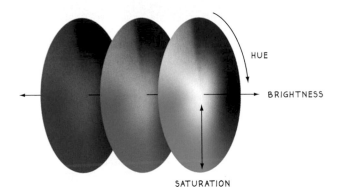

Figure 11.6 *The HSB color space is based on a cylinder.* Hue *refers to the colors of the RGB/CMY color wheel.* Saturation *determines color intensity, as measured from the center of the wheel to the edge.* Brightness *determines how light a color is, ranging from the front of the cylinder to the back.*

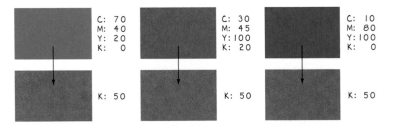

Figure 12.1 *Different colors might possess the same tonal value. These colors might appear distinct, but if you were to convert them to Grayscale mode, they'd appear as identical black values. Keep this relationship in mind as you evaluate an image's overall tonal content.*

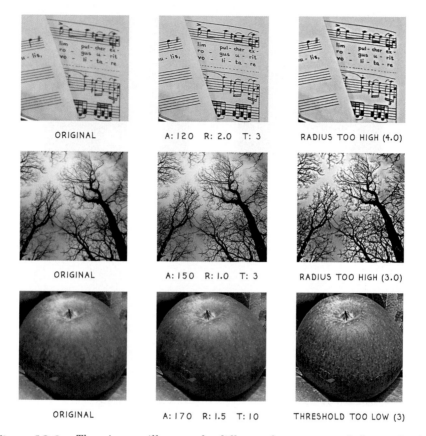

ORIGINAL	A: 120 R: 2.0 T: 3	RADIUS TOO HIGH (4.0)
ORIGINAL	A: 150 R: 1.0 T: 3	RADIUS TOO HIGH (3.0)
ORIGINAL	A: 170 R: 1.5 T: 10	THRESHOLD TOO LOW (3)

Figure 12.9 *These images illustrate the difference between normal, fine, and subtle detail. Each type has its own sharpening requirements. Normal detail (top) can tolerate a higher Radius and lower Threshold, with less possibility of artifacting or lost detail. Fine detail (center) requires a lower Radius—higher settings might obliterate the vital info. Subtle detail (bottom) requires a higher Threshold—if every pixel is sharpened, the image appears textured and unnatural.*

| ORIGINAL | GLOBALLY SHARPENED | ONLY CYAN AND BLACK CHANNELS SHARPENED |

Figure 12.10 *Globally sharpening fleshtones often results in an over-accentuated, sickly appearance. By sharpening the channels containing the least amount of fleshtone data, you emphasize important details without adding texture to the skin.*

PLUGGED SHADOWS   BLOWN HIGHLIGHTS

SUFFICIENT DETAIL

Figure 12.11 *If an image initially suffers from blown-out highlights or plugged shadows, no amount of correcting can save it. Compare these two scans: The colors of both are reasonably balanced, but only one contains the necessary highlight and shadow detail.*

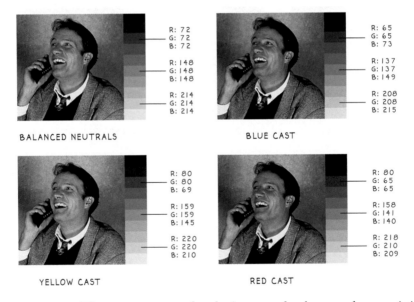

BALANCED NEUTRALS

R: 72
G: 72
B: 72

R: 148
G: 148
B: 148

R: 214
G: 214
B: 214

BLUE CAST

R: 65
G: 65
B: 73

R: 137
G: 137
B: 149

R: 208
G: 208
B: 215

YELLOW CAST

R: 80
G: 80
B: 69

R: 159
G: 159
B: 145

R: 220
G: 220
B: 210

RED CAST

R: 80
G: 65
B: 65

R: 158
G: 141
B: 140

R: 218
G: 210
B: 209

Figure 12.12 *When you assess a value that's supposed to be neutral, any existing color cast becomes immediately apparent. To better illustrate the effect of a cast, I've included a gray ramp next to each image.*

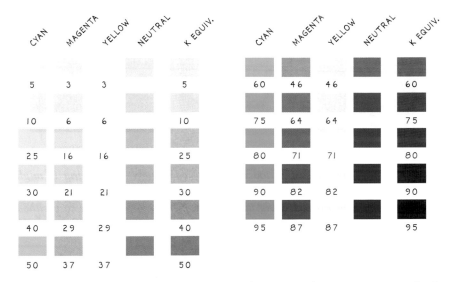

CYAN	MAGENTA	YELLOW	NEUTRAL	K EQUIV.		CYAN	MAGENTA	YELLOW	NEUTRAL	K EQUIV.
5	3	3		5		60	46	46		60
10	6	6		10		75	64	64		75
25	16	16		25		80	71	71		80
30	21	21		30		90	82	82		90
40	29	29		40		95	87	87		95
50	37	37		50						

Figure 12.13 *After colors exist as CMYK values, neutrality requires a special relationship. Due to impurities found in all process inks, each neutral gray requires more cyan than magenta and yellow. When determining the equivalent black value of a neutral, let the cyan percentage be your guide.*

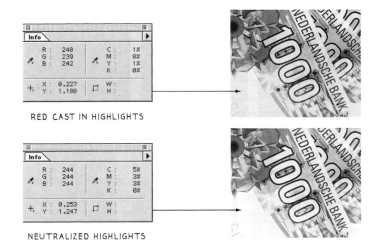

RED CAST IN HIGHLIGHTS

NEUTRALIZED HIGHLIGHTS

Figure 12.18 *Above and beyond ensuring printable shadows and highlights, neutral endpoints will correct a large part of any existing color casts. In this example, the highlights are too light for printing and contain a red bias. After I remap the endpoints, the highlights are neutralized (affecting the red cast all the way up to the midtones), and contain satisfactory dot sizes for printing.*

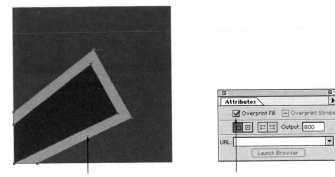

NEW SHAPE PROVIDES TRAP   FILL AUTOMATICALLY OVERPRINTS

Figure 15.24 *The Trap filters of Illustrator and FreeHand create new, overprinting shapes instead of applying strokes.*

Step 2: Set the Appropriate Resolution

Line art scans are unique. They're the only type of image that isn't *screened* during output, or converted to halftone dots. Instead, the information outputs exactly they way it appears in the image—as a series of tiny, solid black squares. Therefore, when you set the resolution of a line art scan, you must be sure the pixels are small enough to avoid detection by the human eye.

Many people hear the term "300ppi" kicked around a lot, not realizing that it pertains only to halftone and color images. If line art exists at any resolution less than 900ppi, the black pixels will become visible as a series of tiny, jagged lines. The lower the resolution, the more visible they are, and the less detail the scan will contain (see Figure 10.13). The industry standard value is 1,200ppi. Higher values than that don't really increase the image quality—they just produce larger files that take longer to process.

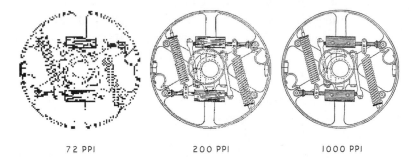

72 PPI   200 PPI   1000 PPI

Figure 10.13 *The resolution of line art scans has to be high enough so the human eye can't detect any individual pixels. If it's too low, details appear jagged and pixelated. Keep in mind that increasing the size of line art in a page layout program essentially lowers the resolution, which might produce jagged results (see Chapter 14 for more info).*

Step 3: Preview the Scan

Every scanner interface features a Preview option, enabling it to quickly capture a small image of the entire glass. After the preview appears, you can drag a marquee around the specific item you want to scan. This lets the scanner focus only on the info you need, and ignore the rest.

Many people try to crop the image as closely as they can during the preview stage, placing the marquee borders right up against the edges of the artwork. However, you have only a low-res thumbnail to work with. If the marquee overlaps any of the artwork, it won't be acquired during the scan, and you'll waste precious minutes capturing the image again. For the best results, leave an eighth- to a quarter-inch of space between the marquee edges and the artwork, and then crop it again in Photoshop. [13]

Step 4: Acquire the Scan

To acquire the image, click the Scan button. This prompts the scanner to read the information you've enclosed with a marquee, and create pixels based on the established settings. When scanning is complete, the image opens in Photoshop, awaiting further edits.

Step 5: Evaluate the Image

Before you apply any edits, check to see whether the initial scan was successful. Did you capture the entire artwork? Are the details well represented? There are two ways to check the scan's quality: Print a copy to compare to the original, and examine the pixels at a 100% view percentage.

Printing a Test Copy

Immediately after the scan opens in Photoshop, print it to your laser printer and compare it to the original artwork. Even if your output device is only 600dpi (half the resolution of the scan), it will still give you a good idea of the scan's overall quality. If the shapes appear jagged, the resolution is probably too low. If the fine details are clogged or blown out, you might need to use a different scanning technique (see "Preparing Detailed Line Art," later this chapter.) If the printout looks acceptable, you're ready to move on.

FOOTNOTE

[13] Many people fall under the impression that the scan preview is some sort of live-action surveillance video of their scanner bed. It's not—it's an actual scan, used for onscreen purposes. More often than not, your scanner software will retain the last-generated preview and marquee, even when you quit and relaunch the software. If you reposition the artwork in the scanner, replace it with another item, or pull it out to evaluate it and then put it back in, these changes are not automatically reflected in the preview. (I don't know how many times I've created a preview as part of a scanning class, removed the artwork to make a point, and then clicked "Scan" while holding the item in my hand.) Whenever you touch the artwork, create a new preview and drag a new marquee if necessary.

Examining the Pixels

Printing a scan to a lower-res output device might not properly show the results of any scanner noise or ultrafine detail. To fully examine the scan, set the view percentage to 100% (by choosing View: **Actual Pixels** or double-clicking the Zoom tool).

If you've ever used a page layout or vector-based graphics program, you're familiar with the concept of view percentage. When you set the view to 100% in those applications, a file displays at its actual size, or the dimensions at which it will print. In Photoshop, however, "100%" has a different meaning. Here, it displays the image pixels at exactly the same size as the pixels that appear on your monitor's screen.

This is an important distinction. Many people prefer to view a scan in its entirety, which invariably requires a percentage of less than 100%. At these smaller view sizes, Photoshop (and your monitor) cannot display every image pixel—an approximation is used instead. Tiny elements such as scanner noise and fine detail, which can be as small as a single pixel, are easily hidden this way (see Figure 10.14). If you don't know the information is there, you can't make accurate editing decisions. [14]

Scans might appear absurdly large at 100% (especially line art). Their resolutions are high, which means their pixels sizes are very small. To display the pixels at the same size as the monitor grid, they must be enlarged onscreen.

You'll be able to examine only a small part of the image at once. It'll be tempting to scroll around or reposition the contents of the window using the Hand tool, but this makes it too easy to miss part of the image. Instead, use this simple strategy whenever you evaluate an image:

FOOTNOTE

[14] Back when I produced my very first line art scans, I had no idea of the relationship between the image and monitor pixels. I evaluated the scans onscreen at their print size, thought they looked pretty good, and then handed the files to the client. After the project was run on-press, the client appeared at my desk and pointed to one printed scan after another. They were filled with thousands of minuscule spots, the result of dust and scanner noise. If I had inspected the image at 100%, I would have seen this information and removed it during the cleanup stage. As it was, the dirty images only told the world who had produced them—an amateur who didn't know any better.

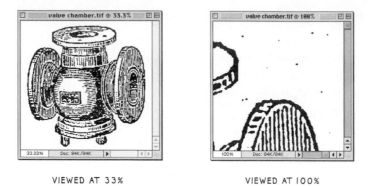

VIEWED AT 33%   VIEWED AT 100%

Figure 10.14 *When you view a line art scan at its print size, it might look as clean as can be (left). When you set the view percentage to 100%, it reveals any dirt or noise that has to be cleaned up (right).*

1. Set the View to 100%.

2. Press the Home key on your keyboard to automatically scroll to the upper-left corner of the image. Check the contents of the window for any random pixels or noise.

3. Press the Page Down key, which scrolls down the height of one window. Again, check the contents of the window.

4. When you reach the bottom of the image, click once in the scrollbar on the bottom of the window, to the right of the page icon. This scrolls the width of the image window to the right.

5. Press the Page Up key to scroll to the top of the image. When you get there, click the bottom scrollbar again, as described in the previous step.

6. Repeat steps 3–5 until you reach the bottom-right corner of the image.

When you evaluate the image this way, you're able to form a plan of attack. Is the image far too dirty? Try cleaning the glass and scanning again. Was too much detail lost? Use the technique discussed in "Preparing Detailed Line Art," later this chapter. Does the scan have adequate detail and minimal noise? Proceed to the next step.

Step 6: Crop and Clean Up the Image

Before focusing on the image pixels, take some time to crop away any extraneous image areas by using Photoshop's Crop tool. Doing so will reduce the file size, and enable you to position the image more precisely when you import into a page layout.

Cleaning up a line art scan is easy: If any stray black pixels appear in the white areas, change them to white; if any stray white pixels appear in the black areas, change them to black. The most common approach is to use the Pencil tool, which enables you to paint with black or white information using a variety of brush sizes. As you scroll through the image (following the steps described in step 5), use the following techniques: [15]

- After choosing the Pencil tool, choose Window: **Show Brushes** to access the Brushes palette. Choose a brush size appropriate for the level of detail you need. If you're removing black pixels from an expansive field of white, use a large brush. If you're working close to the actual artwork, choose a smaller brush. (Your cursor should appear as a circle that illustrates the current brush size—see the "Display & Cursors" preferences earlier in this chapter.)

- To paint with black pixels, set black as the foreground color. To paint with white pixels, set white as the foreground color. Toggle between black and white by pressing the "X" key.

- If desired, use the Pencil tool's Auto Erase function (available in the Pencil Options palette). Here, instead of toggling between black and white, the color is applied automatically: If you click on black pixels, the Pencil tool applies white; if you click on white pixels, the tool applies black.

- If you make a mistake—for example, if you accidentally erase an important part of the image—immediately press (Command-Z) [Control-Z] to reverse it. This keystroke will undo only the most recent edit. If you happen to click the screen before you apply it, you won't get the results you

---

FOOTNOTE

[15] It's easy to obsess when you start cleaning up a line art scan. When you view the image at 100%, the pixels appear huge and looming. Many people dwell on the smallest details, twiddling with the curve of a fine line just so, not realizing that the pixels are so small that many such edits have no effect on the image's printed appearance. Even if an otherwise straight line contains a few pixels clinging to the edge, remember that they're only 1/1,200 of an inch big. Focus your efforts on the obvious flaws: stray pixels, large blotches, any information that's not supposed to be included with the artwork.

want. Fortunately, Photoshop's History palette enables you to simulate the effect of multiple undo levels: Press (Option-Command-Z) [Alt-Control-Z] to cycle backward through your past edits, and (Command-Shift-Z) [Control-Shift-Z] to cycle forward again. (See Chapter 13 for more info.)

Step 7: Save the File

After you've scanned, evaluated, and cleaned up your line art, you must save it in a format that you can import and output. [16] The majority of line art files are saved as TIFFs. Not only does this format produce small file sizes, it enables you to recolor the image after you've imported it into a layout document (see Chapter 14 for more info).

As you save the image, the TIFF Options dialog box appears. Choose the Byte Order option that dovetails with the platform that will receive the image (IBM PC or Macintosh), and check the LZW Compression box, which results in a greatly reduced file size (see Figure 10.15).

Figure 10.15 *When saving a TIFF, choose the Byte Order that matches the file's target platform. Using LZW compression is usually a safe bet; it's compatible in most printing environments. However, some older RIPs or specialized printing needs might disallow this option. If so, just leave it unchecked whenever you save a TIFF.*

FOOTNOTE

[16] Although saving a file is the last logical step in the production process, you shouldn't wait until editing is complete to save. Most people save the image immediately after they scan it, in case they need to revert to the original form. Save the image every time you apply a round of edits, such as cropping or cleaning up. At the very least, if your computer freezes or the power goes out, you won't have to start from scratch.

Preparing Detailed Line Art

Many flatbed scanners do a poor-to-fair job of capturing finely detailed line art. Depending on the scanner's sensitivity and its Threshold setting, details are either filled in with black or blown out to white. After you open a 1-bit color image in Photoshop, there's nothing you can do to recapture this information. Fortunately, you can work around this limitation by scanning the line art as a Grayscale file. From there, you can use Photoshop's tools to generate line art that retains far more detail than your scanner could ever produce (see Figure 10.16).

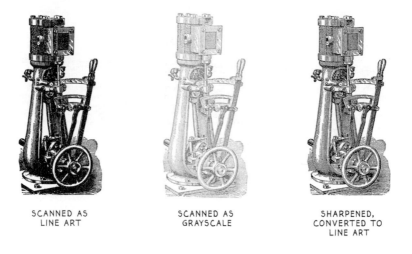

SCANNED AS
LINE ART

SCANNED AS
GRAYSCALE

SHARPENED,
CONVERTED TO
LINE ART

Figure 10.16 *The artwork on the left was scanned by using the best Line Art settings I could establish. I scanned the same image as a Grayscale file (center), applied a few settings to exaggerate the detail, and the resulting artwork shows exactly how much detail was retained (right).*

Scanning Line Art in Grayscale Mode

When you scan line art in Grayscale mode, the image exists as a series of tones, instead of absolute black and white. This will enable you to exaggerate the differences between light and dark pixels before converting to a Bitmap file—something your scanner doesn't do very well.

The thing to remember is that even though you're initially scanning in Grayscale, the image will ultimately become black-and-white line art. Therefore, you must scan at a resolution appropriate for line art: 800 to

1,200ppi. If you don't, the final resolution will be too low for accurate line art reproduction. [17]

Sharpening the Image

To accentuate the fine image details, sharpen the image by choosing Filter: Sharpen: **Unsharp Mask**. (This command is covered in depth under "Scanning and Adjusting Halftones," later this chapter.) In this instance, you don't even have to know what the controls mean. Enter an Amount of 400%, a Radius of 5, and a Threshold of 1. Apply the filter twice, using the same values (see Figure 10.17).

NOT SHARPENED BEFORE CONVERTING   SHARPENED BEFORE CONVERTING

Figure 10.17   *It's possible to generate decent 1-bit artwork if you bypass the Unsharp Mask filter and simply use the Threshold command (left). However, Unsharp Mask is a crucial step if you want to capture as much detail as possible.*

Applying the Threshold Command

The Threshold command (available under the Image: Adjust submenu) converts the tonal information of the Grayscale image to pure black and white. Rather than do a quick conversion, it enables you to move a slider that determines the breakpoint between black and white. Low values produce a lighter, more "open" image; higher values produce darker line art (see Figure 10.18).

F O O T N O T E

[17]   At first, this will result in an exceptionally large Grayscale image. For example, when a 3×5-inch Grayscale image is scanned at 300ppi (the standard for halftoning), its size is roughly 1.3MB. At 1,200ppi, the same image exceeds 20MB. The inflated size is only temporary. After you convert it to 1-bit color and save it as an LZW-compressed TIFF, the file size reduces to as low as a couple hundred kilobytes.

The best approach is to move the slider back and forth, as you preview the effects onscreen. Pinpoint the value at which fine detail is nice and open, but solid black areas aren't speckled with white pixels.

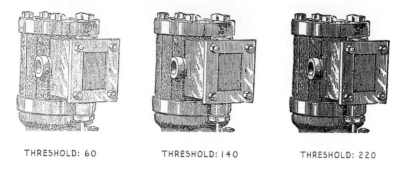

THRESHOLD: 60   THRESHOLD: 140   THRESHOLD: 220

Figure 10.18   *The Threshold command ultimately determines how light or dark the final artwork is. Here, I adjusted the same scan using three different Threshold settings, from low values (lighter) to high (darker). The value will depend on your preference as much as the original artwork.*

For the best results, be sure your view percentage is 100%, which enables you to see every image pixel. To evaluate different parts of the artwork while the Threshold dialog box is open, hold down the spacebar and click-drag the image.

Converting to Bitmap Mode

The Threshold command produces an image that *looks* exactly like a 1-bit line art file, but you're not done yet. The image still exists in Grayscale mode. If you save it at this point, it will be eight times larger than it needs to be. If you import and print it, your page layout program will attempt to screen it (just like any other Grayscale image), which results in a fuzzy dot pattern applied to the edges of the black shapes.

Convert the image to 1-bit color by choosing Image: Mode: **Bitmap**. In the Bitmap dialog box, be sure the Output resolution is the same as the Input value, and select the 50% Threshold method (see Figure 10.19).

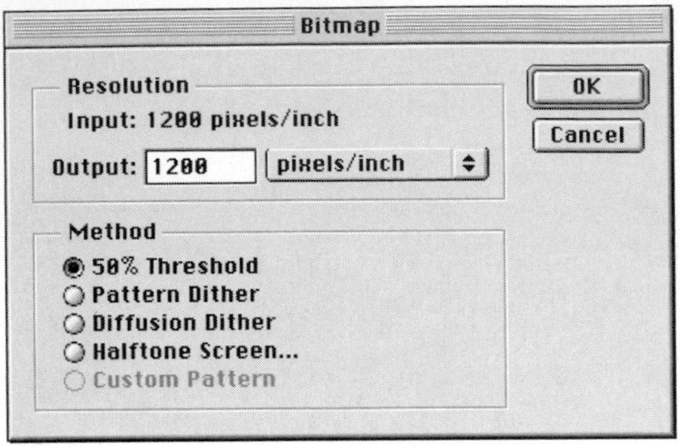

```
┌──────────────── Bitmap ════════════════┐
│  ┌─ Resolution ────────────────┐  ┌────────┐ │
│  │  Input: 1200 pixels/inch     │  │   OK   │ │
│  │                              │  └────────┘ │
│  │  Output: [1200  ]  [ pixels/inch  ◆]  ┌────────┐ │
│  │                              │  │ Cancel │ │
│  └──────────────────────────────┘  └────────┘ │
│  ┌─ Method ─────────────────────┐           │
│  │  ◉ 50% Threshold             │           │
│  │  ○ Pattern Dither            │           │
│  │  ○ Diffusion Dither          │           │
│  │  ○ Halftone Screen...        │           │
│  │  ○ Custom Pattern            │           │
│  └──────────────────────────────┘           │
└──────────────────────────────────────────────┘
```

Figure 10.19 *If you don't convert the image to Bitmap mode, it won't behave as a 1-bit line art file during output. In the Bitmap dialog box, be sure the resolution is consistent and use the 50% Threshold option.*

Cleaning Up and Saving the Image

At this point, you might still have to clean up some stray pixels before saving the image as a TIFF. For more information, refer to "Step 6: Crop and Clean Up the Image" and "Step 7: Save the File," earlier in this section.

Scanning and Adjusting Halftones

In Chapter 9, I described how an output device converts a continuous tone image to halftone dots. However, *generating* the dots is the easy part—it's done automatically by the printer. In this section, you'll learn how to optimize the tonal range of a scan, enabling those dots to reproduce an image that matches the original item as closely as possible.

In a perfect world, you could simply shoot, scan, and print. Images would require no additional adjustments to run beautifully on-press. Unfortunately, the very act of scanning and printing prevents that from happening: [18]

- Scanning flattens the tonal depth and slightly blurs the detail of any image. This is a natural byproduct of the scanning process, and the extent to which it occurs depends on the sensitivity of your input device.

- No printing press on Earth is capable of reproducing every tone between 0% and 100% black. Each press has its own limit, and you must compress the range of image tones to make them fit.

- Halftone dots will expand slightly as ink is absorbed by the paper stock (a phenomenon known as *dot gain*). Unless you account for this change during the editing stage, your image will always reproduce darker than you expect.

- If the previous issues weren't enough, every time you adjust an image to compensate for them, you reduce the number of available tones and obliterate detail. It's all too easy to overadjust a scan, which results in a thin, washed-out appearance.

The natural impulse is to adjust an image so it looks good on your monitor or laser printer. This misconception results in more editing problems than anything else. First, every monitor displays information differently, and the tones that display really have no bearing on what ultimately prints. Second, when an image is properly adjusted for press, a proof is going to look deceivingly lighter and thinner than you expect. If it looks "perfect"—especially if you've output it to RC paper or made a contact proof—the on-press result will always be too dark.

FOOTNOTE

[18] When you think about it, the entire scanning and halftoning process is a lesson in managed loss. You start with a photograph that contains a full, rich range of tones and an ultrafine grain. When you scan it, you reduce it to 256 levels of gray. As you adjust the endpoints, add contrast, compensate for dot gain, and sharpen the detail, you discard anywhere from 20–40% of the tonal range. When you output the image, the continuous tones are further reduced to a series of dots of only one color. Finally, a printing press can reproduce the appearance of only 50 or 60 tones per color—the rest is lost due to spreading ink, lightened highlights, and other imperfections of the process.

A full photographic range reduced to 60 tones. Luckily, the halftoning process can be quite forgiving, as long as you stick to the editing guidelines covered in this section.

Rather than edit on-the-fly, develop a consistent plan for scanning and adjusting your images. You can use the same approach on all scans, but the exact number of steps ultimately depends on the content of each image. A typical strategy looks like this:

1. Assess the original image and learn its purpose.

2. Preview, measure, and adjust your scan.

3. Acquire the scan.

4. Assess the scan, rescan if necessary, and save.

5. Crop and fix any glaring problems.

6. Sharpen the image.

7. Check and adjust the endpoints for press.

8. Adjust for contrast.

9. Retouch any minor flaws.

10. Compensate for dot gain.

11. Review, proof, and massage as needed.

Let's take a closer look at the issues involved in each step.

Step 1: Assess the Original Image

Get to know your original. Thoroughly appraising something before you scan it will identify potential trouble spots, prevent you from wasting your time scanning dirty artwork, and otherwise ground your future corrections in reality. For example, if the object you're scanning has no highlight information, there's no use trying to accentuate it at the time of the scan.

As you examine the original, look for the following:

- **The distribution of tones throughout the image.** Where are the highlights? Where are the shadows?

- **The overall composition of the image.** Try to estimate the values you'll read when you measure the image onscreen.

- **Potentially problematic areas.** What parts of the image will be most difficult to correct? Deep, impenetrable shadows? Thinly varying highlights? Diffuse lighting that renders the midtones flat? You might be able to compensate for these at the time of the scan.

- **The most important part of the image.** Scanning is often a trade-off; to properly focus on the subject, you might have to sacrifice the quality of less vital areas. Identify the area that requires the best results and fight to protect it.

You're also scanning the image for a specific printing method, and you must know what it is. For example, if the image will be reproduced at 150lpi, you must scan at the appropriate resolution: 225 to 300ppi (1.5 to 2 times the target linescreen). On the other hand, low linescreen requests (65 to 85lpi) indicate that you'll be dealing with other problems, such as very high dot gain and an extremely restricted tonal range. Find out this information before you scan.

As pressing as these issues are now, they're even more important when you scan color images. Get used to thinking about them.

Step 2: Preview, Measure, and Adjust

As discussed earlier in this chapter, scanning software typically offers a preview mode that displays an overview of the scanning bed. More robust interfaces also feature a Prescan function, which generates a full-size onscreen version of an image prior to the final scan. The prescan serves two purposes. First, it gives you a good, close look at the image, enabling you to make more accurate decisions about any tonal adjustments performed at the time of the scan. You can use the onscreen densitometer (a floating palette similar to Photoshop's Info palette) to double-check the pixel values, ensuring that no vital data will be lost. Second, most scanners can use the prescan to reevaluate the image data, resulting in a better scan. [19]

FOOTNOTE

[19] It's easy to confuse the prescan with the final scan. For all intents and purposes, they look the same onscreen. Most scanning software enables you to save the prescan, which results in many people simply saving this intermediary image and opening it in Photoshop for further edits. Remember that you *have* to generate a final scan—it's the only way to apply any prescan corrections, and the only way to capture the fullest range of values. Save the prescan image only when you want to compare it to future prescans.

If desired, use your scanning software's tonal editing controls to tweak and enhance the image prior to scanning. For the best results, you'll be using controls similar to Photoshop's Levels and Curves commands (covered in depth later this chapter). The closer you get to final image quality at the time of the scan, the less work you have to do in Photoshop. If you're uncomfortable with the prescan settings—as many people are when they first start out—just do your best to capture as wide a range of tones as possible, following the steps described under "Testing Grayscale Scans," earlier this chapter.

Step 3: Scan and Save

You might want to scan the same image a number of times, using a series of different settings. If your scanner software features *batch scanning* (the capability to set up and generate multiple scans at once), this is easy work. If not, it might seem like a waste of time to produce more than one scan. However, doing so enables you to make a round of quality decisions as you select the most successful image. With a little practice, you'll usually be able to produce an acceptable Grayscale scan on the first try. When you're scanning a difficult item, having a few options to choose from will prove valuable.

As soon as you create the scan, save the file. This way, you'll always be able to revert to its original form if you need to. You can also employ some History palette techniques in Photoshop to build a series of "back doors" into your scan, enabling you to undo certain effects without completely reverting. (See Chapter 13 for more info.)

Step 4: Assess the Scan

After the scan opens in Photoshop, you have to decide whether you want to keep it. A quick comparison between the original and the scan should give you the answer.

In Step 1, you identified the shadows and highlights in the original. Zoom into the image's shadow information. Without clicking, move the cursor over the darkest areas. In the Info palette, you should see the K value flash through a changing series of percentages. This indicates that tonal differences have been captured, and the necessary detail has been captured by the scanner. If the percentages don't change, you have a problem—the shadows have been averaged to a single value, and the shadows will reproduce as a solid blotch. Next, zoom into the highlight areas. Look for the same varying pixel values, and be sure no areas are blown out to 0% black. If your scan doesn't contain the necessary detail, acquire it again with a different round of settings. [20]

As you assess the image for detail and tone, keep your eyes open for any defects. If there's an excess of dust or other particulates, clean the scanner bed and/or the original and scan it again. Rescanning almost always takes less time than trying to manually repair the defects in Photoshop.

Before you move on, make a mental list of an image's potential trouble spots and where they're located. This will act as a checklist to review after you've adjusted the image for press conditions.

Step 5: Crop and Fix Any Glaring Problems

Before you apply any tonal adjustments, use Photoshop's Crop tool to trim the image down to the exact dimensions you need. Leaving any unwanted data in the image might make it harder to read and adjust the tonal range. For example, if the image includes a sliver of the scanner cover, the bright white values will give you misleading results when you target the endpoints. When you adjust an image, you want to work only with the data that matters.

If the image requires any radical changes, such as including part of another image, removing a head from a group shot, or repairing a wrinkle or tear, now's the time to do it. Also, if you're running a technique such as descreening a preprinted image, you should always do it before sharpening and tonal adjustment. Before you optimize any image for print, it must contain all the

---

FOOTNOTE

[20] The best Grayscale scans don't contain wide areas of the same value. For example, you shouldn't see large patches of 60% black in a still-life photograph. Even image areas that appear solid, such as a blue wall or white snow, should be comprised of subtly varying pixel values. There's no such thing as a truly "solid" color in nature; everything we see is affected by light, shadows, and textures. When tone patches appear in a halftone, they're usually the result of a bad scan or over-adjustment, which posterizes the image tones. Ranges of the exact same dot size are picked up by the eye, and recognized as unnatural. Minor pixel variations produce an ever-so-slight difference in halftone dot sizes, which imbues the printed image with a much more organic feel.

necessary information. For example, say you've already optimized an image of a group shot. If you add a new head later on, the addition won't contain the same balance of tones and sharpness, and the difference will be noticeable after printing.

Don't confuse the glaring problems with the standard touch-up techniques discussed under Step 9. Look at it this way: If you have to change the content of the image, do it here. If you have to remove any dust or specks, do it later.

Step 6: Sharpen the Image

The majority of scanned material has to be *sharpened*, which compensates for the slight blurring that invariably results from the scanning process. Contrary to popular belief, sharpening doesn't *add* detail to an image—instead, it exaggerates the differences between adjoining pixels, which creates the *appearance* of increased detail (see Figure 10.20).

Figure 10.20 *Most often, details are slightly blurred during the scanning process (top). The Unsharp Mask filter creates the illusion of increased detail by exaggerating the difference between light and dark pixels (bottom).*

Some scanning software can sharpen the image at the time of the scan. If you use this feature with any degree of success, there's no need to sharpen the image again. However, Photoshop's Unsharp Mask filter typically does a much better job than your scanner. Most scanner-based sharpening (as well as Photoshop's remaining Sharpen filters, which you should never use) applies only a single, even-handed value to the scan. As you'll see, Unsharp Mask gives you three independent controls, enabling you to apply a unique value to each image. [21]

There has been some confusion over where sharpening should take place in a scanning workflow. In conventional printing, sharpening is the last step in the cycle. In digital printing, that would be a mistake. The hallmark of a sharpened image is that dark pixels become darker, light pixels become lighter; this pixel-level contrast is what creates the appearance of increased detail. If you sharpen an image after you've adjusted the tones, you'll more than likely push several pixels beyond the reproducible range of the printing press.

To access the filter, choose Filter: Sharpen: **Unsharp Mask**. The dialog box contains three values: Amount, Radius, and Threshold (see Figure 10.21).

Amount (1% to 500%)

This setting determines the degree that pixels are lightened or darkened. Higher values produce more contrast; lower values produce less. The exact amount of sharpening varies from pixel to pixel, and is affected by the Radius and Threshold settings.

The amount of sharpening an image requires depends on the size and the content of the image. An image with a higher resolution might require a higher Amount than the same image at a lower resolution, because the effects of the filter are spread out over a wider range of pixels.

FOOTNOTE

[21] "Unsharp Mask" sounds like an inaccurate name, because it's actually used to *sharpen* an image. It dates back to a conventional prepress technique, in which a reverse mask of an image was laid over the original to produce a sharpened effect on a third set of films. The mask itself was slightly blurred, or "unsharp," hence the term. Photoshop's filter uses a similar approach: It duplicates the image and applies a Gaussian Blur to it. The blurred data is never visible—instead, it's used as a mask that protects and exposes certain parts of the original image. The filter compares the two images, and the differences determine the amount of sharpening applied to each pixel. The greatest amount occurs where the two images differ most. Little sharpening occurs in the most similar areas.

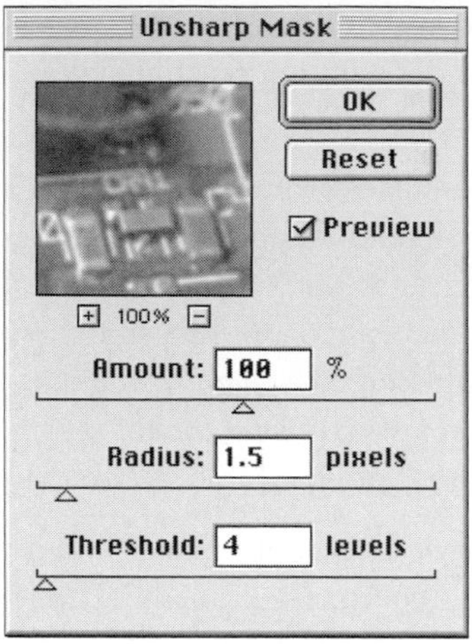

Figure 10.21 *In the Unsharp Mask dialog box, you control the intensity of the effect using three different controls. Until you become more familiar with the effects of the different values, set the Amount to 100%, the Radius to 1.5, and the Threshold to 4, then move the Amount slider to achieve the desired sharpening.*

Radius (.1 pixel to 250 pixels)

This setting determines the amount of blurring applied to the invisible mask image. Low settings result in sharper edges between contrasting colors, while pixel values that vary slightly are only minimally affected. At high settings, the entire mask image differs from the original image, and sharpening occurs more evenly throughout the image.

Threshold (0 to 255 levels)

This setting determines how much two adjacent pixels have to differ before they are sharpened. The range is measured in brightness levels. (See Chapter 9 for more info.) When two pixels fall within the Threshold range, they're not sharpened. For example, if the Threshold is set to 10 and two pixels differ by only 5 brightness level, they're ignored by the filter; if they differ by more than 10 levels, they're sharpened. A Threshold of 0 sharpens everything. A Threshold of 255 sharpens nothing, regardless of the remaining settings.

Raising the Threshold is useful to protect tones you don't want sharpened. Film grain, for example, consists of small patches of pixels that differ slightly from their adjacent neighbors. Sharpening such an image with a low

Threshold tends to turn the subtle grain into unwanted texture. Similarly, sharpening areas of subtle tonal change, such as flesh tones, can destroy the subtle changes and create artifacts or banding. An increased Threshold will protect those areas.

Unsharp Masking Strategies

The goal of sharpening is to make an image look realistic, without adding so much contrast that things look textured or unnatural. Keep the following tips in mind:

- Images that already have crisp details typically require little or no additional sharpening.

- Unsharp Mask provides a full-image preview that displays the exact effects before applying any changes. To take full advantage of this, set the view percentage to 100% before accessing the filter. Other percentages can blur the image preview and lead to oversharpening.

- Each image can conceivably require different Unsharp Mask settings. As a starting point (on a 300ppi continuous tone Grayscale image), set the Amount to 100%, the Radius to 1.5, and the Threshold to 4. Move the Amount slider up or down, as needed.

- It's difficult to anticipate how the onscreen appearance of a sharpened image will translate into printed form. Over time, you'll begin to see the relationship between the two. Until then, follow this rule of thumb: When it looks like you've sharpened the image just a *little bit too much*, it's probably just about right.

- Setting the Amount value too high results in *artifacts*, or light and dark pixels that obviously stand out from the surrounding information. Setting the Radius value too low results in *halos*, or visible rings encircling darker pixels.

- Apply this filter only once. If you don't like the results of the last setting, undo it before applying the command again. If you apply separate rounds of sharpening, you'll quickly oversharpen the image. (The effect of looking at an oversharpened image is similar to trying on someone's prescription eyeglasses; the image appears overfocused and unnatural.)

Step 7: Check and Adjust Endpoints for Press

The *endpoints* are the darkest and lightest pixel values of an image. [22] However, no printing press can successfully reproduce all the tones that Photoshop can display. When editing a Grayscale image, you work with dot sizes that range from 1% and 99% (0% and 100%, white and black, are not made of halftone dots). The average press can tolerate dot sizes between 8% and 90%. Values lower than 8% break down to white, while values higher than 90% fill in to black. For the unadjusted image, this results in poor highlight and shadow reproduction (see Figure 10.22). [23]

First, you must target the endpoints, or locate the diffuse highlight and shadow pixels, and be sure they fall within the printable range of the press. If they don't, you must compress the tonal range, or reposition the endpoints to accommodate the limitation.

FOOTNOTE

[22] In the case of the lightest endpoint, you must make a further distinction. An area with no information, which results in pure white paper, is said to be a *specular highlight*. Most often, a specular highlight is a small, intensely bright part of an image, such as a flash on chrome or a gleam in someone's eye. The lightest part of an image that actually carries detail is the *diffuse highlight*. The difference between the two is important. For the most part, a specular highlight is a unique and focused effect, and is present only when a particular scan requires it. The diffuse highlight determines the value of the lightest information in *any* image. If it falls outside the range of the press, the dot structure breaks down, resulting in irregular patches of white. Even a picture of snow doesn't appear as white paper; if you examine it closely, you'll see a fine screen of halftone dots.

[23] Each press has its own reproducible range. For example, a well-maintained press handling coated paper might tolerate 5–95%; a press used for newsprint might handle only 12–80%. If you're unsure of what the press you're going to use will handle, ask your printer. If they're unsure, ask them to run a test strip, or one black film plate that you can create in a page layout program.

In one-percent increments, create a series of half-inch squares ranging from 1% to 30% and 70% to 99%. Output this file to film on a well-calibrated imagesetter. (If you will be using a digital press, process it using the actual press.) After running the chart on-press, evaluate the printed tones with a loupe. The first values that don't break down or fill in are the endpoints for that press.

Determining the precise range of every press isn't always practical. When scanning and adjusting halftones, many professionals use the average values of 8% and 90% black until a specific project demands more exact values.

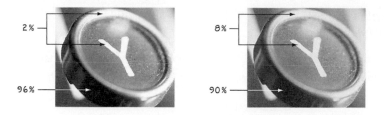

Figure 10.22 *If you don't reset the endpoints, parts of your image might blow out to white or fill in to solid black (left). When you set the endpoints appropriately, the halftone doesn't contain any black or white, which produces a much more appealing effect.*

Targeting the Endpoints

Targeting endpoints is as easy as finding the darkest and lightest pixels. If you want to, you can move the cursor all over the image, reading every pixel value in the Info palette, until you find the right ones. Here's an easier method, using the Levels dialog box:

1. Be sure Video LUT Animation is turned on under the File: Preferences: **Display & Cursors** panel. (Refer to "Setting Photoshop's Preferences," earlier this chapter.)

2. Choose Image: Adjust: **Levels** to access the Levels dialog box.

3. Uncheck the Preview box.

4. Hold down the (Option) [Alt] key and grab the white slider just beneath the histogram. The image appears to turn black.

5. Move the slider to the left. As soon as you reach the point in the histogram that represents the lightest tones, those pixels in the image appear to turn white. These are the lightest image pixels, or the current highlight endpoint (see Figure 10.23).

6. Move the white slider back to its original position.

7. Hold down the (Option) [Alt] key and grab the black slider. The image appears to turn white.

8. Move the slider to the right. As soon as you reach the point in the histogram that represents the darkest tones, those pixels in the image appear to turn black. These are the darkest image pixels, or the current shadow endpoint (see Figure 10.24).

9. Move the black slider back to its original position and click Cancel to close the dialog box.

Armed with this information, you'll know where to go to measure the endpoints using the Info palette.

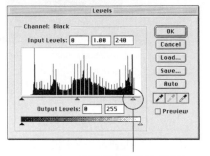

OPTION (OR ALT)-DRAG

HIGHLIGHT INFO

Figure 10.23 *When targeting the highlight endpoint, the white pixels that first appear when you (Option-drag) [Alt-drag] the white slider indicate the lightest image tones.*

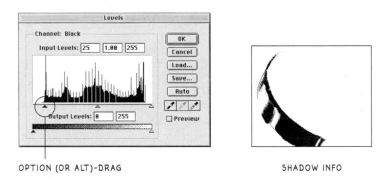

OPTION (OR ALT)-DRAG   SHADOW INFO

Figure 10.24 *When targeting the shadow endpoint, the black pixels that first appear when you (Option-drag) [Alt-drag] the black slider indicate the darkest image tones.*

Resetting the Endpoints

Before you can reset the endpoints, you must enter the reproducible range in Photoshop. For this example, assume you've already determined that the press will tolerate a range from 8% to 90%. Follow these steps:

1. Choose Image: Adjust: **Curves** to open the Curves dialog box. [24]

2. To set the shadow dot, double-click the black eyedropper button. The color picker appears.

3. Enter C:0, M:0, Y:0, K:90 in the CMYK fields, and then click OK (see Figure 10.25).

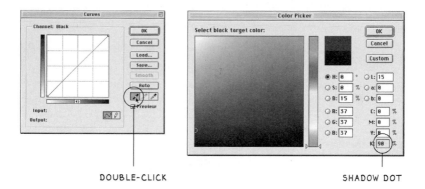

DOUBLE-CLICK   SHADOW DOT

Figure 10.25   *To set the shadow dot value, double-click the black eyedropper in the Curves dialog box, and then enter the value in the CMYK fields of the color picker.*

4. To set the highlight dot, double-click the white eyedropper button. The color picker appears again.

5. Enter C:0, M:0, Y:0, K:8 in the CMYK fields, and then click OK (see Figure 10.26).

F O O T N O T E

[24] The endpoint controls covered in this technique are also available in the Levels dialog box. However, you'll be applying the majority of your tonal edits using Curves, so it pays to become more familiar with this command. For more info on Levels-based adjustment techniques, see Chapter 13.

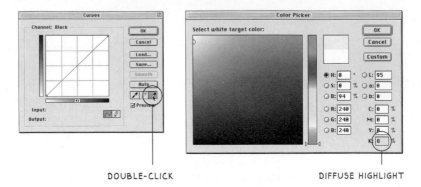

DOUBLE-CLICK   DIFFUSE HIGHLIGHT

Figure 10.26 *To set the diffuse highlight dot value, double-click the white eye-dropper in the Curves dialog box, and then enter the value in the CMYK fields of the color picker.*

After you enter these values, they remain there until you manually change them again. If your press requirements will never change, You can set this value once and leave it. If you routinely adjust images for different printing methods, you'll have to set the right values for each round of scans.

There are three ways to apply these values to the image. The first two are automatic: You can click the Auto button in the Curves dialog box, or you can close the dialog box and choose Image: Adjust: **Auto Levels**. Avoid these options. They simply hunt down the lightest and darkest pixels and arbitrarily apply the dot values. You don't have any control over which pixels are used—in particular, Photoshop doesn't know the difference between a specular and a diffuse highlight. If the image contains a small, bright flash that you want to reduce to 0% black, the Auto Levels command will set those pixels to 8%, which skews the remaining tones. For the best results, set the endpoints manually:

1. To set the shadow dot, click once on the black eyedropper in the Curves dialog box.

2. Using the Info palette as a guide, move the cursor over the image until you find the darkest value. (You've already pinpointed its location, using the technique described under "Targeting the Endpoints.")

3. Click the darkest pixel.

4. To set the highlight dot, select the white eyedropper.

5. Using the Info Palette as a guide, move the cursor over the image until you find the diffuse highlight.

6. Click the lightest pixel.

If you feel you've clicked in error, hold down the (Option) [Alt] key. The dialog box's Cancel button changes to Reset, and clicking it removes any edits you've made while the command was open.

After you reset the endpoints, an image usually appears to flatten considerably. This is natural, and you'll compensate for it by adding contrast in Step 8. Also, you might notice an occasional pixel falling outside the established limits. Unless it occurs in a wide area, it won't impact the final print quality.

Step 8: Adjust for Contrast

Two stages of the imaging process reduce the overall contrast of an image: the act of scanning, and repositioning the endpoints. To compensate for this loss of information, you must use the Curves dialog box to restore some contrast. Essentially, contrast involves making the light tones lighter and the dark tones darker.

Before we get into specifics, let's take a quick look at the controls featured in the Curves dialog box, and how you'll use them to adjust an image.

Understanding Curves

The Curves command is Photoshop's most powerful tool for *remapping* pixels, or changing their values from one percentage to another. Other commands enable you to do the same thing, but this command is by far the most comprehensive; when used properly, you can change the value of one pixel to virtually any other. In the sections that follow, I describe the most pertinent options in the Curves dialog box (see Figure 10.27).

The Channel Pop-Up

When you adjust a Grayscale image, you're actually editing the contents of the Black channel. When you use Curves to edit a color image, however, you'll be able to target individual color channels, or the entire image at once. (See Chapter 12 for more info.)

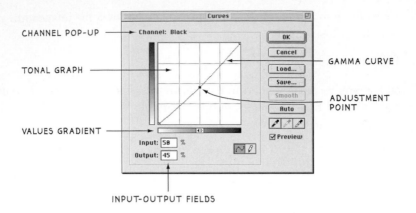

Figure 10.27 *The Curves dialog box contains Photoshop's most powerful and comprehensive color and tonal adjusting tools.*

The Values Gradient

The bar below the graph is a gray ramp that displays all the tones from black to white. By looking at this, you know which end of your curve represents shadows and which represents highlights. More importantly, it determines whether the command uses brightness values or output percentages. Photoshop defaults to brightness values, which many users prefer for reading RGB color. Most print professionals prefer reading values in terms of halftone dot sizes. If the Input/Output fields don't display black percentages when you move the cursor over the graph, click once on the values gradient.

The Tonal Graph

The tonal graph is the crux of the Curves command. Here, two forms of tonal information are plotted against each other. The horizontal axis represents *input levels*, or the values that existed before you opened the dialog box. The vertical axis represents *output levels*, or color values that will exist after you apply a curve. By default, the graph is divided into a four-by-four grid. This makes it easier to target the primary image tones: highlights, quarter tones, midtones, three-quarter tones, and shadows. If you like, you can (Option-click) [Alt-click] the graph to switch it to a 10-by-10 grid.

The Gamma Curve

The gamma curve enables you to remap the pixel values, using the tonal graph as a basis of measurement (see Figure 10.28). [25] This line represents all the possible tones from lightest to darkest, even though your image might contain a shorter range. Although the line initially appears straight, it bends into a curved shape as you make corrections, which distributes your changes more smoothly throughout the rest of the image, thus avoiding jarring results such as posterizing and unexpected tonal shifts.

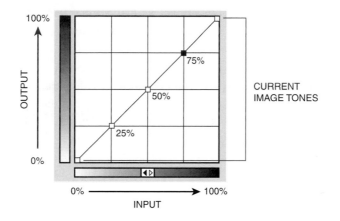

Figure 10.28 *The tonal graph enables you to gauge changes in pixel values as you manipulate the gamma curve. In this example, I've placed points at 25%, 50%, and 75%. To change the tonal distribution, drag one of these points up (to darken) or down (to lighten).*

Adjustment Point

To edit the shape of the curve, click it once to place an adjustment point. Drag the point above its original position to lighten or below to darken the

---

F O O T N O T E

[25] *Gamma* is an expression of change. In this case, it refers to the ratio between input and output values. This relationship can be expressed as a chart, such as the shape of the curve against the tonal graph, or as a number. A gamma of 1 means no change; a higher gamma produces a lighter result, and a lower gamma produces a darker result. For example, if you change a 50% black pixel to 27% black, the input/output ratio is 50/27, or 1.8. If you change the 50% black pixel to 62% black, the ratio is 50/62, or .8. The Curves command uses this math whenever you plot new values on the graph.

tones of the image. Refer to the Input/Output values at the bottom of the dialog box to track your changes.

Adjustment points have two uses. They can adjust tone and color, which happens when you drag a point from one spot to another, remapping the values. You can also use them to anchor the curve, allowing you to target one part of the tonal range. For example, if you only want to edit the highlights, click to add points at 25%, 50%, and 75%. Now, when you edit the lightest values, you don't affect the remaining tones.

You can add as many as 14 adjustment points to a single curve, in addition to the existing endpoints. Remove a point by dragging it off the graph.

The Input/Output Fields

As you manipulate the curve, the before-and-after values represented by the current point appear in these fields. The Input field displays the tonal values that existed before you applied the edit. The Output field displays the remapped values that will exist after you apply the curve. As soon as you place a point, the fields become editable. If desired, you can select a point by clicking it, and then enter a new value in the field.

The Point and Pencil Tools

The Curves command defaults to the Point tool, which enables you to click-drag points, as described previously. You can use the Pencil tool to manually draw curves on the graph. Usually, this option is casually dismissed as just another special effect. While it's true that you can create off-the-wall tonal adjustments, you can also switch to the Pencil option to make discreet edits that might be more difficult with the Point tool.

Using Gamma Curves

When you use the Curves command to adjust image tones, keep the following tips in mind:

- Beware of applying curves that are too steep. Even changes of 2–3% produce a noticeable effect. Most of your adjustments will be around 5% or less.

- Don't apply too many curves. For example, don't apply a contrast curve, decide it wasn't enough, and then apply another one. If necessary, undo the last command and start over. Each change reduces the number of available tones, and overadjusting the image eventually causes it to become washed out or posterized.

- If unsure of a particular tonal value, move the cursor onto the image. It changes to an eyedropper. When you click on the image, a small feedback circle appears, indicating the click-point's position on the curve.

- To add a point to the curve based on the image information, (Command-click) [Control-click] the image. For example, if you (Command-click) [Control-click] on a 63% black pixel, a point is automatically placed on the curve at 63%. This enables you to pinpoint the values of a specific image area.

- When you apply an adjustment and then open the dialog box again, the gamma curve appears straight again. The curve doesn't *track* the tones of an image; it's only used to *change* them. Sometimes, it's useful to know the last-applied curve, especially if it wasn't quite right and you want to fine-tune it. If you choose (Option-Command-M) [Alt-Control-M], the Curves dialog box appears displaying the most recent adjustment. (If you want to fine-tune the curve, don't forget to choose Edit: **Undo** before recalling the curve—otherwise, you'll adjust the image twice.)

The "Classic" Contrast Curve

This technique illustrates the most commonly used contrast curve. It's a straightforward adjustment, suitable for a wide range of image types (see Figure 10.29). Follow these steps:

1. Choose Image: Adjust: **Curves**. (Be sure the Input/Output values read as percentages. If not, click the values gradient.)

2. Move the cursor to the three-quarter tones portion of the gamma curve. When both Input/Output fields read 75%, click to add a point.

3. Drag this point straight up until the Output value reads 80%. The Input value should still read 75%.

4. Move the cursor to the quarter tones portion of the gamma curve. When both Input/Output fields read 25%, click to add a point.

5. Drag this point straight down until the Output value reads 20%. The Input value should still read 25%.

6. Click OK and save.

BEFORE CONTRAST   AFTER CONTRAST

CONTRAST CURVE

Figure 10.29 *When you lighten the quarter tones and darken the three-quarter tones, a simple S-shaped curve adds contrast to the entire image.*

These values are just guides—let the content of the image dictate your actual behavior. For example, one image might require a lesser adjustment in the quarter tones than the three-quarter tones; another might need a greater adjustment in the shadows. Whatever the case, you won't know until you inspect the image.

Step 9: Retouch Any Minor Flaws

Back in the "Scanning Line Art" section (earlier this chapter), I explained how to examine every pixel in the image, and then clean up any stray specks, dirt, or scratches that appeared in the scan. Grayscale images require more effort to clean up. Instead of simply painting with white or black pixels, you'll retouch each flaw by sampling and cloning with the Rubber Stamp tool. [26]

Sampling and cloning is a two-step process. When you sample, you specify the pixels that you'll use to conceal the defect. When you clone, you apply the sampled pixels. When this is done correctly, it looks as if the flaw never existed. Let's take a look at this in action:

1. Set your view percentage to 100% and choose the Rubber Stamp tool.

2. In the Brushes palette, select a brush that best accommodates the amount of data you need to sample and clone. If you're retouching a small flaw, choose a small brush. For the best results, use a brush with a thin, anti-aliased edge—the broad, soft-edged brushes produce a muddy effect.

3. Pinpoint what you want to retouch. In this example, it's a small speck.

4. To sample, hold down the (Option) [Alt] key and click the image. Don't click on the flaw, and don't click on some random spot. Instead, click near the defect, on an area that contains similar pixel values.

5. Release the (Option) [Alt] key. (If you don't, you'll just create a new sample the next time you click the image.)

6. Click directly on the defect. Two things happen: A small crosshair appears where you originally sampled from, and the defect is concealed by the source pixels (see Figure 10.30).

7. If unsatisfied with the results, choose Edit: **Undo** and try again. If everything looks good, move on to the next flaw.

F O O T N O T E

[26] Photoshop includes a "Dust & Scratches" filter, which theoretically removes any minor specks and flaws from the image. Some people apply this command to the entire image, attempting to repair it in a single pass, which is a mistake. By blurring the information between narrow areas of lighter or darker pixels, the filter will indeed remove minor flaws. Unfortunately, it affects the entire image, producing slightly fuzzy, less-detailed results. This filter is only acceptable in situations where getting the job done quickly is more important than image quality. It's not a substitute for removing dust and scratches using the Rubber Stamp tool.

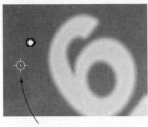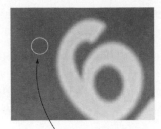

OPTION (OR ALT)-CLICK
TO SAMPLE

CLICK OVER DEFECT
TO RETOUCH

Figure 10.30 *When you sample and clone, you copy pixels from one point and apply them over an image defect. As you clone, you'll see a crosshair briefly appear over the original sample point.*

Using the Rubber Stamp Tool

When you use the Rubber Stamp tool to retouch an image, keep the following tips in mind:

- The Rubber Stamp tool is not well-suited for cloning a specific image element, such as a tree or rock. To create multiple copies of an existing element, you're much better off using one of the Selection tools to isolate the desired pixels, and copying it to a new layer. From there, it's much easier to duplicate and reposition the item. However, if your intent is to *remove* the rock or tree, the Rubber Stamp tool is the most effective option.

- Resist the temptation to *paint* with the Rubber Stamp tool, or clone pixels in sweeping brushstrokes. For example, if you're retouching a long scratch or errant hair, don't create a single sample and then drag the length of the flaw. It might seem easier, but it will more than likely produce noticeable streaking or tonal variations. For the best results, follow a zipper-style pattern, sampling pixels on either side of the scratch as you move along. Take a piece from here and a piece from there, and carefully dab them into place (see Figure 10.31).

- Don't sample too close to the defect. Depending on the size of your brush, you might include the flaw in the sampled area. When this happens, it creates the effect of the flaw jumping around onscreen as you reapply it click after click.

LENGTHY DEFECT

SAMPLING AND CLONING
FOLLOWING "ZIPPER" PATTERN

Figure 10.31 *When retouching a long scratch, don't "paint" with the Rubber Stamp tool. Instead, take samples from either side of the defect as you move down its length, following a sort of zipper pattern. This will prevent you from producing any visible artifacts, patterns, or tonal variations.*

- The Rubber Stamp Tool can read information from a separate image. To do this, open both images at once. (Option-click) [Alt-click] to define a sample area in the first image, and then click in the second to apply the pixels.

- If you're working with multiple image layers, the effect of the Rubber Stamp tool will depend on the settings in the Rubber Stamp Options palette. When the Use All Layers box is unchecked, you can only sample the pixels of the active layer. When the box is checked, you can sample pixels from all visible layers.

Step 10: Compensate for Dot Gain

After you've tweaked, adjusted, and retouched the image, only one task remains. You must lighten the overall image to compensate for the dot gain that will occur on-press. The idea is simple: Because dot gain results in a darker halftone, printing a deliberately lightened image will result in the tones falling right into place. [27]

FOOTNOTE

[27] You only have to manually adjust for dot gain when editing a Grayscale image. When you convert an RGB image to CMYK mode, Photoshop accounts for dot gain automatically.

Before you apply the adjustment, you must know how much dot gain to expect. It all depends on the printing method and the type of paper stock used. The more absorbent the paper, the higher dot gain you can expect. Because dot gain affects the midtones more than any other part of an image, you'll focus the adjustment on the 50% value.

Dot gain is measured as a percentage, which can lead to some confusion. For example, when your print shop says you can expect a 25% dot gain, it doesn't mean that your 50% dot will jump to 75%. Instead, it means that the 50% dot will expand by 25% of its original size, to roughly 62%. In the following table, I've listed four printing options, their usual dot gain values, and the extent to which you should adjust the midtones to compensate for it.

Printing Method	Dot Gain	Reduce 50% To...
Web/coated stock	15–25%	44–40%
Sheetfed/coated stock	10–15%	46–44%
Sheetfed/uncoated stock	18–25%	43–40%
Newsprint	30–45%	39–35%

There are two ways to apply the adjustment—the one you choose depends on whether you want to change the actual contents of the image.

Manually Compensating for Dot Gain

When you manually adjust the image, you're irreversibly editing the tonal range, which makes it more difficult to repurpose the same image for other printing methods. For example, assume you've already adjusted an image for newsprint. If you print the same image in the future on high-quality coated paper, the image will reproduce too lightly on-press. If necessary, save a copy of the original image, including the dot gain adjustment in the filename.

In this example, I lighten the midtones to accommodate an expected 15% dot gain:

1. Open a Grayscale image that you've already adjusted for press limitations and contrast.

2. Choose Image: Adjust: **Curves**.

3. Move the cursor to the midtones and click to add a point at 50%.

4. Drag this point straight down until the Output value reads 44% (see Figure 10.32).

NO DOT GAIN COMPENSATION

ADJUSTED FOR 20% DOT GAIN

Figure 10.32 *When you don't compensate for dot gain, the image darkens on-press, particularly in the midtones (left). By lightening the image, you can predict the effect of dot gain.*

5. Click OK and save.

The image will appear much lighter than you want it to be, especially when you proof it on a laser printer. This is supposed to happen; rest assured, it will darken on-press.

Building a Transfer Function

If you need to retain the original image values (and you don't want to produce different copies of the same image), your only option is build a *transfer curve*, or a tonal adjustment that affects the image only during output. This option does have some limitations. You have to save it as an EPS file, which are larger than TIFFs, and you won't be able to recolor the halftone in a page layout program.

In this example, I build a transfer curve to accommodate a 15% dot gain:

1. Open a Grayscale image that you've already adjusted for press limitations and contrast.

2. Select File: **Page Setup** to access Photoshop's Page Setup dialog box.

3. Click the Transfer button to access the Transfer Functions dialog box.

4. Apply your compensation curve. The graph is similar to the one that appears in the Curves command, but you can also use the editable fields to enter your own output values. For this example, I entered 44% in the

50% field—this is the same as dragging the midpoint of the curve down to 44% (see Figure 10.33).

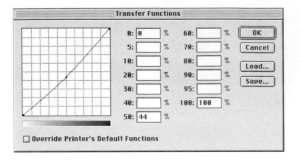

Figure 10.33   *To create the transfer curve, I entered 44% in the 50% field, telling the dialog box to reduce the 50% value to 44% black. The image itself doesn't change— instead, the adjustment is applied by the output device when you print the file.*

5.   Save the image as a Photoshop EPS file. In the EPS Options dialog box, check the Include Transfer Functions box. If you don't, the correction will not be applied during output (see Figure 10.34).

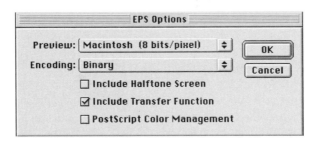

Figure 10.34   *Images with a transfer curve must be saved as EPS files. In the EPS Options dialog box, check the Transfer Functions box—otherwise, the output device will not be triggered to apply the adjustment.*

When you open the image in the future, the original tones haven't been pre-lightened for dot gain. If desired, you can change the transfer curve and resave the image as an EPS, or apply a manual compensation and save the image as a TIFF.

Step 11: Review, Massage, and Save

After you've completed your round of adjustments, sit back and review your work. Can some image areas use a little more help? How did you do on your mental correction checklist? Compare the original with the scan and critically assess your work with the printing press in the back of your mind. If you need to tweak the image any further, do it using the smallest of steps. If the image is satisfactory, move on to the next one.

Summary

When you first start grappling with the issues and techniques, acquiring line art and Grayscale images for print seems a pretty daunting task. Success depends on setting up a consistent and predictable scanning environment, and understanding the press-related issues that invariably impact your images:

- Before you even turn on your scanner, be sure Photoshop's extensive preferences are set to accommodate the scanning, adjusting, and onscreen preview process.

- Take some time to test your input device, to ensure it's sensitive enough to capture the necessary range of tones. Does it capture enough detail in your line art? If not, adjust the software's Threshold setting. If that doesn't work, you'll have to scan and adjust the artwork as a Grayscale image, then convert it to line art. Does it capture a wide enough range of gray levels for halftone reproduction? If not, try adjusting the levels or contrast controls of the scanner software. If that doesn't work, you might have to invest in a higher-quality device.

- The quality of any halftone is measured by its tone, detail, contrast, and sharpness. The scanning process, by its very nature, inhibits these qualities. It's up to you to enhance them intelligently by using Photoshop's controls.

- Always adjust an image with the target printing method in mind. Be sure the tonal range falls within the reproducible limit of the press, and bear in mind that dot gain will always darken your images.

In the end, you'll find that it's not as complex as it seems. After you absorb the issues, it will take only a few minutes to scan, evaluate, and adjust each image.

The more complicated world of high-res color is grounded in the same core issues that govern halftone reproduction. Whatever you learn during your work with Grayscale images will prepare you well for tackling the issues of a four-color environment. Keep these lessons in mind as you explore Chapter 11, "Color Spaces and Printing," and Chapter 12, "Scanning and Adjusting Color Images."

COLOR SPACES AND PRINTING

It's easy to underestimate the issues of working with full-color images. After investing in the hardware and software required to produce digital files for print, many people assume that such expensive tools will somehow handle color automatically. However, reproducing colors accurately on-press has always been the most complex and demanding task in the industry. The advent of digital technologies, for the most part, have succeeded only in making the equation more complicated.

To get a feel for working with color in a production environment, imagine the last time you parallel parked. If your work doesn't require dead-on color, you have plenty of room to maneuver, and you can slide in with relative ease. When color accuracy is important, you're trying to squeeze in between a Cadillac and a Lexus, hoping beyond hope that you don't leave a scratch (and if you're under deadline pressure, there's someone right behind you, flashing their lights and honking their horn, waiting to get past). No matter how much you spend on your car, it will never park itself. Like parallel parking, successful color editing always requires practice, a good eye, and the kind of judgment that only experience can develop.

When compared to the issues of scanning and adjusting halftones, the complexity of working in full color increases geometrically. It's not an impossible task, however, as evidenced by the enormous variety of high-quality printed images around you. [1] All you need to start is a solid footing in the issues of color and how they relate to ink-on-paper. This chapter covers the following:

- The nature of color itself, and how matters as simple as lighting and emotional response influence its appearance.

- The standard models used by Photoshop to describe different ranges of color.

- The all-important relationship between RGB and CMYK color spaces.

- The role of ICC profiles in a color-adjusting workflow.

- Establishing settings that control color separations for different press conditions.

The Variability of Color

Let's take a moment to consider color in the natural world. Put simply, color is a form of light energy transmitted in waves. The length of each wave determines its intensity, which corresponds directly to its appearance. Some can't be seen by the human eye—for example, the wavelengths of infrared light are too long to be detected, and the wavelengths of X-rays are too short. In between, you find the visual spectrum you learned about in 9th grade physics. The colors of the spectrum are continuous, but for the sake of convenience, the color spectrum is divided into a series of fundamental values: red, orange, yellow, green, blue, indigo, and violet. The dominant colors are red, green, and blue.

FOOTNOTE

[1] It's important to note that many designers and production specialists don't necessarily require an in-depth knowledge of color and the appropriate adjustment techniques. For example, if you work only with pre-corrected stock CD-ROM images, or you routinely turn your scans over to a service provider, or you mainly output files that have already been corrected and proofed, you may well get by without a full understanding of the nature of digital color. In fact, you're better off focusing your efforts on software techniques more specific to the work at hand. Ultimately, however, getting your head around this info always pays off in the end. You'll have a better understanding of your images, be able to pursue more intensive artistic directions, and, if desired, assume more responsibility for currently outsourced work. (The fact that it will increase your market value doesn't hurt, either.)

Color as a Physical Phenomenon

When people think of color, they tend to envision physical objects, like green grass, a black Honda Civic, or a blue baseball cap. What you interpret as "color" is actually the result of absorbed and reflected light waves, which stimulate sensors in your eye and trigger associations in your brain. Three physical factors influence the appearance of a given color: the light source, the surrounding information, and even your eyes.

The Influence of Light

White light is the combination of every wavelength in the visual spectrum. When that light strikes a non-luminous object (such as paper or ink), some wavelengths are absorbed by the material, some bounce off, and the subtracted waves produce the appearance of color. If the light shines through transparent material (like a slide), the light is filtered rather than absorbed, but the effect is the same. The wavelengths of visible light are changed somehow, producing the color experience.

Differences in the quality of light that strikes an object can strongly impact the resulting light waves, and therefore, your color experience. For example, assume you're viewing a single color swatch under two different light sources. Because the swatch is constant, it absorbs the same light waves from each source. However, because the original light waves were different, the reflected waves differ as well, resulting in the appearance of a different color.

This is easy to see for yourself. Next time you're at the supermarket, examine a box of Wheaties in the cereal aisle, then inspect it again when you take it home. The overhead florescents at the supermarket are quite unlike the soft 60-watt bulb in your living room; they transmit different combinations of light energy. The cereal box remains constant, but its color appears different in each location because the light source has changed. In mathematical terms, light X minus object Y produces a different waveform than light Z minus object Y (see Figure 11.1).

Measuring Light

Most people not directly involved with the creation and reproduction of color images don't give a fig about the scientific rationale behind varying light sources, nor should they; they know that some light gives them headaches, some light creates a warm mood, and so forth. The rest of us—photographers, artists, and color specialists alike—must be able to gauge the quality of light somehow, in an effort to create standardized constant.

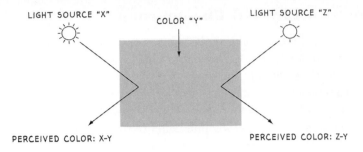

Figure 11.1 *The varying waves of different light sources directly influence the way you perceive a color. The same object always absorbs the same levels of light; your eyes can only detect what's left over.*

This is done by measuring the temperature of a light source, or its *chromaticity*. Color scientists use the Kelvin scale, which starts at absolute zero (-273°C), the point at which all molecular motion stops. The idea of pairing light and temperature may seem odd at first, but it makes a certain sense. Imagine heating up an iron rod. As the temperature increases, it glows red, then white, and then eventually blue. If you were to describe each color stage with the corresponding temperature, you begin to get the idea.

In nature, the temperature of light ranges from 1900K (that's *Kelvins*, not kilobytes) for weak candlelight to 7500K for bright daylight. For the purpose of viewing color in a production environment, 5000K has long been the industry standard. Ideally, this means that everyone involved in making color decisions should be able to evaluate materials under identical lighting conditions. When multiple environments have the same lighting, the color corrector at the service bureau and the designer at his studio can examine the same proof with fewer variables impeding their communication and understanding of the colors at hand.

So, if light is so important to color, why not proof under the same conditions that materials will be viewed? Why not proof an item destined for the supermarket under yellow florescent lights, or a magazine cover under daylight? The problem is standardization. Would the lighting standard for supermarkets take into account different light bulbs or ceiling height, or the difference between a small corner store and a mega-mart warehouse? What about when that box of Wheaties comes home? Reproducing the lighting conditions for every viewing scenario would be so monumental and counterproductive, it may as well be impossible. Instead, you'll rely on a single, universal standard, and make adjustments only as situations warrant.

The Influence of Surroundings

Even under a single light source, a color sample is also affected by its surroundings, further complicating the task of correcting colors. For example,
if a pale blue swatch sits on a dark brown table, it appears slightly different
than if you hold it against a bright green wall (see Figure 11.2). One way or
another, this discrepancy must be accounted for as you plan and execute a
project. This is one of the reasons that you proof entire pages, instead of
only the component images; their appearance is likely affected by other
design elements.

Figure 11.2   *The same color appears to change when placed against differently
colored surroundings (see color insert).*

The Influence of Your Eye

The last physical variable of the color experience cannot be overcome by
any amount of correction. The cones in your retinas, the photoreceptors of
the human eye, are more inclined to recognize reds, greens, and blues than
other, less dominant colors. As far as your brain is concerned, color is a
neural response, triggered when your cones are stimulated by light. Slight
genetic differences in these microscopic cells explain how two people looking at the same item under the same conditions can each see it differently.

Color as a Psychological Phenomenon

The human eye can detect an amazing range of light energy, but what happens to it from there is a matter of physio-psychology, and not necessarily
color science. Color represents a strong part of our emotional association
fields, a sort of resonant touchstone to which we tie ideas and subconscious
feelings. Studies have shown that a person's overall mood and perception of
events can be influenced by the colors of their surroundings.

If you ask most people their favorite color, they'll tell you it's a shade of blue. But why? The intonation applied to these colors is entirely based on individual perception. To some, blue connotes peace, wisdom, or depth; to others, it suggests depression or distance. The soft values you associate with colors not only determines how you respond to them, but tempers their appearance in your eyes and mind.

Even societal pressures influence your perception of color. Different countries have their own cultural references and color expectations. Some use different printing inks, which adds a different shape to the range of reproducible colors. Others follow different light source standards for viewing photos and proofs.

Memory Colors

Next to your sense of smell, color is the most powerful memory trigger. When you view a color you've seen many times before, you tend to accept it as a sort of proxy for the color embedded in your mind. Essentially, you "see" the color by remembering a different value. As you interact with the world, you do this automatically and instinctively. Think of the last time you stretched out in a grassy field. Do you remember the *precise* shade of green? Could you pick the *exact* blue of the sky out of a line-up? Probably not. You've seen these images thousands of times in your life. Right now, your brain is substituting something close, a reasonable estimate that satisfies your need to complete the memory (see Figure 11.3).

Figure 11.3   *These three images contain a slightly different colored sky. Which one is correct? They all are. As long as a memory color is well-balanced and isn't contrary to what you expect to see, your eyes and brain accept it as natural (see color insert).*

If you're color correcting, however, these *memory colors* pose certain difficulties. If an image of a grassy field and blue sky don't come reasonably close to what the viewer expects to see, it can destroy the illusion of photography.

If the sky doesn't look like *sky*, it influences the appearance of the remaining image colors, and the job more than likely will be rejected.

Color in the Digital Workflow

Your monitor is another variable that complicates the interpretation of color. In most monitors, a cathode ray tube beams red, green, and blue light at a sheet of glass coated with florescent phosphors. When charged electrons strike the phosphors, they vibrate and glow. The speed of the vibrations—determined by the varying wavelengths projected by the CRT—produces the different colors displayed by the unit. This sounds simple enough (your television uses the same process), but from a color accuracy standpoint, there are some inherent problems:

- Variability in the mechanics of the CRT and phosphors result in color discrepancies.

- The high color temperature of a monitor is near the blue end of the spectrum and tends to give images a bluish cast.

- The glass of most monitors is slightly curved, which produces slight viewing and color abnormalities.

- An aging (or low-quality) CRT can lead to monitor misregistration and an overall lack of sharpness.

- Monitors themselves are unstable; the same unit will produce unexpected color shifts throughout its life, and even as it warms up throughout the day.

These issues apply only to CRT-based monitors, which are used almost exclusively in the production environment. Flat LCD monitors may one day enable you to avoid some of these problems, but to date, they haven't proven effective enough for widespread acceptance. (Refer to Chapter 2, "Creating Your Work Environment," for more info.)

Understanding Color Models

Now that you have an idea of the complexity of color, it's time to address how it's handled in your images. I've already explained that Photoshop uses different file structures called *color modes* to display and output certain pixel values (refer to Chapter 9, "Digital Imaging Fundamentals," for more info). This is only part of the equation. Each mode is based on a *color model*, or a mathematically defined color space.

In an effort to compensate for our subjective perception of color info, each model renders a specific range of colors as a two- or three-dimensional space. From there, each value is defined as a position within that space—in essence, each color exists as a set of numerical coordinates. This method enables color information to be communicated between your computers, software, and peripheral devices. [2]

Color models are only used by Photoshop to generate full-color images, and this section lists the most prevalent ones you'll encounter. Images with 256 colors or fewer—including those in Bitmap, Grayscale, Duotone, and Indexed Color mode—are not based on any particular color model. (Instead, these files refer to a built-in color table that contains all the available values.)

The RGB/CMY Model

The RGB model is used to reproduce the spectrum of visible light, and it represents anything that transmits, filters, or senses light waves (such as your monitor, scanner, or eyes). It's commonly described as the *additive primary* model. The absence of all light is black; to create different colors, you must add levels of the primary colors (red, green, and blue). [3]

F O O T N O T E

[2]   Color models aren't a Photoshop creation; they've been conceived and refined throughout the centuries by physicists, such as Sir Isaac Newton; organizations, such as the *Commission Internationale d'Eclairage* (CIE) and the National Television Standards Committee (NTSC); software companies, such as Adobe; and hardware manufacturers, such as Apple. Photoshop refers to these models for two reasons. First, and most prominently, to determine which colors will display in a given color mode. Second, if you've implemented a color managed workflow, to determine the range that displays on your monitor. (For more info, see "Establishing a Viewing Standard," later this chapter.)

[3]   RGB is the most commonly used color space, and it has one strength and one weakness. On one hand, this model is extremely useful for high-res image editing. It displays a wide range of values, and images in RGB mode can take advantage of nearly all of Photoshop's commands and filters. On the other hand, RGB is *device dependent*, meaning that regardless of a color's numerical definition, the way it appears depends entirely on the hardware used to display it. Environmental factors, such as monitor age and the amount of ambient light, make displaying color consistently on multiple devices almost impossible.

You can't discuss RGB color without mentioning its opposite, the CMY model. This model represents *reflected* light, or the colors you see in printed inks, photographic dyes, and colored toner. CMY is described as the *subtractive primary* model. Here, full values of the primary colors (pure cyan, magenta, and yellow) produce black; to produce different colors, you must *reduce* the levels of the primaries (see Figure 11.4).

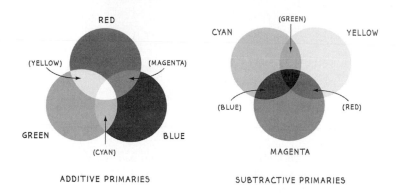

ADDITIVE PRIMARIES   SUBTRACTIVE PRIMARIES

Figure 11.4 *When you combine full values of the additive primary colors (the basis for transmitted light), the result is white. When you combine full values of the subtractive primary colors (the basis for reflected light), the result is black. Note how two primaries of one model combine to produce a primary in the other (see color insert).*

Because RGB and CMY are the inverse of each other, they share a special relationship. When you display this information as a single color wheel, the colors alternate between RGB and CMY (see Figure 11.5). If you combine two RGB colors, you produce a CMY value; if you combine two CMY colors, you produce an RGB value. For example, in the CMY model, red is described as the combination of magenta and yellow. In the RGB model, magenta is described as the combination of red and blue.

Complementary Colors

Take another look at the RGB/CMY color wheel. When two colors of one model are combined to create a color of the other, there's one left over. This is known as the new color's *complement*. For example, magenta and yellow combine to produce red; therefore, the complement of red is cyan. As you can see in the color wheel, cyan appears as the direct opposite of red.

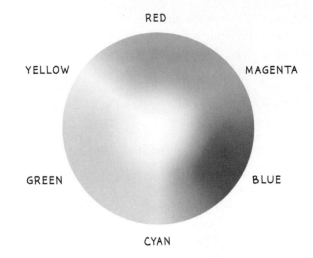

RED

YELLOW   MAGENTA

GREEN   BLUE

CYAN

Figure 11.5 *The RGB/CMY color wheel alternates between the additive and sub-tractive primaries. To determine a color's complement, look for the value directly across from it (see color insert).*

Understanding component and complementary colors is useful when work-ing with a color image. For example, assume you're scanning an item that you perceive to be too yellow. You want to reduce the amount of yellow at the time of the scan, but your scanning software doesn't contain any controls for yellow—only red, green, and blue. You have two ways to address this problem. First, according to the color wheel, yellow is a combination of red and green. Reducing these colors during scanning produces the same effect as reducing yellow. Second, the complement of yellow is blue. Increasing blue is the same as reducing yellow. Given these choices, the former is usu-ally more effective. It's easier to compensate by pulling color out, as opposed to pushing it in. Complementary colors are important to an image's tone and sharpness; if you create too steep an imbalance during scanning, you may not be able to correct it afterward.

The following table lists the component and complementary colors of the RGB/CMY primaries:

Color	Components	Complement
Red	Yellow + Magenta	Cyan
Green	Cyan + Yellow	Magenta
Blue	Magenta + Cyan	Yellow
Cyan	Blue + Green	Red
Magenta	Red + Blue	Green
Yellow	Green + Red	Blue

The CMYK Model

The very laws of physics prevent you from printing RGB colors. One way or another, when you have an RGB image destined for print, you must convert its additive color values to CMY, a purely subtractive state.

The CMYK color model represents the four colors used to reproduce full-color images: cyan, magenta, yellow, and black. In theory, CMY inks are sufficient to reproduce the full range of colors—in fact, color photography is *trichromatic*, meaning cyan, magenta, and yellow dyes are pure enough to produce a full range of color. However, this is impossible in print. CMY inks always contain slight impurities, and different types of paper stock absorb different levels of light, further affecting your perception of color. As a result, combining 100% levels of CMY inks produces more of a muddy brown color instead of black. To compensate, black ink is added to balance the range of colors. [4]

Because CMYK represents a much smaller range of color than RGB, it is impossible to reproduce all the colors that appear on your monitor. When you convert an RGB image to CMYK in order to reproduce the colors in print, many of the values will change. (For more info, see "Color Gamut," later this chapter.)

F O O T N O T E

[4] You may have noticed that black is represented by a "K" in the CMYK acronym, instead of a "B". Many people assume that this was done to avoid confusion with the blue of RGB color. Not so. When printers started using black ink as a full-color component, it was referred to as the "key" color. Black was the first ink laid down on paper, providing the basis for registering the remaining inks.

The HSB Model

This model defines color using three criteria that people recognize intuitively: hue, saturation, and brightness. (In the earliest versions of Photoshop, there was actually an HSB color mode. It no longer exists, but you can see HSB in action by temporarily setting the Apple color picker in Photoshop's File: Preferences: **General** panel.)

Hue refers to a particular color, such as purple, orange, or red. When HSB space is represented as a 3D cylinder, the visible spectrum of colors encircles its circumference, with each color assigned an angle (see Figure 11.6). Red is positioned at 0°, and the remaining colors are arranged the same as the RGB/CMY color wheel: yellow is at 60°, green at 120°, cyan at 180°, blue at 240°, and magenta at 300°.

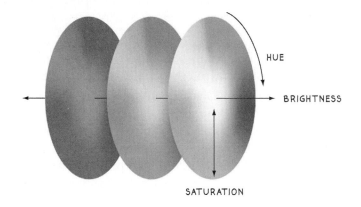

Figure 11.6 *The HSB color space is based on a cylinder.* Hue *refers to the colors of the RGB/CMY color wheel.* Saturation *determines color intensity, as measured from the center of the wheel to the edge.* Brightness *determines how light a color is, ranging from the front of the cylinder to the back (see color insert).*

Saturation refers to a color's intensity. For example, a soft pastel orange has a low saturation value; the blaze orange of a traffic cone is highly saturated. In the HSB cylinder, colors in the center have a saturation value of 0, which produces a gray tone. As a color moves closer to the outer edge, the saturation increases.

Brightness (color) refers to a color's tone, or how light or dark it appears. Lower brightness values darken a color, creating what you perceive to be a deeper tone. In the cylindrical model, brightness moves from front to back. At one end, brightness is at full value; at the other, all colors are reduced to black.

HSB is referential, as opposed to the RGB and CMYK spaces. Those color models are actually instructions that tell a monitor or printer how to construct a color. However, you can use hue, saturation, and brightness as the basis for creating adjustments in every color mode. They're available in Photoshop's color picker and the Image: Adjust: **Hue/Saturation** and **Replace Color** commands.

The Lab Model

The Lab model was developed in 1976 (and continues to be refined) by the Commission Internationale d'Eclairage, a scientific organization whose main concern is measuring color. This model is unique in that it's *device independent*. The RGB and CMYK models describe colors by component values (how they're *supposed* to appear), but cannot accommodate the variability of your hardware and environment (which determines how they *ultimately* appear). The Lab model is constructed according to how color actually exists and how it is perceived in different environments.

The basic idea is this: Although your eye is most sensitive to red, green, and blue, you cannot detect different colors until three additional neural responses register in your brain: a magenta-green relationship, a yellow-blue relationship, and a lightness (or black-white) relationship. Magenta contains no green; yellow contains no blue; white contains no black. The Lab model correctly assumes that any conceivable color can be described by quantifying its position between these complements. When a Lab specification is told to account for certain lighting conditions, it can further refine a color value based on how the human eye would respond to it.

Lab is actually an acronym for the three components of the color space. The "L" represents Lightness, or how bright a color is. The "a" represents a color's position between magenta and green. The "b" represents the position between yellow and blue.

You probably don't realize it, but Lab is one of the most commonly used models in the print industry. Whenever you convert an image from one color mode to another, Photoshop internally converts to Lab first. As you set your printing and separation preferences (as described later this chapter), Photoshop uses Lab space to determine the correlating RGB and CMYK values, and then builds a database called a *look-up table* (LUT). During conversions, Photoshop uses this table to produce the necessary colors.

Lab is a superlative model for communicating color information between machines. Most device-independent color management systems and many scanners use Lab in their reckoning of color. Kodak's YCC color space (which it developed for its PhotoCD system) is also based on Lab space. Entire books have been written about Lab by esteemed color scientists, and a small cadre of hard-core, high-end specialists swear that it's the only way to go.

Does this mean you should consider performing your color adjustments in Lab Color mode? Absolutely not. Being abstract and highly mathematical, it does a horrible job of describing color to ordinary human beings. (Try telling your printer that you need to boost an image's "a" component sometime, and see what response you get.) It's difficult to comprehend, let alone master. Your time is better spent focusing on the relationship between RGB and CMYK color; pursue Lab only if the demands of your workplace specifically require it.

Color Gamut

Every color model embodies a unique range of colors, known as the *gamut*. Of the models described in this section, Lab color has the largest gamut, encompassing all the colors of RGB space, and then some. In turn, RGB contains more colors than CMYK, the smallest gamut.

Gamut becomes an issue when you convert an image from one color space to another, particularly when you convert from Lab or RGB to CMYK. When this happens (and one way or another, it has to if you want to reproduce an image on press), Photoshop must re-describe the colors of one range with combinations of CMYK values, based on the information established in the CMYK Setup dialog box. If a color falls outside the CMYK range and cannot be described, it's pushed back to the closest borderline color.

Unfortunately, this causes two problems. First, many shades and subtle differences in tone are lost. Extreme colors, such as bright blues and vivid greens, flatten and darken considerably. Two slightly different RGB colors can even be changed to the same CMYK value. Second, you get only one chance to move between color spaces. Converting to CMYK irreversibly clips any out-of-gamut colors—you cannot regain them by switching back to the previous model.

This phenomenon poses one of the greatest challenges of color correcting. Not only must you balance the colors of an image to match the original material, you must do so in a space that contains far fewer colors than your eyes can see, a camera can recognize, and your scanner can capture. Like working with halftones, it's an illusion, a process of highly managed loss.

Establishing a Viewing Standard

When you edit color images in Photoshop, you must establish a few settings that contribute to a consistent viewing environment. At this point, it's important to understand Photoshop's current approach to color images.

Starting with version 5, Photoshop is compatible with *ICC profiles*, the hardware descriptions used by Apple ColorSync to track consistent color values from image acquisition through final output. In theory, profiles make device-independent color possible. For example, by profiling your scanner, monitor, proofing device, and press type, you can alter image colors to accommodate their unique ranges and limitations. This would enable you to work with consistent color values as you acquire, view, proof, and print an image.

This enhanced function is not intended for every Photoshop user. First of all, profiling is considered impossible in a Windows-based environment, due to the widespread lack of unified hardware standards. (In fact, industry development in this area has essentially stopped.) Profiles are ultimately used by graphics professionals in a large-scale, color-managed workflow. The best candidates are closed-loop environments, such as magazines and newspapers, which have total control over every stage of the production process, from scanning to printing. It is *not* a viable solution for individual users or smaller companies who use a variety of vendors.

If you don't have the resources to invest in such an undertaking, or if it simply doesn't fit your current methodology, don't worry about establishing an ICC-based process. However, profiles play a limited role even in an uncalibrated environment, and you're bound to encounter some of the issues described in this section if you work with old images or client files.

Using ICC Profiles

Although most devices are based on a common color space (RGB), they don't interpret the same source values alike. For example, the green filter in your scanner doesn't match the green phosphors of your monitor. This discrepancy means that the colors you scan aren't necessarily the colors you view. To make matters worse, image colors appear to change when they're imported into another application. For example, you may adjust an image perfectly in Photoshop, but when you bring it into XPress, the program only imports a low-resolution preview. This makes it difficult to proof your work accurately onscreen.

When you profile your devices, their unique ranges are compared to a standardized reference space. This enables ICC-aware programs like Photoshop and XPress to calculate the values needed to match colors from device to device, and application to application. Contrary to popular belief, this method doesn't produce flawless front-to-back color. Instead, it's meant to get you as close as possible, using a consistent standard based on the limitations of your particular tools.

There are three kinds of profiles. An *input* (or *source*) profile describes the range of a device used to capture images, such as a scanner or digital camera. A *display* profile describes the onscreen color space of a specific monitor. An *output* (or *destination*) profile describes the range of a device used to reproduce an image, such as a high-end color printer, laminate proof system, or printing press. You can also use output profiles to soft-proof, or display final colors onscreen before printing.

Profiles are not specific to Photoshop. They're separate files that reside in your system folder and require a conversion engine (like ColorSync), which applies the profile to an image like a sort of filter. To be implemented successfully, profiles must be generated by dedicated software and hardware, the only way to target the colors of your devices with any sort of objectivity. It's also the main reason that creating a color-managed workflow is expensive and time-consuming, requiring constant evaluation and maintenance. Before you even consider establishing such a workflow, complete the following tasks:

- Determine your working color space. In printing, it's a decision between CMYK and RGB. If you edit in RGB, it's wiser to choose a space other than the working range of your own monitor (like Adobe RGB). Because the values of these spaces are already known and tabulated, the same image can be successfully viewed and edited on different monitors within the same color-managed workflow. (For more info, see "Establishing the RGB Workspace," later this chapter.)

- Determine the color space used by your *legacy files*, or older images that were initially created using no particular profile. (Most often, they're Photoshop 4 images, which are based on the device-dependent RGB space of your monitor.) Photoshop enables you to convert these images to your established color space, or you can tell it to apply a specific profile. These settings are established in the dialog box that appears when you choose File: Color Settings: **Profile Setup**. (For more info, see "Handling Embedded Profiles and Legacy Files," later this chapter.)

- Determine whether you will embed profiles in your images. You'll almost always want to do this in a color-managed workflow. The only time you would not embed a profile is when actual color values are more important than the way they are visually perceived. For example, if you're producing a test image for calibration purposes, you must be able to refer to specific numerical values to characterize a device.

Creating a Consistent Viewing Environment

Before you characterize your monitor and establish Photoshop's viewing settings, take control of the factor that wreaks the most havoc on onscreen colors: your physical environment. Most full-blown color correcting departments rightfully take this concept to the extreme. They seal off all the windows in the room, turn off all overhead lighting, use 5000K bulbs for every light source, and even paint the walls a neutral gray. This approach maximizes the brightness of your monitor, protects your eyes from any aberrant stray light, and otherwise ensures that color is displayed under identical conditions at any hour of the day.

Of course, this isn't feasible for every workplace. However, you can do a few things to create a more consistent environment for viewing and evaluating onscreen colors:

- Turn your monitor away from any direct light sources, moving your desk away from the window if necessary.

- Turn off any overhead lights when performing any critical color corrections.

- Install a 5000K light box for viewing originals and proofs.

- If you work in a room with windows (or you can't routinely dim the lights), shield your light source and monitor from any ambient light. You can purchase inexpensive hoods from any graphics supply store, or even make one yourself out of black cardboard.

- Set your desktop to a neutral gray, to avoid any influencing casts. Some operating system versions include such a value in the Appearances control panel. If not, create an RGB image in Photoshop, color it R:128, G:128, B:128, and load it as a repeating pattern.

Characterizing Your Monitor

Characterizing your monitor is different than *calibrating* it. Calibration was an attempt to make all monitors adhere to a single standard; when you characterize your monitor, you create a profile that describes every aspect of its unique physical state. In turn, Photoshop uses the profile to ensure that image colors display as consistently as possible, based on your monitor's parameters. [5]

There are two ways to produce a monitor profile. First, you can use a hardware-based measuring system, which uses a suction cup to affix a spectrophotometer to your screen. This device is driven by a dedicated software package; it cycles through a predefined series of colors that the device reads and compares to the original values. The software calculates the difference between what's *supposed* to appear and what *actually* appears, and the resulting profile is used to bring the onscreen colors back to an acceptable spec. The success of this approach depends in part on your monitor. Some units, like the Radius PressView series, contain built-in support for this process, enabling the profile to gather much more accurate information. Most off-the-shelf monitors don't have this feature, so the resulting characterization is built on a slightly less specific standard.

The second way to build a profile is less accurate, but doesn't require additional hardware. The new Adobe Gamma utility walks you through a series of screens, requesting input based on your visual judgment, and writes a profile based on your decisions. (Be aware that this method is entirely dependent on your viewing environment; if your lighting conditions change over time, you'll have to run the utility again to keep the info up-to-date.)

FOOTNOTE

[5] It's important to note that you don't have to characterize or calibrate your monitor. Visually, you won't be able to rely as much on the colors that display in Photoshop, but you can still refer to the RGB and CMYK values listed in the Info palette (just as you should under any editing conditions). If this is the case—or if you're bypassing the use of profiles altogether, which many users do with a good degree of success—make sure you turn off the Display Using Monitor Compensation option in the RGB Setup dialog box.

When you first launch Photoshop 5.5, Adobe Gamma appears automatically. Otherwise, you can choose it from your Control Panels submenu. [6]

Two of the major issues characterization attempts to establish is your monitor's white point and gamma. The standard for Macintosh is a white point of D50 (which dovetails with the 5000K lighting standard) and a gamma of 1.8. Because the monitors of a PC workstation tend to display information darker than a Mac does, the accepted standard is different: Most users set the white point to D65, and the gamma to 2.2.

After you generate a profile of your monitor, it has to be loaded into your system. If you used the Adobe Gamma utility, Photoshop loads the profile automatically. If you created a profile using third-party software and hardware, follow the instructions that shipped with the product.

Establishing the RGB Workspace

In Photoshop 4, the range of available colors was equal to the displayable range of your monitor. In theory, this made sense. Assuming you entered the correct settings in the Monitor Setup dialog box, Photoshop would be aware of the exact space of your monitor and display colors appropriately. However, this method was plagued with problems:

• All monitors are slightly different, and even the same unit changes over time as it ages. If two monitors embody two different ranges of color, there's no way they can display the same image consistently.

• The RGB space of a typical monitor is still smaller than the range captured by film, a scanner, or a digital camera. When you opened such an image in Photoshop 4, its colors were compressed to fit within the monitor's smaller gamut. If you later converted the image to CMYK color, the lost values probably weren't apparent; if you intended to burn an RGB image onto a slide using a film recorder, they most certainly were.

F O O T N O T E

[6] The Adobe Gamma utility is designed to completely replace the original Gamma control panel. If you've upgraded to Photoshop 5 or 5.5, don't use the old version— delete it before characterizing your monitor with the new utility. Likewise, if you're using third-party products to create a display profile, ignore the Adobe Gamma utility completely. Running it will replace the current profile.

- Even though CMYK has a smaller gamut than RGB, most monitors cannot accurately display *every* CMYK value, particularly in vivid blue areas. If you can't see all the values, you can't take full advantage of Photoshop's editing tools.

In response, Photoshop 5 features a considerably revamped set of viewing controls. Most importantly, you can now bypass the limited range of your monitor, choosing a new RGB workspace from a set of clearly defined options. Loading a separate color space has two great advantages. First, you ensure that the available gamut is large enough to display all the values of RGB and CMYK images. Second, you can standardize your workflow by loading the same space on each workstation. [7]

With this in mind, you're ready to configure the settings in the dialog box that appears when you choose File: Color Settings: **RGB Setup** (see Figure 11.7).

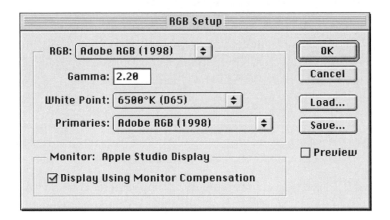

Figure 11.7   *You establish your RGB workspace in the RGB Setup dialog box.*

FOOTNOTE

[7]   Of course, even when you choose to *work* within a larger color space, your monitor still cannot *display* all the colors. Setting a new RGB workspace goes hand-in-hand with creating a monitor profile; it makes no sense to do one without the other. Think of the workspace as all the possible colors an image can contain. Think of the profile as a filter that displays those colors as accurately as possible, taking into account the quirks and limitations of your particular monitor. Remember, the goal isn't to magically create perfect color—it's to create reasonable color that displays consistently.

The RGB Pop-Up Menu

In the RGB pop-up menu, you choose the desired RGB workspace. The available options are numerical models developed by third-party color groups. The one you choose is ultimately based on the nature of your work; for most printing purposes, Adobe RGB (1998) or ColorMatch RGB are perfectly adequate. When you choose a predefined option, Photoshop automatically loads values for Gamma, White Point, and Primaries. (If you change any of those settings to match the needs of your workplace, the pop-up menu reads "Custom," indicating that the base settings have been altered.) Choose from the following options:

- **Monitor RGB.** When you choose this option, Photoshop defaults to the color space of your monitor, just like it did in version 4.

- **sRGB.** Short for "standard RGB," this option represents the color space of most PC monitors and is promoted primarily by Hewlett-Packard and Microsoft. If you're not part of a workflow using this space, there is little need for it. Its range is smaller than the color space used by earlier versions of Photoshop. Many CMYK values fall outside the sRGB gamut, making it a poor choice for print professionals. (In Photoshop 5.0 and 5.0.2, this option initially appears as the default setting—unless you need it, change it immediately.)

- **Adobe RGB (1998) ("SMPTE-240M" in version 5.0).** Adobe produced this color space to have the largest gamut possible, making it the best option for prepress and printing. It's interesting to note that its gamut includes many values that can't even display, let alone print. This means that some similar colors either will be clipped or averaged into a single value. This phenomenon is rarely noticeable in print—in fact, it allows for a little more flexibility when adjusting color.

- **Apple RGB.** This space is based on the range of a 13-inch Apple RGB monitor, the default used by Photoshop 2.0. Its range is only slightly larger than sRGB, making it less than useful.

- **SMPTE-C.** This option is the current broadcast television standard used in the United States. Use it only when producing images for video broadcast.

- **PAL/SECAM.** This option is the current broadcast television standard used in Europe. Again, use it only when producing images for video broadcast.

- **ColorMatch RGB.** This option represents the range of a Radius PressView monitor.

- **Wide Gamut RGB.** This option is based on pure primary colors (instead of the primaries used by a specific device) and therefore offers the widest available range. However, the range is so broad that most of its colors cannot be displayed or reproduced, and even minor adjustments produce unpredictable effects.

- **CIE RGB.** This option is the RGB space developed by the Commission Internationale d'Eclairage. No longer considered a print standard, it's still referenced by some workflow systems.

- **NTSC (1953).** This option is the original broadcast color space adopted by the National Television Standards Committee. No longer considered a video standard, it's still referenced by some workflow systems.

Gamma

This value is different than the gamma that describes your actual monitor. For example, if your monitor has a measured gamma of 1.8, you don't have to set the *color space* to the same value. Here, the gamma value applies an overall correction applied to your monitor's contrast. Most print-oriented RGB workspaces work best with a gamma of 2.2.

White Point

This value determines the *white point* of the established working space, or the projected value of pure white. Like Gamma, it's different than the white point of your actual monitor, and the two do not have to be identical. Most print-oriented color spaces default to 6500°K (D65).

Primaries

This option determines how Photoshop handles the primary colors generated by the electron guns inside your monitor. Because the methods used to produce red, green, and blue differ from medium to medium, setting the appropriate item duplicates the desired effect.

Monitor

This field displays the profile currently referred to by Photoshop. To change it, use the appropriate ColorSync or ICM 2.0 utility, or create a new profile of your monitor with the Adobe Gamma control panel.

Display Using Monitor Compensation

When this option is checked, Photoshop optimizes open images to display within the established color space. When you're not using profiles or a particular color space, turn this option off.

Establishing Separation Preferences

All the work you've done so far addresses only how images appear onscreen in Photoshop. You still have to determine how Photoshop converts an image into CMYK components. [8]

Converting an RGB image to CMYK seems simple enough—choose Image: Mode: **CMYK Color**, and all the image colors now exist as percentages of cyan, magenta, yellow, and black. However, how will dot gain be addressed? How much black ink will be used to reproduce shadow detail? What is the maximum limit of ink percentages? These requirements change from job to job, depending on how an image will be reproduced. The target paper stock, ink types, and type of printing press all contribute to the necessary separation settings.

The CMYK Setup dialog box that appears when you choose File: Color Settings: **CMYK Setup** contains the most intensive separation values in

---

FOOTNOTE

[8]   To be fair, Photoshop also uses the CMYK Setup dialog box to *display* CMYK images. An image may be based on cyan, magenta, yellow, and black information, but as long as you view it onscreen, Photoshop has to render the image using the RGB values of your working space. To produce the most accurate representation, it refers to the separation settings to understand the color breakdowns, and then displays the image accordingly.

The colors of your workspace may be constant, but the separation values of your image will change, depending on the factors of the current job.

Photoshop (see Figure 11.8). Understanding the issues they represent will make or break the quality of your printed images. [9]

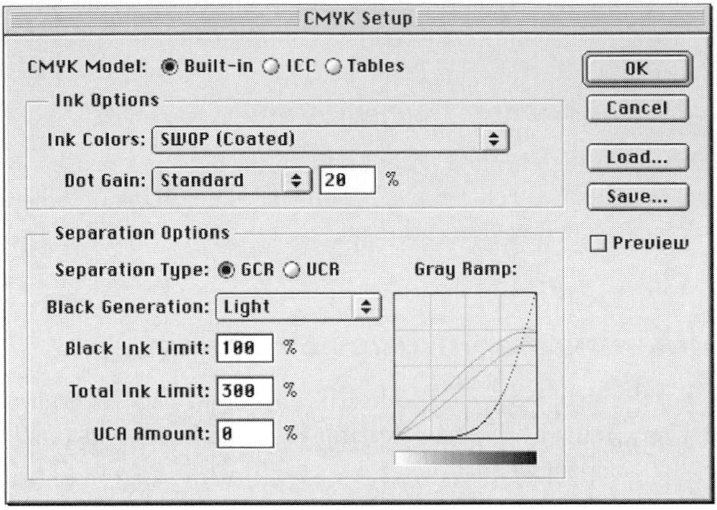

Figure 11.8 *The CMYK Setup dialog box, where you establish the settings that determine how RGB (and Lab Color) images convert to CMYK.*

CMYK Model

The CMYK Setup dialog box is much more expansive than it initially appears. There are actually three ways to establish separation settings in Photoshop: using Photoshop's built-in tools, using an ICC profile, and loading an existing separation table. The bulk of this section is dedicated to the built-in values, but the remaining options are briefly discussed in the following sections.

ICC

The ICC option enables you to load the values of an output profile. This file contains the reproducible range of a specific output device or printing press.

FOOTNOTE

9   The changes you make in the CMYK Setup dialog box are not specific to a single image. They remain in effect until you manually change them again.

When the image is separated, its colors are compressed to fit accurately within the targeted space. In theory, the same image can be tailored to reproduce optimally using a variety of methods under a variety of conditions.

In reality, this method is more complex than it sounds. Many manufacturers offer factory-made profiles for each of their color output devices. They may or may not be accurate; it will require considerable testing on your part. If not, you'll have to use dedicated hardware and software to create a custom profile. Unless you work in an environment with stringent control over your printers and presses, and have the time and money to invest in endless testing and refining, you'll likely find more success using Photoshop's traditional separation scenario.

Tables

The Tables option offers two functions. First, you can load separation settings that were established and saved from an older image. When you do, the values are automatically entered in the Built-in portion of the CMYK Setup dialog box.

You can also save the current settings of the CMYK Setup dialog box as an ICC profile. After establishing the desired values in the Built-in section, click Tables: **Save**. The resulting file can be used with any other application that uses ICC profiles. To enter the values of an existing profile, click Tables: **Load**.

Ink Colors

By choosing an ink set, you enable Photoshop to refer to an internal model of how those inks should appear. The default is *SWOP* (Specifications for Web Offset Printing), the North American standard—but it's not universal. For example, Japan uses the Toyo set, Europe uses Eurostandard. If there is any question about the type of ink used to reproduce an image on-press, consult your printer. Each standard has a setting for coated paper, uncoated paper, and newsprint. Selecting one automatically resets the Dot Gain value.

Dot Gain

Dot gain is the tendency of printed halftone dots to expand slightly as the ink is absorbed into the paper. If ignored, dot gain darkens any full-color reproduced on-press. The amount of the darkening depends on the absorbency of the paper—coated paper absorbs the least, uncoated paper absorbs a little more, and newsprint absorbs the most.

Selecting an ink standard automatically enters a value for dot gain. When a full-color image is converted to CMYK from RGB, you don't see this change—Photoshop uses this value to slightly darken the onscreen appearance of the image, so you can make editing decisions based on its interpretation of the printed colors. When the separations are output, the midtones are lightened to compensate for the on-press gain.

You can set this value independently of the Ink Colors pop-up. You can enter a new percentage, letting Photoshop distribute the change throughout the four inks, or you can write your own curves. Producing your own curves may offer the best way to tailor the compensation to a particular press, but it requires considerable testing, reading hundreds of printed swatches with a densitometer. Either way, changing the dot gain value involves considerable input from your print shop and press operators.

Separation Type: UCR

Short for *under color removal*, UCR replaces neutral grays with a black screen (literally removing color from a gray area). Equal values of cyan, magenta, and yellow produce a neutral gray; UCR replaces them with an equivalent black value. For example, a color consisting of 85% cyan, 85% magenta, and 85% yellow is replaced with 85% black. UCR typically removes unneeded ink in the shadow areas, leaving the remaining image info full of CMY values. Because it focuses only on shadow detail, images affected by UCR are usually more difficult to control on-press.

Separation Type: GCR

Short for *gray component replacement*, GCR takes UCR one step further. It replaces gray values throughout the image, exchanging any neutral grays with a black equivalent. For example, consider a color that exists as 50% cyan, 30% magenta, and 20% yellow. They all share at least a 20% percentage, which Photoshop interprets as a neutral value. When GCR is applied, the same color can appear as 30% cyan, 10% magenta, and 20% black.

This produces a more even-handed gray replacement throughout the image and greatly reduces the amount of ink required to reproduce it. However, if not handled properly, it can be quite destructive to the image quality. If you replaced every last gray value with black ink, your eye will start to detect the difference in the lightest image tones. The remaining controls compensate for this effect.

Black Generation

This setting determines the *black highlight*, or the point at which gray substitution begins. For example, if you choose Medium (the default), the starting point is 20%. This means that relative grays lighter than 20% are ignored by the GCR command, and values above 20% are substituted with black ink. The values for each option are as follows:

- **None.** Here, no black information at all is generated when you convert an image to CMYK. All colors are based on CMY combinations.

- **Light.** Black generation starts at 40%. This option is best suited for most offset printing purposes.

- **Medium.** Black generation starts at 20%. This option tends to work better for newsprint images.

- **Heavy.** Black generation starts at 10%.

- **Maximum.** Here, black is substituted for all colors, producing the highest amount of black information.

Some specialized printing processes may require a customized black generation curve. If so, choose Custom from the pop-up menu. In the Black Generation dialog box, you can manually determine the degree that black replaces the remaining CMY components. Typically, these are created for difficult-to-print high-key images (like snowy mountain tops), which tend to lack color, or low-key images (like dark cityscapes), which tend to be too rich in black. Don't treat this command lightly; it has enormous impact on the separated values of your images, and an incorrect curve will produce impossible-to-correct colors. Custom curves always require serious input from the print shop, and it may take a few on-press proofs to get it right.

Black Ink Limit

This setting determines the darkest possible value of black that Photoshop will produce. Essentially, where Black Generation defined the black highlight, Black Ink Limit describes the black shadow. Most often, the only time to reduce this value is when you reduce the Total Ink Limit. Otherwise, leave it at 100%, making any necessary changes during the color correction stage.

Total Ink Limit

Total ink refers to the combined CMYK percentages. For example, when a color is 80% cyan, 50% magenta, 20% yellow, and 10% black, the total ink value is 160; if you combine 100% values of all four colors, the total ink is 400. The Total Ink Limit determines the maximum ink density that Photoshop will produce in a CMYK image. If the limit is set too high, too much ink will be applied to the paper, and it may bleed through. If it's too low, the image will not be as rich as it could be. If this value is set below 300, consider reducing the Black Ink Limit. For example, many service bureaus set their default Total Ink Limit value to 280, which accommodates a wider range of paper stocks. In this case, the Black Ink Limit should be reduced to 90%.

UCA Amount

Short for *under color addition*, UCA compensates for the rather severe effects of GCR by replacing some of the black removed from neutral shadow areas. Even at the highest value, it only affects values darker than 50%, so you still receive the benefit of reduced ink coverage. Typically, UCA values from 5–15% are sufficient.

Typical CMYK Conversion Setups

Your print shop should be able to assist you with any uncertainty concerning your separation settings. The following list of typical printing types is a strong starting point:

Coated Stock

Ink Colors	SWOP (Coated)
Dot Gain	15–25%
Separation Type	GCR
Black Generation	Light
Black Limit	90–100%
Total Ink	290–340% (less for web press, more for sheetfed)
UCA	0–10% (typically 0%)

Uncoated Stock

Ink Colors	SWOP (Uncoated)
Dot Gain	18–25%
Separation Type	GCR
Black Generation	Light
Black Limit	90–100%
Total Ink	270–300% (less for web press, more for sheetfed)
UCA	0–10% (typically 0%)

Newsprint (GCR)

Ink Colors	SWOP (Newsprint)
Dot Gain	30–40%
Separation Type	GCR
Black Generation	Medium
Black Limit	90–100%
Total Ink	250–280% (less for web press, more for sheetfed)
UCA	0–10% (typically 0%)

Newsprint (UCR)

Ink Colors	SWOP (Newsprint)
Dot Gain	30–40%
Separation Type	UCR
Black Generation	N/A
Black Limit	70–80%
Total Ink	250–280% (less for web press, more for sheetfed)
UCA	N/A

Non-Standard Printing Inks

Some projects require printing with a non-standard ink, or an ink that replaces cyan, magenta, yellow, or black. I once worked with a newspaper's production department who had replaced their magenta with a bright red spot ink. This produced a crisp, snappier red when they used it for boxes, headlines, and rules, but caused all sorts of problems when they tried to use it to reproduce a CMYK image. Because it made economical sense for them to continue using the red ink, the best they could do was make Photoshop aware of the ink's properties by resetting its brightness values in the Ink Colors dialog box. Follow these steps:

1. Print some test bars of the ink in question.

2. Measure the bars with a colorimeter.

3. In the CMYK Setup dialog box, choose Custom from the Ink Colors pop-up. The Ink Colors dialog box appears (see Figure 11.9).

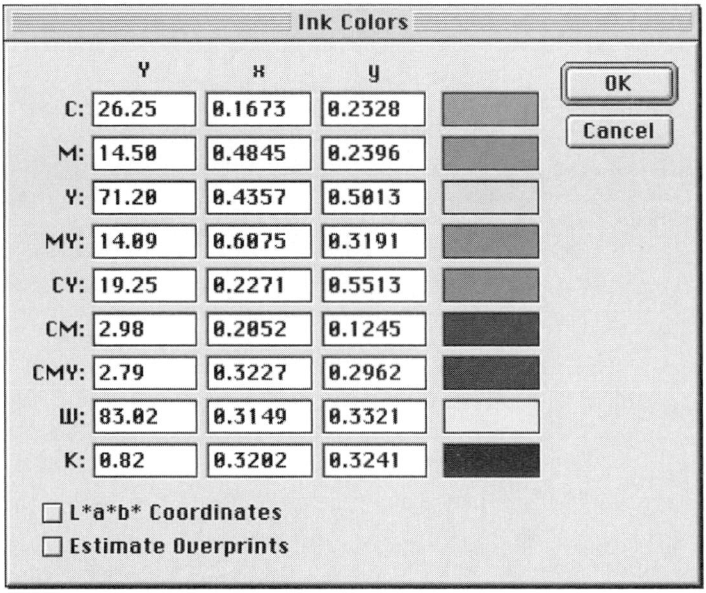

	Y	x	y		
Ink Colors					OK
					Cancel
C:	26.25	0.1673	0.2328		
M:	14.50	0.4845	0.2396		
Y:	71.20	0.4357	0.5013		
MY:	14.09	0.6075	0.3191		
CY:	19.25	0.2271	0.5513		
CM:	2.98	0.2052	0.1245		
CMY:	2.79	0.3227	0.2962		
W:	83.02	0.3149	0.3321		
K:	0.82	0.3202	0.3241		

☐ L*a*b* Coordinates
☐ Estimate Overprints

Figure 11.9 *The Ink Colors dialog box awaits the measured Yxy values for your non-standard ink.*

4. In the fields for the ink that's being replaced, enter the Yxy values (which you received from the colorimeter) for the new ink.

If the replacement ink is from the PANTONE system, you can avoid using the colorimeter. Follow these steps:

1. Open the color picker in Photoshop.

2. Click the Custom button and enter the desired PANTONE catalog number.

3. After finding the color, click the Picker button to return to the standard color picker.

4. Write down the values that appear in the three Lab fields.

5. In the CMYK Setup dialog box, choose Custom from the Ink Colors pop-up.

6. At the bottom of the Ink Colors dialog box, check the L*a*b* Coordinates box (see Figure 11.10).

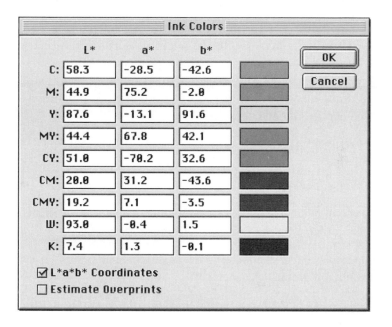

Figure 11.10 *If you're replacing one of your process components with a PANTONE spot ink, you don't need a colorimeter. Instead, enter the Lab values in the Ink Colors dialog box.*

7. In the fields for the ink that's being replaced, enter the Lab values for the PANTONE ink.

8. After returning to the CMYK Setup dialog box, save the setting to avoid repeating these steps in the future.

Handling Embedded Profiles and Legacy Files

ICC profiles can cause as many problems as they purportedly resolve. One of the most common issues is embedded profiles. First, you must determine whether your images will contain built-in profile information. Second, if you receive an image with an embedded profile (or if you provide such an image to another user), you must determine how that information will be handled. Finally, when you open any old images that were created in Photoshop 4 (which didn't use profiles), you must determine whether you will convert the image to adhere to your current profile.

This is important, because profiles were never intended to be swapped around with wanton abandon. If you mistakenly convert an image tagged with one profile to another, you literally change its color content, which results in unexpected on-press color shifts. Fortunately, Photoshop includes a series of roadblocks that alert you when a potential conflict arises. From there, you can make any necessary changes.

The Profile Setup dialog box handles most of these issues by controlling three things:

- Whether or not you embed a display profile into an image.

- Photoshop's course of action whenever you open an image that contains a display profile different from your current working space.

- Photoshop's course of action whenever you open an older image that does not contain a profile.

If you work in a closed-loop environment and don't use profiles at all, you don't have to worry about these settings. Uncheck all the Embed Profiles boxes, set the Assumed Profiles pop-up menus to None, and set the Profile Mismatch Handling pop-up menus to Ignore. This way, you don't include any profile information in the images you save, and any images you open adhere to the settings in your RGB Setup dialog box.

However, if you're working with a device profile or routinely accept images that contain embedded profile information, you'll have to pay closer attention to the options in the Profile Setup dialog box (see Figure 11.11).

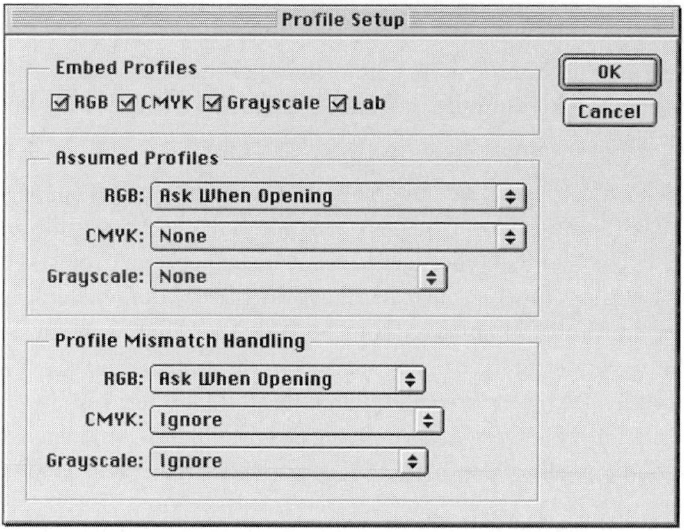

Figure 11.11   *The Profile Setup dialog box, where you determine how Photoshop handles images with different settings than your RGB Setup dialog box.*

Embed Profiles

These boxes enable you to build a profile into any color image that you save. Only images that contain color channels can contain a profile (images in Bitmap, Duotone, Indexed Color, and Multichannel mode are excluded from this feature).

By default, Photoshop enables all four of the options. This means that when you save an RGB image, the settings in the RGB Setup dialog box are included in the file. When you save a CMYK image, the settings in the CMYK Setup dialog box are included. When you save a Grayscale image, the settings in the Grayscale Setup dialog box are included. When you save a Lab Color image, Photoshop includes its internal D50 Lab profile.

Most users choose to leave these options enabled, which is the safest bet. If a client or vendor requests that you send an image without an embedded profile, re-open the image in Photoshop, uncheck the box that dovetails with the image's color mode, and resave. Also, if you're saving any images to be used for calibration or characterization purposes (like test strips and color bars), make sure you save them without a profile.

Assumed Profiles

These options determine how Photoshop handles an image that doesn't include an embedded profile. For most purposes, the following settings are sufficient:

- **RGB.** In this pop-up menu, choose the same RGB workspace you set in the RGB Setup dialog box. This ensures that the legacy file opens in a space consistent with your more recent images. Some people set this item to Ask When Opening, instead. This way, instead of converting to a new space, the Profile Mismatch dialog box appears when you open the image, enabling you to set the desired space. For example, if you're opening RGB legacy files that were created on a calibrated monitor, you'll want to keep the original profile. Instead of setting the profile here, you can set it in the Profile Mismatch dialog box.

- **CMYK.** If you've gone through the work of correcting the colors of a CMYK image, you don't want to convert them to a different color space. Therefore, set this pop-up menu to None.

- **Grayscale.** Like the CMYK option, this pop-up menu is most often set to None, because the majority of Grayscale images are destined (and therefore adjusted) for print.

Profile Mismatch Handling

These options determine how Photoshop responds when you open an image that contains profile info different than your RGB Setup and CMYK Setup dialog boxes. Unlike the Assumed Profile pop-up menus, which are largely advisory, these settings can actually convert the color content of an image. If they're set up improperly, you can destroy the balanced colors of an image by simply opening it. For most purposes, the following settings are sufficient:

- **RGB.** When you open an image with a conflicting profile, you'll *probably* want to convert it to your current RGB workspace (by choosing Convert to RGB), but you can't assume you'll want to do it every time. Instead, set Ask When Opening in this pop-up menu.

- **CMYK.** Set this pop-up menu to Ignore, to maintain the existing separation values of the image.

- **Grayscale.** Like the CMYK option, set this pop-up menu to Ignore to maintain the tones of a Grayscale image.

Missing and Mismatched Profiles

The settings I've recommended for the Profile Setup dialog box do not automatically apply any profile conversions. When you open legacy files or client-provided images, you're bound to encounter the Missing Profile dialog box or the Profile Mismatch dialog box (see Figure 11.12).

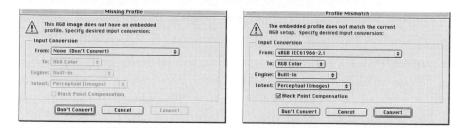

Figure 11.12 *When you open a legacy file with no embedded profile, the Missing Profile dialog box appears (left). When you open an image that contains a different profile than your current RGB workspace, the Profile Mismatch dialog box appears. Both options enable you either to assign your current profile or to bypass the conversion process altogether.*

When either dialog box appears depends on the profile content of the opened image. However, they both do the same thing: They enable you either to assign a new profile to the image or to bypass conversion altogether.

If you're opening a CMYK or Grayscale image, you'll almost always want to click the Don't Convert button. This preserves the color and tonal content of the image, as opposed to re-assigning the values to adhere to a new color space. (The only time you should do otherwise is if you want to convert a CMYK or Grayscale image to RGB, which has little use in a print environment.)

If you're opening an RGB image, you'll probably want to apply the current settings in the RGB Setup dialog box. Assuming you've set a color space with a wide gamut (like Adobe RGB), this results in minimal color shifts. In both dialog boxes, use the following settings:

- **From.** If the image contains an embedded profile, it appears in this pop-up automatically. If it doesn't contain a profile, this pop-up defaults to None (Don't Convert).

- **To.** Set this pop-up menu to RGB Color. This way, the RGB image is opened into the RGB workspace currently set in the RGB Setup dialog box.

- **Engine.** This option refers to the rendering engine that will perform the profile conversion. It defaults to Built-in, Photoshop's internal engine, which is the recommended choice.

- **Intent.** This pop-up menu contains different conversion methods. Because you'll be working primarily with scanned images, set it to Perceptual (Images). Here, when you convert to the target color space, the relative color values of the original image are maintained. The overall color may change, but the visual relationship between them is preserved.

- **Black Point Compensation.** This option determines how the darkest image information will be handled during conversion. In almost every instance, you'll want to leave it checked. This way, the darkest neutral color of the original color space is mapped to the darkest neutral color of the new color space. Otherwise, the darkest neutral color is simply mapped to black, which may push the overall colors out of balance.

Summary

If you haven't guessed by now, working with full-color images is no easy task. Throughout the years, a number of manufacturers have come and gone, making promises of "one-click color" as if there were only a few minor variables to master. These dreams have never been realized, and it's unlikely that they ever will.

The most important thing to understand is that color consists of an incredible range of variables. Humans perceive it differently. Scanners read it differently. Monitors display it differently. Printers output it differently. Even the same project reproduces differently from press to press.

Instead of solving the color issue, you have to roll with it, resolving whatever variables you can and learning to work around the ones you can't. Establishing a flexible and consistent editing environment, as you've read about in this chapter, is half the battle. The rest comes with experience, using the techniques covered in Chapter 12, "Scanning and Adjusting Color Images."

SCANNING AND ADJUSTING COLOR IMAGES

Whenever I think of all the variables involved in evaluating and adjusting color, I'm reminded of my colleague Steve.

A few years ago, he hit a roadblock while color correcting a particularly tricky image. He'd fought with the scan late into the evening, trying in vain make the colors match the original slide. But the yellows were still too saturated; the greens were too blue. Every adjustment he made, it seemed, pushed another part of the image out of balance. Finally, he resigned himself to calling the client with the bad news that the work was behind deadline.

The client was understandably upset, but agreed to visit the shop in the morning. In the meantime, Steve fussed with the image, pouring more non-billable time into a file he still couldn't correct to his satisfaction. When the client finally arrived, Steve was apologetic, but he knew he had achieved the best color that technology would allow. To set the stage for his tale of woe, he opened the original scan to show how far he had come, all things considered. Before he could continue, the client cut him off. "That looks great!" he exclaimed. "Do you have a proof?" The original, uncorrected proof was pulled from the bottom of a pile. And the client loved it. And that was that. Steve never even had a chance to open the image he'd labored so fruitlessly to correct.

No one was really at fault here. Steve did more than what was expected of a color corrector, and the client—although you may question his judgement—walked away satisfied. Nonetheless, it illustrates two of the more frustrating issues you'll encounter when working in full color. First, it's never an automated process. Each image is subject to the same core issues, but the initial color content is always different. To achieve optimal color values, every image will require a unique series of techniques and adjustments. Second, there's no guarantee that the color you produce will be accepted or even understood by the client. You'll always play two roles: above and beyond color correcting, you must also act as a sort of mediator, creating a bridge between what a client wants, what he expects, and what's realistically possible.

Space prohibits a detailed discussion of every variable and technique involved in adjusting color. However, understanding the component issues, required tools, and fundamental approaches creates the right foundation for future experience. This chapter covers the following:

- The need to establish the client's expectation of color quality before you start the work

- Photoshop's most powerful color-correcting tools, and where they're most appropriately applied

- The concept of neutral grays, and how to use them as a benchmark for most of your color correcting

- How to address critical colors by reading their component values

As you'll see, understanding color issues and being able to communicate them are equally important to anyone who assumes the role of color corrector.

Establishing Color Expectations

Not only must you understand the how-to of color editing, you have to cope with the realities of a product that two people are unlikely to see the same way. Communicating and defining client expectations is important in any industry, but nowhere are the variables more subjective than digital color. The level of acceptable quality differs from client to client, and project to project. Some people are satisfied if the colors are simply bright in the right places, while others will request proof after proof before they consider signing off on the job. And even then, they might reject it.

Determine the level of color accuracy the client requires before accepting a job. If the work is color-critical (requiring the highest level of accuracy), you'll usually find out right at the start. If that's not the case, feel out the client by examining pieces they've produced in the past, and gauging how satisfied they were with the results. Benchmarking a client's color needs serves two purposes: If it's not critical, you'll avoid wasting your time achieving an unnecessary level of quality; if it is critical, you'll avoid unpleasant confrontations and rounds of additional proofing down the road. (Refer to Chapter 7, "Project Planning," for more info on color requirements.)

The process of establishing client expectations ultimately involves a color specialist, but it often starts with a sales representative. How well your sales staff can communicate the complexities of color will make or break the success of the project. Consider this example. An artist once brought several paintings to a local service bureau, wanting a series of film separations. She was a potentially big client; if she liked the proofs, she would turn over all the color work for a nationally distributed book. The account exec, eager to make the sale, assured her that the artwork would be reproduced to her satisfaction. Four rounds of scanning, correcting, proofing, and rescanning later, she still wasn't satisfied. No one had discussed limitations and expectations with her, and being an artist, she was extremely sensitive to the smallest color variations. It was also her first experience with digital imaging, and she wasn't prepared for the stark realities of the process. She finally left the service bureau believing she'd wasted her time. No sale.

To be fair, the proofs were quite accurate. However, the paintings featured some vivid colors that simply could not be reproduced with CMYK inks. Clearly, the sales rep—with the assistance of a specialist, if necessary—should have taken the time to address her expectations, explain the imaging process, and properly frame the issues of scanning and correction. It would have saved untold hours, dollars, and raw materials—not to mention the resulting bad feelings, frustration, and negative word of mouth.

This is not to suggest that some clients will accept inferior work. Instead, meeting their expectations is the key to keeping them happy, which in turn keeps them on your client list. If someone's needs are basic, they might appreciate the extra work that goes into producing dead-on color—but not if they're billed for the extra time. It also ensures that you remain profitable. Images that go through three or four unbillable rounds of correction, when they only need one, quickly drain your resources.

The world of color is full of fuzzy boundaries; whatever you can do to firm them up will only help in the end. Provide samples of every stage of the correction process—many clients find changes in form and media somewhat confusing. For example, it's not uncommon for a proofing system to oversell an image. Many color proofs look crisp and unnaturally vivid, and the client may expect them to perfectly match the on-press results. The printed job might look shabby in comparison, especially if it was run on cheap or uncoated stock. Unless the client knows what to expect, he might blame your films instead of the printing method. If possible, show printed samples that roughly equal the intended project.

Any Client Input Is Good Client Input

Some clients will be more knowledgeable than others, and that will help the process considerably. If a designer has spent the last few years seeing projects through to print, he'll have a reasonably clear understanding of what he needs and what's required to achieve it. Others may not have that background. Maybe they're new to the industry, or they've worked exclusively in one or two colors, or they've only recently assumed the responsibilities of project management. Maybe the art director suddenly quit, and the network manager is filling in as a last-minute replacement. Whatever the situation, if you feel a person doesn't have enough experience to make color decisions, don't brush them aside, assuming you know best. Their images are being scanned for a purpose—even if they don't know the ins and outs of color science, they do have an idea of what they want.

Imaging is often a give-and-take process; you might have to sacrifice one part of the image to better emphasize another. Any input you receive about the subject of an image will inform decisions that affect the initial scan as much as the final round of correction. Even simple, ambiguous instructions like "the sweater needs to be really blue" or "this thing needs to be darker" provide a necessary starting point. The goal of color correcting is usually to match the original item, but that's not always the case. Unless you know that you need to correct a defect, or boost the colors of an underdeveloped original, or remove some of the red from an oversaturated sunset, you're basing your edits on guesswork alone.

Scanning and Adjusting Checklist

Working on color without a plan is like cutting hair with electric clippers and no comb. You focus on one section, and another looks off-balance; you try to fix another section, and the first part looks wrong. Pretty soon you have nothing left but a bad haircut that no amount of trimming can repair.

It's important to base your scanning and color correcting on a consistent, step-by-step workflow. Build a checklist and stick with it. Every time you make an edit in Photoshop, tones and colors are clipped from the image. If you don't follow consistent guidelines, you'll soon find yourself with too much hair on the floor and no way to put it back. If you follow a steady procedure, you'll enjoy speedier turnarounds and fewer mistakes, and if necessary, your checklist will be able to evolve as your experience increases.

The following list is a typical approach for color scanning and correction. You might find that it varies, depending on your particular workflow and personal style. Except where noted, feel free to make alterations. The important thing is to attend to the image in a systematic fashion that makes the most intuitive sense to you and the needs of your production environment:

1. **Evaluate the original material and determine its purpose.** How will it be printed? What's the target linescreen and paper stock? Are the colors critical, or do they just need to be balanced and appealing? This usually requires meeting with the client or art director of a project.

2. **Preview, measure, and adjust the image using your scanner's software.** These options ultimately depend on the make and quality of your scanner and its software.

3. **Acquire the image.** After you scan the image, open it in Photoshop (if your scanning software doesn't do it automatically).

4. **Evaluate the scan.** Make sure the range of colors and tones were captured adequately by the scanner, by examining the Histogram or Levels dialog boxes. If not, scan again. If so, save the image.

5. **Prepare the RGB to CMYK separation settings.** These options are found in the File: Color Settings: **CMYK Setup** dialog box (refer to Chapter 11, "Color Spaces and Printing," for more info).

6. **Repair any obvious image defects.** These are the big ones, like a tear in the original material, an element that must be removed, or any image compositing.

7. **Sharpen the image.** Always use the Unsharp Mask filter. (For more info, refer to Chapter 10, "Scanning Line Art and Halftones.")

8. **Retouch the smaller image flaws.** Use the Rubber Stamp tool to remove scratches, dirt, and other small imperfections. (For more info, refer to Chapter 10.)

9. **Evaluate and adjust the endpoints for press.** This prevents the highlight areas from burning out and the shadows from filling in during

printing. It will also enable you to ensure the endpoints are neutral, removing the possibility of a color cast. (For more info, refer to Chapter 10.)

10. **Adjust the tones.** This refers to the image's overall lightness, darkness, and contrast. (For more info, refer to Chapter 10.)

11. **Adjust the overall color content of the image.** Here, you tweak the image colors to either match the original material as closely as possible, or emphasize a particular element.

12. **Review and massage.** Proof the image, making any necessary corrections, and save the file for further use.

For many of these steps, you can follow the same regimen described in the "Scanning and Adjusting Halftones" section in Chapter 10:

- **Steps 2 and 3.** As you gain familiarity with your scanner software, you'll be able to make a basic round of corrections by manipulating the onscreen controls. For example, if your scans routinely appear with an initial blue cast, you'll be able to reduce the blue information by adjusting a curve in your scanner interface. If your scans initially appear too flat, you'll be able to add a small boost in contrast. This will require considerable testing, proofing, and frequent saving of prescan settings to get it right, but it ultimately produces images much closer to the desired color state. Unfortunately, due to the enormous variety of available input technology, software interfaces, and workflow conditions, space prohibits a thorough explanation of this process. Understand that whatever pre-adjustments you need to make will be done using tools and concepts quite similar to the remaining info covered in this chapter.

- **Step 4.** You'll use the same methods to evaluate a scan, determining the distribution of tones before applying any additional adjustments. As with Grayscale files, make sure you set the view percentage to 100%, which enables you to assess the quality of every pixel in the image.

- **Steps 6 and 8.** Repairing and retouching a color image use the same essential tools and techniques used for Grayscale images. For example, the Rubber Stamp tool works just the same in a color image as it does in a black-and-white halftone.

The issues involved in the remaining steps, although closely related to the methods explained in Chapter 10, require further explanation to accommodate the complexity of color images.

The Conversion Question

You might have noticed that the list doesn't contain an item for converting from RGB to CMYK color. This step will depend on whether you scan an image yourself, the type of scanning equipment used, and other workflow considerations.

Most people find themselves correcting images in RGB as well as CMYK mode. The advantages to correcting in RGB include faster processing times, a greater variety of available tools in Photoshop, and of course, its wider color gamut. The advantages to correcting in CMYK are fewer unexpected color shifts and more intuitive, print-oriented color values.

Ideally, the bulk of correcting should take place in RGB. Convert to CMYK only after the most intensive adjustments are made, and it's time to generate a proof. In the adjustment checklist, this step would appear between steps 11 (adjusting colors) and 12 (proofing and fine-tuning). If the image requires any subtle tweaks after proofing, make the corrections in CMYK. [1]

Incorrect Conversion Strategies

It's vitally important that you don't attempt to convert from CMYK back to RGB. After an image exists in CMYK mode, you cannot regain the values that were clipped by converting to the smaller color space. When you convert back to CMYK, the separation settings are re-applied, which results in different levels of information written to the black plate. The color shifts will

---

FOOTNOTE

[1] This idea presupposes that you have an RGB image to begin with, and that you actually want to convert it. Many high-end scanners convert the image to CMYK color on the fly, using internal settings similar to the Photoshop preferences discussed in Chapter 11. If you've contracted a vendor to generate your scans, your images will probably arrive already converted to CMYK, based on a series of general settings. You can request that they be provided in corrected RGB mode (if you're paying for scans by the megabyte, you'll likely save a few dollars.) When I outsource my scans, I often prefer to receive RGB files instead of pre-converted CMYK. This way, I can convert the same image for several different reproduction methods, fine-tune the black generation values, even repurpose the image for RGB-based uses, such as multimedia and the Web. However, when I understand that an image will only used for importing and printing, I seldom bother with obtaining RGB data. The CMYK info from a high-end scanner is usually better than the RGB info from a low-end scanner.

be unpredictable at best, and it's highly unlikely they'll reproduce accurately on-press. The only time to consider doing such a thing is when you need to repurpose a CMYK image for RGB use, such as a Web graphic.

Many people find CMYK values much more intuitive than RGB, which often leads to a serious mistake. As soon as they receive an RGB image, they immediately convert it to CMYK before applying any adjustments. If you have the opportunity to correct an image in RGB, take advantage of it. By working in the larger color space, it's much easier to maximize the range of colors when you convert down to CMYK. Otherwise, you start with a greatly reduced color range, which you must try to expand within the smaller gamut. Also, when you work in RGB, you cannot exceed the maximum black values entered in the CMYK Setup dialog box—those values are only applied at the time you convert to CMYK. If the image already exists in CMYK mode, a large color adjustment can easily deepen the shadows up to a 400% total ink coverage—far too much for on-press reproduction.

Of course, if all you have to work with is a CMYK image, you'll just have to exercise caution as you edit. Keep your adjustments small, and always use the Info palette to track your changes (see "The Info Palette," later this chapter).

Elements of Color Quality

You can infer from the issues described so far that overall color quality is based on several factors. Some of them are obvious, some seem unimportant at first, but if any of them are ignored, poorly executed, or incorrectly communicated, the proofs will likely be rejected by the client. The major correction points are detail, tone, gray balance, and memory colors.

Detail

Detail is often related to image sharpness. The goal of sharpening is discrete: By emphasizing the right amount of detail, you're adding realism by making the image appear as if it hadn't been scanned. Too little sharpening, and the image is soft and out of focus; too much, and it looks exaggerated and unnatural. Detail is also a function of color scanning and correcting. As you'll see, incorrect color balancing can wash out much of your detail, and improper endpoint placement can destroy it altogether. The best image reproduction captures all the inherent detail, then compensates for the damage that naturally results from scanning, correcting, and printing.

Tone

Tone is the distribution of light and dark values throughout the image. The right tonal balance plays a strong role in ensuring a realistic, three-dimensional appearance. Tone is most often associated with *contrast*, the relationship that exists between light and dark information. The greater the difference between two tones, the higher the contrast. This applies to an image in two ways: the overall contrast, and the specific contrast between abutting colored areas.

The most obvious example is a Grayscale image. It contains only one color (black), so the image you see is based on lighter and darker pixel values—in essence, it's comprised entirely of tone. Color has tone, as well—regardless of the specific values, each color has a relative lightness or darkness associated with it. It can be difficult to recognize the various tones in a color image. You may perceive one color to be lighter or darker than another, when in fact their tonal values are identical (see Figure 12.1). For example, a high level of yellow is the tonal equivalent of a low level of cyan. If you were to convert a 100% yellow swatch and a 15% cyan swatch to Grayscale, the black values of both would be 7%.

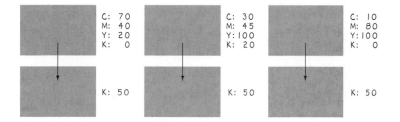

Figure 12.1 *Different colors might possess the same tonal value. These colors may appear distinct, but if you were to convert them to Grayscale mode, they'd appear as identical black values. Keep this relationship in mind as you evaluate an image's overall tonal content (see color insert).*

One of the best ways to understand the role of tone is to gain extensive experience adjusting Grayscale images for print. Also, when editing a color image, try setting part of the Info palette to display Grayscale values. As you measure different parts of the image, you'll get an idea of the relative tonality of colored areas. (For more info, see "The Info Palette," later this chapter.)

Gray Balance

Gray balance refers to the CMYK percentages that combine to form neutral gray values on-press. Neutral grays can appear in every portion of the image, from the diffuse highlight to the darkest shadows. This color relationship is a special one, and must be carefully addressed. When the grays are out of balance, the neutral values acquire a color *cast*, or a slight bias. For example, if a neutral value contains too much magenta information, even a percentage point or two, it produces a pinkish cast throughout the image. Not only will the cast appear in the printed version, it will affect your perception of the remaining colors as you attempt to correct them onscreen. Maintaining neutral grays is a fundamental goal of any color-correcting effort, intrinsic to the production of professional results.

In RGB color space, equal values of red, green, and blue produce an unbiased gray. Once you convert to CMYK, however, the relationship changes. Impurities in the inks mean that you cannot create a neutral gray using equal values of cyan, magenta, and yellow. As you'll see, creating neutrality will require the presence of a higher level of cyan. (For more info, see "Assessing Gray Balance and Color Casts," later this chapter.)

Memory Colors

A *memory color* is any value that a person recognizes instinctively, such as blue sky or green grass. No one needs a proof to tell them what color an orange should be, and as long as the printed result closely matches what the viewer expects, the colors are acceptable.

Some memory colors give you a certain degree of latitude. For example, if an image doesn't require that you perfectly match the values of the sky, there is a tolerable range of "skies" that the viewer will intuitively accept. The average blue values can shift somewhat as you focus on the subject of the image. However, when the colors fall outside the acceptable range—for example, if the sky has a greenish cast—the viewer will reject it, because it doesn't match his preconceived notion of how the sky should appear.

Other memory colors are more strict. Take white, for example. Everyone knows how white is supposed to appear. If an image element is supposed to be white (often represented by the neutral diffuse highlight value) but has even the slightest color bias, it looks plain wrong to the viewer. Equally strict are corporate colors, such as a logo, or universally recognized objects, like the red of a can of Coca-Cola. In each case, properly identifying and correcting these colors is a key issue that determines whether a job is accepted or rejected by the client. (For more info, see "Adjusting Non-Neutral Colors," later this chapter.)

Photoshop's Color Adjustment Tools

Successfully adjusting a color scan in Photoshop requires the use of several tools and commands. The most vitally important are the Info palette, the Curves and Levels command, the Unsharp Mask filter, and the Rubber Stamp tool. Below, I describe their roles in a color-correcting environment, and cover a series of issues and techniques that you can put to immediate use in your workflow.

The Info Palette

The Info palette is Photoshop's onscreen densitometer, easily the most important tool for tracking color changes. Keep this palette visible at all times—I've learned to keep it separate from any other palettes, never moving it from the upper-right corner of my monitor. When used properly, the Info palette performs three vital tasks for the color adjuster:

- It displays the current pixel values of the image, which appear as you move the cursor over different color areas.

- At the same time, it displays the relative pixel values of another color mode. For example, when editing in RGB, you can display the values that will exist after converting to CMYK.

- When you're making adjustments in a dialog box, the Info palette enables you to gauge their effect by displaying before-and-after values. As long as the dialog box is open, the original and new values are separated by a slash.

Although the Info palette is divided into four quadrants, only the top two display color values. To set the readout units, click one of the small eyedropper icons. A pop-up menu appears, listing the following options:

- **Actual Color.** The default setting, its values are based on the image's current color mode.

- **Grayscale.** This option displays the tonal values of the image. When editing a Grayscale image, it stands for the black percentages that will output when you print the file. (For more info, refer to Chapter 10.) If the current image is in color, it displays the values that would result if you converted to Grayscale mode.

- **RGB Color.** This option displays color values as brightness levels, or the 256 tones of the Grayscale spectrum. When the current image is in RGB mode, it displays the tonal values of the red, green, and blue channels for each pixel. If the image is in Grayscale mode, the three values are always equal, indicating neutrality. If the image is in Lab Color mode, the values display what the exact colors will be when the image is converted to RGB. If the image is in CMYK mode, however, this readout is of little use. (For more info, refer to Chapter 11.)

- **HSB Color.** This option displays color values in terms of hue, saturation, and brightness. Hue values, or a pixel's particular color, range from 0° to 360°, indicating its position on the RGB/CMY color wheel. Saturation values, or color intensity, range from 0% (gray) to 100% (full intensity). The Brightness value refers to how light or dark the color is, and ranges from 0% (black) to 100% (full brightness). (For more info, refer to Chapter 11.)

- **CMYK Color.** When the current image is in CMYK mode, this option displays the cyan, magenta, yellow, and black information of each pixel. If the image is in any other color mode, it displays the values that will appear after converting to CMYK. These values can change, depending on the current settings in the CMYK Setup dialog box. (For more info, refer to Chapter 11.)

- **Lab Color.** This option displays the values found in the three Lab channels. The L stands for Lightness, similar to HSB's Brightness, and ranges from 0 (black) to 100 (full lightness). The a and b values are positions in the Lab Color space, and range from –128 to 127. The a value represents a color's location between magenta and green, and the b value represents its location between yellow and blue. (For more info, refer to Chapter 11.)

- **Total Ink.** This option displays the total ink density of a particular color, or its combined CMYK percentages. If this option is selected for a non-CMYK image, the value represents the ink density that will result when you convert to CMYK. The Total Ink Limit, or the maximum allowable amount, is determined in the CMYK Setup dialog box, and is applied when an image is converted from RGB or Lab Color to CMYK. Once in CMYK mode, it's possible to increase the Total Ink value beyond the specified limit, so this option provides a way to keep track of your darkest colors.

- **Opacity.** This option displays the combined opacity levels of all layers in particular area. If the background layer is visible, it will always read 100%. To get a more accurate reading of your image layers, hide the background layer.

Editing RGB Images

When editing an RGB image for print, set the first Info palette quadrant to RGB Color (or Actual Color), and the second to CMYK Color. This way, you can always read the values that will ultimately appear after converting to CMYK (see Figure 12.2).

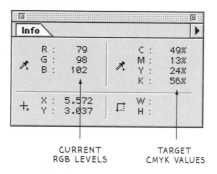

CURRENT
RGB LEVELS

TARGET
CMYK VALUES

Figure 12.2 *When adjusting an image in RGB color, set one color readout of the Info palette to display RGB values, and the other to display CMYK. This enables you to predict the values that will exist after you convert the image to CMYK mode. (As long as you're in RGB mode, the CMYK values might change, depending on the current settings in the CMYK Setup dialog box.)*

There's another advantage to this setup. Whenever you target an RGB value that falls outside the CMYK gamut, the CMYK readouts will be followed by an exclamation point. This will let you know where the most prominent color shifts will occur when you finally convert to CMYK.

Editing CMYK Images

When editing a CMYK image for print, set the first Info palette quadrant to CMYK Color (or Actual Color), and the second to Total Ink. This way, you can easily read the current color content, while keeping an eye on the combined ink percentages in the darkest areas (see Figure 12.3). If any adjustment forces the values above the tolerance of the target printing method, you can undo the command or reduce the intended settings.

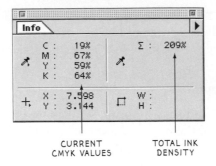

CURRENT
CMYK VALUES

TOTAL INK
DENSITY

Figure 12.3   *After an image exists in CMYK color, it doesn't matter what the equivalent RGB values are. Instead, set one color readout of the palette to display CMYK
values, and the other to display the Total Ink density. This way, you can keep an eye
on your shadows, making sure your adjustments don't push them beyond the limit
established in the CMYK Setup dialog box.*

The Eyedropper Tools

Most people are already familiar with the standard Eyedropper tool, which
you can use to set the foreground or background color by clicking the image.
Whenever you're in a color adjustment dialog box, such as Curves or
Hue/Saturation, Photoshop enables you to use the same tool to target values
for more specific editing. As you move the cursor over the image, it changes
to a small eyedropper icon.

The Eyedropper Options palette contains a single setting, Sample Size,
which determines the method used by the eyedropper to read color values
(see Figure 12.4). There are three options:

- **Point Sample.** Here, the tool reads the value of the single pixel beneath
  the cursor. Some seasoned pros prefer this option because it gives them a
  true reading of actual pixel values. If you use it, always make sure the view
  percentage of the image is set to 100%—otherwise, the onscreen pixels
  are anti-aliased, which results in inaccurate readings.

- **3 by 3 Average.** Here, the tool reads the average color value of a nine-
  pixel square that surrounds the targeted pixel. This is particularly useful
  when sampling a range of colors, because it softens the effect of any aberrant pixels (such as white or black scanner noise). This option is used most
  often by color professionals.

- **5 by 5 Average.** Here, the tool reads the average color value of a 25-pixel
  square that surrounds the targeted pixel. Ordinarily, this range is too wide for

accurate color samples, but some people prefer it when editing extremely high-resolution color images (400ppi and up).

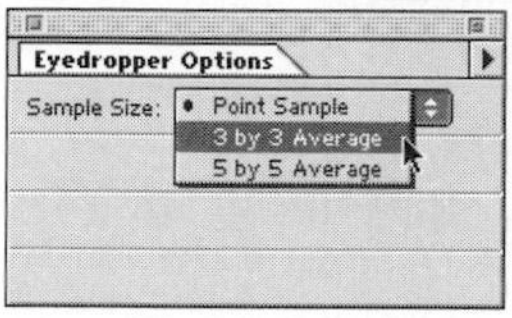

Figure 12.4 *In the Eyedropper Options palette, set the Sample Size to 3 by 3 Average (unless you have a specific need to choose a different option). This will give you more accurate color readings, reducing the possibility of being misled by an aberrant light or dark pixel. This palette affects all the eyedroppers available throughout Photoshop.*

After you choose an option, it affects every eyedropper in Photoshop: the standard Eyedropper tool, the color adjustment dialogs, the Color Range selection command, and so forth. The option also affects the readout of any color samplers contained in the image.

Placing Color Samplers

Photoshop's eyedroppers can only sample one color at a time, making it difficult to track changes throughout an image. To compensate, Photoshop 5 introduced the capability to place up to four *color samplers* to each image. A sampler is a sort of evaluation target, a way to continually monitor the effects of your color adjustments on critical or sensitive portions of the image.

Place a sampler by clicking the image with the Color Sampler tool (found in the same location as the standard Eyedropper tool in the Tools palette). After you add a sampler, the Info palette expands to display the values directly beneath it. To hide the samplers from view, choose Hide Color Samplers from the Info palette submenu. To delete a color sampler, (Option)[Alt]-click it with the Color Sampler tool.

Although it's not necessary to place samplers, most people find them quite helpful. Try this strategy: Place one on the diffuse highlight, one on a neutral midtone, and one on a dark neutral value. This way, you can tell if any of your adjustments add a slight cast to the image. Reserve the fourth sampler for any specific color you're trying to adjust or preserve (see Figure 12.5).

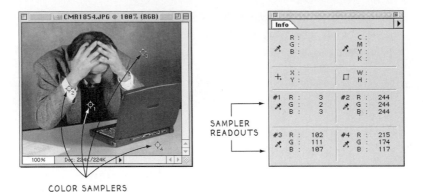

Figure 12.5 *Here, I've placed four color samplers throughout my image—one for each of my targeted neutrals, and one to read the values I'm currently adjusting.*

The Curves Command

Photoshop's Curves is without a doubt the most flexible and powerful color-adjustment tool. Other color-editing commands may be available, but Curves can duplicate nearly all of their features, and it usually does a better job. The basic function of the Curves dialog box was described in Chapter 10. When editing color images, though, its feature set grows to accommodate the increased range of information. Most importantly, it enables you to edit the content of individual color channels, as well as the image as a whole.

To illustrate, assume the current image is in RGB mode. When you first open the Curves dialog box, the Channels pop-up menu is set to RGB. Any adjustments you apply to the curve are applied equally to the red, green, and blue channels. If you set the pop-up menu to Red, any curve adjustment is applied only to the red channel. Each item in the pop-up menu can contain different curves at the same time. For example, you can lighten the shadows by making an RGB adjustment, and then switch to Blue to remove a slight cast in the highlights, without first having to apply the original curve (see Figure 12.6).

Follow these guidelines: When addressing the *entire tonal content* of the image—for example, adding some contrast, opening up the shadows, or boosting the midtones—make your adjustments to the RGB or CMYK channel; when addressing a specific color, such as removing a green or red cast, make your adjustments to the appropriate color channel.

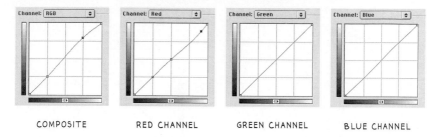

Figure 12.6 *The Curves command enables you to edit the individual color chan-nels, or all of them at once. Use the composite channel for tonal adjustments, and the color channels for specific color edits. Note how you can edit each of the items inde-pendently. (In this example, I've adjusted the overall shadows, as you can see in the composite channel, and the red highlights, as you can see in the red channel.)*

RGB Versus CMYK Adjustments

Using the Curves command to adjust a CMYK image is similar to adjusting a Grayscale image for print. Always make sure the dialog box displays out-put values, or percentages from 0% to 100%. If the Input/Output fields are showing brightness levels, click the Values Gradient at the bottom of the graph (refer to Chapter 10).

When editing an RGB image, though, you don't want to use output values. If you do, the numbers you read in the dialog box don't relate to the values displayed in the Info palette. Remember, an RGB image is based on trans-mitted light, not reflected light. Therefore, the output values that describe halftone dot sizes have no bearing here. There is no such thing as "50% red" or "75% blue." By basing your adjustments on brightness levels, which range from 0 to 255, you use the same values referred to by your monitor to display the image. If the Input/Output fields are showing output values, click the Values Gradient at the bottom of the graph. (Refer to Chapter 9, "Digital Imaging Fundamentals," for more info.)

The most important thing to remember is that RGB is the inverse of CMYK. The tonal values mapped in the Curves dialog box are opposite, as well. For example, to lighten the midtones of a CMYK image, place a point in the cen-ter of the curve and drag downward. To lighten the midtones of an RGB image, place a point in the center of the curve and drag upward. In a CMYK image, like a Grayscale, the highlight info is found in the lower left of the graph; the shadows are found in the upper right. In an RGB image, the highlights are in the upper right and the shadows in the lower left (see Figure 12.7).

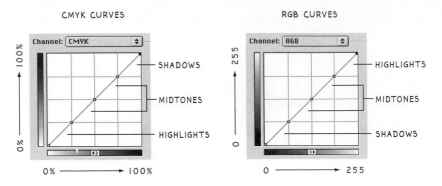

Figure 12.7 *When you move between RGB and CMYK images, the Curves command might seem awkward at first. Just as RGB and CMYK are inverse color models, their curves share an inverse relationship, as well.*

Keep this inverse relationship in mind when adjusting colors, too. The following table illustrates the basic relationships you'll encounter when editing RGB and CMYK images, and provides a starting point for your adjustments. (Refer to Chapter 11 for more info.)

Adjustment	RGB Image	CMYK Image
Subtract red	Pull down red curve (or pull up green and blue curves)	Pull up cyan curve (or pull down magenta and yellow curves)
Subtract green	Pull down green curve (or pull up red and blue curves)	Pull up magenta curve (or pull down cyan and yellow curves)
Subtract blue	Pull down blue curve (or pull up red and green curves)	Pull up yellow curve (or pull down cyan and magenta curves)
Add red	Pull up red curve (or pull down green and blue curves)	Pull down cyan curve (or pull up magenta and yellow curves)
Add green	Pull up green curve (or pull down red and blue curves)	Pull down magenta curve (or pull up cyan and yellow curves)
Add blue	Pull up blue curve (or pull down red and green curves)	Pull down yellow curve (or pull up cyan and magenta curves)
Subtract cyan	Pull up red curve (or pull down green and blue curves)	Pull down cyan curve (or pull up magenta and yellow curves)
Subtract magenta	Pull up green curve (or pull down red and blue curves)	Pull down magenta curve (or pull up cyan and yellow curves)
Subtract yellow	Pull up blue curve (or pull down red and green curves)	Pull down yellow curve (or pull up cyan and magenta curves)

Adjustment	RGB Image	CMYK Image
Add cyan	Pull down red curve (or pull up green and blue curves)	Pull up cyan curve (or pull down magenta and yellow curves)
Add magenta	Pull down green curve (or pull up red and blue curves)	Pull up yellow curve (or pull down cyan and magenta curves)
Add yellow	Pull down blue curve (or pull up red and green curves)	Pull up cyan curve (or pull down magenta and yellow curves)

Targeting Colors

One of the most useful features of the Curves dialog box is the capability to target a specific color or tone. As you move the cursor onto the image, it changes to an eyedropper. When you hold down the mouse button, a small feedback circle appears on the curve, indicating the pixel's value. This enables you to pinpoint the right part of the curve to edit (see Figure 12.8).

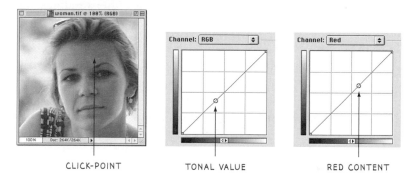

CLICK-POINT   TONAL VALUE   RED CONTENT

Figure 12.8   *Click the image while the Curves dialog box is open to pinpoint a value's position on the curve. For example, to determine the overall tone of an RGB color, click while in the RGB channel. To determine the location of a color's red component, click while in the Red channel.*

The circle's exact meaning depends on the item currently set in the Channels pop-up menu. For example, if you're editing the Red channel, the circle indicates the red component of whatever color you've clicked. If you're editing the RGB channel, the circle indicates the color's overall tonal content. [2]

By holding down (Command)[Control], you can add points directly to the curve. As long as you hold down the mouse button, the feedback circle appears. When you release it, the circle is replaced with an adjustable point. If you (Command-Shift-click)[Control-Shift-click], you add a point to each color channel, at the precise location of each component value.

The Unsharp Mask Filter

As described in Chapter 10, sharpening an image exaggerates the differences between colored pixels, producing the illusion of crisper detail. However, a color image contains many more variables than a halftone—or most notably, it contains three or four 8-bit channels for the color info, as opposed to the single black channel of a Grayscale file. Successfully sharpening a color image requires a closer evaluation of the most important detail, a greater understanding of the Unsharp Mask filter's settings, and the occasional use of some more advanced techniques.

If the bulk of your color work consists of small images (2×2 inches and under), you can probably make do with a single Unsharp Mask setting—the effect of the filter will be less apparent. When you work with larger images, detail becomes more important, variances between color channels are more apparent, and a more-sensitive approach to the Unsharp Mask filter is required.

Is Sharpening Necessary?

One way or another, every image needs to be sharpened. The process of translating real-life materials to digital pixels always results in lost detail, no matter how sensitive or expensive the device. Whether you're the one who does the sharpening depends on your equipment and your workflow.

F O O T N O T E

2   When editing an RGB image, you can use the feedback circle on any channel, including the RGB composite. When editing a CMYK image, you can only use the feedback circle in the individual color channels—it will not appear when "CMYK" is set in the Channels pop-up menu. This is mainly due to the complexity of calculating an accurate onscreen tonal value from CMYK percentages.

If you're using a CCD-based device, such as a flatbed scanner, avoid using the sharpening controls in the scanner software. First, these controls typically offer only one setting (usually a percentage), as opposed to the Unsharp Mask filter, which offers three. Sharpening the image in Photoshop will almost always give you better results. Additionally, these devices tend to include a certain level of noise to the scan, either in the shadows or the blue channel. Sharpening at the time of the scan will exaggerate this noise, and future sharpening might destroy the image detail.

On the other hand, if you're working with images generated by a high-quality drum scanner, you probably don't need to apply any additional sharpening. The software for these devices offer a greater range of tools, and the sharpening effect is automatically applied as the image is converted to CMYK color. Far less noise is introduced than with CCD-based devices, and future sharpening may exaggerate the film grain of the original material.

Evaluating and Sharpening Detail

The best way to approach sharpening is to make a distinction between *fine* detail and *subtle* detail (see Figure 12.9). Fine detail is clearly visible: Tree branches interweaved against the sky, hair blowing in the wind, and the criss-cross pattern of plaid fabric are all good examples. Subtle detail is less obvious: Fleshtones, the skin of an apple, and blades of grass in a manicured lawn are all based on the slightest tonal and color variations. Of course, some images possess neither fine nor subtle detail. For example, a product shot of a telephone primarily consists of well-defined, simple shapes. Unsharp Mask settings that work well one type of detail will either obliterate or have no effect on the other.

It's impossible to recommend only one or two Unsharp Mask settings for a wide variety of color images. However, you can start with a basic methodology:

- **Normal detail.** When the image detail consists of bold, clean lines against a reasonably contrasting background, start with a higher Radius (between 1.5 and 3 pixels, depending on the image resolution) and a lower Threshold (between 2 and 5 levels). This produces a more pronounced effect that includes most of the image pixels.

- **Fine detail.** Areas of fine detail typically require a low Radius (between .5 and 1.5 pixels) and low Threshold (between 2 and 5 levels). This way, no detail is obliterated by the halo produced by a large Radius, and more pixels are included in the overall effect.

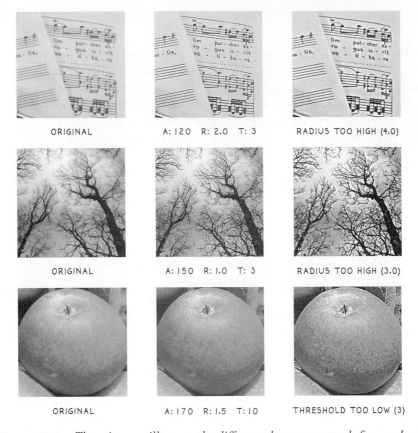

ORIGINAL   A: 120 R: 2.0 T: 3   RADIUS TOO HIGH (4.0)

ORIGINAL   A: 150 R: 1.0 T: 3   RADIUS TOO HIGH (3.0)

ORIGINAL   A: 170 R: 1.5 T: 10   THRESHOLD TOO LOW (3)

Figure 12.9 *These images illustrate the difference between normal, fine, and subtle detail. Each type has its own sharpening requirements. Normal detail (top) can tolerate a higher Radius and lower Threshold, with a less possibility of artifacting or lost detail. Fine detail (center) requires a lower Radius—higher settings may obliterate the vital info. Subtle detail (bottom) requires a higher Threshold—if every pixel is sharpened, the image appears textured and unnatural (see color insert).*

- **Subtle detail.** Areas of subtle detail typically require a higher Radius value (between 1 and 3 pixels) and a higher Threshold (between 6 and 15 levels). This emphasizes the more contrasting ranges, while ensuring that slightly varying values are unaffected.

These relationships are only starting points—the content of each image will determine the final settings. Also, notice I didn't include an Amount setting. That value simply determines the degree of lightening and darkening applied by the Unsharp Mask filter. Because detail is most affected by the Radius and Threshold, establish those settings before setting the Amount.

If you have difficulty pinpointing the effect of Radius and Threshold, try this technique:

1. Set the view percentage to 100% and open the Unsharp Mask dialog box.

2. Make sure the Preview box is checked.

3. Set the Amount slider all the way to 500%.

4. Set the Radius and Threshold sliders all the way down. At first, the image will not appear to sharpen.

5. Slowly raise the Radius value. (If desired, highlight the Radius field and press the up arrow on your keyboard to move in .1-pixel increments.) The high Amount value will over-exaggerate the effect, but you'll immediately see which pixels are affected by the setting. Stop when the resulting halo starts to obliterate any detail, or appears obviously wide.

6. Slowly raise the Threshold value. (Highlight the field and press the up arrow to move in 1-level increments.) As the value increases, you'll see more and more subtle detail ignored by the command. Stop when you're sure that sharpening will not cause any artifacting or over-emphasized grain.

7. Reduce the Amount setting. Don't be afraid to use a value over 100%—in fact, many images require percentages up to 200% or 250%. The same guideline for sharpening halftones applies: As soon as it looks like you've sharpened just a little too much, the Amount setting is probably appropriate.

8. Click OK to apply the unsharp mask. Leaving the view percentage at 100%, choose (Command-Z)[Control-Z] a couple of times to evaluate the before-and-after effect. If you need to try again, make sure you've undone the effect before choosing Unsharp Mask.

Channel-Based Sharpening

Some images are difficult (if not impossible) to sharpen in one even-handed pass. This is especially true in two cases: images produced by a lower-end RGB scanner, and fleshtones. If you cannot get balanced, satisfying results by sharpening the composite channel, you'll likely do better by sharpening one or more of the color channels.

The trick is to sharpen the channels that contain the least amount of detail. In most RGB scans, the blue channel contains most of the detail, as well as a little bit of scanner noise. If you oversharpen this channel, you can quickly introduce visible artifacts and halos to the image. By sharpening only the red and green channels, you can emphasize the image detail without exaggerating these aberrant pixels. [3]

If the image has already been converted to CMYK, you'll have to examine the channels more closely. If the original image contained blue channel noise, most of it will carry over to the yellow channel—avoid sharpening this one. However, the content of the remaining channels will determine your next actions. If the subject matter is predominantly green, the cyan channel will contain considerable detail. In this case, sharpen the magenta and black plates. If it's predominantly red, the magenta channel will contain considerable detail. Here, sharpen the cyan and black plates. [4]

Sharpening Fleshtones

Fleshtones have their own sharpening requirements. If these details are overexaggerated, the subject picks up an unsightly pattern, as if he had an unfortunate skin condition. (Also, glossy red lips tend to look unnatural when you sharpen them, regardless of the settings used.) When the Unsharp Mask filter doesn't give satisfactory results when applied to the composite channel, these images are the perfect candidates for channel-specific sharpening.

FOOTNOTE

[3] In cases where a large amount of noise exists in the blue channel, you'll benefit by applying Filter: Noise: **Despeckle** to the channel before sharpening the red and green channels. This will slightly smooth out the level of noise, reducing its visibility in the composite channel.

[4] There are no recommended settings for sharpening individual channels, and the best results will require some trial and error. Make things easier on yourself by doing two things. First, always work from a duplicate of the original image. Second, before sharpening, create a preview image by choosing View: **New View**. This command appears to duplicate the image, but it doesn't—the window enables you to see the same image using different view settings. Set its view to 100%, reduce the window size, and position the image so the most important detail is visible. This way, when you select a channel in the first copy and manipulate the sliders in the Unsharp Mask dialog box, you can preview the effect on the overall image.

When printed, fleshtones are predominantly composed of magenta and yellow. In an RGB image, this means the details are contained in the green and blue channels (green and blue, if you recall, being the complements of magenta and yellow). Here, you can focus the bulk of your sharpening on the red channel (see Figure 12.10).

ORIGINAL   GLOBALLY SHARPENED   ONLY CYAN AND BLACK
                                          CHANNELS SHARPENED

Figure 12.10   *Globally sharpening fleshtones often results in an over-accentuated, sickly appearance. By sharpening the channels containing the least amount of fleshtone data, you emphasize important details without adding texture to the skin (see color insert).*

An image comprised mostly of fleshtones—for example, a close-up head shot—is one of the few occasions where it is preferable to sharpen after converting to CMYK color. Here, it's easier to ignore the magenta and yellow channels completely, focusing your edits on the cyan and black info. Because details such as wrinkles, acne scars, pores, and gleaming lips are far less likely to appear on these channels, you can typically use more intensive Unsharp Mask settings.

Sharpening Selected Areas

Many users attempt to use different Unsharp Mask settings on different parts of an image, working with either selections or complex masks. They might want to apply softer settings to the subject's face, and then apply higher, crisper settings to hair and other details. If you've found you can do this successfully, congratulations—but I don't recommend it. It's far too easy to create a noticeable imbalance, where it's clear to the viewer that portions of the image have been singled out. Whenever something appears to be wrong with the focus, your Unsharp Masking efforts have failed. It's usually better to sacrifice one part of the image for another—for example, losing a little detail in the hair to better accentuate the face—than to force the image to give you something it isn't willing to hand over without a fight.

Color Adjustment and Correction

Most image colors are not critical; instead of precisely matching the original, your goal is to create balanced, appealing colors that look natural to the viewer.

For the most part, critical correction is accomplished only in the most rigidly controlled environments. Unless you have access to well-maintained equipment, calibrated viewing and proofing devices, and a high-end scanning workflow dedicated to generating the highest-quality initial images, you'll have considerable difficulty producing color images that equal their photographic originals. However, even if your workplace falls short of this expansive (and costly) ideal, you can use an approach that will prove more important than trusting what you see onscreen: working by the numbers.

The techniques in this section revolve around the relationships between color values, in RGB as well as CMYK. Every monitor on the planet might display the same image differently, but the Info palette never lies. Whether assessing highlights, identifying neutral values, or determining how to balance unsightly fleshtones, every decision will be based on either brightness levels or output percentages. The colors you view onscreen will eventually be of secondary importance. [5]

Every image you tackle, regardless of its color content, will benefit from the following approach:

FOOTNOTE

[5]   There are as many theories and methods for adjusting color as there are self-proclaimed "experts." Some people prefer to make the bulk of their corrections in the composite channels of the Curves dialog box; others avoid those curves altogether. Some people edit the individual color channels minimally; others use them exclusively. Some people swear that commands like Color Balance, Hue/Saturation, and Levels offer more intuitive controls; others claim that anything other than Curves produces inferior results. Some people insist that color correcting can only take place in a controlled environment; others claim the ability to adjust colors on a black and white monitor, using only the color values as a guide. Which is the right approach? None of them. All of them. Although most of my edits involve the Curves command, you may ultimately find success using other tools and techniques. The only thing that matters is the final result: an image properly targeted for press, with balanced neutrals, crisp details, and colors acceptable to the client. As long as you meet these requirements, it doesn't matter if you used only the Eraser tool and a deck of tarot cards.

1. Assess the individual channels, making sure they contain enough detail in the shadows and highlights to continue editing.

2. Evaluate the neutral grays to identify any color casts.

3. Identify the endpoints.

4. Use the Curves command to set the endpoints for press and balance the neutrals, removing any cast.

5. Target and adjust the most important color areas.

Let's take a closer look at the issues involved in each step.

Evaluating the Shadows and Highlights

Before you spend any time adjusting color, make sure the image is worth the effort. This is similar to assessing a Grayscale image: The highlights should not be blown out to white, and the shadows should not be filled in to black. The highlights are easier to examine—if any patches are colored solid white, it's likely a fair amount of detail has been lost. The shadows may be trickier, because it's more difficult for the eye to discern any subtle differences. To see if there is an acceptable level of shadow detail, move the cursor over the image areas and keep an eye on the Info palette. If the values change, it indicates the existence of a certain level of detail. If the palette shows a constant value, the area exists as a solid color, containing no detail (see Figure 12.11).

PLUGGED   BLOWN
SHADOWS   HIGHLIGHTS   SUFFICIENT DETAIL

Figure 12.11 *If an image initially suffers from blown-out highlights or plugged shadows, no amount of correcting can save it. Compare these two scans: The colors of both are reasonably balanced, but only one contains the necessary highlight and shadow detail (see color insert).*

The next step is to evaluate the overall tone of the shadows and highlights. Here, you must refer to the original material. If the original contains very light info—for example, snow or a white shirt—the image highlights should contain similar values. If the image values are initially too dark, the overall contrast is thrown off balance, making the image more difficult to correct. Likewise, if the shadows initially appear as a sort of dark, washed-out gray, you might be fighting a losing battle. You can correct these imbalances, true, but doing so will expand the tonal content of the color channels. This causes two problems. First, it reduces the flexibility you have in applying future color adjustments, since less information will be available in the file. Second, if the expansion is too great, your colors will look washed out or posterized.

These issues are usually the result of improper scanning—or worse, an incapable scanner. Most midrange and high-end devices give you the ability to manually target the endpoints, or the lightest and darkest image values. This way, the tones and colors are better distributed during the time of the scan. As you evaluate the image, make sure the image endpoints match what you see in the original. When these values are set incorrectly (or not at all) during the prescan stage, the final scan will suffer from lost detail or bad contrast. You're better off scanning again, paying closer attention to the endpoints.

Assessing Gray Balance and Color Casts

Some unbalanced colors are easy to spot—you can simply look at the screen and see that something is off. Maybe the clouds have a pinkish tinge, or someone's flesh looks more jaundiced than rosy. Others are less visible, and cannot be identified until you evaluate a laminate proof. It's unrealistic to assume you can identify the core problem by reading the colored elements. Do you have some ancestral memory of the precise magenta content of the sky? Do you instinctively know how much yellow is supposed to appear in these particular fleshtones? Of course not—these values will differ from image to image. Instead, you can assess something that isn't supposed to have any color bias whatsoever: neutral grays.

Every image contains neutral values. They might be obvious, like a gray sweater, a slab of granite, or a concrete wall. Or they might be subtle, appearing only in the diffuse highlight, or in the edge of a shadow stretching across a white tablecloth. However they occur, they provide one of your most important color adjustment benchmarks. Most scanners introduce a slight cast into each image, or a bias toward one color or another. If you can identify the values that are supposed to be neutral, you can determine the extent of the cast and take measures to remove it. [6]

Reading RGB Neutrals

It's easy to identify neutrals in an RGB image: Equal amounts of red, green, and blue produce a neutral gray. Therefore, when you evaluate what you presume to be a neutral color, the values should be the same. If any of the values are off, you've identified a cast. For example, assume a gray midtone reads as R:127, G:127, B:135 in the Info palette; the neutral contains too much blue data, which indicates that the image contains a slight blue cast. On the other hand, if the same midtone reads as R:127, G:127, B:120, the neutral doesn't contain enough blue data, which indicates a slight yellow cast. Therein lies the beauty of using neutral values to identify color casts—if a neutral contains a bias, you can be sure the remaining colors are affected by it, as well (see Figure 12.12).

Reading CMYK Neutrals

Reading neutrals in a CMYK image is more difficult. In theory, equal amounts of cyan, magenta, and yellow produce a neutral gray. In reality, this cannot happen, due to impurities in the printing inks. If you do the bulk of your corrections in RGB, Photoshop automatically maintains the status of any neutral values when you convert to CMYK color. (The exact percentages will depend on the current settings in the CMYK Setup dialog box.) If you have to compensate for a color cast in a CMYK image, you must become familiar with the basic relationships between the inks. Put simply, neutral values must contain more cyan than magenta and yellow. How much more depends on whether the neutral is a shadow, midtone, or highlight (see Figure 12.13).

FOOTNOTE

[6] Most color casts appear during the scanning stage. To determine the extent introduced by your specific device, scan a *gray wedge* (available at your local photographic supply shop), a thin strip that contains perfectly neutral shadow, midtone, and highlight info. When you assess the image in Photoshop, you can identify the predominant casts, as well as the tones they affect most. For example, you might see that a red cast consistently appears in the midtones and highlights.

This accomplishes two things. First, whenever you generate a scan, you'll know how and where to begin your adjustments. Second, you can use this information to create a pre-adjustment curve in your scanning software, which compensates for the cast at the time of the scan. (If you're using a midrange to high-end flatbed, try positioning the gray wedge next to the original as you scan. This will give you some easy neutral values to evaluate, before you crop the info away and continue your edits.)

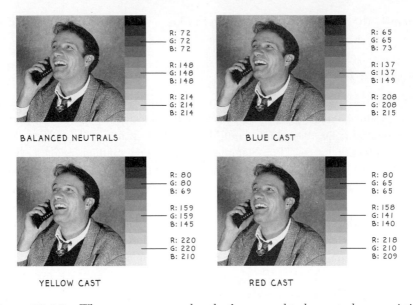

Figure 12.12 *When you assess a value that's supposed to be neutral, any existing color cast becomes immediately apparent. To better illustrate the effect of a cast, I've included a gray ramp next to each image (see color insert).*

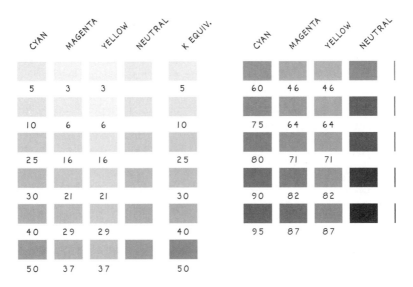

Figure 12.13 *After colors exist as CMYK values, neutrality requires a special relationship. Due to impurities found in all process inks, each neutral gray requires more cyan than magenta and yellow. When determining the equivalent black value of a neutral, let the cyan percentage be your guide (see color insert).*

Think of the values in Figure 12.13 as a guide, not gospel. The important point is the relationship between cyan and the remaining inks. As you can see, a neutral value contains equal amounts of magenta and yellow, but the amount of additional cyan changes as you move along the gray ramp. It typically works like this:

Tone	Additional Cyan
Highlights	2–3%
Quarter tones	7–10%
Midtones	12–15%
Three-quarter tones	8–12%
Shadows	7–10%

Don't worry if a value is off by a point or two. For example, the magenta and yellow might differ by 1%, or the cyan value might appear a notch above or below the recommended amount. Such subtle variations cannot be seen when the image is run on-press.

Identifying the Endpoints

Before you can properly map the extreme shadow and diffuse highlight values for print, you need to identify their locations in the image. You'll ultimately pinpoint these areas by examining the image with the cursor and Info palette, but you need some way to narrow down the field.

In Chapter 10, you learned how to use the Levels command to target the shadow and highlight pixels in a Grayscale file. That technique is of little use with color images. When the image is in RGB color, (Option-dragging) [Alt-dragging] the sliders in the Levels dialog box produces a confusing rainbow effect. When the image is in CMYK color, it produces no effect at all. Follow these steps instead (they work equally well on RGB and CMYK images):

1. Open the image you want to target.

2. Choose Image: Adjust: **Threshold**.

3. In the Threshold dialog box, make sure the Preview option is checked and move the slider all the way to the right (the image appears to turn white).

4. Slowly increase the Threshold value (highlight the Threshold Value field and press the up arrow on your keyboard to raise the value in increments

of 1). The first pixels to appear as black are the image's darkest shadows (see Figure 12.14).

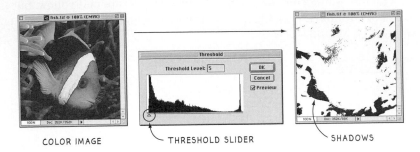

Figure 12.14   *To locate an image's darkest shadow areas, move the Threshold slider all the way to the left and gradually increase the value. The first pixels that turn black are the shadows.*

5. Move the slider all the way to the right (the image appears to turn black).

6. Slowly decrease the Threshold value. The first pixels to turn white are the image's lightest highlights (see Figure 12.15).

7. Click Cancel to close the Threshold command.

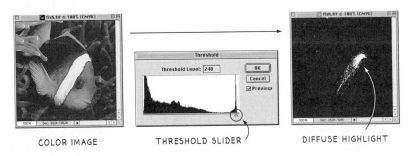

Figure 12.15   *To locate an image's diffuse highlight, move the Threshold slider all the way to the right and gradually decrease the value. The first pixels that turn white are the lightest values. (Make sure you ignore any specular highlights—they'll appear to turn white first.)*

Take note of the shadow and highlight locations. You'll soon return to them, using the Curves command to set their values for printing.

Setting Neutral Endpoints

In Chapter 10, you learned how to set a Grayscale image's endpoints for printing. There, you had one concern: making sure the lightest and darkest pixel values fit within the reproducible range of the target press. In a color image, the endpoints involve two issues. First, like a Grayscale image, they must fit the range of the printing press. Second, they must exist as neutral values. When the extreme shadow and diffuse highlight are unbalanced, the resulting cast more than likely affects the entire image.

In a sense, you'll use the eyedroppers in the Curves dialog box as color correcting tools. By remapping the endpoints to neutral values (that also match the press requirements), the changes impact the entire image; the remaining gray levels are automatically drawn one step closer to neutrality.

Setting Default Endpoint Values

Before you can reset an image's endpoints, you must enter the desired values in the Curves dialog box.

Normally, Photoshop sets the shadow dot value automatically. You can see this when you double-click the shadow eyedropper in the Curves dialog box—the CMYK fields in the Color Picker are already filled with the default black percentages. However, if you already set the shadow dot for Grayscale images, you'll notice that those values still exist (most likely, only a K percentage appears in the CMYK fields). Don't bother figuring out the CMYK shadow values in your head. Instead, follow these steps:

1. Open the Curves dialog box.

2. Double-click the black eyedropper.

3. In the Color Picker, move the cursor to the colored field in the left half of the dialog box.

4. Click-drag, moving the cursor all the way to the lower left of the field. The default black values are automatically entered in the CMYK fields (see Figure 12.16).

5. Click OK to close the Color Picker.

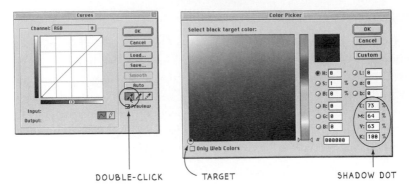

DOUBLE-CLICK   TARGET   SHADOW DOT

Figure 12.16   *When setting the desired shadow dot value, enter Photoshop's default black value. (Here, I dragged the indicator all the way to the lower left of the color field.)*

Even if you're editing an RGB image, focus on the CMYK values when setting the shadow dot. Simply entering zeros in the RGB fields may not be enough to trigger the appropriate CMYK percentages. For example, if the CMYK fields read C:0, M:0, Y:0, K:100, the RGB fields already contain zeros. Re-entering the same values has no affect. However, if the CMYK fields read C:0, M:0, Y:0, K:95, entering zeros in the RGB fields will automatically set the default CMYK black. Err on the safe side and use the above technique to enter the desired values. [7]

To set the diffuse highlight value, double-click the white eyedropper to access the Color Picker again. Here, you must enter a neutral value that retains its dot structure on-press. When printing onto coated paper, the best place to start is C:5, M:3, Y:3, K:0, which produces the visual equivalent of a 5% gray dot (see Figure 12.17). As the quality of your paper (and the tolerance of your printing method) decreases, you may need to raise this value, based on the advice of your printer.

F O O T N O T E

[7]   Photoshop's default black is based on the current settings in the CMYK Setup dialog box. To create it, Photoshop subtracts the Black Ink Limit from the Total Ink Limit, then distributes the remaining values between cyan, magenta, and yellow, in the form of a neutral gray. For example, assume the Total Ink Limit is 300% and the Black Ink Limit is 100%. The default black, therefore, would be C:73, M:64, Y:63, K:100. (The neutral CMY values total 200—add the 100% black, and you meet the Total Ink Limit.) Note that this equation will change somewhat if you increase the level of Black Generation beyond the Light setting. (Refer to Chapter 11 for more info.)

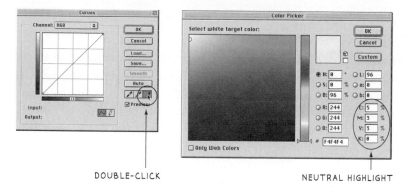

DOUBLE-CLICK   NEUTRAL HIGHLIGHT

Figure 12.17 *The diffuse highlight value requires a light neutral gray. The exact value depends on the printable tolerance of your target press. In this example, I've entered C:5, M:3, Y:3, K:0, a common standard for coated paper.*

If you're unsure of the exact percentages involved in a darker neutral, try entering a series of identical values in the RGB fields of the Color Picker. Photoshop knows to preserve the neutral relationship between RGB's brightness levels and CMYK's output percentages. For example, assume you've optimized the CMYK Setup dialog box for sheetfed printing onto uncoated paper (as described in Chapter 11). If you enter 244 in each of the RGB fields, C:5, M:3, Y:3, K:0 automatically appears in the CMYK fields. If you enter 238 in the RGB fields, the CMYK values change to C:8, M:5, Y:5, K:0—a neutral value that equals an 8% gray dot. Set them to 233, and the CMYK values change to C:10, M:6, Y:7, K:0.

If you work in a closed-loop environment, producing color images for a single printing method, you can set these values once and leave them—they'll remain until you manually change them again. If you routinely produce images for a variety of printing methods, you'll have to evaluate the press requirements and enter appropriate endpoint values for every project.

Applying Neutral Endpoint Values

At this point, you've already determined the location of the darkest and lightest image pixels, and you've entered the desired endpoint values in the Curves dialog box. Before you apply them, take a moment to compare the current image values to the original material. Pay particular attention to the diffuse highlight—you must be sure that this part of the image is supposed to be neutral. For example, if the original photo was taken using colored gels or filters, the highlights will have a deliberate cast. If you remap a non-neutral color to a neutral gray, the resulting color shifts will likely be too extreme in the rest of the image.

Fortunately, most images require a neutral highlight. Most often, the current highlight will be close to neutral, but will either contain a slight cast, or be too light for the target press (see Figure 12.18). If you're adjusting an image with a non-neutral highlight, you can still attack a scanner-induced cast using a different round of techniques. (For more info, see "Half-Cast Removals," later this chapter.)

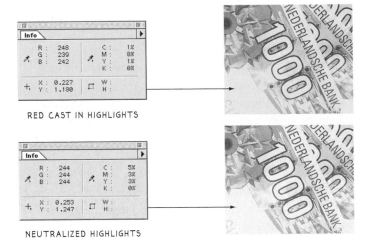

Figure 12.18 *Above and beyond ensuring printable shadows and highlights, neutral endpoints will correct a large part of any existing color casts. In this example, the highlights are too light for printing and contain a red bias. After I remap the endpoints, the highlights are neutralized (affecting the red cast all the way up to the midtones) and contain satisfactory dot sizes for printing (see color insert).*

Follow these steps to remap the endpoints (they assume you've already targeted the image's highlight and shadow, as described in "Identifying the Endpoints," earlier this section): 8

1. Open the Curves dialog box.

2. Click the white eyedropper.

3. Move the cursor over the actual image, referring to the Info palette, until you locate the lightest pixel value.

4. Click with the eyedropper.

To set the shadow endpoint, leave the Curves dialog box open and follow these steps:

1. Click the black eyedropper.

2. Move the cursor over the actual image, referring to the Info palette, until you locate the darkest pixel value.

3. Click with the eyedropper.

The effect of these adjustments is far more predictable when you apply them to an RGB image. This is mainly due to the fact that the black plate hasn't yet been generated, giving Photoshop much more flexibility in remapping the overall image tones. If you're adjusting a CMYK image, ask yourself if you need to reset the endpoints. If the scan was made using a high-end flatbed or drum scanner, a savvy operator will have set the endpoints during the prescan stage. If the endpoints (especially in the highlights) are off by only a couple of points, you might be better off applying small curve adjustments, as opposed to using the eyedroppers.

F O O T N O T E

8 Remember the difference between the *diffuse* and *specular* highlights, as described in Chapter 10. The diffuse highlight represents the lightest printed tone. The specular highlight represents any info that you want reduced to pure white on-press. Common examples include a glint in someone's eye, or a bright flash on a metallic object. Speculars are almost always small pinpoints, and should be ignored when applying your endpoints (they're not found in every image, either). When targeting the desired spot, look for the lightest printable dot, such as a white shirt collar, a light patch of snow, or the shiniest tooth in a smile. If you map a specular highlight to a gray tone, it will slightly darken the rest of the image, reducing the overall contrast.

better to decrease the level of red, as opposed to increasing the levels of green and blue. The only exception to this rule is if the colored area is rather washed–out or weak, and rescanning is not an option.

- Photographic subjects illuminated with different light sources may suffer from multiple casts. It will be extremely difficult to fix them with a single global correction. Focus your efforts on the predominant cast. In extreme cases, use the Color Range selection command to isolate one of the biased areas, make a subtle adjustment, then invert the selection to adjust the remaining tones. (See Chapter 13 for more info.)

- Don't assume that every diffuse highlight should be set at the lightest print-able value. Again, this will depend on the content of the original image, as well as any art direction provided by the client. For example, instead of set-ting the neutral highlight to the equivalent of a 5% dot (C:5, M:3, Y:3, K:0), the original may require a highlight of 20% (C:20, M:13, Y:13, K:0). If you remap a quarter tone down to a highlight, the entire tonal range of the image is expanded. True, a greater disparity between lights and darks increases the overall contrast. That's generally a good thing, but not if the photographer intended otherwise. Among other things, unnatural contrast can destroy the impact of specular highlights.

Half-Cast Removals

Completely neutralizing a cast may move the overall colors too far away from their intended appearance. This frequently occurs when the image doesn't contain obvious neutrals to use as a reference. Your screen (or more often, your proofs) will display an apparent cast, but if you totally remove it, the remaining colors look too clean, even unnatural. These cases are best addressed by a *half-cast removal*. Here, as the name implies, you determine the degree of change required for a full cast correction, then remove half the necessary amount.

For example, if a neutral value reads as R:130, G:130, B:125, it's easy to identify and compensate for the cast; increase the level of blue in the mid-tones, and you're in business. However, if the same area reads as R:140, G:130, B:106, the strategy isn't as clear. Granted, it indicates that a yellow-ish cast exists, but completely neutralizing it would have an extreme effect on the surrounding colors. The optimal correction will depend on the image at hand, but this example is well suited for a half-cast correction. Determine the adjustments required for full neutralization, then cut them in half. In this example, this means reducing the level of red by 5, and increasing the level of blue by 12. A value of R:135, G:130, B:118 will still have a slight cast, but the results will be more appealing than a full correction (see Figure 12.21).

When adjusting a CMYK image, your correction strategy will depend on your ability to identify neutrals (see "Reading CMYK Neutrals," earlier this chapter). The following table illustrates two examples:

Casted	Closest Neutral Values	Difference	Corrected Values
Example 1			
C:25	C:25	0	C:25 (no change)
M:18	M:16	2	M:17 (16+1)
Y:12	Y:16	4	Y:14 (12+2)
Example 2			
C:84	C:80	4	C:82 (80+2)
M:71	M:71	0	M:71 (no change)
Y:69	Y:71	2	Y:70 (69+1)

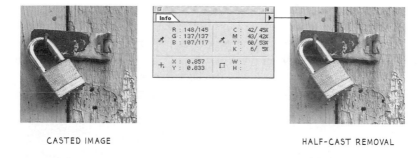

CASTED IMAGE   HALF-CAST REMOVAL

Figure 12.21 *When a cast is too dominant, completely neutralizing it may adversely affect the remaining image colors. By applying a half-cast removal, I bring the cast halfway to neutral, clearing up the most offensive aspect of the cast without compromising the remaining colors (see color insert).*

Adjusting Non-Neutral Colors

The trick behind color correcting is understanding how cyan, magenta, yellow, and black inks work together. Even if you routinely adjust RGB images, you must learn to "think" in terms of CMYK. Why? Because most people can visualize a color based on CMYK percentages; far fewer have the same intuitive grasp of RGB. For example, if you're interested in a color consisting of 50% magenta and 100% yellow, it's relatively easy to envision how it might appear. If you ask for 218 red, 155 green, and 35 blue, few people automatically think "orange."

The relationships involved in neutral colors were easy ones—you could even follow a chart that illustrated the rigid distribution of cyan, magenta, and yellow ink. The values of non-neutral colors will never be so organized. It's impossible to provide targeted values for every color you'll encounter—there are simply too many. However, by knowing how your inks behave, by understanding what happens when they combine to create colors, you can develop a more intuitive approach to your adjustments.

Assume each color is based on a cyan, magenta, and yellow value—even if one of the values is 0%. The dominant ink, or the one with the highest percentage, is described as the *primary* component. In the earlier example (M:50, Y:100), yellow is the primary component. This ink drives the color's hue, or its starting position along the RGB/CMY color wheel. The *secondary* component refines the first color, deepening its tone and adding depth. In the same example, the lesser amount of magenta gives the yellow its orange color.

The *tertiary* (or third) component reduces the overall purity of the color, adding an element of gray into the mix. For example, if you add 20% cyan to our sample orange, the result is a less intense version of the same basic hue. (If you hear a color described as too "dirty," a high amount of the tertiary component is the likely culprit.) Although the third value is sometimes called the "unwanted" color, it's of utmost importance to image reproduction: It adds detail and texture, and a level of control over the color's saturation.

Black generally isn't used to create colors; instead, it helps the tertiary component carry detail, and adds strength to the shadows (see Figure 12.22). It's also used to replace CMY inks on-press (via UCR or GCR), and printers occasionally use it to replace a certain amount of the tertiary color, depending on the reproduction method. In the vast majority of images, the black plate carries the least amount of information.

So how do these concepts apply to a correction strategy? Identify a color's primary and secondary components, and base your initial adjustments on the tertiary. Consider these brief examples:

- The primary component of Caucasian flesh is yellow, and the secondary is magenta—start by evaluating the cyan levels.

- The primary component of sky is cyan, and the secondary is magenta— start by evaluating the yellow content.

- The primary component of green leaves is yellow, and the secondary is cyan— start by evaluating the magenta.

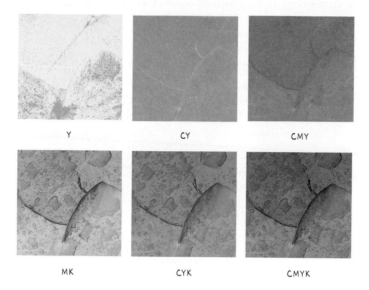

Figure 12.22 *In the greens of this image, yellow is the primary component, and cyan is the secondary. Magenta, the tertiary component, adds tone and detail, and black carries the shadows. Here, these relationships are illustrated by printing one, two, or three inks at a time (see color insert).*

The necessary adjustments will depend on the content of the image. If the amount of the tertiary component is too high, the colors will look dingy and gray. If the levels are too low, the colors will appear oversaturated and lack detail.

Keep these component relationships in mind as you fine-tune the colors of a CMYK image. In the following sections, I discuss the issues involved in some of the most frequently encountered memory colors. As you'll see, the knowledge of how your colors are built will be the most powerful tool for correcting the values that stray. This type of correction is best done on a selective basis; after making tonal adjustments, applying neutral endpoints, and removing any overall casts, you can zone in on the colors that require specific attention.

Fleshtones

Fleshtones are among the most critical colors. Clients tend to become upset when they're given scans—especially of themselves—that appear sunburned, jaundiced, or ashen. When you assess these values, take several readings throughout the important subject area, avoiding any hot spots or dark shadows. Make sure your evaluation is based on a wide sampling of colors.

The primary fleshtone component, regardless of race, is usually yellow. Magenta is the secondary, typically lagging behind yellow by up to 10%. This makes cyan the tertiary, with values often consisting of one-third to one-half the magenta dot. Of course, these values will vary, depending on the person, the lighting, even the curves of someone's face. The important thing is the relationship between the colors. When it's unbalanced, the flesh will appear off somehow to the viewer. Too much yellow, and that sickly jaundiced look sets in. Too much magenta, and someone spent too much time at the beach. Too much cyan, and the colors lose their vitality. The following table illustrates the basic CMYK relationships between the predominant fleshtones:

	Cyan	Magenta	Yellow	Black
African	35%	45%	50%	Up to 30%
Asian	15	43	53	0
Caucasian	10	40	50	0

Use this chart as a reference as you learn to identify and correct these colors. By no means should you try to map any fleshtones to these particular settings. The values you encounter will change from image to image. For example, in the fair skin of a blonde, the relationship between yellow and magenta may change places, due to the nature of her complexion—but the distance between the two values should remain fairly constant. A lighter-skinned African-American will contain less cyan than someone with darker-toned flesh. You must be able to identify any aberrant component values, based in part on the above relationships, and part on the image at hand.

As always, the Curves command is the best tool for targeting and correcting these colors. Work in small steps, reading and re-reading the pixel values as you progress. It's better to apply two or three small adjustments (read: 1–2%) than a single broad and sweeping correction. Over-adjustment will quickly force the remaining image colors out of balance; smaller incremental adjustments will give you more control over the process. [9]

Let's take a look at these ideas at work (see Figure 12.23). The first image is a fair-skinned woman. By taking several samples of her face, I can see that it contains too much magenta, which makes her appear too ruddy and flushed. In the Curves command, I apply a midtone adjustment to the magenta channel, drawing the ink closer to the yellow/magenta relationship appropriate for Caucasian flesh. In the corrected example, you can see that the aberrant redness has been removed, but enough still exists to give her face a natural.

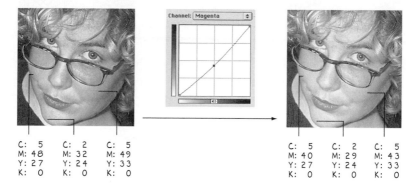

C: 5	C: 2	C: 5		C: 5	C: 2	C: 5
M: 48	M: 32	M: 49		M: 40	M: 29	M: 43
Y: 27	Y: 24	Y: 33		Y: 27	Y: 24	Y: 33
K: 0	K: 0	K: 0		K: 0	K: 0	K: 0

Figure 12.23   *Here, most of the magenta data exists in the midtones. Reducing the overall level takes the "sunburn" out of the subject's skin (see color insert).*

FOOTNOTE

[9] When adjusting fleshtones, always keep an eye on the surrounding image pixels, as well. For example, if you find yourself removing magenta to balance the flesh, you might be pulling important color from another part of the image. When this is the case, try using the Color Range selection command to isolate the fleshtones. This is one of the few cases where correcting the colors of a selected area is advisable; fortunately, flesh tends to stand out in reasonably high contrast from the surrounding colors, making it easier to create a clean selection. Again, it's better to work with small, incremental adjustments. If you overadjust the selected area, it eventually won't fit in with the surrounding colors, and appear as if it was cut and pasted from another image. (For more info on the Color Range command, see Chapter 13.)

In the second image (see Figure 12.24), the background colors are acceptable, but the skin contains a yellow cast in the three-quarter tones. Because I know the yellow content shouldn't be much more than 10% greater than the magenta, I draw a curve for the yellow channel that reduces the level of yellow in the three-quarter tones and shadows, but preserves the content of the highlights and midtones.

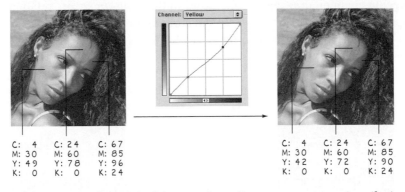

C: 4	C: 24	C: 67		C: 4	C: 24	C: 67
M: 30	M: 60	M: 85		M: 30	M: 60	M: 85
Y: 49	Y: 78	Y: 96		Y: 42	Y: 72	Y: 90
K: 0	K: 0	K: 24		K: 0	K: 0	K: 24

Figure 12.24 *In the original image, the yellow cast appears primarily in the darker areas of the subject's skin. By limiting my adjustment to the tones most severely affected, I can preserve the color content of the rest of the image (see color insert).*

If you lack confidence in your edits, try making slight changes, then proof them to a calibrated color device. Compare each adjustment to the one before it, keeping notes on the targeted values and the corrections you made. This is often the only way to evaluate the cause-and-effect of small (but critical) color edits, and your notes will greatly inform future decisions.

Blue Sky

There's a place in the Southwest where the skies are always blue—at least, that's what the newspaper lets its readers think. It established a standard color combination for blue sky, and demanded that all outdoor photographs be corrected to those values. The result? Every color photo features consistently rich, beautiful skies. (It's a good thing it rarely rains.)

I'm not suggesting that you correct all of your skies to a single standard, regardless of how pleasant the results may seem. However, just like correcting fleshtones, you can develop a strategy to adjust sky blues if you have an idea of how they're comprised. As you might expect, the primary component of sky blue is cyan. The secondary is magenta, which adds richness. You should avoid yellow altogether—it tends to move blue closer to an unnatural teal. If you need to deepen the overall tone, you're much better off adding black as the tertiary component.

The relationship between cyan and magenta shapes the tone and hue of the sky—or as some viewers would claim, its overall mood. In a standard blue, the ratio between cyan and magenta is about 2:1. To create a cooler sky, reduce the level of magenta to as low as 20% of the cyan content—any less than that, and the sky develops an obviously cyan bias. To create a warmer sky, increase the level of magenta to as high as 75% of the cyan content— any more than that, and the sky becomes purple (see Figure 12.25). The following table illustrates the basic relationships:

	Cyan	**Magenta**	**Yellow**	**Black**
Sky blue	60%	25%	0%	0%
Warmer	60	45	0	0
Cooler	60	15	0	0

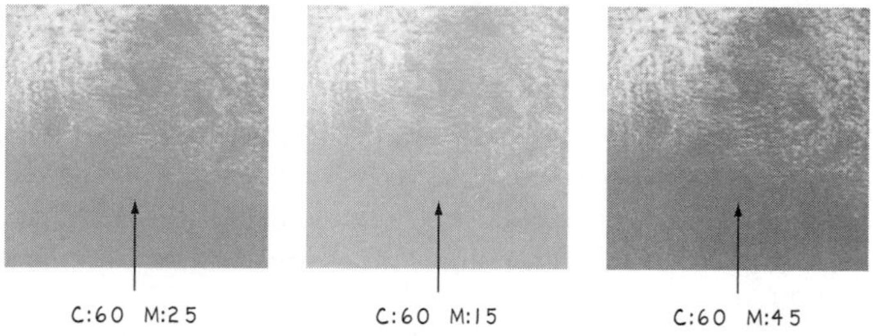

C:60 M:25   C:60 M:15   C:60 M:45

Figure 12.25 *The same sky can be subject to different "moods," depending on the level of the secondary component: magenta (see color insert).*

As with fleshtones, use this chart as a guide, not gospel. Again, the original materials will provide the strongest basis for your decisions. For example, do the clouds contain a reddish cast? This often occurs in nature—if the original contains such a bias, don't attempt to remove it from the image. If the original contains fluffy white clouds, you'll definitely want to reduce the level of magenta—but not so much that the sky becomes unnaturally cool. Remember, it's rare that the sky has to match the original *perfectly*; more important is that it looks natural to the viewer, that it matches his expectation of how a sky should appear.

Common Color Components

As you work with color, keep extensive notes about the values you see and the CMYK percentages that comprise them. This will give you an idea of the colors to expect, given the unique considerations of you workstation, monitor, proofing devices, and printing conditions. You'll eventually learn to apprise colors numerically, instead of allowing yourself to be seduced by what you see onscreen. It's easy to think to yourself, "something doesn't look right." It takes considerable effort on your part to make the jump to thinking, "there is 10% too much magenta in this sky."

The color relationships described in this section are useful, but you can also rely on a wide variety of printed samples. Create your own series of target swatches, proofing them out under the conditions specific to your workplace. Even swatchbooks like Trumatch or PANTONE Process are helpful—they display hundreds of printed samples, and each one lists its CMYK components. Whatever you can evaluate that compares output percentages to actual, printed colors will only enrich your ability to identify them intuitively.

The following figure provides a starting point for some common color combinations (see Figure 12.26). Take note of the primary, secondary, and tertiary components of each one. Create the same colors in Photoshop, then reduce or increase the individual levels, and assess the resulting changes. Produce a four-color proof of the same values and compare them to the color sample provided in this book.

This list could go on forever. However, these examples should provide a solid basis for evaluating many of the values you'll encounter in a color adjusting workflow.

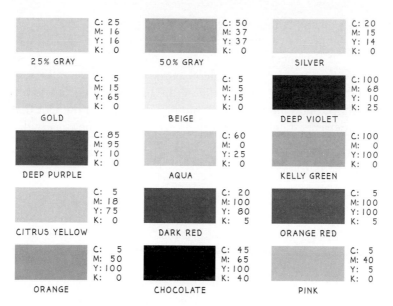

Figure 12.26   *This chart lists the CMYK values for a series of commonly encountered colors. These values are not absolutes; use them as a benchmark for understanding the relationships between the primary, secondary, and tertiary components (see color insert).*

Summary

Color will always be the most complex issue in the realm of print publishing. Some people grasp it immediately, and quickly learn to work miracles with Photoshop's controls. Most people find it more of a "dark art," with an abundance of mysterious rules, but a dearth of specific step-by-step techniques.

Balanced, appealing color requires education, experience, and skill. The issues are framed by the target printing method, and the values are subject to possible change by all the devices involved in your production process. As you read in Chapter 11, you're responsible for correcting colors that no one—clients and specialists alike—sees the same way. Processing cost-effective color day in, day out seems like a daunting task at best.

Fortunately, you're not left to struggle in a vacuum. You can ease the process by clearly defining a client's expectations up front, then paying attention to the fundamental facts of color. Trust the things you know. Examine an image's color channels to locate the most intensive detail. Use neutral values as a guide for identifying and fixing color casts. Understand the component values of the most common memory colors. And most importantly, learn to read the numbers. No single resource can teach you all the ins and outs of color adjustment; once you learn the basics, it's up to you to put in the time, effort, and endless re-evaluation. Take heart in the fact that even the most experienced color specialists learn something new every day.

PHOTOSHOP PRODUCTION
TECHNIQUES

I remember one of my first freelance imaging gigs like it was yesterday. I was still new to the industry, but I'd learned the fundamentals. I could scan a basic image, knew the difference between the Unsharp Mask filter and Sharpen More, and could use the Curves command to adjust the endpoints and add contrast. I was even reasonably adept with the Rubber Stamp tool. I was ready and raring to go.

I arrived to find 25 images on my hard drive, already scanned and corrected. The production manager's notes were extensive: change the color of the canoe from yellow to light blue; sharpen only the buttons on the cardigan sweater; add a soft drop shadow beneath the giant shoe; convert the image to a 20% ghost; create a character mask; draw 15 clipping paths. It quickly dawned on me that there was more to Photoshop than I realized.

Photoshop is arguably the most expansive and powerful program in the graphic arts industry. Many people see it only as a scanning and correction tool, assuming the remaining 90% of its features fall in the realm of high-end artists and illustrators. In a typical workflow, however, your responsibilities don't end after you've adjusted an image for print. Take a look around you. Does every printed image look the same as the originally scanned item? Of course not. Images are tweaked and enhanced, common effects are utilized, elements are removed from their rectangular constraints—in short, the final form of any image depends entirely on the project at hand.

This chapter digs deeper into Photoshop to present a series of techniques that apply to every workplace. It's not a comprehensive list—that information would fill a whole new book. Instead, they address the needs you're most likely to encounter in a production environment:

- Eliminating moiré in your scans.

- Using Photoshop's extensive selection tools, which enable you to target specific parts of an image for editing.

- Working with multiple layers, which enables you to combine images, create editable adjustments, and produce a wide variety of special effects.

- Creating and editing paths, which you can use for anything from customized selections to PostScript masks.

- Isolating image elements by creating silhouettes and clipping paths.

- Using new channels to create intricate masks.

Not only can you use these techniques for immediate profit, they'll form the necessary foundation for any intensive Photoshop work you pursue in the future.

Handling Moiré

One of the most common (and troublesome) adjustment issues is eliminating *moiré*, the blotchy interference pattern that results when overlapping grids of data conflict. Moiré can occur in three different stages of the imaging process: [1]

FOOTNOTE

[1] Some scanning software packages feature a "descreening" command, which attempts to convert halftone dots to continuous tones. Some work very well; many cause as many problems as they attempt to solve. Before applying any anti-moiré techniques, it doesn't hurt to see what your scanner has to offer. Most often, you have to determine the linescreen of the original artwork and then choose the closest value from a "Descreen" pop-up in the scanner interface. (If you have difficulty recognizing the value on sight—as many people do—you can purchase a *linescreen gauge* at your local graphic arts supply shop, which enables you to determine the ruling of a printed image by placing an escalating screen over it.) After you've determined the linescreen, choose the next-highest value from the Descreen pop-up and scan away. If the moiré is significantly reduced, continue editing as usual. If not, refer to the techniques listed in this section.

- **Scanning highly detailed patterns.** The most common example is when you acquire an image of patterned fabric, such as a pinstriped shirt or tweed. Here, many people attribute moiré to the screening process, assuming the halftone dots conflict with the image pattern. Most often, it's the scanner itself that causes the problem—if it's not sensitive enough to adequately read the detail, the resulting moiré is built into the image and is almost always impossible to remove.

- **Outputting incorrect screen angles.** When a multi-color image is output at the wrong screen angles, moiré results when the job is run on-press. Ordinarily, you don't have to worry about screen angles—when you separate a four-color image, they're handled automatically by the output device. Some image types, such as duotones, enable you to define new screen angles. If you don't use the optimal values, moiré is inevitable.

- **Scanning pre-screened images.** When you acquire an image that's already been printed (for example, a photo in a magazine), you're not scanning the same continuous tone information found in a photograph or film transparency—you're scanning halftone dots. The scanner partially recognizes the spaces between the dots, but not well enough to either reproduce them identically or convert them to continuous tones. As a result, the image contains a moiré pattern. In this case, however, you can use several techniques to reduce or eliminate the pattern. Each approach requires that you blur or remove a certain amount of image detail, so the one you use may well depend on the image at hand. They are listed below in the order of least to most damaging to the overall image quality.

Reducing Moiré in a Scanned Halftone

When scanning a prescreened black-and-white halftone, the following steps will often eliminate the spaces between the halftone dots:

1. Scan the image at twice the normal resolution, minus 10 pixels. For example, if you would normally scan a halftone at 300ppi, scan it at 590ppi. (Here, 10 is an arbitrary amount. If you tell Photoshop to reduce the resolution by precisely 25%, 50%, or 75%, it applies an algorithmic "shortcut" to the image, which doesn't create the necessary blurred effect. Because you want Photoshop to re-interpolate the value of every pixel, subtracting after doubling the resolution creates the desired effect.)

2. In Photoshop, choose Filter: Blur: **Gaussian Blur**. This filter is quite damaging to the image, so only apply low values. A radius of .7 to 1.2 pixels should suffice (see Figure 13.1).

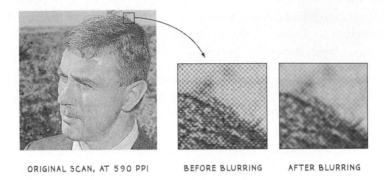

ORIGINAL SCAN, AT 590 PPI   BEFORE BLURRING   AFTER BLURRING

Figure 13.1 *Use the Gaussian Blur filter to ever-so-slightly conceal the dot pattern of a prescreened image. Don't try to eliminate the pattern entirely; if you can reduce it by half, the remaining commands should take care of the rest.*

3. Choose Image: **Image Size**.

4. In the Image Size dialog box, check the Constrain Proportions and Resample Images boxes. This allows you to change the resolution without affecting the width and height. Also, make sure the Interpolation is set to Bicubic.

5. Enter 300 in the Resolution field.

6. Click OK. By cutting the resolution in half, you remove three-quarters of the image pixels. Often, this removes most of the pattern as well (see Figure 13.2).

7. Evaluate the image. If the dots have been sufficiently reduced, continue editing as normal. If not, move on to the next step.

8. Evaluate the image again. If a slight dot pattern still exists, apply the Filter: Noise: **Despeckle** command.

In most cases, the above steps will sufficiently reduce moiré in a scanned halftone. If not, rescan the image using some of the techniques listed below for prescreened color images.

ORIGINAL SCAN   ADJUSTED FOR MOIRÉ

Figure 13.2   *When you reduce the resolution back to the print-oriented value, the interpolation process further removes any remaining dot pattern.*

Beating Moiré by Rotation

When you scan a prescreened color image, dealing with moiré is trickier. Instead of only appearing in one channel (Black), the pattern might appear in one or more of the individual color channels. Over-adjusting the entire image can irreversibly damage the info in a channel that didn't contain any pattern in the first place. Before attempting any channel-specific editing, you should try to eliminate as many of the dot shapes as possible at the time of the scan.

The first technique is similar to swapping the screen angles of the image. Instead of placing the image upright in the scanner bed, place it at a specific angle. (On a flatbed scanner, use an artist's triangle to measure the angle.) This will accomplish two things. First, it will force the scanner to slightly misinterpret the more obvious component colors, such as cyan and black. Second, when you rotate the image in Photoshop, the interpolation process will blur the edges of the dot shapes, producing a more continuous-tone result.

Most people scan at 15°, which is the best place to start. However, scanning the same image at 30° and 45° will give you a variety of choices—when one doesn't work, try the next.

After scanning the image, there are two ways to rotate it. First, choose Image: Rotate Canvas: **Arbitrary**. Enter the angle at which the image was scanned and then crop away any additional canvas that results when you rotate the entire image. Second, you can rotate as you crop the image. (For more info, see "Cropping Scans," later this chapter.)

Beating Moiré by Blurring

The most reliable method of beating a pattern is also the most damaging. Fortunately, by using a series of blurring techniques, this approach presents the most opportunities for user input. The basic steps are as follows:

1. Scan the image at twice the normal resolution, minus 10 pixels (as described under "Reducing Moiré in a Scanned Halftone," earlier this chapter).

2. Blur the entire image.

3. Examine the color channels and blur again as needed.

4. Reduce the resolution to the desired value.

5. Sharpen and continue editing.

Let's take a closer look at the issues involved in each step.

Step 1: Scan at Twice the Normal Resolution

Here, doubling the resolution serves two purposes. First, when you apply the first round of blur filters, the image contains far more information than a standard scan, which results in less damage to important detail. Second, when you later reduce the resolution of the blurred image, more of the conflicting dot structure is likely to be discarded. [2]

Step 2: Blur the Image

When the scan opens in Photoshop, use the Gaussian Blur filter to slightly distort the halftone dot shapes. The goal isn't to remove the pattern entirely.

FOOTNOTE

[2] Scanning at such a high resolution can be time consuming and frustratingly slow, but it's necessary. For example, a 4×5-inch RGB image at 300ppi measures a little over 5MB, but a 590ppi version of the same image exceeds 20MB. If your scanner and workstation are far too slow, remember that most printing methods can tolerate a quality factor of 1.5 to 1. This means that if you're printing an image at 150lpi, the image resolution can be as low as 225ppi. If you scan the same image at 440ppi, the file size is only 11MB—almost half the size of its 590ppi counterpart. If you use this approach, remember to reduce the resolution to the right amount—in this case, 225ppi. Otherwise, it won't produce the necessary blurring effect.

Instead, enter a value that starts to remove the pattern, but not so much that image detail is irreversibly lost. In my experience, I've never applied a blur greater than 1.8 pixels; usually, a value closer to .7 pixels works best. [3]

Step 3: Examine the Color Channels

Most likely, a slight pattern still resides in the image. Examine the color channels by clicking each one in the Channels palette. In many cases, moiré affects only one or two of the channels (see Figure 13.3). If so, you can target your edits more specifically, without hindering the detail of the remaining colors.

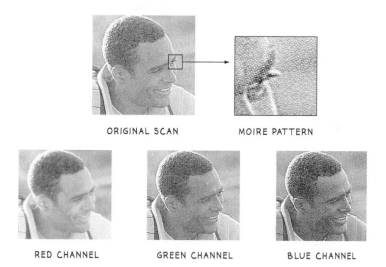

ORIGINAL SCAN   MOIRE PATTERN

RED CHANNEL   GREEN CHANNEL   BLUE CHANNEL

Figure 13.3 *Often, the moiré pattern will be evident in only one or two of the color channels. If so, focus your edits there to retain as much image detail as possible. In this example, the red channel has the least amount of pattern, so you would focus on the green and blue channels.*

FOOTNOTE

[3] Photoshop includes a few other blur filters, such as Blur and Blur More, that should be avoided. The Gaussian Blur filter is superior for two reasons: You can enter precise values, and it applies its effect using *Gaussian Bell Curve* distribution. The Gaussian Bell Curve works by unevenly fading the amount of blur over a distance to create a more natural, aesthetically pleasing effect. The human eye is very sensitive to changes in color. When a blur fades steadily, it appears awkward and computer-generated. By varying the amount of blur, this filter emulates the effects found in nature, such as the edges of shadows.

After you've targeted a problematic channel, try one of two things. First, apply another Gaussian Blur, using the same methods described earlier. Or, apply the Despeckle filter, which seeks out and averages aberrant pixel values. Always keep an eye on the composite channel to make sure your edits in one channel don't cause visible artifacting when you view the image in full color.

Step 4: Reduce the Resolution

After blurring the image, reduce its resolution to the desired value. Do this by choosing Image: **Image Size** (checking the Constrain Proportions and Resample Images boxes) and entering the new value in the Resolution field. As Photoshop interpolates the new resolution, it must recalculate every pixel value, which further reduces the amount of moiré.

The image quality should be considerably improved. If a slight pattern persists, examine the color channels again and lay in another, smaller Gaussian Blur value (.3 to .5 pixels).

Step 5: Sharpen the Image

When you apply the Unsharp Mask filter to a descreened image, you must strike a balance between emphasizing image detail and exaggerating the pattern you worked so hard to remove. It may be difficult to sharpen the image as much as it needs. As you preview the effect of the filter, set the Amount to the point just before the dot pattern starts to stand out.

Cropping Scans

When you crop an image, you mimic the conventional technique of cropping a photograph. There, you mark a photo to specify the portion you want to use. In Photoshop, you do the same thing by drawing a crop marquee around the pixels you want to save, then discarding the data that falls outside its boundaries. [4]

FOOTNOTE

[4] Page layout programs have their own tools to crop imported images. Unlike cropping in Photoshop, they only hide portions of the image from view. This can cause problems during printing, since your output device still has to process the hidden pixels. At the very least, the image takes longer to output. In extreme cases, the file might not output at all. Whenever possible, crop your images in Photoshop. (See Chapter 14, "Page Layout Issues," for more info.)

Create a crop marquee by dragging across the image with the Crop tool. You don't have to drag perfectly the first time; you can easily adjust the shape of the box. Use the following techniques:

- **Resize.** To resize the marquee, drag any of the points on the corners and sides of the outline. To scale the marquee proportionately, Shift-drag one of the points.

- **Move.** To reposition the marquee, place the cursor inside the outline and drag.

- **Rotate.** To rotate the marquee, drag anywhere outside the outline. When you apply the crop, the contents of the marquee rotate to become a vertically rectangular image.

- **Cancel.** To cancel the marquee, press the Escape key.

- **Crop.** To apply the crop command, double-click inside the marquee.

The edge of the crop marquee will automatically snap to the edge of the image when you move it to within an eighth of an inch. Disable this effect by holding down the (Command)[Control] key as you drag.

Straightening a Crooked Scan

It's not always possible to precisely align artwork on your scanner. Unless everything you scan has perfectly squared edges that you can wedge into a corner of the bed, you'll soon encounter an image that needs to be straightened out. The easiest way to right a crooked scan is to rotate a crop marquee. Follow these steps:

1. Using the Crop tool, drag a marquee that encircles the element you want to crop.

2. Move the cursor outside the marquee and drag to rotate the outline.

3. Use the image itself to determine the necessary angle. For example, if it's a photograph, rotate the marquee until the bottom edge is perfectly aligned with the bottom of the photo.

4. If the rotated marquee doesn't include all the important image information, resize the outline appropriately.

5. Double-click inside the marquee to simultaneously crop and rotate the image (see Figure 13.4).

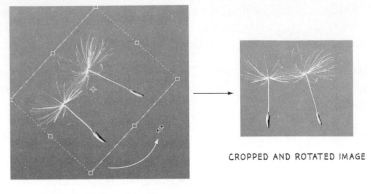

CROPPED AND ROTATED IMAGE

ROTATED CROP MARQUEE

Figure 13.4 *By rotating the crop marquee, you can crop and rotate the image simultaneously.*

Applying Levels-Based Adjustments

Most of the image adjustment techniques in this book involve the Curves command, which offers the greatest control over tone and color. However, many people use the Levels dialog box with a fair degree of success, and the following techniques illustrate how you can use it in your own environment.

Expanding an Image's Tonal Range

In Chapter 10, "Scanning Line Art and Halftones," I described how to use the Levels command to pinpoint the highlight and shadow tones of an image. You can use a slight variation of that technique to compensate for a limited tonal range captured by a scanner:

1. Choose Image: Adjust: **Levels**.

2. Drag the shadow slider to the right, placing it at the start of the image's tonal range (as seen in the histogram). This will remap the lightest pixel value to white.

3. Drag the highlight slider to the left, placing it at the end of the range. This will remap the darkest pixel value to black.

4. Click OK. The existing range expands to encompass the values from black to white, creating the effect of a larger number of image tones (see Figure 13.5).

MOVING IN
THE ENDPOINTS...

TO EXPAND
THE TONAL RANGE

BEFORE

AFTER

Figure 13.5 *By moving the endpoint sliders to the lightest and darkest image tones, you expand the image tones. This technique doesn't increase the number of tones—by redistributing them over a wider range, it can produce the appearance of a fuller scan.*

This technique results in a more appealing onscreen image. If your image is being prepared for print, the endpoints must still be adjusted for press limitations. [5]

Manually Setting Endpoints for Print

You can use the Levels dialog box to reduce the range of image tones, essentially resetting the highlight and shadow endpoints. This method isn't as accurate as using the eyedroppers to apply predefined values, but it can be useful in an automated workflow where quality isn't as high a priority as speed.

To establish the restricted shadow dot, enter a value in the left Output Levels field (or move the black slider at the bottom of the dialog box to the right). To establish the diffuse highlight, enter a value in the right Output Levels field (or move the white slider to the left). When you click OK to apply the adjustment, the tonal range is compressed to fit within the new endpoints (see Figure 13.6).

FOOTNOTE

[5] Be wary of expanding the range of predominantly dark or light images. They were never intended to encompass the entire tonal range, and will appear incorrectly balanced and washed out due to the small number of tones being stretched so far.

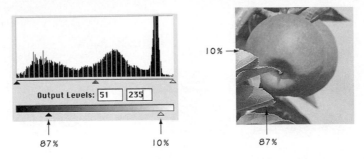

Figure 13.6 *To manually set the endpoints for press, move the Output Levels sliders in to the desired values. Here, they're set to 51 and 235, the equivalent of 87% and 10%.*

Selection Techniques

The most important editing technique you can master doesn't even change a single pixel value. When you work in Photoshop, you always have a choice: Do you apply an edit to the entire image, or do you focus the effect on a specific part of the image? There's only one way to apply a focused adjustment. You have to create a selection.

Selecting in Photoshop is quite different than selecting in a page layout or illustration program. Those applications are object-oriented, meaning every visible element can be individually clicked, edited, layered, and moved. When you select something, its edges are highlighted with a series of dots, indicating that the following commands will affect only that particular item.

That sense of separation doesn't exist in a pixel-based image. For example, Photoshop doesn't know the difference between a piece of fruit and the bowl that holds it, a man and the wall he leans against, or a car and the trees behind it. There's no way to select something by clicking what you only perceive to be a separate object. The only "objects" Photoshop recognizes are the individual pixels that comprise the image. To make a selection, you must create an outline that surrounds the targeted element. A selection is simply a boundary, a kind of mask that enables you to work on one part of an image without accidentally affecting the rest (see Figure 13.7).

There are dozens of ways to create and edit selection outlines. They can be simple, such as dragging a rectangular outline with the Marquee tool; they can be complex, such as saving a selection as a mask channel, editing it like a standard image, and then reloading the info as a selection again. This section covers the basics of Photoshop's extensive selection commands, when they're appropriate, and how to best use them to refine your images.

Figure 13.7 *When you create a selection, you're able to focus your edits on one part of the image while protecting the remaining pixels. (In this example, I applied the eraser tool to a rectangular selection.)*

Using the Marquee Tools

Use the Rectangular and Elliptical Marquee tools to create simple, geometrically shaped selections. When you click-drag across the image, a preview outline extends from the starting point—when you release the mouse button, the preview changes to an active selection. From there, you can edit the selected pixels, or refine the shape of the outline using the following techniques.

New Selection	Marquee Tool Technique
New free-form shape	Click-drag with Marquee tool.
New constrained shape	Hold down Shift key while dragging marquee.
New free-form shape radiating from centerpoint	Hold down (Option)[Alt] key while dragging marquee.
New constrained shape radiating from centerpoint	Hold down (Option-Shift)[Alt-Shift] keys while dragging marquee.

Adding to an Existing Selection	Marquee Tool Technique
Add a free-form shape	Hold down Shift key then drag marquee.
Add a constrained shape	Hold down Shift key and begin dragging marquee (do not release mouse button). Release Shift key. Press Shift key again and continue dragging. The preview outline snaps to a constrained shape.
Add a free-form shape radiating from centerpoint	Hold down Shift key and begin dragging marquee (do not release mouse button). Release Shift key. Press (Option) [Alt] key and continue dragging. The preview outline snaps to a radiating marquee.

Adding to an Existing Selection	Marquee Tool Technique
Add a constrained shape radiating from centerpoint	Hold down Shift key and begin dragging marquee (do not release mouse button). Press (Option)[Alt] key in addition to Shift key and continue dragging. The preview outline snaps to a radiating, constrained shape.

Subtracting from an Existing Selection	Marquee Tool Technique
Subtract a free-form shape	Hold down (Option)[Alt] key then drag marquee.
Subtract a constrained shape	Hold down (Option)[Alt] key and begin dragging marquee (do not release mouse button). Press Shift key in addition to (Option)[Alt] key and continue dragging. The preview marquee snaps to a perfect shape.
Subtract a free-form shape radiating from centerpoint	Hold down (Option)[Alt] key and begin dragging marquee (do not release mouse button). Release (Option)[Alt] key. Hold down (Option)[Alt] key again and continue dragging. The preview snaps to a radiating marquee.
Subtract a constrained shape radiating from centerpoint	Hold down (Option)[Alt] key and begin dragging marquee (do not release mouse button). Release (Option)[Alt] key. Hold down (Option)[Alt] key again. The preview snaps to a radiating marquee. Hold down Shift key in addition to (Option)[Alt] key and continue dragging. The preview snaps to a perfect shape.

Intersecting Selection Outlines

It's possible to create a new selection by *intersecting* two different outlines: The areas where they overlap are converted to a selection, and the areas where they don't overlap are removed. When a selection already exists, hold down the (Option-Shift)[Alt-Shift] keys as you drag the next outline (you'll see a small "x" added to the cursor). Overlap the two outlines as needed. When you release the mouse button, the selection is reduced to the overlapping areas.

Marquee Tool Strategies

Keep the following guidelines in mind as you use the Marquee tools:

- If you want to select the entire image, don't try to drag a rectangular marquee around the very edges. Instead, choose Edit: **Select All**.

- You can use a rectangular marquee to crop an image, similar to using the Crop tool. Drag the desired outline, then choose Image: **Crop**. (This command works only with an unrotated, rectangular marquee—it isn't available when any other selection shape is active.)

- Often, your marquee might not appear exactly where you need it, especially if you're radiating a shape, adding to a selection, or subtracting from one. If you need to reposition the preview outline, hold down the spacebar and continue dragging. (You don't have to release any other keys you may be pressing.) To continue shaping the selection, release the Spacebar.

- You can drag a selection outline only to the edge of the image window. Any pixels that exist beyond that point—for example, if you've added a layer from a larger image—cannot be included in any selection. You can only edit those hidden pixels when you click the appropriate item in the Layers palette(without making a selection).

Using the Lasso Tools

The Lasso and Polygon Lasso tools offer a little more freedom than the Marquee tools, enabling you to draw an outline by hand. They're not perfect solutions—their success depends on your hand-eye coordination, how comfortable you are using a mouse to draw (if you don't have a tablet), and your patience. Even with the most practiced hand, the Lasso tools are appropriate only for quick and simple selections. For the greatest accuracy—as well as the ability to access the same selection over and over again—you're much better off using the Pen tool to create a vector-based outline. (For more info, see "Path Editing Techniques," later this chapter.)

Selecting with the Standard Lasso Tool

Use the standard Lasso tool to encircle the image element you want to select. As you drag, a thin preview line appears. When you release the mouse button, the ends of the line automatically connect, completing the selection. From there, continue editing the selection or apply a command to the selected pixels. For best results, always drag until you end where you started. Otherwise, when the outline is closed, you might cut off part of the image you wanted to select.

Editing an Existing Selection

You can use either Lasso tool to edit the shape of any active selection:

- To add to an existing selection, hold down the Shift key as you draw.

- To subtract from an existing selection, hold down the (Option)[Alt] key as you draw.

- To create a selection based on intersecting outlines, hold down the (Option-Shift)[Alt-Shift] keys as you draw the second outline. When you release the mouse button, only the overlapping areas remain selected.

Including Edge Pixels in a Selection

If you want to include edge pixels in a selection, don't bother trying to drag the Lasso tool along the side of the image—you're bound to drag a crooked line. Instead, move the cursor beyond the edge of the image window. The selection outline traces the edge pixels until you move the cursor back onto the image.

Adding Straight Edges to a Free-Form Selection

As you draw a free-form selection outline, you can use a simple technique to include straight lines (in essence, temporarily mimicking the Polygon Lasso tool):

1. Begin drawing a selection with the Lasso Tool.

2. When you want to begin adding a straight edge, hold down the (Option)[Alt] key.

3. Release the mouse button. As you continue moving the cursor, you don't add to the selection. Instead, a line extends from the click-point to the cursor.

4. Place the cursor wherever you want the straight line to end.

5. Click to add the straight segment to the preview outline (see Figure 13.8).

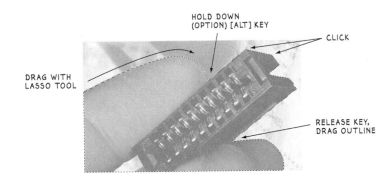

Figure 13.8   *You're not restricted to drawing freehand when you use the Lasso tool. By holding down the (Option)[Alt] key, you can click (without dragging) to place straight selection edges.*

6. At this point, you can do three things: move the cursor and click again to add more straight segments, press the mouse button and release the (Option)[Alt] key to continue drawing a free-form shape, or release all the buttons to convert the preview to a selection.

Using the Polygon Lasso Tool

The Polygon Lasso tool enables you create a selection consisting entirely of straight segments. Unlike the Lasso tool, you don't draw—instead, you place the segments by clicking around the element you want to select. When you move all the way around and click the first spot, the outline is converted to a selection. (If you want, you can double-click anywhere on the image to complete the selection, but this gives you less control over the position of the final segment.)

If you haven't completed a selection with this tool, you can't choose any other tools or access any palettes—the current segment just follows your cursor around, waiting for you to click the next point. Remove a selection in progress by pressing the Escape key.

Including Edge Pixels in a Polygon Selection

To include edge pixels in a polygon selection, you must be able to click just outside the image. If you click along the image itself, you might miss the edgemost pixels. If you click outside the window, you'll activate an application running in the background.

There are two ways to do this. First, choose View: **Show Rulers**. This way, you can click along the rulers and scroll bars to extend the selection to the image edges. Second, if the image is small enough, resize the window so it's larger than the image. When you extend the selection into the gray area that surrounds the image, you automatically include the edge pixels.

Including Free-Form Outlines in a Polygon Selection

As you draw a polygon selection, you can use a simple technique to include free-form edges (in essence, temporarily mimicking the standard Lasso tool):

1. Begin creating a polygon selection.

2. When you want to begin adding a free-form edge, hold down the mouse button.

3. Hold down the (Option)[Alt] key.

4. Draw the outline as you would using the Lasso tool.

5. To click straight lines again, release the mouse button and (Option)[Alt] key.

6. Complete the selection.

Using the Quick Mask Command

A Quick Mask enables you to create a selection by coloring the desired area with one of Photoshop's paint tools. Although you apply brushstrokes directly onto the image, you don't change any pixel values. Instead, when you switch to *Quick Mask mode*, the edits are applied to a temporary mask channel that appears in the Channels palette. When you switch back from Quick Mask mode, the contents of the channel are converted to a selection. People with conventional prepress experience will find this technique similar to using rubylith tape to mask part of an image. [6]

Preparing to Use a Quick Mask

Before you create a selection, it helps to understand the settings in the Quick Mask Options dialog box, accessed by double-clicking either Quick Mask button in the Tools palette (see Figure 13.9).

Figure 13.9   *Here is the Quick Mask Options dialog box, which controls the behavior of Photoshop's Quick Mask mode.*

F O O T N O T E

6   The usefulness of this method falls squarely between manual selections and saved mask channels. On one hand, you can create more complex selections than with the regular selection tools. For example, you can add soft edges and define partial selections, neither of which you can do with the Marquee or Lasso tools. On the other hand, these selections are one-shot deals. They can't be loaded again unless you save them. (See "Saving a Selection," later this chapter.)

Color Indicates

When you "paint" your selection, the mask appears as a semi-transparent overlay. You must determine whether the masked info represents the selected or unselected areas.

Photoshop defaults to Masked Areas. Here, any pixels not colored by the overlay are included in the selection. As you paint, you cover the areas you don't want included in the selection. This method may be more intuitive if you have created opaque masks during conventional stripping or platemaking.

When you choose the Selected Areas option, any pixels colored by the overlay are included in the selection. As you paint, you cover the areas you want included in the selection. (The following examples use this setting.)

Color

This swatch determines the color of the overlay. Photoshop defaults to red, emulating the opaque rubilith tape used in conventional masking. The only time you need to change the overlay color is if it blends too closely to the actual image. To change it, click the swatch and choose a new color in the Color Picker. (The overlay color is only an onscreen reference—changing it has no impact on the final selection.)

Opacity

This value controls the opacity of the overlay. It's set to 50% by default, and there's little need to change it. If the opacity is too high, it obscures the image. If it's too low, the overlay is hard to see.

Creating a New Quick Mask Selection

To paint a new selection, follow these steps:

1. Click the Edit in Quick Mask Mode button. The image doesn't change (although the words "Quick Mask" appear after the filename in the image window).

2. Choose a paint tool and select a brush from the Brushes palette.

3. Set the foreground color to black.

4. Paint the area you want to select.

5. To remove part of the overlay—for example, if you painted beyond the edges of what you wanted to select—switch the foreground color to white.

The paint tool now acts as an eraser, enabling you to refine the overlay as needed.

6. When you're finished, click the Edit in Standard Mode button. The overlay is replaced with an active selection (see Figure 13.10). (Occasionally, the selection might appear to be reversed; this often happens when the wrong Color Indicates option was set in the Quick Mask Options dialog box. If so, choose Select: **Inverse** to reverse the selection area.)

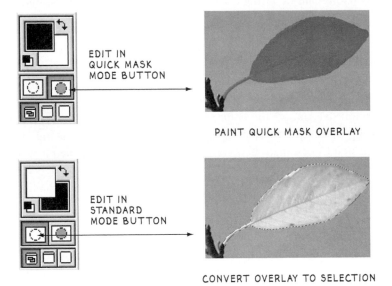

EDIT IN
QUICK MASK
MODE BUTTON

PAINT QUICK MASK OVERLAY

EDIT IN
STANDARD
MODE BUTTON

CONVERT OVERLAY TO SELECTION

Figure 13.10 *When you're finished "painting" the areas you want to select, switch back to standard editing mode to convert the overlay to a selection (see color insert).*

Using Quick Mask to Edit an Existing Selection

You can switch to Quick Mask mode to refine a selection you've already created using any other tool. Follow these steps:

1. Create an initial selection.

2. Click the Edit in Quick Mask Mode button. The active selection is temporarily converted to a semi-transparent overlay.

3. Edit the overlay as needed, using the appropriate paint tool and brush size.

4. When finished, click the Edit in Standard Mode button to convert the overlay back to a selection (see Figure 13.11).

ORIGINAL | SELECTION IN | EDITED QUICK | EDITED
SELECTION | QUICK MASK MODE | MASK OVERLAY | SELECTION

Figure 13.11 *After creating a selection using any other tool, you can switch to Quick Mask mode, refine the outline with any of the paint tools, and switch back to normal editing mode to access the new selection.*

Basic Quick Mask Techniques

Use the following techniques when creating a Quick Mask selection:

- **Creating a selection with hard edges.** To create a selection with no anti-aliasing or feathering, use the Pencil tool in Quick Mask mode.

- **Creating a selection with anti-aliased edges.** To create a selection with a thin, transitional edge, use the Paintbrush tool and choose one of the anti-aliased brush shapes.

- **Creating a selection with feathered edges.** To create a soft-edged selection, use the Paintbrush tool and choose one of the soft-edged brush shapes.

- **Inverting a selection.** To invert the overlay while in Quick Mask mode, choose Image: Adjust: **Invert**. To invert the selection after you've exited Quick Mask mode, choose Select: **Inverse**.

- **Canceling a Quick Mask.** If you don't like the way the selection is working out, don't bother trying to erase everything. Instead, click the Edit in Standard Mode button to create a selection, then choose Select: **Deselect**. If desired, click the Edit in Quick Mask Mode button and try again.

- **Saving a Quick Mask selection.** Ordinarily, Quick Mask selections are temporary—to access the same selection later on, you'd have to paint it again from scratch. To save the selection for future use, choose Select: **Save Selection** immediately after clicking the Edit in Standard Mode button (for more info, see "Saving Selections," later this chapter).

Using the Color Range Command

The Color Range command is the best way to make a selection based on a particular range of tones and colors. Most often, this command is used for selecting details too fine to select by hand, such as hair or lace. It's also a superlative tool for targeting a range of closely related colors, such as flesh-tones or the blue of a sky.

Like any other tool, it has its weaknesses. For the best results, the info you want to select should stand out in high contrast from the surrounding pixels. For example, it's easier to select the branches of a tree if it stands starkly against a pale sky than if it stood in front of another tree. Also, this command cannot produce anti-aliased selections; using it for effects like solid-color fills, extreme color adjustments, and filters will only exaggerate the jagged selection edges.

The Color Range dialog box contains several options, only a few of which are very useful (see Figure 13.12).

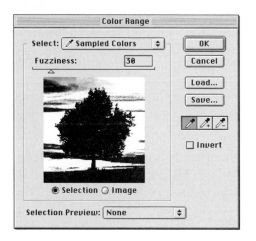

Figure 13.12   *This is the Color Range dialog box, which you can use to create selections based on targeted color areas.*

The Select Pop-Up

You can target a color range manually or automatically. For most selections, the Sampled Colors option works best (it's also the default setting). Here, you create the selection by targeting colors yourself by clicking on the preview image with the Sample eyedropper. Increase or decrease the range by adjusting the Fuzziness slider or by clicking with the Add and Subtract eyedroppers. (When you choose any other option from this pop-up, these editing tools aren't available.)

The remaining options are preset ranges, enabling you to target either a specific color group or tonal range. When you choose one of the color presets, you let the command automatically target a primary color. For example, if you choose Cyans, the command hunts down every color that has Cyan as a primary component. Then it examines the secondary and tertiary color components to determine how "pure" the color is. The purer the color, the more selected it becomes. The result is usually unpredictable.

The tonal ranges are a little more useful, but rarely produce an acceptable selection on their own. These presets compare the Luminance value of each pixel's equivalent Lab color. Photoshop consults an internal chart when determining what represents a highlight, midtone, or shadow, and it works reasonably well. Sometimes, it's useful to use these presets as a starting point, then switch to Quick Mask mode to further refine the selection.

The Out of Gamut option, available only when editing an RGB image, targets all the colors that fall outside the printable range of CMYK inks. In theory, you can select and adjust those values before converting to CMYK, leaving the "safe" colors untouched. Unless the adjustments are very subtle, however, this approach tends to produce visible shifts throughout the image.

The Fuzziness Slider

Use the Fuzziness slider to expand or reduce the range of targeted colors. Starting from the initial sample area, higher values increase the range of colors. In a continuous-tone image, this creates a more widespread and diffuse selection. Lowering the value restricts the range of colors, resulting in a smaller, more focused selection.

"Fuzziness" doesn't really mean anything; it just sounds better than "Relative Deviation" or "Chrominant Variability." It's a friendly way of describing the method Photoshop uses to expand the selection. When you increase the fuzziness, you'll see gray patches appear in the selection preview. They represent partially selected areas, which reduces the possibility of exaggerating the selection edges with any future commands.

The Selection Preview Pop-Up

These options control what type of selection preview, if any, appears in the original image as you target colors with the eyedroppers:

- **None.** This option results in no selection preview. Set it when you need to target very precisely with the eyedroppers.

- **Grayscale.** Here, the selection appears as a series of gray levels. White pixels indicate completely selected areas, gray pixels indicate partially selected areas, and black pixels indicate unselected areas. This option is usually the intuitive choice for users familiar with masking channels.

- **Black Matte.** Here, the image is covered with a black overlay, and only the colors that will be included in the selection are revealed.

- **White Matte.** This option is the same as Black Matte, except the image is covered with a white overlay.

- **Quick Mask.** Here, the preview is similar to a selection created using the Quick Mask tools. By default, it applies a 50% red overlay, which represents either selected or unselected pixels, depending on the current settings of the Quick Mask Options dialog box.

Creating a Color Range Selection

To make the actual selection, start with the following approach, changing the settings only when necessary:

1. Choose Select: **Color Range**. Move the dialog box to the side so you can see the image as well as the controls.

2. Start with these settings: Set the Select pop-up menu to Sampled Colors so you can target your own selection; set the Selection Preview to None; click the Selection radio button so the dialog box's thumbnail displays the selection preview.

3. Set the Fuzziness slider to 30.

4. In the actual image, click the range you want to select. The targeted pixels appear as white areas in the preview.

5. To expand the range, click the image with the Add eyedropper (the one with the "+") or Shift-click with the standard eyedropper. To remove colors from the range, click with the Subtract eyedropper (the one with the "–") or (Option-click)[Alt-click] with the standard eyedropper.

6. After you've targeted the desired range, increase or decrease the Fuzziness value. If you're selecting a specific element, use a lower value.

If you're targeting pixels for a color adjustment, use a higher value (see Figure 13.13).

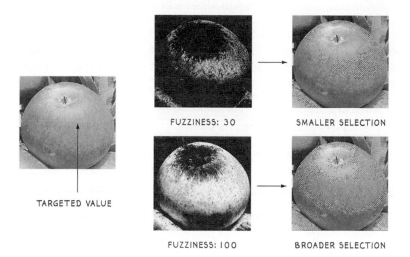

Figure 13.13   *Here are the same targeted colors, with different Fuzziness values. As you can see, higher values produce a more diffuse, widely distributed selection.*

7. Click OK to create the selection.

Use the following techniques to modify or refine a selection:

*   Because the Color Range command recognizes only color info, your selection may include pixels that you don't want to affect. For example, if you're targeting the glaring red in someone's eyes in a bad photograph, the selection will include any other red pixels throughout the image. Don't try to select one range of red over another in the Color Range dialog box— instead, create the selection then manually deselect any unwanted pixels. If you've used a low Fuzziness value, use the Lasso tool. If you've used a high value, use the Quick Mask tools.

*   If you have difficulty using the tiny thumbnail in the dialog box, try swapping the preview functions of the thumbnail and the actual image. Click the Image radio button to display the image as the thumbnail, and choose Grayscale from the Selection Preview pop-up menu. Now you can use the eyedropper to click the small preview and see the targeted results in the larger image.

*   The Color Range command also has the ability to limit its own behavior. For example, maybe you've already done some work selecting an element

from the background, and now you want to desaturate a specific color in the selected area only. If you create a selection before opening the Color Range dialog box, the command will affect only the current selection.

- When using a Color Range selection to make a drastic color change, apply a Feather value to it before editing. After clicking OK to close the dialog box, choose Select: **Feather** and enter a value of 1. This will further conceal the edges of the selection.

Creating Layer-Based Selections

When working with multiple image layers, you can create a selection based on the contents of the Layers Palette. This means you don't have to attempt to select an isolated image element by hand. Use the following techniques:

- **Selecting from an image layer.** Hold down the (Command)[Control] key and click the layer item in the Layers palette. The selection outline is based on the non-transparent contents. Semi-opaque pixels result in partial selections, based on the degree of their opacity.

- **Adding to an existing selection.** To expand the outline of an existing selection, hold down the (Command-Shift)[Control-Shift] keys and click the item in the Layers palette.

- **Subtracting from an existing selection.** To remove the shape of a layered element from an existing selection, hold down the (Option-Command)[Alt-Control] keys and click the item in the Layers palette.

- **Intersecting with an existing selection.** To restrict an existing selection to the area that overlaps a layered element, hold down the (Option-Command-Shift)[Alt-Control-Shift] keys and click the item in the Layers palette.

- **Selecting from a layer mask.** To make a selection based on the contents of a layer mask, hold down the (Command)[Control] key and click the layer mask thumbnail in the Layers palette. Unmasked areas—represented by white pixels—form the basis of the selection. Gray pixels result in partial selections.

Saving a Selection

Creating a complex selection is hard work. When you spend a certain amount of time drawing and refining a selection, ask yourself if you'll need to access it again before completing the image. If you don't like the thought of re-creating a selection from scratch, save it.

Saving a selection has nothing to do with saving the pixels it surrounds; instead, you save the outline itself, including any soft edges that have been added via feathering, Quick Masking, or Fuzziness values. Photoshop does this by creating a *mask channel*, a graphical representation of the selection outline. Here, selected areas are converted into white pixels, and unselected areas are black. Gray tones are treated as partial selections (see Figure 13.14).

ACTIVE SELECTION   SAVED SELECTION   MASK CHANNEL

Figure 13.14   *Here, I saved a feathered selection. As you can see in the mask channel, fully selected areas appear white, and partially selected areas (like the soft edges) appear gray.*

A saved selection appears as an extra item in the Channels palette. As long as it exists in this form, you can reload it at any time, and even edit its contents to change the appearance of the selection. [7]

After you create a selection, there are two ways to save it. First, you can click the Save Selection as Channel button in the Channels palette. Second, you can choose Select: **Save Selection**. This brings up the Save Selection dialog box, which offers you a little more flexibility when creating the mask channel (see Figure 13.15). Pay attention to the following options.

F O O T N O T E

[7] Be aware that saved selections should only hang around during the editing stage of the image. As soon as the image is ready for print, you'll have to delete any extra mask channels. If you don't, you'll experience difficulties when saving or importing the file. For example, you can't save a file containing any mask channels as a Photoshop EPS file. If a TIFF image contains a mask channel, it might not separate properly from a page layout program. To delete a mask channel, select its item in the Channels palette, and then choose Delete Channel from the Channels palette submenu.

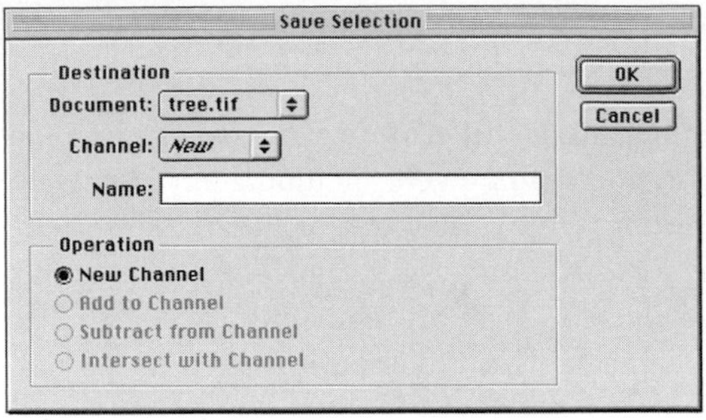

Figure 13.15   *The Save Selection dialog box determines how the new mask channel will appear.*

The Document Pop-Up

These options determine the form of the saved selection. By default, the name of the current image appears here, indicating that the new channel will remain part of the active image.

To save the channel as a separate Grayscale image, choose New from this pop-up. The content is the same as if you'd saved it as a mask channel, and as long as the new image is open, you can easily reload it into another image. This enables people with less-powerful workstations to save a selection without increasing the file size of the current image.

The Channel Pop-Up

These options determine where the mask appears in the image. By default, the selection is simply saved as a new channel. However, if the image already contains at least one other mask channel, you can replace one of them with the new saved selection. Do this by setting the name of the channel you want to replace in this pop-up. There's also an option to turn the selection into a layer mask, but you're much better off using the regular Layer Mask commands to do that (for more info, see "Layer Techniques," later this chapter).

Operation

These options enable you to combine the current selection outline with any existing mask channels. By default, New Channel is chosen, which results in a completely new mask channel. If no other mask channels exist in the image, you can only create a new channel. If other channels are available and you set one in the Channel pop-up menu, you can use the remaining options:

- **Replace Channel.** This option removes the item set in the Channels pop-up menu, replacing it with the current selection.

- **Add to Channel.** This option combines the contents of an existing channel with the new selection.

- **Intersect with Channel.** This option removes any info in an existing mask channel that doesn't overlap the current selection.

Editing a Saved Selection

You can edit a saved selection just as you would any other Grayscale image. Do this by selecting the item in the Channels palette, which displays the selection as a series of black, white, and gray tones. From here, you can apply tonal adjustments, brushstrokes with the paint tools, or filters. When you load the selection again, the new outline embodies whatever changes were made. [8]

Loading a Saved Selection

There are two ways to reload a mask channel as a selection. First, you can use a series of techniques to click the mask channel in the Channels palette:

- **Creating a new selection.** Hold down the (Command) [Control] key and click the mask channel in the Channels palette. (Or, drag the palette item directly onto the Load Channel as Selection button in the Channels palette.)

FOOTNOTE

[8] Remember that whenever you edit a mask channel, you can no longer access the original selection. Before applying any changes, you may want to create a copy of the initial mask channel, and edit that one. That way, if you make a mistake or change your mind, you can readily access the original channel. To duplicate a mask channel, select its item in the Channels palette and choose Duplicate Channel from the palette submenu. (Or, in the Channels palette, drag the mask channel directly onto the New Channel button.)

- **Adding to an existing selection.** To add a saved selection to a current outline, hold down the (Command-Shift) [Control-Shift] keys and click the mask channel in the Channels palette.

- **Subtracting from an existing selection.** To subtract the saved selection from the current outline, hold down the (Option-Shift)[Alt-Shift] keys and click the mask channel in the Channels palette.

- **Intersecting with an existing selection.** To create a new selection based on the overlapping areas of a mask channel and the current selection, hold down the (Option-Command-Shift)[Alt-Control-Shift] keys and click the mask channel in the Channels palette.

The second way to load a saved selection is to choose Select: **Load Selection**. This brings up the Load Selection dialog box, which offers a little more flexibility when loading a mask channel (see Figure 13.16). Pay attention to the following options.

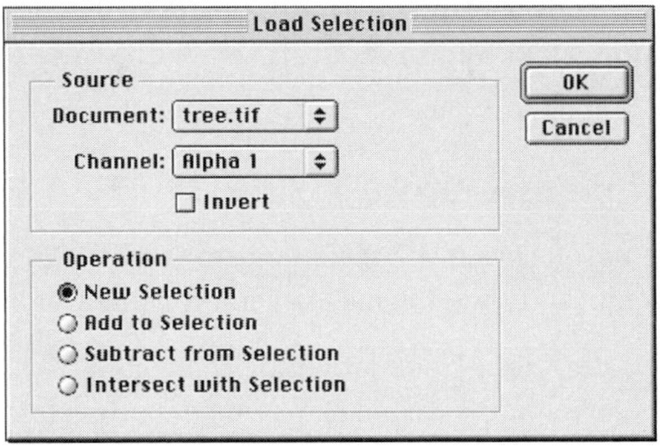

Figure 13.16   *The Load Selection dialog box determines how a mask channel will be converted into a selection.*

By default, the Document pop-up menu is set to the current image. However, if you've saved a selection as a separate file and that file is currently open, you can set it here.

The Channel pop-up menu lists all the mask channels available for loading, based on the image set in the Document pop-up. If an image has multiple mask channels, make sure you've chosen the right one.

When you check the Invert box, the final selection is reversed. The effect is the same as applying a regular selection then choosing Select: **Inverse**.

The Operation options are the same as those listed above when you load selections directly from the Channels palette.

Layer Techniques

Photoshop's layers enable you to work with individual image elements as if they existed on a series of transparent overlays. Without them, you can edit only a flat canvas of pixels; to make focused adjustments or combine multiple image elements, you'd have to use some pretty complicated selection and montage techniques. Working with layers is similar to working in a page layout or illustration program. By isolating a single element, you can make changes without affecting the rest of the image. Using the Layers palette, you can easily rearrange things, whether you move them across the image or change their stacking order (see Figure 13.17).

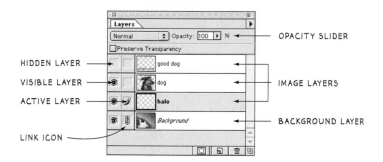

Figure 13.17   *The Layers palette is the focal point for most of Photoshop's layer editing techniques.*

Understanding Layers

Before you begin applying layers-based techniques, it helps to understand the difference between background layers and image layers.

The Background Layer

Consider the background layer the default canvas of an image. It's the bottom level of any layer-editing scenario and the final form of any print-oriented image. It's virtually identical to the single canvas used by the earliest versions of Photoshop (or any other pixel-based graphics program that doesn't support layers).

Most images—such as scans, stock CD-ROM files, and graphics that have already gone through the printing process—initially appear as a background layer. However, you don't have to restrict your edits to it. In fact, the limitations of the background layer can quickly become cumbersome. For example, you can't reposition a background layer, nor can you change the opacity of its contents. If you select part of the image and press the Delete key, the area is filled with the current background color.

Consider the background layer a starting point. If you just need to prep a basic image for print, there's no need to add any more layers. As soon as you need to apply certain effects, combine images, rasterize vector-based artwork, or even use the Type tool, you'll encounter the need for additional layers.

Image Layers

These layers enable you to isolate elements smaller than the image window, giving you independent control over their position and front-to-back arrangement. Each layer appears as a separate item in the Layers palette. As long as an image remains open in Photoshop, it can contain up to 100 separate layers—it doesn't matter whether the image was originally saved in a file format that doesn't support layers, such as TIFF, EPS, or JPEG. However, when an image contains anything more than a single background layer, you can save it only in the native Photoshop file format. To save it in a more appropriate format, you'll have to *flatten* it, or condense the multiple layers into a single background layer (for more info, see "Flattening the Image," later this chapter). [9]

Two features make image layers as powerful and flexible as they are: transparent pixels and the ability to set different opacity levels.

FOOTNOTE

[9] For the most part, you cannot import native Photoshop files into another application. For print purposes, they must be saved as either a TIFF or Photoshop EPS. However, a few programs, such as FreeHand 8, enable you to import an image consisting of multiple layers. There are three reasons to avoid doing this. First, there's no guarantee the image will separate properly. Second, the file size will be much bigger than necessary. Third, if you embed the image in a FreeHand EPS file then import it into Xpress, PageMaker, or InDesign, you'll encounter output problems. For the best results, only import flattened TIFF and EPS images. If you need to retain an unflattened copy, keep one in a different location in your job folder. (See Chapter 5, "File Management," for more info.)

Transparency

When you isolate a single element in an image layer, it's surrounded with *transparent pixels*. These pixels contain no color information at all, enabling you to view any image info that appears on underlying layers. (This effect is sometimes called a *transparency mask*.) When there is no underlying info—for example, if the background layer is hidden, or the file contains only a single image layer—Photoshop displays a checkerboard pattern to indicate transparency (see Figure 13.18). This pattern doesn't print, nor is it recognized by other applications; it's used only to differentiate transparent areas from colored.

Figure 13.18 *Obviously, you can't see transparent pixels. When an element in an image layer is positioned above other info, you can see around it to the underlying pixels (left). When the underlying layers are hidden, the transparent pixels are represented by a checkerboard pattern (right).*

When working with a layer that contains transparent pixels, understand that most Photoshop commands only affect *existing* color info. For example, you can't use the Curves command to change the level of transparency, and you can't use the Add Noise filter to scatter pixels across a transparent area. Transparency can be changed only by commands that add *new* info, such as applying brushstrokes with the paint tools or using filters to distort something that already exists in the layer.

Opacity

The Layers palette contains an Opacity slider, which enables you to add a level of semi-transparency to the pixels it contains. When a layer is 100% opaque, its contents completely obscure any underlying image info. Reducing the opacity produces the effect of fading the layer, allowing the underlying info to show through (see Figure 13.19). At 80% opacity, 80% of the visible info is contained in the layer, and 20% comes from the underlying pixels. If the opacity is set to 50%, the layer and the underlying info appear at equal intensities.

OPACITY: 100%   OPACITY: 80%   OPACITY: 50%

Figure 13.19   *When you reduce the opacity of a layer, you allow some of the underlying information to show through.*

Changing the opacity of a layer only affects its appearance—it doesn't permanently alter the contents until you flatten the image or merge the layer with another one. This means you can reset the opacity at will for as long as the layer exists.

Layering Fundamentals

The following 10 techniques are basic ones, added for your convenience. They're referred to by other layer-specific techniques throughout this chapter.

Creating a New Layer

Depending on your needs and the tools you're using, image layers can be added manually or automatically.

Adding an Empty Layer

There are two ways to insert a layer that contains only transparent pixels. First, you can click the Create New Layer button in the Layers palette. Or, you can choose Layer: New: **Layer**, then click OK when the New Layer dialog box appears. In the Layers palette, the new layer always appears above the currently selected item.

Isolating an Image Element

To place part of an existing image onto a layer for further editing, follow these steps:

1. Select the area you want to isolate, using any of Photoshop's selection tools. (If the image already contains multiple layers, make sure the one that contains the selected info is chosen in the Layers palette.)

2. Choose Layer: New: **Layer Via Copy**. This places a copy of the selected info into a new layer, leaving the original layer untouched (see Figure 13.20). (If you want to remove the info from the original layer, choose Layer: New: **Layer Via Cut**.)

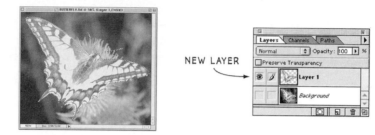

NEW LAYER

Figure 13.20   *After selecting part of the image (left), you can lift it onto a new image layer, where you can edit it independently of the underlying pixels.*

3. Make sure the new layer is chosen in the Layers palette, and continue editing.

Recognizing Automatic Layers

Several commands automatically produce a new layer, with no specific input from the user. The most common instances are as follows:

- **Pasting.** When you copy and paste a selection, whether in the same image or from a different image, the results always appear in a new layer.

- **Rasterizing EPS artwork.** When you convert vector-based info to pixels by opening such a file in Photoshop, the results always appear on an image layer. No background layer exists.

- **Placing a graphic.** When you use the File: **Place** command to import another graphic, it appears on a new layer.

- **Using the Type tool.** When you add type to an image, it initially appears as a *type layer*, a specialized sort of image layer. As long as the type layer exists, you can double-click its Layers palette item to edit and reformat the text characters. (To convert the type layer to a standard image layer, choose Layer: Type: **Render Layer.**)

Converting the Background Layer to an Image Layer

To bypass some of the limitations of the background layer, you can convert it to an image layer. (Bear in mind that it's no longer considered a background layer when you do this—you'll have to flatten the image before saving it as a TIFF or EPS.) There are three ways to do this:

- Drag the background layer with the Move tool.

- Double-click the background layer item in the Layers palette. The Make Layer dialog box appears; enter a new name (if desired) and click OK.

- Duplicate the background layer, either by clicking the item in the Layers palette and choosing Duplicate Layer from the palette submenu, or by dragging the background layer item onto the palette's Create New Layer button. The copy appears as an image layer; from there, you can delete the background layer or hide it, keeping it around in case you need to access any of its info.

Choosing a Layer

Before you can edit a layer, you have to tell Photoshop which one you want to focus on. Do this by clicking the desired item in the Layers palette. You can choose only one layer at a time; to affect the contents of more than one at a time, they must be linked. [10]

FOOTNOTE

[10] It's also possible to select layers using the Move tool. In the Move Options palette, check the Auto Select Layer box. This way, when you click an element onscreen, you automatically activate it in the Layers palette. This is useful when you need to arrange several image elements in quick succession. However, if you want to focus your edits on a specific layer, turn off the auto-select option. Unless you click directly on the element, you'll accidentally activate a different layer.

Linking Layers

Ordinarily, you can select only one layer at a time. By linking multiple image layers, you can drag them as a single unit with the Move tool and affect them simultaneously with transformation commands such as scaling and rotating. Follow these steps to link two layers:

1. Choose one of the layers you want to link by clicking it in the Layers palette.

2. In the second layer, click the empty box to the left of the image thumbnail. A small chain icon appears, indicating the link status.

3. To link additional layers, click their empty box as well. To break the link, click the chain icon to remove it.

Reordering Layers

The Layers palette reflects the front-to-back arrangement of your image layers. The frontmost layer appears at the top of the palette; the bottommost layer appears at the bottom. Change the stacking order of a layer by dragging it to a new position in the Layers palette. When you move the item between two other layers, the line between them is highlighted, indicating the new position.

If desired, activate a layer and use the following keyboard shortcuts:

- **Move the layer all the way to the bottom.** Press (Command-Shift-[) [Control-Shift-[]. If the image contains a background layer, the active layer is placed in front of it.

- **Move the layer all the way to the top.** Press (Command-Shift-]) [Control-Shift-]].

- **Move the layer down one level.** Press (Command-[)[Control-[].

- **Move the layer up one level.** Press (Command-])[Control-]].

Hiding and Revealing Layers

Whenever a layer is visible, a small eyeball icon appears on the left of its Layers palette item. To hide the layer, click the eyeball to remove it. To reveal the layer again, click the empty space to restore the eyeball.

Deleting Layers

When you no longer require a layer, don't simply hide it and forget about it. This can result in several unnecessary layers, which increases the file size and generally creates confusion as you hunt for the layer you want to edit. To delete an unwanted layer, either choose it in the Layers palette and select Delete Layer from the palette submenu, or drag the item directly onto the palette's Delete Current Layer button.

Copying Layers from Image to Image

It's easy to copy a layer from one image to another. For the best results, the two images should be in the same color mode and share a similar width, height, and resolution. Otherwise, the info in the copied layer may change unpredictably. Follow these steps:

1. Open both images in Photoshop, arranging them so both are visible.

2. Activate the image that contains the layer you want to copy.

3. From the Layers palette, drag the layer's item directly onto the second image. When the image's border is highlighted, release the mouse button.

If the two images have the same width and height, the contents of the new layer will appear in the same position. Otherwise, you'll have to position the element manually.

Flattening the Image

Before you save a file for print purposes, you have to *flatten* it, or convert any existing image layers to a single background layer. If you don't flatten an image, the only file format you can save in is native Photoshop.

There are two ways to produce a flattened image. First, you can choose Layer: **Flatten Image**. If any layers are hidden when you choose the command, an alert appears, asking if it's all right to discard them. If so, click Discard to remove the layers. If not, click Cancel and return to the image.

The second method involves saving a flattened copy of the image, leaving the original file open and untouched. Do this by choosing File: **Save a Copy**. In the Save a Copy dialog box, name the file and choose a file format from the available pop-up menu. If you choose a format that doesn't support layers, the saved copy is automatically flattened.

Using Layer Effects

Photoshop's Layer Effects, new to version 5, enable you to quickly create several effects that used to require extensive techniques, such as drop shadows, glow, and beveling. These commands only affect an image layer that contains some sort of information, such as an isolated element or type. You can't use them to affect a background layer.

Layer Effects are so straightforward, they really don't need an in-depth description. To get a feel for the basic use of the command, follow these steps to create a soft-edged drop shadow (see Figure 13.21):

1. In the Layers palette, choose the item you want to cast the shadow.

2. Choose Layer: Effects: **Drop Shadow** to access the Effects dialog box. Make sure the Preview box is checked so you can evaluate the command's effect as you edit the values.

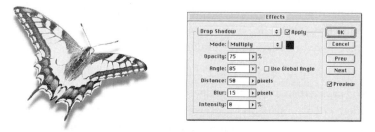

Figure 13.21   *Here, the Layer Effects command automatically adds a drop shadow beneath the active image layer. If I wanted to edit the shadow later on, I could simply double-click its item in the Layers palette to re-open the dialog box.*

3. In the Mode pop-up menu, choose the blend mode you want to affect the shadow. For the best results, set it to Multiply, which best combines the shadow with any underlying colors.

4. Click the small color swatch to define the shadow's color. It defaults to black, the most commonly used color.

5. Set an Opacity value to determine the shadow's transparency. It's rare that a shadow is so dark it obscures all the underlying info. For the best results, use a value between 40% (for light shadows) and 75% (for darker shadows).

6. To place the shadow, set an angle (which determines its direction) and distance (which determines how far away it is from the image). If you have precise values in mind, enter them in the fields. If not, you can place the shadow by dragging it around in the actual image. The fields automatically change to reflect the current position.

7. Determine the edge-softness by adjusting the Blur amount. Lower values produce harder-edged shadows; higher values produce softer-edged shadows. The extent of each value depends on the image's resolution.

8. When you've adjusted the shadow to taste, click OK to close the dialog box.

Layer Effects Guidelines

Keep the following issues in mind whenever you use Layer Effects:

- When an image layer contains a layer effect, a small "*f*" appears next to it in the Layers palette. If you want to re-edit the effect, double-click this symbol to access the Effects dialog box again.

- You can apply more than one Layer Effect to a single layer. For example, if you wanted to bevel the edges of the shape after applying the drop shadow, choose Bevel and Emboss from the Effects pop-up menu after setting the desired shadow values. Check the Apply box to enable the Bevel and Emboss controls. As you'll see in the image preview, the new effect is applied in addition to the shadow.

- If you need to apply the same angle to a series of effects—for example, if you're processing a large number of drop shadows and you want to make them all look the same—use the Global Angle setting. By choosing Layer: Effect: **Global Angle**, you can enter a single value that each layer effect can access. In the future, check an effect's Use Global Angle box to automatically insert the value.

- Although they can produce amazingly complex results, Layer Effects don't do anything you couldn't reproduce yourself using ordinary layer techniques. In fact, Photoshop simply uses a series of concealed layers to display each effect. It's possible to split a Layer Effect into its component parts, revealing all the image layers, groups, and links Photoshop used, enabling you to edit them individually. Do this by selecting the appropriate layer and choosing Layer: Effect: **Create Layers**.

- If you intend to apply the same Layer Effect to a series of images, don't bother applying all the values one image at a time. Instead, apply them once, then click the item in the Layers palette and choose Layer: Effect: **Copy Effects**. To apply the same values to another layer (even one in another image), choose it and apply Layer: Effect: **Paste Effects**.

Creating a Ghosted Image

When you *ghost* an image, you fill all or part of it with semi-opaque white. A popular technique involves ghosting part of a Grayscale or color image, then laying text over it in your page layout program. The faded area appears to be part of the image—you can still see the pixels that comprise the overall graphic—but they're light enough so the text remains legible.

Most often, a ghost is described by the amount of information that remains in the image (see Figure 13.22). For example, a "20% ghost," uses a white area with an opacity value of 80%. Ghosts usually range from 30% to 10%, and the value you use depends on the underlying image. Darker images require a ghost around 10–15%. If you're ghosting a lighter image, high opacity values tend to blow out highlight detail—set a ghost to 20–30%.

30% GHOST   20% GHOST   10% GHOST

Figure 13.22 *Ghosts are defined by how much underlying information shows through the semi-opaque white area. For example, a 20% ghost uses an opacity value of 80% (see color insert).*

To create a ghost, follow these steps:

1. Open the image you want to ghost.

2. Create an empty image layer by choosing Layer: New: **Layer** (or by clicking the Create New Layer button in the Layers palette).

3. Select the area you want to ghost by dragging a rectangle with the Marquee tool. The ghost's dimensions are often determined ahead of time; if so, choose

View: **Show Rulers** and refer to the values in the Info palette as you create the selection. (If you intend to ghost the entire image, don't make a selection.)

4. Fill the selection with white. The quickest way to do this is to reset the default colors (by pressing "D"), then press (Command-Delete)[Control-Backspace].

5. In the Layers palette, set the Opacity slider to the desired value.

6. Use the Info palette to examine the ghosted area, making sure no values have blown out to 0%.

7. Flatten the image and save.

Creating a Resizable Ghost

Once you've created a ghost, the only way to change its position in the image is to produce the effect all over again. If you want the ability to change the orientation of a ghosted area after you've imported the image into a page layout, follow these steps:

1. In Photoshop, open the image you want to ghost.

2. Duplicate the image by choosing Image: **Duplicate**.

3. Close the original image.

4. In the duplicate, apply a ghost to the entire image, following the steps described in the previous technique.

5. Save the ghosted image. Add "ghost" or "gh" to the file name to make sure you don't overwrite the original image.

6. In your page layout program, place and position the original, unghosted image.

7. Import the ghosted image, placing it exactly on top of the original. In QuarkXPress, apply the Item: **Step and Repeat** command to the original image (using no vertical or horizontal offsets), and import the ghosted image into the new picture box. In PageMaker, place the ghosted image, then align the two using the Element: **Align** command. In InDesign, place the image and align the two using the Align palette.

8. Crop the ghosted image to the desired dimensions. As long as you don't move the image, you can change its orientation by using your layout program's cropping functions to manipulate the image edges.

9. When gathering files for final output, make sure you supply both the original and the ghosted image. Many people fail to supply the ghost—if this happens, you'll either get a call from the service bureau, or the image will output at 72ppi.

Using Layer Masks

Layer masks enable you to conceal part of an image layer without deleting any of its information. A layer mask is actually a temporary channel, similar to the ones created by saving a selection or switching to Quick Mask mode. However, Photoshop attaches this channel directly to the layer, and the edits you apply determine the behavior of the mask. Wherever the mask is black, the image is hidden from view. Wherever it's white, the image is fully revealed. Wherever the mask contains gray pixels, the image is semi-transparent.

Creating a Basic Layer Mask

The most intuitive way to create a layer mask is to base it on an active selection. Follow these steps:

1. Select the image layer you want to mask. It has to be an image layer—you can't apply a layer mask to a background layer. (For more info, refer to "Converting the Background Layer to an Image Layer," earlier this chapter.)

2. Draw a selection outline using any of Photoshop's selection tools.

3. Choose Layer: Add Layer Mask: **Reveal Selection**. Two things happen. First, everything that wasn't included in the selection is hidden. Next, another thumbnail appears on the layer's item in the Layers palette. This represents the temporary channel used by the layer mask (see Figure 13.23).

As you plan future edits, you'll have to choose between editing the image layer or the layer mask. It's not enough to choose the layer in the Layers palette—you have to click one of the layer's two thumbnails. To edit the contents of the layer, click the image thumbnail. To edit the layer mask, click the mask thumbnail.

BEFORE MASKING   AFTER MASKING   LAYER MASK

Figure 13.23   *When you base a new layer mask on a selected area, you hide all the unselected pixels. That information still exists, and you can reveal it at any time, by either editing or deleting the layer mask channel. To remove the layer mask (restoring the layer), drag the layer mask thumbnail onto the Layers palette's trash can icon. From there, you can apply the layer mask, which discards the hidden info, or eliminate the mask altogether.*

Unlinking a Layer Mask

By default, an image layer and its layer mask are linked. If you reposition or transform the image layer, the mask is affected as well. To break this link, click the small chain icon that appears between the two thumbnails. Now, you can adjust the image or mask independently of the other—the one you affect depends on which thumbnail you click in the Layers palette.

Creating a Vignette

A *vignette*—a soft-edged, oval-shaped portrait—is a popular technique that has its roots in late-nineteenth-century photography. There are several ways to produce this effect in Photoshop, but the quickest and most flexible technique uses a layer mask. Follow these steps:

1. Open the desired image. There should be adequate space around the subject's head—if the image has been cropped too closely, you might need to rescan it.

2. Make sure the subject exists as an image layer. (For more info, refer to "Converting the Background Layer to an Image Layer," earlier this chapter.)

3. Use the elliptical Marquee tool to draw an oval-shaped selection around the head.

4. Choose Layer: Add Layer Mask: **Reveal Selection**.

5. In the Layers palette, click the layer mask thumbnail (after you create the layer mask, it should be selected by default).

6. Choose Filter: Blur: **Gaussian Blur**. This command softens the edges of the layer mask, producing the vignette effect. Higher blur values produce softer edges, but the exact value you use depends on the image's resolution and your personal preference (see Figure 13.24).

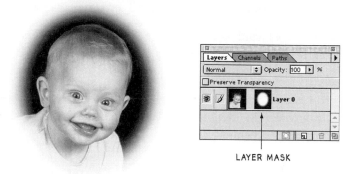

LAYER MASK

Figure 13.24 *By blurring the edges of the layer mask, you soften the edges of the visible image. If you reposition the image inside the mask, make sure you don't reveal the image edge (it will appear as a hard line seen through the soft mask).*

7. If you need to reposition the image inside the vignette, unlink the layer mask, click the image thumbnail in the Layers palette, and drag the image with the Move tool.

8. When you've finished the vignette, flatten the image and save.

Using Adjustment Layers

An adjustment layer doesn't contain any image information—it contains the values of an adjustment command, such as Levels or Curves. The layer acts like a lens, affecting the values of any layer that sits beneath it in the Layers palette.

The main benefit of using adjustment layers is that any color or tonal adjustments aren't set in stone, as they are when you simply apply the commands to an image. As long as the adjustment layer exists, you can tweak the values, even remove them entirely. The effect isn't final until you flatten the image or merge the adjustment layer with any underlying image layers.

To create an adjustment layer, follow these steps:

1. In the Layers palette, choose the top-most layer you want to be affected by the adjustment. (If the image contains only a background layer, you don't need to select anything in the Layers palette.)

2. Choose Layer: New: **Adjustment Layer** to access the New Adjustment Layer dialog box.

3. Set the desired adjustment command in the Type pop-up menu and click OK.

4. If the chosen command has a dialog box, it appears onscreen. (For example, if you set Curves in the Type pop-up, the Curves dialog box appears when you click OK.) Set the desired values here, just as you would if you'd chosen the actual command.

5. Click OK to close the dialog box. The adjustment layer appears in the Layers palette (see Figure 13.25).

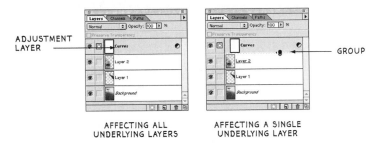

ADJUSTMENT LAYER

GROUP

AFFECTING ALL UNDERLYING LAYERS

AFFECTING A SINGLE UNDERLYING LAYER

Figure 13.25 *An adjustment layer acts like a lens, affecting the colors of any underlying image layers. You can change the values at any time—for example, you can apply a contrast curve without permanently adjusting the image, then change it later on. To restrict the adjustment to a single layer, create a clipping group.*

After you've created an adjustment layer, use the following techniques:

- To restrict the adjustment values to a single image layer, group the two together. There are two ways to do this. To group them as you create the adjustment layer, check the Group With Previous Layer box to group the new layer with the item currently selected in the Layers palette. If you've already created the adjustment layer, move it over the layer you want to group it with, then (Option-click)[Alt-click] the line that separates the two items in the Layers palette.

- To change the values of an adjustment layer, double-click its item in the Layers palette. The adjustment command's dialog box opens again, enabling you to change the settings as necessary.

- You cannot change the command used by an adjustment layer. For example, after you base an adjustment layer on the Levels command, you can't change it to Curves. Instead, you have to delete the first adjustment layer, then create a new one.

Masking an Adjustment Layer

It's possible to restrict the effect of an adjustment layer to a specific part of the image. For example, maybe you only want to apply a Levels adjustment to the eyes of a portrait, or apply a contrast curve to an object in the foreground. To assist you, Photoshop automatically adds a temporary item in the Channels palette whenever you create an adjustment layer. By default, this channel is all white, enabling the adjustment to affect the entire image. To mask the adjustment layer, you must add black pixels to the channel.

There are two ways to do this. The easiest way is to select the area you want to affect before creating the adjustment layer. This way, the new mask channel is entirely black, except for the area inside the original selection. The second technique, masking the areas manually, is a little more intensive:

1. Select the adjustment layer in the Layers palette.

2. Choose the Paintbrush tool and select a hard or soft-edged brush in the Brushes palette.

3. Set the foreground color to black.

4. Paint the image. Wherever you apply black, you remove the effect of the adjustment layer (see Figure 13.26).

It may be difficult to see the areas you're masking because you're not painting with any particular color. In fact, if the adjustment layer contains subtle values, such as a small contrast curve or a slight color bump, you might not be able to see the differences at all.

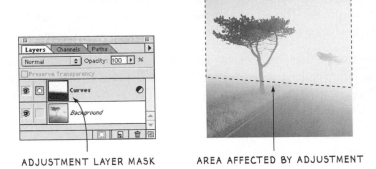

ADJUSTMENT LAYER MASK   AREA AFFECTED BY ADJUSTMENT

Figure 13.26 *Photoshop creates a temporary mask channel whenever you apply an adjustment layer. By painting the channel (or by basing an adjustment layer on a selection), you can apply an adjustment that affects only part of the underlying info.*

Two shortcuts will enable you to see the results of your painted masks. First, you can (Option-click)[Alt-click] the adjustment layer's thumbnail in the Layers palette, which displays the entire contents of the mask channel. (Option-click)[Alt-click] the thumbnail again to return to the normal view. Or, (Option-Shift-click)[Alt-Shift-click] the adjustment layer thumbnail to view the mask as a semi-transparent overlay, similar to the one used in a Quick Mask selection. To hide the overlay, (Option-Shift-click)[Alt-Shift-click] the thumbnail again.

Path Editing Techniques

Like Illustrator and FreeHand, Photoshop features a toolset for drawing paths based on Bézier curves. However, Photoshop's paths are fundamentally different than those found in a vector-based graphics program. Although you still use a Pen tool to place points and segments, you can't print the object-oriented shapes. Instead, you'll force a path to interact with the image somehow, most often as a clipping path or selection. (In fact, once you become proficient with the Pen tool, you'll find it one of the most powerful and flexible selection tools Photoshop has to offer.)

Using Photoshop's Pen tool is almost exactly the same as using Illustrator's or FreeHand's. (Refer to Chapter 8, "Vector-Based Graphics," for more info.) Handling a path after you create it, though, is considerably different. As you work through the following techniques, keep the following issues in mind:

- Paths exist separately from the image, appearing on a sort of transparent overlay. After you create a path, you can hide and reveal it whenever you need to, and edit its shape independently of the underlying pixels.

- Each path appears as an item in the Paths palette, similar to a layer or channel. However, Photoshop uses a slightly different terminology than other programs, which tend to refer to every object-oriented shape as a "path." Photoshop calls each individual shape a *subpath*, because each item in the Paths palette can contain multiple shapes. In turn, each palette item is called a *path*, regardless of how many shapes it contains.

- As soon as you place a single point with the Pen tool, a *work path* appears in the Paths palette, which contains the vector-based information. Work paths are temporary, unsaved items, and shouldn't be left in the palette for very long—if you start creating a new path while the work path is deactivated, the unsaved path is discarded. For the best results, always save a work path by double-clicking its item in the Paths palette.

- After you've saved a path, you don't have to keep saving it whenever you make a change—it updates itself automatically. (Of course, you still need to save the image to retain any new paths for future edits.)

Drawing a Basic Path

The easiest path to create is made entirely out of straight lines—just click around the image without dragging. Most paths require a little curving, though, but many people try to get around it by clicking hundreds of tiny straight lines, hoping they're small enough to escape detection (a technique that never works as well as you hope). Getting the most out of Photoshop's Bézier toolset does require a bit of experience, but you can use the following technique to start drawing simple curves with a minimum of effort. In this example, I use the Pen tool to trace a basic shape (see Figure 13.27):

1. To start the path, click once with the Pen tool (without dragging) to place a single point.

2. Move the cursor a small distance along the shape you're tracing, making sure the next segment you place won't have to curve too steeply.

3. As you click to place the next point, hold the mouse button down and drag in the same direction as the path. This reveals the handles, enabling you to curve the segment.

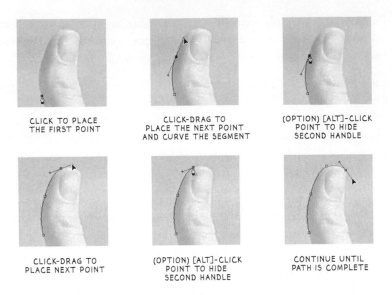

CLICK TO PLACE
THE FIRST POINT

CLICK-DRAG TO
PLACE THE NEXT POINT
AND CURVE THE SEGMENT

(OPTION) [ALT]-CLICK
POINT TO HIDE
SECOND HANDLE

CLICK-DRAG TO
PLACE NEXT POINT

(OPTION) [ALT]-CLICK
POINT TO HIDE
SECOND HANDLE

CONTINUE UNTIL
PATH IS COMPLETE

Figure 13.27 *This simple path-editing technique will satisfy most of your needs in Photoshop, at least until you become more comfortable with the Pen tool.*

4. Move the handle until the segment matches the edge of the shape. (Take your time; as you get accustomed to the handles, it may take a moment or two to get it right.) Release the mouse button.

5. Hold down the (Option)[Alt] key and click the point you just placed. This hides the second curve handle, preventing it from adding any curve to the next segment.

6. Repeat steps 4 through 6 until you complete the path.

The advantage of this technique is that each segment is controlled by only one curve handle, making it much easier to shape the path as you create it. Keep the following issues in mind:

*   If you've determined that you need a closed path, remember to end on the first point you placed.

*   Don't try to get the path perfect the first time around. Just try to get as close as you can. When you've completed the path, you can always tweak it as necessary with the Direct Selection tool.

*   If you click in error, don't try to repair the path on-the-fly (if you're new to the Pen tool, your path can quickly spin out of control). Instead, press (Command-Z)[Control-Z] to undo the last action, and then try again.

- If you're using the Pen tool to trace an image element, try to place the path just inside the element's edge, shaving off a couple of pixels. This way, if you convert the path to a selection or use it as a clipping path, you reduce the chances of including any unwanted background pixels in the outline.

Viewing a Path

To view the contents of a path, click its item in the Paths palette. To hide it from view, click the blank space at the bottom of the Paths palette. You can display the contents of only one path at a time.

Continuing an Existing Open Path

It's possible for a path to become deselected as you're creating it. Usually, this happens as a result of accessing the Direct Selection tool while using the Pen tool (which happens when you hold down the (Command)[Control] key). If you try to continue an unselected path, you actually create two separate subpaths instead, and the shape likely won't behave the way you expect. To reactivate a deselected path, click either end of it with the Pen tool. From there, continue placing new points.

Converting a Path to a Selection

A path is like a saved selection, only without the complexity of a mask channel. You can convert a path to a selection at any time, leaving the original item untouched in the Paths palette. If the selection isn't exactly the way you want it, you can cancel it, edit the path, and try again. Use the following techniques:

- **Creating a new selection.** (Command-click)[Control-click] the desired item in the Paths palette (see Figure 13.28).

- **Adding to an existing selection.** (Command-Shift-click)[Control-Shift-click] the desired palette item.

- **Subtracting from an existing selection.** (Option-Command-click)[Alt-Control-click] the desired palette item.

- **Intersecting with an existing selection.** (Option-Command-Shift-click)[Alt-Control-Shift-click] the desired palette item.

PATH   (COMMAND) [CONTROL]-CLICK   SELECTION
PALETTE ITEM

Figure 13.28 *After you create a path, you can convert it to a selection any time you want. If you need to change its shape, undo the selection, refine the path, and convert it again. In this way, a path is like a saved selection.*

For a little more control (such as the ability to feather the edges of the selection), you can click the desired item in the Paths palette, and then choose Make Selection from the palette submenu.

Converting a Selection to a Path

Photoshop enables you to convert a selection to a path. After creating an outline using any of the selection tools, choose Make Work Path from the Paths palette submenu (see Figure 13.29). The Make Work Path dialog appears, asking for a Tolerance value, which determines how closely the outline will be traced. Lower values produce a path that follows the outline more tightly, but uses a greater number of points. Higher values use fewer points, producing a smoother, looser shape. When you click OK, a new item appears in the Paths palette. [11]

F O O T N O T E

[11]   This method seems like a useful way to create complex paths, but it's riddled with problems. First, unless the selection consists entirely of straight lines, this command will never match the outline perfectly. Low-tolerance paths are distorted and jagged, and higher-tolerance paths are unruly at best. One way or another, you'll have to edit the new path with the Direct Selection tool. More often than not, it takes less time to create a new path using the Pen tool than it does to repair a sloppy, automatic path.

Second, the path will not recognize any soft edges or partially selected areas. It will literally trace the visible selection outline and ignore many of the finer details. If you need to retain this info, you're better off choosing Select: **Save Selection** to create a mask channel (for more info, refer to "Saving a Selection," earlier this chapter).

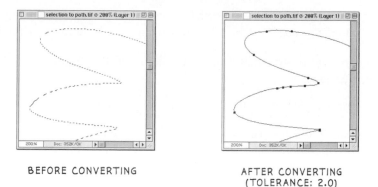

BEFORE CONVERTING

AFTER CONVERTING
(TOLERANCE: 2.0)

Figure 13.29 *Although you can convert a selection into a path, make sure you evaluate it closely before using it for any further editing. More often than not, these paths either have too many points (making the edges jagged and distorted) or too few points (making the edges loose and inaccurate).*

Exchanging Paths with Illustrator

The paths used by Photoshop and Illustrator are so closely related, you can freely copy and paste them from one application to another. (As you'll see, this relationship isn't as strong with FreeHand.) This enables you to produce a variety of effects, including the following:

- **Converting pixels to vectors.** Use Photoshop's Pen tool to trace an element from a scan, such as the outline of a leaf or a black and white logo. By pasting the paths into Illustrator, you can continue editing the item like any other vector-based artwork and save it as a scalable EPS file.

- **Bringing complex paths into Photoshop.** Illustrator enables you to create much more detailed and accurate path shapes. For example, you can convert formatted type to paths, producing outlines that match the character shapes perfectly. (In Photoshop, you can do this only by converting type to a selection, then converting the selection to a work path, which produces unsatisfactory shapes.) By pasting these shapes into Photoshop, you're essentially using Illustrator's powerful toolset to edit a pixel-based image.

- **Aligning customized type.** Photoshop's Type tool is particularly weak and doesn't enable you to flow text along a path. However, you can draw the desired path in Photoshop, and then copy and paste it into Illustrator. Enter and format the type you need, then copy and paste the entire element back into Photoshop. Use the original path as a guide for aligning the new type.

To copy and paste a path from Photoshop into Illustrator or FreeHand, follow these steps:

1. Create a path in Photoshop. Saving the path is advised, but not necessary.

2. Select the entire path, making sure every anchor point is activated. Do this by (Option-clicking)[Alt-clicking] the item in the Paths palette.

3. Choose Edit: **Copy**.

4. In Illustrator or FreeHand, choose Edit: **Paste**. Remember that Photoshop paths have no stroke or fill, so they may not be visible after pasting. In Illustrator, choose View: **Artwork** to display the path outlines; in FreeHand, choose View: **Preview** to disable the Preview mode.

5. Continue editing the path using the tools in Illustrator or FreeHand.

To copy and paste a path from Illustrator or FreeHand into Photoshop, follow these steps:

1. Select an existing path in Illustrator or FreeHand, making sure every anchor point is activated. Do this by clicking it with the Selection tool.

2. Choose Edit: **Copy**.

3. In Photoshop, choose Edit: **Paste**. The Paste dialog box appears, giving you the option to Paste as Pixels or Paste as Paths.

4. To convert the shapes to pixels and insert them into a new image layer, choose Paste as Pixels and click OK. To retain the vector-based outlines and insert them into the Paths palette, choose Paste as Paths and click OK. (Although you can select the Paste as Paths option when you've copied FreeHand outlines, Photoshop will not recognize them. You can paste FreeHand shapes only as pixels.)

5. Continue editing the new information using Photoshop's tools.

Using Silhouettes and Clipping Paths

The most common non-adjustment technique in Photoshop is to remove an image element from its rectangular confines. For example, if you want to place a tree without the background sky, or a head without the connected body, you must isolate that part of the image somehow.

The right method to use depends on how the image will appear in a page layout. If the image will sit alone on an empty white field, you can create a *silhouette*, which surrounds the element with white pixels. If you intend to place the element on top of other objects in your page layout, you must use a *clipping path*, or a vector-based mask.

Creating a Simple Silhouette

Most silhouettes involve simple shapes with hard edges, such as a piece of fruit or a product shot for a catalog. Extracting the image from its surrounding pixels is as easy as drawing a selection. Follow these steps:

1. Scan and adjust the image for print.

2. Select the image element you want to silhouette. You can use the Lasso tool to draw an outline manually, but the Pen tool enables you to create a more flexible, reusable path. If you use a path, convert it to a selection by (Command-clicking)[Control-clicking] its item in the Paths palette.

3. After the image is selected, choose Layer: New: **Layer Via Copy** to lift the element into a new image layer.

4. Preview the silhouette by hiding the underlying layer that contained the original image. You should see only the isolated element, surrounded by transparent pixels (see Figure 13.30).

SELECTED ELEMENT   ISOLATED ELEMENT   NEW LAYER

Figure 13.30 *Here, I've copied a hard-edged selection into a new layer, then hidden the underlying layer to make sure my selection was accurate.*

5. If the selection wasn't perfect—for example, if you included any background pixels or shaved off any info you wanted to use—delete the new image layer and try again.

6. If the silhouette is satisfactory, delete the hidden original layer.

7. Flatten the layers by choosing Layer: **Flatten Image**. This converts the transparent pixels to white, completing the silhouette effect (see Figure 13.31).

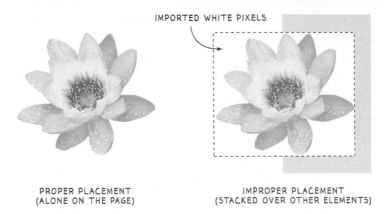

IMPORTED WHITE PIXELS

PROPER PLACEMENT
(ALONE ON THE PAGE)

IMPROPER PLACEMENT
(STACKED OVER OTHER ELEMENTS)

Figure 13.31 *When you import the silhouette, understand that you can only place it alone on the page. The white pixels are still recognized by your software.*

8. Save the image as a TIFF and import it into your page layout.

Creating a Complex Silhouette

If an image element contains fine details along the edges, such as hair or the nap of a sweater, it may be impossible to include them in a selection outline. Here, you have three choices. First, if these details aren't essential to the image, you can exclude them from the selection and use the steps described in the previous technique. Second, you can use a mask channel to isolate the image (for more info, see "Creating Complex Masks," later this chapter). Finally, you can try Photoshop's Extract command, new to version 5.5, which does a reasonable job of isolating finely detailed edge information. Follow these steps:

1. Scan and adjust the image for print. For the best results, the edge detail should appear in high contrast against the background pixels.

2. Choose Image: **Extract**. The image appears in the center of the Extract dialog box.

3. Use the Edge Highlighter tool to target the edges of the image. Don't try to paint the exact details. Instead, for wispy details (such as the fur in this example), use a larger brush size to include the detail area as well as the surrounding pixels. For harder edges (such as the dog's ears and nose), use a smaller brush size to define the area more precisely (see Figure 13.32). Change the brush size on-the-fly by moving the dialog box's Brush Size slider.

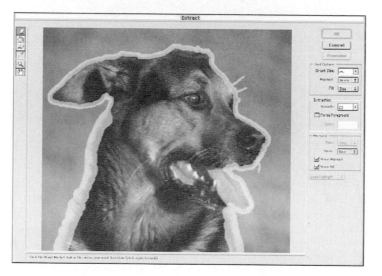

Figure 13.32 *To define the edges of a complex silhouette, I used a large brush shape to include all the tricky details and a small shape to include the well-defined edges.*

4. When you've painted the entire outer edge, choose the Paint Bucket tool and click inside the highlighted area. This enables you to define the primary element of the silhouette (see Figure 13.33).

5. Set a value using the Smooth slider. This will determine how accurately the edge details are lifted from the surrounding pixels. Start with a low value, gradually increasing it if necessary.

6. Click the Preview button to evaluate the extraction. If any pixels are being excluded or if the edge detail is retaining too much of the background pixels, change the Smooth value or edit the mask. You can edit and preview the image as many times as you need to.

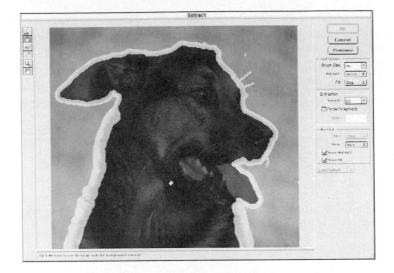

Figure 13.33 *Before you can preview the extraction, you must click the main body of the silhouette with the Paint Bucket tool. Only the inside of the highlighted edges should become colored; if the entire image fills up, there's an open area somewhere around the edges. (Option-click)[Alt-click] the painted area with the Paint Bucket tool to remove the color, then fix the edge with the Edge Highlighter tool.*

7. When the silhouette is satisfactory, click OK to apply the Extract command. The image element is now surrounded by transparent pixels (see Figure 13.34).

BEFORE EXTRACTING   AFTER EXTRACTING

Figure 13.34 *The extracted image should be very close to the desired effect. If a couple of areas have dropped out, you can restore them with the History Brush tool.*

8. Examine the silhouette, making sure the edges don't require additional refining. If they do, see "Touching Up an Extracted Silhouette," later this section. If not, proceed to the next step.

9. Flatten the layers by choosing Layer: **Flatten Image**. This converts the transparent pixels to white, completing the silhouette effect.

10. Save the image as a TIFF and import it into your page layout.

As you isolate an image in the Extract dialog box, keep the following techniques in mind:

- Always use a smaller brush size to define hard edges. If you don't, the edges might drop out or include fringe pixels when you apply the command. Use larger brush sizes only when highlighting complex, highly-detailed edges.

- When extracting a clearly defined element, always make sure the item is completely enclosed by the Edge Highlighter tool. Wherever an element touches the image boundaries, you don't have to highlight the edges. You have to highlight only up to the edge.

- To remove highlighted edge pixels, paint them with the Eraser tool. You can also erase the highlight by (Option-dragging)[Alt-dragging] with the Edge Highlighter tool.

- You can use Photoshop's standard zoom and scroll shortcuts in the Extract dialog box. To zoom in, hold down the (Control)[Command] key and the spacebar, and click the image. To scroll through the image, hold down the spacebar and drag the image. To zoom out, hold down the (Option-Command)[Alt-Control] keys and the spacebar, and click the image.

- To preview the extraction against a colored background, set a color in the Show pop-up menu, in the Preview section of the dialog box. To see how the image will appear as a silhouette, choose White Matte. If the pixels are too light to see clearly, choose Gray Matte or Black Matte.

Touching Up an Extracted Silhouette

More often than not, the Extract command gets *close*, but doesn't go all the way. For example, if the edges of the element shared any similar values to the background pixels—particularly in the harder edges—the command might exclude them. Also, if the Smooth value was set too low, it may have included fringe pixels that you need to erase.

After extracting an image, always zoom in and examine the edges. Use the following techniques, depending on what you find.

Restoring Excluded Pixels

The most common problem with the Extract command is that parts of the image are dropped out. The easiest way to restore them is to use the History Brush tool. By default, the History palette retains a snapshot of the image in its original form. [12] The History Brush tool enables you to apply this information, painting it onto the current layer like any other color. Follow these steps:

1. Choose the History Brush tool.

2. In the Brushes palette, choose a brush type that matches the info you're trying to restore. If you're refining a hard edge, choose an anti-aliased brush. If you're refining a feathered edge, choose a soft-edged brush.

3. Zoom into the image and target the area you want to restore.

4. Paint in small strokes, from the existing image outward. As you paint over the excluded areas, their original content is restored (see Figure 13.35). (Make sure you don't include any of the original background pixels.)

Erasing Unwanted Pixels

Perhaps the Exclude command included some of the background pixels; maybe it masked some of the detailed info poorly, and you simply want to remove parts of it altogether. Follow these steps:

1. Choose the Eraser tool.

FOOTNOTE

[12] If you've changed an image's color mode, dimensions, or resolution since it was scanned, you won't be able to use the default snapshot in the History palette. When this is the case, you must create a new snapshot before extracting the silhouette. Do two things: Choose New Snapshot from the History palette submenu, and then immediately click the paint box next to its palette item. This way, you can use the History Brush tool to restore any missing pixels from the extracted image.

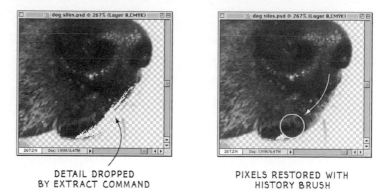

DETAIL DROPPED
BY EXTRACT COMMAND

PIXELS RESTORED WITH
HISTORY BRUSH

Figure 13.35   *Here, I use the History Brush tool to restore some of the info that was dropped by the Extract command. If you accidentally reveal some of the background pixels, choose undo and try again or remove them with the Eraser tool.*

2. In the Eraser Options palette, set Paintbrush in the available pop-up menu.

3. In the Brushes palette, choose the desired brush type. To produce a hard edge, choose an anti-aliased brush. For a feathered edge, choose a soft-edged brush.

4. Zoom into the image and target the area you want to remove.

5. Paint in small strokes, making sure you don't accidentally erase any part of the silhouette you want to keep.

Some stray pixels might be too light to see onscreen, but will be visible after the image is printed. If necessary, create a new image layer, positioning it underneath the silhouette. Fill it with black to emphasize the errant pixels. After erasing them, delete the black layer.

Creating a Clipping Path

If you intend to stack an imported image over other elements in a page lay-out, silhouettes pose a problem. Because you've surrounded the image with white pixels, they obscure any information that sits underneath them. If you want to produce the effect of a silhouette, but be able to place the image over a colored background in your layout document, you must create a vector-based mask called a *clipping path* (see Figure 13.36). By encircling the desired element with a Photoshop path, your layout program will recognize only the pixels inside the path, and ignore any other info. Follow these steps:

SILHOUETTE   CLIPPING PATH

Figure 13.36   *In my page layout, I've imported the same image as a silhouette and a clipping path. As you can see, I can place the clipping path over other elements.*

1. Trace the desired image element with the Pen tool.

2. Save the path.

3. Choose Clipping Path from the Paths palette submenu.

4. In the Clipping Path dialog box, set the saved item in the Path pop-up menu (see Figure 13.37). [13]

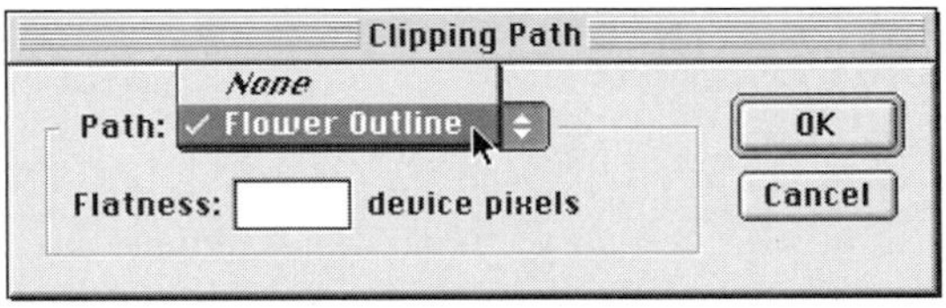

Figure 13.37   *The Clipping Path dialog box enables you to set an existing path as a clipping path.*

FOOTNOTE

[13]   The Clipping Path dialog box contains a field for a Flatness value. You don't have to enter a value here—the only reason to do so is to shorten output times. By default, your output device reproduces the curves of the path using the highest detail possible. By entering a Flatness value, you reduce the curves to a series of tiny straight lines. Values can range from 0.2 to 100 device pixels, which represents the length of each line, as measured in printer dots. For example, if you output a Flatness value of 16 to a 2,400dpi imagesetter, each line segment is 1/144 of an inch, or a half-point long. If you must enter a Flatness amount, use a value of 6 or less to avoid visible lines.

5. Save the image as a Photoshop EPS file. (If you save it as a TIFF, the clipping path command will not take effect.)

6. Import the image into your page layout.

Keep the following issues in mind whenever you create a clipping path:

- **Crop the image before creating the path.** Even though your output device will print only the info inside the path, it still has to process any masked pixels.

- **Use a closed path.** If you define an open path as a clipping path, the two endpoints are automatically connected by a straight line, which might exclude part of the image you wanted to use. For the best results, use only closed shapes for clipping paths.

- **Use simple paths.** Paths that contain a multitude of points take longer to output. Most often, a manually drawn path contains fewer points (and causes fewer output-oriented problems) than a path you created by converting a selection outline.

- **Using multiple subpaths.** If your clipping path contains multiple subpaths, each one acts as a masking element.

- **Using intersecting paths.** If your clipping path contains overlapping subpaths, the intersecting areas are masked. For example, assume you have a small circular path inside a larger square path. The information inside the square will display and print, but the info inside the circle will not appear.

Creating Complex Masks

Sometimes, a simple selection isn't enough. Often, you'll need to target part of an image for additional color correcting, or protect it as you adjust the surrounding pixels. If it has clear, crisp edges, you can use one of the regular selection tools. If it has finely detailed edges, your only option may be to create a complex mask channel based on the existing image information. This will enable you to load a selection that precisely matches the shape of the element.

Masking with the Extract Command

If the element sits in high contrast against the surrounding pixels, you can use the Extract command to create the mask channel using steps similar to creating a silhouette. Follow these steps:

1. Open the image that contains the element you want to mask.

2. Duplicate the layer.

3. Using the steps described under "Creating a Complex Silhouette" (earlier this chapter), use the Extract command to isolate the element, then refine it as necessary.

4. Convert the isolated element to a selection by (Command-clicking) [Control-clicking] its item in the Layers palette.

5. Choose Select: **Save Selection** to convert the selection outline to a mask channel (see Figure 13.38).

EXTRACTED LAYER,
CONVERTED TO A SELECTION

THE SAVED SELECTION
APPEARS AS A MASK CHANNEL

Figure 13.38 *After extracting a copy of the targeted element, I convert the new layer into a selection. From there, I choose Select:* **Save Selection** *to convert the selection into a mask channel.*

6. Choose Select: **Deselect** to deactivate the selection.

7. Delete the layer that contains the isolated element.

8. In the Channels palette, click the new mask channel. It should display the shape of the targeted element.

9. If any stray pixels appear inside the white shape, remove them with the Paintbrush tool (see Figure 13.39).

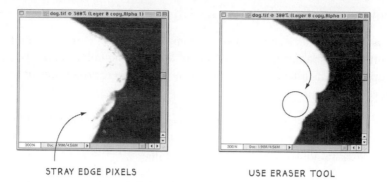

STRAY EDGE PIXELS   USE ERASER TOOL

Figure 13.39 *You must make sure that no pixels have been dropped out of the selection, which sometimes occurs with the Extract command. Fix them by painting them white.*

10. Return to the full-color image by clicking the composite item in the Channels palette.

11. Load the selection by (Command-clicking)[Control-clicking] the mask item in the Channels palette.

12. If you need to adjust the targeted image, apply the commands now (see Figure 13.40). If you need to adjust the surrounding pixels, reverse the selection by choosing Select: **Inverse**, then apply the commands.

ORIGINAL IMAGE   DESATURATED BACKGROUND

Figure 13.40 *After loading the selection, you can edit the targeted element (or its surrounding pixels, if you inverse the selection) without polluting the edge details. Here, I desaturated the background, leaving the colors of the dog untouched (see color insert).*

13. When you're through with the mask channel, delete it by clicking it in the Channels palette and choosing Delete Channel from the palette submenu.

Masking with an Existing Channel

If the image you need to target is too complex for the Extract command, you can often create a mask based on one of the existing color channels. In this example, I want to isolate a detailed tree so I can edit the tones of the sky. Follow these steps:

1. Click through the items in the Channels palette, examining the contents of each color channel. Look for the one that has the most contrast between the targeted image and the surrounding pixels (see Figure 13.41).

CYAN CHANNEL   MAGENTA CHANNEL

ORIGINAL IMAGE

YELLOW CHANNEL   BLACK CHANNEL

Figure 13.41   *Here, I want to mask the tree and ground of a CMYK image. When I inspect the channels, I see that the yellow channel offers the best distinction between the sky and the tree.*

2. To convert the color channel to a mask channel, drag it directly onto the Create New Channel button in the Channels palette.

3. In the new channel—making sure you don't edit the color channel by mistake—you must refine the masking element by removing any pixels that aren't part of the targeted image. Start by applying the Unsharp Mask filter to better define the edge detail (see Figure 13.42). (In this example, my Unsharp Mask values were Amount: 100%, Radius: 4, and Threshold: 18.)

BEFORE SHARPENING   AFTER SHARPENING

Figure 13.42 *To better delineate the target item from the surrounding pixels, I sharpened the mask channel. This will make it easier to remove any lingering tones in the sky, which I want to reduce to white.*

4. Use the Levels command to reduce the amount of gray in the mask channel. The goal is to end up with as much white in the background and black in the image as possible. For best results, move both the shadow and highlight slider toward the center of the histogram (see Figure 13.43). Pay attention to the edge details, making sure they stay consistent with the targeted image. Click OK when finished.

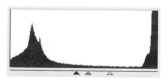

EXTREME LEVELS ADJUSTMENT

CHANNEL TONES PUSHED
CLOSER TO BLACK AND WHITE

Figure 13.43 *By applying a radical Levels adjustment, I exaggerate the darkest mask tones, while blowing most of the unwanted pixels to white.*

5. Touch up the mask channel with the Lasso and Eraser tools, removing any lingering gray ranges and stray pixels (see Figure 13.44).

UNMASKED DETAIL   FIX WITH PAINTBRUSH TOOL

Figure 13.44 *Here, I removed the remaining tones from the sky by using the Paintbrush tool to paint them white. I also solidified my masked areas by painting any stray pixels black.*

6. Return to the full-color image by clicking the composite item in the Channels palette.

7. Load the selection by (Command-clicking)[Control-clicking] the mask item in the Channels palette. In my example, the tree and ground are masked, leaving the sky selected. If you need to reverse the selection, choose Select: **Inverse**.

8. Apply the desired adjustment (see Figure 13.45). (To make your edits easier to see, choose Select: **Hide Edges** to hide the active selection outline.)

ORIGINAL IMAGE   MASKED TREE, ADJUSTED SKY

Figure 13.45 *After loading my mask channel as a selection, I can edit the sky without touching the fine details of the tree. Here, I lightened the overall tones, making the tree stand out in even higher contrast (see color insert).*

9. When you're through with the mask channel, delete it by clicking it in the Channels palette and choosing Delete Channel from the palette submenu.

Summary

It's easy to assume that images are handled by two distinct camps: production (which scans and color corrects) and design (which adds special effects and manipulations). But the responsibility for these tasks has blurred in recent years. Just as more designers are now required to understand scanning issues, more production specialists are being called upon to execute design-oriented techniques. Whatever your job description, understanding the nuts and bolts of the entire operation has tangible benefits.

Editing in Photoshop is the pivotal stage of the production cycle. This program can accomplish more tasks in different ways than any other on your computer. As pertinent and profit-oriented as they are, the techniques listed in this chapter (as well as in Chapters 9 through 12) only scratch the surface of what this marvelous tool can do. Accept them for what they are: a rock-solid foundation for all your future work.

PAGE LAYOUT ISSUES

The page layout program is the final destination of all text and graphics in a project.

At this point, let's assume that you've already entered and edited your text in a more comfortable word processing program, created and modified your vector-based artwork in the appropriate program, and scanned and corrected your halftones in Photoshop. The page layout program is the "drawing board" where you combine all of these disparate elements, creating a cohesive product.

In this chapter, I focus on the three industry-standard page layout applications: QuarkXPress, Adobe PageMaker, and Adobe InDesign. The reason I emphasize these programs for the purposes of page layout is simple: They were specifically designed for layout and color separation. Because they are used by the majority of designers, today's prepress professional is expected to have a working knowledge of all them. Here's why:

- **They are proven commodities.** Their standards have established what we expect from page layout software—their features are not just tacked to a preexisting application with a different purpose.

- **They have the widest user base.** There will never be a question about whether a service bureau will accept your files.

- **Using industry standard software means less risk and lower costs.** Software becomes an industry standard for a reason. Design and prepress professionals owe it to themselves (and their clients) to seek the path of least resistance and proven success.

This isn't to say you can't create complex (multiple page) layouts in a program like FreeHand or Canvas and successfully create color separations. Sure you can. Based on my experience, however, you're taking your chances. The further you deviate from the most widely proven and accepted software, the more you risk problems with output, compatibility, troubleshooting, and a host of other issues. The few hundred bucks you'll spend on a layout program will pay for itself with the first one or two large jobs that output successfully.

This chapter is not about all the minute details that comprise the immense power of XPress, PageMaker, and InDesign. (Indeed, I could write an 800-page book about each one.) Rather, it's about the most fundamental production-specific features and techniques involved in the science of page layout. It's a chapter designed to get you working as efficiently and quickly as possible, while ensuring that your documents will output properly. If you've been enraged or frustrated by the process of page layout, you may recognize some of the following circumstances:

- You must continually set and reset your preferences.

- You must continually redefine or reapply commonly used type, color, and image characteristics.

- Uniform document-wide type changes are difficult, if not impossible

- Your PMS colors output as CMYK percentages, or vice versa.

- Your scanned images take forever to output.

- Your images look jagged and pixelated when scaled, or fail to output at all.

- Elements that appear on more than one document page are inconsistently placed.

- Attempts to impose your pages for printing fail repeatedly.

Once again, I'll present a working system that helps you avoid these traditionally problematic areas. After reading this chapter, you'll understand the following issues: [1]

- Application and document preferences, to better tailor your programs to your specific work.

- Setting up your initial document to ensure that every step is geared toward efficiency and a quality press run.

- Properly defining, applying, and outputting spot and process colors.

- Priming your text for easiest importing, layout, and formatting.

- Working with master pages.

- Handling and outputting scanned and vector-based graphics.

Just as important as low costs and high quality, it's my belief that you should spend as *little* time as possible in the software of each stage of the production process. Working in a page layout program should be like a Navy SEAL mission: Draft a plan, pool your resources, and make your strike with surgical precision. A repetitive task or inefficient operation may only require 60 seconds or so—but if you have to do it 30 times a day (a conservative estimate, when you think about it), that equals 125 squandered, nonbillable hours every year. Five whole days! If your company bills these services at $80 an hour, that's upward of $10,000 that may never see the light of your bank account. Now apply that figure to a staff of five. Or ten. Or twenty. At the very least, spend the time you save with your loved ones.

FOOTNOTE

[1] The sections in this chapter actually reflect the stages of document construction. When creating a page layout, follow a basic methodology. First, set up your document, including the necessary page measurements and orientation. Second, define the document colors. Third, define the desired style sheets (they may require defined colors). Fourth, design your master pages (they may require colors and style sheets). Finally, design the individial pages, which utilizes the results of all the previous steps.

Of course, you can skip one or more of the steps if necessary. For example, one-page layouts don't need master pages, and you don't have to define any colors for a black and white project. The trick is not having to backtrack or repeat yourself when creating the foundation for a document.

Before You Begin: Setting Preferences

Hundreds of values can be entered into all the tools and commands of a page layout program. These values range from line thickness, to color menus, to default fonts. Every program ships with a set of default values, or starting points, for all the tools and commands contained within. These are flexible values, which you can change to best suit your work.

Once again, I ask you to keep a keen eye on your work. Keep a notebook at your workstation. Keep a record of any task you do over and over again. For example: Whenever you draw a line in XPress, it appears as 1 pt thick. Because you prefer a half-point line, you find yourself manually changing the thickness of every line you draw. You can rectify many issues like this one by adjusting the values in the Preferences menus.

Some users fear changing these settings. They feel like they're tampering with the guts of the application, as if they were irreversibly editing its life-sensitive code. Others are frustrated because no matter how many times they change those settings, the settings always revert to the original numbers. The first thing to realize is that there are two types of Preferences: Document and Application.

Document and Application Preferences

There are two ways to establish preferences (or *prefs*, to those in the know). If you change any default settings when a document is open, the changes are specific to that document only. When the document is closed, the defaults revert to what they were before. When you open the document again, the settings shift to changes that were made earlier. These settings, known as *document prefs*, are always included with a document, whether or not you make any changes.

In each application, you can access the preferences dialog boxes when there are *no* documents open. When you set values this way, the changes are permanent, and are applied to every new document created thereafter. These are known as *application prefs*, and the trick is to tailor these settings as closely as possible to your work environment.

Open XPress, PageMaker, or InDesign without opening a document (or creating a new one). Examine the menus and the floating palettes. Menu items and palette controls that are not grayed out are most likely the ones that you can adjust. Because there are potentially hundreds of settings available in every program, I will only focus on the most production-intensive ones.

Recommended QuarkXPress 4.04 Preferences

Of the three layout programs, XPress has the most flexible and production-specific preferences. This dovetails with XPress's long-held reputation of being the strongest production page layout program, although recent upgrades to PageMaker (not to mention the release of InDesign) have leveled the playing field considerably.

Application Preferences

Access the Application Preferences dialog box by choosing Edit: Preferences: **Application**. The settings appear under four tabs: Display, Interactive, Save and XTensions. (In partial contradiction to what I said earlier, you can change the settings of the Application preferences with or without documents open—either way, the settings become defaults.)

In the Display panel, set the following (see Figure 14.1):

- Check Full-Screen Documents to take advantage of every square inch of onscreen real estate.

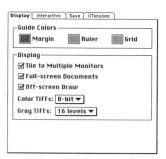

Figure 14.1 *The Display panel of XPress's Applications preferences dialog box.*

- If you use anything but the fastest computer, set Color TIFFs and Gray TIFFs to the lowest values. Doing so allows the screen to redraw more quickly, and it's safe to assume that color and tonality are not going to be adjusted in XPress. The page layout program is the wrong place to correct for color. (Refer to Chapter 12, "Scanning and Adjusting Color Images," for more info.)

In the Interactive panel, set the following (see Figure 14.2):

- Check Smart Quotes, and choose the standard typographer's quotes in the Format pop-up. If you ever need to enter inch and foot marks, hold down the Control key while typing an apostrophe.

- If you need to expand your Pasteboard Width (the work area around the onscreen page) to beyond 100%, you'll need an extra piece of software. Be careful, though. A while ago, an XTension called Pasteboard XT began circulating throughout the industry. Early versions of this program caused problems. Although it did allow you to expand the area to the left and right of the document, if you sent the file to a designer or service bureau who did not have the XTension, they couldn't open the file. Later versions of Pasteboard fixed this problem, but I recommend another XTension: Pasteboard XTerminator. This does not enlarge your pasteboard, but if your responsibility is working with client files, you won't need the larger pasteboard anyway. XTerminator just strips away all traces of the original Pasteboard XT, if it exists in a document. The Pasteboard family of XTensions is available for free at www.markzware.com.

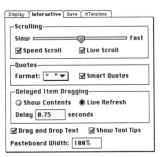

Figure 14.2   *The Interactive panel of XPress's Applications preferences dialog box.*

In the Save panel, set the following (see Figure 14.3):

- Uncheck Auto Save and Auto Backup. In my experience, these features can cause application crashes. Losing your work is hardly autosaving.

- Check Auto Library Save. If you use image libraries, they will automatically save whenever you add or delete an item.

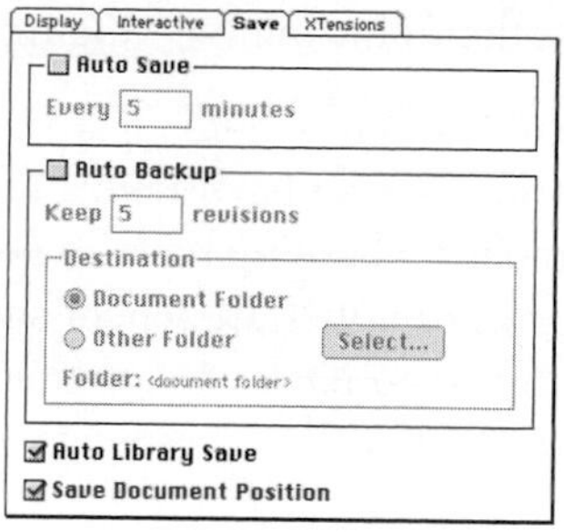

Figure 14.3   *The Save panel of XPress's Applications preferences dialog box.*

In the XTensions panel select the When option, and check Error Loading XTensions Occurs (see Figure 14.4). This way, the XTensions Manager—the dialog box that controls which XTensions load during application startup—appears only if an XTension cannot load. For example, if you try to use an XTension that is only compatible with version 3.32, you'll be aware that its functions will not be available.

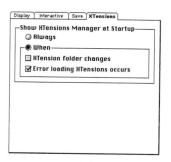

Figure 14.4   *The XTensions panel of XPress's applications Preferences dialog box.*

Document Preferences

Access the Document Preferences dialog box by choosing Edit: Preferences: **Document**. The settings appear under five tabs: General, Paragraph, Character, Tool, and Trapping. (Although XPress refers to these settings as "Document," you can still establish them as application prefs by changing the values with no documents open.)

In the General panel, set the following (see Figure 14.5):

- Horizontal and Vertical Measures default to Inches. Change them to the more accurate (and printer's standard) Points or Picas. Many users spurn points and picas for inches, claiming that the conventional units are used only by print throwbacks or elitist art school snobs. Once you start using them, however, it's hard to go back. Ask yourself: Is it easier to think of object placement in terms of 14 pt increments, or .194 inches?

- Set Framing to Inside. This controls whether a frame applied to a text or picture box is placed on the inside or outside of the box (as opposed to illustration programs, which straddle a path with any stroke value). Placing frames on the inside ensures that your imported high-res images trap properly into the frame. Also, because most frames are black, XPress's "keepaway" function prevents any C, M, or Y inks from creating a multicolored halo around the frame.

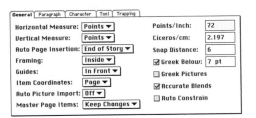

Figure 14.5 *The General panel of XPress's Document preferences dialog box.*

- Set Guides to In Front. It's painful to place a guide, only to have it obscured by everything on the page.

- Set Auto Picture Import to Off. Turning it on will automatically update any modified image in your document. Updating these images manually ensures that you are aware of any modifications accepted into the document.

The Tool panel requires some extra attention, because some of most infuriating factory defaults exist there. By selecting the tools one at a time, you can reset the available preferences for each one by clicking the Modify button (see Figure 14.6).

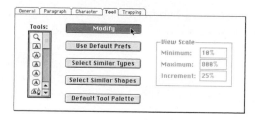

Figure 14.6 *The Tool panel of XPress's Applications preferences dialog box.*

Line Tool Prefs

By setting this value, every line you draw in the future appears at the desired thickness. I typically prefer a half-point line when I use these tools, but it's totally up to you. Beware, though: Do not, under any circumstances, select Hairline as a default for any standard line tool. It may look like a quarter-point line onscreen, or even when sent to a 600 dpi laser printer. It actually outputs at .125 pt, and it's difficult to successfully reproduce or (heaven forbid) trap a line like this. For best results, don't set any line thickness lower than .25 pts. The only time the Hairline option is sufficient is when the actual line produced by the tool will be invisible, as with the Text Path tools. (XPress 3.3 users take note: In older XPress versions, Hairline was a command to reproduce a line as thin as the target output device could produce. In version 4 and above, this value has been changed to the fixed width described previously.)

Picture Box Tools Prefs

With tools, the most problematic settings are Runaround and the background color. By default, XPress adds an Item runaround to every box tool. To remove this value, select a box tool, click Modify, and click the Runaround tab. Select None from the Type pop-up. You should only apply a runaround when you need one, and in my experience, I *don't* need one far more often than I *do*. When every box you draw contains a runaround value, it's all too easy to drag one of its edges onto an existing text box. This could cause your text to change position or reflow.

The background color question is less intuitive. It defaults to white, but you don't have to leave it that way. If you recall, XPress 3.32 had some serious problems with this issue. Back then, if you imported a grayscale or CMYK image into box with a background color of None, XPress had a tendency to lose track of very light pixels. The resulting pixelated fringe, known as "garbage mask" was most apparent when you imported a silhouetted image. To avoid this effect, you had to set the background color of the picture box to white. The only time you could set the box to None—which enabled you to see past the image edges to the underlying page info—was when the image contained a clipping path, or if it was created in a vector-based graphics application.

Fortunately, XPress has addressed this shortcoming, and it now recognizes the lightest-colored image pixels, even when the picture box is colored None. If desired, you can change the default color of all picture boxes to None, which will allow you to stack imported images with a vector-based edge. Change the background color as required in your documents.

Text Box Tool Preferences

On these boxes, it is perfectly safe to set the background color to None, because all text is vector-based. Set the Runaround to None, as well.

Default Colors

Examine your Colors Palette. Chances are that Red, Blue, and Green all share space there. Also, you'll notice that Black and Registration look exactly the same. Let's make some changes.

Red, Blue, and Green have no place in your color menu. You should not, under any circumstances, apply these colors to any element on your page, so why leave them there? They actually pose a risk, because they are defined as Spot Colors. If you apply Red in a CMYK document, five plates will output when you separate the file: Cyan, Magenta, Yellow, Black, and Red. If you apply Red in a two-color job—especially if you've used another red like PANTONE 185 CV in any vector-based graphics—you'll wind up with a third plate during separation. Remove Red, Green, and Blue permanently. Select Colors from the Edit menu (with no documents open) and delete the offending items.

Similar confusion can occur with Black and Registration. Black is just that: 100% black. Registration is a command that applies 100% of all document colors (think of registration marks—they print as solids on every plate). Because registration *looks* black, it's easy to mistake one for the other. Applying it will leave you with a black that is far too dense to reproduce successfully, especially in a four-color job. If you ever define your own crop or registration marks, coloring them black will leave you with only one usable plate. Avoid this problem by changing the onscreen appearance of registration. In the same Colors dialog box:

1. Choose Registration and select Edit.

2. Choose another color from the color wheel, preferably one you'll never use, like pink or bright purple. This changes the onscreen color and leaves the Registration command untouched.

Also, if you find yourself using a few different colors in most of your work— perhaps you only design with the corporate colors—you can add them as permanent items in the Colors Palette.

Default Fonts

The default font in XPress is defined as the Normal style sheet. To reset your default font:

1. Choose Edit: **Style Sheets**.

2. Select Normal, and make the appropriate changes.

I recommend, however, that text in any document be defined as a separate style sheet. Don't attempt to apply type characteristics using the Normal style sheet. The safest bet is setting your default to one of the universal system fonts such as Chicago or Geneva, or leaving it at the universal default: Helvetica. That way, your documents won't inadvertently trigger any "missing font" messages at the service bureau.

Copying XPress Preferences

Whereas all document preferences are stored in the document file, [2] all application prefs are kept in XPress's Preferences file, located in the application folder. XPress is one of the only major programs that keeps its preferences file here, instead of the Preferences Folder inside the System Folder. A quick way to unify all the preferences in a department (read: any place with more than one computer) is as follows:

1. Make all your careful adjustments on one workstation.

2. Copy the XPress Preferences file onto a disk or access it over a network.

3. Replace all other XPress Preferences files with the new copy.

This way, you only need to set your preferences once. The next time the other versions of XPress are launched, they'll start up with the new settings.

Recommended Adobe PageMaker 6.5 Preferences

PageMaker's Preferences dialog box is not as robust as XPress's, but you can still gain most of the control you need through other available menu items.

General Preferences

Access the Preferences dialog box by choosing File: Preferences: **General** (see Figure 14.8). Set the following:

• Reset your measurements and ruler units to Picas.

FOOTNOTE

[2] Just as you build your preferences into a document, so is every other designer using XPress. When you open a document created by someone else (or, using a different copy of XPress), you need to determine how your version of XPress is going to read the document prefs. A dialog box appears, asking you to choose between Use XPress Preferences and Keep Document Settings (see Figure 14.7). Whenever you work with someone else's file, always keep the document preferences. This way, information such as trapping values and custom tracking and kerning information is preserved. The only time you should override the document preferences is when you are certain you want to use the defaults of your specific version of XPress. This often happens when a designer accepts a project halfway through completion, or when an output specialist knows for certain that there are erroneous preferences built into the file.

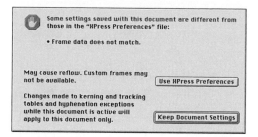

Figure 14.7   *The Preferences Request alert, which almost always appears when you open a client file.*

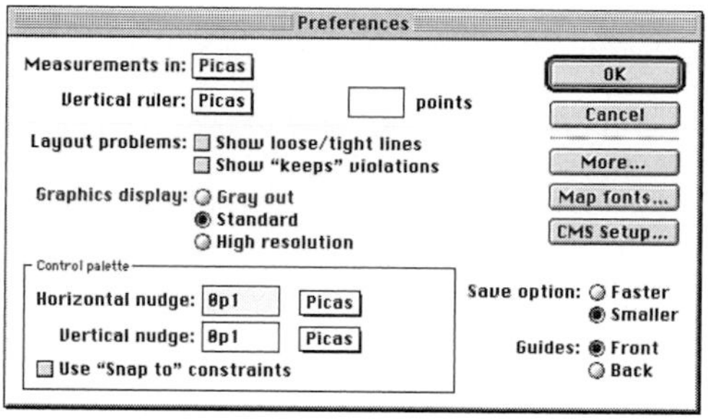

Figure 14.8   *PageMaker's General Preferences dialog box.*

- Keep the graphics display on Standard. This gives a low-resolution display of imported graphics. High Resolution gives 256-color displays, which are good for onscreen proofing by clients and the like, but slows down your redraw time considerably.

- Under Save Option, choose Smaller. This may require a little more time to save a file, but the result is a smaller file. If you choose Faster, PageMaker will not purge a document's internal record of document changes, which can cause the file size to balloon.

- Under Guides, choose Front. This ensures that you have constant, easy access to guides. Unlike XPress, you can lock the guides to prevent accidentally moving them (choose View: **Lock Guides**).

In the same dialog box, click the More button (see Figure 14.9):

- Under Text, turn on Use Typographer's Quotes. To enter inch and foot marks, press (Option-Command-apostrophe).

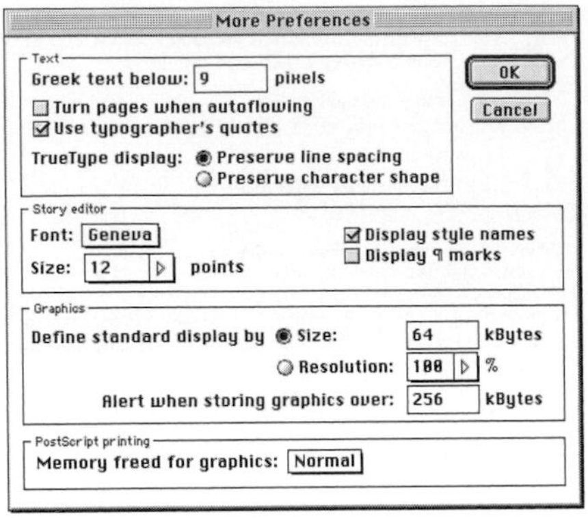

Figure 14.9 *PageMaker's More Preferences dialog box.*

- Under Graphics, look for Alert When Storing Graphics Over. This setting dovetails with the Links Options setting (under the Element menu). As far as importing graphics goes, there are two ways to handle the information. The preferred method is to import a low-res preview of an image, maintaining a connection to the high-res information in the original graphics file. This is called *linking*. (XPress handles graphics this way.) PageMaker's default is to import all high-res information into the document (this explains the sometimes enormous PageMaker file sizes). The alert setting defaults to 256K. This means graphics under that size are imported totally, without links. Graphics larger than that trigger a dialog box offering a choice: create a link or import all the high-res information. I recommend linking *all* graphics files, regardless of their size. If you don't, it's too tempting to send a project to the service bureau without the ancillary graphics files. Theoretically, you don't need to, if all the information was imported into the file. But reality steps in if any of your graphics demand adjusting. Link all your graphics by doing the following:

  1. With no documents open, select Link Options under the Elements menu (see Figure 14.10).

  2. Under Graphics, turn off Store Copy in Publication.

  3. Ignore the Graphics alert in the preferences dialog box.

  4. Always supply all graphics files with your document.

Figure 14.10   *PageMaker's Link Options: Defaults dialog box.*

Line and Fill Defaults

Because PageMaker doesn't use picture boxes (like XPress), the demands here are slightly different:

- Determine your most commonly used line width, and select it from the Element menu, under Stroke. Do not use the Hairline width. If you prefer a thin line, use .5 or .25 pt as your default.

- Leave your default fill at None. It's better to have to define a fill whenever you need one, than to accidentally leave a Paper fill (read: white) where it doesn't belong.

Default Colors

As with XPress, delete Red, Green, and Blue from your color menu. PageMaker, however, does not let you change the onscreen color of Registration. You also find that you can delete cyan, magenta, and yellow from the default menu, but don't worry if you do. Four-color images still separate.

Copying PageMaker Preferences

PageMaker prefs are stored in the Preferences folder, which is located in the System folder. Once your preferences are set for one copy of PageMaker, copy this file into the Preferences folders of your remaining workstations.

Recommended InDesign Preferences

Access InDesign's preferences dialog box by choosing an option from the File: **Preferences** submenu. From there, you can choose from seven available panels.

General Preferences

Set the following preferences:

- In the General panel (see Figure 14.11), set Full Resolution Images in the Images Display pop-up. This gives you the smoothest, most enhanced representation of your imported pixel-based images. If your computer runs at a slower speed (or if you notice a slow down, particularly when working with numerous high-res graphics), choose Proxy Images to reduce the resolution of any imported preview.

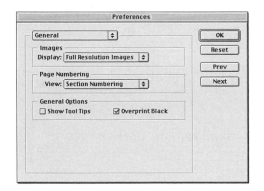

Figure 14.11   *InDesign's General Preferences panel.*

- If your document is divided into sections (using the Sections Options command in the Pages palette submenu), set the Page Numbering View pop-up to Section Numbering. This way, InDesign displays the intended page numbering in the document. To display numbering based on the pages as they appear in the document, choose Absolute Numbering.

- Check the Overprint Black box to force all occurrences of 100% black to overprint.

- In the Text panel (see Figure 14.12), check the Use Typographer's Quotes box.

- If desired (and if your computer has the horsepower), check Anti-Alias Type to render your text more smoothly onscreen. This method is useful when showing a project-in-progress to a client.

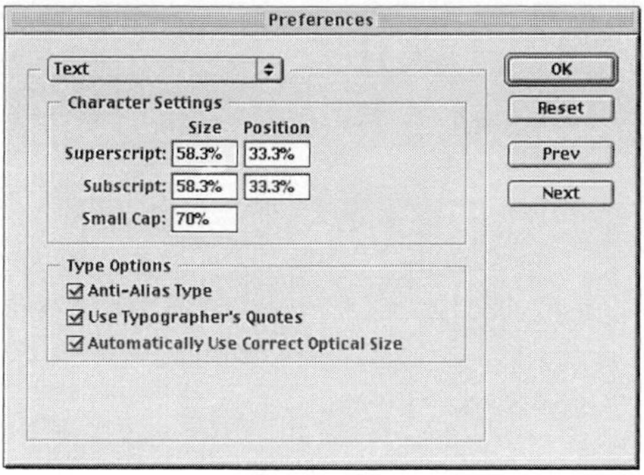

Figure 14.12   *InDesign's Text Preferences panel.*

- In the Composition panel (see Figure 14.13), check the Substituted Fonts box. This way, you are notified whenever and wherever font substitution takes place, allowing you to acquire the necessary font files.

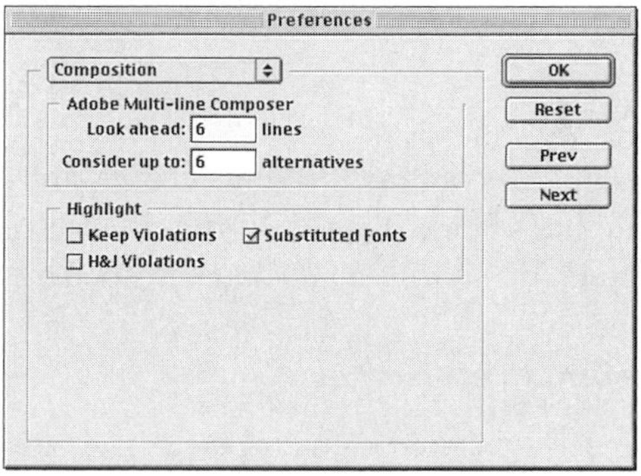

Figure 14.13   *InDesign's Composition Preferences panel.*

- In the Units & Increments panel (see Figure 14.14), set the ruler units to Points or Picas.

Fill and Stroke Defaults

To change the default settings for fill and stroke, do the following:

1. Launch InDesign, but do not open any documents.

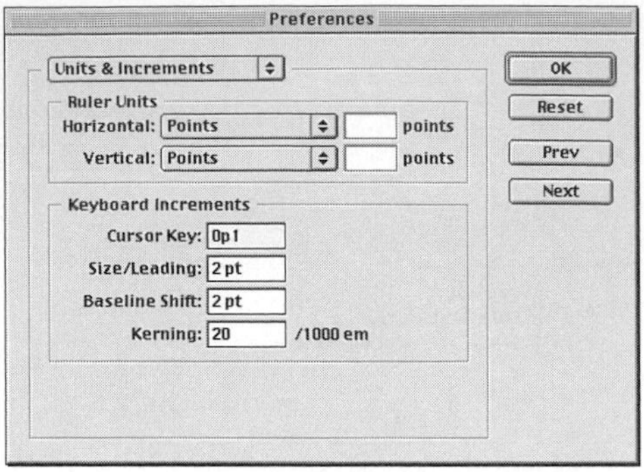

Figure 14.14   *InDesign's Units & Increments Preferences panel.*

2. To change the default stroke, enter the desired value in the Stroke palette. Remember to press the Enter or Return key—otherwise the new value won't "stick."

3. To change the default fill, mix the desired value in the Color palette.

Default Colors

Fortunately, InDesign does not include any superfluous colors in its default palette—it only includes None, Paper (White), Black, and Registration. To add colors as defaults, do so with no documents open.

Copying InDesign Preferences

InDesign's preferences are stored in the InDesign Defaults file, located in the application folder. Once your preferences are set for one copy of InDesign, copy this file into the application folders of your remaining workstations.

Setting Up a Document

Assuming your document has been appropriately planned (refer to Chapter 7, "Project Planning," for more info), it's time to create the foundation of your layout. Proper document setup consists of the following:

*   Setting the proper page dimensions.

*   Determining whether to use Facing Pages.

*   Adding the appropriate number of pages.

These steps require that you understand:

- The New dialog boxes of all three applications (and some additional setup commands).

- The difference between printer and reader spreads.

- The basics of page imposition.

- The conditions surrounding bleeds and crossovers.

- What size press will be used to reproduce your document.

Page Dimensions

Determining your page size is one of the most fundamental elements of page layout. [3] Some people design with nothing but 8.5×11-inch paper in mind, and if that's the only size you'll ever print to, fine. The moment you plan a different size, things become more complex. Use these dimensions from the very start, and only change them if absolutely necessary. Bear in mind the following issues:

- Page dimensions determine the placement of crop and registration marks. Using ruler guides, for example, to design a 9×6-inch booklet on letter-sized pages results in output that cannot be used by your printer (see Figure 14.15).

- Changing page dimensions halfway through a project means having to reposition your page elements. The more these elements are moved around manually, the higher the risk of human error.

FOOTNOTE

[3] Although I've mentioned that the standard unit of measurement in the print industry is points and picas, it doesn't apply to page sizes. When describing a document page or a larger sheet being fed through a press, the standard unit is still inches. However, if you've set the measurement units of PageMaker or InDesign to points/picas, the page dimension values in the New dialog box appear that way as well. (XPress displays these values as inches, regardless of the default settings.) Never fear—just enter the desired values in the horizontal and vertical fields followed by inch marks, and the program automatically converts to points/picas.

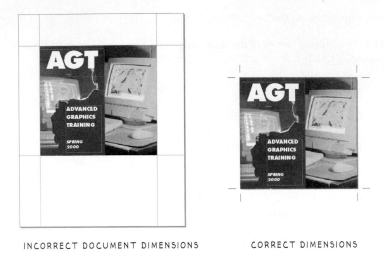

INCORRECT DOCUMENT DIMENSIONS   CORRECT DIMENSIONS

Figure 14.15 *Avoid designing pages on a larger document size (left). Be sure the document page dimensions match the intended page size of your project (right).*

- Don't forget to factor in elements such as perforated mailing cards or covers with the edges folded in. These must be added to the overall page size, but be careful. Depending on the size of your original document, the added inches may make your piece too large to print efficiently (or at all) on the intended press.

Page dimensions are set the same way in XPress, PageMaker, and InDesign:

1. Launch the application and choose File: **New**.

2. Enter the *exact* measurements for a single page of your document (for a 9×6-inch document, enter 9 inches and 6 inches). Don't try creating spreads on a single page (see "Facing Pages," next). You'll only hate yourself later, and so will your printer.

3. If you need to change your page size, select File: **Document Setup**.

4. Avoid creating multipage documents in any program that lets you design with more than one page size at a time. In FreeHand, for example, you can apply different dimensions to all 8 (or 24, or 64) of your pages, if you wanted to. The logistics behind outputting and printing a file like this are nightmarish. I don't describe them here, but don't worry. When some unfortunate output specialist is pushed over the edge, takes a hostage, and leads police on a cross-country rampage, you can read all about it in the

supermarket tabloids. For now, if you need different page sizes within the same document, create new documents and output them separately.

Facing Pages

A *spread* is a relationship between two pages in a document. As you work, you must design and produce with both *printer spreads* and *reader spreads* in mind. To illustrate what I mean, try this exercise:

1. Pick up a co-worker's magazine and flip through it. Page 2 is next to page 3, page 76 is next to page 77, and so on. This natural, side-by-side arrangement of pages is a Reader Spread.

2. Now pull the staples out and examine a single sheet of paper. You'll see that page 2 is printed on the same sheet as page 87, page 33 is on the same sheet as 68. These are Printer Spreads, the result of imposing the individual pages so they appear in the proper order after printing and binding (see Figure 14.16).

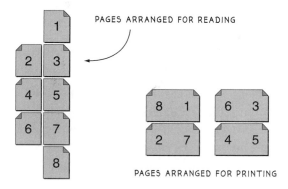

Figure 14.16 *Reader spreads (left) and printer spreads.*

All layout programs enable you to create documents using a feature called Facing Pages.

The upside: when you design a multipage document, facing pages enable you to design using reader spreads. This is more intuitive and efficient, because you have a better idea how the printed piece will look and feel. Facing pages also give you the capability to output spreads, or two side-by-side pages with one set of crop and registration marks.

The downside: you can create simple (and insufficient) page impositions by manually moving the pages into the proper order. Also, many people are compelled to use more complex page elements, including bleeds and crossovers, not realizing how they impact final page imposition and printing.

Imposition refers to the arrangement of page films that ensures the correct order after the printed sheet is folded and trimmed. Unfortunately, imposing pages by computer is extremely complex. So many factors, conditions, and measurements unique to each press are involved, there's no way to develop a standardized approach. In the time it takes to speak with the necessary people, get the right specs, run test sheets, calibrate the imposition software, and output final films, a job can be output as individual page films, stripped conventionally, and run on press. Eventually, digital presses will become so common, imposition will occur automatically, if desired. For now, the people most interested in electronic imposition are designers (many of whom do not understand how difficult it is) and service bureaus (many of which output films that are simply cut up and re-imposed on the stripper's table). The surest technique is to output individual page films and turn them over to the printer.

A technique I often employ takes place just before final output:

1. After designing a file using facing pages, turn the facing pages command off (under File: **Document Setup**).

2. Extend your bleeds—the image information that runs off the page edge— to 9 points beyond the page boundaries. This includes any information that occupies space on another page. These are called *crossovers*, and again, leave them to a stripper. Be sure the crossover image appears on both pages (see Figure 14.17). Switching back to single pages does not place duplicates.

3. Output all pages as single pages (no spreads). The only exceptions are pages that naturally occur as spreads, like covers and center spreads. Output these pages separately with the Spreads command turned on.

4. Group all films by page and turn them over to the printer with explicit instructions and a hard-copy mock-up.

Adding Pages

Add all the pages you need when you first create the document. Avoid simply adding them as you need them. Page count is based on two things: the amount of content and the budget. Because budget almost always wins, the page count in the approved job estimate should be adhered to as closely as possible. Adding another four pages to a job (remember the magazine—four pages to a sheet) adds considerable cost, especially when printing four colors to quality paper in high volumes.

Figure 14.17 *Using nonfacing pages to compensate for bleeds and crossovers prior to output results in a cleaner match when the pages are printed.*

PageMaker and InDesign enable you to enter the number of pages when you create the new document. Add exactly the number of pages you need. In XPress, you must create the document first, then add the remaining pages using the Insert Page command. At this point, you'll already have one page, so add the number of pages you want in your document minus one. (For example, if working on an eight-page document, add another seven pages.)

Even though you won't be numbering them, covers and inserts count as pages. Many designers prefer to keep these items in one document, the guts of a publication in another. This allows for more efficient applications of special treatments, such as crossovers, spreads, and custom page sizes.

Multiple-Page Spreads

In XPress, you can create spreads based on three or more pages. Do this by dragging page icons next to each other in the Document Layout palette. As long as the width does not exceed 48 inches (XPress's page size limit), it doesn't matter how many pages you move together. This technique is particularly handy for double-fold covers and the like.

InDesign refers to these layouts as "island spreads." To create an island spread, select a page icon in the Pages Palette (one you want to include in the spread), and choose Set As Island Spread from the palette submenu. Note: If your document is using facing pages and you want to convert two of them to an island spread, you must select both page icons before applying the command.

Defining and Applying Document Colors

Define your colors before you create or import anything. That way, you can apply color as you introduce elements into your page layout. Existing colors are also required in later stages of the layout process, when defining style sheets and master pages.

There are three golden rules when working with color in a page layout application:

1. Choose colors properly.

2. Define colors accurately.

3. Apply colors wisely.

These have nothing to do with what colors you actually choose. If your brochure is green and brown, or your skies are bronze, or your oceans run red, I don't care—as long as they're the colors you want. Successfully pulling this off depends on your understanding of these issues:

- How to determine which colors to use.

- The nature of spot and process color.

- Naming the colors you define.

- How colors defined in other programs impact your page layout.

- Defining accurate tints for spot and process color.

Using Spot and Process Color

These two ink types live on opposite sides of the zoo. The most important difference is that spot inks are opaque and process inks are transparent. When you combine (or overprint) transparent CMYK inks, the visible light that reflects through them results in a variety of colors. When you overprint opaque inks, the result is a sort of a muddy pigment stew. So of course, CMYK inks are the standard for what we have deemed photorealistic full-color print reproduction. If you find yourself defining spot colors in your document, it's likely for one of these reasons:

- **Budget.** Your project consists of only one or two colors, which cost less to reproduce.

- **Color fidelity.** You add spot inks to your four-color job, compensating for the colors that cannot be accurately reproduced with CMYK combinations. Bright orange, vivid green, and metallic inks are good examples. Note that only 10–15% of the PANTONE library can be accurately reproduced using CMYK percentages.

- **Style.** You intentionally create a job consisting of multiple spot colors.

Because you have these two disparate ink types, the methods you employ when selecting, defining, and applying them determine your ultimate success. One mistake, and you're left with colors that don't separate or reproduce with any degree of accuracy.

Choosing Colors Properly

The only time you don't specifically define the colors used in a document is when scanning full-color images. Sure, you have great control over the colors of a scan, but there you rely as much on hardware, software, and proofing (and sometimes luck) as you do on precisely defining the output percentages. Everything else in your document—boxes, bars, backgrounds, type, rules, colored line art and halftones—is based on color values that you specifically define.

The only accurate way to choose these colors is by referring to a swatchbook. For $50–100, you can purchase the following:

- Actual samples of spot ink libraries. These are printed using the same custom inks that will be used when printing your job. PANTONE is the American standard.

- Process ink combinations that dovetail with the predefined libraries you can access in the color menus of your graphics software. Trumatch and PANTONE Process are two widely used process swatchbooks.

There are other ways to choose colors, of course, but they range from mildly inaccurate to downright folly. Devices such as Light Source's Colortron II provide a decent starting point for color by calculating the RGB values of preprinted or preexisting objects. These values are never absolute, but it beats starting from scratch, especially if you don't have a vast history of color science. The worst thing you can do is choose your colors based on what appears onscreen in your color menus. In a typical environment, your software can't even display *cyan* consistently, let alone custom inks or subtle process combinations. It's worth buying a swatchbook just to hold samples up to your monitor to see the difference between onscreen and printed colors. Cracks me up every time.

Follow these basic steps when choosing colors:

1. Determine the ink type—spot or process.

2. As you plan your document, determine which elements will be colored.

3. Refer to an appropriate swatchbook to select the colors that will be used. Don't use a spot color guide to define process colors (or vice versa), even though your programs let you do so.

4. Define the colors. It's easy to change color definitions down the road, if needed. Every application will allow you to globally replace one color with another.

Defining Colors Accurately

Defining a color means adding it to the color menu of your document. To nitpick a little, let me say that you don't really define a *color*—you define an *output command.* This command determines the information that prints to each plate when a document is separated. This is obviously important: if you reproduce a logo or a line of type using PANTONE 287 ink, it means you want that information printing to a plate film titled "PANTONE 287." If you're creating bright red headline type in a four-color file, you want the letters to print appropriately to the magenta and yellow plates. If information appears on the wrong plate or plates, you can't expect the piece to print accurately on press.

Two issues cause the most problems: naming your colors and determining whether they will be process or spot separations.

Importance of Color Names

Naming requirements are different for spot and process colors. For spot colors, naming is everything. You may have noticed that the names of your spot colors are exactly the same as those that appear at the top of the separated page films. That's right: Whatever you name a custom color is the name of the plate that ultimately separates.

Always name a spot color by its library number. PANTONE inks are mixed at the print shop from a series of fundamental components. For example, mixing four parts of PANTONE Process Blue and 12 parts PANTONE Transparent White creates PANTONE 306. Unless the printer knows the exact ink you want to use, he cannot reference the necessary "recipe." For this reason, avoid naming your spot colors with such general terms as Gold or Sky Blue.

Then there are the naming conventions used by your applications: The same ink may be named PANTONE 306 CV, PANTONE 306 CVC, or PANTONE 306 CVU. The "CV" stands for Color Video, in reference to the onscreen library used by the application. The other two stand for Color Video Coated and Color Video Uncoated, respectively. You may have noticed that in your swatchbook, the PANTONE library is printed twice—once on coated stock, once on uncoated. This is done to give you a better idea how the same ink will appear when printed on different paper types. Most applications enable you to choose between a Coated and Uncoated PANTONE library, and may add the CVC or CVU tag at the end of the color name. The only difference between them is a slightly different onscreen appearance, a half-hearted attempt to show the different results when printing to coated or uncoated stock. Your PANTONE swatchbook illustrates that a hundred times better by giving you real-life printed samples.

In earlier versions of the software, this naming quirk posed a serious problem. For example, if you imported a FreeHand graphic containing PANTONE 306 CVC into an XPress document already containing PANTONE 306 CV, the color would appear twice in the Color Palette. With the latest versions, however, these problems have been ironed out. A PANTONE ink defined in one application will conform to the PANTONE ink defined in the page layout program. If it doesn't, you must go back to the original program, change the color name to conform to the layout program's method, and reimport the graphic. Delete the conflicting color name from the page layout program's color menu if it still appears there.

For process colors, the naming requirements are less severe. It doesn't matter what you name these colors, because the components are always the same: cyan, magenta, yellow, and black. Even if you access colors from the Trumatch library, you could ignore the numerical color titles and change them to something more descriptive, like "Rich Black," "Red Headline Type," or "The Brown of My Sweetie's Eyes." Because you can create thousands more colors using process inks than by using a couple of spot inks, it's easy to define dozens of different colors. Name them as concisely as you please, with no worries of creating erroneous separation plates. Most users employ the following naming methods:

- If you choose a color from a process library (such as Trumatch or PAN-TONE Process), leave the catalog name as-is. This way, if you redefine the color, the name will change accordingly.

- If you enter your own CMYK values, use the component percentages as the color name (for example, "55C, 10M, 80Y" or "80M, 60Y, 15K"). If you redefine the color, be sure you change the name.

How Will Your Colors Separate?

Whether a color separates as spot or process is determined when the color is defined. Unless a color is told to separate into its four-color components, it will output as a spot color: onto its own plate, even if the plate is titled Trumatch 36-a7 (a color from a process library). Likewise, if you tell a spot color to separate into process components, that's just what you'll get, whether you want it or not.

Choosing Separation Types in XPress

In XPress 4.04, the ultimate success of your color separations rests on one little button. As you define a color, take special note of the Spot Color box in the Edit Color dialog box (see Figure 14.18):

- If you are defining a spot color, be sure the box is checked.

- If you are defining a process color (including colors from process libraries like Trumatch and PANTONE ProSim), be sure the box is *not* checked. Even if you switch to CMYK mode and manually define your own percentages, you need to uncheck the Spot Color option.

Always review the Spot Color option when defining a color. You'd think the right setting would be built right into the color library selection, but it's not. The only information you tap into when choosing a color from an electronic library is the color name and its process components. This command, like many commands in today's software, lingers. Rather than reverting to a default setting after you close the program, it clings to the most recently applied choice. This is most evident when you move from a two-color to a four-color job.

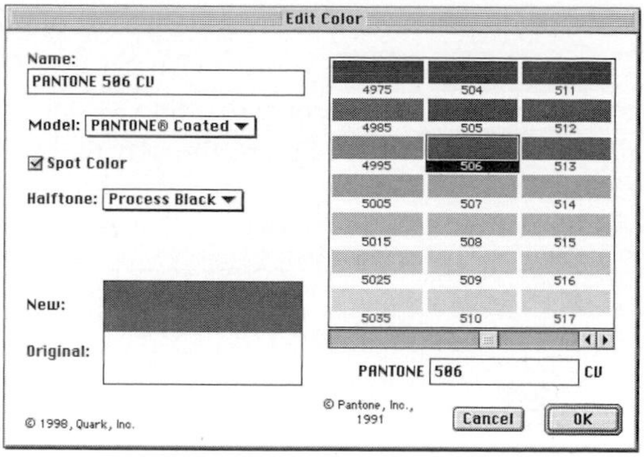

Figure 14.18   *Double-check the Spot Color box when defining a spot color.*

Choosing Separation Types in PageMaker

When defining a color in PageMaker, pay attention to the Type pop-up menu in the Color Options dialog box (see Figure 14.19):

- If you are defining a spot color, be sure Spot is chosen from this menu.

- If you are defining a process color, be sure Process is chosen from the Type menu, as well as CMYK from the Model menu just below. PageMaker has an edge here. It should automatically set these two menus when you choose a color from a built-in library.

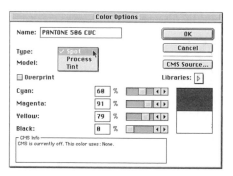

Figure 14.19   *Select the appropriate type in PageMaker's Color Options dialog box for spot or process colors.*

Choosing Separation Types in InDesign

When you add a color from the PANTONE library to the Swatches palette, it automatically appears as a spot color. Likewise, when you add a color from a process library, such as Trumatch, it automatically appears as a process color. This is evident when you choose Swatch Options from the Swatches palette submenu: The appropriate item is set in the Color Type pop-up (see Figure 14.20). You can change the setting by choosing another item there.

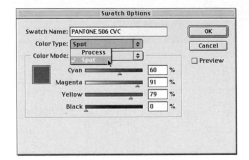

Figure 14.20   *Determining whether a color is spot or process in InDesign's Swatch Options dialog box.*

Applying Color Wisely

Again, this has little to do with the actual colors you choose. Rather, it has to do with what colors you apply to which objects. It also concerns many trapping issues, but that issue is covered in-depth in the next chapter. As you'll see, there are always some restrictions on what you can color, the colors you can apply, and how accurate your printed result is.

You can apply color to six elements in a layout document: [4]

- Type

- Rules

- Frames and Background color in XPress (Line and Fill in PageMaker, Fill and Stroke in InDesign)

- Imported line art (1-bit TIFF)

- Imported halftones (grayscale TIFF)

There are two ways to color these six elements:

- Apply a solid color (100%)

- Apply a tint of a color (1–99%)

Let's cover the issues involved in each of these six elements.

Coloring Type

When colors are improperly applied to small type sizes (14 points and under), the result can be unreadable. When very thin areas are colored—as with thin, serif type—three things can happen:

FOOTNOTE

[4] Two items cannot be recolored in a page layout: high-res pixel-based images and EPS files.

Presumably, the color of a high-res image is adjusted and corrected before you import it. Although some layout programs allow you to adjust colors and tones using rudimentary tools, these commands have proven worthless in a high-end environment, and should be avoided.

Encapsulated PostScript (EPS) files can be vector-based images from Illustrator, duotones from Photoshop, five-part DCS files, or even a page from XPress. Theoretically, a page layout program cannot touch the color content of these images. PageMaker, for some inexplicable reason, allows you to apply a color to an EPS file. It replaces all colors in the image with only the one, and the change doesn't appear onscreen, so you can only tell if the change exists by referring to the Colors palette. If you need to make any changes to an EPS file, open it up in the original application and do it there. This way, you can also read or apply any trapping information, if necessary.

- Areas colored with process inks are invariably comprised of overlapping screen values. If the linescreen is too low, the individual dots of the halftone screen will be larger than the thinner parts of the type characters. This renders the otherwise crisp lines of the characters indistinct and difficult to read. Solution: Color body text 100% black whenever possible. Only color text over 14 points with process combinations.

- If the slightest misregistration occurs on press, the effects will be grossly exaggerated by the fine details of the type. Solution: Again, color body text 100% black whenever possible.

- If you place body text of one spot color on a background of a second spot color, trapping is next to impossible. If you trap the type, the thin shapes will enlarge or reduce much more noticeably. If you try to avoid this by deciding not to trap, any misregistration will be clearly evident. Solution: Use either drop-out (white) type on a colored background, or use colored type on a white background. Trapping small type using spot colors is always next to impossible.

Coloring Rules

The guidelines described for small type apply here as well:

- If a rule is too thin and colored with either a tint or process combination, then low linescreens and misregistration could well be the kiss of death. Solution: Color rules 100% black if you want a nice, thin line. If you want colored rules, use at least a one-point width.

- When using at least two spot colors, don't place thin rules of one color on top of another. If you apply a .5 pt line then apply a trap value of .3 pt, you'll have rules that either spread to over a point in width or choke to nonexistence. Solution: When using rules in a two-color job, keep the colors separate.

Coloring Frames and Backgrounds (Line and Fill)

When using thin frames or borders, the same guidelines discussed in the previous items apply. For best results when trapping a full-color image, use black frames in XPress, black line values in PageMaker, or black stroke values in InDesign.

Coloring Imported Line Art (1-bit TIFF)

You can recolor black and white line art in all three applications, using spot or color process colors. The original image file isn't touched—the image that resides in the document is told to output to different plates.

Some people recolor line art by creating a monotone in Photoshop and saving the file as an EPS. This is not recommended because of your inability to change the color in the layout file (you'd have to go back into Photoshop and respec the monotone). Also bear in mind that standard line art, which outputs at 100% black, automatically overprints. As soon as the line art is reduced to a tint or recolored, it knocks out, and a program's trapping functions will apply to the recolored image. Solution: Line art that sits untouched by any other color never has to be trapped. Or, if using process colors, be sure to create a process bridge. (See Chapter 15, "Trapping," for more info on process bridges.)

Coloring Imported Halftones (Grayscale TIFF)

The techniques and issues here are essentially the same as imported line art files, except that halftones do not automatically overprint when you first place them.

- Again, color these images in your layout program instead of Photoshop. This gives you the flexibility to change colors at the drop of a hat.

- Do not confuse coloring a halftone with creating a duotone or quadtone. If accurately reproducing the deep tonal range of your halftones is paramount, then by all means define a multitone image in Photoshop (Refer to Chapter 12 for more info.)

Defining Tints

Unless you have a printed sample from which to work, defining a tint is based on guesswork. Fortunately, help and resources are nearby:

- PANTONE has released a swatchbook based not only on its custom inks, but different printed tint values. Referring to this guide is a great help in choosing the right percentage. Beyond that, choosing a tint is as easy as entering a percentage in the color palettes of XPress, PageMaker, or InDesign.

- Process tints require greater care. For example, applying a 50% tint of a PANTONE process color may result in an unsatisfying color. This is because each process component is scaled back by 50%, regardless of its initial value—it doesn't scale proportionately, like single spot colors do. You can either settle on the inaccurate (but easier to define) tints or use a swatchbook like Trumatch, which is based on initial colors and relative tint values.

Working with Text, Type, and Style Sheets

The written content of any project exists in three stages:

- First, the raw information is entered, either in a word processing program (to be imported later) or directly in the document.

- Next, you determine all the formatting characteristics that you'll apply throughout the document. You build these definitions into a series of *style sheets*, a quick and fluid way of applying, reapplying, and changing text attributes.

- Finally, you arrange and format the text as desired, in essence converting the raw text into *type*.

Working successfully with text involves the following issues:

- Determining whether your layout program can recognize the text files you want to import.

- Understanding the difference between local and global formatting.

- Knowing when and how to use style sheets.

Entering Text

If any text exists in your document, it was either manually entered or imported from a word processing file. Many projects involve both of these techniques. Typically, shorter items such as headlines, captions, copyright tags, and other brief lengths of text are entered by hand. Longer stretches of text—stories, columns, book chapters, articles—are more efficiently created and edited in a word processing program, such as Microsoft Word. In fact, I recommend that everyone use Word for entering large amounts of text, and the reasons are clear:

- In Word, the only focus is on typing and editing. In a layout program, the focus is on formatting and positioning.

- Entering text in a word processing program is easier on the eyes and head, because the program was specifically designed to perform this function most efficiently.

- Your end-user options are much more flexible. After creating the text file, it can go to someone using XPress, PageMaker, or any other program that accepts that type of file. In fact, Microsoft Word (as you might expect) is the most universally accepted text file format.

- Word's editing tools—spell check, grammar check, thesauruses, and dictionaries—are more powerful.

- Word can open many text files that simply leave XPress and PageMaker confused. A client once gave me a document originally created on an Atari computer. I mean, it was written in about 1981, then transferred from a 5 1/4-inch floppy to a standard 3 1/2-inch disk by a high school kid with an ancient workstation. When I finally cracked it open in Word, it was chock-full of crazy symbols and textual garbage, but it only took a few minutes of editing to clean up. I saved the document as a Word file, and immediately imported it into PageMaker.

- Word is indispensable if you need to save your text into a different text file format, such as RTF, ASCII, or WordPerfect. Word can save into 16 different text formats, as opposed to XPress's 13, PageMaker's 9, and InDesign's 4.

Don't be put off just because you're introducing yet another application in your production process. Word is easy to learn (because you're only using it for rudimentary tasks and some built-in features), and the time and frustration saved by not performing this work in a page layout program more than pays for the extra cost. Just be aware of two issues.

First, avoid formatting type in a word processing program, if possible. Unless you're working with long documents (this book was written in Word, for example, and I used a set of style sheets that were imported into and redefined in the long-doc software used by the publisher), only enter the textual information. Like many other apps, more word processing programs are including incongruous features like vector-based illustration and page layout. These are fine if it's the only application you have, and if you're printing to the office laser printer. Otherwise, ignore them.

Second, your page layout program must have a *filter* (a small piece of software) that enables it to recognize your text file. XPress's filters reside in the XTensions folder, inside the XPress application folder. PageMaker's Filters folder is located in the application folder, in the RSRC folder. InDesign's Filters folder is located in the Plug-Ins folder, in the application folder. If you've just upgraded to Word 8 (known as Word 97 on Windows, Word 98 on Mac), you may have noticed that XPress no longer recognizes your text files. Because Word 8 was not released before your version of XPress, you need to download the free Word 8 filter from Quark's Web site (www.quark.com). Install it in the XTensions folder, relaunch XPress, and you're golden.

Microsoft Word and Your Prepress Environment

Word's role in a productive workflow is hotly debated. When asked for his input, a colleague responded: "Word? Oh please! Its only benefit is the fact that everybody uses it. This poorly designed bloatware is an abomination! Of course, it's the only word processor I use." Regardless of the advice you read in this book, the time will come when you are asked to process or output a Microsoft Word document. The following info will help:

- **Document Reflow.** The line and page breaks of Word 6 docs (and earlier) are defined by the target output device. This means that the same file may output differently from printer to printer. The layout of Word 97 docs (Word 98 on the Mac) and above are based on the *fonts* used, rather than the printer. These docs maintain their original appearance regardless of the computer or printer used, provided the fonts remain unchanged. Embedding TrueType fonts into a document will reduce the need for font substitution, and therefore the occurrence of text reflow. Unfortunately, this only affects a doc created in Word 97/98, and will not necessarily help a file created in an earlier version.

- **Embedding TrueType fonts.** If the client used TrueType fonts when creating the document, they must embed that info into the file itself. This way, I can view, modify, and print the document with the original fonts, even if the fonts aren't installed on my computers. When you save a document, check the Embed TrueType Fonts box in the Save dialog box.

- **Outputting Word Files.** If you routinely accept Word documents from a client, strongly encourage them to upgrade to Word 97/98. Keep the default print settings, making sure the Use Printer Metrics to Lay Out Document option is unchecked in the Print dialog box. Be sure the client has embedded the fonts in the document, and they have provided the fonts with the file.

- **Consider a PDF file.** To preserve all the line breaks and font info of the document, have the client convert the doc to a PDF file. It will be difficult to make any edits to the content, but it will provide a platform-independent means to view and output the info.

- **Invest in a file-conversion utility.** DataViz's MacLink Plus is one example of this utility (see `www.dataviz.com`). It will help considerably when accepting text files from multiple programs and platforms. This utility converts any format of text, spreadsheet, or database file—PC or Mac—to any other, and it also allows for batch processing. Word opens almost any other text file type, but MacLink Plus converts an even wider range, and you can export converted files into nearly any other format.

Converting Text into Type

After you've imported text into your document, you stand at a crossroads. Should you format the text locally or globally? You'll almost always do a little of both, and I'll get to that later in this chapter.

Most likely, the first page layout technique you learned was how to format type. You remember: highlight the text, choose a font, set a point size, change the line spacing, set the alignment, and so on. This is the essence of *local formatting*—any change you make is specific only to the text you've highlighted. It seems an intuitive way to set type. After all, you know exactly what text is being changed, when it's changed, and you walk step-by-step through every attribute. There's a catch, of course. All it takes is one multipage document, and you realize that localized formatting is difficult and time-consuming, and creates a minefield of potential errors and miscalculation:

- You quickly discover that your simple, eight-page document may have dozens of text fields. These all have to be formatted individually.

- If you apply an average of seven text attributes to an area of formatted text (for example, font, size, leading, alignment, color, track, space after), and you average ten areas that need formatting per page (headlines, subheads, captions, text columns, headers, footers, page numbers, and so on), that's 70 formatting commands per page. Eight pages require 560 commands. 48 pages: 3,360. A 300-page book? Forget it. Unless you're Dustin Hoffman starring in *Rain Man*, you'll miss something.

- There's no way to make any quick, universal changes to your text formatting. If you change your mind about any attribute, you have to make that same change by hand throughout the document.

- Unless all of your text—even spaces—is selected when you change fonts, the layout program "remembers" the original font and possibly calls for it when the job is opened at the service bureau. This wastes valuable time at the precise moment you can't afford to.

There are only two occasions when you can safely and efficiently apply local formatting:

- **When you're working on a simple, one-page document.** Examples include a poster or business card. If you just don't have that much text, it's easy enough to get away with lightning-strike formatting.

- **When you locally format text that already has a style sheet applied to it.** This is unavoidable if you want to italicize, boldface, color, or otherwise format individual words. If a style sheet has been applied to text and you've formatted parts of it locally, then those words will retain the "extra" formatting whenever you edit the style. Just remember to supply entire font families with your document (as discussed in Chapter 4, "Font Management").

Beyond these examples, work under the assumption that you'll use style sheets as the basis for all of your type formatting.

Using Style Sheets

Those of you who have worked with conventional typography systems already realize the term "style sheets" is a bit of a misnomer. There, the formatting applied to a single paragraph is called a *style*, and when all the styles of a document are made into a list, it's called a *style sheet*. XPress, PageMaker, and InDesign refer to any automated formatting tags as a style sheet, presumably to avoid confusion with type styles, and other uses of the word.

The premise of style sheets is simple. Rather than format your text by hand, you set the attributes for each style ahead of time, store a list of these attributes in a readily available floating palette, and apply them at will at the click of a button. There are three fundamental but important reasons for doing this:

- Styles are applied in a single stroke, unlike localized formatting.

- Once style sheets are applied, you only have to go back to the original style definition to make changes that automatically appear throughout the document.

- If a style needs to be changed after a document has left your control (or after it has fallen into your hands), the change can be made intuitively and at lower risk.

If style sheets still seem unfamiliar, pick up a publication and scan a couple of pages. Note how the formatting generally remains consistent from page to page. Body text remains the same. Figure callouts, too. Headers and page numbers, pull-quotes and captions, any style that appears *more than once* is best suited for style sheet formatting. The process for defining and applying a series of styles is easy, and I'll take you step-by-step through creating and applying basic style sheets in XPress, PageMaker, and InDesign.

There are two types of style sheet: paragraph styles and character styles. Paragraph styles affect any text that appears between two carriage returns, whether it's a single letter, a 14-page Faulknerian sentence, or a 30,000-word novella. Any attempt to apply a style sheet to a smaller part of a paragraph such as a letter or word will just change the style of the entire paragraph. Character styles, on the other hand, allow you to apply formatting attributes to a highlighted range of text, whether it's a single letter, word, or sentence. [5]

Character styles are applied in addition to paragraph styles. While a paragraph style allows you to define a font, point size, letter spacing and so forth, it also allows you to define leading, space before or after a paragraph, rules above or below a paragraph, indents, and other paragraph-specific attributes. Character styles only affect nonparagraph values such as font, size, type styles, and spacing. A common example of using the two style sheets together is a *run-in head*, where the first sentence of a paragraph appears in a different typeface and color than the rest of the text (see Figure 14.21). The entire paragraph is formatted using the Body Text paragraph style; the first sentence is formatted using the Run-In Head character style.

Before I get into the specifics of each program, let's cover some global style sheet issues:

FOOTNOTE

[5] Both XPress and InDesign feature paragraph and character styles. PageMaker uses only paragraph styles.

CHARACTER STYLE

He thinks it's a change machine. *He inserts a dollar but receives only 35¢. He punches the machine. A can falls out. He slips on the can and falls on his butt. People appear as if out of nowhere, pointing and laughing. He cries himself to sleep. He wakes up, confused, dimly aware that he still needs change. He inserts another dollar in the machine.*

PARAGRAPH STYLE

Figure 14.21 *This entire sample is formatted with a paragraph style, but the run-in head is formatted with a character style.*

- **Type does not have to be highlighted to apply a paragraph style.** Inserting the flashing text cursor anywhere in a paragraph is enough. Character styles, on the other hand, require a highlighted range of text.
- **Avoid entering empty returns.** Using extra returns to provide space between paragraphs throws a couple of obstacles in your path. First, the spaces are only one size, usually the point size of the leading value. Changing the size either involves local formatting or extra spaces. Second, those extra spaces misalign your text if one of them spills over to the next column. Always use a Space Before or Space After value to provide the necessary breathing room between paragraphs (see Figure 14.22). When a style sheet contains a Space After value, you can always press Shift+Return to add a line break without the additional space (this is known as a *soft return*).

A·common·technique·for·producing your·own·fonts:¶
¶
1.→ Draw·an·alphabet,·using·black·ink on·bright·white·paper.¶
¶
2.→ Scan·the·alphabet·at·150·ppi.¶
¶
3.→ Trace·the·characters·in·Adobe· Streamline.¶
¶
4.→ Open·the·traced·alphabet·in· Illustrator·or·Freehand·and·make· any·necessary·fine·adjustments.·¶
¶
5.·Open·Macromedia·Fontographer...·

A·common·technique·for·producing your·own·fonts:¶
1.→ Draw·an·alphabet,·using·black·ink on·bright·white·paper.¶
2.→ Scan·the·alphabet·at·150·ppi.¶
3.→ Trace·the·characters·in·Adobe· Streamline.¶
4.→ Open·the·traced·alphabet·in· Illustrator·or·Freehand·and·make· any·necessary·fine·adjustments.·¶
5.·Open·Macromedia·Fontographer...·

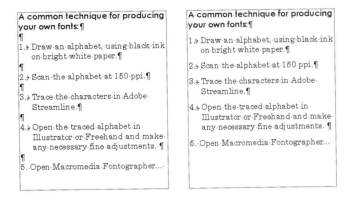

Figure 14.22 *The paragraphs on the left are separated using extra returns; the paragraphs on the right are formatted using a Space After value.*

- **Each program lists "No Style" in its Style Sheets palette.** It means exactly what it says—text with no applied style sheets. You'll see this tag in two situations: imported text and type from which you've manually stripped the style information. It's not a style sheet. It's the absence of a style sheet. It cannot be edited, so don't work under the assumption that you can somehow apply text attributes by changing the No Style tag.

- **Each program lets you create a new style based on a current selection.** This is an intuitive way to create a style. Enter some sample text, format it locally as desired, and highlight it. When you choose the New Style Sheet command, the characteristics are automatically plugged in. Name the style sheet, double-check the values, and you're ready to go. Just remember that the new style is not automatically applied to the original sample text—if necessary, you'll need to apply the new style yourself.

- **Use style sheets when placing tab spaces.** This is especially important when similarly formatted type requires different tab spaces. For example, you may need to create a two-column table on page 3 of your document, and a four-column table on page 6. If the tables retain the same essential formatting as your Body text style, it's tempting to add the desired tab spaces by locally formatting the tables. Instead, use the Based On option to create variations of a basic style, and name the new style sheets appropriately. For example, variations of a style named "Body Text" might be called "Body Text/2-Col Table" or "Body Text/4-Col Table."

Defining Style Sheets in XPress

Follow these steps to create a paragraph style:

1. Access the style sheet dialog box by selecting Edit: **Style Sheets,** or (Command-click) an existing item in the Style Sheets palette (see Figure 14.23).

2. In the New pop-up, choose Paragraph or double-click the New button.

3. Name the style sheet (applying a Keyboard Equivalent, if desired).

4. To define the character attributes, click the Edit button in the Edit Paragraph Style dialog box. One by one, click the tabs for Format, Rule, and Tab and enter the desired settings.

5. Click OK to switch back to the original dialog box.

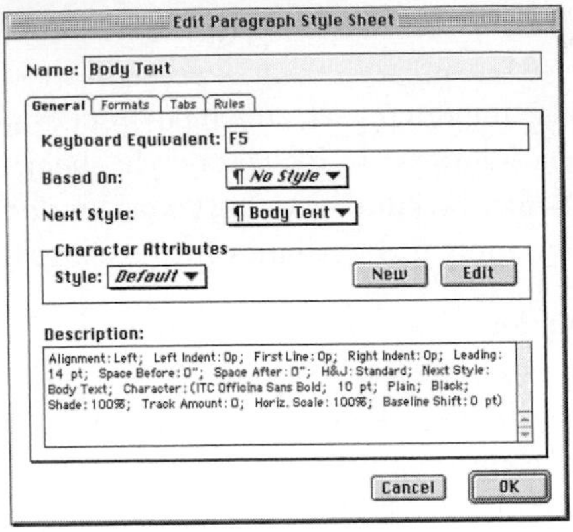

Figure 14.23   *XPress's Style Sheets dialog box.*

6. If you need to define another style, click New and repeat the process. If you need to make any changes, select a style from the window and choose Edit. When you're finished, click Save.

Paragraph styles appear in the top half of the Style Sheets palette, preceded by a paragraph symbol (¶) (see Figure 14.24).

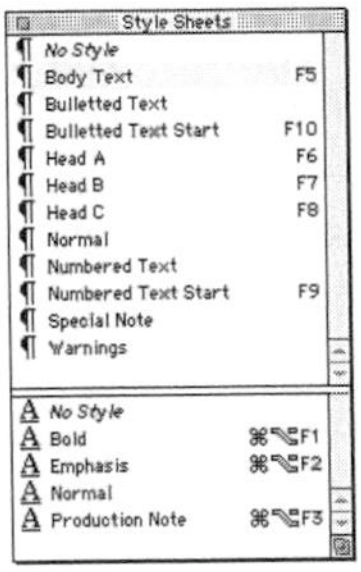

Figure 14.24   *The XPress Style Sheets palette, containing paragraph and character styles.*

Follow these steps to create a character style:

1. Choose Edit: **Style Sheets**.

2. In the New pop-up, choose Character.

3. Name the style sheet (applying a Keyboard Equivalent, if desired).

4. In the Edit Character Style Sheet dialog box, enter the desired character attributes.

5. Click OK to switch back to the original dialog box.

6. If you need to define another style, click New and repeat the process. If you need to make any changes, select a style from the window and choose Edit. When you're finished, click Save.

Character styles appear in the lower half of the Style Sheets palette, preceded by a capital A.

Creating Based On Paragraph Styles in XPress

Follow these steps to base one style sheet on another:

1. Define a basic style, as mentioned previously.

2. In the Style Sheet dialog box, duplicate the basic style.

3. Select the duplicate item and click Edit. You'll notice that all the values and settings are the same as the original.

4. Make the necessary changes. (The examples I mentioned earlier contained subtle differences in Tab spaces.)

5. In the Based On pop-up, choose the original style sheet (see Figure 14.25). This creates a connection between the two style sheets. Not only are the settings largely the same, but any changes you make down the road to the original style sheet (such as font, point size, leading, and so on) will automatically apply to any styles based upon it.

6. Click OK and save the styles.

Importing Style Sheets in XPress

If you've already defined a set of style sheets once, why do it again? If a set of styles that you need already exists in another document, there's no need to define them all over again. You can easily import the style sheets from that already-formatted document.

1. Choose Edit: **Style Sheets**.

2. Instead of choosing New, click Append.

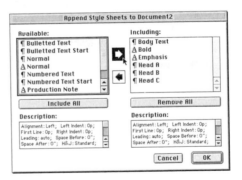

Figure 14.25 *Creating a Based On style sheet in XPress links one style sheet to another so that changes made in the parent style are automatically applied to the related ones.*

3. In the navigational dialog box that appears, find and open the document that contains the styles you want.

4. In the Append Style Sheets dialog box, the style sheets you can copy appear in the Available window. Double-click the paragraph and character styles you want to copy (see Figure 14.26).

5. Click Save.

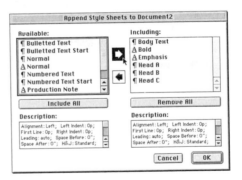

Figure 14.26 *Appending, or copying style sheets from one XPress document to another.*

Avoid simply copying all the available styles. Doing so copies the document's Normal style as well, and you'll get a potentially confusing dialog box that alerts you to a conflict. It doesn't really matter (because you shouldn't be using the Normal style sheet), but the process is much cleaner if you only choose the styles you need.

Applying Styles in XPress

There are two ways to apply styles in XPress:

- **Click the desired item in the Style Sheets palette.** To apply a paragraph style, highlight the desired range of paragraphs and click the appropriate item in the Style Sheet palette. (Because paragraph styles automatically affect an entire paragraph, you also can place the flashing cursor before choosing the style.) To apply a character style, highlight the desired range of text and click the desired item in the Style Sheets palette.

- **Use a Keyboard Equivalent (KE).** KEs are fine things. They enable you to assign a style at the punch of a key instead of always having to refer to a floating palette. Use the F keys on the top of your extended keyboard (I use F5–F12, so I can continue using the F-key shortcuts for Cut, Copy, and Paste). You also can hold down the (Option)[Alt] or (Command)[Control] keys when choosing an F key to expand the range of possibilities. Avoid using the numeric keypad for this purpose (unless you use an additional modifier key). Doing so prevents you from using the keypad to type numbers when entering text.

Defining Style Sheets in PageMaker

PageMaker 6.5 has wisely incorporated Photoshop's palette system for its style sheets, layers, colors, and master pages. To edit styles and permanently delete the default settings, go to the Define Styles dialog box, under the Type menu.

Follow these steps to create a paragraph style:

1. Choose New Style from the Styles palette submenu (see Figure 14.27).

2. Name the style appropriately.

3. One by one, enter the values for Character, Paragraph, Tabs, and Hyphenation. Note: you XPress users will find Rules as an option under Paragraph.

4. Click OK to add the style to the palette.

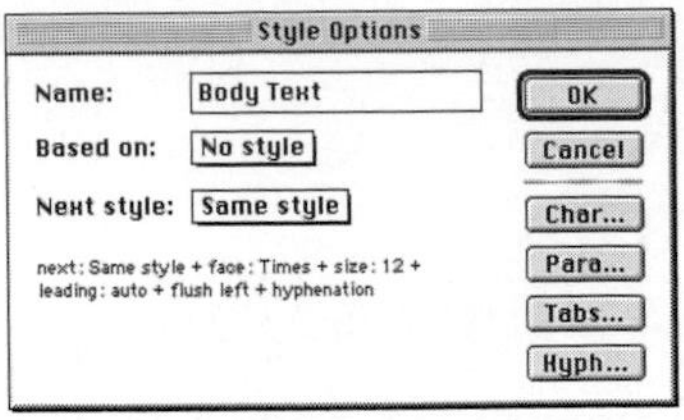

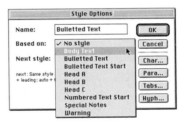

Figure 14.27 *PageMaker's Style Options dialog box.*

Using Based On Paragraph Styles in PageMaker

Follow these steps to base one style sheet on another:

1. Select the original style in the Styles palette.

2. Select Duplicate in the Styles palette submenu.

3. Name the new style accurately.

4. Make the necessary changes.

5. Under the Based On pop-up menu, select the name of the original style (see Figure 14.28).

Figure 14.28 *Creating a Based On style sheet in PageMaker.*

6. Click OK to save the style.

Importing Style Sheets in PageMaker

There are two ways to import styles from another PageMaker document:

1. Open the Define Styles dialog box (see Figure 14.29).

2. Click Import.

Figure 14.29 *Copying style sheets from one PageMaker document to another.*

3. In the navigational dialog box that appears, find and open the document containing the styles you want.

4. Click OK.

Or try the following:

1. Choose Import Styles from the Styles palette submenu.

2. In the navigational dialog box that appears, find and open the document containing the styles you want.

3. Click OK.

Applying Styles in PageMaker

PageMaker has no Keyboard Equivalent function. You can only apply a style by highlighting text (or inserting the cursor in a paragraph) and clicking the desired item in the Styles palette.

Defining Style Sheets in InDesign

Display the Paragraph Style or Character Style palettes by choosing the desired item from the Type menu.

Follow these steps to create a paragraph style:

1. Choose New Style from the Paragraph Style palette submenu (see Figure 14.30).

2. In the New Paragraph Style dialog box, enter a name for the style (adding a Shortcut, if desired).

3. The settings you can apply are contained in 11 different panels. You can choose them one by one from the pop-up at the top of the dialog box (it defaults to General), or you can click the Next and Prev buttons to scroll through them. Enter the desired settings.

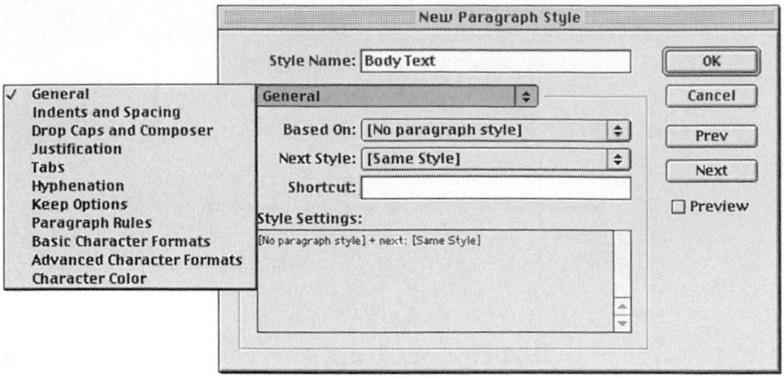

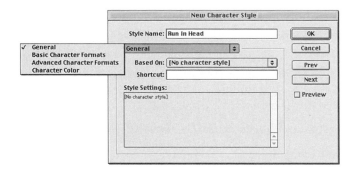

Figure 14.30 *InDesign's New Paragraph Style dialog box.*

4. Click OK to close the dialog box. The item appears in the Paragraph Styles palette.

Follow these steps to create a character style:

1. Choose New Style from the Character Style palette submenu (see Figure 14.31).

Figure 14.31 *InDesign's New Character Style dialog box.*

2. In the New Character Style dialog box, enter a name for the style (adding a Shortcut, if desired).

3. The settings you can apply are contained in four different panels. These panels also appear in the New Paragraph Style dialog box—but because you're only defining character attributes here the choices are limited. Enter the desired settings.

4. Click OK to close the dialog box. The item appears in the Character Styles palette.

To edit a paragraph or character style definition, highlight it in the palette and choose Style Options from the palette submenu. The same dialog box used to define the original style appears, allowing you to make the desired changes.

Using Based On Styles in InDesign

Follow these steps to base one style sheet on another:

1. Define a basic style, as described previously.

2. Duplicate this style by selecting it in the palette and choosing Duplicate Style in the palette submenu.

3. In the Duplicate Paragraph Style dialog box, you'll notice that the original style automatically appears in the Based On pop-up (see Figure 14.32). [6]

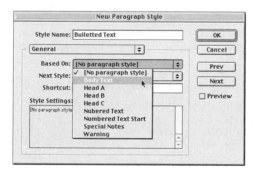

Figure 14.32   *Creating a Based On style sheet in InDesign.*

4. Rename the style (it's originally listed as a copy of the original), and make the necessary changes.

5. Click OK to save the style.

FOOTNOTE

[6] If any style is selected in the Paragraph Styles or Character Styles palette when you choose New Style from the palette submenu, it appears in the Based On pop-up. Avoid this by clicking at the bottom of the palette (away from any styles) before choosing New Style.

Importing Style Sheets in InDesign

Follow these steps to import styles into an InDesign document:

1. Choose Load Paragraph Styles from the Paragraph Styles submenu (see Figure 14.33). If you want to import a set of character styles, you must choose Load Character Styles from the Character Styles palette submenu.

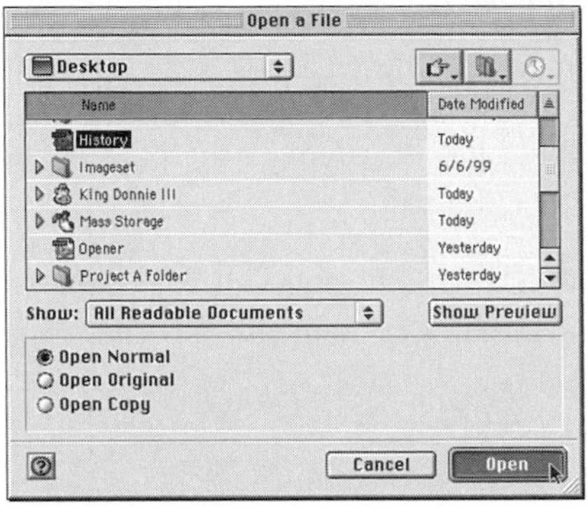

Figure 14.33   *Copying style sheets from one InDesign document to another.*

2. In the navigational dialog box that appears, locate the document that contains the styles you with to copy.

3. Open the document. The styles are automatically added to the palette.

Applying Styles in InDesign

There are two ways to apply styles in InDesign:

- **Click the desired item in the Paragraph Style or Character Style Palette.** To apply a paragraph style, highlight the desired range of paragraphs and click the appropriate item in the Paragraph Styles palette. (Because paragraph styles automatically affect an entire paragraph, you can also simply place the flashing cursor before choosing the style.) To apply a character style, highlight the desired range of text and click the desired item in the Character Styles palette.

- **Use a Shortcut.** Shortcuts are similar to XPress's Keyboard Equivalents. After entering the desired keystroke in the Shortcuts field, you can apply styles simply and efficiently, without having to click the styles palette.

Designing Master Pages

Start layout of your project only after you've defined your document setup, colors, and style sheets. Before you start designing individual pages, however, there's one more thing to take care of. You need to import and position any repeating page elements that appear in your layout:

- Headers (information at the top of pages, usually in the margin area. Often include publication titles, chapter numbers, page numbers, and rules)

- Footers (the same as headers, only at the bottom of a page)

- Siders (typically found on the outside edge of pages, to avoid being obscured by binding)

- Page numbers

- Borders

- Any logo or graphic appearing on all (or many) pages

Of course, there are two ways you can import and position these repeating page elements.

You can manually place each repeating element on every page, carefully measuring and positioning them all, eyeing and nudging everything into place. If you change your mind about something, repeat the entire process. Place page numbers manually, hoping you don't have to add, subtract, or rearrange any pages down the road. And when the piece comes off press, you can obsess madly over the one or two items that escaped your lunatic eye.

Or you can define master pages. These are actually page templates that reside inside your document, and work with your page designs in much the same way that style sheets work with your type. This way, you only have to import and position these repeating elements once. Later on, if you have to make any changes, you can change the templates.

Regardless of which application you use, the rules and restrictions of setting up master pages are almost the same as laying out regular pages. There are some slight differences though, so follow these guidelines:

- Not every document requires the use of master pages. If you're not designing with any repeating items, you don't even have to think about them. Few things become more cumbersome than attempting to use features you do not need. A good rule of thumb is to look for any item that appears in the same place on different pages three or more times.

- Master pages are *templates*, so only place elements on them that can be used on the pages to which they're ultimately applied. Elements that belong only on one page or another should be placed on the actual page, not the master pages.

- The most popular master page item is page numbering. To have a page number automatically appear on a page, you must enter a special character in the desired position on your master pages (see Figure 14.34). In XPress, press Command-3 to enter the character. The symbol looks like <#>, but don't try typing in those three characters. In PageMaker, press Command-Option-P. The character appears as either "LM" or "RM", depending on whether it's entered on a left or right master page. In InDesign, make your box and choose Layout: **Insert Page Number** (or Control-click/right-click the box to access the command from a contextual menu). Here, the master page's prefix is used as the special character. Once entered, you can format the symbol like any other character.

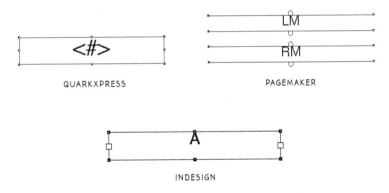

QUARKXPRESS   PAGEMAKER

INDESIGN

Figure 14.34 *The automatic page number symbol, as entered on an XPress (top left), PageMaker (top right), and InDesign (bottom) master page.*

- All three programs allow you to define more than one master page. You also can apply no master page at all, depending on your need. You have two choices when applying master pages. You can apply them at the time you insert the new pages, or you can apply them individually, after all your pages have been created. I prefer to apply my master pages one at a time, after I've defined the number of pages I'll use. It takes only a couple minutes longer, and it gives me more exacting control over my pages.

- Avoid using *crossovers* on your master pages, or items that extend across two pages. The image does not automatically impose on output, and in most cases, the image appears on only one page. In either case, the crossover image does not output with the appropriate bleed. Whenever you design using crossovers, you must place a unique image on both pages, and crop as necessary.

XPress Master Page Issues

Bear in mind the following issues when working with XPress's master pages:

- Automatic page numbering applies to your pages in the order they appear in your document, so your world will temporarily crumble if you reposition your pages using the Document Layout palette. So, if you're imposing a simple job and want to move page 8 so it's next to page 1, you'll quickly find it renumbered page 2—thereby causing your pages to be misnumbered after folding and trimming. In this case, the numbers have to be replaced with *hard* page numbers, which involves highlighting the current page number and typing the desired digit.

- XPress's master page items are actually copied onto each page to which they're applied. This means you can edit any of these elements when you're working on the regular pages. Warning: As soon as you edit any master page item, that page no longer adheres to the master page. It may look like it for the most part, but editing the items placed there by the master page severs the connection. This means that if you edit the original master page, you must reapply it to the individual page. And if you do that, you'll have to double-check it for duplicate items. If all this stresses you out, you can lock all of the elements in your master pages (select the elements and choose Item: **Lock**). This keeps you from accidentally editing the wrong stuff, and you can simply select and unlock anything you want to change.

- XPress's Automatic Text Box is really an internally linked text box located on the initial master page. Although the Auto Text Box is great for importing long stretches of text (like books), it too often gets in the way. I prefer to eschew the Auto Text Box in favor of placing an unlinked text box on the master pages, then taking a moment or two to manually create my links. This sounds like it takes a long time, until you zoom out to 20% or 30%, Option-Select the Link tool, and proceed to link like mad.

PageMaker Master Page Issues

Bear in mind the following issues when working with PageMaker's master pages:

- PageMaker's master pages act like more of an overlay. All the items appear on the regular pages they're applied to, but you cannot edit or delete them.

- You can create a series of master pages, even though only icons for the default set ("L" and "R") appear in the lower left of the window. All master page sets are visible in the Master Pages palette, and can be accessed or applied at any time.

InDesign Master Page Issues

Bear in mind the following issues when working with InDesign's master pages:

- At first, it seems like you can't select or edit any master page items that appear on regular pages, just like PageMaker. But you can, if you (Command-Shift-drag) [Control-Shift-drag] one of these items with the Direct Selection (white arrow) tool. This is known as a *local override*. Once you do this, the elements are no longer considered master page items. For example, if you edit such a shape on a regular page, it will not be affected by future edits to the master page it's based on. Fortunately, there is a way to remove the local override. To revert a single element back to it's status as a master page item, select it and choose Remove Selected Local Overrides from the Master Pages palette submenu. To revert all the over-ridden elements on a page, don't select anything and choose Remove All Local Overrides from the same location.

- You can base the contents of one set of master pages on an existing set. When you choose New Master from the Pages palette submenu, the New Master dialog box contains a Based on Master pop-up. When you choose a master page here, its contents are automatically placed on the new set, allowing you to expand the design as needed. In the future, when you edit the original master pages, the changes are applied globally to any based-on sets as well.

- You can convert a regular page into a master page. After designing the regular page as desired, choose Save As Master from the Pages palette submenu. A new set of master pages is created, based entirely on the original page elements. However, note that this command does not automatically apply the new master page to the regular page you just designed. To do this, you'll still have to delete the original elements and choose Apply Master to Pages from the Pages palette submenu. In the Apply Master dialog box, set the new master page item in the Apply Master pop-up.

- Master pages can contain up to ten individual pages. However, they're not necessary unless your document design specifically calls for it.

Designing Individual Pages

Although this book focuses entirely on production-oriented issues, prepress walks hand in hand with design. Unfortunately, design is the single most common cause of problem files. The more "challenging" a file is to create, the higher the potential for problematic output and printing. The work created by a designer must be *responsible* as well as attractive and effective. This means not succumbing to the following myth: if you can see it on a computer screen, you can make it happen in real life.

Successful output invariably depends on how well you place and handle your graphics files, which depends on your knowledge of the following:

- Importing different graphics styles

- Scaling graphics

- Rotating graphics

- Cropping graphics

- Layering (or stacking) graphics

I'll also discuss some timesaving techniques for those of you who use the same information in many different documents:

- Image libraries

- Color libraries

- Style sheet libraries

Importing Graphics

If anything causes your file to misprint, chances are it's a graphic. That's no big surprise, when you think about it. A document is only a combination of words and pictures, and those pictures come from at least three different programs (Illustrator, FreeHand, and Photoshop), two different forms (pixels and vectors), and two file formats (TIFF and EPS). How you handle these files is just as important as how you create them. The following sections cover the most common output-related problems that occur when importing graphics into a page layout document.

The first and most important rule concerning the use of graphics in a page layout program is this: create and adjust your graphics in the appropriate programs. Don't create graphs in XPress or PageMaker; Illustrator has a Graph tool, and any vector-based drawing program is more adept at fine linework. Don't use a layout program's so-called image editing tools to adjust a halftone; that's what Photoshop is for. All three major layout programs ship with simple graphics tools—circles, rules, boxes, and so forth— but these are only for minor page flourishes and supplementary graphics. As soon as you require something more complex than those things, go to another program. There, you can create the graphic with infinitely more precision. After you import it into the page layout program, your only concerns are working with the single element.

Scaling Graphics

Although the question of scaling graphics has been asked and answered countless times, there still remains an air of mystery about it. The degree to which a graphic can be scaled in a page layout program depends almost entirely on whether it's a vector- or pixel-based image.

Vector-based images can be scaled with wanton abandon, because the lines and shapes comprising the image have no resolution until they are sent to an output device. Beyond that, there are still a few guidelines to follow:

- Although PageMaker and InDesign let you scale practically to infinity, XPress only scales graphics up to 1000%. If you need to enlarge a vector-based image more than that, scale it first in its original program, then import it for fine-tuning.

- If your Illustrator or FreeHand artwork contains an embedded pixel-based image, you can't scale to the same extremes. You're essentially limited to pixel-based scaling restrictions. The best solutions are to avoid graphics with embedded pixel-based images, trace any pixel-based images and incorporate them into the vector-based artwork, or avoid scaling too much by creating the original graphic closer to the intended size (see Figure 14.35).

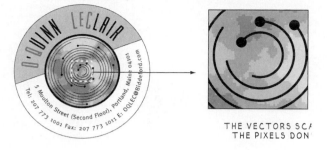

THE VECTORS SC/
THE PIXELS DON

Figure 14.35 *Even though this image was created in a vector-based editing program, the embedded pixel-based info is still subject to scaling restrictions. At 100% (left), the image appears and outputs with no problems. If it is scaled too high (right), the pixel-based data appears jagged, even though the vector-based lines output smoothly.*

- And if you auto-trace an image, nothing points out flaws like massive scaling. In the original program, be sure you zoom in close to double-check the smoothness and shape of your lines.

Pixel-based images, though, are often shrouded in confusion. The scale window on these graphics is considerably smaller because of the relationship that must exist between file resolution and the target linescreen value. Simply put, there must be enough pixel information to satisfy the needs of the halftone cells. Conventional wisdom states that a resolution-to-linescreen ratio of 2:1 satisfies this requirement (that's why service bureaus ask a client for the target linescreen when they have images scanned—they double that number and scan at that resolution). In truth, you can have a 1:1 ratio between resolution and linescreen and output successfully. But if you increased the scale by the tiniest bit, the images would begin to pixelate. The 2:1 ratio was developed to give designers a little elbow room once they received their scans. However, this does not give you free reign to scale with abandon:

- The more you scale up or down, the more likely the possibility of misprinting occurs. Remember the basic rule: increasing scale decreases resolution, decreasing scale increases resolution. Too little resolution, and your image becomes jagged. Too much, and you could have a PostScript error (see Figure 14.36). It's a lot like vitamin C: Too much or too little inevitably causes problems. I prefer keeping the scale window between 75–125%.

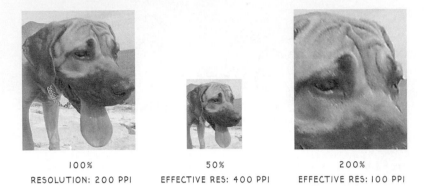

| 100% | 50% | 200% |
| RESOLUTION: 200 PPI | EFFECTIVE RES: 400 PPI | EFFECTIVE RES: 100 PPI |

Figure 14.36   *A 200ppi pixel-based image at 100% (left), 50% (middle), and 200% (right).*

- Scaled pixel-based graphics take longer to output. Between establishing a scale percentage at the time of the scan and using Photoshop's tools to set image size, you should be able to nail the intended image size and reduce your output times.

It's interesting to note that some service providers and printers will flatly refuse to accept graphics that do not meet the 2:1 ppi/lpi ratio. Sometimes, they may not necessarily understand why—they only know that it's a common requirement, as proclaimed by book after book, resource upon resource. You may have to sign an accountability waiver if you want them to accept your images.

Rotating Graphics

Rotating a graphic, like scaling, is considered an image-editing issue, and should be done whenever possible in Photoshop. This isn't as big a deal with most vector-based illustrations, but it can be with medium to large scans. Again, a rotated graphic results in increased output time, and can sometimes lead to PostScript errors. I recommend using the page layout program to determine what degree of rotation needs to be applied (by rotating the imported graphic), then applying that value to the original image in Photoshop. Reimport the image, and you'll immediately see faster redraw and output times.

Cropping Graphics

The process of cropping an image in a page layout program is similar to cropping conventionally. Only instead of marking a photo with crop lines for the stripper to handle, you crop by literally hiding the portions of the image you don't want. Unfortunately, cropping in a layout program is not the same as cropping in Photoshop, Illustrator, or FreeHand. In Photoshop, for example, the information cropped away is discarded, gone forever. In XPress and PageMaker, the information is still there; it's just not showing. This means that even if you import a full-page image and crop it down to the size of a postage stamp, the rest of the image has to be processed. (Adobe claims that this does not apply to InDesign, that the program only sends the visible data to the output device. Just the same, the image still occupies space on the transport media and lengthens copying times, so it's still a good idea to crop in Photoshop whenever possible.)

Consider this worst-case scenario: A designer was attempting to output a one-page document, and failing miserably at every turn. The layout contained perhaps 20 small photographs, head-shots culled from an old group photo. When I examined the file, I found that the designer had scanned the letter-sized photo and then imported it 20 times, cropping each one to show a single head. Instead of working with 20 small images of perhaps 300K apiece (about 6MB total), he was attempting to output over 350MB of information. Just imagine if he had been designing a multipage document.

Whenever possible, crop your images in Photoshop. This step should be part of your established image-editing methodology.

The most common cropping problems include the following:

- When creating vector-based illustrations, many designers create different versions of the artwork, leave them all on the same page for easy reference, and crop away the unwanted ones after they import the file into their layout. This causes untold problems, because the person processing the file has no idea what could have been done to the items not visible. Maybe they contain an imported RGB TIFF. Maybe one item is comprised of six billion points. Maybe another was tagged with one of those awful, nonreproducible, error-generating custom patterns. Solution: one file, one graphic. Make a special copy to contain the extra information, if necessary.

- If you need to crop a scanned image, there are two places to do so before importing it. First, crop as closely as you can at the time of the scan (if you're the one making the scan). Second, use Photoshop's tools to crop more closely. Cropping in your page layout should be kept to a minimum.

- Whenever cropping an image, be sure you leave enough exposed image area to accommodate for any bleeds.

Stacking Graphics

Stacking refers to the process of placing one graphic on top of another in a page layout. For example, you may want to place a logo over an imported scan, or place an isolated Photoshop image over a colored box. This process isn't as straightforward as it seems. Each graphic type you work with is subject to a different set of requirements.

Line Art

Wherever you place imported black-and-white line art, it outputs as overprinting black. As long as the file is saved as a 1-bit TIFF, the whites remain transparent, allowing any background information to show through. If, for whatever reason, you save the file as an EPS, you must check the Transparent Whites box to achieve this effect. Otherwise, the file will behave as a grayscale file—the whites inside and around the image will import as white. Note, however, that line art saved as an EPS does not automatically overprint, nor can you apply a new color in the page layout.

Silhouettes and Clipping Paths

You create a silhouette in Photoshop by isolating an image element from its surrounding pixels. Trouble is, even though the edge pixels of the image are white, you don't really *delete* anything. Those white pixels are imported right into your document. If you don't place the image on top of any other page element, even a colored background, you'll be just fine. As soon as you do, you'll see those white pixels getting in the way. You'll also see the primary reason for defining a clipping path.

When you want to place a silhouetted Photoshop image on top of other page elements in your final document, you have to define a clipping path. This technique is based on the use of vector-based paths made with Photoshop's Pen tool. A clipping path works as a mask on the image, revealing only the part of the image you want visible (see Figure 14.37). (See Chapter 13, "Photoshop Production Techniques," for more on silhouettes and clipping paths.)

Vector-Based Artwork

When you import vector-based artwork, you import only the objects that were created or placed in that file. Some of the differences between imported illustrations and scans include the following:

SILHOUETTE   CLIPPING PATH

Figure 14.37 *When you attempt to place a simple silhouette on a colored background, the white pixels surrounding the image obscure the underlying information (left). To achieve this effect, you must surround the image with a clipping path in Photoshop (right). Created using Photoshop's Pen Tool, a clipping path acts as a vector-based mask, allowing only the pixels inside of it to appear in the layout.*

- The color white has to be intentionally applied. Although white isn't really a color (it's a "print no ink here" command), it appears as an item in the color menus of all applications. Also, there is no white "box" around the image, like a silhouette from Photoshop.

- Before saving the final version of the graphic, be sure to select and delete all stray points and guides. Although they may not be seen on your page, they will affect the placement of the image when it's imported.

- One of the most common uses for these programs is creating customized type. Whenever you create type in an illustration file, always convert that type to paths (or outlines) before saving and importing. This removes the font information, allowing you to avoid having to deal with missing fonts during output.

Summary

The importance of the page layout stage cannot be overemphasized. Ignoring the issues I've discussed is much like spending lots of time and money on building materials for a house, only to pour a substandard foundation.

Often, page layout takes place at the very end of a project, after you've planned, delegated, scanned, corrected, illustrated, and otherwise generated the content for a project. As this material is generated, it's your responsibility to prepare the page layout document to receive this information as easily as possible:

- Set your default preferences, making sure they dovetail with your output and press requirements.

- Properly set your page dimensions, making sure they fall within the reproducible range of the target press.

- Define the colors to be used in your documents, making sure that the names are consistent throughout all of your graphics files.

- Use style sheets to format your type quickly and consistently.

- Apply colors thoughtfully throughout your page layouts, making sure no fine details are lost or obscured through difficult trapping.

- Define master pages to be sure you have an easy, consistent method of applying images on multiple pages.

- Import and position your graphics, making sure you scale, crop, rotate, and layer them in a way that doesn't hinder successful output.

Not so long ago, there were some very compelling reasons to choose one layout program over another, similar to the arguments heard when choosing the Boston Red Sox over the New York Yankees. Nowadays, the industry-leading layout programs are so close to each other in terms of capabilities and ease-of-use, it becomes almost pointless to recommend one in particular.

As a result, all programs will be in widespread use for many years to come. The smartest thing any graphics professional can do is become familiar with XPress, PageMaker, and InDesign. Use one primarily for the projects you create, but be secure in the knowledge that you can step up and win one for the Gipper using another. At the very least, you'll increase your market value. At best, you'll improve the efficiency of your production environment, saving untold hours and dollars every day.

TRAPPING

A printing press is not the perfect reproduction tool you'd like it to be. Rollers and plates spin madly, drawing paper through the works at up to 2,200 feet per minute. Ink is applied faster than the human eye can track. Paper stretches slightly as it's moistened by ink and water. Even on a multi-million dollar press, paper or plates may shift ever so slightly. These factors may result in colors falling out of *register*, or out of alignment. Misregistered inks result in gaps and color shifts between adjacent page elements. Humans have tried for centuries to create a press that consistently holds its register. They've come close, but you still have to compensate for the basic laws of motion and force naturally involved in on-press reproduction.

You have one strategy to combat this phenomenon: trapping. When you trap, you compensate for misregistration by slightly expanding one color into its adjacent color. This way, even though a shift may take place, the overlapping inks conceal any resulting flaws without distorting the shapes of the objects. Until recently, trapping was a mysterious process best left to conventional prepress professionals. While this often remains the best option, today's desktop trapping tools and techniques are more powerful than ever. With a little time, experience, and forethought, you can assume the responsibility of trapping your files digitally.

But be careful: desktop tools have not simplified the issues of trapping. Your colors are subject to the same laws of physics as ever, and trapping is never the result of a single mouse-click. Successful trapping requires a knowledge of process and spot color, thoughtful design, and an awareness of each object in your layout.

Some work will not require any trapping:

- Documents that contain elements of isolated, solid colors don't need to be trapped. There are no adjacent colors, so no gaps would show if misregistration occurs (see Figure 15.1).

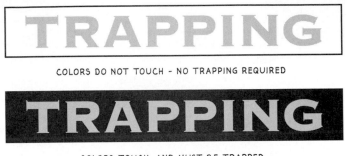

COLORS DO NOT TOUCH - NO TRAPPING REQUIRED

COLORS TOUCH, AND MUST BE TRAPPED

Figure 15.1 *Trapping is not required when colored elements do not touch. Because the word "Trapping" has a white outline in the image on the right, it does not need to be trapped (see color insert).*

- Overprinting black information, such as small text or thin lines, compensates for misregistration because of the underlying inks.

- Images using an abundance of thick black outlines, such as cartoon drawings, may not need to be trapped (see Figure 15.2).

Figure 15.2 *Four-color artwork with heavy black outlines doesn't require trapping if the black is based on multiple inks (see color insert).*

- A publication comprised of process colors does not need trapping if adjacent colors share high enough percentages of process components. (See "Building a Process Bridge," later this chapter, for more info.)

One of the best ways to deal with trapping is to avoid the need altogether. Designing your work so that trapping is kept to a minimum should always be an option. When your trapping needs become more complex, your entire job becomes more complex:

- **The document takes longer to prepare.** Even though your page layout programs have "automatic" trapping features, none of them is thorough enough to stand alone, untouched by the user. Also, imported vector-based graphics are not affected by these commands, so nearly every job will require some sort of manual trapping.

- **The file takes longer to process.** The trapping commands in a page layout program add to a project's output time. If a program like Imation TrapWise is used, there's no telling *how* long the file will take to process. (See "Dedicated Trapping Software," later this chapter, for more info.)

- **The file can cost more money to produce.** Many designers hand trapping responsibilities over to the service provider, who can charge upward of $80 an hour.

- **The margin for error increases.** Incorrect values are applied, images are left untrapped, lack of communication results in strippers misreading your film. The more variables you add to your work, the more likely it is that one of them will be mishandled. This isn't pessimism—it's the fundamental building block of human error.

Does that mean you shouldn't attempt to control these values on your own? Of course not. As long as you understand the need for trapping, how much you are able to do, and which applications will give you the best results, you can trap with the best of us.

Trapping values are established in three places:

- **In your page layout program.** These commands affect anything created within the actual program, such as type, rules, and boxes.

- **In your illustration program.** A page layout program cannot trap an imported EPS file. In Chapter 8, "Vector-Based Graphics," I discussed how you can't edit the internal contents of one of these files. Editing trap means editing color information, and the EPS file structure prevents that. You'll have to establish these traps in Illustrator or FreeHand.

- **In a dedicated trapping application.** Imation TrapWise, the most popular example, does nothing but trap, trap, trap. This sounds like a wonderful solution and it is—sometimes. Typically, this is the best option for difficult traps (like gradients-on-gradients) or establishing extensive and precise trapping values geared to a specific press. Otherwise, TrapWise falls short of a panacea. It's expensive, and requires a dedicated Windows NT workstation.

In this chapter, I focus on the issues involved in manually trapping images in your page layout and illustration programs, including the following:

- Compensating for deficiencies inherent in the color black.

- Maintaining a process bridge in your four-color work, often eliminating the need for additional trapping values.

- Manually trapping artwork in Illustrator or FreeHand.

- Properly establishing trapping preferences in XPress, PageMaker, and InDesign.

Throughout each section, I'll also offer advice on how to best avoid the need for trapping altogether.

Trapping Essentials

There are two types of digital trap. When you apply a *spread*, you expand an object's edge into the surrounding colors. When printed, the expanded edge overprints the background inks, creating the necessary overlap. When you apply a *choke*, you expand the adjoining edge of the colors that surround an object. When printed, this edge overprints the object, creating the necessary overlap.

Chokes and spreads are essentially the same thing—in both, one color extends slightly into another. The only difference is the direction that the edge expands. One simple rule applies: lighter colors always expand into darker colors. This maintains the integrity of your shapes as best as possible. By expanding the lighter colors into darker colors, the overlap is less apparent to the eye. If the darker-colored object is expanded, the change of shape is more obvious.

For example, picture a foreground and a background object, such as a circle within a circle. The background circle is colored PMS 287 (a dark blue), and the foreground circle is colored PMS 185 (a bright red). Because red is the lighter color, it will expand (or spread) into the blue.

Now switch the colors. This time, the lighter background object expands (or chokes) into the darker foreground shape. By trapping the lighter colors into the darker, the printed result is much more subtle and appealing (see Figure 15.3).

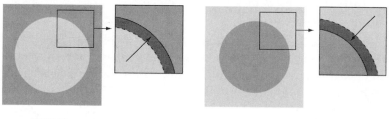

SPREAD   CHOKE

Figure 15.3   *Whether spreading or choking, lighter colors expand into darker colors to minimize the change in the trapped object's shape (see color insert).*

Building a Process Bridge

When you work with spot colors, the need for trapping is ever-present. Do the colors touch? If so, they must be trapped.

When coloring adjacent objects with CYMK combinations, plan to use colors that share ink percentages sufficient to create a *process bridge*. A bridge occurs when two objects share at least 20% of one component color (cyan, magenta, yellow, or black). Generally, this eliminates the possibility of the white gaps that appear as a result of misregistered plates. The most that can be revealed is an ink common to both objects, and this is much less visible to the eye. Depending on the adjacent colors in question, however, additional trapping may be necessary:

- When one adjoining color contains a significantly higher percentage of one component ink, trapping may be required. Misregistration may reveal a visible third color (see Figure 15.4).

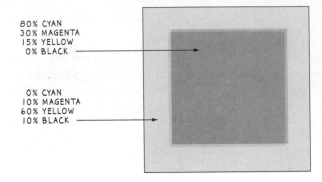

80% CYAN
30% MAGENTA
15% YELLOW
0% BLACK

0% CYAN
10% MAGENTA
60% YELLOW
10% BLACK

Figure 15.4 *Due to the sharp difference in cyan percentages, this process bridge is insufficient (see color insert).*

- If two objects share high percentages of more than one component color, additional trapping isn't required. Any third color revealed during misregistration isn't visually distracting (see Figure 15.5).

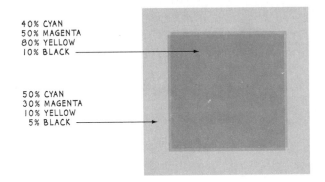

40% CYAN
50% MAGENTA
80% YELLOW
10% BLACK

50% CYAN
30% MAGENTA
10% YELLOW
5% BLACK

Figure 15.5 *Even though the difference in yellow percentages is sharp, the high levels of cyan and magenta make this process bridge sufficient (see color insert).*

- Typically, if all the CMYK percentages of one color are higher than the adjoining color, trapping is not required (see Figure 15.6).

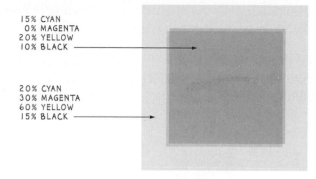

15% CYAN
0% MAGENTA
20% YELLOW
10% BLACK

20% CYAN
30% MAGENTA
60% YELLOW
15% BLACK

Figure 15.6 *Since all the ink levels of one shape are higher than the other, this process bridge is sufficient (see color insert).*

The Limitations of Black Ink

When you think of a color, you could be referencing thousands of possible shades. Light blue, dark green, medium red with cool purple undertones, *all* the colors you work with can be described accurately only by precise mathematical numbers (or an abundance of adjectives). The exception is, one would assume, black. We've come to believe that black means black. Absolute darkness. The absence of all light. There is only one *black*, and when you apply it in a document, you expect it to behave that way.

Unfortunately, it doesn't. The black ink used in four-color printing is transparent, like all process inks. It cannot cover ink or paper as thoroughly as you'd like. Take a close look at a four-color publication and check for the following traits:

- **Unimpressive knockout blacks.** Here, the paper grain shows through large areas of black, and you don't need a microscope to see that it looks a little on the thin side. Ink transparency prevents robust coverage, which becomes even more noticeable when compared to denser blacks.

- **Unimpressive overprinting blacks.** Theoretically, overprinting a black element eliminates the need for trapping. Yet if you overprint a large area—a big, black box placed over part of a high-res image, for example—the underlying inks are visible through the black.

The solution is not as simple as using an opaque black ink during printing. This would wreak havoc on any color or high-res image containing black tints. Instead, you must improvise by adding new and improved process blacks to your color menus. How you define them will depend on how and where the black is applied. This technique is often referred to as creating an *enriched black*. To be more specific, I describe two types of enriched black: *rich black* and *super black* (see Figure 15.7).

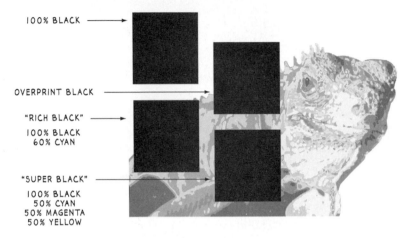

Figure 15.7 *The effects of black, overprinting black, rich black, and super black. Isolated black shapes (upper left) generally don't require enriching. When a 100% black shape overprints other colors (upper right), the underlying info may be visible through the transparent black ink. Black shapes that straddle colored info (lower left) benefit from the addition of one process component, which elimiates any show-through. Black shapes surrounded by colored info (lower right) can tolerate the three remaining process components, which creates the darkest possible black with no additional trapping requirements (see color insert).*

Rich Black

Rich black is a combination of process black and one other process ink. The second ink increases the density of the black, making it appear fuller and darker—in short, blacker. A rich black is appropriate on two occasions:

- When the edges of a black object are fully exposed. A black box on a white field, especially if the paper is high-grain, is a common example (see Figure 15.8).

Figure 15.8 *A rich black is suitable when the edges of a black object are exposed. Smaller black elements don't necessarily require it, but larger elements may benefit considerably (see color insert).*

- When a black object straddles other image information. A black box placed so that half is over a white area and half is over a high-res image is a common example (see Figure 15.9).

Figure 15.9 *A rich black is suitable when a black object straddles another object. It will prevent any underlying colors from showing through after the project is printed (see color insert).*

Avoid the temptation to use enriched blacks for *all* your black objects. While it's true that it results in more satisfying blacks, it's only appropriate for objects at least a quarter-inch thick. Applying a multicolor black to type, rules, or finely detailed line art will almost certainly result in fringe during reproduction. Fortunately, the weaknesses of process black are far less apparent when applied to very thin elements.

Traditionally, a rich black is created by defining a new color comprised of 100% black and 60% cyan (the second ink is referred to as the *undercolor*). If all the edges of a black object are exposed and there are no adjoining colors, this approach is generally acceptable. If adjacent colors are present, however, cyan may not be the best choice. Choose an undercolor that creates a sufficient process bridge with the surrounding image area. For example, if the object straddles an image of a bright red flower, magenta or yellow (depending on the dominant ink) would be the more successful undercolor.

Those exposed edges are the reason you only add one undercolor. If you add more than one extra ink to a black area with exposed edges, any misregistration may result in *fringe,* or one or more of the undercolors peeking from the sides of the object like a multicolored halo (see Figure 15.10). The trapping features in all three major page layout programs have a built-in function called *keepaway*. This automatic command dictates that whenever an object is colored 100% black, the edges of any undercolors are drawn in by the default Auto Trapping value. This way, if misregistration should occur, the undercolor is still covered by the black area. The process bridge and the keepaway function take care of any trapping needs, and any extra inks just increase the likelihood of fringe.

Figure 15.10 *Misregistration can result in fringe around the edges of a black object. In this exaggerated example, the three process components in a super black have misregistered (see color insert).*

Defining a Rich Black in XPress

Follow these steps to add a rich black to XPress's Colors palette:

1. Choose Edit: **Colors**.

2. Click New in the Edit Colors dialog box.

3. Choose Multi-Ink from the Model pop-up.

4. Highlight Process Black in the Ink window.

5. Choose 100% from the Shade pop-up.

6. Highlight Process Cyan (or another desired undercolor) in the Ink window.

7. Choose 60% from the Shade pop-up (see Figure 15.11).

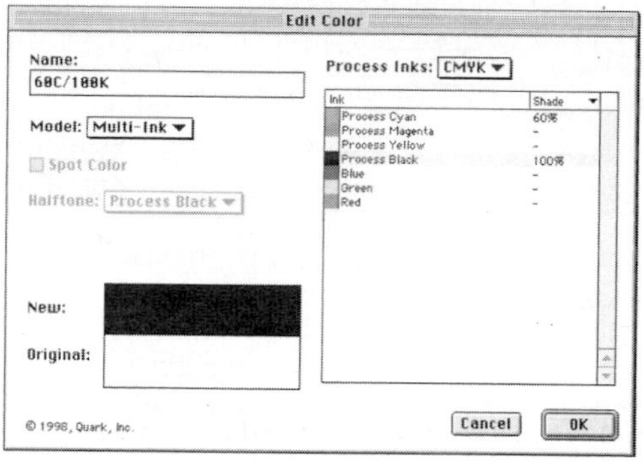

Figure 15.11   *Creating rich black in XPress*

8. Name the color clearly. "Rich Black" is fine, but on occasion I've named the new color "K:100 C:60", so I can be absolutely certain about the inks I apply when editing a document.

9. Click OK to save the color.

You also can define a rich black by choosing CMYK from the Model pop-up, and entering the desired values in the CMYK fields. Be sure the Spot Color box is unchecked before clicking OK.

Defining a Rich Black in PageMaker

Follow these steps to add a rich black to PageMaker's Colors palette:

1. Choose Utilities: **Define Colors**.

2. Click New in the Define Colors dialog box. (You can also access this dialog by choosing New Color from the Colors Palette submenu.)

3. Choose Process from the Type pop-up.

4. Choose CMYK from the Model pop-up.

5. Type in 100% black and 60% cyan or your desired undercolor (see Figure 15.12).

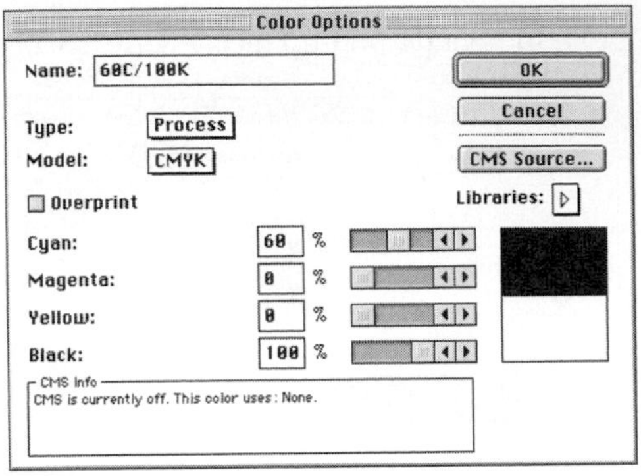

Figure 15.12   *Creating rich black in PageMaker.*

6. Name the color clearly.

7. Click OK to save the color.

Defining a Rich Black in InDesign

Follow these steps to add a rich black to InDesign's Swatches palette:

1. Choose New Color Swatch from the Swatches palette submenu.

2. Choose Process from the Type pop-up.

3. Choose CMYK from the Model pop-up.

4. Type in 100% black and 60% cyan or your desired undercolor (see Figure 15.13).

5. Name the color clearly.

6. Click OK to save the color.

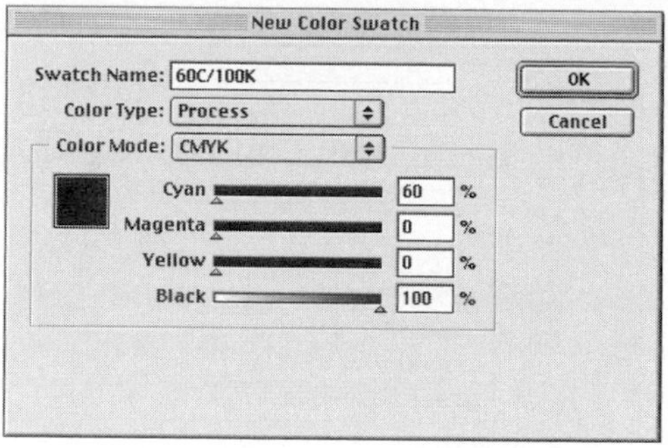

Figure 15.13   *Creating rich black in InDesign.*

Rich Blacks in Illustrator and FreeHand

If you create an object in Illustrator or FreeHand that meets the preceding criterion for rich black, you must define and apply this color in the original application. However, when you import a rich black item, the page layout program cannot trap it, which means the keepaway function will not be applied. You're faced with a choice: simply apply your rich black and take your chances on-press (which many people do, with a fair degree of success), or apply a manual keepaway value to the object as you color it. This involves applying a simple trap using vector-based tools. Use the steps in the next section to create a rich black in Illustrator and FreeHand. See "Vector-Based Trapping Tools," later in this chapter, to apply the manual trap.

Defining a Rich Black in Illustrator

Follow these steps to add a rich black to Illustrator's Swatches palette:

1. Choose New Color Swatch from the Swatches palette submenu.

2. Choose Process from the Type pop-up.

3. Choose CMYK from the Color Mode pop-up.

4. Type in 100% black and 60% cyan or your desired undercolor (see Figure 15.14).

5. Name the color clearly.

6. Click OK to save the color.

7. As you apply the color, be sure Overprint Fill is *not* checked in the Attributes palette.

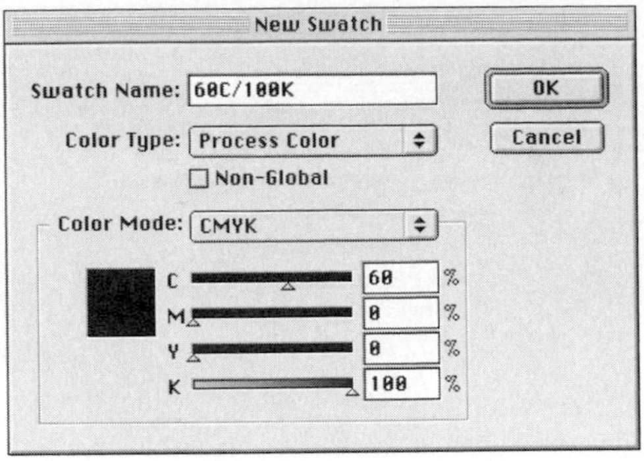

Figure 15.14 *Creating rich black in Illustrator.*

Because all blacks look alike when displayed onscreen, choose Name from the Swatches palette submenu. Doing so lists all colors by name, making it much easier to discern the rich black from the default black.

Defining a Rich Black in FreeHand

Follow these steps to add a rich black to FreeHand's Colors palette:

1. In the Mixer palette, enter 100% black and 60% cyan (or you desired undercolor).

2. Click the Add to Color List button, in the upper right of the palette (see Figure 15.15).

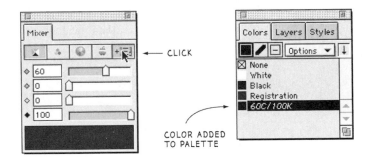

Figure 15.15 *Creating rich black in FreeHand.*

3. In the Add to Color List dialog, select the Process option and click OK.

You can also add the color by dragging the swatch in the lower right of the Mixer palette directly onto the Colors palette.

Super Black

A *super black* is black combined with three undercolors: 50% cyan, 50% magenta, and 50% yellow. This provides the deepest, most satisfying process black you can reproduce on-press.

Super blacks are not for all occasions. Apply them when all the object edges are within other colors, or bleed off the edge of the page. There is no possibility of fringe here, because no edges will be hanging over that vulnerable white landscape. Otherwise, the addition of three inks (as opposed to one, in a rich black) increases the possibility of visible fringe.

The ink density (or combined percentages) of a super black is 250, which is enough for almost all paper and press types. Do not increase the recommended percentages of the undercolors. When ink density is too high, a job takes much longer to dry, and can even result in a sticky mess that has to be replated and run again. This problem often isn't discovered until the job is being printed. When using thin, highly absorbent, or other specialty papers, consult with your printer before using super black.

Defining a Super Black in XPress

Follow these steps to add super black to XPress's Colors palette:

1. Choose Edit: **Colors**.

2. Click New in the Edit Color dialog box.

3. Choose Multi-Ink from the Model pop-up.

4. Highlight Process Black in the Ink window, and choose 100% from the Shade pop-up.

5. Highlight Process Cyan in the Ink window, and choose 50% from the Shade pop-up.

6. Repeat the step 5 for Process Magenta and Process Yellow (see Figure 15.16).

7. Name the color clearly.

8. Click OK to save the color.

You also can define super black by choosing CMYK from the Model pop-up, and entering the desired values in the CMYK fields. Be sure the Spot Color box is unchecked before clicking OK.

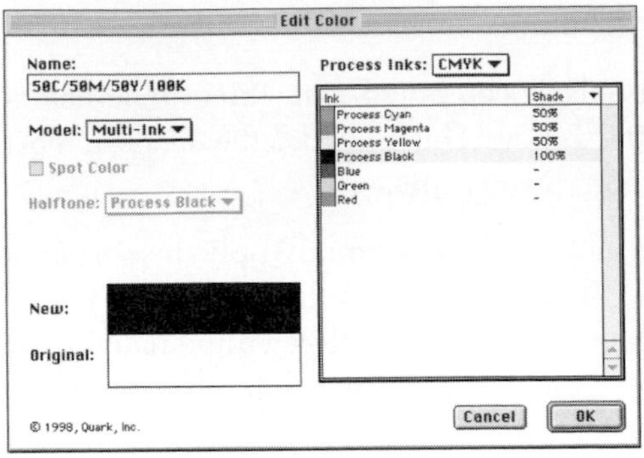

Figure 15.16 *Creating super black in XPress.*

Defining a Super Black in PageMaker

Follow these steps to add super black to PageMaker's Colors palette:

1. Choose Utilities: **Define Colors.**

2. Click New in the Define Colors dialog box. The Color Options dialog box appears. (You can also access this dialog by choosing New Color from the Colors Palette submenu.)

3. Choose Process from the Type pop-up.

4. Choose CMYK from the Model pop-up.

5. In the CMYK fields, enter 50% Cyan, 50% Magenta, 50% Yellow, and 100% Black (see Figure 15.17).

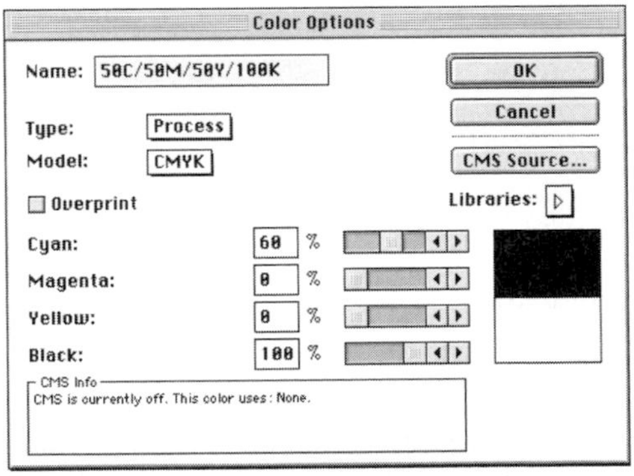

Figure 15.17 *Creating super black in PageMaker.*

6. Name the color clearly.

7. Click OK to save the color.

Defining a Super Black in InDesign

Follow these steps to add super black to InDesign's Swatches palette:

1. Choose New Color Swatch from the Swatches palette submenu.

2. Choose Process from the Color Type pop-up.

3. Choose CMYK from the Color Mode pop-up.

4. In the CMYK fields, enter 50% Cyan, 50% Magenta, 50% Yellow, and 100% Black (see Figure 15.18).

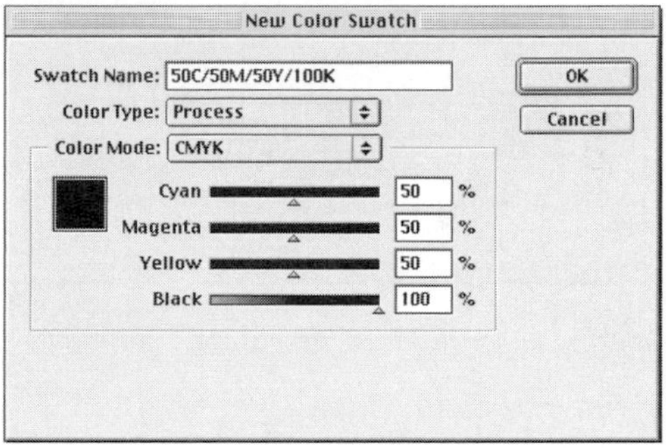

Figure 15.18   *Creating super black in InDesign.*

5. Name the color clearly.

6. Click OK to save the color.

Super Black in Illustrator and FreeHand

Like I stated in the Rich Black section, if you create an object in Illustrator or FreeHand that meets the preceding criterion for super black, you must define and apply this color in the original application. Use the steps that follow to create super black in Illustrator and FreeHand. See "Vector-Based Trapping Tools," later in this chapter, to apply any necessary manual trapping.

Defining Super Black in Illustrator

Follow these steps to add a rich black to Illustrator's Swatches palette:

1. Choose New Color Swatch from the Swatches palette submenu.

2. Choose Process from the Color Type pop-up.

3. Choose CMYK from the Color Mode pop-up.

4. In the CMYK fields, enter 50% Cyan, 50% Magenta, 50% Yellow, and 100% Black (see Figure 15.19).

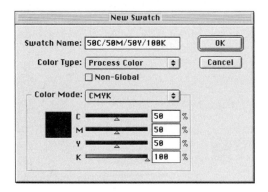

Figure 15.19   *Creating super black in Illustrator.*

5. Name the color clearly.

6. Click OK to save the color.

7. As you apply the color, be sure Overprint Fill is *not* checked in the Attributes palette.

Because all blacks look alike when displayed onscreen, choose Name from the Swatches palette submenu. Doing so lists all colors by name, making it much easier to discern the rich black from the default black.

Defining a Super Black in FreeHand

Follow these steps to add a super black to FreeHand's Colors palette:

1. In the Mixer palette, enter 50% Cyan, 50% Magenta, 50% Yellow, and 100% Black.

2. Click the Add to Color List button, in the upper-right corner of the palette (see Figure 15.20).

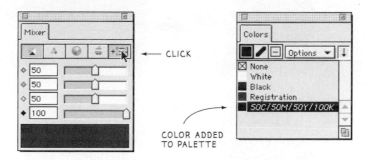

Figure 15.20 *Creating super black in FreeHand.*

3. In the Add to Color List dialog box, select the Process option and click OK.

You also can add the color by dragging the swatch in the lower right of the Mixer palette directly onto the Colors palette.

Knockouts and Overprints

When you place one element on top of another, its color will either knock out or overprint. Most often, an element knocks out, which means that it doesn't mix with any underlying inks. The knockout behavior is automatically applied to every color you define (with some exceptions for black—refer to "The Limitations of Black Ink," earlier this chapter). For example, if you place a red circle on top of a blue square, no blue ink will print within the outline of the circle. When you spec a color to *overprint*, you tell it to combine with the inks of all underlying shapes. Overprinting always results in color shifts (see Figure 15.21).

One hundred percent black is the only color that successfully overprints: when black prints on top of other inks, it remains black. Overprinting any other color—whether a spot ink or process combination—always results in a different color. Overprinting black also removes the need for trapping, which is essential for certain page elements. Depending on the program you use, however, some black objects will automatically overprint, and others will not. You may need to build in any desired overprinting behavior.

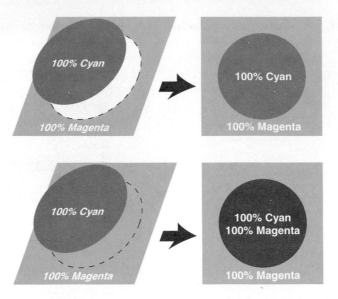

Figure 15.21 *The behavior of objects with knockout (top) and overprinting colors. When a shape knocks out, any color info beneath it is prevented from printing. When the shape overprints, the inks that define it combine with the underlying colors (see color insert).*

Black Type

In the three page layout programs I've been using in my examples, black text automatically overprints. This is one of the primary reasons that black text, particularly at small sizes, is preferable to any other color. Trapping 12-pt body text is impossible. Black text in Illustrator or FreeHand, however, automatically knocks out. The overprint command must be applied in the original program and saved as part of the graphic file.

Black Line Art

Line art files from Photoshop (1-bit TIFFs) automatically overprint when placed in a page layout program. Applying any other color to those files, even 99% black, forces the image to knock out. Black line work from a vector-based program automatically knocks out. As with type, the overprint command for the black shapes has to be turned on and saved into the file.

You can easily incorporate a process bridge into either form of line art. For an imported 1-bit TIFF, simply define and apply one of the enriched blacks I discussed earlier. For Illustrator or FreeHand line work, define an enriched black, apply it as needed, save the file, and import. In this case, it doesn't matter if the image is told to overprint or not, because the bridge assimilates the line art into the adjacent colors.

Vector-Based Trapping Tools

I cannot repeat often enough that color information in an imported EPS file is uneditable. As far as I'm concerned, the graphic is locked in a transparent room with no windows, no door, no way in. We can only gaze upon its contents from our distant vantage point. Therefore, all trapping commands must be applied in the original program *before* the graphic is imported and the document is output.

Illustrator and FreeHand require the same techniques to create simple traps. If the image is constructed using process inks, I encourage designers to choose colors that form a process bridge. (Refer to "Building a Process Bridge," earlier this chapter.) For spot colors and process combinations that don't form a bridge, you must create your own trapping value. This involves applying extremely thin overprinting strokes to objects filled with knockout colors.

A Simple Trap, Manually Applied

The color of a vector-based shape is defined by *fill* and *stroke*. Fill refers to the color of the area within the path, and stroke refers to the color applied to the path itself. Unless forced to do otherwise, a stroke always straddles the path. This means that half the stroke-width falls inside the path, and half falls outside. Understanding this concept is important if you intend to establish your own traps.

The following steps describe how to create a simple trap in a vector-based illustration program:

1. Create a foreground and background object. This example uses a red (PMS 185) star on top of a blue (PMS 287) square.

2. Determine if the foreground color is lighter or darker than the background. The red is lighter than the blue, so you know that you must spread the red into the surrounding blue.

3. Apply an overprinting stroke to the foreground object. Because you're spreading, make the stroke the same color as the foreground object. Force the stroke to overprint by checking theOverprint box. (Note that

in both illustration and page layout programs, only foreground objects receive trapping values.)

4. Set the stroke to *double* your intended trap width. Because only half the stroke width will spread into the adjoining color, you must double the width to achieve the proper value. So to set a trap value of .3 pt—a suitable amount for most offset printing presses—apply a .6-pt stroke (see Figure 15.22).

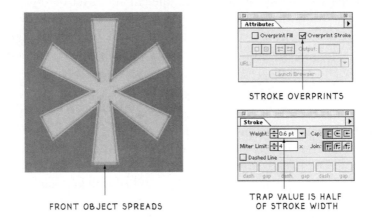

STROKE OVERPRINTS

FRONT OBJECT SPREADS

TRAP VALUE IS HALF
OF STROKE WIDTH

Figure 15.22   *Vector-based traps are created using an overprinting stroke (see color insert).*

5. Save and import the graphic. The shapes are trapped and ready for output.

If the foreground object must be choked instead of spread, color the stroke with the background color. To illustrate, swap the colors used in the previous example, creating a blue star on top of a red square. Because the blue is darker than the red, you don't want to spread the blue shape. As I described in the beginning of this chapter, you always want to expand lighter colors into darker colors. In this case, apply an overprinting red stroke to the blue shape. This way, the stroke-width *inside* the shape overprints, in effect expanding the background color into the foreground shape (see Figure 15.23).

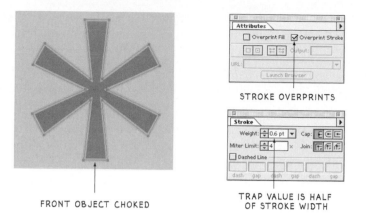

STROKE OVERPRINTS

FRONT OBJECT CHOKED

TRAP VALUE IS HALF
OF STROKE WIDTH

Figure 15.23 *Reverse the stroke color to reverse the direction of the trap (see color insert).*

A Simple Trap, Automatically Applied

FreeHand and Illustrator can automatically trap objects with surprisingly similar plug-ins. Illustrator uses a filter called Trap, found under the Path-finder palette. FreeHand uses an Xtra called Trap, found under the Create submenu.

This trapping method is different than the manual trap I just described. Instead of establishing a series of overprinting *strokes*, these trapping filters create new, narrow shapes that hug the contours of the foreground objects, and their colored *fills* are set to overprint (see Figure 15.24). This method of trapping has benefits and drawbacks.

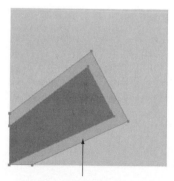

NEW SHAPE PROVIDES TRAP   FILL AUTOMATICALLY OVERPRINTS

Figure 15.24 *The Trap filters of Illustrator and FreeHand create new, overprinting shapes instead of applying strokes (see color insert).*

There are two primary benefits to trapping this way. First, more complex elements, such as multiple shapes of different colors, are much more easily trapped. Second, these tools are fairly intelligent when it comes to determining what needs to be trapped and what doesn't. If two process colors share enough of a common ink, for example, no trapping will be applied.

The automatic method also has some drawbacks. First, only flat, solid fills can be trapped. You cannot use these tools to trap gradations, strokes, patterns, imported images, and other complex attributes. Also, all new objects placed to create the traps make it more difficult to edit the graphic later. If you change your mind after applying the filter, each shape will have to be deleted before you can move on.

After you've decided to use the trapping filters, you only have to understand the values before selecting objects and applying your traps (see Figure 15.25):

- **Thickness** (Illustrator/FreeHand). The most important value in the dialog box, this controls the width of the overprinting path made by the filter. The default is .25 points, which is a little on the thin side (but much better than XPress's .144-point default). Increase the value to between .3 points and .5 points, depending on the registration of the target press, a value you should get from your printer.

- **Tint Reduction** (Illustrator/FreeHand). When trapping spot colors, these filters fill the traps with the lighter color. This value determines the tint of the overprinting fill. Even though these tinted shapes look a little funny onscreen, the fact that they overprint means they will not affect the lighter-colored object and will only darken the other color slightly upon printing, like any good trap should.

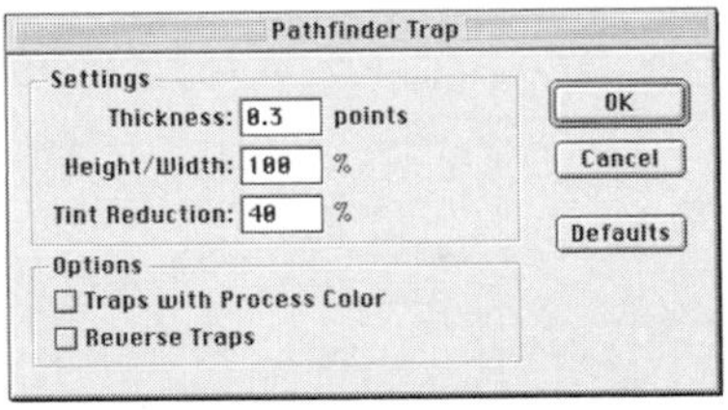

ILLUSTRATOR'S PATHFINDER TRAP 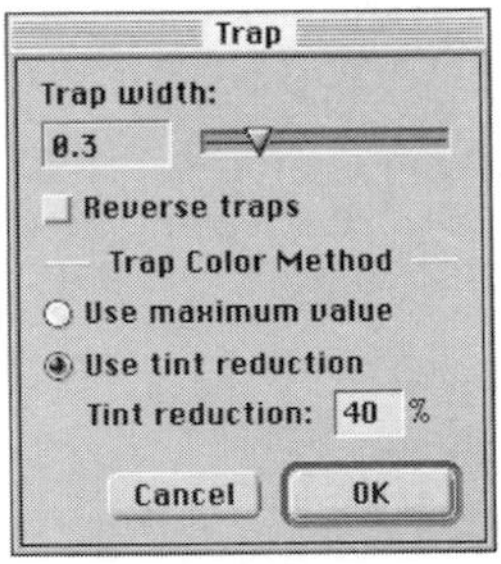   FREEHAND'S TRAP XTRA

Figure 15.25   *The trap dialog boxes of Illustrator (left) and FreeHand (right).*

- **Reverse Traps** (Illustrator/FreeHand). This option changes the direction of the traps, forcing the program to fill traps with the darker color instead of the lighter. Select this option if you do not agree with the filter's decision about which color is darker.

- **Convert Custom Colors to Process** (Illustrator). This automatically fills the trap with process color, regardless of the colors used in the original objects. Usually, this option is left off. If you're trapping spot colors, you want a spot trap. This option is most useful when trapping a spot color into a process color and the screen angle of the spot color might interfere with the underlying process tints.

These tools only trap selected objects. After you've plugged in the necessary information and clicked OK, you'll immediately notice the new shapes appearing on your image. Because further editing gets a little harder from this point on, leave trapping until the very end.

Complex Vector-Based Traps

Some elements just can't be effectively trapped in page layout or illustration programs. The demands of gradients-on-gradients, custom fills, patterns, and complex arrangements of objects can all exceed the meager range of your manual and automatic trapping tools. In these cases, you have three choices:

- Ignore trapping and take your chances. Not a pretty option, but still an option.

- Avoid these situations altogether. Designing around the need for trapping can always relieve more headaches than Tylenol and Advil combined.

- Use a dedicated trapping program like Imation TrapWise. For the most complex traps, this is often the only solution.

Page Layout Trapping Tools

XPress, PageMaker, and InDesign all have built-in trapping features. XPress's are the best known, mainly because they've been around the longest. It's true that XPress has the most extensive capabilities, but no program is the trapping utopia we wish they were. For example, no program will touch an imported EPS graphic. In addition, trapping an object to a gradient is still done primitively, by simply spreading the foreground color. And the default trapping preferences in all programs will always need to be tailored to best suit your work.

Page layout programs only trap the following information:

- Multiple items created in the layout program, such as text, rules, and boxes. As I mentioned earlier, trapping is a relationship between two or more elements. The upper element always receives the trap value, based on the color of the underlying element.

- Objects created in the layout program that overlap imported bitmap TIFF images. No program traps the imported image itself—only the objects placed on top of it.

As I discuss trapping in these page layout programs, I must assume that your imported graphics have already been properly trapped. I'll say it once more: any imported item must have the necessary trapping commands built into the graphic and this can only be done in the original application.

Trapping in XPress

Trapping in XPress can be controlled three different ways:

- **Automatic Trapping.** This means you let XPress trap how it may during output, based on the settings in the Trapping Preferences dialog box. For better or worse, this is the most common approach.

- **Trapping Color-to-Color.** Here, you build trapping behavior directly into a color definition. These values override the automatic settings.

- **Trapping Object-to-Object.** Here, you use the floating Trap Information palette to change or reapply trapping values to individual objects in your document. These settings override both automatic and color-to-color traps.

Each method has its own appropriate time and place, and it's rare that all three are applied in a single document. Often, XPress's automatic settings will suffice, with maybe a little double-checking or tweaking from the Trap Information palette. If you trap color-to-color, you're ignoring the automatic settings. Most often, you'll be better off using the Trap Information palette for any exceptions to your self-imposed trapping rules. Finally, never rely solely on trapping object-to-object. Think about the hundreds or thousands of colored elements in a single project, and it's easy to understand how trapping every object individually becomes prohibitively time-consuming.

Automatic Trapping

These are the trapping values that XPress applies when left to its own devices. You may have noticed that trapping values are never visible in your page layout like they are in Illustrator or FreeHand. All trapping values in XPress, automatic or otherwise, do not officially exist until the file is output. Automatic trapping is always turned on. Unless you tell it to behave otherwise, the current trapping values are always applied to a document.

To access the trapping preferences, choose Edit: Preferences: **Document**, and click the Trapping tab. As with XPress's other preferences (described in Chapter 14, "Page Layout Issues"), you must edit this dialog box with no documents open to set new default values. The Trapping panel contains the following options (see Figure 15.26).

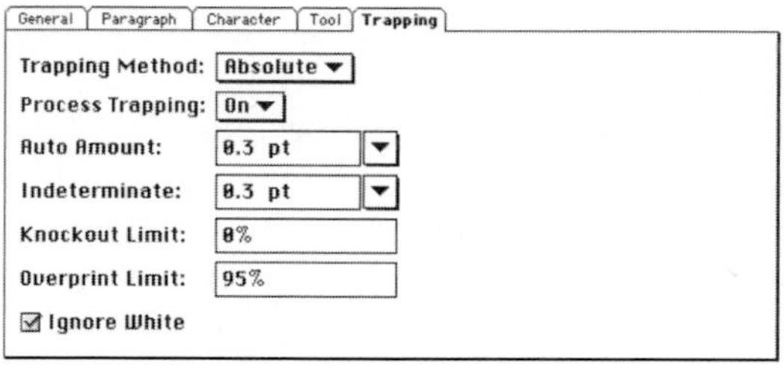

Figure 15.26   *XPress's Trapping Preferences panel.*

Trapping Method

This pop-up determines the method used by XPress when it traps automatically. It contains the following items:

- **Absolute.** This item uses the values in the Auto Amount and Indeterminate fields. Chokes and spreads are based on how light or dark a color appears in relation to any underlying shapes. This method is most similar to the techniques used in conventional trapping, and is by far the most commonly used option.

- **Proportional.** This option results in more variable trap widths. XPress compares the *luminosity* (brightness) of abutting colors. The trap width is determined by multiplying the difference in luminosity by the Auto Amount value. For example, if the luminosity of a blue shape is 90% and a red shape is 30%, the difference is 60% (or .6). If the Auto Amount value is .3 pt, the resulting trap is .18 pt (.6 × .3 = .18).

The idea is that higher-contrast colors receive thicker traps, and lower-contrast colors receive thinner traps. Because this method isn't based on how a color actually *appears*—not to mention that it's difficult to manually calculate luminosity values—it's virtually impossible to predict how your elements will trap.

- **Knockout All.** Choosing this option is the same as turning trapping off. The remaining values are unavailable, any trapping values built into color definitions are ignored, and the Trap Information Palette displays all relationships as knockouts. Select this item only when you're positive you want all colors to knock out. For example, some dedicated trapping programs require that no automatic traps be built into the PostScript file generated from an XPress document. To knockout specific items in a document while trapping others, use the Trap Information Palette.

Process Trapping

When this option is turned off, XPress treats the CMYK components of an object as a single color, and traps according to its overall lightness or darkness in comparison to a background color. When turned on, XPress recognizes the individual CMYK inks in each color. Most often, this option results in smoother process traps, because the chokes and spreads are divided between four plates for each trapped color. Unless you receive specific instructions from your printer, leave this option on.

Auto Amount

This value is the width applied by XPress's automatic trapping. The default is .144 pt—too thin for virtually all printing methods, especially when applied to spot inks. Most presses tolerate between .25 pt and .5 pt, and certain flexographic processes may require a width of as many as several points. Many users permanently set this value to between .25 pt and .4 pt, but you should ask your printer or service bureau for optimal values before each project is output.

Indeterminate

XPress can't trap an object when the underlying info contains many different (and often conflicting) colors, such as a multicolor blend, imported halftone, or imported high-res image. Instead, it treats these items as a single color, called Indeterminate. Therefore, when you place an object over any of these complex colors, it is trapped using the Indeterminate value. Most users use the same value for this and the Auto Amount option.

Knockout Limit

This option establishes a cutoff point at which an object may or may not be forced to knock out. It's based on a comparison of luminosity values. When it's set to 0% (the default), a color that shares the same luminosity value as the background knocks out. If this value is set to 5%, the tolerance increases: Colors with a luminosity within 5% or less of the underlying info knock out. Most users leave this value at 0%, and manually set any desired knockouts using the Trap Information palette.

Overprint Limit

This option establishes a cutoff point at which an object may or may not be forced to overprint. It's based on a tint percentage. For example, 100% black objects always overprint. If you apply a tint of black that falls below the Overprint Limit, the object will not overprint—instead, it traps using the Auto Amount values. Likewise, if a spot color is set to overprint in the Trap Specifications dialog, it will not overprint if its tint falls below the Overprint Limit.

Ignore White

When this box is checked, the color white (which includes the blank page background, or an area of no ink coverage) is ignored by the automatic trapping commands. XPress only considers actual colored background objects when determining trap width. When unchecked, XPress regards white areas—as well as any additional underlying colors—as indeterminate, and applies the trap width entered in the Indeterminate field. This may result in more noticeable trap lines, depending on the colors in question and the direction of the trap. Bear this in mind and examine any colored object that overlays white information when you proof your laser separations.

Auto Trapping Considerations

Theoretically, if your color usage is well-planned, you've considered the presence of a process bridge, and you've taken care of your blacks and vector-based trapping, the automatic trapping settings should be enough to trap the remaining layout-file elements. Still, auto trapping cannot adequately address the following situations:

- **Small type.** If you have to place small type on a colored background, color it black. (Or if the background is dark, use white type.) Black type overprints and is easiest to read. If you attempt to trap spot-colored type under 24 points against another spot-colored background, the result will be sloppy, poorly-formed, and difficult to read. If you need to color small-sized type, place it on a white background whenever possible.

- **Thin rules.** These items are subject to the same guidelines described in the previous paragraph. Fine details are always distorted by trapping.

Trapping Color to Color

Don't like the idea of simply letting a program auto-trap your document? Want more control over the trapping values sent to your output device? XPress allows you to build specific trapping relationships into a color definition. Right up front, understand that this method of trapping is the one *least* used by designers. You're not expected to manipulate these values every time you want to take control of your own trapping. Many users rely on the automatic trapping tools with a clear conscience, and they'll do the trick when combined with good color planning.

There are three reasons to use this trapping method:

- To change the automatic trap relationship between two colors, as specifically instructed by your print shop.

- To expand or shrink the automatic trap value of only one color, while letting the other color be subject to the automatic settings.

- To build automatic overprint or knockout commands into a single color. Because the commands take effect whenever and wherever you apply a color, you will not have to use the Trap Information palette.

Access these controls in the Edit: **Colors** dialog box. Select the color you wish to edit, and click the Edit Trap button. The Trap Specifications dialog box appears, which contains the following options (see Figure 15.27).

Background Color

When defining a color-to-color relationship, you determine how the current color will behave whenever it appears atop the color you select from this list. Although "Background Color" suggests that these traps only apply when the current color on top of another, the -?- and Reverse settings can make the trapping relationships reciprocal (see "Trap Dependency (-?-)" later in this section). White and Registration don't appear on this list, because XPress cannot trap or otherwise adjust these colors.

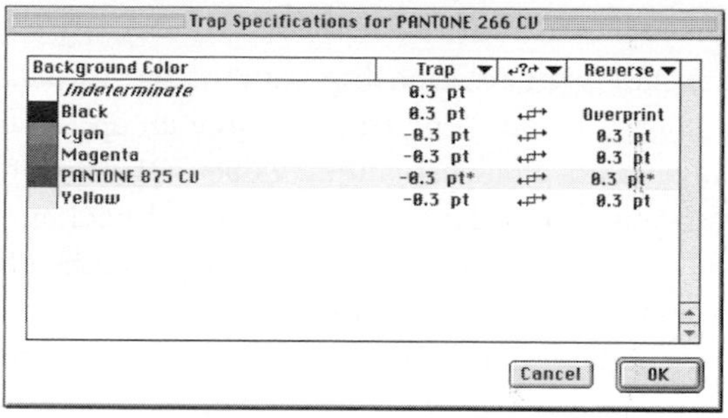

Figure 15.27   *XPress's Trap Specifications dialog box.*

Trap

After selecting a background color, you must choose one of five methods from this pop-up. Default applies XPress's auto trapping values. Positive numbers indicate a spread; negative numbers indicate a choke.

- **Knockout.** This option prevents any trapping from occurring whenever the current color is placed over the selected background color.

- **Overprint.** F This option forces the current color to overprint whenever it overlaps the selected background color.

- **Auto Amount (+).** This option spreads the current color, using the Auto Amount value. If the default trap is already a spread, this item has no effect. If the default trap is a choke, it is reversed.

- **Auto Amount (–).** This option chokes the current color, using the Auto Amount value. If the default trap is already a choke, this item has no effect. If the default trap is a spread, it is reversed.

- **Custom.** This option allows you to manually enter a value from –36 to 36 pt. Enter a positive value to create a spread; enter a negative value to create a choke.

Reverse

This pop-up determines the trapping that occurs when an object colored with the background color appears on top of the current color. Setting a value here simply allows you to avoid opening the Edit Trap dialog box twice for each two-color relationship. The pop-up items are the same as under Trap (see the preceding item).

Trap Dependency (–?–)

This pop-up determines the relationship between the Trap and Reverse values. When you choose Dependent Traps, setting an option in the Trap column automatically enters a corresponding value in the Reverse column, and vice versa. When you choose Knockout from one, Knockout appears in the other. When you choose Auto Amount (+) or (–) in one, the other value is set to the opposite amount. When you enter a Custom value in one, the opposite value appears in the other. However, when you set one to Overprint, the other remains unchanged. To set both columns to Overprint, switch to Independent Traps, then choose Overprint from the Trap and Reverse pop-ups. When you choose Independent Traps, setting a Trap item has no effect on the Reverse value. Likewise, setting a Reverse item has no effect on the Trap value. You must set both pop-ups separately.

Trapping Object-to-Object

XPress's Trap Information palette is used for two purposes. First, you can *review* an item's current trap value by selecting it and examining the palette. Second, you can *apply a new trapping value* by selecting an item and entering the desired values in the palette. (This is sometimes referred to as object-level or item-to-item trapping.) You can examine or manually trap only one item at a time.

Like XPress's other trapping controls, the Trap Information palette can only affect elements that were created in the application, such as boxes, lines, and type. The options that appear in the palette depend on the selected element. The pop-up attached to each option—which allow you to change the current trap value—contains the following items (see Figure 15.28):

- **Default.** This item indicates that no manual trapping has been applied. Instead, the item is trapped according to the values entered in the Trap Specifications dialog box or the Trapping Preferences panel, in that order. The current trap value is displayed to the right of the pop-up.

- **Overprint.** This item indicates that the selected object overprints the underlying colors.

- **Knockout.** This item indicates that the selected object will knock out of the underlying colors.

- **Auto Amount (+).** This item indicates that the selected object is spread by the current Auto Amount value, as entered in the Trapping Preferences panel.

Figure 15.28 *The pop-up available in XPress's Trap Information palette.*

- **Auto Amount (–).** This item indicates that the selected object is choked by the current Auto Amount value.

- **Custom.** When you choose this item, the field to the right of the pop-up changes to Knockout. From there, you can enter your own trap value from –36 pt to 36 pt, in .001 increments. Negative values choke, positive values spread. As long as this item appears in the pop-up, you can edit the trap value as often as you like.

When an object hasn't been adjusted using the Trap Information palette, the Default Info button appears to the right of each available option. Click and hold this button to review the current trap values. As soon as you apply a new trap value, this button is no longer available, because the default settings are being overridden (see Figure 15.29).

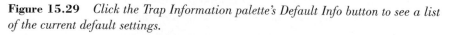

Figure 15.29 *Click the Trap Information palette's Default Info button to see a list of the current default settings.*

Trapping a Text Box

When you select a text box, the Trap Information palette displays the following options (see Figure 15.30):

- **Background.** This option displays the trap applied to a colored box. It is not available if the box has a frame, or if the box is colored None.

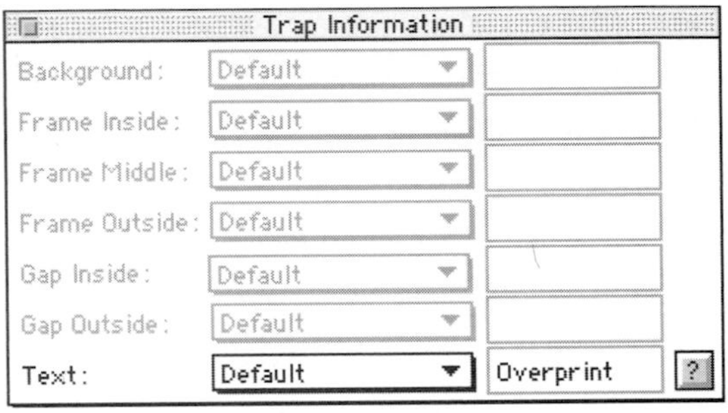

Figure 15.30   *The Trap Information palette, when a text box is selected.*

- **Frame Inside.** The Frame values are only available when the selected box contains a frame. This option refers to the trap between the inner edge of the frame and the background color of the text box. If the background is set to None, it displays the trap between the inner edge of the frame and any underlying colors.

- **Frame Middle.** This option appears when the frame has been modified with XPress's Dashes & Stripes. With dashes, the field displays the trap that exists between the endcaps of each dash and the underlying colors. With stripes, it displays the trap between the inner frame edges and the underlying colors. When frame consists of a dotted line, it displays the trap between each dot and the underlying colors.

- **Frame Outside.** This option indicates the trap between the outer edge of the frame and the underlying colors.

- **Gap Inside.** The gap options appear when a dashed frame contains a gap color, as specified in XPress's Item: Frame dialog box. This option displays the trap between the inner edge of the gap color and the background color of the text box. If the background is colored None, this option indicates the trap between the inner edge of the frame and any underlying colors.

- **Gap Outside.** This option displays the trap between the outer edge of the gap color and any underlying colors.

- **Text.** This option only appears when text is highlighted. It indicates the trap between colored text and the background color of the box. If the background is colored None, it indicates the trap between text and any underlying colors.

Trapping a Picture Box

When you select a picture box, the Trap Information palette displays the following options (see Figure 15.31):

- **Background.** This option displays the trap applied to a colored box. It is not available if the box has a frame, or if the box is colored None.

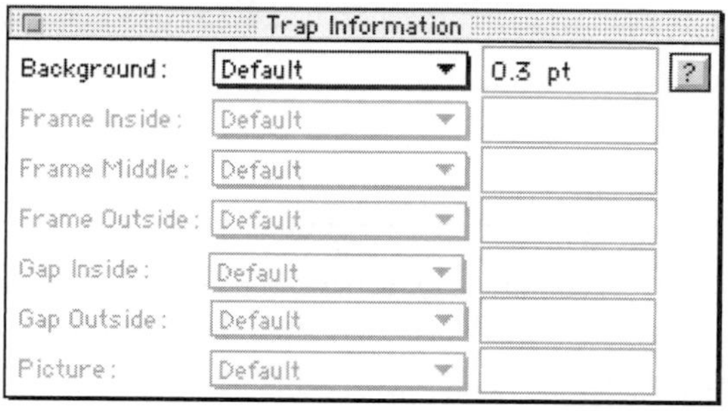

Figure 15.31 *The Trap Information palette, when a picture box is selected.*

- **Frame Options.** The Frame values are only available when the selected box contains a frame. The Frame Inside option indicates the trap between the inner edge of the frame and either the background color or the image inside the box. Otherwise, the options are the same as described previously.

- **Gap Options.** The gap options are only available when a dashed frame contains a gap color. When a gap is applied, Gap Inside indicates the trap between the gap color and either the background color or the image inside the box. Otherwise, the options are the same as described previously.

- **Picture.** This option is unavailable when the box contains a vector-based or Photoshop EPS. When you import any other pixel-based image, the pop-up displays Knockout by default. The only other option is Overprint.

Trapping a Line or Bézier Path

When you select a line or Bézier path, the Trap Information palette displays the following options (see Figure 15.32):

- **Line.** When a solid line is selected, this value displays the trap between the line edges (including the endcaps) and any underlying colors. When a striped line is selected, it displays the trap between the outermost edges of the line and the underlying colors. When a dashed line is selected, it displays the trap between the outer dash edges and the underlying colors.

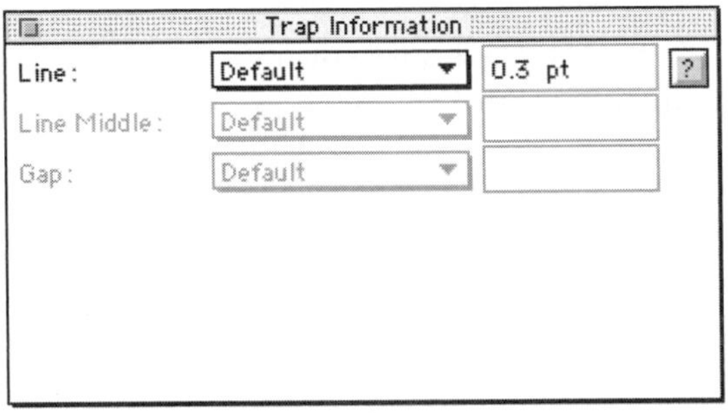

Figure 15.32 *The Trap Information palette, when a line or Bézier path is selected.*

- **Line Middle.** When a striped line is selected, this value displays the trap between the inner line edges and any underlying colors. When a dashed line is selected, it displays the trap between the dash endcaps and the underlying colors. When a gap color is applied, it displays the trap between the gap color and the line color.

- **Gap.** On a striped line, this value displays the trap between the exposed ends of the line and the underlying colors. On a dashed line, it displays the trap between the outer edges of the gap color and the underlying colors.

Trapping a Text Path

When you select a text path, the Trap Information palette displays the following options (see Figure 15.33):

- **Line, Line Middle, and Gap.** These options are the same as described in the previous section, "Trapping a Line or Bézier Path."

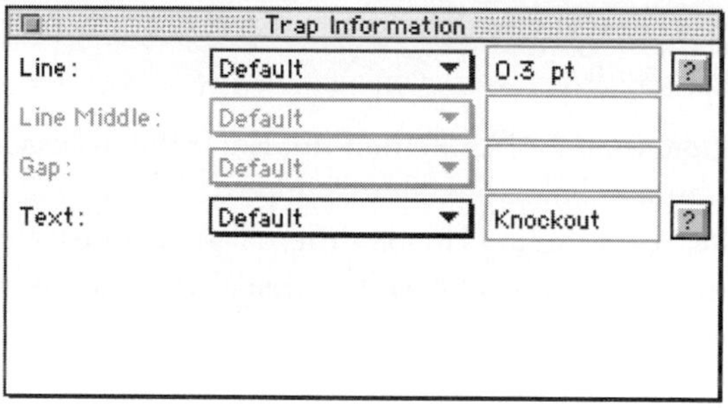

Figure 15.33 *The Trap Information palette, when a text path is selected.*

- **Text.** Only available when text is highlighted, this option displays the trap between colored text and the underlying colors.

Trapping in PageMaker

PageMaker's trapping tools are far less robust than those found in XPress. There are two available trapping methods: You can trap simple objects manually, or you can rely on PageMaker's automatic trapping controls.

Creating a Manual Trap in PageMaker

Create a manual trap by using the Fill and Stroke dialog to apply an overprinting stroke to a shape, picture box, or line. This technique is only appropriate for simple objects, such as overlapping geometric shapes. The approach is similar to using Illustrator or FreeHand, but with one difference: In those applications, a stroke *straddles* the outline of a shape; in PageMaker, the stroke falls entirely *within* the outline of a shape. Bear this distinction in mind when entering your desired trap width.

For example, picture a blue (PMS 287) circle on top of a red (PMS 185) square. Follow these steps to create a simple trap:

1. Select the blue circle.

2. Choose Element: **Fill and Stroke**.

3. Because blue is the darker color, you must choke the circle with the red ink. In the right side of the Fill and Stroke dialog box, set PMS 185 in the Color pop-up.

4. If desired, you can reduce the Tint to 40–50%, which results in a less-apparent color shift.

5. Choose Custom from the Stroke pop-up. Enter the necessary trap width in the Custom Stroke dialog box. For example, to apply a .3 pt trap, enter .3 in the Stroke Width field. (This is different from Illustrator or FreeHand, where you must apply a stroke width twice as thick as your intended trap.) Click OK.

6. Check the Overprint box.

7. Click OK to apply the trap.

To spread the selected object, apply the object's color to the new stroke. For example, if the colors in this example were reversed, you would apply a red stroke to the red circle.

Use this method for only the most basic overlapping shapes. Even then, most users rely on PageMaker's automatic trapping tools, described in the next section.

Auto Trapping in PageMaker

PageMaker's automatic trapping info is controlled from the Trapping Preferences dialog box. For all intents and purposes, this is the only area where you can define trap values in PageMaker, and any chance of trapping successfully ultimately suffers. You can't build trap values into color definitions, nor can you edit objects one by one, adding new settings as you go.

To review and adjust PageMaker's current trap settings, choose File: Preferences: **Trapping**. The Trapping Preferences dialog box contains the following options (see Figure 15.34):

- **Enable Trapping for Publication.** Check this box to turn trapping on. When unchecked, no trapping will be applied when the document is output.

- **Default.** This value determines the trap width applied to all colors (except solid black).

- **Black Width.** This value specifies the trap width for trapping colors next to or under solid blacks. The Black Width is generally set to 1.5 to 2 times the value of the default trap width.

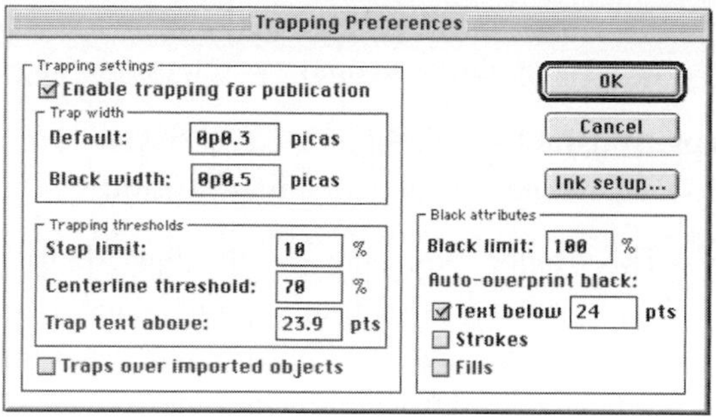

Figure 15.34 *PageMaker's Trapping Preferences dialog box.*

- **Step Limit.** Some jobs only require trapping on extreme color changes, while others require traps for even the slightest color changes. The Step Limit determines the point at which PageMaker considers trapping necessary. Increasing or decreasing this value determines how much the component inks must differ before PageMaker applies trapping. The lower the percentage, the more colors are trapped. To trap only high-contrast colors, raise the value. Otherwise, leave it at the default setting.

- **Centerline Threshold.** Centerline traps use only the highest-percentage process components of abutting colors. When inks have similar neutral densities, neither color defines the edge. Instead of simply spreading the lighter color into the darker, the trap will straddle the centerline (or point of abutment). At 0%, all traps default to centerline. At 100%, centerline trapping is turned off, resulting in a full spread or choke. Most users leave this value at the default setting.

- **Trap Text Above.** This value determines how large type must be before PageMaker applies trapping. For example, the default is 23.9 pt—here, PageMaker only traps type at 24 pt and above.

- **Traps Over Imported Objects.** Checking this box is similar to XPress's Indeterminate color, which is used to apply one flat trap setting into an underlying imported image, regardless of its component inks.

- **Black Limit.** The setting for Black Limit determines what PageMaker considers a solid black or enriched black. The default is 100%, which states that only colors containing 100% black will be treated as solid or rich blacks. When PageMaker encounters a color with a black percentage the same or higher than the Black Limit, PageMaker applies the Black Width trap value, and applies a keepaway function to any undercolors.

- **Auto-Overprint Black.** This option enables you to determine which occurrences of 100% black automatically overprint.

- **Ink Setup.** This dialog box controls the ink density settings that PageMaker refers to when making trapping decisions. Because these values are based on widely accepted industry standards, they should be left alone unless you have a good reason for changing them. This occurs in two fairly common instances. First, if a project requires using a nonstandard ink in a process printing job, you must adjust its density to match the replaced color. For example, one company demanded that Magenta be replaced with PANTONE 213 (their corporate color) in their four-color printing. To keep PageMaker's trapping consistent, the density of PMS 213 was changed from 0.82 to 0.76, the density of Magenta. Second, when some designers use a specialty ink (a metallic, for example), they do not want the ink to be affected by any auto trapping values. By raising its density to a value higher than black, all other document colors would be forced to trap into this ink.

Trapping in InDesign

InDesign 1.0 does not feature any built-in trapping tools. However, PostScript files generated from InDesign documents are recognized by all major dedicated trapping applications. Also, Adobe anticipates a major shift toward in-RIP trapping, which would effectively eliminate the use of program-specific trapping tools. (For more info, see "The Future: Adobe Trapping," later this chapter.)

Trapping in Photoshop

Photoshop features a single trapping tool—the Image: Trap command. Because a page layout program cannot trap the contents of an imported pixel-based image, the question of whether you need to use this command is a good one. The majority of CMYK images are either original artwork consisting of colors that share multiple CMYK components or continuous-tone images (like scanned photographs) that contain a wide and varied range of cyan, magenta, yellow, and black inks.

It's quite rare that a CMYK image requires additional trapping, due to the *process bridge* that naturally occurs. The only time you need to access the Trap dialog box is when an image contains colors that do not share a process component. For example, a pure cyan shape abutting a pure black shape needs to be manually trapped, because they share no component inks.

Once applied, the Trap command targets all abutting image colors and traces them with a thin, colored line. Because trapping always consists of one color expanding into another, Photoshop follows these guidelines:

* Lighter colors expand into darker colors.

* All colors expand into black.

* Yellow expands into cyan, magenta, and black.

* Pure cyan and pure magenta expand into each other equally.

You must determine the width of the overlapping line in the Trap dialog box. Choose points, pixels, or millimeters as a measurement unit. Other programs with trapping functions use points, so this may be the most intuitive unit.

Trapping Vector-Based Artwork Imported into Photoshop

When you import a vector-based image into Photoshop, you convert its component objects into pixels. The color information translates as well, so whether you need to trap such an image depends on how the colors are originally handled. First and foremost, an illustration created using process colors must be imported as a CMYK image. Importing it as RGB and then converting to CMYK alters all the color values. Beyond that, most trapping needs can be resolved before you import the image:

* If the object colors share a process bridge, they do not require additional trapping.

* If you added manual traps to a vector-based illustration before importing it into Photoshop, those color commands translate into the new image.

* If the image contains black outlines—such as a cartoon character or a box with a frame—set them to Overprint before importing the image.

Dedicated Trapping Software

Dedicated digital trapping systems have been available to publishers for years. Until recently, such systems were enormously expensive and complex, and therefore out of the reach of most professionals. In the past couple of years, trapping software packages such as Imation TrapWise and Island Trapper have been garnering favor in the industry, with the promise of flawless, effortless traps.

In a typical scenario, a trapping application processes PostScript files on a separate workstation. TrapWise, for example, requires a dedicated Windows NT server. The file is rasterized (or converted to the pixel information that will be sent to the imagesetter's RIP), then makes trapping decisions based on all the adjacent colored bitmaps. Using this technique, it can trap information that programs like XPress and PageMaker cannot, like adjacent gradients and imported EPS graphics. The user has control over the finest details, and can tailor the values of each output job to the most unique on-press demands.

Service bureaus and print shops using a dedicated trapping program often charge additional output fees for the service. Some may add a percentage of the cost-per-page (25–50% more, for example), while others charge by the processed square inch. Many companies charge between 5 and 8 cents per square inch—for example, at 7 cents, the client is billed an additional $6.50 per trapped letter-sized page. The client must be made aware of these charges before a file is processed.

Two things make dedicated trapping software less appealing to many designers and service providers: time and money.

This software is expensive. Complete packages can run as high as $5,000 (and they're hardware-protected, so don't get any ideas). Plus, the program requires its own dedicated workstation to run most efficiently, which adds thousands of dollars to the initial cost. And this doesn't account for the fact that high-volume shops typically require a well-trained employee whose sole job is to drive the workstation.

Trapping software is also notorious for its wildly unpredictable processing times. A twenty-four page publication may take 30 minutes; a tabloid-sized poster might take all day. It all depends on the graphic types used in a document, the trap settings for a particular job, and the output settings applied when the file is processed. In other words, you usually don't know how long it will take until you download the information and start checking your watch.

Many professionals benefit greatly from the proper use of dedicated trapping software. Many service bureaus use it as a potent weapon in the battle for successful document output. Service bureaus also benefit financially if the demand for trapping services is high. As more and more print shops become proficient in digital technologies, they desire to gain more control over the files that they output for reproduction on their own presses. Trapping software, if used properly, gives them much more flexibility.

But a design firm, on the other hand, shouldn't bother investing in the equipment and training for such a system if they just send the files offsite for output. Many small print shops who are either new to digital prepress or don't have the intense need for exacting control can also afford to pass on dedicated software, at least until client demand forces their hand.

When and Where Trapping Is Required

Refer to the following table for guidance on utilizing appropriate trapping methods:

	Illustration Software	Page Layout Software	Dedicated Trapping Software
Purpose	Creates simple traps manually or automatically.	Traps elements created in layout program.	Typically traps rasterized PostScript file.
Item does not overlap any colored objects.	N/A	N/A	N/A
Item overlaps one other colored object (2 spot colors)	Create simple manual trap.	Auto trap in PageMaker; auto trap or set trap specifications in XPress.	Auto traps where necessary.
Item overlaps multiple objects	Trap with built-in tools: Trap filter in Illustrator, Trap Xtra in FreeHand.	Auto trap in PageMaker; auto trap or set trap specifications in XPress (mult. colors referred to as Indeterminate).	Auto traps where necessary.

continues

continued

	Illustration Software	Page Layout Software	Dedicated Trapping Software
Item overlaps imported image	Use overprinting strokes on image edge to create trap.	Turn on Traps Over Imported Objects in PageMaker; define Indeterminate trap specs in XPress.	Allows user more control when items trap to underlying image.
Item overlaps gradient fill	Use overprinting strokes on image edge to create trap.	Cannot trap in PageMaker; use Indeterminate settings in XPress.	Auto traps, adjusting edge color and position.
Enriched Black item	Add overprinting 100% black stroke to build in trap.	XPress and PageMaker both keep undercolor from the black edge (keepaway).	Applies adjustable keepaway value.
Imported EPS graphics	Cannot trap.	Cannot trap.	Automatically traps, but with wildly varying processing times.

The Future: Adobe Trapping

In anticipation of an all-digital workflow, Adobe is developing a trapping system that could eliminate the need for application-level adjustments. Largely contingent on widespread installation of PostScript Level 3—the latest incarnation of Adobe's page description language—this process will offer the following advantages:

- Trapping will take place on the RIP level, or when a document is output. This way, any established workflow will not have to change to accommodate the addition of trapping values. Documents will trap as they are interpreted by the PostScript print engine.

- You will be able to trap PDF files, which currently cannot be handled by dedicated trapping software.

- There will be one universal set of trap settings, easily accessed in all major applications.

- Speed will be greatly increased, because these commands are integrated in the output device's RIP.

Some environments have begun working with this method. Although it is too early to recommend this process, you can download a free PageMaker plug-in for in-RIP trapping at www.adobe.com. An XTension for QuarkXPress is available from equipment manufacturers who license Adobe's in-RIP trapping.

Summary

Trapping is a tip of the hat to the laws of physics that affect every project during printing, and it has to be considered every time you create a color document. In fact, there are only two ways to avoid the need for trapping altogether: you can only create colored items that never touch, or you can design and print with only one color ink. As any designer can tell you, those are two big restrictions.

Successful trapping, on the other hand, can only be accomplished with the following:

- **An understanding of spot and process color.** These two color types have different trapping considerations. Whenever two spot colors touch, trapping is required. If two process colors touch, they may or may not need to be trapped. If you choose your colors wisely, if your adjacent process colors share enough CMYK components to form a process bridge, trapping is less of a concern.

- **Thoughtful design.** The need for trap should rest at the center of all your design decisions. Whenever possible, design to avoid trapping. If you can't, then be sure that the ultimate trapping values will not degrade any fine details or obscure any type.

- **An awareness of every object in your layout.** Be prepared to double-check each page, object, and color in your document to ensure that all trapping guidelines are being met.

Your best resource for trapping assistance is always the print shop and service bureau. They can tell you the values that best suit your job, or they can trap your work digitally or conventionally. Don't feel obliged to assume control of your trapping if you are not prepared.

PREFLIGHT AND FILE PREP

Your deadlines leave no room for wasted time. Unfortunately, anyone involved in digital graphics can relate to at least one of the following situations:

- You stand by the door, holding a stack of worthless page films, watching the FedEx truck drive away.

- You miss print dates because you need to output a job again.

- You absorb the cost of repairing files and re-outputting films for your clients.

- You find out too late that your traps are wrong, your fonts defaulted to Courier, your text reflowed, and your colors separated incorrectly.

- You find out too late that your file can't be output at all.

- You're on the phone with a client, attempting to explain any of these issues, wondering where on earth you put the Rolaids.

Preflight is more than an official-sounding term copped from NASA. At the core of the preflight process is a method of quality-control that will help you avoid the previous scenarios. For the designer, it ensures successful document output and reduces extra "file fix" charges by the printer or service bureau. For the production specialist, it means shorter processing times, conservation of resources, and a more satisfied client base. For both parties, it's quite possibly the most important profit-oriented strategy in the prepress workflow.

Preflight involves more than simply handing over fonts and graphics with an output job. For designers and service bureaus alike, it's a tangible system to incorporate into your work environment. From organizing project files, to properly transporting them to the service bureau, to outputting test separations and checking traps and bleeds, preflight and everything it stands for should be on your mind during every stage of handling a document and its component files. This chapter discusses the following:

- The three stages of successfully preflighting a digital file: gathering information, reviewing the file, and outputting paper proofs.

- The issues involved in establishing a preflight system.

- The client and vendor issues that arise when instituting these new output requirements.

- The hardware and software required in a successful preflight department.

- Available software packages that automate the preflight process.

The History of Preflight

Back in the Dark Ages of digital prepress, production specialists were held prisoner by an undefined industry, an uneducated designer base, and the desire to please their clients no matter what the cost. Viable color PostScript publishing was still relatively new, and most people responsible for creating electronic documents didn't realize how complex a science it really was. Service providers acted like they could easily output any client file, but the truth was, they couldn't. In fact, a service bureau I worked with conducted a study. They randomly pulled and examined 100 jobs, only to find that 96 of them needed some sort of extra work or adjustment to output successfully.

If other service bureaus were experiencing the same phenomenon—if 96 percent of all output jobs needed some sort of "massaging"—who was responsible for doing the work? The service bureau, almost every time. They quickly found that most clients got upset if a job was refused, or if they were billed for the time it took to make their file output-ready. Because no guidelines existed for demanding print-ready files from their clients, a service bureau would either put in the time free of charge or risk losing the client to another company willing to do the work. For a while, most service bureaus were willing to "take that extra step," thinking they were maintaining their customer base. In reality, they were getting reamed by the costs hidden in that endless stream of poorly constructed files. Eventually, an industry hung in the balance.

On one side were designers, and most of them were already stretched to the limit by being forced to learn the new digital tools required to continue their craft. Their job, it was widely believed, was simply to design the file and leave the finer points of film separations up to the output specialists. "My service bureau bends over backward for me," they said. "Why on earth would I want to change that?"

On the other side were the service bureaus, who had to choose between losing customers (by refusing to process inadequate files) or losing profits (by accepting responsibility for them).

Partial relief came from Scitex, who released their CREF (Computer Ready Electronic Files) standards, creating a platform for designers and output specialists alike to follow when constructing documents. Trouble is, it's one thing for a file to be *computer* ready; it's quite another for a file to be *print* ready. Any file can display on a computer monitor. Not every file can output successfully.

We needed a method to ensure a document's printability *before* the information was downloaded to an imagesetter. To the eternal thanks of graphics professionals everywhere, the preflight process arose.

The ultimate goal of preflighting is to produce composite and separated versions of a file on a PostScript laser printer. Composites (comps) are document printouts with no color separations, which give the viewer a feel for the overall layout. Separations (seps) are document printouts separated into their component color plates. When performed by both designers and output specialists, this task accomplishes the following:

- It proves that a file can be successfully output to a PostScript imaging device. The majority of printers, from laser printers to imagesetters, are PostScript-based. Separating a file on one is the surest indication it will separate on another.

- It places responsibility for an unprintable file back in the hands of its creator, where it belongs. If a file cannot be output to a designer's PostScript printer, you can safely assume it will not output to an imagesetter. Troubleshooting can begin before the file is handed over.

- It proves that all graphics files and fonts were in place and linked at least once before being handed over to a service bureau.

- It lets output specialists ensure that all graphics files and fonts have been provided by the client.

- It allows a final, last-minute proof of bleeds, text flow, font use, color breaks, and trap.

A trend has started over the last few years. Service bureaus now can firmly request all output jobs be handed over with accompanying laser comps and separations. If they receive them, they accept responsibility for outputting separations. If they do not, then the client accepts responsibility for all cost overruns, hours spent repairing bad files, and wasted film. To provide a transition into this requirement, many companies outputting film for clients offer a small discount—from five to ten percent—for a short period of time to encourage their clients to put the extra attention into their work.

The benefits of preflight go beyond the savings of time, money, resources, and customer relations. It's made us all smarter. As the graphics industry evolves, becoming more complex and thorough, so do we. We all gain a better understanding of the issues and techniques required of successful file construction. We flex our minds, become more open to new ideas, and continually strive to improve ourselves and our work.

Before I begin describing the elements of what preflight *is,* let's first consider what it's *not:*

- It's not the time for last-minute changes and tweaks at the request of the client.

- It's not the place for graphic design or additional production techniques.

- It's not the forum for quick, well-intentioned freebies by an output staff. Remember the two benefits: designers are encouraged to learn more about output-specific issues, and service bureaus stop giving away their valuable time.

Stage One: Gathering Information

Think about all the components of your average four-color project. A 48-page color catalog can easily contain 100 color images. An annual report may use several dozen vector-based graphs. Even a simple newsletter can involve a lengthy series of logos, halftones, fonts, and supplementary graphics. Unless you have a way to account for all—and I mean *all*—a file's vital information, you can't expect it to output successfully, whether in-house or at the service bureau.

For the Designer

Whoever creates an electronic file is responsible for tracking its components. This process begins when you first plan your document, and continues until you hand over the project files to a service provider. Throughout the entire project, keep a detailed report of all the settings, parameters, and special instructions pertaining to your document and the ultimate print run. As you generate the supplemental files, you can develop a system to collect these details into a form most easily transported to a service provider and used by an output specialist.

Maintaining a Project Report

On the surface, creating a project report sounds like just another time-consuming activity that distracts designers from their *real* jobs. Actually, maintaining this kind of document serves two vital purposes:

- **It forces you to see your project from your vendors' perspective.** Good design is an equal blend of visual acuity and realistic production demands. By extending your mind's eye beyond the computer screen and into the realm of what can and cannot be printed, you add untold value to your work.

- **It gives your output specialist and printer a better understanding of your expectations.** The more accurately you can communicate your desires, the closer to your vision the final product will be.

For small projects, you may want to output thumbnails and write your information in the margin of the single page (see Figure 16.1).

When working with multipage documents, print lasers of every page, number them, and write down the pertinent info on each one. Include any blank pages that'll be included in the final print run.

Avoid planting any surprises in the report that may be missed by the reader. There should be no new, last-minute instructions. Keep it down to a short series of notes for each page of your document.

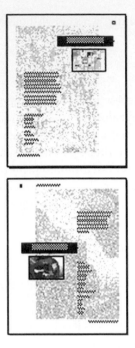

Page 1

Fonts: Simoncini Gar., Futura Condensed
Background graphic: Press/ghost.tiff (PMS 266)
Duotone: Roller.eps (PMS 875, Black)
Header: Charcoal Bar.eps (Black)

Page 2

Fonts: Simoncini Gar., Futura Condensed

BG Graphic: Circuit board/ghost.tiff (PMS 875)
Duotone: Circuit.eps (PMS 266, Black)
Header: Charcoal Bar.eps

Ink order: Black, 875, 266

Figure 16.1 *A project report based on page thumbnails. When you document info such as page breaks, colors, graphic file names, and special print instructions, you give your printer an important resource that helps assure the successful reproduction of your project.*

Include the following topics in your reports:

- **Output settings.** Assuming that you have already consulted with your commercial printer and service provider, include such information as line-screen value, output resolution, UCR/GCR settings, and trap tolerance. Indicate whether your film will be positive or negative, and list the emulsion reading. If necessary, list any color management system or color profiles used.

- **Detailed page information.** List all the pages in the document, including blank pages and page numbers. Use the page numbers to reference any special needs on the pages. In longer documents, list sections, chapters, and any other breaks.

- **Graphics files and folder names.** This includes the name of the page layout document and its location on the transport media (if more than one layout document is handed over, be sure to list the name of every one). List the name and location of each graphics file used in the project, as well as the file format and original application. If you've organized your work adequately, print the window of the folder containing the graphics for your project and staple it to your report.

- **Colors and separation.** For each page, list the colors used, whether they're spot or process, and the specific number of seps to be output for each page. Also list any spot varnishes that have been defined.

- **Fonts.** List all the font families used in the document, as well as any that might have been embedded in imported EPS artwork.

- **Special notes.** List any special needs on each page, including bleeds, crossovers, and any images to be manually stripped. Also describe items that have been trapped, as well as those that still need to be by the service provider.

The project report doesn't take the place of the output request form—it supplements it. As you create this report, you'll likely notice that the information changes as your project evolves. Keep the report up-to-date by outputting fresh pages and noting the most recent changes. This report should always be close by, allowing you immediate access to all the nuances of your printed project. You never know—printers call, contractors call, service bureaus call, and you'll need to be able to talk succinctly about your project and note any new conditions.

Many designers scrap this idea in the interest of saving time in an already crisis-driven environment, not realizing that keeping such a record allows them to avoid many crises right from the start. In essence, the project report is your little Bible, to be read, believed, interpreted, fought over, and revised. Around it, wars will be waged, your spirit will be nurtured, and your faith will be tested. Ultimately, if you follow the teachings, guidelines, and laws, you will find salvation—which lasts all the way to the *next* project.

Assembling the Elements

Before you hand over a project to a service provider, you need to be sure all the necessary information is organized, easy to find, and ready to use. In a perfect world, collecting the project files would be a snap. Just imagine this scenario:

1. At the start of a project, you create a folder with the job number included in the title.

2. When you create the page layout document, you save it directly into this job folder.

3. As graphics, scans, and FPOs are generated by the designers and service bureaus, you place them into the project folder *before* importing them into your page layouts.

4. When the layout is completed, you output and check your laser proofs.

5. Before the job folder is copied to transport media, you place copies of all the same fonts in the project into a folder called "Project Fonts," placing this folder in the job folder.

6. You copy the single job folder containing all the necessary project information onto a universally accepted disk, such as an Iomega Zip or Jaz.

7. You hand the entire bundle—disk, proofs, and your own report—over to your service provider.

Unfortunately, our complex world is riddled with imperfections. We import images stored in different locations on our hard drive. We download FPOs from file servers. We use images and fonts stored on Zips and DAT. We feel we don't have enough time to output comps and seps of the most recent document version. We forget to convert RGB images to CMYK. We forget to hand over an image or font.

If you haven't placed all your graphics in a single job folder, you're faced with a choice. Either hunt down every single graphics file by hand, or utilize a more automated process. Fortunately, XPress, PageMaker and InDesign offer features that enable you to collect document graphics into a single folder. Each program generates small reports that provide the original location of any graphic imported from an external source. This report also lists information such as style sheet definitions, fonts used, and built-in trap values—but it should not be considered a replacement for the project report I discussed earlier. Information it won't include are conversations that you have with your printer, customized page settings, bleed and crossover instructions, and so forth.

In XPress, this function is called Collect for Output. This command copies all linked images into a single folder, adds a copy of the layout document, and includes a written summary of the file components. In PageMaker, the Save As dialog box contains the options for copying the document and graphics, and the summary is created by a PageMaker plug-in. In InDesign, you'll use the File: Package command. (InDesign also features a helpful Preflight command, which I'll cover shortly.) In each application, your project must be completely finished before using these commands.

Collecting for Output in XPress

To use XPress's Collect for Output command, follow these steps:

1. Open your completed document.

2. Choose File: **Collect for Output**. If you've made any changes to the document since opening it, you are prompted to save. If any graphics links have been broken, you are asked to reestablish them, if you can.

3. If you have not already created a job folder, click the New Folder button in the Collect for Output dialog box (see Figure 16.2). Name the folder, determine its location on the hard drive, and click Create. The folder you choose—whether or not you create a new one—receives the project information. Keep track of its location.

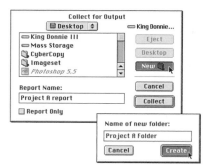

Figure 16.2   *Creating a new project folder using XPress's Collect for Output dialog box. If you use a system of folders similar to the one described in Chapter 5, "File Management," it's likely that this step is unnecessary; the document, project graphics, and fonts are already stored in a central location, and you can copy them directly to your transport media. However, if you've imported graphics that are scattered over many disks or mounted servers, collect them into a new folder.*

4. Click Collect. As illustrated by the progress bar, copies of all imported graphics are placed inside the target folder. This is important to note—the original graphics files are not moved around on the hard drive. [1]

5. Examine the folder. Copies of the document and all currently linked graphics now exist there, as well as a single text file that contains the document summary. If any of your graphics were not linked when you chose this command—for example, if they are stored on removable storage media—they will not copy to the target folder. The summary contains their original location.

6. If necessary, copy any unlinked graphics files into the job folder.

7. No fonts are automatically copied into the target folder. Fonts are never touched by this function, so you must place copies into the job folder manually. (Be sure you don't simply move the fonts from your type library into the folder. To make duplicates as you move the items, Option-drag on a Mac, Control-drag in Windows.)

To create a copy of the report without generating copies of the document or graphics files, check the Report Only box in the Collect for Output dialog box.

Collecting for Output in PageMaker

To collect the document and graphics in PageMaker, follow these steps:

1. Create a job folder on your desktop.

2. Open your completed document.

3. Choose Save As from the File menu.

4. In the Save As dialog box, navigate to the job folder (see Figure 16.3).

5. Under Save As, select Publication.

FOOTNOTE

[1] XPress's Collect for Output does not recognize embedded images. For example, if you import a Photoshop TIFF into an Illustrator graphic, then import the Illustrator EPS into an XPress document, you must manually include the Photoshop file on your transport media.

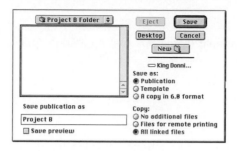

Figure 16.3 *Collecting for output using PageMaker's Save As dialog box. If necessary, click the New Folder button to create a folder that will contain the new elements.*

6. Under Copy, choose All Linked Files.

7. Click Save.

8. Examine the folder. Just like XPress, the document as well as all currently linked graphics are copied into the folder. The fonts have to be copied manually.

PageMaker does not automatically add a document summary when you collect for output. Instead, you must follow these steps to generate a report:

1. Choose Utilities: Plug-ins: **Pub Info**.

2. Under Display, choose the information you want included in the summary: fonts, links, and/or styles (see Figure 16.4).

Pub info	Save...	Done
Document: King Donnie III:Desktop Folder:Project B:Project B Folder:Proje...		

Font:	In Pub	In System
Times	Y	Y
Geneva	Y	Y
BI Times BoldItalic	N	Y
I Times Italic	N	Y
B Times Bold	N	Y
BI Courier BoldOblique	N	Y

Display: ☑ Fonts ☑ Links ☑ Styles

Figure 16.4 *Since PageMaker does not automatically create a project report when you collect for output, you must access the Pub Info dialog box, which contains document info that you can save as a text file.*

3. Click Save.

4. Use the navigational dialog box that appears to place the summary into your job folder.

5. Click Done.

Collecting for Output in InDesign

To collect the document and graphics in InDesign, follow these steps:

1. Open your completed document.

2. Choose File: **Package**. You are prompted to save the document.

3. Before you can access the packaging controls, the Printing Information dialog box appears. It requests basic contact info and special project notes. You can bypass this dialog box if you want to—the info you enter only appears at the start of the project report generated by the command. When you're finished, click Continue.

4. In the Create Package Folder dialog box, navigate to your target job folder (see Figure 16.5). If you haven't already created one, click the New Folder button and name the new item accordingly.

Figure 16.5 *InDesign's Create Package Folder dialog box.*

5. Under Copy, select the items you want to copy into the folder.

6. Click Package.

7. Examine the folder. Copies of all the linked graphics and fonts should now reside there, but check closely. InDesign does not copy entire font families to the job folder, and although it is supposed to recognize any fonts embedded in an imported graphic, it does so inconsistently. Stay on the safe side by copying your font families manually.

Although these features are convenient and usually helpful, you must double-check your work every time you use them. I prefer to greet any so-called "automated" process with a certain degree of doubt and scorn. These guidelines result in the most accurate transport of project documents and support files:

- Any files not linked while collecting for output must be gathered manually.

- Fonts must be gathered manually.

- The document summaries are never adequate replacements for your detailed reports.

- Always open the document that was copied into the new job folder and check the links before copying the information to your transport media.

Handing Over the Project to the Service Provider

As long as your ducks are properly lined up, this is the simplest part of the process. Hand over your project to a service provider only after the following:

- Your graphics and document have been created, copied, and tested.

- All reports and summaries have been completed.

- All laser comps and seps have been produced.

- You've acquired a removable media device accepted by your service provider.

The only issue you have to worry about here is whether to use file compression. My recommendation here is simple: You don't need to compress, so don't bother. These days, removable media is so cheap and abundant, you don't have to be nearly as uptight about space considerations as you used to. File compression also can lead to unnecessary delays in two ways.

First, compressing and decompressing information takes time. Not much, perhaps, but if space is not a huge consideration, save yourself and your output specialists those few precious minutes.

Second, let's say you send compressed files, but you don't save them as self-expanding archives. If your service provider does not have the same compression program (or the same version or higher as yours), all progress stops while they contact you for the software.

Service Provider: Using Your Output Request Form

When processing a client project, a service bureau's most important organizational tool is the output request form. This form is the only documentation of all the parameters of an output job, which makes it an invaluable source of project info. Unless it is completely and accurately filled out, it's of little use. Every last job that crosses the desk of an output specialist should be accompanied by a completed job ticket, with no exceptions—even if the job was designed in-house.

The output request form is typically filled out by one of the following people (in descending order of preference):

- **A trained customer service representative.** Not long ago, I dropped off a simple job at a service bureau across town. I was met at the door with a smile, and I wasn't even allowed to touch the output request form. I was taken through the process item-by-item, and it was probably the most complete form I'd ever seen. Even a well-trained designer can forget or misunderstand parts of these forms—after all, they're invariably filled out at the end of a long and grueling project. Having a customer service rep fill out the forms not only ensures that each item gets the attention it deserves, it provides blessed relief for clients with too much on their mind.

- **The client.** This person is probably most intimate with the components of the file, the profiles of the intended printed piece, and any special instructions. However, the form they fill out is only as good as their knowledge of the issues covered. If necessary, offer to train your clients on the meaning and importance of each item on the form. Many service bureaus routinely hold free preflighting seminars for their clients, and this trend is a good one. Any cost of conducting a class will be quickly recouped by reduced file construction errors.

- **A sales representative.** Often, sales reps pick up jobs from their accounts and fill out the output request form for them, as a service. Unless your sales reps are well-trained in the issues of digital prepress, the form may as well be a paper airplane. Most account reps take the time to understand the changing nature of the services they sell, realizing the importance of being able to speak intelligently with their clients. Some reps, unaware that they lack a solid footing in graphics issues, may see their work suffer. Over time, they tend to promise services or products that their company can't deliver, receive lower scores on customer satisfaction surveys, even lose clients to other AEs (or other companies). Many progressive graphics businesses avert this problem by offering monthly classes, where employees from different departments keep the knowledge base of the sales staff up to date.

The output request form should request all the information pertaining to the method of output, including the following (see Figure 16.6):

- **Platform.** Includes choices between Mac OS 7.x, Mac OS 8.x, Windows 3.1, Windows 95, or Windows 98.

- **Application.** Lists the program (and its version) used to create the final document.

- **Pages to Print.** The page range (include an option for "All") and the number of copies of each page to print.

- **Fonts.** Allows the client to list all the fonts used in the project by name. Also lists whether the fonts are PostScript or TrueType.

- **Graphics.** Lists whether client supplies graphics files or low-res FPOs.

- **File Saved As.** Lists whether a working document or PostScript file has been supplied.

- **Colors.** Offers a choice between Spot, Process, or Both. Also includes space to list any custom color names.

- **Trapping.** Lists whether the client has trapped the file or wants the service bureau to trap it. Space is usually provided for special trapping instructions.

- **Proofing.** Lists the type of proof desired by the client, if any.

OUTPUT ORDER FORM

Billing Information

Name.. Phone..

Company .... Account Number ....

Address .... City.................................... State .... ZIP ....

PO #/Job Title.. Date..

Payment Method: ☐ Account ☐ COD ☐ MC/Visa: ....

Shipping
☐ Same as above

Name.. Phone..

Company ....

Address .... City.................................... State .... ZIP ....

Turnaround ☐ Standard ☐ Rush ☐ Same Day

Delivery Method ☐ Hold at location ☐ Courier ☐ FedEx (list acct #): ....

Other..

File Information

Please use a separate form for each file type.

☐ Mac System 6
☐ Mac System 7
☐ DOS/Windows
☐ FTP Transfer
☐ Modem

File 1 Name ....

Application/version.. Pages to print: from .... to .... copies of each: ......

File 2 Name ....

Application/version.. Pages to print: from .... to .... copies of each: ......

File 3 Name ....

Application/version.. Pages to print: from .... to .... copies of each: ......

Fonts and Support Files

☐ TrueType fonts

Typefaces (and vendor) used..

Support Files (TIFF, EPS, PICT, etc.): ☐ Included ☐ Not included (FPO)

Printing Instructions

Accurate laser-printed proofs are required with every output order.

Please check your output when job is completed and received. We assume no liability for any cost incurred using our output.

Please send backups of your work—do not send original disks.

Output Type	☐ Imagesetting		☐ Color Printing		☐ Film Recording/Slides
Media	☐ RC Paper ☐ Film: Emulsion:	☐ pos. ☐ neg. ☐ up ☐ down	☐ Canon Paper ☐ IRIS Paper ☐ Large Format	☐ IRIS trans.	☐ 35 mm Slides (non-PostScript) ☐ 35 mm Slides (PostScript) ☐ 4x5 Transparency
Resolution	☐ 1200 dpi ☐ 2400 dpi ☐ 3600 dpi				
Page Size	☐ Letter ☐ Legal ☐ Tabloid ☐ Other:		☐ Letter ☐ Tabloid ☐ Other:		
Separations	☐ None ☐ Process (4-color) ☐ Spot (list under Special Instructions) ☐ Overprint (list under Special Instructions) ☐ Knockout (list under Special Instructions) ☐ Trap (turnaround by quote)				
Options	☐ Crop/registration marks ☐ Reduce/enlarge: % ☐ Screen ruling: lpi ☐ Link to in-house scans		☐ Crop/registration marks ☐ Reduce/enlarge: % ☐ Laminate ☐ Link to in-house scans		☐ Photo overhead ☐ Reduce/enlarge: % ☐ No mounts ☐ Plastic mounts ☐ Glass mounts (additional cost)
Proofing	☐ Blueline ☐ Contact ☐ 4C laminate ☐ Dry laminate				

Special Instructions ....

Figure 16.6 *A sample output request form. One way or another, every item on this form must be filled out before a job is loaded into the queue. More money and time is lost during the output process than anywhere else in the workflow—a complete form will help avoid the most obvious problems.*

- **Output Type.** This typically lists a choice between imagesetters, color printers, and film recorders.

- **Media.** For imagesetting, this lists choices between media type (RC paper or film), exposure (positive or negative), and emulsion (up or down). For color printing, this lists choices between printers and output stock. For film recording, this lists slide and transparency sizes.

- **Resolution.** Lists various imagesetter resolutions, usually 1,200, 2,400, and 3,600dpi.

- **Page Size.** Lists standard and custom page sizes.

- **Separations.** Lists choices between None, Process, or Spot. Space is typically provided for special instructions concerning overprint and knockout commands.

- **Options.** For imagesetting, this includes information on crop and registration marks, reduction or enlargement percentages, and linescreen values. For color printing, it includes options for crop/registration marks, reduction/enlargement, and lamination.

- **Preflight Requirements.** States whether the client has supplied laser composite and separations or if the service bureau is to do so. There should be an option for "running blind," which means that the client requests that the file be processed without any laser proofs. This option effectively releases the service provider from any responsibility for unusable film.

This form is the primary source of information specific to an output job. It is used closely with all other written forms and reports provided by the client, but it is essential that all the most important output-oriented facts are kept in one easy-to-read location.

Stage Two: Reviewing the File

The review stage takes place just before laser comps and separations are printed. This process should be completed by both the designer and the output specialist on the same job. Before copying the job folder to transport media, the designer must review its contents and output preflight pages. This ensures that the most recently saved version of the document is used during preflighting. Immediately after receiving the job, the output specialist must also review the file and output preflight pages—even though the client has handed over their own laser-printed pages. It may seem redundant, but this is an important safety measure: it ensures that the project can be printed from the output workstation, and that all the information has transferred successfully to the hard drive. The second printouts should be identical to the ones turned in by the client.

Creating Optimum Preflight Conditions

When you open a client job on an output or preflight workstation, you must do your best to duplicate the conditions in effect when the file was created. You'll mimic the designer's workstation by doing the following:

1. Copy the project folder to the hard drive of the output station. Resist the temptation to leave it on the transport media.

2. Turn off all the fonts currently open on the workstation, using your font management utility. (Refer to Chapter 4, "Font Management," for more info.)

3. Turn on only the fonts supplied by the client. This accomplishes two things. First, it ensures that the *identical* font information is used when outputting the document. Second, if any fonts have not been supplied, you will avoid any erroneous font substitution.

4. Open the project document. Now, you're flagged if any graphics or fonts are missing, eliminating the need to rely on paper proofs for this particular information. (See "Opening and Examining the Document," next, for more info.)

Opening and Examining the Document

This is where you review the contents of the transport media supplied by the client. The simplest way to do this is to open the document. Presumably, all the information has been copied to the hard drive, the fonts have been turned on, and all the graphics are present. When you open the document, you'll be alerted if any fonts and graphics are missing. You can then take the necessary steps to acquire the info from the client before printing the file.

Reviewing an XPress Document

The first thing you should see when opening a client's XPress document is the Preferences Request alert (see Figure 16.7). It indicates that the document was created on a different copy of XPress (the designer's versus the output specialist's), and some settings in the Preferences dialog boxes are inconsistent.

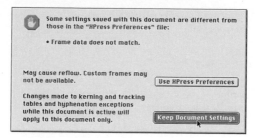

Figure 16.7 *Unless you are opening a file created on your own workstation, XPress's Preferences Request alert should appear whenever you open an XPress document. Always click the Keep Document Settings button—if you don't, you could lose important client-set info such as trapping, tracking, and kerning values.*

Whenever you see this dialog box, click the Keep Document Settings button. Every time. Doing so maintains all the prefs that were in place while the file was created. Clicking Use XPress Preferences overrides the document prefs, and some of the original settings may be replaced. This puts values such as automatic trapping, custom tracking, and kern tables at risk. (Refer to Chapter 14, "Page Layout Issues," for more info on preferences.)

Checking Fonts

After you decide to keep the document settings, you are notified if any fonts are missing. If the Missing Fonts alert appears, do the following (see Figure 16.8):

1. Write down the missing font titles. Most often, this occurs because a client did not supply entire font families, opting to send individual fonts.

2. Double-check the transport media. Perhaps the files are stored in a different location.

3. If the font is not available, contact the client and have them bring (or transfer via email) the entire font family of each missing font. Do not replace fonts with your own versions or other typefaces without written consent of the client. Have them fax their approval, if necessary.

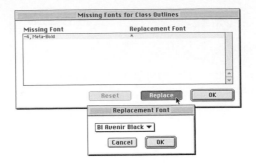

Figure 16.8 *Although you can replace any missing font with one currently open on your system, you must resist the tempation when you see the Missing Fonts alert. Even if you're positive you have the same font in-house, contact the client and get a copy of theirs. Fonts are upgraded just like software, and extremely subtle differences between two versions of Helvetica, for example, can be enough to cause text reflow.*

Checking Graphics

XPress will not automatically notify you if any graphics links are broken, unless you are printing or collecting for output. To check links when opening a file, do the following:

1. Choose Utilities: **Usage**.

2. In the Usage dialog box, click the Pictures tab (see Figure 16.9).

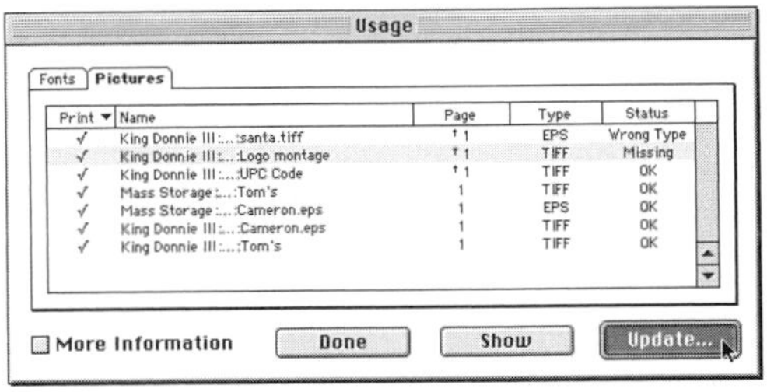

Figure 16.9 *Check graphics links with XPress's Pictures Usage panel. You're notified whether their status is OK, Modified, Wrong Type, or Missing. If anything other than OK appears, you must select the item and click the Update button to reestablish the link.*

3. Scroll down the window, checking the status column. Hopefully, everything reads OK, indicating that all graphics are present and linked. Other messages include Modified (the graphic was updated somehow since the

last time the document was open), Wrong Type (the graphic's file format was changed since the last time the document was opened), and Missing (no link is currently established).

4. If any graphics are read as Modified or Wrong Type, they can be updated by selecting the graphic and clicking Update. Be sure to check each graphic's position in the document. If necessary, contact the designer to be sure you are updating the correct images.

5. If any graphic is listed as Missing, double-check the transport media to see if any files were moved out of the project folder. [2]

6. If a graphic has not been supplied, contact the client immediately and arrange to have the file transferred, dropped off, or shipped.

Reviewing a PageMaker Document

Because PageMaker's preferences are not as intensive as those in XPress, you won't see a dialog box that asks you to choose between document or application preferences. The document preferences are maintained when the file is opened into PageMaker.

Fonts

When you open the document, you are notified if any fonts are missing by the Font Matching Results dialog box (see Figure 16.10).

If it appears, do not accept the suggested changes. Do the following instead:

1. Write down the missing font titles. Most often, this occurs because a client did not supply entire font families, opting to send individual fonts.

2. Double-check the transport media—perhaps the files are stored in a different location.

FOOTNOTE

2   Often, the act of copying a project to a removable disk and then another hard drive will break all the graphic links in the document. In the Picture Usage panel, the status of every item will be listed as Missing. Don't panic—just start updating the files, linking to the files that shipped with the project. If all the graphics are stored in the same folder, linking the first one will trigger XPress to automatically re-link the rest.

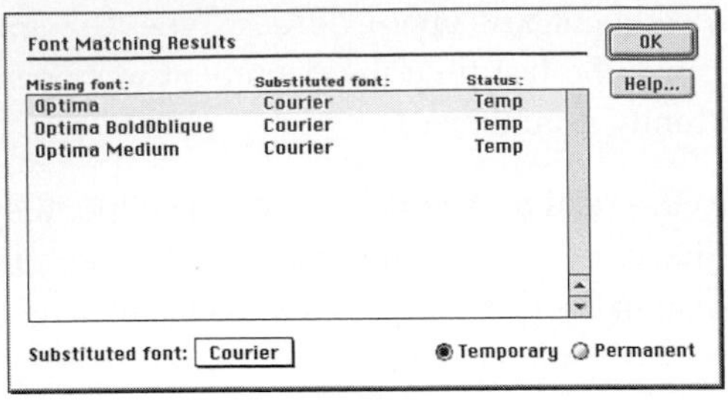

Figure 16.10 *When PageMaker's Font Matching Results dialog box appears, do not replace any fonts. Instead, take note of the missing items, acquire the files from the client, load them onto your system, and open the document again.*

3. If the font is not available, contact the client and have them bring (or transfer via email) the entire font family of each missing font. Do not replace fonts with your own versions or other typefaces without written consent of the client. Have them fax their approval, if necessary.

Graphics

PageMaker will not automatically notify you if any links have been broken, unless you are printing. To examine links while opening a file, do the following:

1. Choose File: **Links Manager** (see Figure 16.11).

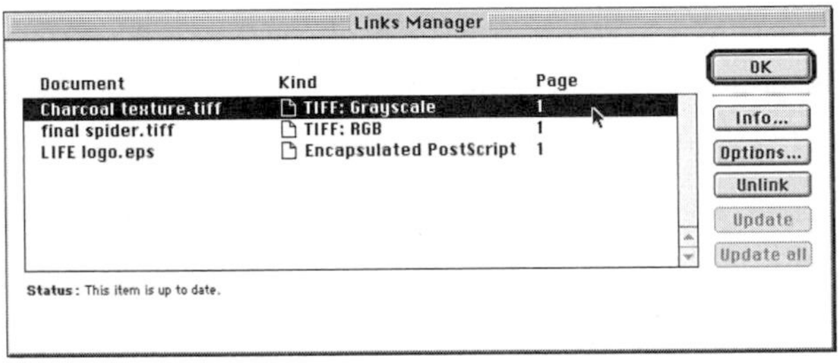

Figure 16.11 *Examining graphics links in PageMaker's Links Manager dialog box.*

2. Scroll down the window. Any graphic starting with a question mark is an unlinked file. Select an individual graphic to reveal its Status down below.

3. If any graphics are unlinked, they can be updated by selecting the graphic, clicking Info, and directing PageMaker to the proper file. Be sure to check each graphic's position in the main document.

4. If any graphic is missing, double-check the transport media to see if any files were moved out of the project folder.

5. If a graphic has not been supplied, contact the client immediately and arrange to have the file transferred, dropped off, or shipped.

Reviewing an InDesign Document

To review the contents of an InDesign document, use the File: **Preflight** command. After InDesign scans the document, the Preflight dialog box presents the info in five panels (choose the panels from the available pop-up, or navigate through them by clicking the Next and Prev buttons). To generate a printed report containing the info found in the following panels, click the Report button in the Preflight dialog box.

The Summary Panel

This panel displays a brief description of the four remaining screens (see Figure 16.12).

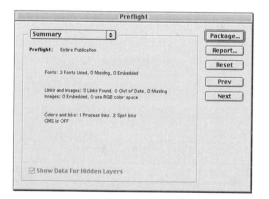

Figure 16.12   *The Summary panel of InDesign's Preflight dialog box displays a synopsis of the document info found in the remaining four panels.*

The Fonts Panel

This panel displays every typeface used in the document (including those embedded in an imported graphic). The font names appear in a scrolling window, followed by their type (Type 1, Type 3, or TrueType) and status (see Figure 16.13). To see if any fonts are missing, check the Show Problems Only box. This way, only the document fonts not currently available are listed.

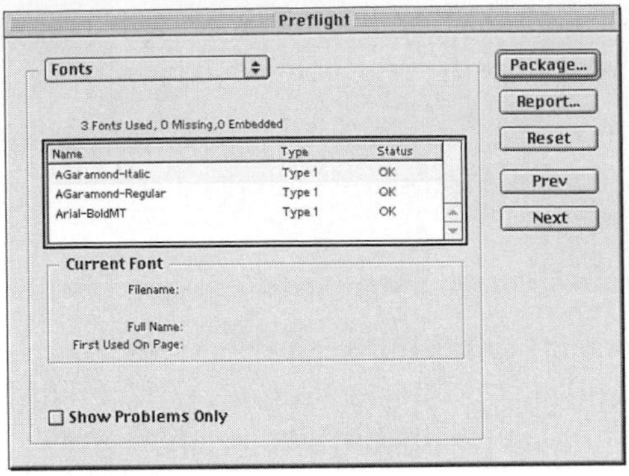

Figure 16.13   *The Fonts panel of the Preflight dialog box displays every font used in the document—including any embedded in an EPS graphic.*

The Links and Images Panel

This panel displays a list of every imported graphic. The filenames appear in a scrolling window, followed by the type (file format), the page on which they appear, the link status, and the name of any attached ICC profiles (see Figure 16.14). If any links have been broken, select the item and click the Update button. As with fonts, you can display only the problematic graphics by checking the Show Problems Only box.

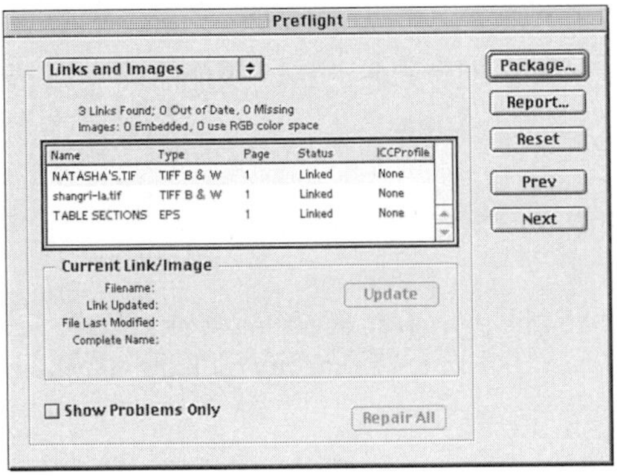

Figure 16.14   *The Links and Images panel of the Preflight dialog box displays the link status of every imported image.*

The Color and Inks Panel

This panel displays all colors applied in the document (see Figure 16.15). If the project is based on CMYK colors, then only cyan, magenta, yellow, and black should appear here. If the project is based on spot colors, only their names should appear.

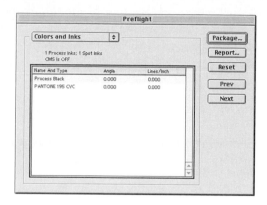

Figure 16.15 *The Colors and Inks panel of the Preflight dialog box displays all colors defined in the document. When designing with spot inks, be sure their name appears here. When working with process inks, only Cyan, Magenta, Yellow, and Black should appear.*

Print Settings Panel

This panel displays the current settings in the Print dialog box (see Figure 16.16). This info is especially useful in a fast-paced enviroment connected to multiple output devices.

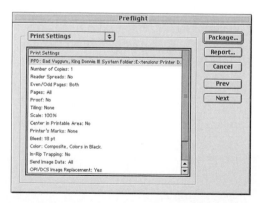

Figure 16.16 *The Print Settings panel of the Preflight dialog box displays the current settings in the Print dialog box.*

Stage Three: Outputting Paper Proofs

Printing laser proofs is the last and most important stage of the preflight process. Always print two sets of proofs: composites and separations. The composite proof is a noncolor separated printout and is used to examine your overall page geometry, bleeds, crossovers, and text. The separations are used to check that colors are printing to the appropriate plates. Both printouts prove as much as possible that the document can be successfully output to a film plotting device.

Outputting these proofs is the responsibility of both the designer and the output specialist. When designers hand these proofs over to their service provider, they're saying, "I've done all I possibly can to make a file that will print right the first time." When output specialists output the file again to laser proofs, they're saying, "I have duplicated your paper proofs. We will now accept responsibility for outputting this file to film."

Necessary Hardware

Before you can output laser proofs, you must have the appropriate tools. Substandard equipment has inhibited the success of many a preflight department.

The Laser Printer

The laser printer is the most important component of your preflight department. Many people bypass preflighting because their printer takes too long to output separations, and they feel that their productivity is being compromised. Usually, this happens because a laser printer is the technological equivalent of an old dog. It's ancient, it hardly works, and it makes a mess more often than it should. You know deep down that you should do the right thing and put it out of its misery, but you've been through so much together, you've developed a bond with it.

If your laser printer is more than five or six years old—or, heaven forbid, you're still using that archaic LaserWriter II—it may be time to upgrade. Newer laser printers are faster, cheaper, and more capable than ever, and the accompanying rise in productivity will pay for a new printer in weeks or months. [3] Look for the following features:

- **PostScript Level 2 (or Level 3).** This refers to Adobe's page description language, and is the platform that drives this very industry. Compared to PS Level 1 laser printers, Level 2 is the Six Million Dollar Man: better, stronger, faster. On these printers, there is virtually no ceiling on the number of points in a vector-based path (including clipping paths), separations output at more than twice the speed, and composite print times positively scream. Plus, you can buy a letter-size Level 2 laser printer for under $1,000 nowadays (compare that to the $7,000 price tag of Apple's first LaserWriter). PostScript Level 3 is starting to become commonplace, and differs from Level 2 only in that it features increased efficiency and speed. One note: be sure the printer uses true PostScript, not a PostScript emulator. Many

---

FOOTNOTE

[3] Upgrading a printer may seem a difficult and costly task, but consider this example: An advertising agency I recently worked with suffered from terribly slow print times. They never suspected their printer, because they purchased it less than three years ago for over $6,000. At that money, they naturally assumed they were getting top performance. Sure, it output tabloid-sized pages at 1,200dpi, but when they tried to separate a 24-page CMYK catalog, it took over two hours *per page*. After contacting the manufacturer for an explanation, I found two problems. First, the printer wasn't even PostScript-based; it used a PostScript *emulator*, or a platform that attempts to simulate the tasks of true PostScript. Second, the emulator was only based on PostScript Level 1, the first and least capable version. There were no plans to offer an upgrade path, because the original manufacturer had been acquired by another company and the line had been discontinued. We had no choice but to retire the printer. I installed an Apple LaserWriter 8500: a 600dpi, PostScript Level 3 device that handles page sizes up to 12×18 inches (and, I might add, cost only $1,600). I output the same 24-page document, and produced laser seps at less than four minutes per page. The original printer was last seen holding open a stockroom door.

This experience illustrates two important points. First, even though your current printer may have been expensive, the slowdown it imposes on your production may be causing you to lose more than you spent. Second, you must research any new printer before you buy. Accept only true PostScript Level 2 or 3, and don't be seduced by superfluously high resolutions (which are always more expensive) or the bold claims of any less-established manufacturers.

manufacturers—such as LaserMaster, NewGen, and Hewlett-Packard—use an emulator in lieu of true PostScript. Some emulators work quite well; others do not. I prefer to bypass the entire issue by investing only in true PostScript technology (you can find this information in a printer's Product Specs—look for the Printer Language item).

- **600 dots per inch.** These days, 300dpi simply isn't enough. 600dpi enables you to check traps and fine type, and your printouts output more crisply and accurately overall. For preflight and proofing purposes, 600dpi is just fine. Although some laser printers offer resolutions of up to 1,200dpi, these smaller dot sizes do not translate directly into higher quality. Most designers and service bureaus use their laser printers primarily for proofing, and a resolution of 600dpi is perfectly suited for this task. However, some print shops use paper output as the basis for producing plates for their own in-house presses. In this case, a 1,200dpi printer offers crisper type, particularly at small sizes.

- **RAM.** Increasing the amount of RAM in your printer (not to be confused with the RAM in your computer) can radically expedite the printing process. Some lower-end models only have room for 2MB–4MB of printer RAM. Consider this the barest minimum. Your best bet, especially if much of your work consists of process separation, is to have between 8MB and 16MB of RAM installed. Many printers, depending on your workload, can be upgraded to 32MB and beyond. When purchasing your printer, check the amount of on-board RAM, how high it can be upgraded, and factor in the amount and type of work you will be sending to it. At the extreme minimum, your printer should have 8MB of RAM. Any less, and complex docs won't print, nothing will spool, and it will be too slow for serious production work.

- **Paper Size.** As far as preflighting goes, a letter-sized printer will suffice. Your comps and seps can be tiled or scaled, depending on the document's overall size. Larger laser printers, usually 11×17 or 12×18 (for tabloid-sized printouts with registration and crop marks), are considerably more expensive and should be purchased only when a tangible need beyond simple preflighting exists. Service providers typically have both letter- and tabloid-sized printers to generate the most accurate paper proofs as a service to their clients. Designers usually get by with a letter-sized printer, unless their needs include full-sized mock-ups or two-page camera-ready art.

- **Ethernet.** Purchase a printer with built-in Ethernet. Using this method of networking to transfer the information to your printer gets the job done roughly 10 times faster than LocalTalk.

The CPU and Storage

An output workstation must have enough speed and storage space to deal with large volumes of client traffic. The goal of these workstations is to open, review, preflight, and output files as quickly as possible. At the very least, a PowerMac G3 (or Pentium III PC) running at 266MHz has enough raw horsepower to efficiently work with this amount of information.

Have at least 2GB of available storage space on every output station. This gives you the capability to copy large files onto your own drive, as well as hang onto a few jobs that might need to be reprinted in the near future. Note that I said *available* space, not *total* space. Programs like Photoshop and Illustrator require at least 500MB of free space for scratch disk purposes (1GB, if possible). If you don't have the space, buy an additional drive. Four-gigabyte hard drives are available for under $300, and the return on this small investment is almost immediate.

Software

The process here is simple. Decide what software you will support, purchase legal copies, install them on each workstation, train your operators, and stick to your guns. If a client insists on handing over a document created in an unsupported application—say, CorelDRAW or MacDraw—accept the file only if the following is true:

- The client enables you to temporarily install their software on your workstation for the express purpose of outputting their file.

- The client understands you cannot guarantee final output if the software used is not a supported industry standard.

In almost all situations, the supported software is what I have covered in this book: QuarkXPress, Adobe PageMaker, Adobe InDesign, Adobe Illustrator, Macromedia FreeHand, and Adobe Photoshop. These software packages have the widest user base, the highest number of trained operators, and the highest rate of proven output success. Service providers will occasionally expand their range of supported software to include programs like Adobe FrameMaker or Deneba Canvas, which have an established user base, but not necessarily as large or as well-proven as the others.

If you do add new software packages to your list of supported programs, be sure you have at least one trained and knowledgeable output specialist in-house. Of course, purchase legal copies of the software.

As you promote your supported software, mention specific version numbers when necessary. Not all current applications can successfully translate documents that were created in earlier versions. Page layout programs have the strongest limitations. For example, PageMaker 6.5 can easily open a PageMaker 6.0 document, but often has difficulty converting a PageMaker 5.0 or 4.2 file. (The latest versions of Illustrator, FreeHand, and Photoshop can successfully open graphics created in every earlier version, so the issue does not apply to these programs.) As a result, service providers typically support the two most recent versions of each page layout program. A list of supported software might read as follows:

- **Page Layout.** QuarkXPress 4.04 and 3.32; Adobe PageMaker 6.5 and 6.0; Adobe InDesign 1.0.

- **Illustration.** Adobe Illustrator; Macromedia FreeHand.

- **Image Editing.** Adobe Photoshop.

If you routinely accept documents created in older program versions, you're opening a potentially frightful can of worms. If you open these files in the new versions, page information may be skewed. If you save one of these files as a document of the latest version and give it back to the client, they may not be able to open it. Encourage your client base to upgrade as soon as a new version becomes supported and viable. Many companies offer free training seminars when a new version is released.

Output Laser Proofs

Now you begin the process of ensuring the integrity of the final film output. As you prepare to output your comps and seps, follow these guidelines:

- Your laser proofs should match the file going to film. If you've made any changes to the document after making laser proofs, you should output it again.

- Scale your pages no less than 75% of the final output size. If necessary, leave the scale value at 100% and tile the pages to your laser printer, rather than scale the pages so small that it makes proofing impossible.

- Be clear about which images are FPOs, which are live scans, and which images are the low-res PICTs of a series of DCS files.

- Delete all unnecessary pages from your multipage documents.

Outputting Laser Composites from XPress

Follow these steps to output nonseparated comps from XPress:

1. Open the document to be output.

2. Choose File: **Print**.

3. Click the Document tab.

4. Be sure Separation is unchecked, and Include Blank pages is checked (see Figure 16.17).

Figure 16.17 *The Document panel of XPress's Print dialog box, with Separations unchecked for printing comps.*

5. Click the Setup tab.

6. In the Printer Description pop-up, set the PPD file for your target laser printer (see Figure 16.18). PPD's contain information that allows for optimal printing to a specific PostScript output device, and setting the wrong one can lead to a PostScript error.

7. If you need to scale your output for preflight, enter the value in the Reduce or Enlarge field. Otherwise, use the Tile function in the Document panel.

8. Choose the appropriate Orientation icon.

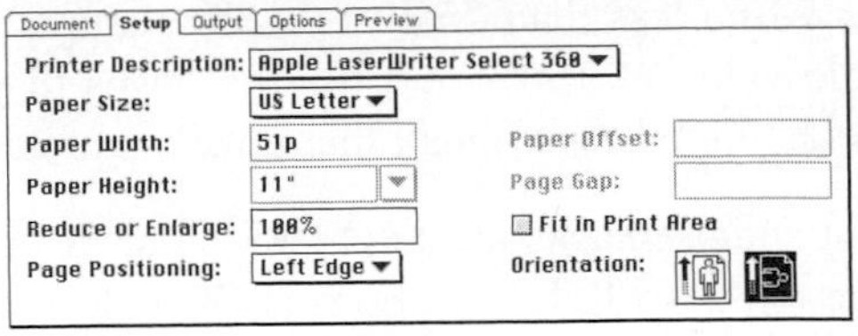

Document | **Setup** | Output | Options | Preview

Printer Description: | Apple LaserWriter Select 360 ▼
Paper Size: | US Letter ▼
Paper Width: | 51p | | Paper Offset:
Paper Height: | 11" ▼ | | Page Gap:
Reduce or Enlarge: | 100% | | ☐ Fit in Print Area
Page Positioning: | Left Edge ▼ | | Orientation:

Figure 16.18 *The Setup panel, after setting the PPD, scale value, and orientation.*

9. Click the Output tab.

10. In the Print Colors pop-up, choose Grayscale (see Figure 16.19). This option outputs black tints based on overall brightness values, rather than flat percentages. The printed result is easier to read—for example, 100% magenta outputs as a lighter tint than 100% cyan.

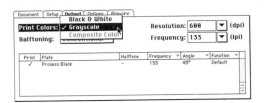

Figure 16.19 *The Output panel, after choosing Grayscale and setting the line-screen value.*

11. In the Frequency field, set your target halftone screen value. It doesn't matter at this stage whether your laser printer can accurately reproduce higher linescreens. You need to be sure they can be output by a PostScript device in general.

12. Click the Preview tab.

13. In the small preview window, be sure your document will not be clipped during output.

14. Click Print.

Outputting Laser Separations from XPress

Follow these steps to output separations from XPress:

1. Open the document to be output.

2. Choose File: **Print**.

3. Click the Document tab.

4. Check the Separations and Include Blank Pages boxes (see Figure 16.20).

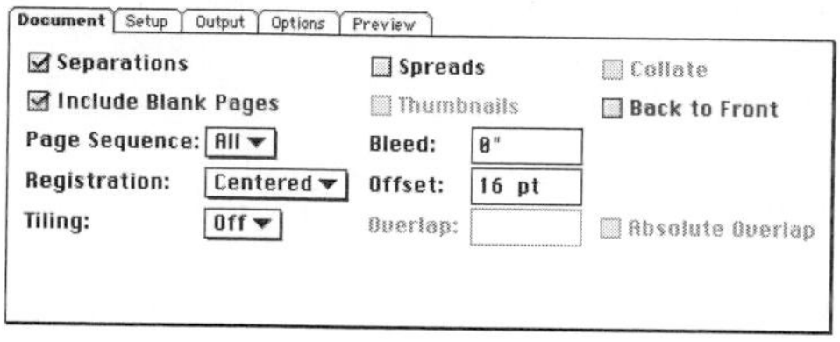

Figure 16.20   *The Document panel of XPress's Print dialog box, with Separations checked for printing seps.*

5. Choose Centered or Off Centered from the Registration pop-up. When enabled, this option adds plate names, crop marks, and registration marks on each separated page.

6. If the document contains bleeds, enter a value in the Bleeds field (usually between .125 and .25 inches). Otherwise, the information will clip at the page edge.

7. Click the Setup tab.

8. Select the appropriate PPD file from the Printer Description pop-up.

9. If you need to scale your output for preflight, enter the value in the Reduce or Enlarge field. Otherwise, use the Tile function in the Document panel.

10. Choose the appropriate Orientation icon.

11. Click the Output tab.

12. Set your target halftone screen value.

13. Click the Preview tab.

14. In the small preview window, be sure your document will not be clipped during output.

15. Click Print.

Outputting Laser Comps from PageMaker

Follow these steps to output nonseparated comps from PageMaker:

1. Open the document to be output.

2. Choose File: **Print**.

3. Click the Document button.

4. Select the appropriate PPD from the Type pop-up (see Figure 16.21).

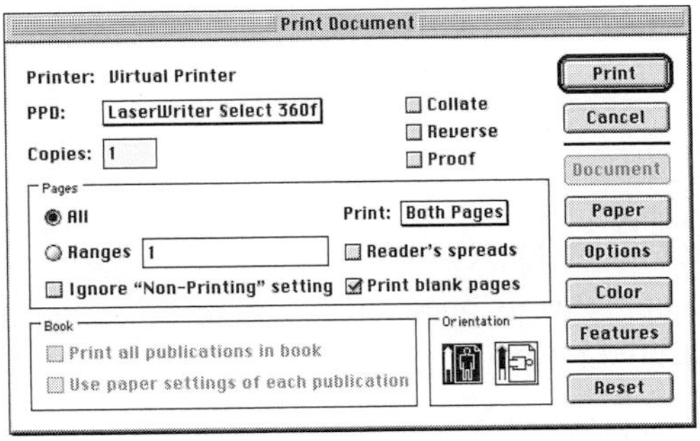

Figure 16.21   *The Document panel of PageMaker's Print dialog box, after setting the desired PPD.*

5. Check the Print Blank Pages box.

6. Click the Paper button.

7. Set the scale value, if necessary. Otherwise, turn tiling on and set the Auto: Overlap to .5 inches (see Figure 16.22).

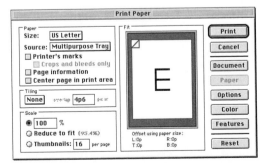

Figure 16.22   *The Paper panel, after setting scale and disabling printer's marks.*

8. Turn Printer's Marks and Page Information off.

9. Click the Options button.

10. Under Graphics, select Normal.

11. Under PostScript, turn Include PostScript Error Handler off (see Figure 16.23).

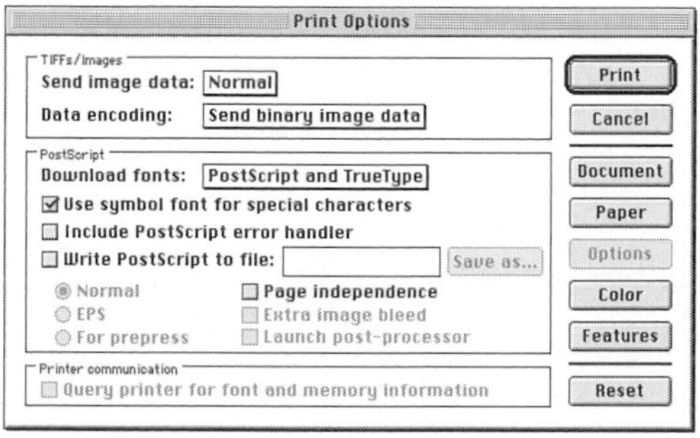

Figure 16.23   *The Options panel, after choosing Normal Graphics and disabling the PostScript Error Handler.*

12. Click the Color button (see Figure 16.24).

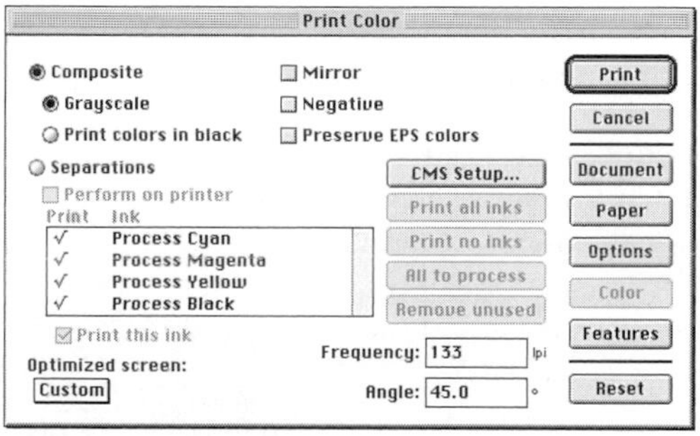

Figure 16.24   *The Color panel, after setting the screen frequency and selecting Grayscale.*

13. Set the halftone screen in the Ruling field.

14. Under Composite, select Grayscale.

15. Click Print.

Outputting Laser Separations from PageMaker

Follow these steps to output separations from PageMaker:

1. Open the document to be output.

2. Choose File: **Print**.

3. Click the Document button.

4. Select the appropriate PPD from the Type pop-up.

5. Turn Blank Pages on.

6. Click the Paper button.

7. Set the scale value, if necessary. Otherwise, turn tiling on and set the Auto: Overlap to .5 inches.

8. Under Paper, turn Printer's Marks and Page Information on.

9. Click the Options button.

10. Under Graphics, select Optimized.

11. Under PostScript, turn off Include PostScript Error Handler.

12. Click the Color button.

13. Set the halftone screen in the Ruling field.

14. Choose Separations (see Figure 16.25).

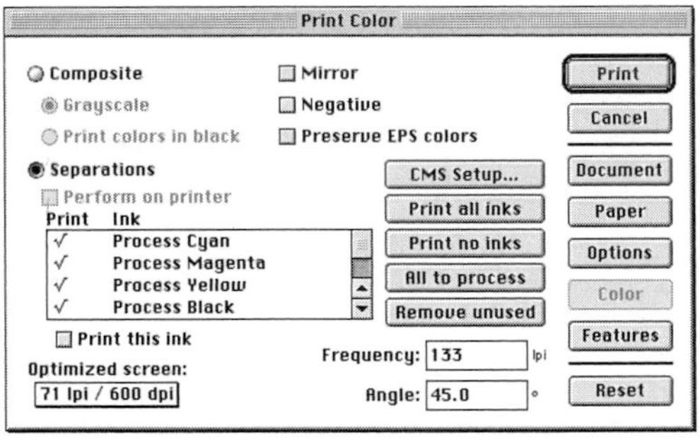

Figure 16.25   *The Color panel, with Separations enabled.*

15. Examine the inks printed in the scrolling field. Be sure only the document colors are checked.

16. Click Print.

Outputting Laser Composites from InDesign

To print from InDesign, you must use the Adobe PS 8.6 driver. Follow these steps to output nonseparated comps:

1. Open the document to be output.

2. Choose File: **Print**.

3. Select Color from the available pop-up.

4. Select the Composites option (see Figure 16.26).

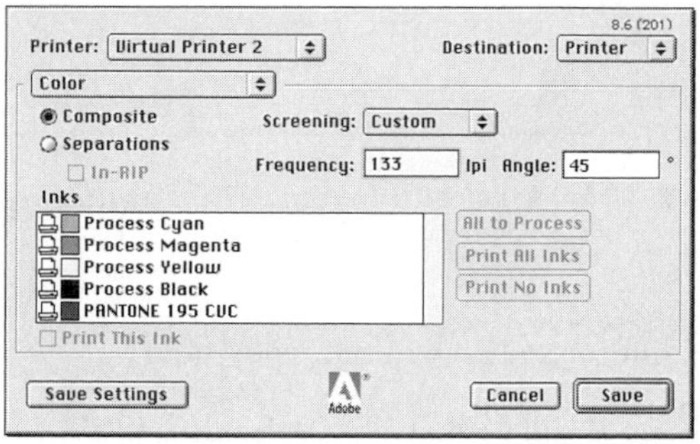

Figure 16.26 *The Color panel of InDesign's Print dialog box, with Composite enabled.*

5. Set the target linescreen in the Frequency field.

6. Examine the scrolling color list; be sure only the intended colors appear.

7. If you need to set a scale value, choose Scale and Fit from the pop-up and enter the desired value in the Width and Height field. If desired, click the Scale to Fit option to reduce the document to fit the target paper size. If the Scale to Fit percentage falls below 75%, bypass it and choose an option from the Tiling pop-up.

8. Click Print.

Outputting Laser Separations from InDesign

Follow these steps to output laser separations from InDesign:

1. Open the document to be output.

2. Choose File: **Print**.

3. Select Color from the available pop-up.

4. Select the Separations option (see Figure 16.27).

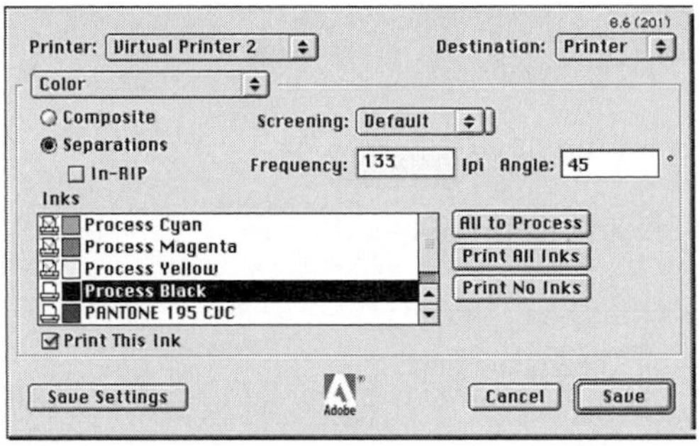

Figure 16.27   *The Color panel of InDesign's Print dialog box, with Separations enabled.*

5. Set the target linescreen in the Frequency field.

6. If you need to set a scale value, choose Scale and Fit from the pop-up and enter the desired value in the Width and Height field. If desired, click the Scale to Fit option to reduce the document to fit the target paper size. If the Scale to Fit percentage falls below 75%, bypass it and choose an option from the Tiling pop-up.

7. Select Page Marks from the pop-up.

8. Check the Crop Marks, Page Information, and Registration Marks boxes. Many users simply check the All Printer's Marks option, which activates all the boxes. This is fine, as long as you understand that the color bars and bleed marks offer little to the preflight process (see Figure 16.28).

9. If your document contains bleeds, enter an accommodating value in the Bleeds field.

10. Click Print.

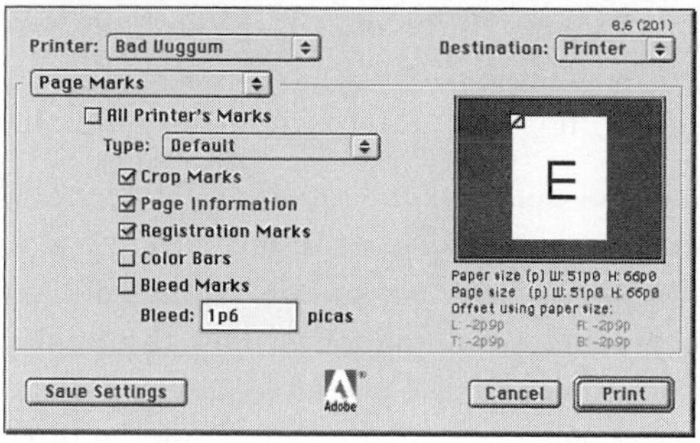

Figure 16.28   *The Page Marks panel, with printer's marks enabled.*

Examining Your Laser Seps

After outputting laser separations, check for the following:

- That all unnecessary pages are deleted from the file.

- That all colors are defined and named correctly. Check for extra plates, spot colors printing as process (and vice versa), and duplicate colors.

- That the proper number of plates are printed for each page.

- That your bleed allowances are satisfactory—at least an eighth of an inch.

- That crossover images appear in the appropriate places on the right pages.

- That your trap specifications are accurate. This may require placing your proofs on a light table, registering them, and examining them through at least an 8x loupe.

- That every graphic is output at the appropriate resolution, with no jagged edges or pixelization.

- That your text did not reflow or default to Courier.

- That your clipping paths actually clipped, and that no silhouettes were placed on top of colored backgrounds.

- That pages are appropriately numbered.

If you need to make any changes based on what you read in the proofs, output new separations of the edited pages. At the very least, if you're pressed for time and the changes are not extensive, note them on the latest proof.

Designers must hand these comps and seps over to the service provider with their transport media. The preflight proofs created by the output specialist should be included with the material sent back to the client.

Preflight lasers do not replace an important problem-solving device: the *dummy*, or project mock-up. Whenever you design a document with more than one or two pages, output comps of every page and glue, staple, or fold them together to produce a simulation of how the final piece will appear. Some ambitious designers even use a glue-stick or spray adhesive to affix pages back-to-back before trimming, folding, and stapling. Turn the mock-up over to your printer, so he will know *exactly* how you intended the project.

Troubleshooting

You can't ignore the fact that problems will occur. PostScript errors halt the printing process; graphics output badly; clipping paths and duotones don't separate properly; the file appears to print, but nothing comes out the other end.

Literally thousands of variables can cause a file to misprint. You may have noticed that no one has written a book listing all the problems and solutions, and there's a good reason. As soon as a new operating system is released, an application is upgraded, a computer model is unveiled, or new technology is hyped, the rules change.

Never fear, though. A wise man once let me in on the Secret of PostScript Troubleshooting, and I share it with you now: "Learn everything there is to know," he said. "Then go fix the problem." Although he laughed then, there's more than a grain of truth here. There are two approaches to troubleshooting a problem file:

- Acquire a library of resources (including this book), that describes the most common prepress techniques, skill-set requirements, problems, and solutions. Use this library as a basis for learning to address (or better yet, *avoid*) output-related problems.

- Work in the industry for years, make lots of costly mistakes, talk to hundreds of professionals, output thousands of files, and work hands-on with millions of problems. Keep detailed journals and strive to improve your knowledge base. Share what you know with others, never hoard your secrets, and always be ready to learn something new.

I suggested keeping detailed journals. I mean that in two ways.

Keep a personal record of the problems you encounter. It's sort of like those chemistry labs in high school: Describe all the variables, what was supposed to happen and didn't, and the ultimate solution. If you think you can retain all the myriad output problems you'll encounter in your head, you're wrong. There are simply too many. Keep a record of problems that recur in a client's work. Clients who continually commit the same file construction errors should be trained in those issues, making everyone's lives more pleasant.

Your work will always consist of a combination of these approaches. Take it from me. In my ten years of graphics experience, I shudder to think of the multitude of costly screw-ups I've made. Even though I've worked as a designer, output specialist, training director, art director, consultant, and author of after-market books, I can still make a mistake that drags the progress of a job to a screeching halt. That only tells me that there is always more to learn, a process to refine, a way to improve. My most valuable resources are always my project notes and my colleagues.

Billing Practices

Repairing a misprinting file takes time. For all intents and purposes, this is billable time and the industry-standard hourly wage for this service runs between $70 and $125. Of course, no one likes to see a surprise charge on their invoice, regardless of how lifesaving the service might have been.

The only recourse a service provider has in successfully billing for file repair is the following:

- Announce your preflight requirements to all clients. Do this when they drop off jobs, have your sales staff explain it concisely to their accounts, send out mailers with your invoices, and announce it in your newsletter. Explain what the requirements are, why they need to be followed, and how they will benefit everyone.

- Establish a firm date for when the requirements will go into effect.

- Some service providers offer a discount—usually between 5% and 10%—for properly preflighted files.

- Offer all clients the option to supply laser proofs or not, but make it expressly clear that you are not responsible for any wasted or unusable film that results from a non-preflighted file.

- If any repairs need to be made, contact the client immediately and explain the situation. Include a detailed description of the problem, how long it will take to repair, and how much it will cost. The client should either bring in a file that they have repaired (with fresh preflight proofs) or agree to the charges.

- Because it's unlikely that every client will actually be asked to pay for these services, be careful which charges get dropped and which will be billed. Be consistent. Do you drop only certain charges for certain people? Do you just offer a discount? Is only one person responsible for these decisions, or do the output specialists have autonomy? Should your sales staff handle the issue instead?

File repair services are every bit as tangible as graphic design or image acquisition. If you continue to do it for free, you may as well bypass the entire preflight process and the thousands of dollars in potential yearly savings that it offers.

Dedicated Preflight Software

The preflight techniques I've described so far require only the standard applications used to create a project. If you're willing to invest a little more money and training time, there are software packages available that automate much of the preflight process. The two I recommend are Extensis's Preflight Pro (www.extensis.com) and Markzware's FlightCheck (www.markzware.com). Each utility effectively collects document components into a single job folder, allowing you to bypass the collect for output commands in each application. It's important to note that these utilities were released before Adobe InDesign—you'll have to wait for future upgrades for compatibility with this page layout program.

Preflight Pro 2.1 ($399) is one of the most useful utilities I've seen. It's compatible with all the major applications, and works by scanning an open document from within the original program. Its interface is based on a Job Jacket, a sort of onscreen simulation of a typical prepress job ticket. You can establish an extensive range of settings that customize the utility to match a specific work environment. When potential problems are flagged, it lists a series of potential solutions, offering you an easy method of repairing the file. Preflight Pro can also scan multiple files, allowing you to process a multi-document project all at once. After documents are scanned and repaired, you can use this utility to bundle all the project elements—even embedded fonts or graphics—into a single folder, with the option of compressing it into a self-expanding archive (a useful feature when sending projects to a service provider via their FTP site). As a bonus, Preflight Pro can create print-ready PDF files using its own built-in Acrobat Distiller settings.

- **Pros:** Intuitive interface; exhaustive settings; PDF compatibility; Multiple file processing (using drag-and-drop Watched folders); Thorough report generation; Custom job profiles; Problem files automatically moved to separate folders.

- **Cons:** Requires native applications installed on workstation; Mac-compatible only; cannot preflight PDF files.

FlightCheck 3.3 ($349)—the first preflight utility—searches for the same essential information as Preflight Pro, but uses a different method. While its interface may be a little clunkier, it scans a file independently of its native application. For example, QuarkXPress 4 does not need to be installed to preflight an XPress 4 document. Still, it searches for over 140 potential problem areas, directing the user as needed.

- **Pros:** Supports greater number of older application versions; Does not require native applications; Can reference fonts not currently loaded; versions available for Mac and Windows.

- **Cons:** No customizable profiles; Less intuitive interface; Only processes one file at a time; Automation via AppleScript only.

Do these utilities represent some sort of file prep Nirvana? No, not really. Your files still need to be examined manually for design and press-specific issues, and you still need to pore over your individual pages before giving the final okay. As far as automating the more mundane aspects of checking file construction, a preflight utility is a useful tool to add to your collection.

Summary

Until recently, the industry thought of design, production, and output as the only three stages an electronic document journeys through before printing. A couple of years ago, the concept of preflighting arose to gel those three areas into one cohesive, predictable, and profitable industry: digital prepress.

Even though the preflight process seems to be most intensive in the moments just before outputting to film, the responsibility for proper output rests with everyone who ever lays their hands on a file, regardless of the task they perform. Successful file output and printing is only possible if care is taken during every stage of a project to ensure that the appropriate decisions, values, and commands are applied to your work.

Outputting and checking your laser prints should be the easiest and most painless stage of a job. But if you do make an error somewhere along the line, the guidelines in this chapter offer the hope of a safe oasis in a sea of risk and chaos. Only by placing your files to the ultimate test—printing, even if only to a laser printer—can you determine if the file will make it through the rest of the process.

PROOFING METHODS

A large client of a graphic design firm ordered 100,000 brochures to launch a major marketing campaign. The client provided all the text for the project, but someone had unwittingly transposed two digits in the toll-free number. The error passed five separate proofing stages used by the design firm, because the client failed to carefully scrutinize the copy. No one noticed until the completed job sat in boxes at the mailing house, awaiting shipping. All 100,000 pieces went into the trash, and the project had to be reprinted.

A mail-order clothing company prepared a new catalog to mark the coming change of season. Dozens of products were photographed, scanned, and saved to disk. The vendor urged the company to use laminate proofs from output films to evaluate the color. Instead, in an attempt to save money, they requested digital proofs from a high-end ink-jet printer that wasn't calibrated to the target press. As a result, the catalog colors differed from the actual products, and the company lost thousands of dollars in returned clothing.

These real-life experiences illustrate what can go wrong when a project isn't thoroughly proofed. Although you should always check and double-check each facet of a job for accuracy, proofing at the end of the production cycle is arguably the most important stage of the process. It's more than a safe-guard against layout, type, and color errors; it's a way of protecting yourself from any mistakes, omissions, or oversights by the client.

With few exceptions, one person is responsible for proofing: the designer. Many people seem to suffer temporary blindness as they examine one inex-pensive laser-printed proof after another. After films are made, however, their eye kicks into overdrive, and they mark up laminate proofs or bluelines with abandon. The proofing cycle is designed to give you plenty of opportunities to correct errors before final output and printing. Because mistakes can occur in a variety of forms, proofing should cover the following:

- **Copy.** The text must be complete, accurate, easily readable, and free of typos.

- **Page layout and composition.** Page elements should be free of misplaced items, arranged exactly as intended by the designer and client.

- **Laser separations.** Here, you ensure that the document will behave properly during final output. (This process is covered fully in Chapter 16, "Preflight and File Prep.")

- **Color accuracy.** Evaluate color proofs of every scan in the project, making sure the colors match the original materials as closely as required by the project. The method you use will depend on the scope of the job.

- **Press sheets.** As the print shop prepares the final press run, you have one last chance to examine the job and make minor adjustments.

Checking Copy

Nothing calls attention to itself like a typographical error. It boldly proclaims to the world that no matter how talented a designer you are, you never learned how to spell.

One of the greatest advantages of digital technology is that it enables you to examine and revise text at any stage of the process. But the longer you wait before making a correction, the more expensive it becomes to fix. If you proofread using laser printouts, it costs only pennies to make a quick edit and reprint. If you wait until color proofs or films are generated, the cost of a simple edit skyrockets.

Proofreading hasn't changed all that much since the earliest days of printing. Many of the same methods are used to ensure the absence of typos, spelling mistakes, and omissions. It's not enough to give your project a quick onscreen read-through. Use the following guidelines:

- **Run spellcheck.** Every word processor and page layout program has a spellcheck command, and they're a great place to start. They're not perfect tools, though, not by a long shot. For example, they can't detect if you've used the words *mane*, *main*, or *Maine* inappropriately; they can only tell if the words are correctly spelled. Also, they don't particularly care if you click the wrong button, accidentally replacing a misspelled word with an erroneous dictionary suggestion. For example, Microsoft Word and QuarkXPress don't recognize the word "PageMaker." If someone had clicked incorrectly during spellcheck, you might be wondering why I spent so much time discussing *pacemakers* in a print publishing book. Use spellcheck to catch any glaring typos, but always be prepared to read through the material again.

- **Print it out.** When you output the text to a laser printer, you give yourself a chance to read it in a different context. You've already spent hours or days staring at the work onscreen, and you're accustomed to looking through the words, to the page geometry, the images, and so forth. It also enables you to mark up the text, noting the need for any edits or rewrites. If necessary, suppress the graphics during printing, which shortens the output time considerably.

- **Read it out loud.** Force yourself to read each word exactly as it's written. It's too easy to skim through the text, especially if you're already familiar with it. Your brain will paraphrase as you read, making it all too easy to miss the most obvious errors.

- **Sleep on it.** Give yourself some time away from the text before attempting to proofread it. When you put a little distance between yourself and the copy, you can approach it more objectively.

- **Have someone else read it.** It's difficult at best to proofread your own work. If you were responsible for entering and formatting the text, you've already looked at it for too long. Hand it over to a fresh pair of eyes. Enlist another designer, someone from another department, anyone with decent skills who can spare the necessary time. For larger projects, consider hiring a freelance proofreader, or ask your print shop. Often, some of their employees have years of typesetting experience, and they tend to be excellent proofreaders.

- **Get formal client approval.** After you've proofed and revised the text to the best of your ability, give laser printouts to the client. Tell them to read the material very carefully, that any future revisions will result in extra charges. Make sure that every person involved in the approval process signs the proof—*do not accept a verbal approval*. This will protect you in case a vital piece of information (such as the toll-free number mentioned earlier) was originally mishandled by the client.

Proofing Layout and Composition

Most designers spend more time looking at the individual pages of a document than any other facet of the project. The layout file is the centerpiece of the design process; here, text and graphics are combined to create the final look and feel of the printed material. However, *designing* the pages is not the same as *proofing* them. When you drag that final element into place, it's easy to assume that the job is finished, that you're ready to preflight the document and jump directly to the output stage. Give yourself time to scrutinize each element and make any last-minute adjustments. Not only does it give you the opportunity to catch anything you overlooked during the frenzy of design, it enables you to get final client approval for the overall composition before expensive color proofs are generated.

Proof the layout separately from the copy or color. Focus on two things: the physical placement of the elements on each page, and how each page interacts with its neighbors. Use the following techniques. (For a full description of production-oriented problem areas, refer to Chapter 14, "Page Layout Issues.")

- **Examine and tweak.** Evaluate each page onscreen. Check the placement of each element, and make sure their alignment is consistent from page to page. Keep an eye out for potential trouble spots, such as large images that are cropped or rotated, EPS graphics that may have embedded fonts, miscolored objects, and so forth. This isn't the time to redesign anything—if you have to make any major changes, start the proofing process again when you're finished.

- **Print thumbnails.** XPress, PageMaker, and InDesign enable you to print a document as thumbnails. Here, every page is shrunk down, and several pages are stacked on each printout. Thumbnails are the quickest way to evaluate the overall composition of the project. If your document was built using facing pages, output using the Spreads option, which arranges left- and right-facing pages side-by-side.

- **Print laser composites.** Print composite laser proofs to examine the placement of your elements in a physical form. It's not important that they don't appear in full-color—instead, they enable you to focus on the page geometry alone. (If your page dimensions are larger than the capacity of your printer, either scale them down until they fit, or use your layout program's Tile function to use multiple sheets of paper to reproduce each page.) Mark up the printouts as necessary, make any required changes, and print them again. Repeat this step until the pages are completely error-free.

- **Create a mock-up (or "dummy").** Here, you do your best to mimic the document's printed and bound form. Use black-and-white lasers or inexpensive color output. Output every page, then use tape or glue to double-side them as needed. Include any custom folds, and clearly mark any perforations or dye-cuts. Use staples to emulate the binding, and trim the results to match the final dimensions. The mock-up satisfies three important needs. First, it lets you examine the project in its intended form. Second, it enables the client to see exactly what they're paying for, at a time when revisions are still possible. Finally, it tells the print shop the precise composition you have in mind; they will endeavor to match what you give them as they prepare films and flats for the press run.

- **Get formal client approval.** Graphic design is a subjective business. The only way to ensure that the clients are satisfied with your efforts is to hand over the final laser printouts or mock-up. Have them examine every page. If they request changes, provide fresh proofs after completing the edits. If they're satisfied, get their approval in writing.

Proofing Color

The only way to see the exact colors of a printed project is to run the job on-press. Of course, this method is a little like building a house in order to approve the blueprints. Fortunately, you can choose from several proofing types that enable you to get closer to the final print run. The appropriate one depends on the specifications of the job at hand:

- Do the image colors only need to be balanced and appealing, or must they match the original scanning materials?

- Does your project contain full-color scans, black-and-white halftones only, or no images at all?

- Will it be printed using process or spot inks?

- Will you be outputting film separations, or using a no-film reproduction method, such as a digital press, direct-to-plate output, or short-run color lasers?

If your project colors are even remotely critical, the goal of the color proofing stage is the *contract proof*—the final, end-all proof that the printer will attempt to match on-press. The contract proof enables you to evaluate the overall project integrity, copy, layout, trapping, screening, tone and color reproduction, and size. It's the only way to ensure that the project was correctly manufactured. After a designer approves a contract proof, the output vendor cannot be held accountable for the final results.

It's not as easy as it sounds—you can't bring in any color printout and expect the pressman to match the colors. Instead, each reproduction method has a corresponding proofing type. For example, if you're outputting film separations, a laminate proof will provide the most accurate results. If you're printing to a digital press, a film-based proof would be a waste of time and money. Instead, you'll require a digital color proof, generated from an output device specifically calibrated for that particular press. If you use the wrong proofing method, you inject a wide range of variables into the process, and it becomes extremely difficult to predict the printed colors. [1]

Consider this example. A major printing company recently switched to an all-digital press workflow. Their proofing methods, however, were never upgraded. Composite proofs are created on uncalibrated color laser printers, which the clients use to get an overall feel for composition and layout. To generate the contract proofs, the printing company actually outputs film separations and creates a laminate proof. After the client approves the proof, the films are discarded and the project is sent to the digital press. This process is essentially the same as using no proofing at all. Because no calibrated digital proof is created, there is no standardized way to match the on-press colors. (The printing company justifies it by claiming its clients are "more comfortable" reading a film-based proof, ignoring the fact that in this case, the laminate proof is just as ineffective as the cheap color lasers.)

FOOTNOTE

[1] Color proofing is essentially a lie. No matter how "accurate" a proofing method is, it will never *precisely* match the printed results. There are too many issues that impact the final colors, including (but not limited to) paper stock considerations, dot gain, press types, halftone dots, even the competence of the pressman. The more critical your colors are, the more work is required beyond a physical proof. You must plan to attend the press check, to make any last-second adjustments to the distribution of inks. If necessary, bring a densitometer and your contract proof to ensure that the values match as closely as possible. Many designers, when printing super-critical color, actually bring products to the press check, to compare the printed values against the real thing.

Color Proofing Methods

The most common color proofing methods—and the work for which they're most appropriate—are listed below.

Soft Proofing

Soft proofing describes the process of evaluating project colors onscreen. It is the least expensive method, because no physical materials are involved. It also tends to be the least accurate—after all, the fact that monitors cannot display accurate values is the very reason color proofing exists in the first place.

This proofing type is appropriate in two cases. First, it's suitable if your color needs are obviously non-critical. For example, if your document colors were selected from a printed swatchbook (such as Pantone for spot inks or Trumatch for process inks), and you don't require a physical proof to examine the values, you might opt for the speed and cost savings of an onscreen proof. Many documents that don't contain full-color scans are reasonable candidates for this method. The client can examine the project at the designer's workstation, or they can evaluate a PDF file at their own location.

The ability to proof *accurate* colors onscreen requires at least one ICC-calibrated workstation. This way, the user can load a profile for a specific output method, which shapes the way image colors appear on the monitor. Most often, this approach is employed by closed-loop production workflows, where it is easier to measure and profile the in-house printers and presses. It is also used by many service bureaus and print shops, which already have color-managed workstations in-house for scanning and correcting purposes. If these vendors routinely use the same presses, they can generate the necessary profiles for onscreen proofing. In theory, the ICC-based method makes *remote proofing* possible. Assuming the client has the same rigidly calibrated system as the vendor, files can be transmitted back and forth for quick onscreen viewing. This requires constant input on behalf of the vendor, who usually is responsible for setting up and maintaining the client workstation. (Refer to Chapter 11, "Color Spaces and Printing," for more info.)

Digital Color Proofs

The advent of digital presses and direct-to-plate printing have made digital color proofs more important than ever. Here, a proof is generated by a color printer, bypassing any film separations.

It's important to make a distinction between a color proof and regular, every-day color output. Color printers are available for as little as a couple of hundred dollars. You can purchase color laser printouts for under a dollar per page. These are completely *uncalibrated* proofs. They're a good, cheap way to get a general feel for your color decisions, and many people prefer proofing layout and composition using color instead of black-and-white laser output. The only time to use one of these devices for a final proof is if the project will be printed on the same machine. For example, if you're planning to run 500 pieces on a color laser printer instead of a press, create your proofs on the same machine. This way, what you see is definitely what you'll get. Otherwise, never accept this type of output as a contract proof.

Digital color proofs are run on costly, capable machines. Optimally, they're calibrated to a specific press, whether digital or conventional. The high-end units, from companies such as Iris, Kodak, and Imation, enable you to proof color based on halftone dots, with compensation for dot gain and other press conditions. Many devices can print directly onto your desired paper stock, giving you an excellent indication of the final results. It comes at a price: The cost of a four-color proof can exceed $45 for a single 8.5×11-inch page.

Many users are switching to digital proofs, even if their job ultimately will be separated to film. (Compared to a laminate proof, the cost is typically 40–60% less per page.) Other users distrust digital printouts, believing only the results of film that they can see and feel. Again, it will depend on how critical your colors are. If your accuracy needs are medium, a well-calibrated digital proof will likely suffice for a film-based print run. If the need for accuracy is high to super-critical, laminate proofs are still the best way to go.

The variables of digital proofs are too extensive for a single chapter in a book. The best thing you can do is ask your vendor for samples from its particular devices and cost breakdowns. Also get detailed information on how well the vendor will suit your workflow. Seek the advice of other designers who have used different digital proofing methods—their successes and failures will give you an excellent direction to pursue.

Film-Based Laminate Proofs

More than 60% of all materials generated by the print industry are based on lithographic film. All-digital workflows are slowly but surely taking a bite out of that number, but the practice of outputting and proofing a film-based project is sure to be an established one for years to come.

The most accurate method of proofing the colors of a film-based project is to create a laminate proof (also known as *off-machine proofing*). This method emulates the actual printing process, using the film separations for each page. A paper substrate holds the proof, and the operator uses cyan, magenta, yellow, and black gel laminates to simulate the CMYK inks. It works like this. The cyan laminate is fused to the substrate. The cyan film plate is placed over the laminate, and the entire unit is exposed to ultraviolet light, which binds the visible laminate areas to the substrate. The proof is run through a chemical bath, which washes away the unexposed areas (in a *dry* system, the laminate is simply peeled away, leaving only the exposed areas). The magenta laminate is then fused to the substrate, the magenta film plate is registered to the existing info, and the proof is again exposed to UV light and run through the chemical bath. The process repeats for the remaining colors. After the final color has been applied, the operator can apply a gloss or matte finish, to mimic the appearance of coated or uncoated paper.

Laminate proofs are expensive. The cost (including the film output) can exceed $110 for an 8.5×11-inch page. However, they enable you to proof your project in a way that digital proofs do not. You can immediately evaluate the integrity of the film, checking for flaws that would otherwise appear during the press run. With an 8-power loupe, you can examine traps and registration on a light table. If you're using custom screen angles (or you've scanned prescreened artwork), you can easily identify any instances of moiré. The proofs aren't perfect; you cannot evaluate dot gain, because the substrate doesn't absorb the laminate the way that paper absorbs ink. Nonetheless, these proofs provide the most accurate color possible for a film-based project, and remain the most successful option for a contract proof.

Wet Proofing

Consider wet proofing (also known as *machine proofing*) "near printing." It uses film, plates, and a printing mechanism that emulates the target press. The operator uses your final film separations to burn a set of plates, hangs them on the mechanism, and hand-feeds sheets of paper to produce the proof.

The main advantage to wet proofing is accuracy. By duplicating the conditions of the press run, the resulting press sheet resembles the final product more closely than any other proofing method. The disadvantage is cost (it's the most expensive option—prices vary according to the print shop and reproduction method) and the required time. Many designers consider this option before committing super-critical color to high-volume print run.

Evaluating a Color Proof

The color proofing stage is typically broken into two phases. First, you examine your images after they're scanned and pass through the first round of corrections. Second, you proof entire pages, images and all, just prior to the press run. The considerations and techniques differ slightly with each approach.

Scatter Proofs

When you first turn materials over to a scanning vendor, you have the option of requesting a laminate or calibrated digital proof (the difference will be reflected in the price). Choose the method that dovetails with your color requirements. When the vendor provides a scatter proof, your images are ganged up on a single page. They enable you to evaluate the content of the scans before the document pages are completely designed and output. This is your chance to request additional adjustments, rescans, or other work before the deadline looms too near. If you wait until page proofs are produced before requesting these changes, it might be too late.

Examine the scatters thoroughly, under a controlled light source—use the vendor's facilities. Look for the following problems:

- **Color content.** Compare the proofs to your originals. Look for extreme or unpleasant variances. Pay particular attention to skin tones, memory colors, and the focal point of the image.

- **Contrast.** The tones should be balanced and appealing, not flat or over-exaggerated.

- **Burned-out highlights.** The diffuse highlight should contain dot structure and detail. Keep an eye out for all-white details or patches of solid color.

- **Plugged-up shadows.** There shouldn't be any solid blacks. Shadows should contain an identifiable dot structure, and carry visible detail.

- **Poor detail.** Detail should be crisp and well-sharpened. Check for overt blurriness, which can result from bad scanning over over-correction.

- **Alignment problems.** Look for visible color fringes, whether along the edges of the image edges or the colored shapes within. If this occurs when the registration marks are perfectly aligned, the image must be rescanned.

- **Visible artifacts.** Look for any dust or scratches that the retoucher might have missed, as well as any blips or inconsistencies that result from poor retouching and editing.

- **Moiré.** Screen patterns can result from scanning prescreened objects, conflicting screen angles, and images such as fabric with a detailed pattern.

- **Orientation.** If originals are mounted incorrectly during the scanning process, they'll appear backwards or reversed.

Don't be timid about requesting any changes. Many of these problems can be corrected, and if they are the result of vendor error, the images will be rescanned and adjusted free of charge. After the scatters are corrected and approved, the images are re-inserted into the production cycle for placement, layout, and future page proofs.

Color Page Proofs

Page proofs give you one last opportunity to examine your project for errors or necessary adjustments. They should be produced only after you've proofed the copy, layout, and document composition. Optimally, there should be no errors found at this stage.

These proofs, whether produced digitally or via film-based laminates, should appear as close to the final printed piece as possible. In fact, if you were to trim these proofs, staple the pages together, and view it beside the finished piece, you should see no appreciable differences. In addition to the problems you looked for in the scatter proof (which you'll want to double check), examine the following page items:

- **Printer's marks.** These include crop marks, trim lines, fold lines, perforation lines, and so forth.

- **Tints and screens.** Make sure any large expanses of solid color aren't mottled or blotchy. Any tints should appear at the desired level, not darker or lighter than intended.

- **Color consistency.** Areas colored with the same values should appear the same on every page; there should be no shifts or variances.

- **Bleeds.** If any page information is intended to run to the edge of the trimmed piece, it must extend beyond the crop marks on the page proof. Most printers require a bleed of at least an eighth of an inch.

- **Trapping.** You'll likely have to examine traps with a loupe and a light table. Beware of elements that appear to abut perfectly, with no slight overlap.

- **Pagination.** Your pages should appear in the correct order, properly numbered.

- **Crossovers.** When a single element extends from one page to another, the two parts must line up when the two page proofs are aligned. Most printers require a bleed on both pages.

After you've approved the page proofs, pack them up and send them to the printer along with your films, digital files, mock-up, and whatever else they require. [2]

Marking a Proof for Revisions

Whether examining scatters or page proofs, you need to communicate any desired changes as clearly as possible. Mark the changes directly on the proof—even if you're the one who will be making the changes. Use the following guidelines:

- Leave nothing up to chance, and never assume that someone else will spot an error that seems obvious to you. Mark everything that seems questionable.

- Circle the particular element in question.

- Whenever possible, use CMYK terms when requesting changes. Instead of saying something is "too green," try to pinpoint the problematic component.

- Avoid unspecific adjectives like "warm" or "cool." Describe your problem with the colors as best you can.

F O O T N O T E

[2] If you're printing direct-to-plate or to a digital press, you may have to examine the page proofs during the press check. Make sure you allocate the necessary time for a thorough examination, and triple-check your laser proofs to minimize the possibility of a major error.

- Don't simply refer people to the original materials. Define the difference between what you see and what you want to see. For example, "The detail is missing in the mountaintops" is far more useful than "See the transparency."

- Avoid ambiguous commands such as "brighten," "improve," and "correct," unless you can provide specifics.

- Use plus (+) and minus (–) signs to indicate an increase or decrease of the CMYK inks. For example, write "–M" to state a desire to reduce the level of magenta.

Proofing Spot Colors

Most of the information presented so far has revolved around process color. This is mainly due to the enormous variability involved in viewing, interpreting, and printing in full-color. Spot inks do not require as stringent an approach to proofing. Their colors are constant, chosen from a printed catalog, so their values are unlikely to change between the proofing and printing stages.

You're not off the hook, however. You might not need to scrutinize each occurrence of a custom ink, but your active involvement is required in the following areas:

- **Ink selection.** Many designers choose spot colors that appear to go well together when they compare the swatches, but look horrible when actually printed. (I was once responsible for producing a quarterly calendar for a print broker, which consisted of a large full-color image surrounded by a thick colored border. Because of the reproduction method used by the print shop, the border had to appear as a 50% tint of a custom ink. As often as not, what seemed like a decent selection in my PANTONE swatchbook completely mismatched the colors of the image when run on-press. Each time, I was able to replace the first custom ink with another, more appropriate selection.) Such experiences are rare, but can be salvaged with some quick thinking at the press check. At the very least, ask the print shop to provide a *draw down* at the start of the project, where they smear samples of the target inks on the intended paper stock.

- **Ink integrity.** Your print shop might be using old inks, or they might be mixed improperly, or the wrong one might be used altogether. A print shop I know once swapped one metallic gold ink for another, because they "already had it mixed." Bring your swatchbook to the press check.

- **Duotones.** Spot ink duotones are difficult to create, and nearly impossible to proof. A few digital proofers (such as the 3M Rainbow) enable you to proof the colors of a duotone, but they don't address the screen angles. If necessary, you can request a laminate proof. The colors will be wrong, but if you've used custom screen angles, any unintended moiré will become immediately apparent.

- **Trapping.** Unlike process colors, you cannot build a bridge with spot colors to reduce the need for trapping. This significantly increases the need to proof your traps before the project is run on-press.

Digital printers rarely offer true spot color proofs. Instead, they typically create a process simulation of the spot ink. Because most spot inks cannot be reproduced with process components, it is difficult at best to expect a color-accurate proof. Most laminate systems have available spot laminates, but you can expect to pay a lot more for them (assuming you can find a vendor willing to order and produce them). For the most color-sensitive jobs, particularly high-volume runs containing duotones, wet proofing quickly becomes an attractive proofing option.

The Press Check

The press check is your last opportunity to affect the outcome of the print process. Here, you make arrangements to visit the print shop as the job is readied for printing. After the plates are hung and the rollers are inked, the press is kicked into gear. The press crew burns through a few hundred sheets of paper (or dozens of yards, on a web press), called *make ready*, as they make adjustments to the machinery. When they feel they've sufficiently matched the contract proof, they shut down the works and bring you a press sheet to approve.

This is not the time to discover a typo, or decide you want to increase the thickness of a line. Instead, you make sure that no defects exist in the film or plates, and see that the colors are as accurate as you requested. Always have the contract proof at hand for ready comparison. If slight color imbalances exist, the press operator can make slight adjustments by increasing or decreasing the amount of an ink applied to a given part of the page.

When examining the press sheet, look for the following:

- **Contrast.** If too much or too little ink is laid down, the tonal range of your images will appear flattened or exaggerated.

- **Tints.** Areas of solid color should appear evenly screened, with no blotches or mottled areas.

- **Colors.** The same colors should appear consistent from page to page, and on different parts of the same page.

- **Crossovers.** Elements that run from one page to the next should line up when the pages are aligned.

- **Slurring.** The product of insufficient *tack* (viscosity) of the ink, slurring results in unevenly shaped halftone dots and a soft, blurry appearance.

- **Picking.** When tack of the ink is too high for the target stock, the rollers might pull up little threads of paper. (You should be warned in advance of this problem when you select your stock, by either a sales rep or the print shop.)

- **Smearing.** If the paper stock shifts on its way through the press, printed matter will smear, producing blurred images and type.

- **Hickeys.** If a speck of dust, a blob of ink or water, or a tiny piece of paper gets onto the plate during the run, a small spot appears on the press sheet.

- **Ghosting.** If the ink on the plate is depleted because of heavy coverage on one part of the sheet, a ghosted (or thin) area may appear on other images or colors behind it.

- **Bleedthrough.** Some paper stock is too thin for heavy ink coverage, particularly on both sides of the page. The ink may soak through the paper, appearing as a blotch or inconsistency on the other side.

- **Misregistration.** Examine the registration marks, making sure the plates are perfectly aligned.

As you examine the press sheet, circle any problem areas, just as you do with a color proof. Discuss them with the pressman. Remember that the press crew wants your project to look its best. If you're unsure of anything, ask for their input. After making any adjustments, the operator runs a few more sheets and provides another press sheet. This process continues until you're satisfied with the results. After you sign the sheet (indicating your approval), the press runs at full speed until the run is completed.

Summary

The proofing cycle is the quality-assurance stage of the production process. No matter how much conscious effort you put into the design process, you can never assume that you've paid attention to every detail. At various stages of the game, you must turn a stern, objective eye toward your project:

- Copyedit the text, to make sure that no typos or formatting errors exist.

- Proof the layout, to make sure that each element is in the right place, and each page appears in the proper location and form. Create a mock-up of the entire project for the client and print shop.

- Evaluate the colors of your document, using a proofing type appropriate for your method reproduction, to make sure the colors will reproduce as you intend.

- Preflight the document, to make sure it can be properly separated by an imagesetter or digital press.

- Attend the press check, to make sure the colors, pages, printer's marks, and inks will behave as necessary to create the final piece.

- Get formal client approval at every phase of the process, to make sure you're not held accountable for any errors.

As you can see, the operative phrase here is "to make sure." You can spend ages editing a project onscreen, using all the software techniques, design methods, and knowledge resources the industry has to offer. Until you complete the proofing stage, you'll never know what to expect on-press.

IMAGE CREDITS

With only a few exceptions, the images appearing in this book are from the excellent and extensive John Foxx Images library. For full-size, full-color previews of the entire series, please visit its Web site (www.johnfoxx.com).

The following table lists the images I used, along with their reference code and CD volume. Any image not credited here is from my personal archives.

Figure	Image	Volume	CD Title
8.1	AN 2058	SS 17	*Unique Images of Animals*
8.70	AN 2046	SS 17	*Unique Images of Animals*
9.1	CM 1825	SS 04	*People & Computers*
9.10	IN 1894	SS 10	*Industry*
9.11	IN 1896	SS 10	*Industry*
9.12	IN 1894	SS 10	*Industry*
9.15	AN 2074	SS 17	*Unique Images of Animals*
9.18	AN 2044	SS 17	*Unique Images of Animals*
9.19	AN 2045	SS 17	*Unique Images of Animals*
9.21	AN 2082	SS 17	*Unique Images of Animals*
10.10	CM 1869 (#1)	SS 05	*Computer Elements*
	CM 1872 (#7)	SS 05	*Computer Elements*

continues

continued

Figure	Image	Volume	CD Title
10.11	CM 1895	SS 05	*Computer Elements*
10.20	CM 1892	SS 05	*Computer Elements*
10.22	DB 1856	SS 06	*Business Details*
10.23	DB 1856	SS 06	*Business Details*
10.24	DB 1856	SS 06	*Business Details*
10.28	DB 1884	SS 06	*Business Details*
10.31	DB 1886	SS 06	*Business Details*
11.2	CL 1805 (left)	BS 24	*Clouds, Skies, & Aerial Views*
	CL 1808 (center)	BS 24	*Clouds, Skies, & Aerial Views*
	CL 1809 (right)	BS 24	*Clouds, Skies, & Aerial Views*
12.5	CM 1854	SS 04	*People & Computers*
12.8	PE 2134	SS 13	*Lifestyles Today 2*
12.9	NA 2085 (apples)	SS 18	*Unique Images of Nature*
	NA 2072 (tree)	SS 18	*Unique Images of Nature*
	ST 1952 (music)	SS 16	*Concepts & Ideas*
12.10	PA 2036	SS 02	*Women in Business*
12.11	PA 2056	SS 02	*Women in Business*
12.12	CM 1806	SS 02	*Women in Business*
12.14	NA 1999	SS 19	*Unique Images of Water*
12.15	NA 1999	SS 19	*Unique Images of Water*
12.18	FI 1880	BS 03	*Money Backgrounds*
12.19	AR 1880	BS 07	*Architectural Elements*
12.20	AS 1904	BS 07	*Architectural Elements*
12.21	ST 1904	SS 16	*Concepts & Ideas*
12.22	FL 1908	BS 25	*Colourful Flowers*
12.23	PE 2125	SS 13	*Lifestyles Today 2*

Figure	Image	Volume	CD Title
12.24	PE 2148	SS 13	*Lifestyles Today 2*
12.25	CL 1804	BS 24	*Clouds, Skies, & Aerial Views*
13.5	NA 2043	SS 18	*Unique Images of Nature*
13.6	NA 2080	SS 18	*Unique Images of Nature*
13.7	NA 2085	SS 18	*Unique Images of Nature*
13.8	NA 2047	SS 18	*Unique Images of Nature*
13.9	NA 2049	SS 18	*Unique Images of Nature*
13.10	CM 1819	SS 04	*People & Computers*
13.12	NA 2062	SS 18	*Unique Images of Nature*
13.14	NA 2057	SS 18	*Unique Images of Nature*
13.15	NA 2085	SS 18	*Unique Images of Nature*
13.20	MG 0014 (dog)	Vol. 20	*Mini GoldDisc*
	NA 2097 (beach)	SS 18	*Unique Images of Nature*
13.21	NA 2042	SS 18	*Unique Images of Nature*
13.22	AN 2045	SS 17	*Unique Images of Animals*
13.23	AN 2045	SS 17	*Unique Images of Animals*
13.24	MT 1886 (hand)	DS 02	*Metallic Hands*
	IN 1887 (fire)	SS 10	*Industry*
13.25	WS 1803	BS 27	*Wood Structures*
13.26	TG 1847	BS 13	*Typographic Backgrounds*
13.27	BA 1972	SS 14	*Natural Babies & Children*
13.28	BA 1946 (baby)	SS 14	*Natural Babies & Children*
	NA 1970 (sky)	SS 20	*The Golden Beauty of Nature*
13.29	ST 1897	SS 16	*Concepts & Ideas*
13.31	ST 1912	SS 16	*Concepts & Ideas*
13.32, 13.33	ST 1897	SS 16	*Concepts & Ideas*

continues

continued

Figure	Image	Volume	CD Title
13.35, 13.36	FL 1908	BS 25	*Colourful Flowers*
13.37–40	MG 0014	Vol. 20	*Mini GoldDisc*
13.42	FL 1908	BS 25	*Colourful Flowers*
13.43–45	MG 0014	Vol. 20	*Mini GoldDisc*
13.46–50	NA 2041	SS 18	*Unique Images of Nature*
15.8	CM 1865	SS 05	*Computer Elements*
15.20	ST 1955	SS 16	*Concepts & Ideas*
15.41	ST 1909	SS 16	*Concepts & Ideas*
15.42	ST 1947	SS 16	*Concepts & Ideas*
15.43	PA 1930	SS 03	*Business & Transportation*
16.8, 16.9	MG 0008	Vol. 20	*Mini GoldDisc*

INDEX

Symbols

1-bit Color (Bitmap mode), 317

8-bit Color (Grayscale mode), 317-318

10BASE-2, 207

10BASE-5, 207

10BASE-F, 207

10BASE-T, 207

24-bit Color (RGB mode), 317-319

100BASE-T Ethernet, 208

130MB EZ drives, 185

600 dots per inch (upgrading printers), 700

A

absolute option (XPress trapping method), 653

accelerated graphics cards, 40-41

acquiring

halftone scans, 384

scans, line art, 372

Acrobat Distiller, watched folders, 157

activating fonts (ATM Deluxe), 136

Actual Pixels command (View menu), 373

Add Anchor Point tool, 244

Add Layer Mask: Reveal Selection command (Layer menu), 537

Add to Color List button, 285

Add to Color List dialog box, 285

add-on cards, 338

adding. *See also* inserting

empty layers, 528

straight edges to free-form selection (Standard Lasso tool), 510-511

additive primary model, 416

Adjust: Auto Levels command (Image menu), 394

Adjust: Curves command (Image menu), 393, 399

Adjust: Equalize command (Image menu), 368

Adjust: Levels command (Image menu), 504

Adjust: Threshold command (Image menu), 378, 475

adjusting

color, 470

adjusting non-neutral colors, 485-492

gray balance and color casts, 472-475

identifying endpoints, 475-476

neutralization in practice, 483-485

setting neutral endpoints, 477-479, 481-483

shadows and highlights, 471-472

contrast (halftone scans), 395-400

endpoints (halftone scans), 390

resetting endpoints, 393-395

targeting endpoints, 391-392

halftone scans, 383-384

adjustment layers, 539-542

adjustment points (curves), 397-398

adjustment tools, color, 455

Curves command (Photoshop), 460-464

Eyedropper (Photoshop), 458-460

Info Palette (Photoshop), 455-458

Unsharp Mask Filter (Photoshop), 464-469

Adobe

Acrobat Distiller, watched folders, 157, 236

Font Folio, 126

Illustrator, 44, 231, 281

InDesign 1.0 page layout program, 45

PageMaker 6.5 page layout program, 45

PostScript, 110

RGB option (RGB pop-up menu), 429

Streamline, 235, 300

Type Reunion, 91

Web site, 55

after-market books, 52-53

Align Center button, 271

Align command (Element menu), 536

alignment, scatter proofs, 726

All Linked Files command (Copy menu), 683

AM screening (amplitude modulated), 335

Angle field (Fill Inspector palette), 297

annual reports, examples of quality, 225

Anti-Alias Postscript (On) option (General panel of Photoshop's Preferences), 353

Anti-Alias Type, 580

anti-aliased edges (Quick Mask command technique), 515

anti-aliasing (rasterizing), 306

antistatic brushes, 369

Antivirus utilities, 91

Append File Extension (On) option (Saving Files panel of Photoshop's Preferences), 354-355

Apple

Authorized technicians, 106

PostScript, 110

RGB option (RGB pop-up menu), 429

application

colors, 594-595

defining tints, 597

frames/backgrounds, 596

imported halftones, 597

imported line art, 597

lines, 596

fill and stroke

FreeHand, 280-281

Illustrator, 278-280

levels-based adjustments (cropping scans), 504

expanding tonal range, 504

manually setting endpoints for print, 505-506

preferences, 351, 568

QuarkXPress, 569-571

scratch disk space, 80

servers, 211

support (scanner software), 344

archiving

CD-R media, 199

DLT media, 202

file management, 168

magneto-optical media, 201

storage media, 187

Area Type tool, 267

Arrange: Bring to Front command (Object menu), 251

artifacts

pixels, 389

scatter proofs, 727

Artwork command (View menu), 548

assembling the elements (preflight process), 679-681

collecting for output in InDesign, 684-685

collecting for output in PageMaker, 682-684

collecting for output in XPress, 681-682

assessing

halftone scans, 384-385

images when scanning halftones, 382-383

Assumed Profiles option (Profile Setup dialog box), 442

ATA drives, 193

ATM, 114-115

optimizing, 91

Type 3 fonts, 116

ATM Deluxe, 115, 133-136, 145

activating/deactivating fonts, 136

cataloging, 145

sets, 134-136

Attach to Path button, 269

auto amount option (XPress Trapping Preference panel), 654

Auto Backup, 163

Auto button, 394

Auto Erase function (Pencil tool), 375

Auto Overprint Black option (trapping), 666

automatic

applying simple traps, 649-651

backups, 168

layers, 529-530

page numbering, master pages (QuarkXPress), 617

tracing of pixel-based images, 300-301

trapping

   PageMaker, 664-666

   XPress, 653-656

Automatic Text Box, master pages, 617

AutoStart virus, 92

available space, 701

Awaiting Approval folder, 160

B

background color

   QuarkXPress preferences, 573

   trapping color-to-color in XPress, 656-657

Background layer, 525

   converting to Imagebacking up, 530

   file management, 166

      automatic, 168

      manual, 167

   In-House Type folder, 157

   media dexterity, 176

   previous versions folder, 163

   storage media, 187

   unneeded software, 83

banding, gradients, 292

baseband signaling, 207

Based On style sheets

   InDesign, 613

   PageMaker, 610

   QuarkXPress, 607

Baseline Shift option (Character palette), 273

batch scanning (scanner software), 345, 384

beds (scanners), mapping, 368-369

Beep When Done (Off) option (General panel of Photoshop's Preferences), 353

Bernoulli drive, 184

Bézier curves, 238-239

   curve handles, 241-242

   drawing curved paths in FreeHand, 245-246

      adding points, 246-247

      deleting points, 247

   drawing curved paths in Illustrator, 242-243

      adding points, 244

      deleting points, 244

   points and segments, 239-240

   straight-line paths, 240-241

   trapping in XPress, 662

Bézier, Pierre (engineer for Renault), 238

"Big Brother" utilities, 158

billable hours (project costs), 222

billing practices, troubleshooting PostScript, 713-714

binding printer spreads, 585

bit depth

   scanners, 342-343

   versus pixel depth, 316

bitmap fonts, 113

Bitmap mode (1-bit Color), 317

Bitmap mode (preparing detailed line art), 379-380

black

   color (default color), 282

   highlight, converting images into CMYK components, 435

   line art, 624

   QuarkXPress preferences, 575

Black Generation dialog box, 435

black ink, 633-634

   enriched black, 634

      rich black, 634-640

      super black, 641-645

   limit, converting images into CMYK components, 435-436

   overprinting and knockouts, 645

      black line art, 646-647

      black type, 646

Black Limit value (trapping), 665

Black Width (trapping), 664

black-and-white line art, reproduction of images in Bitmap mode, 317

bleeds, color page proofs, 727

bleedthroughs, press check, 731

blends, 292

   color-to-color, 292

   None, 293

blue horizontal bars, 269

blue sky, adjusting non-neutral colors, 490-491

Blur: Gaussian Blur command (Filter menu), 498

blurring moiré, 500

   blurring the image, 500

   color channels, 501-502

reducing resolution, 502

scanning at twice the normal resolution, 500

sharpening the image, 502

bridges, process (trapping), 631-633

brightness levels, reading pixel values, 320-321

browsers, file management, 155

Brushes palette, 375

budgeting projects, 222

buses, 36-37

Button View, 94

buttons

Add to Color List, 285

Align Center, 271

Attach to Path, 269

Auto, 394

Choose, 358

CMYK, 285

Corner Point, 246

Create New Channel, 560

Create New Layer, 528

Delete Current Layer, 532

Document, 706

Edit (Quick Mask Mode), 513

Edit (Standard Mode), 514

Edit Trap, 656

Flow Inside Path, 268

Keep Document Settings, 691

Load Channel as Selection, 523

Paper, 706

Picker, 439

Process Black, 636

Process Cyan, 637

Report, 695

Reset Palette Locations to Default, 354

Reverse Path Direction, 249

RGB, 285

Scan, 372

Byte Order option (TIFF Options dialog box), 376

C

cable modems, 215

cache buffer, 182

Cache Levels option (Image Cache panel of Photoshop's Preferences), 359

Calculate Folder Sizes setting, 94

calibrating monitors, 426

canceling

Quick Mask command technique, 515

scan cropping, 503

Castlewood ORB drive, 197

casts, color adjustment, 472

reading CMYK neutrals, 473-475

reading RGB neutrals, 473-474

catalogs, examples of quality, 225

CCD sensors (charged-coupled devices), 339

CD-R drives, 198

CD-ROMs

archiving, 169

backups, 167

training, 53-54

CD-RW drives, 199

cell size (halftones)

lpi, 327-329

pixel values, 329

cells (grid of squares), 326

Center Alignment option (Paragraph palette), 270

Centerline Threshold (trapping), 665

central processing units (CPUs), 25

chairs, 71

Channel Pop-Up (curves), 395

Channel Pop-Up options (saving selections), 522

channel-based sharpening (Unsharp Mask Filter), 467-468

channel-specific settings (scanner software), 345

channels, color, 316

character masks

FreeHand, 255

Illustrator, 252-253

Character palette, 273

character styles, 603

characterizing monitors, 426-427

charge-coupled devices. *See* CCD sensors

checking copies (proofing), 718-719

formal client approval, 719

have someone else read it, 719

printing it out, 719

reading aloud, 719

sleeping on it, 719

spellcheck, 718

chokes (trapping), 630-631

Choose button, 358

choosing
layers, 530
pixel color modes, 320
editing tools available, 320
number of available colors, 320
ultimate use of the image, 320
processors, 32
scanners, 346-347
chromaticity, 412
CIE RGB option (RGB pop-up menu), 430
circles
FreeHand, 274-275
Illustrator, 271-274
Clean Install, 81
cleaning scanners, 369-370
client approval, color expectations, 446-448
client lists, 52
clipped highlights/shadows (scanners), 365
Clipping Path dialog box, 556
clipping paths
creating, 555-557
stacking graphics, 624
clock speed, 31
closed paths, 239, 557
CMOS sensors (complementary metal-oxide semiconductor), 339
CMYK button, 285
CMYK color model (cyan, magenta, yellow, and black), 419
converting images to CMYK components, 431-432
black highlight, 435
black ink limit, 435-436

CMYK conversion setups, 436-437
dot gain, 433-434
GCR, 434-435
ICC option, 432-433
ink colors, 433
non-standard printing inks, 437-439
Tables option, 433
total ink limit, 436
UCA amount, 436
UCR, 434
CMYK command (Model menu), 637
CMYK images, editing color of images, 457-458
CMYK mode (24-bit Color), 319
CMYK Setup dialog box, 432
co-worker resources, 55-57
coated stock printing, 436
coaxial cable, 207
codes (PostScript), 232
Collect for Output command (File menu), 681
Collect for Output command (XPress), 165
Collect for Output dialog box, 681
collecting for output
InDesign, 684-685
Pagemaker, 682-684
XPress, 681-682
collection commands, file management, 165
color
adjustment and correction, 470
adjusting non-neutral colors, 485-492
gray balance and color casts, 472-475

identifying endpoints, 475-476
neutralization in practice, 483-485
setting neutral endpoints, 477-483
shadows and highlights, 471-472
adjustment tools, 455
Curves command (Photoshop), 460-464
Eyedropper (Photoshop), 458-460
Info Palette (Photoshop), 455-458
Unsharp Mask Filter (Photoshop), 464-469
black ink, 633-634
enriched black, 634-645
overprinting and knockouts, 645-647
channels, 316
blurring moiré, 501-502
composite view (Photoshop), 316
corrector, digital prepress design, 16-17
Desktop settings, 86
establishing client expectations, 446-448
gradients, 291-292
creating in FreeHand, 296-297
creating in Illustrator, 293-295
InDesign preferences, 582
knockouts, 290

models, 415

  CMYK, 419

  gamut, 422

  HSB, 420-421

  Lab, 421-422

  RGB/CMY, 416-417

modes, pixels, 315-316

  Bitmap, 317

  choosing color modes, 320

  CMYK, 319

  Grayscale, 317-318

  pixel depth, 315-316

  RGB, 317, 319

monitors, 415

overprints, 290

page layout, 588

  applying, 594-597

  choosing, 589

  defining, 590

  naming, 590-591

  separations, 592

  separations in InDesign, 593

  separations in PageMaker, 593

  separations in QuarkXPress, 592

  spot/process, 588

PageMaker preferences, 579

physical phenomenon, 411

  environment influence, 413

  eye influence, 413

  light influence, 411-412

proofing, 721-723

  choosing service providers, 228

  color page proofs, 727-728

  digital color proofs, 723-724

  film-based laminate proofs, 724-725

  marking for revisions, 728-729

  scatter proofs, 726-727

  soft, 723

  spot colors, 729-730

  wet, 725-726

psychological phenomenon, 413-415

quality, 452

  detail, 452

  gray balance, 454

  memory colors, 454-455

  requirements, 224

  tone, 453

QuarkXPress preferences, 574-575

RGB (QuarkXPress preferences), 574

samplers, placing with Eyedropper tool, 459-460

scanning and adjusting checklist, 448-452

undercolors, 636

vector-based objects, 278

  applying fill and stroke in FreeHand, 280-281

  applying fill and stroke in Illustrator, 278-280

  converting colors between ink types, 290

  creating tints, 287-288

  default colors, 281-283

  defining colors, 283-286

  deleting unnecessary colors, 288-290

  naming colors, 286

viewing standards, 423

  characterizing monitors, 426-427

  consistent viewing environment, 425

  ICC profiles, 423-425

  RGB workspace, 427-431

Color and Inks panel (InDesign's Preflight dialog box), 697

Color Channels in Color (Off) option (Display and Cursors panel of Photoshop's Preferences), 355-356

Color Depth option, 90

Color Indicates option (Quick Mask command), 513

Color List

  creating in FreeHand, 285-286

  creating in Illustrator, 283

color mode (rasterizing), 306

Color option (Quick Mask command), 513

color page proofs, 727-728

Color palette, 278

Color Picker, 477

Color Picker option (General panel of Photoshop's Preferences), 352

Color Range command, 516

  creating a color range selection, 518-520

  Fuzziness Slider option, 517

  Select Pop-Up option, 516-517

  Selection Preview Pop-Up option, 517-518

Color Range dialog box, 516

Color Settings: CMYK Setup command (File menu), 431

Color Settings: Profile Setup command (File menu), 424

Color Settings: RGB Setup command (File menu), 428

Color Video, 591

color-to-color blends, 292

color-to-color trapping (XPress), 656

   background color, 656-657

   reverse, 657

   trap dependency, 658

ColorMatch RGB option (RGB pop-up menu), 430

Colors command (Edit menu), 636

Colors Palette (QuarkXPress preferences), 574

Colors Palette submenu, 637

ColorSync, 87

ColorSync Profile option, 91

Colortron II, 589

Combine options (FreeHand), 262

   Crop, 263

   Divide, 262

   Intersect, 263

   Punch, 263

   Union, 262

Combine submenu (Modify menu), 262

combining shapes, 247

   compound paths, 247-250

Comfort Keyboard System, 74

commands

   Copy menu, All Linked Files, 683

   Edit menu

      Colors, 636

      Copy Attributes, 281

      Cut, 253

      Cut Contents, 257

      Paste Attributes, 281

      Paste Behind, 254

      Paste in Front, 254

      Paste Inside, 254

      Preferences: Document, 653

      Select All, 277, 508

      Select: Masks, 252

      Select: None, 246

      Undo, 234, 399

   Element menu

      Align, 536

      Fill and Stroke, 663

   File menu

      Collect for Output, 681

      Color Settings: CMYK Setup, 431

      Color Settings: Profile Setup, 424

      Color Settings: RGB Setup, 428

      Export, 302

      Export: Paths to Illustrator, 300

      Links Manager, 694

      Open, 308

      Package, 684

      Place, 353, 529

      Preferences, 235

      Preferences: Trapping, 664

      Save, 281

      Save a Copy, 532

      Save As, 302

   Filter menu

      Blur: Gaussian Blur, 498

      Noise: Despeckle, 498

      Sharpen: Unsharp Mask, 378, 387

   Format menu, Illustrator EPS, 302

   Graphics menu, Normal, 707

   Image menu

      Adjust: Auto Levels, 394

      Adjust: Curves, 393, 399

      Adjust: Equalize, 368

      Adjust: Levels, 504

      Adjust: Threshold, 378, 475

      Crop, 508

      Duplicate, 536

      Extract, 550

      Histogram, 364

      Image Size, 498

      Levels, 391

      Mode, 364

      Mode: Bitmap, 379

      Mode: CMYK Color, 431

      Rotate Canvas: Arbitrary, 499

   Item menu, Step and Repeat, 536

   Layer menu

      Add Layer Mask: Reveal Selection, 537

      Effects: Copy Effects, 535

      Effects: Create Layers, 534

      Effects: Drop Shadow, 533

      Effects: Global Angle, 534

      Effects: Paste Effects, 535

      Flatten Image, 532

      New: Adjustment Layer, 540

      New: Layer, 528

      New: Layer Via Copy, 529

      New: Layer Via Cut, 529

      Type: Render Layer, 530

   Model menu

      CMYK, 637

      Multi Ink, 641

Modify menu

   Combine submenu, 262

   Join, 249, 255

   Rasterize, 307

   Split, 250

   Ungroup, 247

Object menu

   Arrange: Bring to Front, 251

   Compound Paths: Make, 249

   Compound Paths: Release, 249

   Create Gradient Mesh, 295

   Group, 273

   Masks: Lock, 252

   Masks: Make, 251-252

   Masks: Unlock, 252

   Rasterize, 296, 306

Select menu

   Color Range, 518

   Deselect, 558

   Feather, 520

   Hide Edges, 562

   Inverse, 524

   Load Selection, 524

   Save Selection, 521

Text menu

   Convert to Outlines, 255

   Effect submenu, 266

Type menu

   Create Outlines, 253, 277

   Linear, 293

   Process, 637

   Radial, 293

Utilities menu

   Define Colors, 637

   Plug-Ins: Pub Info, 683

   Usage, 692

View menu

   Actual Pixels, 373

   Artwork, 548

   Show Rulers, 511

Windows menu

   Panels: Color List, 285

   Panels: Color Mixer, 285

   Panels: Tints, 288

   Show Attributes, 249

   Show Brushes, 375

   Show Swatches, 283

   Swatch Libraries submenu, 283

   Xtras: Operations, 262

Commission Internationale d'Eclairage, 421

communication role for digital prepress, 19-20

compatibility, storage media, 187

compensating, dot gain (halftone scans), 403

   manually, 404-405

   transfer function, 405-406

complementary colors (RGB/CMY color model), 417-419

complementary metal-oxide semiconductor (CMOS) sensors, 339

Completed folder, 160

complex masks, creating, 557

   existing channels, 560-563

   Extract command, 558-559

complex silhouettes, creating, 550-553

complex traps, vector-based, 651

Composite view (Photoshop), 316

composition proofing, 720-721

   creating a mock-up, 721

   formal client approval, 721

   printing laser composites, 720

   printing thumbnails, 720

compound masks (Illustrator), 252

compound paths, 247-248

   combining separate shapes, 248

   creating in Freehand, 249-250

   creating in Illustrator, 249

   editing customized type, 248

   facilitating merge commands, 248

   punching holes in shapes, 248

   versus grouped items, 247

Compound Paths: Make command (Object menu), 249

Compound Paths: Release command (Object menu), 249

compressed air, 369

Computer Ready Electronic Files (CREF), 675

computer role for digital prepress, 19

computer technology, 25

   MacOS versus Windows 98, 26-29

   Windows NT, 29-30

concepting

   conventional prepress, 10

   digital prepress, 13

consistency of color, color page proofs, 727

Context box, 256

contract proofs, 721

contrast, 453

  adjusting (halftone scans), 395-400

  press check, 731

  scatter proofs, 726

Contrast curves, 399-400

Control Panels, 85

  appearance, 86

  ColorSync, 87

  general controls, 87

  installing software, 98

  memory, 87

    Disk Cache, 88

    RAM Disk, 89

    Virtual Memory, 88

  monitors and sounds, 89

conventional prepress, 10

  concepting and design, 10

  image acquisition, 11-12

  page composition and paste-up, 12

  proofing and revising, 12-13

  stripping and imposition, 12

  typesetting, 11

Convert Custom Colors to Process option (Trap dialog box), 651

Convert to Outlines command (Edit menu), 255

converting

  Background layer to Image layer, 530

  colors between ink types (vector-based objects), 290

    FreeHand, 290

    Illustrator, 290

  images into CMYK components, 431-432

    black highlight, 435

    black ink limit, 435-436

    CMYK conversion setups, 436-437

    dot gain, 433-434

    GCR, 434-435

    ICC option, 432-433

    ink colors, 433

    non-standard printing inks, 437-439

    Tables option, 433

    total ink limit, 436

    UCA amount, 436

    UCR, 434

  paths to selections, 545-546

  RGB to CMYK, color scanning, 451-452

  selections to paths, 546

  type to paths, 275-277

    FreeHand, 277-278

    Illustrator, 277

CoolScan III (Nikon), 339

Copy Attributes command (Edit menu), 281

Copy menu commands, All Linked Files, 683

copying

  InDesign preferences, 582

  layers from image to image, 532

  PageMaker preferences, 579

  QuarkXPress preferences, 576-577

CorelDRAW, 701

Corner Point button, 246

correcting color, 470

  adjusting non-neutral colors, 485-492

  gray balance and color casts, 472-475

  identifying endpoints, 475-476

  neutralization in practice, 483-485

  setting neutral endpoints, 477-483

  shadows and highlights, 471-472

cost-per-megabyte, 183

course outlines, 49

CPUs (central processing units), 25

crashes, superfluous Extensions, 83

Create Gradient Mesh command (Object menu), 295

Create New Channel button, 560

Create New Layer button, 528

Create Outlines command (Type menu), 253, 277

Create Package Folder dialog box, 684

creating

  clipping paths, 555-557

  color range selections, 518-520

  complex masks, 557

    existing channels, 560-563

    Extract command, 558-559

  complex silhouettes, 550-553

  compound paths in Freehand, 249-250

  compound paths in Illustrator, 249

  ghosted images, 535-536

    resizable, 536-537

  layer masks, 537

  layer-based selections, 520

  layers, 528

  masks in FreeHand, 254

    adding items, 256-257

    character masks, 255

coloring masked elements, *255*

moving masked items, *255*

releasing, *257*

selecting masked items, *255*

transforming, *256*

masks in Illustrator, 251-252

character masks, *252-253*

coloring masked elements, *252*

compound masks, *252*

locking, *251*

releasing, *254*

selecting masked items, *252*

mock-ups (proofing), 721

Quick Mask selection, 513-514

simple silhouettes, 549-550

tints (vector-based objects), 287

FreeHand, 288

Illustrator, 287-288

vignettes, 538-539

work environment, 23-24

hardware, 24-42

software, 42-47

CREF (Computer Ready Electronic Files), 675

crooked scans, straightening, 503-504

Crop command (Image menu), 508

Crop Marks box, 710

Crop option (FreeHand Combine), 263

Crop option (Illustrator Pathfinders), 261

Crop tool, 374, 385, 503

cropping

glares, halftone scans, 385-386

graphics

page design, 622-623

problems with, 623

line art scan images, 374-376

scans, 502

applying Crop command, 503

applying levels-based adjustments, 504-506

canceling, 503

repositioning, 503

resizing, 503

rotating, 503

straightening a crooked scan, 503-504

CrossFont, 119

crossovers, 586

color page proofs, 728

master pages, 617

press check, 731

CTS (carpal tunnel syndrome), 69

Curie point, 200

curve handles, 241-242

curved paths

drawing in FreeHand, 245-246

adding points, 246-247

deleting points, 247

drawing in Illustrator, 242-243

adding points, 244

deleting points, 244

curves

adjusting contrast of halftone scans, 395

adjustment points, 397-398

Channel Pop-Up, 395

Contrast curves, 399-400

Gamma curves, 398-399

Input/Output Fields, 398

Point/Pencil Tools, 398

Tonal Graph, 396-397

Values Gradient, 396

Bézier, 238-239

curve handles, 241-242

drawing curved paths in FreeHand, 245-247

drawing curved paths in Illustrator, 242-244

points and segments, 239-240

straight-line paths, 240-241

transfer, 405

Curves command (Photoshop), color adjustment tool, 460

RGB versus CMYK adjustments, 461-463

targeting colors, 463-464

Curves dialog box, 393

custom fills, vector-based objects, 291

gradients, 291-297

patterns, 298-299

Custom Stroke dialog box, 664

customized type, editing with compound paths, 248

customizing system, 81

Cut command (Edit menu), 253

Cut Contents command (Edit menu), 257

D

DAT, 202

data servers, 211

Datahand, 75

DataViz, MacLink Plus, 601

de Casteljau, Paul (engineer for Citro), 238

deactivating fonts (ATM Deluxe), 136

default colors (vector-based objects), 281

black, 282

none and white, 281-282

registration output, 282-283

default endpoint values, 477-479

default value (Trapping), 664

Defaults file, 582

Define Colors command (Utilities menu), 637

Define Colors dialog box, 637

defining colors (vector-based objects), 283

creating Color List in FreeHand, 285-286

creating Color List in Illustrator, 283

Delete Anchor Point tool, 244

Delete Current Layer button, 532

Delete key, 244

deleting

layers, 532

points from curved paths in FreeHand, 247

points from curved paths in Illustrator, 244

unnecessary colors (vector-based objects), 288

FreeHand, 289-290

Illustrator, 289

unwanted pixels (silhouette touch up), 554-555

Deneba Canvas, 702

densitometers, 344, 383, 455

density. *See* dynamic range

density ink, 641

descreening function (scanner software), 345

descreening software, 334

Deselect command (Select menu), 558

design

conventional prepress, 10

digital prepress, 13-14

color corrector, 16-17

designer, 14

Illustrator, 15

output specialist, 17

production specialist, 15

scanner operator, 16

pages, 619

cropping graphics, 622-623

importing graphics, 619

rotating graphics, 622

scaling graphics, 620-622

stacking graphics, 624-625

project costs, 222

desks, 72

desktop rebuilding, 96

Desktop Color Separation (DCS) file, 171

Desktop file, 96

Desktop settings (Fonts), 86

Despeckle filter, 502

destination profiles, 424

detail

color quality, 452

radius and threshold, 467

scatter proofs, 726

detailed line art, 377

applying Threshold command, 378-379

converting to Bitmap mode, 379-380

saving the image, 380

scanning in grayscale mode, 377

sharpening the image, 378

device-independent model, 421

dialog boxes

Add to Color List, 285

Black Generation, 435

Clipping Path, 556

CMYK Setup, 432

Collect for Output, 681

Color Range, 516

Create Package Folder, 684

Curves, 393

Custom Stroke, 664

Define Colors, 637

Edit Colors, 636

EPS Options, 406

Export Document, 302

Extract, 550

Fill and Stroke, 663

Font Matching Results, 693

General, 235

Image Size, 498

Ink Colors, 438

Ink Setup, 666

Load Selection, 524

Make Layer, 530

Make Work Path, 546

Missing Profile, 443-444

New Swatch, 283

Preferences, 352

Preflight, 695

Print, 236

Printing Information, 684

Profile Mismatch, 443-444

Profile Setup

   Assumed Profiles option, 442

   Embed Profiles option, 441

   Profile Mismatch Handling option, 442

Quick Mask Options, 512

Rasterize, 306

Rasterize EPS Format, 308

Save a Copy, 532

Save As, 302

Swatches Option, 288

Threshold, 475

TIFF Options, 376

Trap Specifications, 656

Trapping Preferences, 664

Units and Undo, 235

Unsharp Mask, 467

Usage, 692

diffuse highlights, 390

digital cameras, 340-341

   instant-capture models, 341

   scanning-back models, 341

digital color proofs, 723-724

digital prepress, 13

   concepting, 13

   design and production, 13-14

      color corrector, 16-17

      designer, 14

      Illustrator, 15

      output specialist, 17

      production specialist, 15

      scanner operator, 16

   proofing and revising, 17-18

roles and expectations, 18

   changing trends, 20-21

   communication, 19-20

   computers, 19

   troubleshooting, 20

Direct Selection tool, 242

disinfectant, 92

Disk Cache settings, 88

disk drives

   backups, 167

   history of, 178

   media dexterity, 177

   media dexterity stations, 205

   RAID, 194

   reformatting for optimization, 78-80

   rotational speed, 181

   SCSI, 192

   seek time, 181

   transfer rates, 182

Disk First Aid, 96

disk utilities, 97

Display and Cursors panel (Photoshop's Preferences)

   Color Channels in Color (Off) option, 355-356

   Other Cursors (Standard) option, 357

   Painting Cursors (Precise) option, 356

   Use System Palette (Off) option, 356

   Video LUT Animation (On) option, 356

display profiles, 424

Distiller, watched folders, 157

Divide option (FreeHand Combine), 262

Divide option (Illustrator Pathfinders), 259

DLT, 202

   archiving drives, 169

Document button, 706

Document Pop-Up options (saving selections), 522

document preferences, 351, 568

   QuarkXPress, 571-573

      Line Tool, 573

      Picture Box Tools, 573

      Text Box Tool, 574

documents

   local formatting, 601

   MS Word in page layout, 600

   setup, 582

      adding pages, 586

      multi-page spreads, 587

      page dimensions, 583-585

      spreads, 585-587

dot gain, 328, 381

   compensating (halftone scans), 403

      transfer function, 405-406

   converting images into CMYK components, 433-434

dot pitch, choosing monitors, 40

dot shapes (halftone screens), 334-335

downloads, file management, 155

dpi resolution (dots-per-inch), 325

draw programs, 231

drawing

   basic paths, 543-545

   tablets, 76

Drive Converter, 80

Drive Setup, 78

drivers, useless Extensions, 84

drum scanners, 340

dry system (proofing), 725

dummy, 712

duotones

defining screen angles, 334

spot color proofing, 730

Duplicate command (Image menu), 536

Dust and Scratches filter, 401

dynamic range, scanners, 343

E

Edge Highlighter tool, 551

edge pixels

Polygon Lasso tool, 511

Standard Lasso tool, 510

Edit Color dialog box, 592

Edit in Quick Mask Mode button, 513

Edit in Standard Mode button, 514

Edit menu commands

Colors, 636

Convert to Outlines, 255

Copy Attributes, 281

Cut, 253

Cut Contents, 257

Paste Attributes, 281

Paste Behind, 254

Paste in Front, 254

Paste Inside, 254

Preferences: Document, 653

Select All, 277, 508

Select: Masks, 252

Select: None, 246

Undo, 234, 399

Edit Trap button, 656

editing

customized type, compound paths, 248

existing selection

Quick Mask selection, 514-515

Standard Lasso tool, 509-510

path, 542

continuing existing paths, 545

converting a path to a selection, 545-546

converting a selection to a path, 546

drawing a basic path, 543-545

exchanging paths with Illustrator, 547-548

viewing a path, 545

pixel-based programs, 45

saved selections, 523

Effect submenu (Text menu), 266

Effects: Copy Effects command (Layer menu), 535

Effects: Create Layers command (Layer menu), 534

Effects: Drop Shadow command (Layer menu), 533

Effects: Global Angle command (Layer menu), 534

Effects: Paste Effects command (Layer menu), 535

EIDE ports, 38

Element menu commands

Align, 536

Fill and Stroke, 663

Ellipse tool, 242

Elliptical Marquee tools, 507

email, media dexterity, 216

Embed Profiles option (Profile Setup dialog box), 441

embedded images, collecting for output, 682

embedded profiles, 440

Missing Profile dialog box, 443-444

Profile Mismatch dialog box, 443-444

Profile Setup dialog box

Assumed Profiles option, 442

Embed Profiles option, 441

Profile Mismatch Handling option, 442

emergency startup disk, storage media, 187

employee resources, 55-57

empty layers, adding, 528

emulators, 699

Enable Trapping for Publication box, 664

Encapsulated PostScript file. *See* EPS File Format

Ending Color slider, 293

endpoint placement (scanner software), 345

endpoints, 367

adjusting (halftone scans), 390

resetting, 393-395

color adjustment, 475-476

neutralization in practice, 483-485

setting neutral endpoints, 477-483

manually setting for print (cropping scans), 505-506

enriched black, 282, 634

rich black, 634-636

FreeHand, 640

Illustrator, 639-640

InDesign, 638

PageMaker, 637-638

XPress, 636-637

super black, 641

FreeHand, 644-645

Illustrator, 644

InDesign, 643

PageMaker, 642-643

XPress, 641

entire tonal content, 460

environment

creating consistent viewing environment, 425

influence on color, 413

preparing for scanning, 351-359

EPS artwork, rasterizing, 529

EPS File Format (Encapsulated PostScript file), 301

FreeHand, 302-303

Illustrator, 302

line art, stacking graphics, 624

EPS files, 406

coloring in layout, 595

importing graphics, 304

avoiding Matryoshka, 304-305

scaling restrictions, 304-305

EPS Options dialog box, 406

ergonomics, work environment, 68

eye strain, 77

gloves, 76

keyboards, 74-75

pointing devices, 75

RSI, 68-73

taking breaks, 77

wrist rests, 76

Ethernet, 207-208

hubs, 208

upgrading printers, 701

examining laser separations, 711-712

Excel graphs, saving as PostScript files, 236

exchanging paths with Illustrator, 547-548

Exclude option (Illustrator Pathfinders), 258

expansion bays, 35-36

expansion slots, 36-37

expert sets, 120

Export Clipboard option (General panel of Photoshop's Preferences), 353

Export command (File menu), 302

Export Document dialog box, 302

Export: Paths to Illustrator command (File menu), 300

exporting, 301

EPS File Format, 301

FreeHand, 302-303

Illustrator, 302

Native File Format, 301

Extended format, 79

Extension Manager, selecting unneeded Extensions, 83

Extensions

Adobe Type Reunion, 91

installing software, 98

system recovery, 103

Extensions Manager, 81-83

Extensis (Preflight Pro software), 714

Extensis Suitcase, 122-127

client sets, 132-133

in-house set, 129-131

startup set, 128-130

external hardware, peripherals, 25

Extract command (Image menu), 550

creating complex masks, 558-559

Extract dialog box, 550

extracted silhouettes, touching up, 553

erasing unwanted pixels, 554-555

restoring excluded pixels, 554

eye sight, influence on color, 413

eye strain, 77

Eyedropper color adjustment tool (Photoshop), 458

options, 459

placing color samplers, 459-460

Eyedropper tool, 279

F

Fast Ethernet, 208

Fast/Wide SCSI 2, 192

FAT32, 79

FDISK, 79

Feather command (Select menu), 520

feathered edges (Quick Mask command technique), 515

file extensions, naming conventions, 170

file formats

conversion utilities, 601

Word, 599

file management, 149-152
  Application folder, 152-154
  archiving, 168
  backups, 166
    automatic, 168
    manual, 167
  Internet folder, 155
  Libraries folder, 156
  naming, 170
  offsite storage, 171-173
  opening files over networks, 213
  Personal folder, 158
  storage media, 183
  System folder, 152-153
  To Archive folder, 157
  Type Library folder, 154
  Utilities folder, 156
  watched folders, 157
  work folder, 159-166
File menu commands
  Collect for Output, 681
  Color Settings: CMYK Setup, 431
  Color Settings: Profile Setup, 424
  Color Settings: RGB Setup, 428
  Export, 302
  Export: Paths to Illustrator, 300
  Links Manager, 694
  Open, 308
  Package, 684
  Place, 353, 529
  Preferences, 235
  Preferences: General, 352
  Preferences: Trapping, 664

Save, 281
Save a Copy, 532
Save As, 302
file servers, 209
File Sharing Monitor, useless Extensions, 84
files
  EPS, 406
  InDesign Defaults, 582
  legacy, 424, 440
    Missing Profile dialog box, 443-444
    Profile Mismatch dialog box, 443-444
    Profile Setup dialog box, 441-442
  media dexterity, 175
  PDF, converting PostScript files to, 236
  PPD, 703
  QuarkXPress preferences, 576
  saving line art scans, 376
  transferring with FTP, 218
fill, 278
  applying in FreeHand, 280-281
  applying in Illustrator, 278-280
  InDesign preferences, 581
  PageMaker preferences, 579
Fill and Stroke command (Element menu), 663
Fill and Stroke dialog box, 663
fill color, 647
Fill option (Color palette), 278
film
  cleaner, 369
  output, out-sourcing, 227
film-based laminate proofs, 724-725

Filter menu commands
  Blur: Gaussian Blur, 498
  Noise: Despeckle, 498
  Sharpen: Unsharp Mask, 387
  Sharpen: Unsharpen Mask, 378
filters
  Despeckle, 502
  Dust and Scratch, 401
  Gaussian Blur, 500
  page layout, 600
  Trap, 649
fine detail, 465
FireWire drives, 193
fixed array sensors, 339
flatbed scanners, 338-339
flats, 12
Flatten Image command (Layer menu), 532
flattening layer images, 532
flaws, retouching (halftone scans), 400-401
  Rubber Stamp tool, 402-403
fleshtones
  adjusting non-neutral colors, 488-490
  sharpening, 468-469
FlightCheck software, 714-715
floppy disks, 189
floppy drives, 178
Flow Inside Path button, 268
FM screening (frequency modulated), 335-336
  versus AM screening, 335

folders
  Extensions/Control Panels, 82
  file management
    Application folder, 152-154
    Internet folder, 155
    Libraries folder, 156
    Personal folder, 158
    System folder, 152-153
    To Archive folder, 157
    Type Library folder, 154
    Utilities folder, 156
    watched folders, 157
    work folder, 159-166
  font libraries, 124
  Native Graphics, 164
  Placed Graphics, 165
  Previous Versions, 163
  Project Type, 165
  Raw Scans, 164
  sharing, 212
  Text Files, 164
Font Matching Results dialog box, 693
font utilities, 91
FontAgent, 118
FontLab Developers Group, 120
FontMonger, 119
Fontographer, 119
fonts, 46-47, 107
  activating, 129
  ATM, 114-115
  cataloging, 145
  coloring in page layout, 595
  converting between platforms, 119
    Mac-based, 120
    Windows-based, 119

document reflow in Word, 600
expert sets, 120
file management, 165
Fonts folder, 121-124
hinting, 111
history of, 110-112
including for service bureaus, 137-141
libraries, 116, 118-119
licensing, 144
managing libraries, 126
    ATM Deluxe, 133-136
    Extensis Suitcase, 127-133
naming, 126
organizing libraries, 124-126
outline, 114
outputting, 140
paths, stacking graphics in layout, 625
printing, 144
project reports, 679
QuarkXPress preferences, 575
reviewing in PageMaker documents, 693-694
reviewing in XPress documents, 691
screen, 113
storing on network servers, 143
suitcase files, 113
tracking upgrades, 137-141
TrueType, 112
Type 3, removing, 116
types, 110
vector-based graphics, 236
Fonts Control Panel, optimizing performance, 86
Fonts folder, 121-124

Fonts panel (InDesign's Preflight dialog box), 695-696
footers, master pages, 615
formal client approval, proofing, 719-721
Format menu commands, Illustrator EPS, 302
formats, choosing service providers, 227
FPO images, 171
fragmentation, 97
FrameMaker, 702
frames, QuarkXPress preferences, 572
free-form outlines (Polygon Lasso tool), 511-512
FreeHand, 231
  applying fill and stroke, 280-281
  Combine options, 262
    Crop, 263
    Divide, 262
    Intersect, 263
    Punch, 263
    Union, 262
  combining shapes, 247
  converting colors between ink types, 290
  converting type to paths, 277-278
  creating Color List, 285-286
  creating gradients, 296-297
  creating masks, 254
    adding items, 256-257
    character, 255
    coloring masked elements, 255
    moving masked items, 255

releasing, 257

selecting masked items, 255

transforming, 256

creating tints, 288

deleting unnecessary colors, 289-290

drawing curved paths, 245-246

   adding points, 246-247

   deleting points, 247

importing graphics, 303

   avoiding Matryoshka, 304-305

   scaling restrictions, 304-305

   TIFF and EPS files, 304

patterns (custom fills), 299

RAM allocation, 102

rasterizing, 307

renaming colors, 286

rich black, 640

saving an EPS file, 302-303

scaling graphics, 620

super black, 644-645

type along a path, 269

type around a shape, 270-271

type around both sides of a circle, 274-275

type within a shape, 268

FreeHand Document, 301

freelancers, 61-64

freezes, superfluous Extensions, 83

frequency modulated screening (FM screening), 335-336

fringe, 636

FTP, media dexterity, 217

Full-Screen Documents setting, 569

furniture, 71

Fuzziness Slider option (Color Range command), 517

G

Gamma curves, 397-399

gamma option (RGB workspace), 430

gamut of colors, 422

GATF (Graphic Arts Technical Foundation), 363

gathering information (preflight process stage one), 676-677

   assembling the elements, 679-681

      collecting for output in InDesign, 684-685

      collecting for output in PageMaker, 682-684

      collecting for output in XPress, 681-682

   handing over to service provider, 685-686

   maintaining project report, 677-679

      colors and separation, 679

      detailed page information, 678

      fonts, 679

      graphic files, 678

      output settings, 678

      special notes, 679

   service providers, 686-689

Gaussian Blur, 387

Gaussian Blur command (Filter menu), 498

Gaussian Blur filter, 500

GCR (gray component replacement), 434

   converting images into CMYK components, 434-435

General Controls, 87

General dialog box, 235

General panel (Photoshop's Preferences), 352

   Anti-Alias Postscript (On) option, 353

   Beep When Done (Off) option, 353

   Color Picker option, 352

   Export Clipboard option, 353

   Interpolation (Bicubic) option, 352-353

   Save Palette Locations (On) option, 354

   Short PANTONES Names (On) option, 353

   Show Tool Tips (On) option, 353

general preferences

   InDesign, 580-582

   PageMaker, 576-579

ghosted images, creating, 535-536

   resizable, 536-537

ghosting, press check, 731

Gigabit Ethernet, 208

glares, cropping halftone scans, 385-386

glass cleaner, 369

gloves, 76

Gradient palette, 293

gradients, 291-292

   banding, 292

   creating in FreeHand, 296-297

   creating in Illustrator, 293-295

linear, 291

mesh issues, 295-296

radial, 291

Graphic Arts Technical Foundation (GATF), 363

graphic files (project reports), 678

graphics

cards, 40-41

cropping for pages, 622-623

file management, 164-165

importing, 303

avoiding Matryoshka, 304-305

scaling restrictions, 304-305

TIFF and EPS files, 304

importing into pages, 619

PageMaker preferences, 578

reviewing in PageMaker documents, 694-695

reviewing in XPress documents, 692-693

rotating for pages, 622

scaling for pages, 620-622

stacking in pages, 624-625

vector-based, 231-235

Bézier curves, 238-247

features, 233-234

fonts and font characters, 236

graphs, 236

limitations, 236-237

logos, 235

programs, 44-45

refining traced images, 235

stylized typefaces, 235

Graphics menu commands, Normal, 707

graphs

Excel, saving as PostScript files, 236

vector-based graphics, 236

gray balance color

adjustment, 472

reading CMYK neutrals, 473-475

reading RGB neutrals, 473-474

quality, 454

gray component replacement. See GCR

grayscale

scanning line art, 377

testing scans, 362

compensating for lost highlights and shadows, 367-368

evaluating tonal range, 364-367

setting right scanning mode, 363

Grayscale mode (8-bit Color), 317-318

Group command (Object menu), 273

grouped items versus compound paths, 247

H

half-cast removals, 484-485

halftone dots, 313, 326

constructing with printer dots, 330

establishing cell size

lpi, 327-329

pixel values, 329

resolution requirements, 324

halftone screens, 325-326

angles, 332-334

dot shapes, 334-335

frequency modulated, 335-336

halftone dots, 326

constructing with printer dots, 330

establishing cell size via lpi, 327-329

establishing cell size via pixel values, 329

halftones

reducing moiré, 497-498

scaling pixel graphics, 621

scanning, 380-382

acquiring the scan, 384

adjusting contrast, 395-400

adjusting endpoints, 390-395

assessing original image, 382-383

assessing the scan, 384-385

compensating for dot gain, 403-406

cropping glares, 385-386

previewing, adjusting, and measuring scan, 383-384

retouching any flaws, 400-403

reviewing and saving, 407

sharpening the image, 386-389

halos (pixels), 389

hand-held scanning devices, 338

hands-on training, 50

Hard Disk Toolkit, 78

hard drives, Virtual Memory, 88

hard edges (Quick Mask command technique), 515

hardware, 24-35

  computer technology, 25

    MacOS versus Windows 98, 26-29

    Windows NT, 29-30

  expansion bays, 35-36

  expansion slots, 36-37

  monitors, 38-39

    accelerated graphics cards, 40-41

    adding second monitor, 41-42

    viewable image size, 39-40

  peripherals, 25

  ports, 37-38

  processors, 30-31

    choosing, 32

    upgradeable, 32-33

  RAM, 33

    determining amount, 34

    purchasing, 34-35

  requirements, outputting the proofs (preflight process), 698

    CPU and storage, 701

    laser printers, 698-701

headers, master pages, 615

HFS+, 79

hickeys, press check, 731

Hide Edges command (Select menu), 562

hiding layers, 531

highlights

  clipped, 365

  color adjustment, 471-472

  grayscale scans, 367-368

  scatter proofs, 726

hinting, 111

Histogram command (Image menu), 364

History Brush tool, 554

hot points, 269

How, 54

HSB color model (hue, saturation, and brightness), 420-421

Hubs (Ethernet), 208

hue (color), 420

human resources, 55

  employees/co-workers, 55-57

  freelancers, 61-64

  print brokers, 57-59

  print shops, 60-61

  service bureaus, 59-60

  VARs, 64-65

I

ICC option, converting images into CMYK components, 432-433

ICC profiles, 423-425

Icon option (Saving Files panel of Photoshop's Preferences), 354

Icon Size setting, 95

Icon View, 93

IDE drives, 193

Illustrator, 231

  applying fill and stroke, 278-280

  combining shapes, 247

    compound paths, 247-249

  converting colors between ink types, 290

  converting type to paths, 277

  creating Color List, 283

  creating gradients, 293-295

  creating masks, 251-252

    adding items, 253-254

    character masks, 252-253

    coloring masked elements, 252

    compound masks, 252

    locking, 251

    releasing, 254

    selecting masked items, 252

  creating tints, 287-288

  deleting unnecessary colors, 289

  digital prepress design, 15

  drawing curved paths, 242-243

    adding points, 244

    deleting points, 244

  exchanging paths, 547-548

  importing graphics, 303

    avoiding Matryoshka, 304-305

    scaling restrictions, 304-305

    TIFF and EPS files, 304

  Pathfinder options, 257

    Crop, 261

    Divide, 259

    Exclude, 258

    Intersect, 257

    Merge, 260

    Minus Back, 259

    Minus Front, 259

    Outline, 261

    Trim, 260

    Unite, 257

  patterns (custom fills), 298

  RAM allocation, 102

  rasterizing, 306-307

  renaming colors, 286

rich black, 639-640

saving an EPS file, 302

scaling graphics, 620

super black, 644

type along a path, 268-269

type around a shape, 270

type around both sides of a circle, 271-274

type within a shape, 267

Illustrator EPS command (Format menu), 302

iMac, 186

image acquisition, conventional prepress, 11-12

Image Cache panel (Photoshop's Preferences), 358

Cache Levels option, 359

Use Cache for Histograms option, 359

Image layer, 526

converting from Background, 530

opacity, 527-528

transparency, 527

Image menu commands

Adjust: Auto Levels, 394

Adjust: Curves, 393, 399

Adjust: Equalize, 368

Adjust: Levels, 504

Adjust: Threshold, 378, 475

Crop, 508

Duplicate, 536

Extract, 550

Histogram, 364

Image Size, 498

Levels, 391

Mode, 364

Mode: Bitmap, 379

Mode: CMYK Color, 431

Rotate Canvas: Arbitrary, 499

Image Previews option (Saving Files panel of Photoshop's Preferences), 354

image size, choosing monitors, 39

Image Size command (Image menu), 498

Image Size dialog box, 498

images

assessing when scanning halftones, 382-383

blurring (moiré), 500

cropping and cleaning up (line art), 374-376

evaluating (line art), 372

examining the pixels, 373-374

printing test copies, 372

flattening (layers), 532

FPO, 171

ghosted, 535-536

resizable, 536-537

importing, 313

offsite storage, 171-173

sharpening (blurring moiré), 502

sharpening (halftone scans), 386

amount, 387

radius, 388

threshold, 388-389

unsharp masking strate-gies, 389

imagesetters, choosing service providers, 228

imaging

halftone screens, 325-326

dot shapes, 334-335

frequency modulated screens, 335-336

halftone dots, 326-330

screen angles, 332-334

overview of process, 312-314

pixels, 312-314

color modes, 315-320

reading values, 320-323

resolution, 323-325

scanners. *See* scanners

iMation SuperDisk, 190

Imation TrapWise, 630, 668

importing

graphics, 303

avoiding Matryoshka, 304-305

scaling restrictions, 304-305

TIFF and EPS files, 304

images, 313

imposed flats, 12

imposition, 586

In Progress folder, 160

In Proofing folder, 160

Include Composited Image with Layered Files (Off) option (Saving Files panel of Photoshop's Preferences), 355

Include FreeHand Document (EPS box), 303

Include PostScript Error Handler, 708

Include Transfer Functions box, 406

incorrect conversion strategies, 451-452

InDesign

  collecting for output, 684-685

  defining style sheets, 611-614

  document review, 695

    Color and Inks panel, 697

    Fonts panel, 695-696

    Links and Images panel, 696

    Print Settings panel, 697

    Summary panel, 695

  general preferences, 580-582

  laser composites, outputting paper proofs, 709

  laser separations, outputting paper proofs, 710

  master pages, 618

  rich black, 638

  scaling graphics, 620

  separation types, 593

  super black, 643

Indeterminate option (XPress Trapping Preference panel), 654

industry market share, 27

influences on color

  environment, 413

  eyes, 413

  light, 411

Info Palette (Photoshop) color adjustment tool, 455-456

  editing CMYK images, 457-458

  editing RGB images, 457

ink

  black, 633-634

    enriched, 634-645

    overprinting and knock-outs, 645-647

colors, 589

  converting images into CMYK components, 433

  density, 456, 641

  integrity, spot color proofing, 730

  naming colors, 590

  non-standard, 437-439

  selection, spot color proofing, 729

  types, converting colors between, 290

    FreeHand, 290

    Illustrator, 290

Ink Colors dialog box, 438

Ink Setup dialog box, 666

Ink window, 636

input devices, scanners. *See* scanners

input profiles, 424

input sprockets, useless Extensions, 83

Input/Output Fields (curves), 398

inserting

  items to a mask

    FreeHand, 256-257

    Illustrator, 253-254

  points in curved paths

    FreeHand, 246-247

    Illustrator, 244

Insider Software, 118

installing applications, 98

  RAM allocation, 99-102

instant-capture digital cameras, 341

Interactive settings (QuarkXPress), 570

Internet

  cable modems, 215

  FTP, 217

  ISDN, 214

  T1, 215

  training, 54-55

  transmitting data, 217

Internet folder, file management, 155

interpolated resolution, 342

Interpolation (Bicubic) option (General panel of Photoshop's Preferences), 352-353

Intersect option (FreeHand Combine), 263

Intersect option (Illustrator Pathfinders), 257

Intersecting selection outlines (Marquee tools), 508

Inverse command (Select menu), 524

inverting a selection (Quick Mask command technique), 515

Iomega

  Bernoulli drive, 184

  Jaz drives, 197

  Zip drives, 196

ISA expansion slots, 37

ISDN (Integrated Services Digital Network), 214

island spreads, 587

Island Trapper, 668

isolating an image element (layers), 529

J

Jaz drives, 197

  cost-per-megabyte, 183

job tracking, Work folder, 159

Jobs folder

  Native Graphics subfolder, 164

  Placed Graphics subfolder, 165

  Previous Versions subfolder, 163

  Project Type subfolder, 165

  Raw Scans subfolder, 164

  Text Files subfolder, 164

Join command (Modify menu), 249, 255

K

Keep Document Settings button, 691

keepaway (trapping), 636

Kelvin scale, 412

KEs (Keyboard Equivalents), style sheets, 609

keyboards, 74-75

Keyline view, 274

Kingston Web site, 35

Knockout All option (XPress trapping method), 654

Knockout Limit option (XPress Trapping Preference panel), 655

knockouts, 645

  black line art, 646-647

  black type, 646

  colors, 290

knowledge resources, 48

  humans, 55

    employees/co-workers, 55-57

    freelancers, 61-64

    print brokers, 57-59

    print shops, 60-61

    service bureaus, 59-60

    VARs, 64-65

  reference materials, 52

    after-market books, 52-53

    CD-ROMs, 53-54

    Internet, 54-55

    magazines, 54

    videos, 53

  training, 48

    assessing needs, 49

    classroom versus onsite, 50

    determining time formats, 50

    explaining needs, 49

    follow-up availability, 51

    industry ties, 51-52

    requesting client lists, 52

    requesting cours outline, 49

    seeking hands-on training, 50

L

lab color, 456

Lab color model, 421-422

LANs. *See* networks

laser composites

  outputting from InDesign, 709

  outputting from PageMaker, 706-707

  outputting from XPress, 703-704

  printing when proofing, 720

laser printers, requirement for outputting paper proofs (pre-flight process), 698-701

laser separations

  examination, 711-712

  outputting from InDesign, 710

  outputting from PageMaker, 708-709

  outputting from XPress, 704-705

LaserWriters, TrueType fonts, 118

Lasso tools, 509

  Polygon, 511

    edge pixels, 511

    free-form outlines, 511-512

  selecting with Standard Lasso tool, 509

    adding straight edges to free-form selection, 510-511

    edge pixels, 510

    editing existing selection, 509-510

Launcher, useless Extensions, 85

Layer Effects command, 533-534

Layer menu commands

  Add Layer Mask: Reveal Selection, 537

  Effects: Copy Effects, 535

  Effects: Create Layers, 534

  Effects: Drop Shadow, 533

  Effects: Global Angle, 534

  Effects: Paste Effects, 535

  Flatten Image, 532

  New: Adjustment Layer, 540

New: Layer, 528

New: Layer Via Copy, 529

New: Layer Via Cut, 529

Type: Render Layer, 530

layer-based selections, creating, 520

layers, 525-528

adding an empty layer, 528

adjustment, 539-541

masking, 541-542

automatic, 529-530

Background, 525

converting to Image, 530

choosing, 530

copying from image to image, 532

creating, 528

deleting, 532

flattening the image, 532

ghosted images, 535-536

resizable, 536-537

hiding and revealing, 531

Image, 526

converting from Background, 530

opacity, 527-528

transparency, 527

isolating an image element, 529

Layer Effects command, 533-534

linking, 531

masks, 537

creating, 537

unlinking, 538

reordering, 531

vignettes, 538-539

Layers Palette, 520

layout

documents

job folders, 162

naming conventions, 170

proofing, 720-721

creating a mock-up, 721

formal client approval, 721

printing laser composites, 720

printing thumbnails, 720

LeafScan 45 (Scitex), 339

legacy files, 424, 440

Missing Profile dialog box, 443-444

Profile Mismatch dialog box, 443-444

Profile Setup dialog box

Assumed Profiles option, 442

Embed Profiles option, 441

Profile Mismatch Handling option, 442

Level 1, 2, 5 RAIDs, 195

Levels command (Image menu), 391

libraries

fonts

maintaining, 116-119

managing, 126-136

organizing, 124-126

folder, file management, 156

licensing fonts, 144

lights, influence on color, 411

limitations

automatic trapping (XPress), 655-656

vector-based graphics, 236

drawing by hand, 237

extremely complex images, 237

page layout, 237

photo-realistic images, 237

line art

black, overprinting and knockouts, 646-647

coloring in page layout, 597

preparing detailed line art, 377

applying Threshold command, 378-379

converting to Bitmap mode, 379-380

saving the image, 380

scanning in grayscale mode, 377

sharpening the image, 378

resolution requirements, 323

scanning, 370

acquiring the scan, 372

cropping and cleaning up image, 374-376

evaluating the image, 372-374

previewing the scan, 371

saving the file, 376

setting appropriate resolution, 371

setting scanning mode to Line Art, 370

stacking graphics, 624

testing scans, 360-362

line of demarcation. *See* threshold

Line Tool preferences, 573

linear array, 339

Linear command (Type menu), 293

linear frequency (resolution), 323

linear gradients, 291

lines

  coloring in page layout, 596

  PageMaker preferences, 579

  QuarkXPress preferences, 573

  straight, 240-241

  trapping in XPress, 662

lines-per-inch (lpi), halftone dot size, 327-329

linescreen values (resolution), 324-329

linking

  layers, 531

  PageMaker preferences, 578

Links and Images panel (InDesign's Preflight dialog box), 696

Links Manager command (File menu), 694

List View, 93

Load Channel as Selection button, 523

Load Selection command (Select menu), 524

Load Selection dialog box, 524

loading saved selections, 523-525

local formatting, 601

local override, 618

LocalTalk, 206

locking masks in Illustrator, 251

logos, 235

lpi (lines-per-inch), 327-329

LUT (look-up table), 421

  Video LUT Animation (On) option, 356

LZW Compression box, 376

M

MacDraw, 231, 701

machine dots, 330

MacLink Plus, 601

MacOS

  Control Panels, 85

    appearance, 86

    ColorSync, 87

    General Controls, 87

    Memory, 87-89

    Monitors and Sounds, 89

  converting fonts for Windows, 120

  Desktop file, 96

  Extended format, 79

  Extensions Manager, 81-83

  Fonts folder, 121-124

  identifying TrueType fonts, 117

  managing fonts

    ATM Deluxe, 133-136

    Extensis Suitcase, 127-133

  neutral gray background, 86

  System folder, file management, 152

  versus Windows 98, 26-29

MacPaint, 231

Macromedia Fontographer, 119, 236

Macromedia Freehand. *See* FreeHand

MacWrite, 231

magazines, training, 54

magnetic media, 188

  ATA drives, 193

  Castlewood ORB, 197

  floppies, 189

  Iomega Jaz, 197

  Iomega Zip, 196

  RAID, 194

  SCSI hard drives, 192

  SuperDisk, 190

  USB/FireWire drives, 193

magnetic tape, 202

magneto-optical media

  MO, 3.5-inch, 200

  MO, 5.25-inch, 201

maintaining project reports (preflight process), 677-679

  colors and separation, 679

  detailed page information, 678

  fonts, 679

  graphic files, 678

  output settings, 678

  special notes, 679

maintenance utilities (software), 47

Make Layer dialog box, 530

make ready, check press, 730

Make Work Path dialog box, 546

managing font libraries, 126

manual

  application of simple traps, 647-649

  backups, 167

  compensation for dot gain, 404-405

  tracing of pixel-based images, 299-300

  trapping (PageMaker), 663-664

Map, useless Extensions, 85

mapping scanner beds, 368-369

marking proofs for revisions, 728-729

Markzware (FlightCheck software), 714-715

Marquee tools, 507-508

Elliptical, 507

intersecting selection outlines, 508

Rectangular, 507

strategies, 508-509

mask channels, 521

Mask: Lock command (Object menu), 252

Mask: Make command (Object menu), 251-252

Mask: Unlock command (Object menu), 252

masking adjustment layers, 541-542

masks, 247-250

complex, creating, 557-563

FreeHand, 254

adding items, 256-257

character masks, 255

coloring masked elements, 255

moving masked items, 255

releasing, 257

selecting masked items, 255

transforming, 256

Illustrator, 251-252

adding items, 253-254

character masks, 252-253

coloring masked elements, 252

compound masks, 252

locking, 251

releasing, 254

selecting masked items, 252

layers, 537

creating, 537

unlinking, 538

master file, 171

master pages, 615-616

InDesign, 618

local override, 618

PageMaker, 618

QuarkXPress, 617

Matryoshka, avoiding when importing graphics, 304-305

measuring

halftone scans, 383-384

light, 411-412

media dexterity, 175-177

history of, 177-179

Internet

cable modems, 215

ISDN, 214

T1, 215

media types, 187

magnetic, 188-197

magnetic tape, 202

magneto-optical, 200-201

optical, 198-199

modems, 213-215

email, 216

FTP, 217

POTS, 214

networks, 206

connectivity, 212

Ethernet, 207-208

LocalTalk, 206

servers, 209-211

sharing resources, 212

working off network, 213

selecting appropriate media, 179

manufacturer reputation, 179

market penetration, 184-187

product performance, 180-184

standardizing in-house devices, 203

stations, 204

media life, 184

megahertz (MHz), 31

memory

colors, 414-415

quality, 454-455

scratch disk space, 80

Memory Control Panel, 87

Disk Cache, 88

RAM Disk, 89

Virtual Memory, 88

merge commands, compound paths, 248

Merge option (Illustrator Pathfinders), 260

merging shapes, 257

FreeHand's Combine options, 262-263

Illustrator's Pathfinder options, 257-261

mesh objects, gradients, 295-296

MHz (megahertz), 31

Microsoft. See Excel; Office; Word

Minimum Size setting, 101

Minus Back option (Illustrator Pathfinders), 259

Minus Front option (Illustrator Pathfinders), 259

misregistered inks, 627

misregistration, press check, 731

Missing Fonts alert, 691

Missing Profile dialog box, 443-444

Mixer palette, 285

MO drives (magneto-optical)

3.5-inch, 200

5.25-inch, 201

Mode command (Image menu), 364

Mode: Bitmap command (Image menu), 379

Mode: CMYK Color command (Image menu), 431

Model menu commands

CMYK, 637

Multi Ink, 641

modems, media dexterity, 213-215

email, 216

FTP, 217

POTS, 214

Modify menu commands

Combine submenu, 262

Join, 249, 255

Rasterize, 307

Split, 250

Ungroup, 247

moiré, 496

blurring, 500

blurring the image, 500

color channels, 501-502

reducing resolution, 502

scanning at twice the normal resolution, 500

sharpening the image, 502

halftone screen angles, 334

reducing in a scanned halftone, 497-498

rotation, 499

scatter proofs, 727

Monitor RGB option (RGB pop-up menu), 429

monitors, 38-39

accelerated graphics cards, 40-41

adding a second one, 41-42

additional color features, 40

calibrating, 426

characterizing, 426-427

colors, 415

compensation (RGB workspace), 431

dot pitch, 40

dots-per-inch (dpi), 325

pixels-per-inch (ppi), 324-325

resolution, 40

samples-per-inch (spi), 325

spots-per-inch (spi), 325

viewable image size, 39

Monitors and Sounds Control Panel, 89

mouse, reducing RSI, 75

moving masks in FreeHand, 255

multi-sync monitors, 40, 90

Multiple Master Typefaces, 121

N

naming

colors, 590-591

colors (vector-based objects), 286

renaming in FreeHand, 286

renaming in Illustrator, 286

files, file management, 170

fonts, 126

image files, 161

National Television Standards Committee, 430

Native File Format, 301

Native Graphics folder, 164

native resolution, 325

negatives, 314

networks

media dexterity, 176, 206

connectivity, 212

Ethernet, 207-208

LocalTalk, 206

servers, 209-211

sharing resources, 212

working off network, 213

RAIDs, 195

servers, storing fonts, 143

storage media, standardizing, 204

neutral endpoints

setting, 477

default endpoint values, 477-479

neutral endpoint values, 479-482

neutral midtones, 482-483

values, 479-482

neutral gray background, 86

neutral midtones, 482-483

New Swatch dialog box, 283

New: Adjustment Layer command (Layer menu), 540

New: Layer command (Layer menu), 528

New: Layer Via Copy command (Layer menu), 529

New: Layer Via Cut command (Layer menu), 529

newsletters, examples of quality, 225

newsprint

GCR printing, 437

UCR printing, 437

No Style option, 605

Noise: Despeckle command (Filter menu), 498

Non-Global box, 290

non-neutral colors, adjusting, 485-487

blue sky, 490-491

common color components, 492

fleshtones, 488-490

non-standard printing inks, converting images into CMYK components, 437-439

None, blends, 293

none color (default color), 281-282

Normal command (Graphics menu), 707

normal detail, 465

Normal style sheet, 575

NTSC option (RGB pop-up menu), 430

O

Object Inspector palette, 246

Object menu commands

Arrange: Bring to Front, 251

Compound Paths: Make, 249

Compound Paths: Release, 249

Create Gradient Mesh, 295

Group, 273

Mask: Lock, 252

Mask: Make, 251-252

Mask: Unlock, 252

Rasterize, 296, 306

object-to-object trapping (XPress), 658-659

lines and bézier curves, 662

picture boxes, 661

text boxes, 660-661

text paths, 662-663

OCR (optical character recognition), 338

scanner software, 345

off-machine proofing, 725

Office 98 word processor, 44

Office 2000 word processor, 44

offsite storage, 171-173

On Hold folder, 160

onscreen fonts (ATM), 114

onsite training, 50

opacity, 457

Image layer, 527-528

Opacity option (Quick Mask command), 513

Open command (File menu), 308

open paths, 239

operating system (OS), 25

Operations options (saving selections), 522-523

optical character recognition. *See* OCR

optical media, 198

CD-R, 198, 200

CD-RW, 199

optical resolution, 325

optimizing

systems

customizing, 81

formatting disk drives, 78-80

installing, 81

MacOS Control Panels, 85-89

MacOS Extensions Manager, 81-83

work environment, ergonomics, 68

ORB drive, 197

orientation, scatter proofs, 727

OS (operating system), 25

Other Cursors (Standard) option (Display and Cursors panel of Photoshop's Preferences), 357

out-sourcing, 226

outline fonts, 114

Outline option (Illustrator Pathfinders), 261

output

commands, colors, 590

fonts, 140

FPO images, 171

profiles, 424

reliability, 28

request form, service providers, 686-689

list of people completed by, 686-687

requirements, 687-689

settings (project reports), 678

specialist, digital prepress design, 17

tab, 704

values, reading pixel values, 321

outputting paper proofs (preflight process stage three), 698-702

laser composites

  InDesign, 709

  PageMaker, 706-707

  XPress, 703-704

laser separations

  InDesign, 710

  PageMaker, 708-709

  XPress, 704-705

necessary hardware, 698

  CPU and storage, 701

  laser printer, 698-701

necessary software, 701-702

Overprint box, 647

Overprint Limit option (XPress Trapping Preference panel), 655

overprinting, 645

black line art, 646-647

black type, 646

colors, 290

P

Package command (File menu), 684

page composition, conventional prepress, 12

page information (project reports), 678

Page Information box, 710

page layout, 565-567

budgeting pages, 586

colors, 588

  applying, 594-597

  choosing, 589

defining, 590

naming, 590-591

separations, 592

separations in InDesign, 593

separations in PageMaker, 593

separations in QuarkXPress, 592

spot/process, 588

crossovers, 586

designing pages, 619

  cropping graphics, 622-623

  importing graphics, 619

  rotating graphics, 622

  scaling graphics, 620-622

  stacking graphics, 624-625

document setup, 582

  adding pages, 586

  multi-page spreads, 587

  page dimensions, 583-585

  spreads, 585-587

Facing Pages, 585

imposition, 586

master pages, 615-616

  InDesign, 618

  local override, 618

  PageMaker, 618

  QuarkXPress, 617

programs, 265-266

  trapping tools, 651-666

setting preferences, 568

  document/application, 568

  InDesign, 580-582

  PageMaker, 576-579

  QuarkXPress, 569-577

software, 45-46

text, 598

  converting to type, 601-602

  MS Word, 600-601

  style sheets, 602-614

page numbering, master pages, 616

PageMaker

collecting for output, 682-684

coloring EPS files, 595

defining style sheets, 609-611

document review, 693

  fonts, 693-694

  graphics, 694-695

general preferences, 576-579

laser composites, outputting paper proofs, 706-707

laser separations, outputting paper proofs, 708-709

master pages, 618

MS Word filter, 600

rich black, 637-638

scaling graphics, 620

separation types, 593

super black, 642-643

trapping tools, 663-666

  automatic trapping, 664-666

  manual traps, 663-664

Pages Palette, island spreads, 587

pagination, color page proofs, 728

paint programs, 231

Painting Cursors (Precise) option (Display and Cursors panel of Photoshop's Preferences), 356

PAL/SECAM option (RGB pop-up menu), 429

palettes

Brushes, 375

Character, 273

Color, 252, 278

Gradient, 293

Mixer, 285

Object Inspector, 246

Paragraph, 270

Pathfinder, 257

Swatches, 279

Tints, 288

Transform, 256

Panels: Color List command (Windows menu), 285

Panels: Color Mixer command (Windows menu), 285

Panels: Tints command (Windows menu), 288

PANTONE

defining tints, 597

naming colors, 590

spot versus process color, 589

swatchbooks, 589

Paper button, 706

paper size, upgrading printers, 700

Paragraph palette, 270

paragraph styles, 603

Partition Magic, 80

partitioning disk drives, 80

Paste Attributes command (Edit menu), 281

Paste Behind command (Edit menu), 254

Paste in Front command (Edit menu), 254

Paste Inside command (Edit menu), 254

paste-up, conventional pre-press, 12

Pasteboard XT, 570

Pasteboard XTerminator, 570

path editing, 542

continuing existing paths, 545

converting a path to a selection, 545-546

converting a selection to a path, 546

drawing a basic path, 543-545

exchanging paths with Illustrator, 547-548

viewing a path, 545

Path Type tool, 268

Pathfinder options (Illustrator), 257

Crop, 261

Divide, 259

Exclude, 258

Intersect, 257

Merge, 260

Minus Back, 259

Minus Front, 259

Outline, 261

Trim, 260

Unite, 257

Pathfinder palette, 257

paths, 239

clipping, creating, 555-557

closed, 239

compound, 247-248

combining separate shapes, 248

creating in FreeHand, 249-250

creating in Illustrator, 249

editing customized type, 248

facilitating merge commands, 248

punching holes in shapes, 248

converting type to, 275-277

FreeHand, 277-278

Illustrator, 277

curved

FreeHand, 245-247

Illustrator, 242-244

open, 239

stacking grapics in layout, 625

type along in FreeHand, 269

type along in Illustrator, 268-269

pattern brushes, 298

patterns (custom fills), 298

FreeHand, 299

Illustrator, 298

PCI expansion slots, 37

PDF files

converting PostScript files to, 236

MS Word documents, 601

Pen tool, 240

Pencil tool, 375

curves, 398

performance

Application folder, 153

Desktop file, 96

Fonts folder, 122

optimizing systems, 86

print servers, 210

RAID, 194

selecting appropriate storage media, 180

Virtual Memory, 89

peripherals, 25

Personal folder, file management, 158

phonorecord copyright symbol,
236

photo wipes, 369

photomultiplier tubes (PMT
sensors), 340

Photoshop

allocating RAM, 99

cropping, 623

Curves command (color
adjustment tool), 460

*RGB versus CMYK adjust-
ments, 461-463*

targeting colors, 463-464

DCS, 173

Eyedropper (color adjustment
tool), 458

options, 459

*placing color samplers,
459-460*

FPOs, 172

Info Palette (color adjustment
tool), 455-456

*adjusting RGB images,
457*

*editing CMYK images,
457-458*

line art files, overprinting,
646

rasterizing, 307-308

setting Preferences for scanning, 351-352

*Display and Cursors
panel, 355-357*

General panel, 352-354

*Image Cache panel,
358-359*

*Plug-Ins and Scratch
Disk panel, 357-358*

*Saving Files panel,
354-355*

Silhouettes, stacking graphics
in layout, 624

trapping tools, 666-667

Unsharp Mask Filter (color
adjustment tool), 464-465

*channel-based sharpen-
ing, 467-469*

*evaluating and sharpen-
ing detail, 465-467*

*sharpening selected areas,
469*

phototypesetting, 11

Picker button, 439

picking, press check, 731

Picture Box Tools, document
preferences, 573

picture boxes, trapping in
XPress, 661

Pictures tab, 692

pirating fonts, 145

pixel depth, 315

paint programs, 231

versus bit depth, 316

pixel-based editing programs,
45

pixel-based images, 232

coloring in layout, 595

scaling, 621

tracing, 299

automatically, 300-301

manually, 299-300

pixels, 231-314

artifacts, 389

color modes, 315-316

Bitmap, 317

choosing, 320

CMYK, 319

color channels, 316

Grayscale, 317-318

pixel depth, 315-316

RGB, 317-319

examining when evaluating
images, 373-374

halos, 389

rasterizing, 305-306

FreeHand, 307

Illustrator, 306-307

Photoshop, 307-308

reading values, 320-323

brightness levels, 320-321

output values, 321

remapping, 395

resolution, 231, 323-324

dots-per-inch (dpi), 325

*monitor pixels-per-inch
(ppi), 324-325*

*requirements for halftones,
324*

*requirements for line art,
323*

*samples-per-inch (spi),
325*

spots-per-inch (spi), 325

values, establishing halftone
dot size, 329

Place command (File menu),
353, 529

Placed Graphics folder, 165

placing color samplers
(Eyedropper tools), 459-460

platforms, 25

MacOS versus Windows 98,
26-29

Windows NT, 29-30

Plug-and-Play, 29

plug-ins, 357

Plug-Ins and Scratch Disk
panel (Photoshop's
Preferences), 357

Plug-Ins Folder option,
357-358

Scratch Disk option, 358

Plug-Ins Folder option (Plug-Ins and Scratch Disk panel of Photoshop's Preferences), 357-358

Plug-Ins: Pub Info command (Utilities menu), 683

PMT sensors (photomultiplier tubes), 340

Point tool (curves), 398

Pointer tool, 242

pointing devices, 75

points, 239-240

   adding to curved paths

      FreeHand, 246-247

      Illustrator, 244

   deleting from curved paths

      FreeHand, 247

      Illustrator, 244

Polygon Lasso tool, 511

   edge pixels, 511

   free-form outlines, 511-512

ports, 37-38

posterization, 331

PostScript

   code, 232

   converting files to PDF files, 236

   emulators, 699

   fonts, 110

      printer, 114

      screen, 113

   Level 2 or 3 (upgrading printers), 699

   rotated graphics, 622

   troubleshooting, 712-713

      billing practices, 713-714

posture, 70

POTS modem, 214

PPD files, 703

ppi resolution (pixels-per-inch), 324-325

PRAM, zapping, 104

preemptive multitasking, 30

preferences

   page layout, 568

      document/application, 568

      InDesign, 580-582

      PageMaker, 576-579

      QuarkXPress, 569-577

   Photoshop, setting for scanning, 351-352

      Display and Cursors panel, 355-357

      General panel, 352-354

      Image Cache panel, 358-359

      Plug-Ins and Scratch Disk panel, 357-358

      Saving Files panel, 354-355

   XTensions, 571

Preferences command (File menu), 235

Preferences dialog box, 352

Preferences Request alert, 690

Preferences: Document command (Edit menu), 653

Preferences: General command (File menu), 352

Preferences: Trapping command (File menu), 664

Preferred Size setting, 101

Preflight, 165

Preflight dialog box, 695

Preflight Pro software, 714

preflight process, 673

   gathering information, 676-677

      assembling the elements, 679-685

      handing over to service provider, 685-686

      maintain project report, 677-679

      service providers, 686-689

   history, 674-676

   outputting paper proofs, 698-702

      laser composites from InDesign, 709

      laser composites from Pagemaker, 706-707

      laser composites from XPress, 703-704

      laser separations from InDesign, 710

      laser separations from Pagemaker, 708-709

      laser separations from XPress, 704-705

      necessary hardware, 698-701

      necessary software, 701-702

   reviewing the file, 689

      InDesign documents, 695-697

      optimum preflight conditions, 690

      PageMaker documents, 693-695

      XPress documents, 690-693

   software, 714-715

      FlightCheck, 714-715

      Preflight Pro, 714

preparing scanning environment, setting Photoshop's Preferences, 351-352

   Display and Cursors panel, 355-357

   General panel, 352-354

   Image Cache panel, 358-359

   Plug-Ins and Scratch Disk panel, 357-358

   Saving Files panel, 354-355

prepress

conventional, 10

  concepting and design, 10

  image acquisition, 11-12

  page composition and paste-up, 12

  proofing and revising, 12-13

  stripping and imposition, 12

  typesetting, 11

digital, 13

  concepting, 13

  design and production, 13-17

  introduction to, 9-10

  proofing and revising, 17-18

  roles and expectations, 18-21

Prescan function (scanners), 383

Preview tab, 705

previewing

  halftone scans, 383-384

  scans, line art, 371

Previous Versions folder, 163

primaries option (RGB workspace), 430

primary components, 486

Print Blank Pages box, 706

print brokers, 57-59

Print dialog box, 236

print industry focus, 27

print queue, 210

print servers, 210-211

Print Settings panel (InDesign's Preflight dialog box), 697

print shops, 60-61

printer

dots, constructing halftone dots, 330

fonts, 114

marks, color page proofs, 727

resolution

  constructing halftone dots, 330

  linescreen values tolerable before posterization, 332

spreads, 585

printers

choosing, 227-230

laser, requirement for out-putting paper proofs (pre-flight process), 698-701

upgrading, 699

  600 dots per inch (dpi), 700

  Ethernet, 701

  increasing RAM, 700

  paper size, 700

  PostScript Level 2 or 3, 699

useless Extensions, 83

printing

fonts, 144

laser composites (proofing), 720

non-standard inks, 437-439

quality requirements, 223

scaling pixel graphics, 621

test copies when evaluating images, 372

thumbnails (proofing), 720

Printing Information dialog box, 684

Process Black button, 636

process

  bridges (trapping), 631-633

  camera, 12

colors

  naming, 591

  page layout, 588

  trapping option (XPress Trapping Preference panel), 654

Process command (Type menu), 637

Process Cyan button, 637

processors, 30-31

  choosing, 32

  upgradeable, 32-33

  word. *See* word processors

production

  digital prepress, 13-14

  specialist, digital prepress design, 15

Profile Mismatch dialog box, 443-444

Profile Mismatch Handling option (Profile Setup dialog box), 442

Profile Setup dialog box

  Assumed Profiles option, 442

  Embed Profiles option, 441

  Profile Mismatch Handling option, 442

profiles

  display, 424

  input, 424

  output, 424

Programs folder, 152

Project Type folder, 165

projects

  archiving, 169

  job folders, 161-162

  management, 219-221

    assigning responsibilities, 226

    choosing service providers/ printers, 227-230

job requirements, 222-223

page layout, master pages, 615

quality requirements, 223-226

mock-up, 712

planning, 220

proofing

conventional prepress, 12-13

digital prepress, 17-18

loop, Work folder management, 160

proofing methods

checking copies, 718-719

formal client approval, 719

have someone else read it, 719

printing it out, 719

reading aloud, 719

sleeping on it, 719

spellcheck, 718

color, 721-723

color page proofs, 727-728

digital color proofs, 723-724

film-based laminate, 724-725

marking for revisions, 728-729

scatter proofs, 726-727

soft proofing, 723

spot colors, 729-730

wet proofing, 725-726

layout and composition, 720-721

creating a mock-up, 721

formal client approval, 721

printing laser composites, 720

printing thumbnails, 720

press check, 730-732

proportional option (XPress trapping method), 653

protected memory, 30

Punch option (FreeHand Combine), 263

punching holes in shapes, 248

purchasing RAM, 34-35

Q

quality

color, 452

detail, 452

gray balance, 454

memory colors, 454-455

tone, 453

control, preflight process, 673

QuarkXPress

Auto Backup, 163

Collect for Output, 165

collecting for output, 681-682

defining screen angles, 334

defining style sheets, 605-609

document review, 690-691

fonts, 691

graphics, 692-693

laser composites, outputting paper proofs, 703-704

laser separations, outputting paper proofs, 704-705

master pages, 617

MS Word filter, 600

page numbering character, 616

preferences

application, 569-571

copying, 576-577

default colors, 574-575

default fonts, 575

document, 571-574

RAM allocation, 102

rich black, 636-637

scaling graphics, 620

separation types, 592

super black, 641

trapping tools, 652

automatic trapping, 653-656

color-to-color, 656-658

object-to-object, 658-663

QuarkXPress 4.04 page layout program, 45

Quick Mask command, 512

Color Indicates option, 513

Color option, 513

creating a New Quick Mask selection, 513-514

editing existing selection, 514-515

Opacity option, 513

techniques, 515

Quick Mask mode, 512

Quick Mask Options dialog box, 512

QuickDraw 3D, useless Extensions, 84

R

Radial command (Type menu), 293

radial gradients, 291

radius
  detail, 467
  halftone scan image sharp-
    ness, 388
RAID, 194
RAM (random access memory),
  33
  allocating for new software,
    99-102
  determining amount, 34
  Disk Cache, 88
  Disk settings, 89
  increasing when upgrading
    printers, 700
  purchasing, 34-35
random access memory. *See*
  RAM
Rascal Software, 145
Rasterize command (Modify
  menu), 307
Rasterize command (Object
  menu), 296, 306
Rasterize dialog box, 306
Rasterize EPS Format dialog
  box, 308
rasterizing
  EPS artwork, 529
  vectors to pixels, 305-306
    FreeHand, 307
    Illustrator, 306-307
    Photoshop, 307-308
Raw Scans folder, 164
reader spreads, 585
reading
  aloud (proofing), 719
  CMYK neutrals, 473-475
  pixel values, 320-323
    brightness levels, 320-321
    output values, 321
  RGB neutrals, 473-474

readying scanners, 359
  cleaning scanner, 369-370
  mapping scanner beds,
    368-369
  testing grayscale scans, 362
    *compensating for lost
      highlights and shadows,
      367-368*
    *evaluating tonal range,
      364-367*
    *setting right scanning
      mode, 363*
  testing line art scans,
    360-362
rebuilding desktop, 96
recovering from crashes,
  102-105
Rectangular Marquee
  tools, 507
reducing
  resolution (blurring moiré),
    502
  moiré, scanned halftones,
    497-498
redundancy, backups, 167
reference materials, 52
  after-market books, 52-53
  CD-ROMs, 53-54
  Internet, 54-55
  magazines, 54
  videos, 53
refining traced images to
  vector-based graphics, 235
reflected light, 417
reflective
  artwork, flatbed scanners,
    338
  originals (casts), 483
refresh rate, 40
register, 627

registration
  marks, page dimensions, 583
  output (default color),
    282-283
  QuarkXPress preferences,
    575
Registration Marks box, 710
releasing masks
  FreeHand, 257
  Illustrator, 254
remapping pixels, 395
remote proofing, 723
Remove Selected/All Local
  Overrides commands, 618
reordering layers, 531
Report button, 695
Report Only box, 682
repositioning, scan cropping,
  503
requirements
  halftone resolution, 324
  line art resolution, 323
  output request forms,
    687-689
  trapping, 669-670
Resample Images box, 498
researching software, 103
Reset Palette Locations to
  Default button, 354
resetting endpoints (halftone
  scans), 393-395
resizable ghosted images, creating, 536-537
resizing, scan cropping, 503
resolution, 231
  choosing monitors, 40
  dependent images, 231
  independent images, 232
  interpolated, 342
  monitor settings, 90

optical, 341

pixels, 323-324

  dots-per-inch (dpi), 325

  monitor pixels-per-inch (ppi), 324-325

  requirements for halftones, 324

  requirements for line art, 323

  samples-per-inch (spi), 325

  spots-per-inch (spi), 325

reducing (blurring moiré), 502

scanners, 341-342

scanning at twice the normal resolution (blurring moiré), 500

setting when scanning line art, 371

testers (output devices), 360

true, 341

resolution-to-linescreen ratio, scaling pixel graphics, 621

resource forks, Type 3 fonts, 117

resources

  knowledge, 48

    human resources, 55-65

    reference materials, 52-55

    training, 48-52

  sharing, 212

restoring excluded pixels (silhouette touch up), 554

retouching flaws (halftone scans), 400-401

  Rubber Stamp tool, 402-403

Retrospect, 168

return on investment (ROI), 28

returns, style sheets, 604

revealing layers, 531

Reverse option (trapping color-to-color in XPress), 657

Reverse Path Direction button, 249

reviewing halftone scans, 407

reviewing files (preflight process stage two), 689

  creating optimum preflight conditions, 690

  InDesign documents, 695

    Color and Inks panel, 697

    Fonts panel, 695-696

    Links and Images panel, 696

    Print Settings panel, 697

    Summary panel, 695

  PageMaker documents, 693

    fonts, 693-694

    graphics, 694-695

  XPress documents, 690-691

    fonts, 691

    graphics, 692-693

revising

  conventional prepress, 12-13

  digital prepress, 17-18

revisions, marking proofs, 728-729

RGB (red, green, blue)

  images, adjusting color of images, 457

  QuarkXPress preferences, 574

  workspace, 427-428

    gamma, 430

    monitor compensation, 431

    monitor option, 431

    primaries, 430

    RGB pop-up menu, 429-430

    white point, 430

RGB button, 285

RGB mode (24-bit Color), 317, 319

RGB pop-up menu, 429-430

RGB/CMY color model (red, green, blue/pure cyan, magenta, and yellow), 416-417

  complementary colors, 417-419

  converting images to CMYK components, 431-432

    black highlight, 435

    black ink limit, 435-436

    CMYK conversion setups, 436-437

    dot gain, 433-434

    GCR, 434-435

    ICC option, 432-433

    ink colors, 433

    non-standard printing inks, 437-439

    Tables option, 433

    total ink limit, 436

    UCA amount, 436

    UCR, 434

rich black, 634-636

  FreeHand, 640

  Illustrator, 639-640

  InDesign, 638

  PageMaker, 637-638

  XPress, 636-637

ROI (return on investment), 28

Rotate Canvas: Arbitrary command (Image menu), 499

rotation

  latency, 182

  moiré, 499

  scan cropping, 503

  speed, 181

roughs, 10

routing Ethernet hubs, 208

RSI (Repetitive Stress Injury), 68

carpal tunnel syndrome, 69

eye strain, 77

preventing

desks, 72

furniture, 71

posture, 70

stretching, 73

Rubber Stamp tool, 401-403

runarounds (QuarkXPress preferences), 573

S

SAD system (source, attenuator, detector), 338

saturation (color), 420

savable settings (scanner software), 345

Save a Copy command (File menu), 532

Save a Copy dialog box, 532

Save As command (File menu), 302

Save As dialog box, 302

Save command (File menu), 281

Save Palette Locations (On) option (General panel of Photoshop's Preferences), 354

Save Selection command (Select menu), 521

saving, 301

detailed line art images, 380

EPS File Format, 301

FreeHand, 302-303

Illustrator, 302

halftone scans, 384, 407

line art scan images, 376

Native File Format, 301

Quick Mask selection, 515

selections, 520-523

Channel Pop-Up options, 522

Document Pop-Up options, 522

editing saved selections, 523

loading, 523-525

Operations options, 522-523

Saving Files panel (Photoshop's Preferences), 354

Append File Extension (On) option, 354-355

Image Previews options, 354

Include Composited Image with Layered Files (Off) option, 355

scaling restrictions, importing graphics, 304-305

Scan button, 372

ScanDisk, 96

scanners, 337-338

batch scanning, 384

bit depth, 342-343

choosing, 346-347

cleaning kits, 369

clipped highlights/shadows, 365

digital cameras, 340-341

drum, 340

dynamic range, 343

flatbed, 338-339

halftones, 380-382

acquiring the scan, 384

adjusting contrast, 395-400

adjusting endpoints, 390-395

assessing original image, 382-383

assessing the scan, 384-385

compensating for dot gain, 403-406

cropping glares, 385-386

previewing, adjusting, and measuring scan, 383-384

retouching any flaws, 400-403

reviewing and saving, 407

sharpening the image, 386-389

line art, 370

acquiring the scan, 372

cropping and cleaning up image, 374-376

evaluating the image, 372-374

previewing the scan, 371

saving the file, 376

setting appropriate resolution, 371

setting scanning mode to Line Art, 370

maps, 368

operator, digital prepress design, 16

preparing environment, 351

setting Photoshop's Preferences, 351-359

Prescan function, 383

readying, 359

cleaning scanner, 369-370

mapping scanner beds, 368-369

testing grayscale scans, 362-368

testing line art scans, 360-362

resolution, 341-342

SAD system, 338

scanning target, 363

sensors, 339

   CCDs, 339

   CMOS, 339

   PMTs, 340

sheetfed, 338

software, 344-345

   application support, 344

   batch scanning, 345

   channel-specific settings, 345

   densitometer, 344

   descreening function, 345

   endpoint placement, 345

   OCR, 345

   savable settings, 345

   scan modes, 344

   sharpening features, 345

   tonal correction, 344

   transparency adapters, 344

threshold, 361

transparency, 339

wipes, 369

scanning

   back digital cameras, 341

   color, 448-450

   out-sourcing, 226

   Raw Scans job folder, 164

scans

   cropping, 502

     applying Crop command, 503

     applying levels-based adjustments, 504-506

     canceling, 503

     repositioning, 503

     resizing, 503

     rotating, 503

     straightening a crooked scan, 503-504

   modes, 344

scatter proofs, 726-727

Scitex, 675

Scratch Disk option (Plug-Ins and Scratch Disk panel of Photoshop's Preferences), 358

scratch disks, partitioning disk drives, 80

screen

   angles (halftone screens), 332-334

     defining with duotones, 334

     defining with QuarkXPress, 334

     moiré, 334

   fonts, 113

   halftone. *See* halftone screens

   images, 371

screening. *See* tinting

SCSI hard drives, 192

SCSI ports, 38

secondary components, 486

seek time (storage media), 181

segments, 239-240

Select All command (Edit menu), 277, 508

Select menu commands

   Color Range, 518

   Deselect, 558

   Feather, 520

   Hide Edges, 562

   Inverse, 524

   Load Selection, 524

   Save Selection, 521

Select Pop-Up option (Color Range command), 516-517

Select: Masks command (Edit menu), 252

Select: None command (Edit menu), 246

Selecting masks

   FreeHand, 255

   Illustrator, 252

Selection Preview Pop-Up option (Color Range command), 517-518

selection techniques, 506

   Color Range command, 516

     creating a color range selection, 518-520

     Fuzziness Slider option, 517

     Select Pop-Up option, 516-517

     Selection Preview Pop-Up option, 517-518

   creating layer-based selections, 520

   Lasso tools, 509

     Polygon Lasso tool, 511-512

     selecting with Standard Lasso tool, 509-511

   loading selections, 523-525

   Marquee tools, 507-508

     intersecting selection outlines, 508

     strategies, 508-509

   Quick Mask command, 512

     Color Indicates option, 513

     Color option, 513

     creating a New Quick Mask selection, 513-514

     editing existing selection, 514-515

     Opacity option, 513

     techniques, 515

   saving selections, 520-523

     Channel Pop-Up options, 522

     Document Pop-Up options, 522

editing saved selection,
523

Operations options,
522-523

Selection tool, 253

sensors (scanners), 339

CCDs, 339

CMOT, 339

PMTs, 340

separation (project reports),
679

separation preferences,
431-432

black highlight, 435

black ink limit, 435-436

CMYK conversion setups,
436-437

CMYK model, 432

ICC option, 432-433

Tables option, 433

dot gain, 433-434

GCR, 434-435

ink colors, 433

non-standard printing inks,
437-439

total ink limit, 436

UCA amount, 436

UCR, 434

servers, 209

application, 211

data, 211

file, 209

print, 210-211

service bureaus, 59-60

choosing, 227

graphics, scaling requirements, 622

history of, 178

including fonts, 137-141

job estimates, 223

media dexterity, 175

modem transfers, 216

storage media, standardizing,
204

service providers

choosing, 227-230

output request forms,
686-689

list of people completed
by, 686-687

requirements, 687-689

setting Photoshop's Preferences
for scanning, 351-352

Display and Cursors panel,
355-357

General panel, 352-354

Image Cache panel, 358-359

Plug-Ins and Scratch Disk
panel, 357-358

Saving Files panel, 354-355

Setup tab, 703

shade-stepping. *See* banding

shadows

clipped, 365

color adjustment, 471-472

grayscale scans, 367-368

scatter proofs, 726

shapes, 239

combining, 247

compound paths, 247-250

merging, 257

FreeHand's Combine
options, 262-263

Illustrator's Pathfinder
options, 257-261

punching holes in compound
paths, 248

type around

FreeHand, 270-271

Illustrator, 270

type within

FreeHand, 268

Illustrator, 267

sharing resources, 212

Sharpen: Unsharp Mask command (Filter menu), 378, 387

sharpening

features (scanner software),
345

images (blurring moiré), 502

images (halftone scans), 386

amount, 387

radius, 388

threshold, 388-389

unsharp masking strate-
gies, 389

line art images, 378

selected areas (Unsharp
Mask Filter), 469

sheetfed scanners, 338

Short PANTONES Names (On)
option (General panel of
Photoshop's Preferences),
353

shortcuts, style sheets, 614

Show Attributes command
(Windows menu), 249

Show Brushes command
(Window menu), 375

Show Columns setting, 95

Show Problems Only box, 695

Show Rulers command (View
menu), 511

Show Swatches command
(Windows menu), 283

Show Tool Tips (On) option
(General panel of Photoshop's
Preferences), 353

silhouettes, 548

complex, creating, 550-553

simple, creating, 549-550

stacking graphics in layout, 624

touching up extracted ones, 553

erasing unwanted pixels, 554-555

restoring excluded pixels, 554

simple traps

automatically applied, 649-651

manually applied, 647-649

slurring, press check, 731

smearing, press check, 731

SMPTE-C option (RGB pop-up menu), 429

soft proofing, 723

soft returns, style sheets, 604

software, 42-43

defragmentation utilities, 97

fonts, 46-47

installing, 98

RAM allocation, 99-102

maintenance utilities, 47

outputting the proofs (preflight process), 701-702

page layout, 45-46

pixel-based editing programs, 45

preflight process, 714-715

FlightCheck, 714-715

Preflight Pro, 714

scanners, 344-345

application support, 344

batch scanning, 345

channel-specific settings, 345

densitometer, 344

descreening function, 345

endpoint placement, 345

OCR, 345

savable settings, 345

scan modes, 344

sharpening features, 345

tonal correction, 344

transparency adapters, 344

trapping, 668-669

updating, 96

upgrading, 97

vector-based graphics programs, 44-45

word processors, 43-44

source profiles, 424

source, attenuator, detector system. *See* SAD system

special notes (project reports), 679

Specifications for Web Offset Printing (SWOP), 433

specular highlights, 390

spellcheck, 718

spi resolution (samples-per-inch), 325

spi resolution (spots-per-inch), 325

Split command (Modify menu), 250

spoolers, 210

Spot Color box, 637

spot colors

page layout, 588

proofing, 729-730

spreads, 585-587

multi-page, 587

trapping, 630-631

sRGB option (RGB pop-up menu), 429

stacking graphics, page design, 624-625

Standard Lasso tool, 509

adding straight edges to free-form selection, 510-511

edge pixels, 510

editing existing selection, 509-510

standard RGB (sRGB), 429

Standard View Options For setting, 94

standards

page layout measurement, 583

page layout programs, 565

storage media, 184

swatchbooks, 589

Starting Color slider, 293

Startup Set (fonts), 128

Step and Repeat command, 536

Step Limit (trapping), 665

Step-by-Step Design, 54

stochastic screening. *See* FM screening

stop/start time, 182

storage

capacity, 181

history of, 177-179

offsite file management, 171-173

requirement for outputting paper proofs (preflight process), 701

storage media

ATA drives, 193

Castlewood ORB drive, 197

CD-R, 198-199

cost-per-megabyte, 183

emergency startup disks, 187

FireWire drives, 193

life span, 184

magnetic tape, 202

MO, 200-201

proper use of, 187

RAID, 194

SCSI hard drives, 192

standardizing in-house
devices, 203

SuperDisks, 190

types of, 187

> *magnetic, 188-197*
>
> *magnetic tape, 202*
>
> *magneto-optical, 200-201*
>
> *optical, 198-199*

USB drives, 193

straddling strokes, 663

straight edges, adding to free-
form selection (Standard
Lasso tool), 510-511

straight lines, 240-241

straightening crooked scans,
503-504

strategies (Marquee tools),
508-509

stretching, 73

stripping

conventional prepress, 12

out-sourcing, 227

stroke, 278, 647

applying

> *FreeHand, 280-281*
>
> *Illustrator, 278-280*

InDesign preferences, 581

straddling outline of shapes,
663

Stroke option (Color palette),
279

StuffIt Deluxe, watched folders,
158

style sheets, 602-605

defining

> *InDesign, 611-614*
>
> *PageMaker, 609-611*
>
> *QuarkXPress, 605-609*

importing

> *InDesign, 614*
>
> *PageMaker, 610*
>
> *QuarkXPress, 607*

subpaths, 543, 557

Substituted Fonts, 581

subtle detail, 465-466

subtractive primary model, 417

Suggested Size setting, 100

suitcase files, 113

suitcases

adding sets with ATM
Deluxe, 135

maintaining, 115

organizing fonts, 126

Summary panel (InDesign's
Preflight dialog box), 695

super black, 641

FreeHand, 644-645

Illustrator, 644

InDesign, 643

PageMaker, 642-643

XPress, 641

SuperDisks, 190

Swatch Libraries submenu
(Windows menu), 283

swatchbooks

choosing colors, 589

naming colors, 591

Swatches Option dialog box,
288

Swatches palette, 279

SWOP (Specifications for Web
Offset Printing), 433

SyQuest 130MB EZ drives,
184-185

System folder

Control Panels, 82

file management, 152-153

Fonts subfolder, 122

systems

converting fonts between,
119

> *Mac-based, 120*
>
> *Windows-based, 119*

optimizing

> *Antivirus utilities, 91*
>
> *customizing system, 81*
>
> *Disk First Aid, 96*
>
> *disk utilities, 97*
>
> *font utilities, 91*
>
> *formatting disk drives,
> 78-80*
>
> *installing system, 81*
>
> *MacOS Control Panels,
> 85-89*
>
> *MacOS Extensions
> Manager, 81-83*
>
> *rebuilding desktop, 96*
>
> *updating software, 96*
>
> *View settings, 92-95*
>
> *weekly maintenance, 95*

recovery, 102-105

T

T1, 215

tables, when and where trapping is required, 669-670

Tables option, converting
images into CMYK compo-
nents, 433

tabs

Output, 704

Pictures, 692

Preview, 705

Setup, 703

style sheets, 605

Trapping, 653

tack (ink), 731

targeting

colors (Curves command), 463-464

endpoints (halftone scans), 391-392

technical support, selecting appropriate media storage, 180

templates, master pages, 615

tertiary components, 486

test copies, printing when evaluating images, 372

testing

grayscale scans, 362

compensating for lost highlights and shadows, 367-368

evaluating tonal range, 364-367

setting right scanning mode, 363

line art scans, 360-362

text, 265

boxes, trapping in XPress, 660-661

page layout, 598

coloring, 595

converting to type, 601-602

MS Word, 600-601

style sheets, 602-614

paths, trapping in XPress, 662-663

Text Box Tool, document preferences, 574

Text Files folder, 164

Text menu commands, Effect submenu, 266

Text tool, 266

Text toolbar, 268-269

Text-to-Speech, useless Extensions, 84

theTypeBook, 145

thickness option (Trap dialog box), 650

thickwire coaxial cable, 207

thinwire coaxial cable, 207

threshold

detail, 467

halftone scan image sharpness, 388-389

scanners, 361

Threshold command (Image menu), preparing detailed line art, 378-379

Threshold dialog box, 475

Thumbnail option (Saving Files panel of Photoshop's Preferences), 354

thumbnails, printing when proofing, 720

thunking, 30

TIFF files, importing graphics, 304

avoiding Matryoshka, 304-305

scaling restrictions, 304-305

TIFF Options dialog box, 376

time until sleep, 182

Tint Reduction option (Trap dialog box), 650

tint slider, 287

tinting, 327

tints

color page proofs, 727

creating (vector-based objects), 287

FreeHand, 288

Illustrator, 287-288

defining for page layout, 597

press check, 731

Tints palette, 288

To Archive folder

file management, 157

tonal content, 460

tonal correction (scanner software), 344

Tonal Graph (curves), 396-397

tonal range, 317

evaluating when testing grayscale scans, 364-367

expanding (cropping scans), 504

tools

Add Anchor Point, 244

Area Type, 267

color adjustment, 455

Curves command (Photoshop), 460-464

Eyedropper (Photoshop), 458-460

Info Palette (Photoshop), 455-458

Unsharp Mask Filter (Photoshop), 467-469

Crop, 374, 385, 503

Delete Anchor Point, 244

Direct Selection, 242

Edge Highlighter, 551

Ellipse, 242

Eyedropper, 279

History Brush, 554

Path Type, 268

Pen, 240

Pencil, 375

Pointer, 242

QuarkXPress, preferences, 573

Rubber Stamp, 401-403

Selection, 253, 506

selection
  Color Range command, 516-520
  Lasso, 509-512
  Marquee, 507-509
  Quick Mask command, 512-515
Text, 266
trapping, 651-652
  PageMaker, 663-666
  Photoshop, 666-667
  vector-based, 647-651
  XPress, 652-663
Type, 252, 266, 530
total ink density, 456
total ink limit, converting images into CMYK components, 436
total space, 701
touching up
  extracted silhouettes, 553
    erasing unwanted pixels, 554-555
    restoring excluded pixels, 554
  traced images, refining to vector-based graphic, 235
tracing pixel-based images, 299
  automatically, 300-301
  manually, 299-300
trackballs, 76
tracks, 181
training (computers), 48
  assessing needs, 49
  classroom versus onsite, 50
  determining time formats, 50
  explaining needs, 49
  follow-up availability, 51
  industry ties, 51-52
  requesting client lists, 52

requesting course outline, 49
seeking hands-on training, 50
transfer
  curves, 405
  function, dot gain, 405-406
  rates, 182
Transform palette, 256
transforming masks in FreeHand, 256
transmissive originals (casts), 483
transmitting data, 217
transparency
  adapters, 344
  Image layer, 527
  mask, 527
  pixels, 527
  scanners, 339
  units, 338
TransType, 120
trap dependency option (trapping color-to-color in XPress), 658
Trap filter, 649
Trap Specifications dialog box, 656
Trap Text Above Value (trapping), 665
Trap Xtra, 649
trapping, 290, 627-630
  application servers, 212
  chokes, 630-631
  choosing service providers, 228
  color page proofs, 728
  coloring text, 596
  complexities, 629
  future Adobe, 670-671
  items that do not require trapping, 628-629
  out-sourcing, 227

process bridges, 631, 633
software, 668-669
spot color proofing, 730
spreads, 630-631
table of when and where trapping is required, 669-670
tools, 651-652
  PageMaker, 663-666
  Photoshop, 666-667
  vector-based, 647-651
  XPress, 652-663
values, 629-630
Trapping Method option (XPress Trapping Preference panel), 653-654
Trapping Preferences dialog box, 664
Trapping tab, 653
Traps Over Imported Objects box, 665
Trim option (Illustrator Pathfinders), 260
troubleshooting
  digital prepress, 20
  PostScript, 712-713
    billing practices, 713-714
true resolution, 341
TrueType fonts, 112
  converting to Type 1, 119
  maintaining libraries, 117
  MS Word documents, 600
TTConverter, 120
twisted pair, 207
type, 265
  converting to paths, 275-277
    FreeHand, 277-278
    Illustrator, 277
  Customized, editing with compound paths, 248
  style sheets, 604

stylized in vector-based graphics, 235

vector-based techniques, 266

type along a path in FreeHand, 269

type along a path in Illustrator, 268-269

type around a shape in FreeHand, 270-271

type around a shape in Illustrator, 270

type around both sides of a circle in FreeHand, 274-275

type around both sides of a circle in Illustrator, 271-274

type within a shape in FreeHand, 268

type within a shape in Illustrator, 267

Type 1 fonts, 110

Type 3 fonts, 111

converting to Type 1, 119

removing, 116

Type Library folder, file management, 154

Type menu commands

Create Outlines, 253, 277

Linear, 293

Process, 637

Radial, 293

Type Reunion, 134

Type tool, 252, 266, 530

Type: Render Layer command (Layer menu), 530

typefaces, 107

expert sets, 120

families, 108

file management, 165

typesetting, conventional prepress, 11

typestyles, 108

U

ubiquitous mouse, 76

UCA (under color addition), 436

converting images into CMYK components, 436

UCR (under color removal), 434

converting images into CMYK components, 434

uncalibrated proofs, 724

uncoated stock printing, 437

under color addition. *See* UCA

under color removal. *See* UCR

undercolors, 636

Undo command (Edit menu), 234, 399

Ungroup command (Modify menu), 247

Union option (FreeHand Combine), 262

Unite option (Illustrator Pathfinders), 257

Units and Undo dialog box, 235

unlinking layer masks, 538

Unsharp Mask dialog box, 467

Unsharp Mask filter (Photoshop), 386

color adjustment tool, 464-465

channel-based sharpening, 467-469

evaluating and sharpening detail, 465-467

sharpening selected areas, 469

unsharp masking strategies, halftone scans, 389

Updaters subfolder, 156

upgradeable processors, 32-33

upgrading

printers, 699

600 dots per inch (dpi), 700

Ethernet, 701

increasing RAM, 700

paper size, 700

PostScript Level 2 or 3, 699

software, 97

uploading modems, 216

Usage command (Utilities menu), 692

Usage dialog box, 692

USB drives, 193

USB ports, 38

Use Cache for Histograms option (Image Cache panel of Photoshop's Preferences), 359

Use Relative Date setting, 94

Use System Palette (Off) option (Display and Cursors panel of Photoshop's Preferences), 356

Use XPress Preferences, 576

utilities

disk, 97

folder, file management, 156

menu commands

Define Colors, 637

Plug-Ins, Pub Info, 683

Usage, 692

V

value added resellers (VARs), 64-65

values

  pixels, reading, 320-323

  trapping, 629-630

Values Gradient (curves), 396

VARs (value added resellers), 64-65

vector-based applications, draw programs, 231

vector-based graphics, 231-235

  Bézier curves, 238-239

    curve handles, 241-242

    drawing curved paths in FreeHand, 245-247

    drawing curved paths in Illustrator, 242-244

    points and segments, 239-240

    straight-line paths, 240-241

  codes, PostScript, 232

  colors, 278

    applying fill and stroke in FreeHand, 280-281

    applying fill and stroke in Illustrator, 278-280

    converting colors between ink types, 290

    creating tints, 287-288

    default colors, 281-283

    defining colors, 283-286

    deleting unnecessary colors, 288-290

    naming colors, 286

  custom fills, 291

    gradients, 291-297

    patterns, 298-299

features, 233

    easily stacked in a layout document, 234

    infinitely editable, 233

    infinitely scalable, 234

    nondegradable, 233

    print at highest resolution, 234

    small file size, 234

    Undo endlessly, 234

  fonts and font characters, 236

  graphs, 236

  limitations, 236

    drawing by hand, 237

    extremely compex images, 237

    page layout, 237

    photo-realistic images, 237

  logos, 235

  programs, 44-45

  refining traced images, 235

  stacking in layout, 624

  stylized typefaces, 235

  tracing pixel-based images, 299

    automatically, 300-301

    manually, 299-300

vector-based trapping tools, 647

  complex, 651

  simple traps

    automatically applied, 649-651

    manually applied, 647-649

vector-based type, 266

  along a path in FreeHand, 269

  along a path in Illustrator, 268-269

around a shape in FreeHand, 270-271

around a shape in Illustrator, 270

around around both sides of a circle in FreeHand, 274-275

around around both sides of a circle in Illustrator, 271-274

within a shape in FreeHand, 268

within a shape in Illustrator, 267

vectors, rasterizing, 305-306

  FreeHand, 307

  Illustrator, 306-307

  Photoshop, 307-308

Video LUT Animation (On) option (Display and Cursors panel of Photoshop's Preferences), 356

video training, 53

View menu commands

  Actual Pixels, 373

  Artwork, 548

  Show Rulers, 511

viewing

  paths, 545

  standards for viewing colors, 423

    characterizing monitors, 426-427

    consistent viewing environment, 425

    ICC profiles, 423-425

    RGB workspace, 427-431

vignettes, creating, 538-539

Viking Web site, 35

Virtual Memory settings, 88

viruses, 29

  antivirus utilities, 92

VST USB floppy drive, 191

W-Z

Wacom, 76

warranties, selecting appropriate media storage, 180

watched folders

file management, 157

print folders, 210

Web sites

Adobe, 55

data servers, 211

Kingston, 35

selecting appropriate media storage, 180

Viking, 35

weekly maintenance, 95

Weight field (Stroke palette), 279

wet proofing, 725-726

white color (default color), 281-282

white line art, 624

white point option (RGB workspace), 430

Wide Gaunt RGB option (RGB pop-up menu), 430

Win 98 Drive Converter, 80

Winchester technology, 178

Windows

configuring for performance, 86

converting fonts for MacOS, 119

drivers, 82

file extensions, 170

Fonts folder, 122

managing fonts (ATM Deluxe), 133-136

Programs folder, 152

ScanDisk, 96

TrueType fonts, 112

Windows 98 versus MacOS, 26-29

Windows menu commands

Panels: Color List, 285

Panels: Color Mixer, 285

Panels: Tints, 288

Show Attributes, 249

Show Brushes, 375

Show Swatches, 283

Swatch Libraries submenu, 283

Xtras: Operations, 262

Windows NT, 29-30

Word 97/98 word processor, 44, 598-601

word processors, 43-44, 598

incongruous features, 599

work environment, 23-24

ergonomics, 68

eye strain, 77

gloves, 76

hardware, 24-35

computer technology, 25-30

expansion bays, 35-36

expansion slots, 36-37

monitors, 38-42

ports, 37-38

processors, 30-33

RAM, 33-35

keyboards, 74-75

pointing devices, 75

RSI, 68

CTS, 69

preventing, 70-73

software, 42-43

fonts, 46-47

maintenance utilities, 47

page layout, 45-46

pixel-based editing programs, 45

vector-based graphics programs, 44-45

word processors, 43-44

taking breaks, 77

wrist rests, 76

work folder

file management, 159-166

job tracking, 159

work paths, 543

workflow, 149-151

workstations

file management, 150

fonts

Startup Set, 128

storing, 143

Fonts folder, 122

installing software, 98

sharing resources, 212

WORM media, 198

wrist rests, 76

XPress. *See* QuarkXPress

XTensions

Pasteboard XT, 570

preferences, 571

Xtras

Operations command (Windows menu), 262

Trap, 649

zapping PRAM, 104

Zip disks

backups, 167

reformatting hard drives, 79

Zip drives, 196

cost-per-megabyte, 183

efficient use, 183